AFRICAN HISTORY

REVISED EDITION

Edited by
CHIMA KORIEH
Marquette University
and
RAPHAEL CHIJIOKE NJOKU
University of Louisville

Bassim Hamadeh, CEO and Publisher
Christopher Foster, General Vice President
Michael Simpson, Vice President of Acquisitions
Jessica Knott, Managing Editor
Kevin Fahey, Cognella Marketing Manager
Jess Busch, Senior Graphic Designer
Jamie Giganti, Project Editor
Brian Fahey, Licensing Associate

First published in the United States of America in 2013 by Cognella, Inc.

Printed in the United States of America

ISBN: 978-1-63121-012-9 (pbk)/ 978-1-62131-000-6 (br)

CONTENTS

INTRODUCTION

By Raphael Chijioke Njoku and Chima Korieh

African History provides students and instructors with richer source materials that can be used either alone or along with supplementary materials in the teaching and learning of African history. In the past six decades, African history has made remarkable progress as historians continue to thin the field of resilient stereotypes brought to bear by the European scholars and publicists of the eighteenth and nineteenth centuries. Consumed by the successes of the Industrial Revolution in Europe, these writers saw Africa (including other peoples of the world) as profoundly uncivilized. As new books and articles are published every year, they have helped deepen our knowledge and appreciation of the continent's rich and remarkable contributions to our collective human civilization. The findings of the new studies have rendered obsolete the aged debate whether Africa has a rich, vital, and vibrant history. The study of African history with minimum biases and prejudices now presents students with a better and more rewarding opportunity to understand the truth about the continent's people and cultures.

This anthology is not meant to replace the use of other valuable texts that offer the reader an opportunity to explore Africa as a dynamic continent, a region of the world that has been the harbinger of innovations and cultural change. The intent here is to help instructors and students bring to the classroom some of the best essay selections on diverse topics related to Africa's history, culture, and society. This reader is therefore born out of the need for those interested in the study of Africa to draw perspectives from multiple sources and to use these diverse viewpoints to master some crucial historiographical debates. These debates have shaped the development of African history over the past six decades as scholars use diverse disciplinary and paradigmatic approaches to elucidate insights on a plethora of complex sociocultural, political, and economic themes.

This reader contains thirty-six chapters divided into five parts. The three chapters in Part I: "Perspectives on the African Past" offer some critical knowledge about the continent and its people, the early ideas and stereotypes held by outsiders, and how these forms of knowledge have shaped certain prejudices and biases that are difficult to dispel today. This background chapter is also useful in elucidating knowledge about oral tradition as a useful source of African history. In fact, Thomas Spears's discussion on methods remains one of the best approaches to the use of oral tradition for its utilitarian purpose in time and space. Here we appreciate the understanding that oral tradition, especially in the African precolonial context, was meant to serve social function, and that this function was dynamic—hence, orality was also dynamic. Thus, oral traditions can neither be viewed nor evaluated as a text that must, for relevance, meet non-precolonial African standards of record keeping.

Part II: "Early History and Society" contains ten chapters designed to provide students and instructors with a richer and deeper appreciation of early or precolonial history of Africa. The plan is for the reader to use a combination of primary and secondary materials to better access the precolonial history of the continent. With these tools, a text of this nature on African history meaningfully broadens the cusp of historical narrative and the qualities of cultures, which encapsulate their meaning and motivations. In this context, Africa's past could be seen and understood both objectively and subjectively, thus using the benefits of those time-honored eyewitness accounts to purge the subjectivity of skewed historiography, and to see beyond the impulses driving the biased narrative.

Part III: "Europeans in Africa" contains eleven chapters, which together focus on the dramatic and life-altering African encounter with the Europeans. Among other things, it examines the trans-Atlantic slave trade, Christian missionary evangelism, and the pervading impact of the new ideology. Additionally, it covers the colonial military conquest of the continent, consolidation of colonial rule, and the diverse consequences of colonial rule, particularly on women. The gender perspective is crucial, because as the different studies by John Pape and John Oriji show, colonialism affected the genders in different ways, with women suffering the worst aspects of the experience. This view provides us with a better sense of the history of gender relations in the postcolonial state.

The six chapters in Part IV: "Nationalism and Decolonization" cover the short but treacherous road to decolonization from the mid-1940s, when African nationalists began more aggressively to press on the colonial rulers that alien domination had lost its purpose and relevance. Although historians have yet to fully comprehend the details of that phenomenon due to the unavailability of classified documents, its politics of secrecy, ideological brinkmanship, negotiations, and buy-offs—in addition to the twists and turns of Cold War–era politicking—it remains clear that the impact the process has brought to bear on modern Africa will remain for a long time. Now we know that the worst form of colonialism was practiced in South Africa, and that the process of "flag independence" ended with the eventual dismantling of the obstinate white-minority regime in that country.

The last section, Part V: "Postcolonial Africa," contains five chapters exploring issues related to contemporary Africa. From Adu Boahen's impressive appraisal of colonial impact on Africa, through the discussion on the effects of the Cold War in the Congo, China's presence in Africa, Genocide in Rwanda, and to Boaduo's preview on the emerging images of xenophobia and terror on a global scale, the various authors attempt to provide up-to-date readings on some of the most recent topics and how they relate to the continent.

African History cannot possibly meet all the needs and interests of every teacher or student. Combining this reader with some other good texts can surely point the way to mastering a more useful and useable knowledge of African peoples, history, and societies. Above all, it will, no doubt, shed lucre and dispel centuries-old stereotypes that have continued to cast dark shadows of mystery and fictions about Africa, particularly among pessimists.

AFRICAN HISTORY

PART ONE

PERSPECTIVES ON THE AFRICAN PAST

CHANGING OUR MIND ABOUT AFRICA

By Curtis Keim

Most of us who are Americans know little about Africa. We might have studied Africa for a few weeks in school or glanced occasionally at newspaper headlines about genocide, AIDS, malaria, or civil war, but rarely have we actually thought seriously about Africa. If we do want to learn about Africa, it is difficult to find ample and accurate information in our popular media such as television and newspapers. Africa and its people are simply a marginal part of American consciousness.

Africa is, however, very much a part of the American subconscious. Ironically, although we know little about Africa, we carry strong mental images of the continent. Once you begin to notice, you find that Africa appears in the American public space quite frequently. Although it may not figure often in the news, it shows up in advertising, movies, amusement parks, cartoons, and many other corners of our society. And although most Americans do not possess many facts about Africa, we do know certain general truths about the continent. We know, for example, that Africans live in tribes. And we know that Africa is a place of famine, disease, poverty, coups, and large wild animals.

General images are useful and perhaps necessary for our collective consciousness. We can't know everything about the world, so we have to lump some things into big categories that are convenient if lacking detail. Life is too short for most of us to become experts on more than a couple of subjects. Thus, these images help us to organize Africa's place in our collective mind. A war in Congo? Ah, yes, that's more of the "African trouble" category. Elephants being used in a commercial? Yes, wouldn't it be fun to have an elephant wash your car. There are lots of large animals living in the wilds of Africa, aren't there?

If our general categories are reasonably accurate, they help us navigate our complex world. If, however, they are inaccurate, these categories can be both dangerous and exploitative. If, for example, we are wrong about Africa's supposed insignificance, we will be blindsided by political, environmental, or even medical events that affect how we survive. Or, if we think of Africa only as a place of trouble, a large zoo, or a storehouse of strategic minerals rather than as a place where real people live real lives, we will likely be willing to exploit the continent for our own purposes. France's former president François Mitterrand demonstrated this possibility graphically when, speaking to his staff in the early 1990s about Rwanda, he noted that "in some countries, genocide is not really important."[1] Although in the short term the exploitation of Africa might help France or us, in the long term the planet's society and environment will pay dearly for our failure to care.

SPEAKING "AFRICAN"

Anyone who wants to study Africa in depth needs to learn African languages, because language is the major key to understanding how people mentally organize the world around them. Likewise, anyone who wants to understand Americans must examine the words Americans know and use. You can begin to discover American ideas about Africa by trying some free association with the word *Africa*. Ask yourself what words come to mind when you hear *Africa*. Be aware that this is not the time to "clean up your act" and impress yourself with your political correctness. Rather, search for the words your society has given you to describe Africa, some of which will seem positive, some negative, and some neutral.

My students have helped me create lists of words that come to mind during such an exercise. Within a few minutes, a class frequently generates thirty or forty words that Americans associate with Africa. *Native, hut, warrior, shield, tribe, savage, cannibals, jungle, Pygmy, pagan, voodoo,* and *witch doctor* are commonly associated with "traditional" Africa. "Tourism words" include *safari, wild animals, elephant, lion,* and *pyramid.* There are also "news words," including *coup, poverty, ignorance, drought, famine, tragedy,* and *tribalism.* And then there is a group of "change words" (indicating Western-induced change), such as *development, foreign aid, peacekeeping,* and *missionary.* Occasionally, a really honest person will come up with "racist words" he or she has heard, like *spear chucker* or *jungle bunny.*

Although some American words might be positive—*kinship, wisdom,* or *homeland*—the overwhelming impression gained from studying American language about Africa is that Africa is a primitive place, full of trouble and wild animals, and in need of our help. A survey by a major American museum on popular perceptions of Africa found a number of widely held misconceptions, including the following: Africa is just one large country; Africa is all jungle; Africans share a single culture, language, and religion; Africans live in "grass huts"; Africans mainly hunt animals for their subsistence; and Africa has no significant history.

If you think you have escaped these concepts, you are either extraordinarily lucky or you fool yourself easily. The messages that perpetuate such impressions pervade American culture. They are ideas that have deep roots in American history as well as strong branches that entwine our daily lives. At one time in our history, most of white America did not even consider Africans to be equal as humans! By comparison, today's understanding is positively enlightened. Yet historical misperception, ignorance, stereotype, and myth still cast shadows upon our thinking. Once you begin to look for them, you see inaccurate portrayals of Africa that reproduce the blatant old images in subtler, modernized versions. In fact, a worthwhile exercise is to ask yourself where the words listed above have come from. Home? School? Church? Friends? Television? Newspapers? Magazines? Movies? Books? Amusement parks? It is difficult to get complete and balanced views of Africa in everyday American life. This topic will be discussed further in Chapter 2, "How We Learn."

This book investigates the histories of our inaccurate and stereotypical words and ideas and suggests alternatives. For example, Africans are sometimes referred to in everyday America as "natives." You may or may not think that *native* is a negative word, but its use is a legacy of the colonial period in Africa, when words were weapons employed by outsiders to keep Africans in their places. In the first part of the twentieth century, most Americans believed that Africans could be (indeed, *should* be) subjugated because they were primitives, natives. The problem is not the term itself, however. The first dictionary definition *of native* is someone who belongs originally to a place. Thus, "He is a native of Boston" is a neutral and acceptable use of the word. We also use *native* in a positive political way in the term *Native American*, which implies that an "American Indian" has rights and connections that go beyond those belonging to the rest of us who are more recent immigrants. But the term *African native* evokes a negative connotation, whether intended or not, that is a holdover from its colonial meanings of primitive, savage, or unenlightened. Why can we think of Africans as natives, but never the Chinese? The answer is that we have long thought of Africans as primitive and Chinese as civilized. Today, even when we intend no insult to Africans, we have these leftover phrases and connotations that get in the way of conceiving of Africans as real people like ourselves.

You can get around the "African native" and "native African" problem in a number of ways. For example, if you are referring to an African living in a rural area, you can say "a rural African." If you mean someone who is an inhabitant of Africa, just say "an African." If you mean someone who belongs to the Kikuyu ethnic group, use the words "a Kikuyu." These phrases are more precise and therefore less likely to create images that evoke stereotypes. And, to avoid even a hint of insult, you might steer clear of phrases like "He is a native of Cape Town," which in most other contexts would be neutral but in the African context might elicit musings on whether you are referring to the stereotype.

THE USE AND MISUSE OF STEREOTYPES

In an ideal world, we would abandon our stereotypes about Africa and learn to deal with Africans as they really are. Human cognition does not allow this, however. Everybody stereotypes. And we do it about practically everything. The reason for this is, first of all, that we are biologically wired to try to make sense of reality, even when it makes no particular sense. Whether through science, history, literature, religion, or whatever, humans strive to understand and categorize what is in front of them. In fact, not trying to understand apparent reality is so extraordinary that Buddhism, as one example, has made a philosophy out of it. Buddhism's attempt to experience the "is-ness" of reality directly, without thought, promises liberation from ordinary human consciousness and suffering, but such salvation is sought only by a few. Most of us will continue our attempts to make sense of the reality in front of us.

We also stereotype because it is virtually impossible to know everything that is going on in reality, and therefore we are bound to base our judgments on partial information. Like the proverbial blind men and the elephant, we each take our separate, limited experiences and extrapolate to make sense of the whole. Moreover, we often use ideas provided by our culture instead of investigating things for ourselves. If our culture has a pre-made picture of reality for us, we are likely to accept it. One way to think about this is to invert the notion "seeing is believing," making it "believing is seeing." Once we "know" something through our culture, we tend to fit new information into the old categories rather than change the system of categorization.

To say that we inevitably use stereotypes is really to say that we use mental models to think about reality. But the word *stereotype* also implies that our models are so limiting that they deform reality in ways that are offensive, dangerous, or ridiculous. Thus we need to strive to make our mental models as accurate as possible. We should, for example, study African art, history, literature, philosophy, politics, culture, and the like so we can differentiate between Africans. We should also ask ourselves whether we cling to inaccurate models of Africa because they shore up our self-image or allow us to do things otherwise unthinkable.

Following are brief discussions that explore different reasons for the persistence of our misconceptions about Africa. Later in the book I offer extended discussions of many of these topics.

Leftover Racism and Exploitation

During much of American history, a large majority of Americans considered racism and exploitation of Africa acceptable. Although the United States never ruled colonies in Africa, Americans did enslave Africans and maintain both a slavery system and segregation. Moreover, we profited from our businesses in Africa, sent missionaries to change African culture, and did not protest the colonization undertaken by Europeans. This exploitation of Africa, whether direct or indirect, required thinking about Africans as inferiors. In other words, our culture has had a lot of practice, hundreds of years of it, in constructing Africa as inferior. The legacy is obvious in the words and ideas we call to mind when we hear the word *Africa*.

Our legacy of negativity poses a question: Can we attribute a major portion of our modern stereotypes about Africa to our just not having gotten around to changing the myths we inherited from our racist and imperialist past? Perhaps we no longer need most of these myths, but they persist because only a few decades have passed since the end of the colonial period and a similarly brief period since the passage of the US Civil Rights Act of 1964.

A few decades in cultural history is really only a moment in time because cultures have momentum and are slow to change direction. Perhaps our myths about Africa are dying, but slowly.

Support for this view comes from the fact that African independence and the civil rights movement have made it unacceptable for news reporters and commentators to use the most blatantly negative of the words we once associated with race and with Africa. Likewise, schoolbooks are vastly improved in their treatment of Africa. One could argue that with greater sensitivity to the issue and more time, Americans will change. To put this idea another way, shouldn't we give Americans the benefit of the doubt and assume that most people do not consciously intend to exploit or misrepresent Africa? I believe that we should.

Current Racism

I am assuming that most readers are not intentionally racist, because people who are probably wouldn't read this kind of book. But we have to take account of the connection between our stereotypes about Africa and current racism in America. Racism is still alive in America, but the most derogatory images of Africa can no longer appear in public spaces. We must conclude, therefore, that they persist because we learn them in the more private aspects of our lives, from family and friends, and often through jokes or offhand comments. Unfortunately, such private racism is difficult to eradicate, because

continuing efforts like this book can do little for those who would not seriously consider them. Others of us, perhaps most of us, are a different kind of racist, for although we truly want to believe that all humans are equal, we entertain undercurrents of racist doubt in our minds that make us susceptible to more subtle myths about Africa. It is this *real but unintentional* racism that concerns us here, because a deeper consideration of the issues can help us see Africans more clearly.

It would be incorrect, however, to say that all or even most of the public stereotypes about Africa come from unintentional racism. First, each of us has negative stereotypes about others that are not racist. Second, not all of our stereotypes about Africa are negative. Inaccuracy and insensitivity are not necessarily racist, even when they have racist roots and produce racist results. This is a fine distinction to make, especially if you are a victim of racism, but it seems a useful distinction if we are to help decent, willing people to see Africa in new ways.

Current Exploitation

We also perpetuate negative myths about Africa because they help us maintain dominance over Africans. From our perspective in the United States, it is difficult for us to see how globally influential our country actually is. In simple terms, we are a superpower. To wield this kind of might and still think of ourselves as good people, we need powerful myths. Whereas in the past the myth of the racial inferiority of Africans was the major justification for Western control of Africans, now cultural inferiority is a more likely reason. Our news media, for example, are much more likely to inform us about African failures than about African successes. And the successes we do hear about tend to demonstrate that our own perspectives on reality are correct. It doesn't take much imagination to figure out that modern Americans who deal with Africa—bureaucrats, aid workers, businesspeople, missionaries, and others—might have an interest in describing Africa in ways that justify the importance of their own work.

Entertainment

If Africa were portrayed as being "just like us," it would be quite uninteresting. "Man bites dog" sells more newspapers than "Dog bites man." The word *exotic* describes the point; *exotic* portrays African culture as excitingly different. Usually this is at the expense of African culture, an extraordinarily large portion of which is removed from its everyday context in a way that allows us to believe that the wider culture itself is wholly extraordinary. Movies and novels thrive on this sort of thing. America too is often portrayed overseas as exotic, and we are thus frequently mistaken. In his book *American Ways*, for example, Gary Althen describes an international student who was misled by myths about exotic America. Coming to the United States having watched American movies, the student expected to find a lot of women ready for sexual activity with him. Actually, he found them, but it took him nearly two years to figure out that such easy women were also marginal and often disturbed and that more desirable women were not so readily available.[2]

I provide African examples in later chapters, but give a first illustration here. One *National Geographic* issue includes a short article on the gold of the Asantehene, the traditional ruler of the Asante people in Ghana.[3] Ten beautiful photographs show the gold clothing and ornaments of the Asantehene, his court, and his relatives. But the authors make almost no effort to tell us how all of this fits into the life of the Asante or of the modern country of Ghana. Presumably, *National Geographic* does not intend to portray Africans in stereotypical ways. Without (con)text, however, the reader might think almost anything.

This is exoticism. Exoticism portrays only a portion of a culture and allows the imagination to use stereotypes to fill in the missing pieces. Most frequently, when we supply the missing pieces, we extrapolate that other people are more different from us than they are similar. We can too easily sustain our myths about Africans and believe that words such as *mysterious* and *the Dark Continent* actually apply to Africa.

Self-Definition

Sometimes we use other people, including Africans, as a mirror. We want to know about them so we can know about ourselves. This very human activity accounts at least partially for our interest in people-watching in parks and the appeal of television sitcoms, movies, literature, history, and many other cultural phenomena. Yet this is a tricky business. For example, we know that people who spend a lot of time watching soap operas begin to conceive of the world as a soap opera and themselves as characters. And those who watch the local evening news feel that life is much more violent and chaotic than it really is.

In the case of Africa, we might say that many of us want Africans to be a bit savage so we can feel more satisfied with our own lot in life. The *Looney Toons* announcer on the Cartoon Network puts it well: "Without nuts like these, the rest of us look crazy." Perhaps you have never thought of Bugs Bunny, Daffy Duck, and Elmer Fudd as therapists, but doesn't Africa often serve the same function? If we focus on ourselves without comparison to others, don't we look pretty messed up? But if we can see that others are poorer, less educated, or more chaotic, then it is easier to believe that we are fine despite our problems. To put it differently, we can't be rich without the poor, developed without the underdeveloped, saved without the sinner, normal without the abnormal, civilized without the uncivilized, and so forth. Sometimes students tell me that they believe the reason they are required to study other cultures in college is to demonstrate how good we have it in America.

Our culture is especially susceptible to this kind of thinking because of the way we conceive of time. Our idea of time as a continuum from the past to the future—rather than, for example, as a circle returning to a golden age of the past—is embodied in our concept of progress. For us, progress generally means going forward, moving on, getting over it, improving ourselves, growing up, and a whole collection of other ideas implying that the past is negative and the future is positive. Of course, if we believe this to be true, we will expect reality to substantiate the belief. Indeed, one way we perceive African reality reveals this way of thinking. We see African community life as basic, but impossible to *return to* in our own communities. And tribalism is something we *have gotten beyond*. It wouldn't help to find much of use to us in Africa, because that would contradict our understanding of progress.

The same is true for the way we understand nature or daily life. Although we might believe abstractly in the balance of nature, or might desire that our lives resemble a *peaceable* kingdom where friendly lions and lambs coexist, we have been more likely to see our lives in dog-eat-dog terms that conform to the "law of the jungle." Africa as the prototypical jungle is useful as a myth to substantiate our view of daily life as a jungle that we escape when we go home at night.

Positive myths about Africa also serve Western self-definition. Those who are dissatisfied with modern American life might construct Africa to present viable alternatives. Some might search African customs for a more natural way to live. Some might look to Africa for a less racist culture. Some, specifically African Americans, might be looking for their idealized personal and cultural roots.

STEREOTYPES OVER TIME

As Europeans spread across the world from the 1400s onward, they had to make sense of the new peoples and places they encountered. Over time, and for reasons explained later in this book, Africans and Africa became representative of extreme "otherness." They were not the only representatives of difference, of course: there were also Aborigines, Native Americans, and so forth. But Africa certainly became a primary symbol that Europeans and white Americans used to express difference. Even black Americans found Africa's difference useful at times.

This is not all bad, because there is indeed a great deal of difference between African and Western cultures. Moreover, we know that humans tend to think symbolically, so it is natural that Africa

should stand for something, rather than nothing, in our minds. The real problem has been that using Africa as a *symbol* of difference has meant that the continent has been treated as an object. As an object, Africa is described and manipulated, but Africans, as objects, cannot speak for themselves or make comments on who *we* are.

Fortunately, with each passing decade, Americans have been treating Africans with less prejudice. Perhaps we are in the midst of a real withdrawal, however slow, from the myths of primitive Africa. Indeed, we cannot afford such myths. Africa, because of its sheer size, population, resources, and modernization, will play an increasingly important role in the world, whether for good or ill, and will have to be taken seriously. Our long-term interest in our shrinking world is to understand Africa with as little bias as possible.

The point is not that an accurate and whole picture of Africa has to be totally positive. Indeed, such a claim would be a continuation of our stereo typing. What we should strive for is a view of Africa as a continent full of real people, both like us and not like us. On the surface this seems easy: "It's a small world after all!" "Why can't we just get along?" "All we need is love!" "Just leave them alone." But these stereotypical, facile solutions don't automatically work in the real world. As you will see in the pages that follow, seeing others as fully human without desiring to change them into ourselves is exceedingly difficult. It may be, however, the only thing that will make our home—the planet—a safe place to live.

A WORD ABOUT WORDS

Before we go any further, a warning is in order. As I wrote this text, I realized that some of the words I use regularly are problematic. For example, the word *Africa* is used incorrectly throughout the book, because I mean "Africa south of the Sahara." This is a problem that might be helped by replacing all occurrences of *Africa* with *sub-Saharan Africa*. However, that would make reading difficult, and the change would not solve the problem entirely.

For example, not all sub-Saharan Africans are the subjects of the stereotypes discussed in this book, assuming we consider the millions of European Africans in South Africa, Zimbabwe, Kenya, and elsewhere to be Africans. Following the example of other scholars, I have opted to use the convenient expression *Africa* instead of a more accurate term. I assume that readers understand what is meant and will fill in missing qualifiers where needed.

Likewise, terms such as *Westerners* and *Americans*, and the pronouns *we* and *our*, are frequently distortions of the truth. There is, you will agree, no such thing as an average American, just as there is no such thing as an average African. As I wrote this book, I found myself generalizing and perhaps over-generalizing about Americans for the sake of calling attention to "our" stereo typing of Africans. We need to remember, however, that in every era there have been Americans who did not accept the general view and who spoke out on behalf of Africans.

One of the biggest difficulties with generalizing about American views of Africa concerns the inclusion of African American views. The problem is complex because American culture is complex. Until at least the 1960s, for example, it was quite common for African Americans to think of Africans as having primitive cultures. This should not be too surprising, considering the dominance of European culture and the fact that most information about Africa was filtered through European American eyes. Thus when I say that "we Americans" believed Africa to be primitive, it can be taken as somewhat accurate for black as well as white Americans.

On the other hand, African Americans since well before the American Revolution have resisted white efforts to define black reality and therefore they cannot be said to have invented the idea of African primitiveness, even if they believed in portions of it. They were victims in much the same way that Africans have been victims. Moreover, African Americans have largely rejected white American interpretations of race, and many have attempted to teach America about African achievements. Until the mid-twentieth century such teachers

were largely ignored, but their efforts make it more difficult to generalize about "Americans."

In this book, I have usually focused on white American myths about Africa—because they have been the most dominant, the most negative, and the most in need of change. Although I include a brief summary of African American perspectives in Chapter 5, I do not do the subject justice. Unfortunately, as far as I know, no studies since the mid-1970s have attempted to investigate the whole spectrum of contemporary African American attitudes toward Africa. Without such studies, preferably ones undertaken by African Americans, I would not want to write much more than I have already.

What seems most strikingly similar about white and black American perspectives on Africa is that all of us have generally "used Africa to think with." Whether Africa has been constructed in a negative or positive manner, we have used the continent to reflect upon who *we* are in relation to each other and in relation to Africa. Much of this thinking, negative and positive, has stereotyped Africa in ways explained in this book.

PRELUDE: AFRICA AND THE HISTORIANS

By Elizabeth Isichei

After a while the truth of the old tales changed. What was true before, became false afterwards.

A Kuba elder

WRITTEN SOURCES

All history is ideological, because all history reflects the concerns of the individuals and societies which produce it. What is remembered, and, where possible, recorded is what is felt to be of enduring importance. Because of this, we continue rewriting history—not because new facts come to light (though they often do) but because we have learned to understand them in new ways.

A general work of synthesis is the visible apex of a pyramid, based sometimes on original research, but more often on specialised studies written by others. These rest in their turn on many different kinds of evidence. 'African history' is a shorthand for many very different specialisations. The historian of medieval Ethiopia works from manuscripts in Ge'ez—which few non-Ethiopians read—and only Egyptologists (who do not consider themselves historians of Africa) can understand the original records of ancient Egypt. The historian of Benin (the Edo kingdom, not the modern nation) studied records in Portuguese, Italian, French and Dutch, as well as English. There is a vast body of material on the African past in Arabic, much of it written by Africans, and also a corpus of work in African languages, such as Fulfulde, Hausa and Swahili, transcribed in Arabic script. A history written in Arabic by a scholar of Timbuktu in *c.* 1665 is called *Kitab al Fettash, The Book of the Seeker.* It would in many ways be appropriate for the present volume.

Language skills are only part of the expertise required of the historian of Africa; some studies have led their authors into subjects as arcane as the properties of copper oxides and sulphates, or the different 'races' of sorghum. Historians of Africa are perhaps unique in their readiness to absorb the findings of other disciplines—archaeology, linguistics, human palaeontology, botany, animal genetics, and geology—the list is far from complete.

In European sources, we perceive the African past through a glass, darkly. Its authors rarely spoke the languages of the peoples they described (this is also true of many modern academics) and they have always, inevitably, seen Africa through the 'I-glasses' of their own cultures. A nineteenth-century English visitor ketched the bronze pectoral mask which forms part of the regalia of the king of Igala, in central Nigeria. He called it 'not unlike "the man in the moon"' and drew it accordingly. Because this sculpture still survives, we know his drawing is a travesty. But what if the original did not survive? Some of the source material in European languages was written by Africans; much of this, but not all, dates from the nineteenth and twentieth centuries. The autobiography of the Igbo, Olaudah Equiano (1745–97), is a justly celebrated example. He fell victim to the Atlantic slave trade as a child, but won his freedom and settled in England. Narratives from within, of course, are not immune from their own distortions. His account contains a number of literary echoes; his childhood home cannot be identified and its inconsistencies suggest it is a palimpsest of his own memories and those of other Igbo victims of the slave trade.

ORAL LITERATURE

There is a sense in which African studies are somewhat marginal, in universities outside Africa. And yet it has been claimed that African historians have been at the cutting edge of research methodology; those who suggest this are thinking, above all, of oral history. The collection and analysis of oral literature—not only material of an overtly historical character—is of crucial importance in the study of the African past. Many African societies kept no written records, and because the spoken word is more difficult to preserve than the written one, oral traditions are rigorously selected. What is omitted is as revealing as what is preserved, and traditions sometimes speak most eloquently through their silences.

Certain patterns tend to recur. Traditions of origin are preserved as the founding charter of a state's identity. They are often symbolically rather than literally true; their interpretation tends to be obscure and disputed. The Mbundu of Angola have at least three different traditions of origin, and the Kuba of Zaire have no less than seven alternative creation myths. The question we must ask is not 'Which is true?' but 'What kind of truth do these embody?'

In kingdoms, traditions often have a court bias, the justification of a dynasty's right to rule. This often means that facts which run counter to this claim are elided or reinterpreted—a successful usurper becomes a younger son. Whole historical epochs were personalised, and their innovations attributed to a culture hero who is often a king. Shyaam, magician and first king, is such a figure among the Kuba. In the colonial period, traditions were often changed or even invented, to support one or the other claimant to political office, and the process continues. The spread of western education has led to the publication of oral histories, a task pioneered by western-educated Africans in the nineteenth and early twentieth centuries. This has preserved information which might otherwise have been lost, but books of this kind—Johnson's history of the (Oyo) Yoruba, Egharevba on Benin—tend to become an Authorised Version, making the collection of alternative traditions impossible. For, in only too common a paradox, informants trust the printed word rather than the continuation of that oral tradition on which the book was based in the first place.

Historians have tended to concentrate on centralised kingdoms rather than on peoples who lived in small autonomous villages. There are obvious practical reasons for this—it is much easier to write a history of a unified state than of, for instance, the 2,240 village groups of the eastern Igbo! But sometimes they have implied that centralised kingdoms were in some way more advanced than miniature polities—though those who think so would not consider Zaire more developed than Monaco. Historical research tends to focus on large states and major ethnic groups, and the study of small peoples, such as the Yako or Rukuba, is generally left to the anthropologist.

The *History of West Africa to 1800*, edited by Ajayi and Crowder, is a justly celebrated work which has been through three editions, in each of which chapters felt to be out of date have been replaced. But the chapter on 'stateless societies', written by an anthropologist, continues to appear in it—and to be very widely cited—though the approach is ethnographic rather than historic, and it concludes with a discussion of the growth of states. Great States re-emerge, even in a chapter devoted supposedly to the so-called 'stateless' polities. And sadly, papers which set out to make a case for the study of small-scale states sometimes ignore the growing corpus of work in this field, in a most determined fashion. Oral history has often been unconsciously elitist, because it has been collected from professionals, such as griots, who looked to a court patron. A recent valuable paper pointed out that a kingdom consisted of a number of social groups, each with its own oral history. The kingdom of Jaara, in modern Mali, was overthrown by al-Hajj Umar in 1862. Almost half the people in the region where it was located are of slave descent, and women of slave ancestry are the custodians of their oral tradition. It is a profound irony that those who were abruptly cut off from their history by enslavement join the custodians of the history of the captor society. There is a further paradox: the African scholar who drew attention to these traditions does not, as a male, have access to them.

Oral tradition proper refers to testimonies which have been passed down, as distinct from reminiscence. But the latter is a precious source for the history of our own times, recording voices which are otherwise silenced.

Historians who collect oral traditions must also do archival research, but the reverse is not always true. Archival research and fieldwork require different skills and, to some extent, different temperaments. Archival research is solitary; some of its most gifted practitioners feel ill at ease with the constant encounters with strangers which oral history requires. Whatever the reason, an otherwise excellent book such as Freund's *Capital and Labour in the Nigerian Tin Mines* (1981) is marred by his inexplicable failure to interview living tin miners. Some historians obtain a comparable insight into individual experience by studying sources such as the popular press—but only a tiny minority of the African population was literate. Popular songs, folk tales and proverbs speak from the heart; they are a valuable source for cognitive history—the problem is that they are often undatable.

African historians collecting oral history among their own people have great advantages in fieldwork, especially in their command of the appropriate language. They may well not have the language skills or opportunity for research in widely scattered European archives. For most European historians, a facility in different European languages is more readily acquired than competence in a tonal and perhaps little-studied African language. This became evident to me in my years in Africa, in the course of innumerable encounters with historians from abroad grappling with what was then the obligatory *rite de passage* of fieldwork. In the case of some historians, this was a brief sojourn in the field, using interpreters, providing what was essentially a cosmetic veneer for a history in fact based on archival materials. I made attempts to bridge this gap, first in *Igbo Worlds*, an anthology of both oral and archival sources, and later in the series Jos Oral History and Literature Texts.

Some excellent works published in recent years have been based on archival sources alone. The author of one of them suggests an informal division of labour; European historians concentrating on the archives and African historians on fieldwork. Scholars are coming to realise that the polarity between written and oral sources is itself an artificial one. The European authors of published and unpublished accounts of African history or ethnography relied on local informants, whose words are the submerged subtexts of their narratives.

HISTORY AND ANTHROPOLOGY

Both oral historians and anthropologists do fieldwork in Africa, and the relationship between the two is a complex and changing one. In the past, historians were often critical of anthropological writing which was frequently—but not invariably—located in a timeless and imaginary ethnographic present. But anthropologists came much closer than historians to an understanding of African societies in their total complexity, studying variables such as kinship, ritual and culture. The divorce between the two was due less perhaps to doctrinaire considerations than to the impossibility of doing justice simultaneously to both structure and process.

Meanwhile, anthropologists have become increasingly sensitive to the variable of historical change. Some of the finest studies of the African past are the work of anthropologists—Peel's history of Ilesa, Horton's accounts of cognitive change among the Kalabari, Janzen's study of Lemba. Historical writing has become richer and more densely textured, concerned with ecological factors including climate, famine and disease, religion and kinship.

Anthropological analysis has undergone an intensive rethinking from within; much of this has been the work of African specialists, such as Fabian. Hard questions have been asked about fieldwork and it is realised that much anthropological enquiry has been formulaic—a classic instance of an invention of Africa. Vansina points out, with characteristic insight, the remarkable degree of similarity in the vast corpus of published and unpublished ethnographic writing on the Zaire basin. This undoubtedly reflects stereo typing in the questions asked.

FUNCTIONALISTS AND STRUCTURALISTS

Different schools of anthropology have mounted significant challenges to the methodology of the oral historian. The first form this took was functionalist—oral traditions were interpreted as a 'mythical charter' for present social realities. They often undoubtedly do work in this way, but this does not, in itself, invalidate them as a record of past events. Claude Lévi-Strauss is the founding father of structuralist anthropology, a school which was, for a time, immensely influential. He interpreted oral traditions not as more or less accurate mirrors of past events but as statements which embody a different kind of symbolic truth. The mind, he believes, tends universally to perceive reality in terms of paired opposites—such as Nature and Culture (symbolically expressed as the Raw and the Cooked, the title of one of his most famous books), or Life and Death. Legends which apparently tell of the foundation of states, for instance, are really essays in cosmic speculation, and belong rather to the history of ideas (which is not in itself to diminish them—rather the reverse).

Lévi-Strauss worked on Native American mythologies; his ideas were applied to central Africa in an enormously influential study by the Belgian anthropologist Luc de Heusch (see p. 112 below).

Some historians of Africa, notably Christopher Wrigley, absorbed the structuralist viewpoint to a degree which cast doubt on the literal veracity of virtually all historical traditions. J. B. Webster and his collaborators were at the other end of the ideological spectrum, extrapolating the reigns of precisely dated kings far into the past, in a way most of their colleagues found unconvincing.

Some historians are moving towards a more sophisticated synthesis in response to structuralism, where traditions are seen as neither entirely symbolic nor wholly true, but rather as a composite of myth and real event. To disentangle the two is a task requiring great skill and subtlety. It was once assumed that oral traditions comprise a core of truth and a penumbra of myth. But it has been suggested that the core is a cliché, and the accretions mirror real events. But of course the symbols and clichés are also 'real', mirroring landscapes of the mind. Historians' increasing agnosticism about the literal truth of the traditions they collect is mirrored in a recent dictum by the scholar who pioneered the critical use of oral testimonies: 'For the most part [traditions of origin] represent cosmological speculation.' These clichés, or recurrent core symbols, pose many problems of interpretation. Sometimes they are clearly part of a single far-flung complex: the myth of the immigrant hunter-king found throughout Africa's southern savannas is an example. But essentially the same myth is found far away, among various peoples in Nigeria. Woot, the Kuba culture hero, is a Drunken King, insulted by his sons, defended by his daughter. His wife discovers salt when she is a fugitive. Does this story embody echoes of missionary stories which gradually penetrated the Zaire basin from the Atlantic coast or are such stories the great archetypes of the mind which Jungian analysis attributes to the collective unconscious?

Historians are increasingly conscious of the way in which oral traditions are shaped both by the way in which human memory operates and by the fact that they are always related for an audience. The tendency for the concrete rather than the abstract to be remembered contributes to the crystallising of events and processes as clichés. Feedback from an audience helps make the testimony a collective product.

The basic tool of historical research is the quest for independent confirmation from different sources. This is a complex task, for sources are often not truly independent. The king lists of Bunyoro and Buganda, in Uganda, largely confirm each other; a chronology based on them, and other evidence, was hailed as a triumphant step towards locating the African past in a firm temporal context. Later critiques showed first that the Bunyoro list was not truly independent, but was consciously constructed to fit the Buganda data—which itself has come under increasingly critical scrutiny. More profoundly, it has been suggested that the very making of lists is the product of a literate culture. The distortion in the Buganda and Bunyoro king lists seems to be that of lengthening. But the limitations of human memory more commonly result in the telescoping of history. The process of settling in an area and the formation of large political units are entirely distinct phenomena, and the former is undoubtedly in most cases far more ancient. But even remembering this caveat, it is clear that the available evidence leads us to place the origins of many states far too late, and events which really belong to the Early Iron Age are transposed to the fifteenth or sixteenth centuries or even later. This is true of the interlacustrine kingdoms, and of much of Central Africa. It is also demonstrably true of some West African polities. All available evidence suggests that the Igbo have lived in much their present homes since the dawn of human history. But a dense network of mutually consistent family genealogies places the formation of many settlements in the sixteenth or seventeenth centuries.

Where written sources extend far into the past, they provide a precious resource against which oral testimonies can be checked. Where they are lacking, until the nineteenth or even twentieth century, historians tend to rely on linguistic and ethnographic data, as well as a sensitive awareness of the dynamics of the traditions themselves. Where written evidence exists, it sometimes suggests that oral testimonies have a truly astonishing reliability.

It has been suggested that both oral histories and traditional written chronicles focus on political events to the neglect of socio-economic change. Vansina says of the Kuba, in words which are applicable to many other societies as well, 'For the most part, political events dealing with succession, war, law, administration, and the royal personality were remembered.' Yet they do, in fact, preserve much socio-economic data, and these data are particularly valuable because they are not the primary focus. At the present time, the interpretation of oral tradition is at least as individualistic as art criticism. A highly regarded and sophisticated study of the Mbundu of Angola and their neighbours suggests that the people mentioned in historical traditions represent titles in the possession of particular lineages. There is evidence to support it, but it cannot be conclusively proved, and the postulate is the basis on which the whole book rests.

The scholarly community tends to see the oral traditions of any given people through the eyes of its specialists—literally for much of Nigeria (but not Igala), symbolically in Central Africa.

Despite these caveats, oral history is often both remarkably accurate and strikingly truthful. Buganda, at the apogee of its power and influence, preserved traditions, both of its humble origins and of defeats at the hands of Bunyoro.

AFRICA'S HISTORIANS

We have seen how both the written and oral sources for African history are shaped by the conscious or unconscious aims of their authors. This is, of course, equally true of modern historians. Nothing shows the way in which historical and ethnographic literature is shaped by one's preconceptions more clearly than the history and ethnography produced during the colonial period. Its authors were naturally preconditioned to be aware of the creative role of white invaders from the north. It was initially assumed that the stone structures of ruined Great Zimbabwe were the work of Phoenicians or built for the Queen of Sheba. Cecil Rhodes welcomed the theory of its exotic origins as it offered a positive precedent for intruders from afar. Frobenius saw the corpus of Ife sculpture, the relics of its glass industry, as proof that it was the site of an ancient colony of Etruscans, the reality underlying Atlantis. Colonial ethnographers saw traces of Egyptian influence everywhere, bolstering their theories with amateur etymology. The belief that sacred kingship and iron smelting diffused into black Africa from Egypt and Meroe respectively was to have a long history, surviving well into the period of modern scholarship. There were other versions of the so-called Hamitic hypothesis, which attributed the foundation of states in the Western Sudan to a Berber or Arab *héros civilisateur*. Sadly, some African writers welcomed such theories—sadly, because they had internalised the assumption that Egyptian civilisation was superior to that of black Africa. European writers tended to glorify the achievement of ancient Egypt, while they marginalised not only black Africa but also the Maghrib, which a French author called 'one of those rare Mediterranean countries which made no original contribution to civilisation'.

We should not, of course, dismiss the work of colonial ethnographers. The writings of colonial officials such as R. S. Rattray or C. K. Meek contain much of enduring value, and it is a sign of a maturing discipline that historians of Africa are increasingly willing to acknowledge this. A natural reaction against the Hamitic hypothesis led a generation of scholars to emphasise the indigenous roots of everything. Now they are more open to an understanding of black Africa's many linkages with the ecumene. Jan Vansina says—in this case, probably wrongly—of a distinctive theme in Nupe, Benin and Yoruba art, 'The whole motif derives from the Hellenistic Mediterranean.'

It is no coincidence that the study of African history took shape as a serious field of academic endeavour at the time when many African states gained their independence. Both African and expatriate historians shared in the hopes those years engendered. Those historians who chose African history as a research field did so out of a generous sympathy for African aspirations.

The dominant impulse in the 1960s—which I shared—was to prove that black Africa had a history at all, a history as worthy of study as any other. This was a salutary reaction to a historiography which saw Africans as the passive backdrop to the deeds of white proconsuls and missionaries. Not only the ignorant believed that black Africa had no history worthy of study: it was an Oxford historian justly famed for his scholarship who described the discipline as the study of the unrewarding gyrations of barbarous tribes, thus drawing on his head the obloquy of a generation of Africanists. Max Weber, one of the founding fathers of sociology, had made much the same point earlier; he was 'indignant that the history of the Bantus could be studied as much as that of the Greeks'. The great art critic Roger Fry, admiring African sculpture, reflected: 'It is curious that a people who produced such great artists did not produce also a culture in our sense of the word.'

Historians of Africa were critical of colonialism, stressing the violence with which it was imposed, its often unconscious racism, its *immobilisme*. They laid great stress on resistance to its imposition, which was seen, both by scholars and by African politicians, as a prelude to the triumphs of political nationalism. The first generation of politicians in independent Tanzania were the conscious heirs of Maji Maji, the great anti-German uprising in the early years of this century. Historians focussed primarily on political and economic history, studying great states partly to show that Africans were capable of creating and maintaining them. They wrote about long-distance trade, successful entrepreneurs, the rationality of African economic choices, in a conscious corrective to stereotypes of African inertia and backwardness. For similar reasons, they devoted considerable attention to indigenous forms of literacy.

By the late 1970s, something of a crisis had developed in African historical writing. The optimism which had heralded African independence became increasingly difficult to sustain. Civil wars, military coups, a cycle of impoverishment and indebtedness and recurrent famines, had a traumatic impact on a discipline which had been shaped by the exigencies of the present. Many historians—myself among them—interpreted these various afflictions as the (presumably temporary) consequences of particular historical circumstances. Thus political instability could be explained in terms of colonialism's divisive and artificial boundaries, and ethnic conflicts through its invention of ethnicity (pp. 97, 106, 123 below).

The historiography of the 1960s and early 1970s had undoubted weaknesses, including a reluctance to confront the deficiencies of African societies, past and present. However well-intentioned, this produced many imbalances of historical judgement. We have noted one example—the tendency to regard state formation, whatever the cost, as a Good Thing. Nowhere was this more glaring than in studies of the transatlantic slave trade, where the desire to depict the African as *homo economicus* rather than as victim or comprador led to an undoubted tendency to minimise its evils, and stress its positive by-products. Shaka and the marauding captains of the Mfecane were depicted as creative state founders, with minimal emphasis on the enormous misery and loss of life for which they were responsible. There was a tendency to ignore the exploitative aspects of pre-colonial states, and to idealise the traditional rulers who led resistance to colonialism, assuming that their interests were identical to those of the ruled. There was a marked tendency to eulogise African entrepreneurs of all varieties; gradually, the shortcomings of at least some of them became evident, and 'kleptocracy' became part of the vocabulary of academic discourse.

Reductionism was a weakness as fundamental as elitism. The initial focus of Africanist history was political; within this, it tended towards the analysis of Great States, and, in the words of a seventeenth-century visitor to West Africa, to the study of 'Kings, rich men, and prime merchants, exclusive of the inferior sort of *Blacks*'. Peoples organised in small-scale states tended to be overlooked; here my own work, first on the Igbo and later on the Jos plateau, was a corrective.

The Africanists of the 1960s and 1970s were attempting to demolish the mistaken stereotypes on which racism rests. They were also, in a sense, engaged in a conversation which may have been the wrong one to choose. In a partly unconscious endeavour to prove to critics like Trevor-Roper that Africa indeed had a history, they cast their own work in a quasi-European framework. Wilks' vast study of nineteenth-century Asante is a classic example. He was reacting against stereotypes, in early European accounts, which depicted Asante as bloodthirsty and barbaric. He constantly uses words such as bureaucratisation, and the less acceptable face of Asante life—human sacrifice—is interpreted as judicial execution. The work is meticulously documented and researched; it has been criticised on the grounds that by assimilating Asante life to western models, it diminishes and impoverishes it. Looking back on my own 'Africanist' years, I can see that I too was involved in a perpetual dialogue, both with the biases implicit in my sources and with the assumptions of other historians of Africa, who tended to define the African past in terms of Great States. I began *The Ibo People and the Europeans* with a quotation from Margery Perham: 'the groups of the south-east have no history before the coming of the Europeans'. I felt that I needed to prove that the study of Igbo history itself was a valid enterprise. It seems to me now that this essentially defensive attitude was unnecessarily restricting.

The largest single cluster of African historians in the 1960s and 1970s was associated in various ways with the University of Ibadan. All were agreed in denouncing the shortcomings of missionaries and colonial governments. But there were considerable areas of ambiguity. Ajaye and Ayandele wrote books covering a quite similar area, concentrating on Nigeria's early educated Christians, the predecessors and in many cases the ancestors of the nation's later elite. But in a later study, Ayandele denounced them furiously; significantly, it was not for any shortcomings in their social vision, but for their cultural ambiguity, their distance from their African roots. Traditional rulers were sometimes idealised for their opposition to colonialism, sometimes, in a proliferation of studies of Indirect Rule, critiqued for their opposition to the modernisers. To a striking extent, the Ibadan school focussed either on resistance to colonial conquest or on aspects of government; many Nigerian historians came to take an active role in government, often as state commissioners in military regimes. Surprisingly little attention was paid to social history.

THE MARXIST PERSPECTIVE

The most sustained and trenchant attack on 'Africanist' historiography came from Marxists (who often called themselves neo-Marxist, materialist or radical). At their most doctrinaire, they compressed all other historical writing about Africa into a single school, variously termed liberal, bourgeois, nationalist, historicist or Africanist. How sad and inexplicable it would once have seemed that 'Africanist' should become a term of condemnation, or empiricism be rejected as 'nihilism'.

'Liberal' historians of Africa (to use the least pejorative term) do not form and have never formed a single united school. They have often been, very properly, enthusiastically at variance with each other. We have noted Wrigley's critique of Fage; one might equally well note a myriad other controversies, including a famous exchange about the so-called Dar es Salaam school.

Materialist historians, of course, do not form a united school either and beyond the core of those who consider themselves Marxists or neo-Marxists there is a large circle of scholarship, bearing the clear imprint of Marxist insights—as, indeed, the present work does. Iliffe's study, *The Emergence of African Capitalism*, takes Marx as its starting point. Marxist writing on Africa has sometimes been barren and doctrinaire; there was once a sterile quest to accommodate African history to the writings of the Master, whose reflections were based on the experiences of industrial Europe. This led to unpromising lines of enquiry: in the 1960s there was much unprofitable debate concerning whether the African experience was an example of Marx's Asiatic mode of production. In 1972, the French Marxist Coquery-Vidrovich made an interesting attempt to define an African mode of production in terms of the way in which rulers reaped a profit from long-distance trade. This was widely criticised, not least because it emphasised exchange rather than production. The rejection of experience in favour of dogma, somewhat in the style of a medieval theologian, is not entirely dead. In words which became, perhaps, for the historians of the 1980s what Trevor-Roper's sentiments on barbarian tribes were for their predecessors, two Marxists wrote: 'We reject the notion of history as a coherent and worthwhile object for study.' This approach, especially associated with the French Marxist Althusser, provoked in one of Britain's most celebrated Marxist historians a furiously indignant polemic. The forms which the rejection of experience can take are many and strange. A writer on the medical history of Tanzania is an example. 'In a Marxist construction of social reality ... only human agency is causal ... If only human action has causal efficacy, then germs cannot be said to cause disease.'

And yet Marxist insights have inspired some of the most perceptive writing on the African past. A group of French Marxist anthropologists working in West Africa, and especially Claude Meillassoux, have had a great impact on African historical writing. Meillassoux made a plea for a more complex and nuanced study of modes of production, reacting against the (western) stereotypes of classical economics. He focusses on what has been called the politics of reproduction, and in particular on the conflict between village elders and youths over the control of resources in general and wives in particular. Marxist and feminist analysis has shed much light on the division of labour by gender, and created a new awareness of women's role in production. Some have criticised Meillassoux on the grounds that the polarities he describes are not peculiar to Africa. This does not in itself invalidate his insights. Inevitably, he stresses structure rather than process; in a sense he extrapolates the experience of a few West African societies into a generally applicable model. But he has had a transforming effect on historical writing—nowhere more than in South Africa, where, because of both its industrialisation and its class structure, Marxist concepts are most readily applied.

Marxist history has led to a more holistic approach to the African past, a greater awareness of material culture. It is a great strength of 'mode of production' theory that it concentrates attention both on the actual process of wealth creation and on its distribution in society. It is a weakness that the application of the theory over vast areas may lead us to underestimate their differences, the particularities of local historical experience. Different scholars define and locate modes of production somewhat differently. A widely accepted sequence runs as follows: lineage mode of production, tributary mode of production, slave mode of production, merchant and then industrial capitalism. It tends to impose a false sense of a linear and inevitable development.

It is by no means always self-evident who is, and who is not, a Marxist—and it should be noted that *marxisant* is not a term of approval. (I was startled but not displeased, years ago, when a reviewer called me a disciple of Frantz Fanon, something of which I was hitherto unaware!) Wilks described his history of Asante as Marxist. Terray, whose Marxist credentials are indisputable, endorses Wilks' Marxist approach, but a critic pointed out that Marxism first appears on page 700! Even Coquery-Vidrovitch, a central figure in French Marxist writing on Africa, refers to her own intellectual preferences as 'supposedly Marxist'. Klein says of himself, in words many historians of Africa would echo: 'my Marxism is rather diluted. I have difficulty accepting the labour theory of value and find it impossible to reduce all history to class struggle. Nevertheless, I find that the concept of a mode of production is a very powerful tool for historical analysis.'

Another historian endearingly compared his own studies of French Marxist literature with the adventures of Winnie the Pooh in pursuit of a Woozle!

A mode of production has two parts: the *forces* of production (ecology, labour, technology, raw materials) and the *relations* of production (the extraction and distribution of a surplus). Clarence-Smith suggests some detailed questions:

> Who controlled (not owned) the means of production and how? If ... a restricted group, what right of access did the majority of the population have, and in return for what kinds of payment? Was the extracted surplus redistributed, or was it wholly, or partially retained by the restricted group? If it was retained, how was it realised, in economic investment, leisure activities, conspicuous consumption, or the maintenance of repressive political and ideological apparatuses? ... Did the dominant group interfere directly in the process of production?

An awareness of the changing relations of production informs some of the best writing on archaeology. It shapes some outstanding historical monographs: Kea's densely textured work on the seventeenth-century Gold Coast is enormously richer than its 'Trade and Politics' predecessors. The difficulty is that the study of a large number of variables tends to obscure the chronology of events. It is a central problem in multidimensional history. And the model, while shedding light on reality, should not be confused with reality itself. 'Modes of production do not exist.'

Some exponents of Marxism have written as if the world of culture and ideas was simply the reflection of the material base. There are, of course, passages in Marx which say just this: 'The mode of production of material life conditions the social, political and intellectual life process in general. It is not the consciousness of men that determines their being, but, on the contrary, their social being that determines their consciousness.' Marx, however, did say that he was not a Marxist! One of the most important differences between palaeo- and neo-

Marxists is the latter's increasingly sophisticated awareness of the autonomy of cognitive history.

DEPENDENCY THEORY

There is a fundamental division in radical thought about the merits of dependency theory. It draws its inspiration from the writings of Andre Gunder Frank, who was concerned with 'the development of underdevelopment' in Latin America. Frank regarded the impoverishment of the Third World as an ongoing process, the result of the exploitation of the metropolitan countries. The late Walter Rodney and Samir Amin were influential proponents of this viewpoint in the African context. The title of the former's most widely read book, *How Europe Underdeveloped Africa*, still worth reading for all its polemicism and oversimplifications, encapsulates the theory.

Orthodox Marxists are critical of dependency theory on several grounds: that it emphasises trade rather than production, and that it negates Marx's emphasis on the positive aspects of capitalism. They also point out that it tends to replace class with regional conflict.

I was greatly influenced by dependency theory when I worked on the impact of the Atlantic slave trade on the Igbo, since it seemed to cast much light on this encounter. Dependency theory critiques the comprador, the local collaborator who makes external exploitation possible, whether the king who sells slaves, or the modern politician or military ruler who enriches himself by collaboration with the big multinationals. But dependency theory has its limitations. It reduces Africans to the helpless victims of international market forces and sheds no light on the long periods of time when external exploitation was unimportant. International capitalism had no impact at all on the Anaguta of Jos plateau in central Nigeria until the early twentieth century. As late as the 1950s, its impact was insignificant, in part through the conscious choices of the Anaguta themselves. Dependency theory ignores the enormous differences between the different peoples who experienced the impact of international economic forces and responded to them in one of a wide variety of ways. It is profoundly pessimistic about their capacity to transform their own lives. Perhaps, in its own way, it is just as Eurocentric as the Hamitic hypothesis.

The basic inspiration of both Marxists and dependency theorists is concern for the poor. But this has, increasingly, become a central preoccupation of African historical writing in general. It derives, in part, from a tradition of 'history from below' in English scholarship. Often specific insights from historical research elsewhere have fed into African studies; Hobsbawm wrote a famous book on bandits, and in due course, a collection of essays on banditry in Africa appeared. Possibly bandits have replaced Improvers as the historian's romantic heroes. But many historians of Africa who do not consider themselves particularly radical are concerned with the poor and obscure. That monument of scholarship and humanity, Iliffe's *The African Poor: A History*, is a particularly distinguished example of History from Below.

The least satisfactory aspect of some—not all—radical writing was its intolerance of alternative views, its tendency to regard all non-Marxist writing as a 'school' to be condemned. I pointed out long ago that a belief in the verbal inspiration of sacred texts, intolerance of alternative views and conviction of one's own infallibility have long since been unacceptable in theology. Should it be otherwise in African history? But having said this, it is important to acknowledge that some of the most original writing in African history is the result of materialist insights, and its influence is writ large on the pages which follow.

All research is in some sense ideological; facts neither select nor explain themselves. What is important, is that theory should illumine historical research, and never replace it.

Goethe said, 'Grey is every theory, and green and gold is the tree of life.'

ALTERNATIVE MODELS: BRAUDEL AND *LA LONGUE DURÉE*

Fernand Braudel, who died in 1985, was one of Europe's most celebrated historians. His masterpiece was his two-volume study of the Mediterranean in the age of Philip II, a work of great erudition, full of finely observed social detail—the walnut trees which shade villages in the High Atlas, fuel shortages in Cairo. It was immensely influential, not least as an example of history in the round.

Braudel was impatient with sociologists, feeling that they paid too little attention to social change. But he was also critical of 'the history of events: surface disturbances, crests of foam … surface manifestations of these large movements and explicable only in terms of them'. He stressed the importance of social processes occurring over centuries—*la longue durée*. The expression threads its way through his writings, and is echoed in much historical literature which appears to owe little else to his work. It has become part of the baggage of historical writing. There has been a reaction; some notable modern scholars have written in defence of narrative history. Dates and 'events' are necessary points of reference in an otherwise unnavigable sea—and it is notable that part of Braudel's great work was in fact concerned with 'events'.

Braudel paid much attention to the physical environment; scholarship has moved beyond his rather simplistic and static geographical determinism. His book is full of pictures of Mediterranean ships but he does not reflect on the consequences of the timber cut to build them.

Braudel's impact on African studies has been limited. This is partly because he began his research in 1923, and published the first edition of *The Mediterranean* in 1946, relying, therefore, for his North African material on French ethnographers writing in the inter-war period whose work has long since been overtaken by more recent scholarship. Not surprisingly, his influence has been greatest on those working in related fields, that is, on historians of the Maghrib.

LANDSCAPES

In *The Ibo People and the Europeans*, published over twenty years ago, I wrote of 'a people in a landscape', a theme to which I reverted in my *History of Nigeria*. This emphasis grew, not from Braudel, whom I had not at the time read, but from the experience of living successively in very different African environments. The importance of ecology is one of the key insights of contemporary writing on Africa. Book titles and subtitles reflect this—*The Ecology of Survival* or *The Historical Anthropology of an African Landscape*. It grows out of the too evident impact of a deteriorating environment on contemporary human lives. A treatise al-Maghili wrote in the late fifteenth century for the benefit of a king of Kano has a curiously contemporary resonance: 'Cherish the land from the spoiling drought, from the raging wind, the dust-laden storm … and the beating rain.'

Sometimes a failure to locate historical writing firmly in a changing landscape reflects an inadequate familiarity with it; southern Nigeria is often described in books and atlases as located in a belt of 'rainforest'; there is indeed a substantial area of which this is true—the Benin forest—but most of southern Nigeria has been transformed for many generations by human industry. It was said of Yorubaland, in 1891: 'Far and wide, the land has for generations, and indeed for centuries, been cultivated by these industrious natives. The hatchet, the fire and the hoe have removed all traces of the original forest.'

Famine and disease, for obvious reasons, loom large in modern historical writing. Ford's pioneering study of the impact of the tsetse fly, published in 1971, was a precursor.

ALTERNATIVE MODELS: THE FRONTIER

Interesting attempts have been made to adapt Jackson's concept of the frontier, which has been so seminal in American historical writing. In an African context, this becomes less a tide sweeping across a continent than an infinite series of internal frontiers, a recurrent pattern of pioneer settlers who then become 'owners of the land' in relation to later immigrants. Often this movement is essentially conservative—the migrants endeavour to recreate the social structures of the society they have left, but with a more favourable position within it. Like the white settlers of America, the frontierspeople very often moved into areas which were already inhabited.

One strength of this approach is that it moves beyond the invention of watertight and monolithic 'tribes' and finds room for the—often multilingual—people of the borderlands. An alternative, independent form of the model focusses on the Islamic frontier.

THE PROBLEM OF GENDER

Half Africa's people are women. They are responsible for virtually all food preparation and child rearing, and often play a dominant role in agriculture. Crafts are gender-specific, and in many areas women control trade (specific commodities are often sold only by men or only by women). But in much historical writing women are invisible, except for the rare, and sometimes legendary, queen. This is equally true of some of my own earlier work. I felt alienated from the feminist writing of the 1960s and early 1970s because of its white middle-class character–limitations which mainstream western feminism has long since recognised and reacted against. I felt that it was self-indulgent to agitate about matters such as inclusive language in liturgy when millions were threatened by famine. Partly because of the admiration I felt for the vitality and achievements of the Nigerian professional and market women with whom I was in daily contact, I did not sufficiently recognise the way in which colonialism eroded the position of women, or the fact that they are often the poorest of the poor. Women's invisibility in academic writing in the colonial period and later did much to cause their neglect in many development projects, which too often left women both poorer and more burdened than before. This distortion was recognised and in part corrected, largely through the writings of feminist scholars.

Feminist, like radical, scholarship has fed important insights into African studies as a whole, inspiring, for instance, some notable studies of the history of the family. But studies of women and the family have often been compartmentalised—books and papers are either totally concerned with women, or not at all.

There is an increasing awareness of gender in work which is not specifically feminist. The anthropologist van Binsbergen studied the Nkoya, a Zambia people also known as the Mbelwa, and while doing so translated a traditional history by a local pastor, assuming that rulers whose gender was unstated were male. It wss only when he was asked to contribute to a conference on the Position of Women in the Early State that he read the text with new eyes, and came to understand it as describing a transition, from 'a peaceful stateless situation when … women were politically and ritually dominant to male-headed systems in which violence predominated'.

Conventional histories concentrate on political and economic change, and many fine studies focus exclusively on men in positions of authority, the Captains and the Kings. The balance is not to be redressed by concentrating on the rare historical instances of women in authority, such as Nzinga (p. 399 below), but by directing our attention, as Marxist historians urge us to, to the forces of production.

Cultural expression tends to be gender-specific too: men are metal workers, wood carvers or masked dancers; women have their own outlets which vary from culture to culture but may include particular genres of oral art (like the grinding songs of northern Nigeria) or textile design or body painting. These have often been little studied; if they change at all, the process is difficult to document. Much of their communication is non-verbal. Can these unheard voices and unseen symbols find a place in a general study? I grapple with this problem in the pages which follow.

WHOSE DISCOURSE?

African history has been written either by westerners, or by Africans trained in western traditions. It has been suggested that 'the study of Africa, more than of any other continent, has been dominated by aliens and their theories'. A recent pamphlet by a group of eight church leaders in South Africa, six of whom were women, and most of whom were illiterate, made the same point.

> Until now all the research and all the literature about the so-called 'African independent Churches' has been the work of outsiders. Anthropologists, sociologists and theologians from foreign Churches have been studying us for many years and they have published a whole library of books and articles about us. Each of them has had his or her own motives for studying us. Generally, their motives have been purely academic. We have become a fertile field for the kind of research that will enable a person to write an 'interesting' thesis and obtain an academic degree … It is therefore not surprising that we do not recognise ourselves in their writings. We find them seriously misleading and often far from the truth. They are full of misunderstandings, misconceptions and falsehood. In trying to understand us outsiders suffer serious handicaps. They have their own frame of reference, the assumptions of anthropology or sociology or a Western theology. We find ourselves judged in terms of these norms.

These words make sobering reading for a historian of Africa.

Scholars have become aware that all ethnographic description is, in a very real sense, an Invention of Africa. Some peoples—the British, French and Americans among them—conduct ethnographic studies, and others are perpetually studied. Those studied would not recognise themselves in the accounts which are written of them, to which they tend not to have access anyway. The problem is not solved by learning an African language, or entering with great empathy into the world of the Other. We are prisoners of the rationalism taken for granted in the western world. An example makes this clearer. In 1873–4, British forces defeated the Asante. The western historian will explain it in various ways: the disparity in armaments and resources, or various factors which weakened the Asante. Asante tradition has a different explanation: it was caused by the loss of the Asantehene's war charm in the Pra river.

The concept of academic history, its diverse subdivisions—political, economic, social, religious —grew up in the western world. Those who study the African past, myself included, are the prisoners of intellectual categories which did not develop in Africa. The alternative is not to invent a system of 'African thought' and work within its categories. Such endeavours have been made and found wanting. A facile solution is to place everything in inverted commas—'slaves', 'Nguni'—but this becomes little more than a stylistic affectation.

Anthropologists of Africa, rather than its historians, have been influenced by thinkers conveniently called postmodernists or poststructuralists. Some of the best known names are those of Foucault, Derrida, Ricoeur and Toulmain, and the semiotician (and novelist) Eco. They are, in many respects, at variance with each other, but they share certain basic assumptions. A key word in their writing is 'discourse', by which they mean the total system of language and meaning in a given society, which, unconsciously, shapes our thinking from the cradle to the grave. Foucault regarded it as an instrument of coercion, and in studies of the European past used the approach of the 'archaeologist' to resurrect forms of discourse which have been forgotten or marginalised. Foucault was oblivious to the Third World: his vision was not only Eurocentric but francophone, but his insights have been applied to other parts of the world in a number of thought provoking studies. Edward Said wrote of 'orientalism' as the creation of European thought. Its implications for anthropology were explored in a series of important books, where specialists in Africa made major contributions.

'The problem is perhaps most acute in the case of symbolism. A symbol, by its very nature, has many dimensions of meaning. What is the relationship between 'the symbolic universe the scholar analyses in an African people and their own perceptions? The late Victor Turner described the extremely rich symbolic universe he found among the Ndembu. If the Ndembu themselves did not—could not—analyse their own rituals in the same way, does this kind of description truly mirror their own cognitive world? In Mary Douglas' fine study, *Purity and Danger*, she states explicitly, with reference to her account of the Lele pangolin cult: 'The metaphysical implications have not been expressed to me in so many words by Lele … No one member of the society is necessarily aware of the whole pattern.' In other words, she discerns patterns in the Lele experience which are not apparent to the Lele themselves.

We have referred to the increasing readiness of materialist historians to accept the validity of African cognitive maps. An important collection of essays on South African history is subtitled 'African class formation, culture *and consciousness*'. A valuable study of a Zionist church in South Africa describes its thought, often expressed in non-verbal ways, as *appropriate* for its members' life situation.

Religion is often of great importance in African cognitive maps, past and present, though in the holistic universe of the 'traditional' way there was no word for religion, and no concept of it as a distinctive mode of being. 'If a people's behaviour is in part shaped by their own images and concepts, to the degree that these images and concepts are ignored and alien ones imposed or applied, that behaviour will be misunderstood and faultily explained.'

An influential book published in 1980 was called *The Invention of Culture*. It was echoed in the title of a study by a brilliant Zairois scholar, V. Mudimbe, *The Invention of Africa*. Historians and anthropologists have come to realise that we invent cultures, rather than describing them, that their books are 'true fictions'. The anthropologist's field notes describe one social fact but not another. She attends one ceremony but not another held at the same time—or, of course, those held before her arrival or after her departure.

Her informants have their own silences: some are intended, and some reflect the fact that people describe what they think of, what seems important at a particular time. The historian does the same: she takes notes on a tiny fraction of what she reads, selecting those passages which seem significant at that particular time. Studies have been made of the silences in famous texts: the invisibility of Nuer and Dinka women in Evans-Pritchard's writing on the Nuer, Lienhardt's *Divinity and Experience* (on the Dinka).

We have learned to look askance at the academic conventions which once ruled unquestioned. The poststructuralists have not created a new paradigm but have taught us to see the limitations of old ones. They have reminded us of the artificiality of the various academic disciplines into which we divide our interpretation of reality. Neo-Marxists have long symbolised their critique of these divisions by their adoption of the term 'political economy'. Poststructuralists tend to opt for 'ethnography'.

Points are easily scored off the poststructuralists, who sometimes write as if they alone stood outside the discourse of their time. No one does. One may catch glimpses of another cognitive world in a society like nineteenth-century Asante, where the primary documentation is abundant and the secondary literature perhaps uniquely rich. Nothing more.

Societies, like individuals, make a series of decisions, which are often subconscious, about what is important to them; these decisions are reflected in their lives more than in their words. It has been said that the Australian Aborigines have chosen not to accumulate possessions, in order to be free to elaborate complex worlds of religion and art. In Africa, much of the most advanced technology went into bronze sculpture. Iron, smelted at great cost in fuel and labour, was used in sculpture, as well as for utilitarian purposes. Wood carving (with built-in obsolescence in a tropical environment), the energy expended in dance, masking cults, religious rituals, all embody cultural choices. It is difficult to reflect them in a book of this size, but I have attempted to do so, in so far as the existing literature allows. The study that follows is a theme in counterpoint which concentrates, above all, on three variables—the ecological factor, the economic base, which made everything else possible, and the cognitive maps Africans constructed to make their world intelligible.

SILENCES

Oral and written sources sometimes speak most eloquently in their silences. These silences are deafening, but it is not always easy to know what they mean. Historians are becoming aware of the importance of 'listening for silences', aware, too, of a 'past containing many voices, often discordant ones'. The difficulty is that many of these voices can no longer be heard.

Historical texts reflect, not the totality of historical experience, but that small fraction of it which is preserved in various kinds of source material. These sources themselves are often explicit about their silences. In the words of one version of the Sundiata epic:

> If you ask whether in that intervening
> period [between two famous kings] there
> were other kings,
> Of course there were,
> But their names are not known.

In the 1820s, it was said of the Akan, 'Little kingdoms have been … annihilated … whose names have almost become obsolete.' In the words of a modern historian, summarising one dimension of the work of a generation of French post structuralists: 'The historian is never a specialist of past events … He [*sic*] is … a specialist of past signs [sources]. More accurately, he is a specialist of those past signs which have survived into the present.'

We construct our own maps to make sense of both familiar and unfamiliar landscapes. But 'map is not territory'. Of this, we must continue to remind ourselves.

ORAL TRADITIONS: WHOSE HISTORY?

BY THOMAS SPEARS

I

Historians rarely pause to reflect on the history and theory of our own discipline, but it is a salutary exercise, particularly when the discipline is as young as African history. Twenty years ago a majority of African peoples emerged from colonial domination and acquired their independence. In that same year their history was also symbolically liberated from domination by the activities of Europeans in Africa through the inauguration of the *Journal of African History*. And one year later the new African history was given what was to become one of its dominant methodologies with the publication of Jan Vansina's *De la tradition Orale*.[1]

African history was to be the history of Africans, a history that had begun well before the European 'discovery' of Africa. The problem was sources. Western historiography was firmly based on written sources which could be arranged in sequence and analyzed to trace incremental changes and establish cause and effect relationships in evolutionary patterns of change. Unlike written documents which were recorded in the past and passed down unchanged into the present, oral traditions had to be remembered and retold through successive generations to reach the present. Their accuracy was thus subject to lapses in memory and falsification in the long chains of transmission from the initial

report of the event in the past to the tradition told in the present. To overcome these problems Vansina established an elaborate and meticulous methodology by which traditions should be collected and transcribed, their chains of transmission traced and variants compared, and obvious biases and falsifications stripped off to produce primary documents suitable for writing history within the western genre.[2]

The emphasis was on method, as scores of graduate students took to the field clutching Vansina's book and attempted to observe his demanding tenets that they learn the language fluently, master the social structure, collect as many variants as possible of any given oral tradition and traditions at all levels of society, and observe subtle nuances in values and expressions, in addition to dabbling in linguistics, anthropology, and archeology.[3] As the data came in, however, it became apparent that oral traditions were less reliable, in the documentary sense, than had been feared, and a number of once enthusiastic practitioners began to doubt if they had any historical value at all.

This, of course, was what anthropologists had been saying for years. Functionalists, following Malinowski, viewed oral traditions as historical charters which served to validate current social, political, and economic institutions. It was shown, for example, that genealogies were frequently telescoped as people forgot the names of ancestors who did not represent significant nodes in a system of segmentary lineage development. Later we learned that genealogies were also expanded to incorporate strangers who had been adopted into the lineage or clan. Far from being an accurate list of ancestors, then, genealogies often merely reflected existing social relations on the ground. Like other elements of social structure, then, oral traditions were seen as functional, carefully articulated with other aspects of the society and frequently adjusted to reflect changes in institutions. They could hardly be accurate historical records.

Later, structural anthropologists following the pioneering work of Claude Levi-Strauss argued that oral traditions were largely composed of collages of universal symbols artifully constructed according to set patterns of thought to express essential human values. Traditions might tell us something of mankind and its thought, then, but little of individual peoples, societies, or cultures.[4] Historians were sensitive to these criticisms and rapidly incorporated them into their work by stripping from the traditional corpus elements which were obviously charters or symbols. In the case of genealogies, for example, historians found they could be divided into three periods. The earliest ancestors were preterhuman heroes whom God had placed on earth to conquer disorder and establish orderly human society. These were obviously mythical figures which could be dismissed as historical personages. The middle period of genealogies listed only those ancestors who had given rise to major clan and lineage segments in the society, all intervening generations having been forgotten. This period was duly discarded as charter, leaving only the most recent three to four generations as an accurate representation of reality.

Historical traditions revealed the same tripartite pattern. The Kikuyu tradition of Gikuyu and Mumbi is typical of African origin traditions. God created the first man and woman and gave them sheep, goats, and land. The two had nine sons, among whom the land was divided. These were the ancestors of the present Kikuyu clans and these clans still farm the land allocated to them by God. The lesson is simple: man did not evolve, but emerged fully developed as a cultured Kikuyu-speaking member of the Kikuyu people with rights in land.[5] Or there are the traditions of the nine Mijikenda peoples who today live behind the Kenya coast. These traditions start with Muyeye, his two sisters, and their nine sons—Mdigo, Mribe, Mgiriama, etc. They lived at Singwaya in Somalia together with the Oromo until one day the Mijikenda killed an Oromo boy as part of the initiation of their first age-set. The Oromo were furious and drove the Mijikenda from Singwaya down the Somali and Kenya coasts until the Mijikenda met a hunter, Alaa, who showed them nine forested hilltops on which they could hide from the Oromo. Each son was able to establish his village, or *kaya*, on a separate hilltop, bury protective magic brought from Singwaya in the center, divide the area among his sons, and initiate the young men into age-sets. Today the nine Mijikenda peoples still identify with their respective hilltop *kayas*; call themselves Digo, Ribe, Giriama, etc. after the nine brothers; continue to belong to the clans established by the sons of the founding brothers; and maintain close symbiotic relations with the Laa hunters who first befriended them.[6] The earliest period of traditions, then, is a time of genesis, when hero ancestors appeared from nowhere and created the institutions and values of civilized life.

While the period of origins is one of anti-social activities, such as incestuous marriages, murder, and warfare, the middle period of historical traditions consists of uneventful series of social activities. For the Mijikenda people continued to live in the *kayas* while age-sets were initiated at appropriate intervals and clans segmented into sub-clans and lineages. There are no innovations recalled in this period; it was one in which people simply continued to follow the ways of their ancestors in repetitive cycles of orderly social processes.

Disorder returns in the last period of traditions, that period which lies within the recent or living memory of elders, who bemoan the fact that society is falling apart because people no longer follow in the way of the ancestors. For the Mijikenda this is a period of social ferment, as young people moved out of the *kayas* to pursue lucrative trading opportunities available on the plains below. The institutions and values of Mijikenda life were transformed as these wealthy traders gathered local followings around them, the *kayas* declined in social and ritual importance, the *kaya* elders ceased to exercise effective control over Mijikenda life, young men were no longer initiated into age-sets, and local lineages became more important than the clans.

As with genealogies, then, it is only the most recent period that appears to contain any accurate historical information. The period of genesis clearly appears to be mythic, while the middle period just as clearly seems to be charter. It was not quite that simple, however, for I was able to show from other evidence that six of the nine Mijikenda peoples actually did come from Singwaya and had been driven south to their present *kayas* by the Oromo some time in the sixteenth century. And, while the middle and later periods of Mijikenda traditions contrast the earlier unchanging world of the *kayas* with the later individual experiences of the traders, it is clear from other evidence that the Mijikenda did live in *kayas* governed by elders of the senior age-sets up until the mid-nineteenth century. The traditions thus contain an accurate historical narrative over four centuries and continue to describe accurately instititions which have not existed for over 130 years.

It was thus obvious that oral traditions could have different levels of meaning—as myth, charter, and accurate narrative—each amenable to different kinds of analysis. The exclusivist claims of anthropologists that traditions had to be either charter or fact, myth or history, had been countered, although the narrative core remaining once the other elements were stripped away was shrinking.[7] The initial assumption that traditions could simply take the place of written documents was proving false.

We are left with a paradox: increasingly sophisticated methods of source analysis leave us with decreasing amounts of historical data to a far greater extent than is true for written sources. What went wrong? On the one hand, nothing. A vast corpus of traditional data has been collected, analyses of it have become more sophisticated,[8] and the outlines of pre-colonial African history are beginning to emerge from the number of excellent studies that have been completed.[9] On the other hand, however, I believe that we have been approaching the problem from the wrong perspective in seeking to force oral traditions into the mold of documentary sources suitable for western-style history. Traditions are not documents, not even oral ones, they are history, the product of oral historians' attempts to make sense of the past. Trying to write history from them is thus equivalent to attempting to write our history from the secondary or tertiary accounts of historians who have already sifted through the debris of the past, selected from it the items they deem important, and decided their significance, while ignoring the rest. To avoid this we must accept oral traditions as history in their own right and traditional oral historians as our colleagues in the practice of a common craft, seeking to understand their theory and practice of history in order to be able to translate their history, as expressed in their cultural idioms, into our own history in our own cultural idioms. The answer to my question "Whose History?" is thus, initially, "Theirs."

II

Modes of Communication and Historical Thought

To understand traditional history we must first seek to understand the intellectual conditions within which it is composed and how these differ from our own. The main difference is the different modes of communication employed by oral and literate historians.[10] Both start with a present and seek to explain how it developed by delving into the words describing past events and processes which have come to them through history. Whereas the literate historian is able to work directly on the words *of* the past in the form of diaries, letters, and other records, however, the oral historian must work on the words communicated to him orally through one or more generations of ancestors *from* the past. Such words do not come to the oral historian verbatim, but in a series of core images or formulae embedded in a narrative skeleton around which he, like his predecessors before him, weaves a complete tradition.[11] Each retelling of a tradition thus becomes a separate composition, in which the teller creates the tradition anew around the received core formulae and skeleton. Traditions are thus subject to continual reinterpretation as the words from the past take on contemporary meanings in the context of the present, a tendency which is reinforced by the collective response of the audience to each oral performance.[12] In this way oral traditions are continually generated in a manner which ensures that they express a collective cultural conscience, thereby conveying an impression of cultural homeostasis. The words from the past become congruent with the values and self image of the present.

This process contrasts dramatically with the research of the literate historian who finds in the words of the past clear evidence of the differences between past and present. Made aware of such differences, the literate historian is encouraged to analyze the events leading from the past to the present to explain the changes which have obviously taken place. The literate historian is thus made critical and self-aware, while the traditional historian, unable to recognize changes which have occurred, maintains an image of an unchanging past. The differing modes of communication thus have implications for the historical thought of the two types of historians. Since cognitive development is a dialogue between culture and the mind, the ways that cultural values are communicated have a crucial impact on the development of cognitive processes.[13] It is thus important to examine how the oral mode of communication influences the ways in which oral historians view history, how they go about constructing their histories, and how they seek to explain change.

A useful starting point is Robin Horton's article, "African Traditional Thought and Western Science."[14] In this analysis Horton seeks to cut through previous broad characterizations of 'primitive' thought as irrational, pre-logical, superstitious, or mythical when opposed to 'scientific' thought as rational, logical, scientific, or historical in order to establish the precise similarities and differences between the two.[15] Starting from the philosophy of science, Horton demonstrates that both modes of thought seek to explain the diversity, disorder, complexity, and anomalies of experience by the use of abstract analogical models. The content of the two is, of course, very different, but their substance is the same. Whereas western science draws its analogies from the physical realm of experience, traditional thought uses models drawn from human behavior and social organization.[16] All mankind thus draws from its realm of familiar phenomena to construct theoretical models to render puzzling observations orderly and explicable. There is nothing intrinsically less rational in a model of the universe ordered by human forces than one ordered by physical ones. It is simply a different model, internally coherent and consistent when understood on its own terms.

If we carry Horton's analysis into the realm of social science and history, we can see the same similarities between social theory and oral traditions. Both are theories of society. Whereas social scientists use various predictable mechanical and organic models to describe, interpret, and understand social and cultural behavior, traditional historians use models drawn from predictable patterns of society.[17] Lest this seem too fanciful a leap, let us return to the problem of genealogies. The genealogical model is based on the familiar and ubiquitous reproductive processes that connect parent and child, ancestor and descendant. Kinship was the traditional theory of society long before it was discovered by anthropologists. It is the elementary historical model, descent representing both development through time and the close relations that are ideally thought to exist among blood kin, while marriage represents alliances with more distant, non-related groups and implies a more ambiguous set of relations. Kinship is not prescriptive of actual social relations; rather it is a model of social relations in reproductive terms.[18] For the most recent generations a genealogy takes as its model the simple three—or four—generation family which comprises the basic land holding and social community of the village. In the middle period it draws on the structural relations that exist between the lineage of the village and other lineages within the clan and between different clans. And finally, the earliest section of the genealogy explains the creation of human society by means of one or more epical ancestors. Taken together, the genealogy explains the development of society from the beginning to the present in a single elegant model expressing easily remembered truths.

These are obviously different historical truths from the ones which literate historians are familiar with. They are structural truths employing a basic reproductive model to explain the historical development of present social structure. Actual ancestors are as irrelevant to this model as structural elements are to our narrative one. In a fascinating permutation of the genealogical model, the Imbangala of Angola relate lengthy genealogies of male ancestors together with the women they married. On closer inspection, however, none of the items appearing in the genealogies are named individuals; they are titles, and the genealogy relates the development of a series of titles which Imbangala kings bestowed on other lineages to 'marry' them to the royal line.[19] For the oral historian history is thus a way of explaining the structures of his society and the relationships that exist among the elements of those structures. In the case of the Mijikenda, for example, the close social relations and shared culture of the nine peoples is economically explained through the idiom of the nine brothers, while the relative seniority of each brother vis-a-vis the others is used to explain the order of social relationships that exist among the nine peoples.

If oral traditions were simply models, their value for historical reconstruction of anything but the present would be extremely limited. The important point is that they are part of an overall cultural system, a system of meanings which emerges out of a people's historical experience.[20] Myths are not the products of sheer invention. The values expressed in traditions, the structures delineated, and the idioms and models used are all cultural products of history. And what is particularly interesting—and valuable for the historian—is that these cultural patterns often show greater persistence in time than the actual structures or behaviors they represent. Values generated in the past often assume their own historical reality and outlive the circumstances of their creation. There is thus a profound cultural lag built into traditions. For the traditional historian they serve as models of the "world-as-it-was" and "ought-to-be" in contrast to the "way-it-is" now. For the literate historian they are historical survivals from a previous historical period.

The traditional model is thus one which exists in time—or more accurately, times. We have seen that traditions are divided into three periods—recent, middle, and early. Each of these is characterized by a different sense of time. The recent period uses linear time, relating remembered events in roughly the sequence they occurred; the middle period uses repetitive or cyclical time, relating recurring processes of lineage segmentation, age-set initiations, and investitures of rulers as events repeat themselves; while the period of origins is expressed in mythical time, where events of thousands of years are compressed within a single timeless moment.[21] This triparite division in traditional thought is the result of two factors. The first is the process of how traditions are made.[22] Let us start with a current event, the birth of a male child. Observers of the event pass the good news around the neighborhood, relating in detail the particular features of the event—who the parents were, when the baby was born and how, who paid the mother's bridewealth and thus had rights in the child, etc. Soon non-observers pick up the news and pass it further along the oral newswires. As time goes on, however, the particular events of the birth are forgotten, but his name and parentage will continue to be remembered so long as they remain factors in local social organization and landholding.

When the local lineage focused on this individual splits, however, his importance will recede and he may eventually be forgotten. If, however, he left the group and pioneered in the settlement of new land, his name will endure as an important ancestor since he formed his own lineage or clan and endowed it with rights to land. And if, in the longer run, people tracing descent from him come to identify themselves as a separate people, he will assume the status of a mythical folk hero, born of the gods, who created a new social and cultural order. [23]

As the event recedes in time, remembrance of it is increasingly abstracted, details deemed to be unimportant are lost and only its structurally significant elements remain encapsulated in simple verbal formulae. Later the new elements remaining may be restated in different terms, terms which convey the significance of the event more expressively or symbolically and, hence, are more easily remembered and interpreted.[24] Like all history, certain details are selected as important, generalizations are made from these, and eventually the significance of those generalizations is distilled in a simple memorable phrase. What is less usual about oral traditions are the ways they change in form from narrative to formula to myth and in meaning from literal to intended to symbolic as the events they recall recede into the past. This process is precisely what we see when we collect traditions today, the three periods or times being the result of progressive abstraction and transformation as the oral historian delves deeper into the past.

While this process of ever-increasing abstraction is easily seen in the repetitive processes of cultural and social life and their reproduction, the same process also characterizes apparently non-repetitive events. A colleague of mine, Cynthia Brantley, was mystified when her informants repeatedly claimed that a Giriama revolt against the British in 1914 was caused by a rape. She knew there were a range of causal factors, including land alienation, the imposition of tax, and forced labor, that she felt had been responsible for the revolt, but when queried about these, her informants would only acknowledge that those factors were present before they returned to emphasize the story of the rape. It was only when I discovered that a number of earlier wars were also attributed to rapes that we were able to see that the idea of rape was a convenient abstraction denoting a serious social transgression which, when involving outsiders, was a legitimate cause for war. Since the British had made serious transgressions against the Giriama, the Giriama response was legitimate and, hence, caused by a rape. The term encapsulates Mijikenda philosophy on the legitimacy of war. The event, less than sixty years in the past, has already been abstracted to the level of a formula.[25]

The second factor influencing the tripartite division of traditions, embodying three different concepts of time, is traditional thought concerning change. We have seen in our hypothetical example the ordinary birth of a child transformed in time to the miraculous creation of a mythical folk hero. Such figures are commonplace in traditions dealing with the establishment of new social and cultural formations. This phenomenon follows from the difference which Horton finds between "the 'closed' and 'open' predicaments" in traditional and scientific modes of thought and is attributable to the different modes of communication each uses.[26] Western science, he claims, is characterized by the

Traditional Concepts of Time

Period	Time	Content	Form	Meaning
early	mythical	origins: things-as-they became	myth	symbolic
middle	repetitive	cyclical processes: things-as-they-should-be	formula	intended
late	linear	events: things-as-they-are	reminiscences	literal

availability of alternatives and by the acceptance of new ideas; as models lose their explanatory power they are transformed gradually into new models in a process of evolutionary change. Traditional thought, by contrast, is characterized by the lack of alternatives and an unwillingness to consider ideas at variance with the accepted theory. The lack of a written historical record, for example, makes it difficult for pre-literate historians to be aware of differences between the remembered past and what actually occurred. And the normal lack of calendar time makes it hard to place past events in sequence. The image of an unchanging order stretching back to the beginning is thus unchallenged and unchallengeable.

This image of an unchanging past is reinforced by traditional social theory which holds that the social world of people and the physical world of nature are so interrelated that moral and social acts can and do affect the natural order. Men and women are obliged to maintain the social and moral values inherited from their ancestors, who discovered the laws of relationships among these interrelated phenomena, at the risk of bringing on total chaos if they do not. Change can only then be conceived of as the result of amoral and antisocial people disregarding the ways of the ancestors, or responding to new ideas emanating from the ancestral spirits. Both these images are prominent in traditions. The first is epitomized by Shaka, founder of the Zulu nation, who in the course of the tradition is transformed from a warrior king to an inhuman demonic figure who rose above prevailing moral and social conventions to transform them.[27] The second is seen in prophetic figures who introduced changes only after being possessed by ancestral spirits and having new ideas revealed to them.[28] In both cases, change can only be brought about by people possessing, or being possessed by, extraordinary spiritual power. This notion of spiritual power exists in many areas of traditional thought, including witchcraft, sorcery, and possession. Imbedded in all these beliefs is the assumption that in both their human and spirit forms people can exercise power over the forces of nature and society. People can kill or heal, bring or withhold the rains by their moral and social acts. They can also effect revolutionary historical transformations through creation, conquest, or migrations.

Most traditions contain at least one of these images. A people and their culture were created in a far-off land from which they migrated to their present location.[29] Virtually no society simply evolved in situ. Nor did they interact with previous peoples; they assimilated them, destroyed them, or chased them away. If a society does trace its origins through a previous people, outsiders came and imposed the new order through conquest. In this way kingdoms arose among people who had previously been "stateless."[30] Change is thus seen as discontinuous and revolutionary, the archetype of which is the creation of culture out of nature and social order out of antisocial disorder portrayed in countless genesis traditions. Once established, the new order then continued, unchanging, to the present day. When significant changes do occur the tradition is slowly updated through assimilating these back into the period of origins or through the replacement of the original traditions, in which case they will either eventually be forgotten or, possibly, maintained among minority groups, such as conquered peoples or displaced rulers, as testimony to their prior claims.[31]

Traditional history thus has the shape of a self-contained era. Traditions may recount a series of such revolutionary changes or eras, each ostensibly unrelated to the others in a pattern of sequential development, but more commonly they relate only the last such era, that which is associated with the present moral, social, and cultural order. Origin traditions may therefore stem from only the recent past, or like the Mijikenda traditions, extend over 300 to 400 years.

Traditional thought thus views history in terms of a series of discontinuous eras, each a product of preterhuman activity and embodying a distinct conception of the moral, cultural, and social order. Each is a theoretical model of society, employing a personal idiom to explain "how-it-became" and "how-it-ought-to-be" in contrast to "how-it-is." It is the accurate abstraction and conveying of these structural truths which are the most important canons of the traditional historian.

III
_____

STRUCTURE, PROCESS, AND HISTORY

It might well seem that this notion of structural truth is simply a recombination of functionalist and structuralist dogma, and in a sense it is but for the fact that structures are not static; they are processual. Societies and cultures are in a constant state of becoming; so tradition is an ongoing process. Oral traditions are thus closely related to our notion of tradition. They are the representation of cultural traditions stretching back into the past which will continue on into the future, integral parts of the cultural process and history they convey.

Cultural change is dialectical, brought about through interaction between contradictory or opposed values and structures present within a society at any one time. We have already seen how values and ideals generated in the past often assume their own historical reality and outlive the circumstances of the present. We all face the problems of the present with values and structures derived from the past. It is the dialectical interaction between past ideals and present social behavior that generates future cultural syntheses. Thus there can never be the one-to-one functional correspondence between elements of social structure and their validating charters as envisioned by Malinowski. Rather, the past confronts the present in the future. Elders in all societies constantly bemoan the fact that things are no longer "as-they-were" and "ought-to-be." This is why the two most recent periods of traditions are frequently opposed; the middle period is an ideal statement derived from the past of how "things-ought-to-be," while the recent period portrays the "world-as-it-is" in all its vital diversity. Thus the Mijikenda maintain and act on

values from an ideal construct more than 130 years old. These traditions are more than simple relics, as noted earlier; they have been part of the historical dialectic for the past 130 years. An example of this can be seen in the revolt against the British in 1914 mentioned earlier, when internal cleavages within the Giriama between elders still residing in the *kayas* and others who had moved off to the frontier regions of Giriama settlement proved as important in understanding the event as their common opposition to the British.[32] Traditions are thus not simply representations of the past, but also keys to understanding historical process and action.

Inherent in a structure at any one time are also large numbers of other opposed and contradictory values. When one section of an Ndembu lineage refutes basic social values of lineage solidarity to move away, it does so by appealing to alternative values and labelling its opponents anti-social witches.[33] It is in such oppositions and contradictions that the germ of historical practice lies, that determine who a person actually marries, where he or she really lives, and the social group he or she physically interacts with on a daily basis. As Sahlins has noted:

> I am not talking about what 'actually happened.' Yet what I am talking about—indigenous schemes of cosmological proportions—may be even more significant historically ... such schemes are the true organization of historical practice, if not true memories of primordial events.[34]

Willis finds that historical meaning also emerges in such oppositions:

> The purpose of the cognitive relations of opposition ... is not to resolve contradictions but rather to precipitate them. Meaning then emerges as the final product of the tension between opposed aspects of experience. [35]

If our quest as literate historians is for understanding historical action and its meanings, then oral traditions may prove to be even more valuable than we originally thought.

IV

HISTORY AS TRANSLATION OF MEANING

We have seen that oral traditions are not primary documents any more than genealogies are accurate lists, though both may contain accurate historical information, recalling real people and events within an overall framework of traditional historical thought. But any attempts to take them literally, such as calculating average generational, regnal, or age-set lengths to establish absolute chronologies, is bound to fail because they do not obey our historical canons or chrono-logic. They are fully realized histories in their own right.

Our task is thus to seek a more complete understanding of what traditional historians mean when they use certain models, idioms, and formulae, and what canons they themselves observe in composing and assessing the validity of their histories.[36] Whether Muyeye, his two sister-wives, and their nine sons did or did not actually exist (a 'fact' we shall never know), the representation of the relationship reveals an important historical truth of how the Mijikenda view themselves. And even though we do not think that all the Mijikenda peoples came from Singwaya, the fact that all today who have adopted Mijikenda culture and who call themselves Mijikenda claim such origins reveals that what the oral historians are concerned with is the emergence of something definable as Mijikenda-ness, the essence of their culture and self-identity, in the chaotic historical circumstances of bygone eras. Out of that original population movement and subsequent interaction with other peoples in the south emerged a definable group of peoples possessing common institutions and values which are still relevant today.

Such important historical myths are not, of course, unique to Africa. Musing on why Americans still celebrate Columbus Day in spite of the fact that America had long been known to its own inhabitants and the first European to 'discover' the continent may well have been a Viking or Leif Erikson, James Oliver Robinson concludes:

Perhaps because it was a formidable combination of visions and images, hardware, ideals and desires that first appeared on the horizon of the Americas with those three little ships in the autumn of 1492. The elements in the mythology of the New World are, when looked at separately, a chaotic jumble of visions and images, ideals, metaphors. Their repeated associations with one another, in endless tellings and retellings over the hundreds of years since Columbus, have given them the active imperative effect of being logically connected with each other in reasonable, necessary ways.

Through our stories, histories, novels, poems, dramas, and all the other ways we have of learning, we know the New World was fresh, innocent, wild, and empty, in contrast to the decadent, sinful, teeming civilization of the Old World. The New World is Paradise regained, and refurbished it is Utopia, El Dorado, Atlantis, Eden. The Old World by contrast is Paradise lost, the Tower of Babel, and the fleshpots of Rome. ...

The magic of such myths, the force that holds people to belief and drives them to act, comes from all the contradictory images; puny little people on tiny ships making their way by uncharted routes across vast and furious oceans to continents never before dreamt of; strange peoples and fabled cities; great forests, sparkling mountains, rich prairies that invite and defy the efforts of people from the Old World to find them, understand them, and conquer them. The myth is an imperial vision of paradise, of the kingdom of heaven upon earth and made earthly. It gives permission to break the chains of the past and to seek something new, something better. In the New World, there was, and is, and will be, more opportunity for better ends, Thus, in reality, Columbus discovered a new world of the mind. Leif Erikson didn't. … Such a world was as new to Europeans as it was to Incas or Aztecs or Africans or Chinese.[37]

Such times were, in reality as well as in the traditions, periods of dramatic and important changes, so important that the traditions have absorbed both earlier and later changes. The anxiety which Mijikenda feel today in the conflict between the world "as-it-was" and "ought-to-be" and the fragmented world "as-it-is" is acute. This will eventually have to be resolved by assimilating the world of the present to the past, but this will only happen as the slow process of tradition-making abstracts the lessons for the future from the variety of present experience. In the meantime, Mijikenda traditions provide a very real historical picture of the way that it was—the way that is 'really' was—in terms of the historical values and institutions that molded their way of life. If they choose to omit the random facts of day-to-day life, only we, the foreign historians who treasure such ephemera, are the losers. If we choose to neglect the real histories that they compose about the past, then we will be doubly the losers, unable to make any meaningful sense of their past at all.

My point is simple. We must accept that oral traditions exist within an oral mode of thought which, regardless of how irrational it may appear to us, is rational and coherent when understood on its own terms. The task of the historian is not to prune away what we see as irrational, leaving what we judge to be rational, but to accept the whole as rational within a mode of thought that is different from ours and then to try to translate the rationality of that mode into the rationality of ours. The task

of translation is difficult—all translation is—but at least we can hope to capture a holistic image of a coherent body of thought instead of the bits and pieces remaining after we have irrationally (in both our terms and theirs) hacked out the heart from the traditional body. The task is best seen, then, as a problem of translation across the gulf in modes of communication and thought that separate us. No amount of rationalist posturing across that gulf will do anything more than emphasize its breadth. We need to bridge it by trying to be as sensitive to their modes, values, and historical canons as we are to our own. In the end there will be two histories, theirs and ours. Ours will obviously be within a literate mode of historical thought, taking account of all the additional data we can muster to reconstruct sequential, evolutionary patterns of change. It will satisfy us, while theirs continues to satisfy them. The final answer to my question, is thus 'Both of ours.'

NOTES

*   I wish to express my appreciation to David Dorward, Bronwen Douglas, Lindsay Farrall, Joseph Miller, Sheila Spear, Michele Stephen, and Jan Vansina for their support, criticism, and generous sharing of ideas.

1. Tervuren, 1961. English translation: *Oral Tradition* (Chicago, 1965).

2. Aptly described by Joseph Miller as the "documentary analogy" in "The Dynamics of Oral Tradition in Africa" in B. Bernardi, ed., *Fonti Orali* (Milan, 1978), 75–101.

3. For an introduction to African historiography, see Thomas Spear, *Kenya's Past: An Introduction to Historical Method in Africa* (London, in press).

4. For comprehensive analyses of the functionalist and structuralist critiques, see Miller, "Dynamics of Oral Tradition" and P. Pender-Cudlip, "Oral Traditions and Anthropological Analysis: Some Contemporary Myths," *Azania*, 7(1972), 3–24.

5. Godfrey Muriuki, *A History of the Kikuyu, 1500–1900* (Nairobi, 1974), 46–47.

6. Thomas Spear, *The Kaya Complex: A History of the Mi, Likenda Peoples of the Kenya Coast to 1900* (Nairobi, 1978).

7. Pender-Cudlip, "Oral Traditions."

8. See Vansina, *Oral Tradition*, and his frequent frank revisions, such as "Once Upon a Time: Oral Traditions as History in Africa," *Daedalus*, 100(1971), 442–468 and "Traditions of Genesis," *JAH*, 15(1974), 317–22, together with Joseph Miller, ed., *The African Past Speaks* (Folkestone, 1980), the other articles cited here, and the many valuable methodology articles that have appeared in the *Journal of African History and History in Africa* over the years.

9. See, e.g., Steven Feierman, *The Shambaa Kingdom* (Madison, 1974); John Lamphear, *The Traditional History of the Jie of Uganda* (Oxford, 1976); Joseph Miller, *Kings and Kinsmen* (Oxford, 1976); Muriuki, *History of the Kikuyu*, and Vansina, *The Children of Woot* (Madison, 1978).

10. See the stimulating discussion by Jack Goody in his *The Domestication of the Savage Mind* (Cambridge, 1977), an expansion of his and Watt's earlier "The Consequences of Literacy," *Comparative Studies in Society and History*, 5(1963), 304–45.

11. Such a core image or formula is often called a cliche. Alfred B. Lord, *The Singer of Tales* (Cambridge, 1960); Harold Scheub, *The Xhosa Ntsomi* (Oxford, 1975); B. Colby and M. Cole, "Culture, Memory and Narrative" in Robin Horton and Ruth Finnegan, eds., *Modes of Thought* (London, 1973); and J. Goody, "Oral Tradition and the Reconstruction of the Past in Northern Ghana" in Bernardi, *Fonti Orali*, 285–95.

12. Scheub, *Xhosa Ntsomi*; Miller, "Dynamics of Oral Tradition."

13. L.S. Vygotsky, *Mind and Society* (Cambridge, 1978); A.R. Luria, *Cognitive Development* (Cambridge, 1976); J.S. Bruner, et al., *Studies in Cognitive Growth* (New York, 1966); J.W. Berry and P.R. Dasen, eds., *Culture and Cognition* (New York, 1970); and M. Cole and S. Scribner, Culture and Thought (New York, 1974).

14. *Africa*, 37(1967), 50–71, 155–87.

15. In an effort to avoid such meaningless and often inaccurate dicotomies, I differentiate here between the two on the basis of their differing modes of communication. Thus oral historians compose oral tradition (which can thus be called either oral or traditional history), while literate historians write literate history. The two are, of course, ideal types. A wide range of oral traditions are composed within the oral genre, just as numberous kinds of histories are written within the literate one. And, as Goody points out (*Domestication*, 152–60), there is a range of intermediary types between the two.

16. While modes drawn from the social world predominate in traditions, traditional thought also draws its models from the natural world. See, e.g., Victor Turner, *The Forest of Symbols* (Ithaca, 1967) or Roy Willis, *Man and Beast* (London, 1974).

17. This point is elaborated more fully by Miller, "Dynamics of Oral Tradition;" W. MacGaffey, "African History, Anthropology, and the Rationality of Natives," *HA*, 5(1978), 101–20; and M. Sahlins, "The Stranger King, or Dumezil among the Fijians," Presidential Address to the Anthropology Section of Australian and New Zealand Association for the Advancement of Science, 12 May 1980.

18. For kinship as ideology see: M. Bloch, "Moral and Tactical Meaning of Kinship Terms," *Man*, 6(1971), 79–87; and M. Jackson, "The Structure and Significance of Kuranko Clanship," *Africa*, 44(1974), 397–416.

19. Miller, *Kings and Kinsmen*, 16–21.

20. For 'culture' see C. Geertz, *The Interpretation of Cultures* (New York, 1973).

21. R. Willis, *On Historical Reconstruction from Oral Traditional Sources: A Structuralist Approach*, [Twelfth Melville J. Herskovits Memorial Lecture, Northwestern University, 16 February 1976.] (Evanston, 1976).

22. Miller, "Dynamics of Oral Traditions."

23. For an historical account of this process see Muriuki, *History of the Kikuyu*, 62–82.

24. This is not to say that all 'narrative' truth is thereby lost. The narrative may well remain as the structure of the tradition and historical residues commonly remain, as I have shown above.

25. See Brantley, *The Giriama and British Colonialism in Kenya* (forthcoming) for abundant evidence of the fact that detailed and insightful history can, nevertheless, be written from such traditional evidence.

26. Horton, "African Traditional Thought," 155–87. I have reservations about the dichotomy posed here by Horton. For the less than "open" nature of science, see Thomas Kuhn, *The Structure of Scientific Revolutions* (Chicago, 1962) while, for the unsatisfactory nature of the dichotomy itself, see Goody, *Domestication*, 1–9. Nevertheless, Horton's points closely reflect the differences between predominantly oral cultures and those which are predominately literate (ibid., 38–46).

27. The fact that this transformation takes place within the tradition itself makes this particular tradition a fascinating study of the making of mythical heroes. Thomas Mofolo, *Chaka* (London, 1931).

28. Possession and prophecy remain important elements in coping with change today, as shown by the thousands of prophets leading independent churches throughout Africa. See David Barrett, *Schism and Renewal in Africa* (Nairobi, 1968) and John Middleton and John Beattie, eds., *Spirit Mediumship and Society in Africa* (London, 1969), xvii–xxx. Traditional possession and prophecy also remain important, as demonstrated dramatically by Peter Fry, *Spirits of Protest* (Cambridge, 1976).

29. Miller shows how migration traditions are usually "myths of transferal," denoting "transfers of ideology and identity" rather than actual movements of population. "Listening for the African Past" in Miller, *African Past Speaks*, 32–33.

30. The pervasiveness of images of migration and conquest led earlier literate historians to view change in much the same way as traditional historians. The most notable example is the now notorious "Hamitic hypothesis," which combined traditional notions of causation with European racism to attribute the development of all African states to conquering white pastoralists whose ideas about state-craft came originally from Egypt or Southwest Asia. We now read the idiom of 'conquest' as indicating probable interaction between two peoples resulting in syncretic political structures. See B.A. Ogot, "Kingship and Statelessness among the Nilotes" in *The Historian in Tropical Africa*, J. Vansina, et al., eds., (London, 1964), 284–304 and R. Horton, "Stateless Societies in the *History of West Africa*" in History of West Africa, J. Ajayi and M. Crowder, eds., (London, 1971), 1:72–113.

31. Miller, "Listening for the African Past," 39–42.

32. Brantley, *Giriama and British Colonialism*.

33. Victor Turner, *Schism and Continuity in an African Society* (Manchester, 1957), 177.

34. "Stranger King," 5.

35. Willis, *Man and Beast*, 128.

36. Concern for the recovery of meaning features prominently in the collected essays in Miller, *The African Past Speaks*. It is now a feature of other historical schools as well, notably the French *Annales* and the new British and American social history. The literate historian can also learn much about the complex process of decoding and translation from the work of structural anthropologists such as Willis, MacGaffey, and Leach or of symbolists such as Turner.

37. "Good Buy, Columbus," *New York Times*, October 12, 1980.

AFRICAN HISTORY

PART TWO

EARLY HISTORY AND SOCIETY

THE ORIGINS OF AFRICAN SOCIETY

By J. D. Fage

The earliest known evidence anywhere in the world for the existence of man and the emergence of human society comes from East and North-East Africa, from a series of discoveries that stem from Dr Louis Leakey's pioneer excavations at Olduvai Gorge in northern Tanzania. Later finds, by Lake Turkana in Kenya and the river Omo in Ethiopia, for example, have taken the story of human evolution in Africa even further into the past. But the historian need go no further back than the situation disclosed at Olduvai about 1½ to 2 million years ago. Hominids, about 4 feet 6 inches tall, were then living in small groups on lake shores in savannah country, and chipping a rough edge on stones to make crude tools with which they could kill and dismember animal prey. Such tools have been called 'pebble tools', but since stones other than pebbles were also used, most archaeologists now prefer to call them 'choppers'.

The East and North-East African discoveries of Leakey and his successors have taken the story of human evolution right back to the time when man first became distinguishable from other primates. It is usually held that a useful distinction between man and all other animals is man's capacity to make tools, though recently this has become somewhat blurred by the discovery that some apes make what are in effect simple tools. But though the Olduvai hominids had small brains behind their massive faces, they must have possessed a greater ability to learn and to communicate than is normally associated with apes. The use of simple choppers spread throughout the African savannahs and elsewhere in the Old World. However, these implements have not been found in the forest lands of tropical Africa. Earliest man was a creature of the open country. He could not find the game he preyed on in the dense tropical forests, where indeed any kind of movement or of social life would have been very difficult without the use of better tools than he was able to make.

About a million years ago, man began to refine his simple stone choppers, with their single jagged cutting edge, and so evolved better and more specialized stone implements. The most characteristic of these is what was called a 'hand-axe', with two cutting edges meeting in a point; others were scrapers, specialized choppers, and hammerstones. As it happens, hand-axes and the culture represented by them were first recognized in western Europe, and the names which archaeologists gave to them, such as Acheulian, derived from European type-sites. But the earliest hand-axes known today once again come from the Olduvai deposits investigated by Leakey. Thus the first steps towards the evolution of more specialized Stone Age technologies seem also to have been taken by African man. Since this evolution enabled man to become a more efficient hunter, improving his food supply by killing more and larger animals, it became possible for him to live in larger societies.

The African savannahs, with adequate supplies of game animals and with year-round warmth from the sun, seemed to have provided a very suitable environment for early man, at least where there were permanent supplies of water, as on the banks of lakes and rivers. But it could have been the chills of winter which led to the next major technological advance, control of the use of fire, which may have first been discovered in Eurasia. However, by 50,000 to 60,000 years ago, African man was also using fire, a tool with which he could cook and make tender the tougher parts of his prey, and so make a more efficient use of his food supply and allow a further enlargement of the size of his communities.

But over the vast span of hundreds of thousands of years during which man was evolving from his earliest beginnings, there were considerable climatic changes in Africa. The continent did not experience the great Ice Ages which occurred in Europe, but the presence of large ice-caps both to the north and south had an appreciable effect on conditions in Africa. During the last European Ice Age, the Würm glaciation between about 70,000 and 10,000 B.C., for example, the eastern part of sub-Saharan Africa was cooler and wetter than it now is, while the western part was cooler and drier. The balance between forest and grassland was appreciably altered. In the east, evergreen montane forests covered a much larger area than they now do, while in West Africa and the Congo basin the effect was to weaken the hold of the moist, dense tropical forests, and to make them more open and habitable. In this situation man was no longer limited to the open savannahs. Equipped with fire, he began to live in the forests also, finding shelter in caves, and making increasing use of a most versatile new raw material, wood, with which he began to make tools which he used alongside his earlier stone and bone implements. With more permanent homes and an improved technology, there was a further increase in the size and complexity of man's social groups. The result was the cultural tradition which the archaeologists called Sangoan (the type-site being at Sango Bay on Lake Victoria in Uganda), recognizable by distinctive stone tools used on trees and timber as well as on animals and their carcasses.

The Sangoan tradition, with various variants and developments, is widely distributed over most of what we now recognize as Negro Africa. It has not been found, however, north of the Sahara nor in those parts of southern Africa which are today grassland or steppe. In the latter, the old hand-axe tradition survived, presumably because it was still suited to the conditions, and here it developed into what archaeologists called the Fauresmith industry. In North Africa, on the other hand, the hand-axe tradition gave way to a new culture, the Mousterian, which was shared with other parts of the Mediterranean basin and the Near East. Since the Mousterian appears in Africa in a fully developed form, it was presumably intrusive.

Between about 35 000 and 8000 B.C. there occurred the highly significant development by which modern man replaced by natural selection all other types of human. In general terms, the practitioners of the Mousterian and Sangoan Stone Age cultures were distinguishable from modern man by their heavy brow and jaw structures. In North Africa these men are called Neanderthal, in line with their fellows in Europe and Asia, while in Africa south of the Equator they were called 'Rhodesioid'. Although modern man is a single, interbreeding species, variations in his environment coupled with limits to his mobility meant that he evolved into a number of variants. These have provided the foundation for the modern concepts of 'race'. Race is a contentious, indeed emotive, theme, and it is as well to try and clarify some aspects of it as they affect Africa before proceeding further.

In the modern world, human race tends to be primarily defined in terms of skin colour, a sharp distinction usually being made between the 'white' and the 'coloured' races, who in Africa are for the most part dark-skinned, and so are called 'Blacks' (which is to be preferred to the older team 'Negroes'). But this criterion of race creates problems for the historian of Africa. In the first place, the distinction has a sharpness which is not in accordance with reality, and it is one which leads on to assumptions about the relative superiority and inferiority of 'white' and 'black' which can be positively dangerous and cloud historical judgement.

Skin pigmentation is essentially due to the combined influences of climate and breeding. Dark skins afford better protection in conditions of bright sunlight and heat; fairer skins, and other genetically associated traits like lighter coloured eyes, are more suited to more diffused lights and colder climates. Thus by and large men who live in the tropics tend to be dark-skinned. But peoples have been moving, meeting and mixing for many thousands of years, and 'white' and 'black' are extremes which hardly exist. Northern and western Europeans, who tend particularly towards fairness, would be better described as 'pinks', while their more southerly and easterly representatives are often quite dark-skinned. Similarly few African Blacks are wholly 'black', and some in fact have skin tones which are little different from those of the darker Europeans.

These problems of colour and nomenclature become particularly difficult in connection with those inhabitants of Africa, mainly in Mediterranean and north-eastern Africa, who are not called Blacks. Europeans, believing—correctly—that these people belong to the same basic stock, usually called Caucasoid, as themselves, tend to think of them as 'whites', and with this there unfortunately often goes the assumption that they are inherently superior to the 'black' people of Africa. This assumption is, for example, the guiding principle of the interpretation of African history offered in such a standard anthropological introduction as C. G. Seligman's *Races of Africa*. In its more recent editions, this actually goes so far as to call the northern Africans 'Europeans'! Earlier they were always referred to as 'Hamites', and the book is full of examples in which these Hamites are supposed to have exerted their superiority over Blacks, most of which can now be seen not to fit the actual historical circumstances. But one problem here is simply that there is no satisfactory general name in modern use for the men of Caucasoid stock who do not live in Asia or

Europe, as most Caucasoids do, but who are native to Africa in that they have been resident there for many thousands of years.

These Africans who are not Blacks, but who are also not always very fair-skinned, are sometimes called Libyan-Berbers, Libyans being the name given to them by the Greek geographers of the first millennium B.C., and Berbers that provided by the Muslim Arabs who entered North Africa from Syria and Arabia from the seventh century A.D. onwards. Both Greek and Arab geographers made a distinction between the Libyans or Berbers and the more southerly Africans, who were called Ethiopians or *al-Sudan*, the name in each case meaning simply 'dark-skinned men'. The fairly general usage 'Hamites'—from the Biblical Ham— as in Seligman, for example, introduces yet another difficulty, that of confusing race with language and culture. Properly the terms 'Hamite' and 'Hamitic' should be used not of an ethnic stock, but for a group of related languages, including Ancient Egyptian and the Berber languages of the rest of North Africa and of much of the Sahara (the first of which has now wholly, and the remainder of which have now mainly, been superseded by Arabic), the so-called Cushitic family of languages in northeastern Africa (including Beja, Somali and Oromo), and some of the languages spoken south of the Sahara between the Niger and Lake Chad, most notably Hausa. But the speakers of Hausa are now universally accepted as Blacks, so it is at once apparent—as indeed should be obvious—that there need be no direct correlation between ethnic and linguistic stocks.

Even as terms of purely linguistic classification, 'Hamite' and 'Hamitic' present difficulties, and are not now much in favour. The view of modern linguists is that there is little if anything to distinguish the Hamitic languages of Africa as a group from the Semitic languages of Arabia and the Near East. Some of the latter, most notably Arabic, but also Amharic, the dominant language of the Ethiopian highlands, are now, as a result of many centuries of culture contact with and settlement by Semitic-speaking peoples, African languages also. It is therefore increasingly accepted that the so-called Hamitic languages of Africa and the so-called Semitic languages, found both in nearer Asia and in Africa, should be classified together in one major language family, for which the best name is 'Afroasiatic'.

An altogether different kind of problem facing the historian of Africa if skin colour is used as the main denominator of race, is that it is something which does not long survive death and burial. Indeed even a man's bones do not usually survive in the earth as well as some of the things he has made, especially perhaps if these are of stone or pottery. This is particularly true of tropical Africa, where a combination of high humidities and acid soils generally means that organic material is unlikely to survive in the earth for any length of time. This is why, so far in this introductory chapter, the history of man in Africa has been sketched mainly in terms of developments in his culture as revealed by those of his tools that have been found by archaeologists. A human culture cannot be confidently assigned to the activity of a specific type of man unless there is a good amount of adequately preserved skeletal material found in proper archaeological context with the cultural evidence, and this is rare in Africa, especially tropical Africa, until comparatively modern times. There is also the problem that any successful new type of tool of general application —and, indeed, any new generally viable cultural idea—must often have tended to spread more widely and quickly than the particular human type, or the particular group of men, which first developed it. For these reasons, it is not at present possible to give any considered account of the processes by which the Neanderthalers and 'Rhodesioids' gave way in Africa to modern men, whether Black or Caucasoid.

However, the cultural evidence after about 35 000 B.C. suggests that man was now evolving particular technologies which were specifically related to particular climatic and geographical situations. One such was the Aterian (named from a type-site at Bir al-Ater in eastern Algeria), which succeeded the Mousterian in north-west Africa and the Sahara, and other specialized local cultures developed in the African tropics. The skeletal evidence suggests that a type of modern man distinct from the Caucasoids of Asia, Europe and northern Africa, and especially adapted to the conditions of the African tropics, may have appeared in East Africa by about 50,000 B.C., and that over about 10,000 or 20,000 years this type evolved by natural selection in two different directions to meet the needs of two different environments. One result was the Black, adapted to the wet conditions of equatorial and West Africa, and the other was a variant more suited to the drier grasslands and savannahs of eastern and southern Africa. The modern representatives of this variant tend to be rather shorter than the Blacks,[1] and to have yellow or yellowish-brown rather than dark skins; as will be seen, they are best called Khoi or Khoisan. North and north-eastern Africa, on the other hand, with a climate and geography similar to those in adjacent parts of Asia and Europe, were open to settlement by the same stock as these lands.

All these stocks were, of course, inter-breeding, so that many degrees of hybridization were—and are—possible. Initially, too, it would seem that the geographical boundaries between them were not as precise as they appear to be today. The situation in modern times is that North and North-East Africa are practically entirely inhabited by Caucasoids, the Khoisan are practically confined to the arid area in the extreme south-west of the continent, in and around the Kalahari desert, while in all the rest of the continent Blacks are dominant. Even as recently as about five thousand years ago, the situation may have been very different.

Caucasoids were certainly the dominant stock, if not the only one, living in North and North-East Africa, but there is also evidence that some Caucasoids were living further south, in at least the northern half of the open highland country which runs southwards from Ethiopia to South Africa. Two of the clues which lead to this conclusion are that the men who practised a local culture called the Kenya Capsian in the dry zone of central Kenya and northern Tanzania around 7000 B.C. seem to have been of Caucasoid type, while in the same area today, there are islands of remnant people, such as the Iraqw, who speak languages which are classified as Cushitic, and therefore belong to the Afroasiatic family. But most of the population of the open country south and east of the equatorial forest seem to have belonged to the Khoisan branch of African man, genetically linked to the Blacks, but distinguishable from them not only by skin colour and some other physical features, but presumably also by language. Certainly the Khoisan languages today are quite distinct from the family of languages spoken by the Blacks; among other things, their phonology makes an unusual use of click sounds. The Khoisan are often called Bushmen and Hottentots, but these terms refer rather to their cultures than to their ethnic stock. Hottentots are those Khoisan who, when Europeans first met with the stock in South Africa some centuries ago, had cattle but no agriculture, while the Bushmen had neither, being entirely Stone Age hunter–gatherers. Khoisan, made up from the Hottentot and Bushman names for themselves, 'Khoikhoi' and 'San' respectively, is certainly to be preferred. There is a fair amount of skeletal evidence for the earlier wide distribution of the Khoisan peoples, and there is also a Khoisan language, Sandawe, surviving today in central Tanzania alongside the Southern Cushitic remnants.

It is more difficult to be confident about the extent of Black habitation 5000 or so years ago. In the first place, as has already been mentioned, the Black seems to be an adaptation to the hot and wet conditions of equatorial and western Africa, that is to just those conditions least suitable for the preservation in the soil of skeletal evidence. It has already been suggested that the tropical forests which cover much of western and equatorial Africa were not a good environment for early human habitation, and the numbers of Blacks initially living actually within those forests were probably not large. Only one skeleton of Black type of any antiquity (about 9000 B.C.) has so far been found in these conditions—in southern Nigeria. Most of the early skeletal evidence for early Blacks is in fact not very early; it relates to the period roughly 5400–2000 B.C., and it comes from the southern Sahara between about 15° and 25°N. This is no

doubt simply because the dry soils of this area afford much better conditions for the preservation of bones than exist further south.

But Blacks were not the only inhabitants of the Sahara at this time; there were also Caucasoid peoples there. This introduces a second difficulty in defining the area of Black occupation around 3000 B.C.: on the northern fringes of this area, they were certainly mingled with non-Blacks, and it seems that this was the case on other fringes also. The most dramatic evidence comes in fact from the far north, from the Neolithic cemetery at Badari in Upper Egypt, which must date from about the fourth millennium B.C. Skeletons excavated here have been classified as belonging in about equal proportions to Caucasoid, Black and hybrid types. A similar mingling between Blacks and Caucasoids seems almost certainly to have been the case on the eastern fringe of Black occupation, in Uganda and Ethiopia, and it could well have been the case that there was a considerable overlap also southwards and south-eastwards into the Khoisan area. But here it would hardly be detectable because of the subsequent vast expansion into this area of Blacks from West Africa, which led to speakers of the particular group of languages called Bantu becoming the dominant stock of all the southern half of Africa save only the extreme southwest.

This radical alteration in the population map of Africa—and also a somewhat less dramatic shift in the distribution of population in the Sahara—was the consequence of two great changes in the northern half of the continent between about 8000 and 2000 B.C., one climatic and the other cultural. It was not until about the latter date that the Sahara emerged as the great desert it is today. Earlier it had an appreciably wetter climate, with the result that it was typically open grassland, supporting considerable game and, in its highlands, a Mediterranean flora. It had also supported an appreciable human population composed, as has been suggested, apparently about equally of Caucasoids and Blacks. But from about 10,000 B.C. onwards, the Saharan climate began to get appreciably drier, until ultimately the desert took over. The other great change was the spread in northern Africa of a series of exceptionally beneficial cultural innovations which had begun to be evident in a particular environment from about 8000 B.C. onwards. These innovations were to bring to an end the long Stone Age period of man's development, and launched him onto a series of cumulatively ever more rapid technological advances which eventually led to the present world civilization.

The beginnings of this process have commonly been called the Neolithic Revolution. The label is not very apt, since the appearance of a series of much more sophisticated and specialized new stone (i.e., 'neolithic') tools, ground and polished rather than simply chipped or flaked, was only one—and not necessarily the most significant—of a number of vital new technological advances, so that the revolution was plural and not solely Neolithic. Other important innovations were the invention of baskets and pottery, in which foods and liquids and other goods could be stored and transported, and the development of more or less permanent huts for man to live in. The real breakthrough, and the foundation for all subsequent human development, came with the discoveries that animals could be tamed and kept and bred and improved, and not simply hunted, and that seeds and roots could be improved and cultivated, and not merely collected or grubbed up from the wild.

The consequence was that man was no longer limited to small bands roaming the wilderness in search of his needs for food and water. He could live in increasingly larger and more permanent settlements, situated close by the best supplies of water for himself, his animals and his crops. He could be more or less certain that he could produce, store and preserve sufficient supplies of food to last him for a season, more or less independently of droughts and floods. Furthermore, some men could devote at least some of their time to specialized pursuits like the making of pottery and baskets and weapons and tools, or even, ultimately, war or government or scholarship. For the Neolithic Revolution was soon followed by the invention of writing—an admirable device for the accumulation and dissemination of knowledge—and the evolution of metallurgy—how to make implements of metal, first of copper and bronze, and then of iron.

It has usually been supposed that the lead in developing these enormously important new techniques was taken by the Near East, where both agriculture and towns had appeared by about 8000 B.C. or even earlier. But recent archaeology has suggested that adjacent parts of Europe and of Africa were not so far behind the Near East as once was thought, and that they need not have owed all their advancement to diffusions from the Near East. But in any case, as far as Africa is concerned, the northeastern part of the continent is practically part of what Europeans call the Near East. Archaeological activity in Africa was first concentrated mainly on Egypt and the lower Nile valley, and it has long been appreciated that here both animal husbandry and agriculture were established by at least 4000 B.C. More recently it has become apparent that at least some aspects of the Neolithic Revolution extended more or less contemporaneously into other parts of northern Africa. What happened in what is now the Sahara desert and in the region between the Sahara and the northern limits of the tropical forest, the region which is now called the Sudan,[2] had crucial effects on the distribution of races of man almost throughout the continent.

It is now known that the peoples of the Sahara before it became a desert had pottery as early as peoples of the Near East—certainly by about 6000 B.C., and cattle at least as early as the Egyptians—i.e., by about 4000 B.C. But two or three thousand years later the climate of the Sahara had become much what it is today, and conditions for human habitation had become barely tolerable. Human hunting and desiccation had between them destroyed almost all the game, and agriculture was impossible except in a few small areas, the oases, in which there were supplies of underground water. Over most of the Sahara, virtually the only means of human sustenance left was cattle-herding. The cattle competed with agriculture in the oases, greatly to its and their detriment, and eventually cattle herding came to depend mainly on transhumance, a specialized form of nomadic pastoralism by which cattle were taken deep into the desert only during the short seasons when it afforded some grazing, and spent the rest of the year in better pastures either to the north or the south.

The populations which could be supported in this way were obviously small. They were essentially Libyan-Berbers in the western half of the desert and also to the east of the Nile, the westerners—the ancestors of the modern Tuareg—distinguishing themselves by adopting a custom by which their menfolk were never seen in public without a veil covering the face below the eyes. In between, the desert pastoralists were much more Negroid, and presumably spoke languages which—as will be seen later in this chapter—have now been termed 'Nilo-Saharan'. Most of the earlier population of the Sahara, presumably at least partly cultivators, must have emigrated from the desert towards lands of higher rainfall or where there were at least better supplies of permanent water. It was natural that by and large the Caucasoids would choose to move north and north-east towards their fellows established in the Mediterranean coastlands and in the valley and delta of the lower Nile, while the Blacks from the Sahara tended to move southwards into the Sudan. In both cases the result would be to increase population densities, and so to encourage the development of agriculture as the most effective way to use the available land to support the increased population. There is evidence that population had been increasing in this way for some time in the lower valley and delta of the Nile, thus helping to produce the revolutionary situation which led by about 3000 B.C. to the emergence of Pharaonic Egypt, which is discussed in the following chapter.

What needs to be considered here are the subsequent developments in the Sudan. Over and above the increase of population resulting from immigration from the Sahara, the development of agriculture seems to have brought about a substantial increase of population in at least one area, which led to Blacks beginning to settle in the southern half of Africa, where eventually they displaced or absorbed all other populations save only those in the extreme south-west. The sequence of events which led to

this result has begun to be discerned only during about the last twenty years, and is therefore nothing like as well known or understood as the broadly parallel sequence concentrated into a single river valley which gave rise to Pharaonic Egypt. Some parallelisms are obvious enough; for example that the Niger valley and the Lake Chad basin afforded somewhat similar conditions for the growth of population to those in the Nile valley, and that the key process was the development of agriculture. Nevertheless, in the present state of knowledge, some argument by analogy and some speculation are inevitable.

However, one major and often accepted speculation is not necessary. This is that the Blacks of the Sudan experienced a Neolithic Revolution that was separate from the Neolithic Revolution of the Near East and Egypt. This has been argued, for example, most cogently in recent years by the anthropologist G. P. Murdock, who has in particular supposed an independent invention of agriculture by the Mande-speaking group of Blacks of the upper Niger valley. If at the relevant period, which would be broadly within the limits 5000 and 200c B.C., the Sahara had been the desert that it now is, such an argument might be necessary. But—as has been seen—at least at the beginning of this period, the Sahara provided a not unattractive, even in part cultivable, habitat for man, and it was a zone in which Black and Caucasoid peoples met and mingled. The evidence for Saharan agriculture is full of gaps, both chronological and spatial. Nevertheless, as has been pointed out, for example, by the archaeologist Desmond Clark, it is clear enough from the nature of the implements used that the Sahara participated in one single process of agricultural development in common with Egypt and the Near East. There is no reason to suppose that Saharan Blacks did not share in this development equally with Saharan Caucasoids; conceivably perhaps they shared more than equally. The first Saharan potters seem to have been Blacks; furthermore, modern Caucasoids in the Sahara are essentially pastoralists, while such cultivation as there still is, in the oases, is essentially by Blacks.

But the transformation of the Sahara into desert, which was completed by about 2000 B.C., did however mean that thereafter in the Sudan the development of agriculture, and of the Neolithic Revolution generally, did tend to stop being part of the one general Old World process, and became somewhat idiosyncratic. Historians of the west have tended to see this change in terms of sub-Saharan Africa being cut off from a mainstream of development in the Near East and the eastern Mediterranean which ultimately led to their own civilization. But this is neither really true nor really to the point. Contact across the Sahara desert was never impossible. Even if all else failed, which was not the case, transhumance alone would have ensured the continuance of some contact between North Africa and the Black Sudan. But the Blacks did need to adapt to new conditions the legacy they already possessed before the Sahara became a desert. Furthermore, the subsequent filtration—rather than cessation—of contacts with the north occasioned by the establishment of the desert, afforded them the opportunity to select what subsequent innovations pioneered in the Near East and the eastern Mediterranean seemed to be worth accepting and developing in the new situation in which they found themselves.

The essence of the difference between the situation of the Blacks and other Old World peoples who were experiencing the Neolithic Revolution was that the Blacks were the only people to be confined to a large land mass which (except for its remote southern tip) lay wholly within the tropics. This immediately posed problems for the agriculture they possessed before the growth of the desert confined them to the Sudan and to lands to the south of it. The staple crops, wheat and barley, of the farmers of temperate lands would not flourish in the short growing season of the Sudan, and would not grow at all in the wetter conditions further south. The Black farmers therefore had to turn to develop new seed crops from wild grasses indigenous to the Sudan, thus evolving the various grain crops called millets[3], and also domesticating an African rice. The Mande of the upper Niger may have been significant in the development of this African agriculture, but not as original inventors; rather because they inhabited a favourable river rain situation which, like the Nile valley, was unusually close to the Sahara from which some of their ancestors may have come. The evidence does indeed suggest that they were those who first cultivated the African variety of rice, but the major indigenous sub-Saharan grain crops, the millets, seem to have been developed in a number of strains throughout the Sudan. Further south, especially perhaps between modern Ghana and modern Nigeria, where today there is a gap in the tropical forest but where conditions did not favour the development of grain crops, the evolution was probably initially one of vegeculture rather than of agriculture proper. The African species of yams may have been first cultivated in this forest gap.

There is as yet rather little hard evidence for the dating of the progress of agriculture among the Blacks of the Sudan. But such evidence as there is (see, for example, chapter 3, p. 66) tends to the conclusion that the new cereal crops may have been developed in the savannahs between about 4000 and about 1000 B.C.

The next major development arising out of the Neolithic Revolution was the invention of metal tools and weapons to replace or supplement those made of the earlier raw materials, stone, wood and bone. This was certainly pioneered in the Near East, and the filtering effect of the Sahara desert may help to explain why it was that the smelting of iron ore and the forging of iron or steel implements appears in Black Africa at about the same time as the smelting of copper ores and the manufacture of objects of copper. It is known that copper was mined and worked at two localities in the southernmost western and central Sahara during the first half of the first millennium B.C.; iron was being smelted in the nearby Sudan, by people of the culture first recognized around Nok in what is now northern Nigeria, by at least 500 B.C. Thereafter knowledge of the working of the two metals seems to have spread more or less together, and remarkably rapidly, throughout almost all of sub-Saharan Africa, reaching what is now the Republic of South Africa by about A.D. 400. Elsewhere in the world, it was usual in the history of metallurgy for some millennia of copper working to precede the beginning of iron working. This was presumably because, although iron is a much harder and so more useful metal than copper and its alloys, its ores are much less obviously something out of which objects might be made than are some of the sources of copper, and, after it has been smelted, forging or other further treatment is needed before the metal is usable. As the two metals spread through sub-Saharan Africa, tools and weapons seem always to have been made from iron; the softer metal and its alloys being kept for the manufacture of decorative or symbolic objects. It should also be noted that, while deposits of iron ore may be found virtually throughout Black Africa, workable copper ores are relatively scarce, so that they and their products became highly valued. In the Sudan, copper ores hardly exist at all; it looks therefore as though the people of the Sudan may have taken up iron-working without previously having worked copper. It is difficult to imagine an invention of iron-working by people who had not previously worked the softer metal, so it seems likely that knowledge of iron-working must have been introduced into the Sudan from elsewhere. But exactly how this happened is unknown.

The most general hypothesis is that, after the establishment of the regular use of the metal in the Near East by about 1200 B.C., iron implements were introduced to the North African littoral on which the Phoenicians shortly began to colonize. But it is not thought that the manufacture of iron was developed in Africa on any scale until after the conquest of Egypt by iron-using Assyrians in the seventh century B.C. Following this, Nubia, the land above Egypt in the Nile valley, possessing greater resources of iron ore and especially of the timber needed to smelt it than did Egypt, became a major centre of iron-working from which it is thought that the technology was further diffused into sub-Saharan Africa.

But no evidence has yet been found for the diffusion of iron-working from Nubia westwards through the Sudan. Indeed a habitation site at Daima, just to the south of Lake Chad, which was occupied continuously from about the sixth century B.C. to about the twelfth century A.D., does not seem to have known iron until about the fifth or sixth century A.D. This is about ten centuries later than the known date for iron-working in the Nok culture, which lies further to the west, i.e., further from Nubia. It would not do to hang too much on the negative evidence from the one site at Daima, but it does suggest that it is rather more likely that knowledge of iron-working may have come to the western and central Sudan from the north, across the Sahara from the region of Phoenician settlement, than from the Nile valley in the east. Two additional pieces of evidence would seem to support this view. Knowledge of iron-working is probably unlikely to have been transmitted across the desert simply by its transhuman pastoralists who, among other things, had virtually no supplies of fuel for smelting. But it is known that there was a regular use of wheeled vehicles southwards across the western Sahara, conducted by peoples who lived close to its northern edge, by at least the fifth century B.C., while no equivalent traffic is known to have passed westwards from the Nile valley through the lands of the pastoralists of the eastern Sahara.* Secondly, there is the early evidence for copper mining and working in the southernmost western and central Sahara that has already been remarked.

With both wheeled vehicles and copper in the western and central Sahara at the relevant time, it seems plausible to suppose that knowledge of iron-working could have passed from North Africa to the western and central Sudan as quickly as did knowledge of the art of writing and the religion of Islam that brought it in its train. North Africans were hardly converted to Islam before the eighth century, and some West African Blacks were apparently converted by the tenth century at least. Indeed innovations from North Africa seem to have been quickly taken up by the Blacks in the Sudan provided only that they seemed likely to be useful to them in their circumstances. It was doubtless this criterion of utility in the Sudan which explains why the Blacks did *not* adopt the wheel, which other peoples invariably found a most useful invention, and which it seems must certainly have been known to the northernmost Blacks by the fifth century B.C.

As has been seen, the wheel approached West Africa as a means of transport, but though usable on light animal-drawn vehicles in areas of hard-going in the dry Sahara, it must have been much less useful in the Sudan, where wheeled vehicles would have been impracticable in the rainy season without made roads, and where anyway the Senegal and Niger rivers, and Lake Chad and its affluents, were natural waterways affording means for the much more efficient transport of men and goods by canoe. Also, the invention of the equipment to enable animals to be ridden, though appreciably later to the north of the desert than the discovery of how to use animals to draw vehicles, seems to have reached the Sudan hard on its heels. The use of horses and donkeys and, later, of camels for riding and as beasts of burden was much more practicable in the Sudan than their use as draft animals, and so caught on very quickly. It also quickly replaced the use of wheeled vehicles in the Sahara.

The growth of agriculture in the Sudan, reinforced by subsequent technological advances such as iron-working, must have permitted a considerable increase in its population. It is difficult to suppose that, even with the extensive use of land by shifting cultivation, population ever began to outrun the capacity of the land available for farming. But, if aridity was still increasing, or in periods of drought or other natural calamity, it may have become difficult to support people at the new levels of life to which they had become accustomed. On the other hand, the development of food production through agriculture had given time to spare for other pursuits, especially during the dry season between the harvest and the sowing. Bands of restless young men might well use this new leisure to go on excursions into the unknown lands surrounding their villages and farms. While supporting themselves by hunting and fishing, they would naturally keep their eyes open for empty lands and new resources which might offer further opportunities for themselves and their kinsfolk.

There was little scope for exploration, and none for expansion, northwards, where the Sahara desert was becoming ever more firmly established. So, if new lands were to be found for settlement and cultivation, they had to be sought to the south. But, with the one exception of the gap between modern Ghana and Nigeria, the land to the south was covered with thick tropical forest, difficult to penetrate even when iron tools had become available, and where the staple crops of the savannah could hardly be grown. On the wide front, therefore, all that was feasible was for small bands to infiltrate the forest or to explore the possibility of outflanking it to the east. Because increasing desiccation had always inclined the early farmers to concentrate their settlements on the banks of rivers and lakes, where as much of the year might be spent in fishing and canoeing as in actual farming, the key to the success of both enterprises seems likely to have been in the disposition of these major water features. Outflanking the forest to the east would have been facilitated by using affluents of Lake Chad like the river Chari, but in the end it would have run into the waterlogged country of the Upper Nile known as the Sudd, an unpromising region for agricultural settlement. Today the western limits of the Sudd coincide with a major cultural and linguistic boundary, with agricultural peoples speaking Niger-Congo languages to the west and pastoral peoples speaking Nilo-Saharan languages to the east (see below, pp. 22–3). However small bands could infiltrate the forest and make some progress by clearing small plots on the banks of streams, gradually developing crops more suitable to the conditions, and placing the emphasis more on vegetables like yams than on grain crops. In one direction really considerable advances were ultimately possible. Successive generations of pioneers advancing through the forest to the south of the Benue tributary of the Niger would in time come to rivers like the Sanga and the Ubangi, and thus gain access to the major central African drainage system of the Congo basin, so that further exploration would ultimately bring them to the wide savannahs to the south and east of the forest. The evidence suggests that such a movement must have occurred, beginning possibly around 2000 B.C. and reaching the savannahs not later than about 300 B.C., with the ultimate result that the people who today are called the Bantu had become the dominant human stock throughout the southern half of Africa save for the extreme south-west, in and around the Kalahari desert, where rainfall was (and is) inadequate to permit of cultivation.

'Bantu' is strictly speaking a term of linguistic classification. It derives from the facts that in the languages spoken by the Black peoples who today provide almost all the inhabitants of the southern half of Africa, some form of the root *ntu* is in general used to mean 'human being', and that these languages have a system of noun classes in which some form of the prefix *ba* -signifies the plural form of the class denoting persons. The 400 or so Bantu languages spoken in the enormous expanse of territory south of a line which runs roughly from Mt. Cameroun on the Atlantic coast to Mount Elgon in Uganda, and thence to the east coast near Lamu (albeit with a big re-entrant to the south into central Tanzania), are indeed much more alike in vocabulary and in grammatical structure than is usually the case—even with much smaller areas—with the languages of the Sudan. Thus when, about the mid-nineteenth century, African languages began to be the subject of scientific study, Bantu was seen to be a much more obvious language family than any which could be worked out for the other languages of the Blacks. Though in due course a number of groupings for what came to be called the Sudanic languages were proposed and discussed, the plain fact was that any two adjacent Sudanic peoples, even if culturally very similar, could speak languages so markedly different from one another that their date of separation from any presumed common parent language must have taken place many thousands of years in the past. Any one Bantu language, on the other hand, was likely to be partially intelligible to the speakers of nearby languages, and perhaps not wholly unintelligible to speakers of any other Bantu language, even one spoken some distance away.

It was this unusually close interrelationship of the Bantu languages that provided the first indication that the ancestors of their modern speakers must have occupied the whole southern half of Africa relatively recently and relatively quickly. But other early surmises as to what else this close interrelationship might signify were less apt. It was common to think of the Bantu tongues as a family of languages separate from all other language families of the Blacks. Often the Bantu languages were thought to be so distinct from the other African languages that their speakers could not be 'true Blacks'; it was not unusual, indeed, to think of them as 'Hamiticized Blacks', i.e., to suppose that both their similarities among themselves—cultural as well as linguistic—and their separateness from other black Africans were due to processes of conquest by, and mixing with, 'Hamites'.

The second of these conclusions was very much a value judgement, favoured by those, such as Seligman, who believed in the myth of Hamitic superiority. But neither could be overthrown until enough work had been done in reasonable depth on a substantial number of the multitude of languages that are spoken in Africa, so that the nature and extent of interrelationships between them might be assessed on scientific principles. By the late 1940s, the American linguist, Joseph H. Greenberg, considered that enough was known for him to begin the heroic task of trying to work out an overall, genetic scheme of classification for all the languages of Africa. His method was the classic one first used by the pioneers who had recognized the Indo-European language family. From each of the 800 or so languages spoken in Africa for which he could secure dictionaries or word-lists, Greenberg extracted as many as he could find of a sample of some 400 words with quite basic meanings (e.g., the words for the first ten numerals and for parts of the body, or the words for 'sun' and 'bird', or for 'to eat' or 'to die'). He then compared these words, together with available grammatical evidence, with a view to establishing genetical relationships between the languages.

It was immediately apparent to Greenberg that there was no evidence that the Bantu languages were genetically related to 'Hamitic'. Their grammatical behaviour was different, and so too was their basic vocabulary. The most that could be said was that some word-borrowing had occurred in areas where speakers of two entirely separate language traditions had come into cultural contact.

But by the time that Greenberg was writing, this conclusion was less revolutionary than his eventual decision (1963) that there were only four separate and distinct families of languages in the whole continent. Two of these have already been mentioned, Afroasiatic and Khoisan. The others, which were the language families of the Black peoples, he proposed to call 'Nilo-Saharan' and 'Congo-Kordofanian'.

The 'Nilo-Saharan' languages were spoken by dark-skinned peoples living in the eastern Sahara (for example, the Kanuri, the Teda and the Zaghawa), in the valley of the Niger where it bends north into the desert (Songhai), between the river Chari and the Upper Nile (including Nubian and the 'Nilotic' languages such as Shilluk, Acholi and Nuer), and south-eastwards of this to make an indentation into Bantu country in the dry lands of Kenya and Tanzania east of Lake Victoria, the home of what had previously been called 'Nilo-Hamitic' languages (such as Masai and Nandi).

'Congo-Kordofanian' included a few languages spoken by small groups in Kordofan, in the Sudan Republic, but its main grouping was what Greenberg called 'Niger-Congo'. This comprised the languages spoken by all the agricultural peoples in West Africa from Senegal to eastern Nigeria, and all the Bantu languages of central, eastern and southern Africa. Building on earlier work by Diedrich Westermann, Greenberg confidently asserted that within this major family the status of the Bantu languages, despite their number and their vast spread, was merely a branch of the particular sub-family of the languages spoken by the Blacks living between the river Benue and the Cameroons.[5]

The overall genetic scheme proposed by Greenberg was so far-sweeping and radical that immediate and universal acceptance of it by other linguists was hardly to be expected. Some of them, indeed, were critical of his methods, pointing to the small sample of words used to establish genetic

relationships between the languages and to his use of words from vocabularies which all too often had not been rigorously established. But the negative conclusion that the Bantu languages are not in any real sense 'Hamitic' presents no difficulty, nor does the idea that the Bantu languages are related in some way to the Sudanic languages of West Africa. Furthermore, both 'Nilo-Saharan' and 'Niger-Congo' are illuminating concepts for the historian. An outstanding characteristic of the speakers of Nilo-Saharan languages is that they are predominantly pastoralists. It is therefore possible to surmise that they are the descendants of Blacks of the eastern Sahara and Sudan whose experience of the Neolithic Revolution included the development of animal husbandry and of iron-working, but commonly stopped short of much in the way of agriculture. An obvious explanation for this would be that they inhabited territories with annual rainfalls inadequate to allow of cultivation as a major mode of subsistence. With appreciably greater confidence, it can be suggested that the ancestors of the speakers of the Niger-Congo languages were the inhabitants of the western Sudan who experienced the full flood of the agricultural revolution, and who consequently expanded over all available lands to the south and south-east.

Greenberg was led to suppose, indeed, that the peopling by Blacks of the southern half of Africa must have taken the form of an overflowing to the south and east by the nearest West African farmers, those of the Benue-Cameroun border area. As a result, the Bantu languages, despite their subordinate genetic status, had become by far the most widespread group of the whole Niger-Congo family. But hardly had this conclusion been published, than it was apparently challenged by the results of another substantial piece of research, that undertaken by Malcolm Guthrie, an older and more cautious British linguist, and one of those who had been most critical of Greenberg's work.

Whereas Greenberg's purpose had been to classify all the languages of Africa (so that he had no choice but to work from the top down using a select list of 'basic' words), Guthrie was interested in the classification only of the Bantu languages. He was therefore able to work from the bottom upwards, examining material from virtually all the Bantu languages, and in the case of 28 of them, selected in part because their data had been well established but also because geographically they were well distributed over the whole Bantu-speaking area, he took into account their whole known vocabularies. Guthrie ended up by assembling some 22,000 sets of cognates, that is two sets of words, each word coming from a different language, which, when due allowance had been made for shifts of sound and sense according to recognized rules, were sufficiently alike in both respects for it to be confidently asserted that they must descend from a single root in some ancestral language. About 500 of these cognates had a relatively uniform meaning throughout a very wide range of Bantu languages, so that Guthrie concluded that they must be descendants from roots in a language which was the ancestor of all Bantu languages, a 'Proto-Bantu'. A further 1500 were found to exist entirely or predominantly in either westerly or easterly Bantu languages, the inference being that the first split of Proto-Bantu was into western and eastern dialects.

Somewhat to his surprise, Guthrie found that those of his 28 test languages containing the highest proportions, 50 and 54 per cent respectively, of reflexes from the 500 roots common to his Proto-Bantu as a whole, were the languages of the Luba and Bemba, peoples living right in the centre of the present Bantu-speaking area, in southeastern Zaire and adjacent Zambia. He was led to the conclusion that it was in this region, in and around the Shaba province of modern Zaire, that the speakers of Proto-Bantu must have lived, and that it was from there that their descendants must have subsequently spread out, after their tongues had diverged into western and eastern variants, to occupy the rest of what may now be called Bantu Africa. In the process, their languages diverged even further. Whereas east and west of the 'Bantu nucleus' the divergencies were relatively slight, so that both Kongo on the west coast and Swahili on the east coast had retained 44

per cent of the Proto-Bantu roots, they increased as one looked further afield, and particularly in the extreme south-east, where Xhosa had only 26 per cent, and in the far north-west, where the Douala language in Cameroun retained as little as 14 per cent of the roots of Proto-Bantu.

Concerned as he was only with the Bantu languages, Guthrie did not attempt to relate his Proto-Bantu to the Sudanic languages of West Africa. Nevertheless he was in a very general way prepared to accept that there was some connection, and that Proto-Bantu could have had a West African ancestor which might be called 'Pre-Bantu'. But his historical interpretation of the Bantu linguistic pattern which he had discerned, with expansion in all directions—including northwest *towards* West Africa—from a central Shaban nucleus, did not permit him to accept Greenberg's notion of a straightforward overflowing from the Benue-Cameroun border region into what was to become Bantu Africa. He was left with the idea that a few 'Pre-Bantu' must have moved very quickly along the Congo waterways through the forest until they reached the southern savannahs, where their agriculture could flourish again and they became the Proto-Bantu. Then, as their numbers grew, especially following the introduction of metal technology and of south-east Asian food-crops well suited to the wetter parts of their environment, they spread out in all directions into what is now known as Bantu Africa.

Some support for such a hypothesis comes from the presence of canoeing and fishing terms among the 500 or so roots reconstructable for Proto-Bantu, and also from some scraps of very exiguous literary evidence. When the Indian Ocean coast of Africa was first described in writing, in the Greek sailors' guide of about A.D. 100 known as the *Periplus of the Erythraean Sea*, this coast was called Azania, and no 'Ethiopians', dark-skinned people, were mentioned among its inhabitants. They first appear in the largely fourth-century *Geography* ascribed to Claudius Ptolemy of Alexandria, and then only towards the south, probably on the coast of what today is northern Mozambique, i.e., about the latitude of

Guthrie's 'Bantu nucleus'. Cosmas Indicopleustes in the sixth century was to call this southern coast Zingium. After Cosmas, the surviving descriptions of the East African coast are not written in Greek, but in Arabic; Greek-speaking merchants had given way to sea-traders who spoke Arabic, and for them Zingium had become Zanj. Whether Zanj is to be understood as an ethnic or a geographical designation seems to vary with the context in which the name is used; nevertheless, for Mas'udi, a Baghdad geographer of the tenth century, Zanj encompassed the whole known East African coast south of what is now Somalia, i.e. from the present northern limit on the coast of Bantu-speaking Blacks. The inference from these references seems to be, first, that for the early Greek observers, the original 'Azanian' inhabitants of the Indian Coast were not to be distinguished from the peoples they knew on the African shore of the Red Sea, and that therefore they were speakers of Afroasiatic, and most probably Cushitic, languages; and, second, that southwards from Somalia, by the tenth century these Azanians had been replaced by Blacks coming from the south who were presumably ancestors of the modern Bantu-speaking peoples of East Africa.

The suggestion that the spread of the Bantu from a central, Shaban, nucleus was facilitated by the arrival of south-east Asian food-crops is a reasonable one. There is no question but that some of today's most significant sub-Saharan food-crops— including bananas and plantains, the coconut and the sugar-cane, and important varieties of yams and rice—were first brought into cultivation in South-East Asia, and that it was as cultigens that they were introduced into Africa, presumably across its eastern coastline. Some of them had no African equivalents and—more generally—because they had been developed in areas of greater rainfall than most of the sub-Saharan food-crops, they must have made it easier for humans to settle, and to multiply their populations, in the wetter tropical African areas such as the forests and the monsoonal eastern coastlands. Exactly how and when the south-east Asian food-crops came into tropical Africa is not known. However it is plausible to suppose

that one route of introduction would have been connected with the colonization of the great island of Madagascar by Indonesians. Little is known about this colonization beyond the basic fact that the Malagasy language unquestionably belongs to the family of languages spoken in Indonesia. Moreover, since its words for iron and iron-working have cognates in modern Indonesian languages, while on the other hand it shows no evidence of Sanskrit or Hindu influences, there are good grounds for supposing that the colonization of Madagascar must have taken place after the beginning of the Iron Age in Indonesia and before its languages were subjected to influences from India, that is between the limits of about A.D. 300 and A.D. 800. The northern end of Madagascar is in the same latitude as Shaba and Guthrie's presumed Bantu nucleus, and, since the island was settled by Bantu-speaking Blacks as well as by emigrants from Indonesia, it does seem that Madagascar would have provided a suitable route for the transmission of the south-east Asian food crops to the Bantu.

But, attractive though it is, there is really no hard evidence to substantiate the idea (used in the first edition of this book) that a central nucleus of Bantu settlement was encouraged to flourish and expand by the arrival of south-east Asian food-crops. Such a notion starts, indeed, with a misconception, that the nucleus discerned by Guthrie has *historical* significance. Its real significance is rather statistical and geographical, for it is reasonable to expect that the largest common word stock of a widely spread and developing family of languages is more likely to be central rather than peripheral. (Conversely, the languages of the family in which the greatest number of cognates have survived from the original ancestral language are perhaps more likely to be found on the periphery.) Luckily Guthrie published all the data on which his conclusions had been based, and it was therefore possible for other investigators—perhaps most notably Bernd Heine and Alick Henrici—to rework it. It has been shown that his conclusions were least convincing for the north-western Bantu languages, not only in relation to the connection between 'Pre-Bantu' and the Sudanic languages of West Africa, but also, and importantly, in the analysis of the Bantu languages of this quadrant. It is now apparent that the connection with the West African Sudanic languages is much more like that suggested by Greenberg, and that the pattern of relationships among the north-western Bantu languages was much more determined by a southwards drift of peoples from West Africa than by any movement or influences going in the reverse direction. This fits in with the opinion of many anthropologists that there is a considerable degree of cultural continuity from West Africa round the Bight of Biafra to northern Angola.

While there has been general acceptance for Guthrie's concept that the Bantu languages on the eastern side of the continent are sufficiently closely related to mark them off as a group distinct from the others, the later investigators have had difficulty in recognizing any single equivalent grouping for the languages of the western Bantu peoples of the Congo basin and of the savannah lands immediately to its south. It looks as though the expansion in the west must have been by and large slower than expansion in the eastern half of Bantu Africa. Certainly today it is apparent that the eastern languages cover more ground and encompass appreciably more speakers than do the western Bantu languages. Geography does much to explain this. Movement through the Congo basin forest must necessarily have been slower and more piecemeal than movement over the savannah lands characteristic of eastern and south-eastern Africa, and when the westerners came out of the forests, by and large they were faced with drier lands than the easterners, so that ultimately their expansion was totally halted by the Namib and Kalahari deserts. Conversely, the population growth and the expansion of the eastern Bantu is likely to have been helped by the coming of the south-east Asian food-crops to a greater extent than was possible for the western Bantu. But it now seems plain that, if these food-crops did not arrive among the Bantu before somewhere between about A.D. 300 and A.D. 800, it would have been too late to help with their first expansion beyond the Congo basin.

Since the time when Greenberg and Guthrie were working on the linguistic data, a great amount of relevant archaeological evidence has accumulated. Work at a very large number of sites, firmly dated by the radiocarbon technique, has now demonstrated that by about the end of the fourth century A.D. virtually the whole of the present area of Bantu speech from Uganda in the north to as far as the Transvaal in the south was already occupied by iron-working peoples. There is, of course, no means of knowing for certain what languages were spoken by pre-literate iron-workers, but archaeologists have inferred from the pottery and other evidence of their material culture that has survived that in all probability these iron-workers were the ancestors of modern peoples who speak Bantu languages. Guthrie had suggested from his analysis of the linguistic evidence that the Bantu expansion had begun as one of pre-Iron Age fishermen and cultivators, with knowledge of iron working coming in later. The archaeological evidence would seem to support this. Though there are some earlier dates at the end of the B.C. era around Lake Victoria, over almost all the rest of what is now Bantu Africa the dates for the establishment of iron-working lie between about A.D. 100 and about A.D. 400, and the gradient of the dates between north and south is really so slight that it would seem possible that for the most part the people were already *in situ* when knowledge of iron-working reached them. Indeed the coming of iron need not have involved any great migration of people; it could have taken the form of the swift adoption of a valuable new technology by well-established and progressive farming peoples. No more than the south-east Asian crops can knowledge of iron-working be looked to as a primary factor in the Bantu expansion.

It must be appreciated that Bantu-speaking migrants moving out of the Congo basin forests were not moving into uninhabited lands. As has already been remarked (p. 11), the Sandawe survive as an island of Khoisan speech as far north as central Tanzania, and the language of their near neighbours the Hadza may also be classified as Khoisan. In addition it is well known that the south-easternmost

Bantu languages such as Zulu and Xhosa incorporate the click consonants characteristic of Khoisan—the most likely explanation for this being intermarriage between incoming Bantu-speakers and local Khoisan. Indeed, the further south they went, the more it is likely that the advance of the Bantu involved the absorption of earlier, rather thinly spread Khoisan populations. In the north-east, the Bantu entered 'Azanian' lands inhabited by peoples speaking southern Cushitic languages. Indeed this was of some importance because there is firm archaeological evidence that modern Kenya and northern Tanzania were the home of a succession of societies, once known as the 'Stone Bowl' cultures, which from about the middle of the third millennium B.C. onwards had cattle and were developing food-producing techniques well suited to the environment. It is unlikely that the Bantu would have brought large cattle with them through the forest, and their cattle terminology suggests that they acquired cattle from eastern African speakers of Cushitic languages, possibly through the mediation of Khoisan-speaking peoples. There is also linguistic evidence to suggest that at a later stage the Bantu may have borrowed the practice of milking directly from Cushitic-speaking peoples in East Africa.

In conclusion, it can be said that the Bantu expansion seems to have begun as a gradual seepage of small groups through the forests of the Congo basin. The relatively slow and piecemeal nature of this movement in a difficult environment helps to explain the complexity of the pattern and the interrelationship of the languages in the north-western quadrant of present-day Bantu Africa. When the advancing Bantu had penetrated right through the forest, the situation changed. The northeastern Bantu in the forest do not seem to have expanded beyond it, perhaps because to do so would bring them up against Nilo-Saharan societies that were well adapted to an environment that was at best marginal for agriculture. But when the Bantu came to the open savannahs beyond the southerly boundaries of the forest, their expansion seems to have substantially accelerated. Their cereal agriculture could provide the basis for larger populations than already existed there, but at the same time they were also able to absorb useful aspects of the material cultures of, and sometimes also people from, these populations. The earlier societies survived intact only in drier lands which were at best marginal for agriculture. In the north-east, while Nilo-Saharan pastoralists were able to hold on to the salient of arid plains which extend from the south of the modern Sudan Republic into central Tanzania, Cushitic-speaking peoples—except for the small groups like the Iraqw which have survived at the southern end of this salient near the Sandawe and Hatsa—were restricted to an essentially pastoral existence in the hot lowlands of the Horn. In central and southern Africa, although there may have been some Caucasoids, the bulk of the pre-Bantu population seems to have been composed of the culturally weaker Khoisan. Some of these, in contact with early Bantu arrivals, may have adopted their use of agriculture and metals, but in the long run most of them were swamped by, and absorbed into expanding Bantu-speaking populations. Some of the Khoisan, being entirely Stone Age hunter–gatherers, were not really absorbable and in so far as they were not hunted to extinction, survived only by retreat into the arid refuge of the Kalahari.

The Bantu expansion seems to have been most fruitful on the eastern side of the continent. On the western side, the Bantu could do little more than develop their Sudanic inheritance on a new frontier, a frontier which became increasingly less attractive the further south they went towards the desert lands of the Namib and the Kalahari. In the east, on the other hand, the Bantu met with a number of new stimuli. The first of these was contact with the Cushitic pastoralists and food-producers, while later on they would be the first to receive the rewarding new south-east Asian food-crops. In between times, of course, it would seem that it was in the far north-east that what we now know as Bantu first began to make tools and weapons of iron, and it was from there that knowledge of iron-working was spread through most of the rest of Bantu-speaking Africa.

NOTES

1. This may *not* be very significant, as there is a good deal of evidence of the influence of diet on stature.

2. The name comes from the Arabic *Bilad al-Sndan*, i.e., 'the land of the black men', which is equivalent, as has been seen, to the original Greek sense of Ethiopia. There was also an equivalent North African Berber name, *Akal n-Iguinawen*, from which derives the modern term Guinea. But whereas in modern geographic and ethnographic usage, 'Sudan' and 'Sudanic' are applied to the whole belt of territory immediately south of the Sahara which the early Arab geographers saw to be inhabited by Blacks, 'Guinea', because the name came into European languages via the Portuguese, who approached Black Africa from the west by sea, is now used geographically and ethnographically only for the southern, forested zone of the Sudan. Today, of course, both Sudan and Guinea also have much more restricted extents in political usage, since four African republics now bear these names, while Ethiopia is really only used for the state of that name.

3. E.g., the *Sorghum* species ('Great Millet'), the *Digitaria* species ('Small Millet'), and the *Pennisetum* species ('Bulrush' or 'Pearl Millet').

4. Phoenician settlement in North Africa, the development of civilization in Nubia, and the wheeled vehicles in the Sahara are all subjects which are developed further in chapter 2.

5. In this book, the old-fashioned English term 'the Cameroons' refers to the coastal region by the Cameroons river and Mt. Cameroun, while 'Cameroun' is used For the much larger area of the modern republic and the former colony, which was first German (Kamerun) and then French.

THE SEARCH FOR ADAM AND EVE

By John Tiernney, Linda Wright, and Karen Springen

Scientists are calling her Eve, but reluctantly. The name evokes too many wrong images—the weak-willed figure in Genesis, the milk-skinned beauty in Renaissance art, the voluptuary gardener in "Paradise Lost" who was all "softness" and "meek surrender" and waist-length "gold tresses." The scientists' Eve—subject of one of the most provocative anthropological theories in a decade—was more likely a dark-haired, black-skinned woman, roaming a hot savanna in search of food. She was as muscular as Martina Navratilova, maybe stronger; she might have torn animals apart with her hands, although she probably preferred to use stone tools. She was not the only woman on earth, nor necessarily the most attractive or maternal. She was simply the most fruitful, if that is measured by success in propagating a certain set of genes. Hers seem to be in all humans living today: 5 billion blood relatives. She was, by one rough estimate, your 10,000th-great-grandmother.

When scientists announced their "discovery" of Eve last year, they rekindled perhaps the oldest human debate: where did we come from? They also, in some sense, confirmed a belief that existed long before the Bible. Versions of the Adam-and-Eve story date back at least 5,000 years and have been told in cultures from the Mediterranean to the South Pacific to the Americas. The mythmakers spun their tales on the same basic assumption as the scientists:

that at some point we all share an ancestor. The scientists don't claim to have found the first woman, merely a common ancestor—possibly one from the time when modern humans arose. What's startling about this Eve is that she lived 200,000 years ago. This date not only upsets fundamentalists (the Bible's Eve was calculated to have lived 5,992 years ago), it challenges many evolutionists' conviction that the human family tree began much earlier.

Eve has provoked a scientific controversy bitter even by the standards of anthropologists, who have few rivals at scholarly sniping. Their feuds normally begin when someone's grand theory of our lineage is contradicted by the unearthing of a few stones or bones. This time, however, the argument involves a new breed of anthropologists who work in air-conditioned American laboratories instead of dessicated African rift valleys. Trained in molecular biology, they looked at an international assortment of genes and picked up a trail of DNA that led them to a single woman from whom we are all descended. Most evidence so far indicates that Eve lived in sub-Saharan Africa, although a few researchers think her home might have been southern China. Meanwhile, other geneticists are trying to trace our genes back to a scientifically derived Adam, a putative "great father" of us all. As is often the case, paternity is proving harder to establish: the molecular trail to Adam involves a different, more elusive sort of DNA.

The most controversial implication of the geneticists' work is that modern humans didn't slowly and inexorably evolve in different parts of the world, as many anthropologists believed. The evolution from archaic to modern Homo sapiens seems to have occurred in only one place, Eve's family. Then, sometime between 90,000 and 180,000 years ago, a group of her progeny left their homeland endowed apparently with some special advantage over every tribe of early humans they encountered. As they fanned out, Eve's descendants replaced the locals, eventually settling the entire world. Some "stones-and-bones" anthropologists accept this view of evolution, but others refuse to accept this interpretation of the genetic evidence. They think our common ancestor must have lived much farther in the past, at least a million years ago, because that was when humans first left Africa and began spreading out over the world, presumably evolving separately into the modern races. As the veteran excavator Richard Leakey declared in 1977: "There is no single center where modern man was born."

But now geneticists are inclined to believe otherwise, even if they can't agree where the center was. "If it's correct, and I'd put money on it, this idea is tremendously important," says Stephen Jay Gould, the Harvard paleontologist and essayist. "It makes us realize that all human beings, despite differences in external appearance, are really members of a single entity that's had a very recent origin in one place. There is a kind of biological brotherhood that's much more profound than we ever realized."

This brotherhood was not always obvious in Chicago two months ago, when the Eve hypothesis was debated by the American Anthropological Association. Geneticists flashed diagrams of DNA, paleoanthropologists showed slides of skulls and everyone argued with everyone else. "What bothers many of us paleontologists," said Fred Smith of the University of Tennessee, "is the perception that this new data from DNA is so precise and scientific and that we paleontologists are just a bunch of bumbling old fools. But if you listen to the geneticists, you realize they're as divided about their genetic data as we are about the bones. We may be bumbling fools, but we're not any more bumbling than they are." For all their quarrels, though, the two groups left Chicago convinced they're closer than ever to establishing the origin of modern humanity. To make sense of their bumbling toward Eden, it may be best to go back to one ancient relative accepted by all scientists. That would be the chimpanzee.

Until the molecular biologists came along, the role of the chimpanzee in evolution rested on the usual evidence: skeletons. Scientists have relied on bones ever since the 1850s, when Darwin published his theory of evolution and some quarriers unearthed a strange skeleton in Germany's Neander Valley. Was the stooped apelike figure a remnant of an ancient race? Leading scientists thought not. One declared it a Mongolian soldier from the Napoleonic Wars. A prominent anatomist concluded it was a recent "pathological idiot."

But more skeletons kept turning up across Europe and Asia. Anthropologists realized that Neanderthal man was one of many brawny, beetle-browed humans who mysteriously disappeared about 34,000 years ago. These early Homo sapiens, incidentally, were not stooped (that first skeleton was hunched with arthritis). Nor did they fit the stereotype of the savage cave man. Their skulls were thicker than ours, but their brains were as large. Their fossils show that they cared for the infirm elderly and buried the dead. It seemed they might be our ancestors after all.

Meanwhile, fossil hunters in Asia more than a half century ago found the still older bones of Java man and Peking man, who had smaller brains and even more muscular bodies. These skeletons dated back as far as 800,000 years. Perhaps they represented evolutionary dead ends. Or perhaps they, too, were human ancestors, with their descendants evolving into modern Asians while the Neanderthals were becoming modern Europeans—a process of racial differentiation that lasted a million years. Either way, it appeared that all these ancient humans traced their lineage back to Africa, because that was the only place with evidence of humans living more than a million years ago. Stone tools were invented there about 2 million years ago by an ancestor named Homo habilis ("Handy Man"). Before him was Lucy, whose 3 million-year-old skeleton was unearthed in the Ethiopian desert in 1974. (Her discoverers celebrated by staying up all night drinking beer, and they named her after the Beatles' song that kept blaring on the camp's tape player, "Lucy in the Sky with Diamonds.") Lucy was three and a half feet tall and walked erect—not ape, not quite human. At some point her hominid ancestors had begun evolving away from the forebears of our closest relative, the chimpanzee.

But when? Most anthropologists thought it was at least 15 million years ago, because they had found bones from that era of an apelike creature who seemed to be ancestral to humans but not apes. Then, for the first time, geneticists intruded with contradictory evidence, led in 1967 by Vincent Sarich and Allan Wilson of the University of California, Berkeley. They drew blood from baboons, chimps and humans, then looked at the molecular structure of a blood protein that was thought to change at a slow, steady rate as a species evolved. There were major differences between the molecules of chimps and baboons, as expected, since the two species have been evolving separately for 30 million years. But the difference between humans and chimps was surprisingly small—so small, the geneticists concluded, that they must have parted company just 5 million years ago. Other geneticists used different techniques and came up with a figure of 7 million years.

Traditional anthropologists did not appreciate being told their estimates were off by 8 million or 10 million years. The geneticists' calculation was dismissed and ignored for more than a decade, much to Wilson's displeasure. "He was called a lunatic for 10 years. He's still sensitive," recalls Rebecca Cann, a former colleague at Berkeley who is now at the University of Hawaii. But eventually the geneticists were vindicated by the bones themselves. As more fossils turned up, anthropologists realized that the 15 million-year-old bones didn't belong to a human

ancestor and that chimps and humans did indeed diverge much more recently.

Now Wilson, who won a MacArthur "genius grant" in 1986, is once again trying to speed up evolution. The Eve hypothesis, being advanced both by his laboratory and by a group at Emory University, is moving up the date when the races of humanity diverged—and once again Wilson faces resistance. Some anthropologists aren't happy to see Neanderthal and Peking man removed from our lineage, consigned to dead branches of the family tree. Wilson likes to remind the critics of the last fight. "They're being dragged slowly along," he says. "They'll eventually come around."

To find Eve, Cann first had to persuade 147 pregnant women to donate their babies' placentas to science. The placentas were the easiest way to get large samples of body tissue. Working with Wilson and a Berkeley biologist, Mark Stoneking, Cann selected women in America with ancestors from Africa, Europe, the Middle East and Asia. Her collaborators in New Guinea and Australia found Aboriginal women there. The babies were born, the placentas were gathered and frozen, and the tissue analysis began at Wilson's lab in Berkeley. The tissues were ground in a souped-up Waring blender, spun in a centrifuge, mixed with a cell-breaking detergent, dyed flourescent and spun in a centrifuge again. The result was a clear liquid containing pure DNA.

This was not the DNA in the nucleus of the babies' cells—the genes that determine most physical traits. This DNA came from outside the nucleus, in a compartment of the cell called the mitochondrion, which produces nearly all the energy to keep the cell alive. Scientists didn't learn that the mitochondrion contained any genes until the 1960s. Then in the late 1970s they discovered that mitochondrial DNA was useful for tracing family trees because it's inherited only from the mother. It's not a mixture of both parents' genes, like nuclear DNA, so it preserves a family record that isn't scrambled every generation. It's altered only by mutations—random, isolated mistakes in copying the genetic code, which are then passed on to the next generation. Each random mutation produces a new type of DNA as distinctive as a fingerprint. (The odds against two identical mitochondrial DNA's appearing by chance are astronomical because there are so many ways to rearrange the units of the genetic code.)

To study these mutations, the Berkeley researchers cut each sample of DNA into segments that could be compared with the DNA of other babies. The differences were clear but surprisingly small. There weren't even telltale distinctions between races. "We're a young species, and there are really very few genetic differences among cultures," Stoneking says." In terms of our mitochondrial DNA, we're much more closely related than almost any other vertebrate or mammalian species. You find New Guineans whose DNA is closer to other Asians' than to other New Guineans." This may seem odd, given obvious racial differences. In fact, though, many differences represent trivial changes. Skin color, for instance, is a minor adaptation to climate—black in Africa for protection from the sun, white in Europe to absorb ultraviolet radiation that helps produce vitamin D. It takes only a few thousand years of evolution for skin color to change. The important changes—in brain size, for instance—can take hundreds of thousands of years.

The babies' DNA seemed to form a family tree rooted in Africa. The DNA fell into two general categories, one found only in some babies of recent African descent, and a second found in everyone else and the other Africans. There was more diversity among the exclusively African group's DNA, suggesting that it had accumulated more mutations because it had been around longer—and thus was the longest branch of the family tree. Apparently the DNA tree began in Africa, and then at some point a group of Africans emigrated, splitting off to form a second branch of DNA and carrying it to the rest of the world.

All the babies' DNA could be traced back, ultimately, to one woman. In itself that wasn't surprising, at least not to statisticians familiar with the quirks of genetic inheritance. "There must be one lucky mother," Wilson says. "I worry about the term 'Eve' a little bit because of the implication that in her generation there were only two people.

We are not saying that. We're saying that in her generation there was some unknown number of men and women, probably a fairly large number, maybe a few thousand." Many of these other women presumably are also our ancestors, because their nuclear genes would have been passed along to sons and daughters and eventually would have reached us. But at some point these other women's mitochondrial genes disappeared because their descendants failed to have daughters, and so the mitochondrial DNA wasn't passed along. At first glance it may seem inconceivable that the source of all mitochondrial DNA was a single woman, but it's a well established outcome of the laws of probability.

You can get a feel for the mathematics by considering a similar phenomenon: the disappearance of family names. Like mitochondrial DNA, these are generally passed along by only one sex—in this case, male. If a son marries and has two children, there's a one-in-four chance that he'll have two daughters. There's also a chance that he won't have any children. Eventually the odds catch up and a generation passes without a male heir, and the name disappears. "It's an inevitable consequence of reproduction," says John Avise, a geneticist at the University of Georgia. "Lineages will be going extinct all the time." After 20 generations, for instance, it's statistically likely that only 90 out of 100 original surnames will disappear. Avise cites the history of Pitcairn Island in the Pacific, which was settled in 1790 by 13 Tahitian women and six British sailors who had mutinied on the Bounty. After just seven generations, half of the original names have disappeared. If the island remained isolated, eventually everyone would have the same last name. At that point a visitor could conclude that every inhabitant descended from one man—call him the Pitcairn Adam.

So thus there must be a mitochondrial Eve, and even traditional anthropologists can't really argue against her existence. What shocked them about Mitochondrial Mom was her birthday, which the Berkeley researchers calculated by counting the mutations that have occurred to her DNA. They looked at the most distant branches of the family tree—the DNA types most different from one another—and worked backward to figure out how many steps it would have taken for Eve's original DNA to mutate into these different types. They assumed that these mutations occurred at a regular rate—a controversial assumption that might be wrong, but which has been supported by some studies of humans and animals. Over the course of a million years, it appears that 2 to 4 percent of the mitochondrial DNA components will mutate. By this molecular calculus, Eve must have lived about 200,000 years ago (the range is between 140,000 and 290,000 years). This date, published this past January by the Berkeley group, agrees with the estimate of a team of geneticists led by Douglas Wallace of Emory University.

But the Emory researchers think Eve might have lived in Asia. They base their conclusion also on mitochondrial DNA, which they gathered from the blood of about 700 people on four continents. They used different methods in chopping up the DNA and arranging the types in a family tree. Their tree also goes back to one woman, who lived 150,000 to 200,000 years ago, they estimate. Unlike the Berkeley researchers, however, they found that the races have distinctive types of DNA. They also found that the human DNA type most similar to that of apes occurred at the highest frequency in Asia, making that the likely root of the family tree. Wallace's data suggests that Eve can be traced to southeast China, but he cautions that this is only one possible interpretation of the data. "If we make other assumptions, we can run our data through a computer and come up with a family tree starting in Africa," he says. "So I'm not ruling out Africa. I'm just saying that we can't yet decide whether it's Asia or Africa."

The rival geneticists are quick to criticize one another. Wallace faults the Berkeley researchers for getting most of their African DNA samples from American blacks, whose ancestors could have mixed with Europeans and American Indians. The Berkeley researchers insist that their study is better because they chopped the DNA into smaller pieces, enabling them to analyze differences more carefully.

Both groups acknowledge that there's room for improvement, and they're planning to gather more samples and look more closely at the DNA's structure.

At the moment, the evidence seems to favor an African Eve, because other genetic studies (of nuclear DNA) also point to an origin there and because that's where the earliest fossils of modern humans have been found. But wherever Eve's home was, the rival geneticists agree that she lived relatively recently, and this is what provokes anthropologists to start arguing—often with Biblical metaphors of their own.

If Eve lived within the past 200,000 years, she may have been a modern human, perhaps one of the first to appear. In that case she might have looked like a more muscular version of today's Africans. Or maybe it was her descendants who evolved into modern humans. Eve herself might have been our immediate ancestor, an archaic Homo sapiens, and therefore brawnier, with a large, protruding face and a forehead receding behind prominent brow ridges. She was certainly a hunter-gatherer, probably much like today's Bushmen in southern Africa, living in a group of maybe 25, carrying a nursing child across the plains in search of food. Humans around the world—Java man, Peking man—were living like this for hundreds of thousands of years before our mitochondrial Eve.

The question is: what happened to all the other populations around the world? For their women's mitochondrial genes apparently all vanished. The Berkeley biologists conclude that everyone outside Africa stems from a group of Eve's descendants who left their homeland between 90,000 and 180,000 years ago. As they moved across Asia and Europe, they would have encountered Neanderthals and populations of archaic Homo sapiens. They were probably outnumbered in many places. But wherever the daughters of Eve went, only their mitochondrial DNA survived.

Did the immigrants kill the natives? Possibly, but the conquests may have been peaceful. Because they were modern humans, Eve's descendants were less muscular than the archaic natives, but they were more organized, more able to plan ahead. They could make better stone tools. As they prospered and multiplied, consuming more of the local fruit and game, the natives would have suffered; a slight increase in their mortality rate could have led to their extinction in just a thousand years.

The immigrants may have been able to interbreed with the locals. Some anthropologists see physical vestiges of the Neanderthals in modern Europeans, and the Eve hypothesis doesn't rule out the possibility that the Neanderthals' nuclear genes were passed along to us. But the fact remains that the Neanderthals' mitochondrial genes all disappeared after Eve's descendants arrived, so both the Berkeley and Emory biologists suspect there was little or no mixing. Maybe the immigrants were so different that they couldn't interbreed. Or maybe they simply shunned the natives as being too "primitive." The Neanderthals' attempts at courtship presumably suffered if, as some scientists speculate, they lacked modern humans' power of speech.

This question of interbreeding is the crux of the bones-molecules debate. The geneticists' most vehement critic is Milford Wolpoff, a University of Michigan paleoanthropologist who believes our common ancestor lived closer to a million years ago. "The most obvious conclusion from the genetic evidence," he says, "is that Eve's descendants spread out of Africa and weren't incorporated at all into the local populations. I find that incredible. In recorded history, there always has been intermixing as populations moved or villages exchanged wives. I believe we have a long history of people constantly mixing with one another and cooperating with one another and evolving into one great family." Wolpoff finds his version of evolution more satisfying than "this business about Eve showing the common nature of everything." If Eve's descendants wiped out all rivals, Wolpoff suggests, maybe the theory should be named after her murderous son, Cain.

Actually, the more common term for this idea is Noah's Ark, coined by Harvard's W. W. Howells in describing the two classic schools of anthropological thought on the origin of modern humans. One school believes that a small group of modern humans appeared in one place recently—perhaps 100,000 to 200,000 years ago—and colonized the entire world, like the survivors of Noah's ark. The other populations were not inexorably climbing the ladder or the tree of evolution—they were more like twigs on a bush or the arms of a hatrack, branching off to an inglorious end. The idea of a recent common origin for humanity was held by many anthropologists long before DNA provided supporting evidence.

The opposing school believes in what Howells called the "candelabra hypothesis": the different races diverged long ago and evolved independently into modern humans, progressing like the parallel candles of candelabra. This view became prominent in 1962 with Carleton Coon's book "The Origin of Races." He insisted that modern humans did not suddenly appear, "fully formed as from the brow of Zeus," in one place. "I could see that the visible and invisible differences between living races could be explained only in terms of history," wrote Coon, a University of Pennsylvania anthropologist. "Each major race had followed a pathway of its own through the labyrinth of time."

Unfortunately, Coon published his theory along with a speculation that was denounced as racist. He suggested that African civilization was less advanced because black people were the last to evolve into modern humans. Although the first hominids may have arisen in Africa, Coon said, the evolution of modern humans seemed to occur first in Europe and Asia. "If Africa was the cradle of mankind, it was only an indifferent kindergarten." He couldn't have been more wrong. Bones subsequently discovered in Africa are believed to be from modern humans living there about 100,000 years ago. These bones (as well as some from Israel that might be as old) represent the earliest known modern humans. Before their discovery it was assumed that modern humans didn't evolve until 35,000 years ago, which is when they first appear in the European fossil records. So blacks were hardly the last to reach modernity.

Coon's mistake didn't invalidate the basic candelabra hypothesis, which is still popular in a modified version. Wolpoff prefers to think of a trellis: the separate races gradually evolving along parallel lines but connected by a network of genes flowing back and forth. The Neanderthals turned into modern Europeans while Peking man's descendants were becoming modern Chinese. Immigrants brought in new genes, but the natives' basic traits survived. This would explain why both the Neanderthals and the modern Europeans have big noses, why Peking man and current residents of Beijing have flat faces, why today's Aboriginal Australians have flat foreheads like Java man. These similarities presumably wouldn't persist if the ancient natives had disappeared when Eve's descendants arrived.

Other anthropologists, however, find these similarities unconvincing. It might just be a coincidence that modern Europeans have big noses like the Neanderthals. To the Noah's ark school, what's striking are the differences between ancients and moderns. Modern Europeans, for instance, are much less stocky than Neanderthals—their arms and legs are proportioned more like those of humans from the tropics, as Eve's presumably were. And there's no clear sign in the fossil records of a transition from Neanderthal to modern. Some anthropologists cite bones that might belong to hybrids of immigrants and natives, but these interpretations are disputed.

"I don't rule out the possibility that there was interbreeding, but I don't see it in the fossils," says The British Museum's Christopher Stringer. "In the two areas [where] we have the best fossil evidence, Europe and Southwest Asia, the gap between archaic and modern people is very large. The entire skeleton and brain case changed. I think the fossil evidence is clearly signaling replacement of the archaic population. I was delighted to see the DNA results support this view."

Most anthropologists, though, are still skeptical. They don't reject outright the genetic evidence, but they don't accept it flatly, either. After the mistakes of the past, they're leery of any grand new theory about human evolution. They rightly point out that the geneticists' molecular clock could be way off—change a few assumptions and Eve's birthday could move back hundreds of thousands of years, bringing ancients like Peking man back into our lineage. Above all, anthropologists would like to see the corroborating bones.

"We don't know what's going on here," says the University of Pennsylvania's Alan Mann. "Maybe we are dealing with a dramatic jump. Maybe the origin of creatures like us occurred very recently. Certainly the mitochondrial data is a significant advance. But there really isn't any good fossil evidence from that period to back it up. If you look at the fossils, the good evidence on Africa can be placed on the palm of your hand. In this field, a person kicks over a stone in Africa, and we have to rewrite the textbooks."

So the fossil hunters will keep digging—now they have something specific to look for in the sediments of 200,000 years ago. Maybe they'll vindicate the geneticists once again, but the geneticists aren't waiting to find out. They're already trying to expand the Eve theory by finding Adam. Researchers in England, France and the United States have begun looking at the Y chromosome, which is passed along only on the male side. Tracing it is difficult because it's part of the DNA in the cell's nucleus, where there are many more genes than in the mitochondrion. This Adam will be the one lucky father whose descendants always had at least one son every generation. He may have been hunting and gathering while Eve was, or he may have lived at another time (though it would cast doubt on the Eve hypothesis if the time and place of his birth were too distant). The researchers hope to get an answer within several years.

In the meantime, there is one temporary candidate for an Adam—not the one scientists are looking for but one defined simply as a man from whom we are all descended. Since we are all descended from Eve's daughters, any common ancestor of theirs would be a common ancestor to everyone today. This wouldn't necessarily be Eve's husband. For all we know, she may have had more than one. But her daughters all certainly had the same maternal grandfather. So, at least for now, the only safe conclusion is that Adam was Eve's father.

THE LEGACY OF PHARAONIC EGYPT

By R.-El-Nadoury

Pharaonic Egypt's valuable contributions to the world can be traced in many fields including history, economics, science, art, philosophy. Specialists in these, and many other fields, have long realized the importance of this legacy, even though it is often impossible to determine in what way it was passed on to neighbouring or subsequent cultures.

Indeed, that legacy or, at least, the evidence we have of it, which is so important for the history of mankind, was transmitted in large part by classical antiquity (first by the Greeks and later by the Romans) before passing to the Arabs. Now, the pre-Hellenes and Greeks did not come into contact with Egypt before –1600 or thereabouts and close ties were not established until the seventh century before our era, with the spread of Greek adventurers, travellers and, later, settlers into the Mediterranean basin, particularly into Egypt. At the same time, the Greeks and their forerunners in the second and first millennia before our era were in contact with the civilizations of Asia Minor and through them, with the ancient Mesopotamian world of which they were the continuation. It is, accordingly, often very difficult to ascertain the exact cultural milieu, whether Asian or Egyptian, both so closely linked, in which this or that invention or technique first appeared.

In addition, the difficulty of establishing the chronology of the remote periods of antiquity makes attributions of the paternity of ideas very hazardous. Carbon 14 datings are too vague to determine to the nearest century or two whether, in a milieu where knowledge was always rapidly-transmitted, it was the Asian or African world that was the originator. Lastly, the possibility of convergences cannot be disregarded. To cite but one example: there is good reason to believe (see the Introduction) that writing was discovered at about the same time both in Egypt and Mesopotamia without there necessarily having been any influence of one civilization on the other.

For all that, the legacy bequeathed by Egypt to succeeding civilizations, and to the ancient civilizations of Africa in particular, is not to be underestimated.

CONTRIBUTIONS OF PREHISTORIC EGYPT

One of the earliest and most remarkable advances made by Egypt was in the field of economics. At the end of the Neolithic period, around –5000, the ancient Egyptians gradually transformed the Nile valley (see Chapter 1), enabling its inhabitants to progress from a food-gathering economy to a food-producing one, and this important transition in human development in the valley had great consequences, material as well as moral. For the growth of agriculture made it possible for the ancient Egyptian to adopt a settled, integrated village life and this development affected his social and moral development not only in prehistoric but also during the dynastic periods.

It is not certain that Asia played the predominant and unique role in the Neolithic revolution that was formerly attributed to it (see Unesco *General History of Africa*, Vol. I, ch. 27). However that might be, one of the first results of this Neolithic revolution in the valley was that the ancient Egyptian started to think of the natural forces around him. He saw these, especially the sun and the river, as gods, who were symbolized in many forms, especially in the animals and birds with which he was most familiar. In developing agriculture he also established the principle of co-operation within the community, for without such co-operation among the people of the village, agricultural production would have been limited. This led to another important development: the introduction of a new social system within the community; that is, the specialization of labour. Specialized workers appeared in farming, irrigation, agricultural industries, pottery-making and many other related fields and the large number of archaeological remains attest to their long-lasting traditions.

Pharaonic civilization was remarkable for the continuity of its development. Once a thing was acquired, it was passed on, with improvements, from the dawn of the history of Egypt to its close. This was how Neolithic techniques were transmitted and enriched in the predynastic period (−3500 to −3000) and were subsequently preserved when the historical period was in full flower. The art of stone-cutting is sufficient evidence.

As early as −3500, the Egyptians, the heirs to the Neolithic period in the valley, used the flint deposits there, especially those at Thebes, to carve instruments of incomparable quality, of which the Gebel-el-ArakKnife (see Chapter 1) is one example among hundreds. Produced by pressure, the fine and regular grooves of the stone gave the knife an inimitable gently rippled and perfectly polished surface. To make such weapons required uncommon manual dexterity. This art remained alive in Egypt and ascene painted in a tomb at Beni Hasan depicts artisans of the time of the Middle Kingdom (c. −1900) still fashioning these same knives with incurvate blades.

This craftsmanship is also found in the carving of stone vases. Here, too, the technique of the Neolithic period carried through the predynastic period and the Old Kingdom and continued to the end of ancient Egyptian history. The Egyptian stone-carver used every kind of stone, even the hardest varieties, working with basalt, breccia, diorite, granite, porphyryas as readily as with the softer calcareous alabasters, schists, serpentines and soapstones.

From Egypt, stone-carving techniques later passed to the Mediterranean world. The carvers of Cretan vases must surely have learned their skills, if not in Egypt itself, at least in a milieu that was thoroughly steeped in Egyptian culture like the Syro-Palestinian Corridor. Even the shapes of the vases that were carved in ancient Minoa betray their Egyptian origins.

The dexterity of the cutters of hard stone passed to the sculptors. This can be seen in the great Egyptian hard stone sculptures, from the diorite Chefren of Cairo to the large black basalt sarcophagi of the Apis bulls. The skill then passed to the sculptors of the Ptolemaic period and later found expression in the statuary of the Roman empire.

These changes in Neolithic times are characteristically reflected in the growth of town planning in Egypt. A striking example of this can be found in one of the oldest villages in the Nile valley: Merimda Beni Salama on the western edge of the Delta.

In conjunction with the very ancient Egyptian belief in the after-life and immortality, we have here a combination of important cultural and social developments which can be traced throughout the Neolithic and Chalcolithic periods from the predynastic down to the protodynastic period. They led to the establishment and development of the Egyptian Pharaonic tradition.

In the Egyptian Pharaonic civilization of historical times two main currents can be discerned. The first is the material legacy. The second, also descended from the most distant past, is the more abstract cultural legacy. They are inter-related and together comprise the Egyptian cultural phenomenon. The material legacy includes crafts and sciences (geometry, astronomy, chemistry), applied mathematics, medicine, surgery and artistic productions. The cultural side covers religion, literature and philosophic theories.

Craft contributions

The ancient Egyptians' contribution in the crafts can be traced in stone, as we have just seen, but also in metal, wood, glass, ivory, bone and many other materials. They explored and exploited the various natural resources of the country and gradually refined the techniques required in making stone and copper tools such as axes, chisels, mallets and adzes designed with great skill for use in building as well as in industry for such purposes as drilling holes or fixing blocks. They also fashioned bows, arrows, daggers, shields and throwing-clubs.

For a long period, and even during historical times, the tools and arms inherited from the Neolithic period continued to be made of stone. The chalk cliffs bordering the Nile are rich in flints of large size and excellent quality which the Egyptians continued to use long after the discovery of the use of copper and bronze. Furthermore, religious rites often required the use of stone instruments, a fact that contributed largely to the perpetuation of stone-cutting techniques and especially of flint knapping.

Very little use was made of iron for metal vases until the very end of the Pharaonic period, so Egyptian metal-working techniques were confined to the use of gold, silver, copper, and copper alloys such as bronze and brass. Traces of the mining and processing of copper ore by Egyptians have been found in Sinai as well as in Nubia and Buhen where the Pharaohs of the Old Kingdom possessed copper-smelting plants.

In Sinai and in Nubia, the Egyptians worked with the local populations, and the techniques used in the processing of metal could, therefore, pass easily from one culture to the other. This was perhaps the time when Pharaonic script, through the intermediary of proto-Sinaitic script, which it influences, played an important part in the invention of the alphabet. It was perhaps the occasion when copper working became widespread, first in the Nile basin and then beyond.

As long ago as the early dynastic period (*c*. −3000), the Egyptians knew, and employed in making their copper tools, all the basic techniques of metal working such as forging, hammering, casting, stamping, soldering, and riveting techniques which they mastered very rapidly. As well as tools, large Egyptian copper statues have been found which date from −2300. Texts of an earlier time, dating back to −2900, note the existence of statues of the same type, and scenes from mastabas of the very earliest period depict workshops where gold and electrum, which is a blend of gold and silver, are being fashioned into jewellery. Although gold and copper working did not originate in Egypt, there is no doubt that Egypt contributed a great deal to its improvement and extension.

As we stressed at the beginning of this chapter, it is often difficult to determine whether a particular technique originated in an Asian or African culture. But, thanks to the representations found in tombs, Egypt at least provides us with a wealth of information on the techniques used by craftsmen. In the workshops depicted in paintings or bas-reliefs on the tomb walls, both above and below ground, one sees, for example, carpenters and cabinet-makers at work making furniture, weapons and boats, and the tools they used, such as pliers, hammers, saws, drills, adzes, chisels and mallets, all faithfully represented and with infinite detail, as well as the manner in which they used them. As a result, we know that the Egyptian saw was a pull-saw and not a push-saw, like the modern saw. There is a mine of information for students of the history of techniques and the way they came down to us, which has not yet been fully studied.

As well as these pictorial representations the ancient Egyptians left in their tombs models of workshops with model craftsmen making various objects. These models are also invaluable to the historian in interpreting the techniques and the manner in which they developed. Furthermore the large quantities of artisan objects which have been found, manufactured either by hand or with the aid of tools, attest to the variety of industries in ancient Egypt. For example, in the making of jewellery they used precious and semi-precious stones such as gold, silver, felspar, lapis-lazuli, turquoise, amethyst and cornelian, fashioning them with remarkable precision into crowns, necklaces and other items of adornment.

The cultivation of flax rapidly led to great ability in hand-spinning and linen-making. The latter was known from the start of the Neolithic period (c. –5000), and its beginning coincided with the emergence of civilization in the Nile valley. The women spun the linen, doing so with great skill since they frequently handled two spindles simultaneously. Characteristic of Egyptian spinning was the length of the thread produced and this required a technique which placed the spindle some feet away from the raw fibre. To make the distance even greater, the women perched on high stools. Their looms were at first horizontal, and then, beginning in the Middle Empire, vertical which enabled them to produce the very long fabrics required for the loose-fitting everyday clothing, as well as for the funerary ritual mummy wrappings and shrouds.

For the Pharaohs, woven fabrics constituted a commodity particularly appreciated abroad. The finest cloth of all, byssus, was woven in the temples and was especially renowned. The Ptolemies supervised the weaving shops and controlled the quality of the manufacture, and their central administration, doubtless following the pattern set by the earlier Pharaohs, organized sales abroad which brought the king huge revenues because of the superior quality of the goods produced by Egyptian weavers. Here we have a graphic example of one of the ways in which the Egyptian legacy was handed down.

The wood, leather and metal industries were also perfected and the products of these industries have survived in good condition to the present day.

Other objects produced by Egyptian craftsmen included silver vases, wooden coffins, combs and decorated ivory handles. The ancient Egyptians also had a special talent for weaving wild reeds into mats and the spun fibre of the palm-tree made possible the production of sturdy nets and ropes. Pottery manufacture which started in prehistory in a rough form developed into the finer red, black-rimmed pottery, and then polished and incised pottery. These vessels were used for storing various materials but some were for decorative purposes. The Egyptian belief in certain values and especially in eternal life necessitated the manufacture of a great number of often decorated objects for the dead and led to a high standard of perfection and artistic production.

Egypt contributed, if not the invention, at least the distribution of glass-making techniques to world civilization. While it is true that Mesopotamia and the civilizations of the Indus were likewise familiar at a very early time with glazing, the technique which is the basis of glass-making, there is no evidence to suggest that they spread it abroad. The most one can suppose, therefore, is that once again there was a phenomenon of convergence and that glass-making was discovered independently both in Asia and in the Nile valley.

It is certain that the Egyptians demonstrated their aptitude in the art of glass-making in a relatively short time. The presence of glass beads seems to be attested in the predynastic period (c. –3500), although it is not certain that they were deliberately made by the craftsman. Glass, as such, was known in the fifth dynasty (c. –2500) and began to spread from the time of the New Kingdom (c. –1600). It was then used not only for beads but also for vases of a great variety of shapes, from the graceful stemmed chalice to vases in the form of fishes. They were usually polychromatic and always opaque. Transparent glass made its appearance under Tutankhamun (c. −1300). Starting about −700, Egyptian polychromatic glass vases, in the form called alabaster, spread throughout the Mediterranean area. They were copied by the Phoenicians, who developed their manufacture into an industry.

In the later period, hieroglyphic signs, moulded in coloured glass, were set in wood or stone to make inscriptions. The techniques of the Pharaonic glass-makers were handed down to craftsmen of the hellenistic period, who invented blown glass. Alexandria then became the main centre for the manufacture of glass-ware, exporting its products as far as China. Aurelius levied a tax on Egyptian glass-ware imported into Rome. The Meroitic empire later imported some glass-ware from Alexandria but, above all, adopted its manufacturing techniques and spread them to the upper Nile valley.

One of the most important industries was that of the production of papyrus invented by the ancient Egyptians. No plant played a more significant role in Egypt than papyrus. Its fibres were used for boat-making and for caulking, for the wicks of oil lamps, for mats, baskets, ropes and hawsers. The hawsers which served to moor the pontoon bridge that Xerxes tried to lay across the Hellespont were made in Egypt out of papyrus fibres. When tied together in bundles, papyrus stems served as pillars in early architecture until classical architects took them as a model for their simple or clustered columns whose capitals were shaped like closed or open flowers. But, above all, papyrus was used to make 'papyrus', from which the word 'paper' is derived, undoubtedly a cognate of the ancient Egyptian word *paperaâ* which means 'He of-the-Great-Residence' (Royal Palace) which has come down to us from classical antiquity.

Papyrus was made by placing crosswise successive layers of fine strips taken from the stem of the plant which, after pressing and drying, formed a large sheet.

Twenty sheets of papyrus joined together while they were still moist formed a scroll 3 to 6 metres in length. Several scrolls could be joined together and reach a length of 30 or 40 metres. It was this scroll that constituted Egyptian books. They were held in the left hand and unrolled as the reading proceeded. The volumen of classic antiquity is a direct heir of this scroll.

Of all the writing materials employed in antiquity, papyrus was certainly the most practical. It was supple and light. Its sole drawback was its fragility. Over a long period it stood up poorly to humidity, and it burnt very easily. It has been estimated that to maintain the inventory of a small Egyptian temple, 10 metres of papyrus were required each month. Provincial notaries, during the Ptolemaic dynasty, used from six to thirteen scrolls or 25–57 metres *each day*. Every large estate and royal palace and all the temples maintained registers, inventories and libraries, which indicates that hundreds of kilometres of papyrus must have existed at that time whereas only a few hundreds of metres have been rediscovered.

The papyrus used in Egypt from the time of the first dynasty (c. −3000) until the end of the Pharaonic period was later adopted by the Greeks, the Romans, the Copts, the Byzantines, the Aramaeans and the Arabs. A large part of Greek and Latin literature has come down to us on papyrus. Papyrus scrolls were one of the principal exports of Egypt. Papyrus was, unquestionably, one of the major legacies bequeathed to civilization by Pharaonic Egypt.

All these industries depended on techniques and skills and led to the creation of a body of artisans and improved techniques. The museums and private collections throughout the world contain hundreds, even thousands, of archaeological examples of the various products of ancient Egypt.

Not the least of their technical contributions to the world were their tradition and ability in stonemasonry. It was no easy task to transform huge blocks of granite, limestone, basalt and diorite from raw material into well-shaped polished masonry required by various architectural designs.

Moreover, the search for stone to build their monuments, no less than prospection for ores and efforts to discover fibres, semi-precious stones and coloured pigments, contributed to the spread of Egyptian techniques to Asia and Africa.

The Egyptians did not hesitate to fetch their stone from the open desert, sometimes going as far as 100 kilometres from the Nile. The quarry from which the diorite came for the famous statue of Chephren in the Cairo Museum lies in the Nubian desert some 65 kilometres to the north-west of Abu Simbel. Quarries were worked from the dawn of Egyptian history (c. –2800).

Egyptian quarrying techniques depended on the kind of stone being extracted. For limestone, they hollowed out galleries in the broad band of Eocene cliffs that border the Nile and extracted the magnificent blocks of fine stone used to construct the Great Pyramids which were then faced with blocks of granite. The sandstone deposits in the region of ElKob, in Upper Egypt and in Nubia, were mined by open-face techniques. For hard stone, the quarriers first cut a groove around the block to be extracted, and then at various points along the groove made deep notches into which they inserted wooden wedges. These they wet and the swelling of the wood was sufficient to split the block along the groove. This technique is still used today in granite quarries. Is it a legacy from Egypt?

The only tools used by the Egyptian stone worker were the wooden mallet and copper chisel for soft stones like limestone and sandstone, and the pick, chisel and hard stone hammer for metamorphic rocks like granite, gneiss, diorite and basalt. When the quarry was located far from the Nile, an expedition was launched with sometimes as many as 14000 men comprising officers and soldiers, porters and quarrymen, scribes and doctors. Such expeditions were equipped to remain for long periods out of Egypt and must have contributed to the spread of Egyptian civilization, especially in Africa.

The skills acquired by stoneworkers in the early dynastic period led the Egyptians, by the time of the Old Kingdom (c. –2400), to hew their final resting-places in solid rock. Much before this date, from –3000 to –2400, the building of tombs, planned as the dwelling-places of the dead, had already led them to build imposing super structures which, in time, with the changes which occurred in architecture, led first to the step pyramid and then to the pyramid proper.

The Egyptian expertise in woodworking is brilliantly manifested in their ship building. The necessities of daily life in the Nile valley, where the river is the only convenient thoroughfare, made expert boatmen of the Egyptians from the earliest times. Boats occupied a prominent position in their earliest works of art from prehistoric times on. Since in their belief an after-life was closely modelled on earthly life, it is not surprising that they placed models of boats in the tombs, or represented scenes of boat construction and river scenes on tomb walls. They would even sometimes bury actual boats near the tombs ready for use by the dead. This was the case at Heluan in a burial ground of the first two dynasties, and at Dahshur, near the pyramid of Sesostris III. But a more recent, discovery is extraordinary. In 1952, two great pits dug into the rock and covered with huge limestone slabs were discovered along the southern side of the Great Pyramid. In the pits, partially disassembled, but complete with oars, cabins, and rudders, were discovered the very boats used by Cheops. One of these boats has been removed from the pit and restored. The other one is still waiting to be taken out of its tomb.

Cheops' boat, now in a special museum, has been rebuilt. When found it consisted of 1224 pieces of wood which had been partially disassembled and stacked in thirteen successive layers in the pit. The boat measures 43.4 metres long, 5.9 metres wide, and has a capacity of about 40 tons. The side planks are between 13 and 14 centimetres thick. Its draught is difficult to calculate precisely, but was clearly very slight in relation to the ship's mass. Although it does possess a rudimentary frame of timbers, Cheops' boat has no keel, and is flat-bottomed and narrow. The most remarkable fact is that it was built without any nails: the pieces of wood are held together solely by the use of tenon and mortise joints. The constituent elements, planks, timbers and cross members, are tied to each other with ropes. This facilitated their reassembly. The ship contained a large, spacious central cabin, as well as a covered shelter in the bow. There was no mast, and it was either propelled by oars or was towed, even though the sail had been in use in Egypt long before Cheops' reign. Amphibious military expeditions far from Egypt on the Red Sea and the Euphrates were made possible by this method of construction, assembling separate sections which were then tied to one another. In fact, the Egyptian army carried with it, in a piecemeal form, the boats which it might need.

We can see from their width in relation to their length and from their shallow draught, that these Egyptian boats were designed for use on the river. Their primary object was to achieve maximum capacity while avoiding running aground. None the less, beginning with the fifth dynasty, and probably even before, the Egyptians knew how to adapt their ships for ocean-going voyages. The boats of Sahure show that for use at sea the height of the prow and the poop were greatly reduced. In Cheops' boat, these were raised high above the waterline. This made the ship difficult to manage in the waves of the Mediterranean or the Red Sea. In addition, Egyptian naval engineers lent great solidity to the whole structure by equipping the ship with a torsion-cable passing over the bridge and tyingthe stern firmly to the bow. This cable also acted as a keel, ensuring the rigidity of the entire structure and reducing the danger of its breaking in the middle.

With these modifications, the Egyptian ship was capable of plying the farthest maritime routes opened up by the Pharaohs, whether on the Mediterranean in the direction of Palestine, Syria, Cyprus and Crete, or on the Red Sea towards the distant country of Punt. There is no reason to believe that the Egyptians had been influenced by the Phoenicians in this field. On the contrary, it is quite possible, although it cannot be proved, given the current level of knowledge, that it was the Egyptians who pioneered the use of sails in maritime voyages (Egyptian yards and sails were adjustable, allowing various speeds) and invented the rudder. Certainly from the time of the Old Kingdom the large directional oars located in the stern were provided with vertical bars, transforming them in effect into rudders.

SCIENTIFIC CONTRIBUTIONS

The Pharaonic contribution to science and applied mathematics has left a valuable legacy in the fields of physics, chemistry, zoology, geology, medicine, pharmacology, geometry and applied mathematics. In fact, they gave to humanity a large store of experience in each of these fields, some of which were combined in order to execute a specific project.

Mummification

One outstanding example of the genius of the ancient Egyptians is mummification. It shows their mastery of a number of sciences including physics, chemistry, medicine and surgery. Their ability in each branch was an accumulation of long experience. For example, they exploited their discovery of the chemical characteristic of natron, which was found in certain areas of Egypt, particularly in the Wadi el Natrun, by using the chemical attributes of this substance for use in the practical fulfilment of the demands of their beliefs in the after-life. For the ancient Egyptians believed in the continuity of life after death and emphasized this belief in a practical way by preserving the human body. The compounds of natron have been analysed in modern times as a mixture of sodium carbonate, sodium bicarbonate, salt and sodium sulphate. The ancient Egyptian, therefore, was aware of the chemical functions of these substances. In the process of mummification he soaked the body in natron for seventy days. He drew the brain out through the nostrils and he also removed the intestines through an incision made in the side of the body. Such operations as these necessitated an accurate knowledge of anatomy and the good state of preservation of the mummies illustrates this intimate knowledge.

Surgery

It was, undoubtedly, the knowledge they acquired from mummification that enabled the Egyptians to develop surgical techniques at a very early period in their history. We have quite a good knowledge of Egyptian surgery, in fact, thanks to the Smith Papyrus, a copy of an original which was composed under the Old Kingdom, between –2600 and –2400. This papyrus is virtually a treatise on bone surgery and external pathology. Forty-eight cases are examined systematically. In each case, the author of the treatise begins his account under a general heading: 'Instructions concerning [such and such a case]'; followed by a clinical description: 'If you observe [such symptoms]'. The descriptions are always precise and incisive. They are followed by the diagnosis: 'You will say in this connection a case of [this or that wound]', and, depending on the case, 'a case that I can treat' or 'the case is without remedy'. If the surgeon can treat the patient, the treatment to be administered is then described in detail, for example: 'the first day you will apply a bandage with a piece of meat; afterwards you will place two strips of cloth in such a way as to join the lips of the wound together ' …

Several of the treatments indicated in the Smith Papyrus are still used today. Egyptian surgeons knew how to stitch up wounds and to set a fracture using wooden or pasteboard splints. And there were times when the surgeon simply advised that nature should be allowed to take its own course. In two instances, the Smith Papyrus instructs the patient to maintain his regular diet.

Of the cases studied by the Smith Papyrus, the majority concerned superficial lacerations of the skull or face. Others concerned lesions of the bones or joints such as contusions of the cervical or spinal vertebrae, dislocations, perforations of the skull or sternum, and sundry fractures affecting the nose, jaw, collar-bone, humerus, ribs, skull and vertebrae. Examination of mummies has revealed traces of surgery, such as the jaw dating from the Old Kingdom which has two holes bored to drain an abscess, or the skull fractured by a blow from an axe or sword and successfully reset. There is also evidence of dental work such as fillings done with a mineral cement, and one mummy had a kind of bridge of gold wire joining two shaky teeth.

By its methodical approach, the Smith Papyrus bears testimony to the skill of the surgeons of ancient Egypt, skill which it would be fair to assume was handed on gradually, in Africa as well as in Asia and to classical antiquity, by the doctors who were always attached to Egyptian expeditions to foreign lands. Moreover, it is known that foreign sovereigns, like the Asian prince of Bakhtan, Bactria, or Cambyses himself, brought in Egyptian doctors, that Hippocrates 'had access to the library of the Imhotep temple at Memphis' and that other Greek physicians later followed his example.

Medicine

Medical knowledge can be considered as one of the most important early scientific contributions of the ancient Egyptian to the history of man. Documents show in detail the titles of Egyptian physicians and their different fields of specialization. In fact the civilizations of the ancient Near East and the classical world recognized the ability and reputation of the ancient Egyptians in medicine and pharmacology. One of the most significant personalities in the history of medicine is Imhotep, the vizier, architect and physician of King Zoser of the third dynasty. His fame survived throughout Egyptian ancient history and through to Greek times. Deified by the Egyptians under the name Imouthes, he was assimilated by the Greeks to Askelepios, the god of medicine. In fact, Egyptian influence on the Greek world in both medicine and pharmacology is easily recognizable in remedies and prescriptions. Some medical instruments used in surgical operations have been discovered during excavations.

Written evidence of ancient Egyptian medicine comes in medical documents such as the Ebers Papyrus, the Berlin Papyrus, the Edwin Smith Surgical Papyrus and many others which illustrate the techniques of the operations and detail the prescribed cures.

These texts are copies of originals dating back to the Old Kingdom (c –2500). In contrast to the Edwin Smith Surgical Papyrus, which is highly scientific, the purely medical texts were based on magic. The Egyptians regarded sickness as the work of the gods or malevolent spirits, which provided justification for resorting to magic and which explains why some of the remedies prescribed on the Ebers Papyrus, for example, resemble more a magical incantation than a medical prescription.

Despite this aspect, common to other ancient civilizations as well, Egyptian medicine was a not inconsiderable science which contained the beginnings of a methodical approach, especially in the observation of symptoms, and this method doubtless passed to posterity by reason of its importance. The Egyptian doctor examined his patient and determined the symptoms of his complaint. He then made his diagnosis and prescribed treatment. All the extant texts describe this sequence, from which it may be concluded that it was standard procedure. The examination was made in two stages some days apart if the case was unclear. Among the ailments identified and competently described and treated by Egyptian doctors were gastric disorders, stomach swelling, skin cancer, coryza, laryngitis, angina pectoris, diabetes, constipation, haemorrhoids, bronchitis, retention and incontinence of urine, bilharzia, ophthalmia, etc.

The Egyptian doctor treated his patient using suppositories, ointments, syrups, potions, oils, massages, enemas, purges, poultices, and even inhalants whose use they taught to the Greeks. Their pharmacopoeia contained a large variety of medicinal herbs, the names of which, unfortunately, elude translation. Egyptian medical techniques and medicines enjoyed great prestige in antiquity, as we know from Herodotus. The names of nearly one hundred ancient Egyptian physicians have been passed down to us through these texts. Among them are oculists and dentists, of whom Hesy-Re, who lived around –2600 under the fourth dynasty, could be considered as one of the most ancient. Among the specialists were also veterinarians. The physicians used a variety of instruments in their work.

Mathematics (arithmetic, algebra and geometry)

Mathematics is an important field of science in which the ancient Egyptians worked. The accurate measurements of their enormous architectural and sculptural monuments are worthy proof of their preoccupation with precision. They would never have been able to reach this pitch of perfection without a minimum of mathematical capacity.

Two important mathematical papyri have come down to us from the Middle Kingdom (–2000 to –1750), those of Moscow and Rhind. The Egyptian method of numeration, based on the decimal system, consisted of repeating the symbols for numbers (ones, tens, hundreds, thousands) as many times as necessary to obtain the desired figure. There was no zero. It is interesting to note that the Egyptian symbols for the fractions 1/2, 1/3, 1/4, and so on originate in the myth of Horus and Seth, in which one of Horus' falcon eyes was torn out and cut into pieces by Seth. It is these pieces that symbolize certain fractions.

Egyptian mathematics may be considered under the three headings of arithmetic, algebra and geometry.

Egyptian administrative organization required a knowledge of arithmetic. The efficiency of the highly centralized administration depended on knowing exactly what was happening in each province, in all spheres of activity. It is not surprising, then, that the scribes spent an enormous amount of time keeping records of the area of land under cultivation, the quantities of products available and their distribution, the size and quality of the staff, and so on.

The Egyptian method of calculation was simple. They reduced all operations to a series of multiplications and divisions by two (duplication), a slow process which requires little memorization and makes multiplication tables unnecessary. In divisions, whenever the dividend was not exactly divisible by the divider, the scribe introduced fractions, but the system used only fractions whose numerator was the number 1. The operations on fractions were also done by systematic doubling. The texts contain numerous examples of proportional shares obtained in this way, with the scribe adding at the end of his calculations the formula 'it is exactly that', which is equivalent to our 'QED'.

All the problems posed and solved in Egyptian treatises on arithmetic have one trait in common: they are all material problems of the type that a scribe, isolated in some remote outpost, would have to solve daily, like the apportioning of seven loaves of bread among ten men in proportion to their rank in the hierarchy, or the calculation of the number of bricks required to build an inclined plane. It was, then, basically an empirical system, with little in it of an abstract nature. It is difficult to judge what elements of such a system might have passed into neighbouring cultures.

It is not exactly clear whether one may properly speak of an Egyptian algebra and specialists in the history of science hold different views on this matter. Certain problems described in the Rhind Papyrus are formulated as follows: 'A quantity [ahâ in Egyptian] to which is added [or subtracted] this or that increment (n) results in quantity (N). What is this quantity?' x Algebraically, this would be expressed as $x \pm \frac{x}{n} = N$, which has led some historians of science to conclude that the Egyptians used algebraic calculations. However, the solutions proposed by the scribe of the Rhind Papyrus to this type of problem are always reached by simple arithmetic, and the only instance in which algebra might have been used is a problem of division which implies the existence of a quadratic equation. The scribe solved this problem as a modern algebraist would do, but instead of taking an abstract symbol like x as the basis of calculation, he took the number I. The question whether Egyptian algebra existed or not depends therefore on whether one accepts or rejects the possibility of doing algebra without abstract symbols.

The Greek writers Herodotus and Strabo concur in the view that geometry was invented by the Egyptians. The need to calculate the area of the land eroded or added each year by the flooding of the Nile apparently led them to its discovery. As a matter of fact, Egyptian geometry, like mathematics, was empirical. In ancient treatises, the task was first and foremost to provide the scribe with a formula that would enable him to find rapidly the area of a field, the volume of grain in a silo or the number of bricks required for a building project. The scribe never applied abstract reasoning to the solution of a particular problem but just provided the practical means in the shape figures. None the less, the Egyptians knew perfectly well how to calculate the area of a triangle or a circle, the volume of a cylinder, of a pyramid or a truncated pyramid, and probably that of a hemisphere. Their greatest success was the calculation of the area of a circle. They proceeded by reducing the diameter by one-ninth and squaring the result which was equivalent to assigning a value of 3.1605 to π, which *is* much more precise *than the value* 3 given *to* π by other ancient peoples.

Knowledge of geometry proved of considerable practical use in land-surveying, which played a significant role in Egypt. There are many tombs with paintings showing teams of surveyors busy checking that the boundary-stones of fields have not been shifted and then measuring with a knotted cord, the fore runner of our surveyor's chain, the area of the cultivated field. The surveyor's cord or *nouh* is mentioned in the earliest texts (*c.* –2800). The central government possessed a cadastral office, the records of which were ransacked during the Memphite revolution (*c.* –2150) but were restored to order during the Middle Kingdom (*c.* –1990).

Astronomy

The documentation we possess on Egyptian astronomy is not at all comparable to the material available on mathematics (the Rhind and the Moscow papyri) or surgery and medicine (the Edwin Smith and the Ebers papyri). There is reason to believe, however, that treatises on astronomy did exist. Although the Carlsberg 9 Papyrus, which describes a method for determining the phases of the moon, was undoubtedly written during the

Roman period, it derives from much earlier sources and is devoid of any hellenistic influence; the same is true of the Carlsberg I Papyrus. Unfortunately the earlier sources are not extant and the Egyptian contribution to astronomy must therefore be deduced from practical applications made on the basis of observations. This contribution is, however, far from insignificant.

As we have seen (see Introduction), the Egyptian calendar year was divided into three seasons of four months, each having thirty days; to these 360 days, five were added at the end of the year. The 365-day calendar year, the most accurate known in antiquity, is at the origin of our own calendar year in as much as it served as the basis of the Julian reform (–47) and of the Gregorian reform of 1582. Side by side with this civil calendar, the Egyptians also used a religious, lunar calendar and were able to predict the moon's phases with adequate accuracy.

Ever since the Napoleonic expedition to Egypt, Europeans have been struck by the accuracy of the alignment of structures built at the time of the Pharaohs, particularly the pyramids, the four façades of which face the four cardinal points. The Great Pyramids deviate from true North by less than one degree. Such accuracy could have been achieved only by astronomical observation either of the direction of the Pole Star at the time; or the culmination of a fixed star; or the bisectrix of the angle formed by the direction of a star at twelve-hour intervals, the bisectrix of the angle of the rising and setting of a fixed star; or the observation of the maximum deviations of a fixed star (which would have been 7 fromUrsa Major, according to Z. Zorba). In all these cases, precise astronomical observation is required to calculate the alignment. The Egyptians were perfectly capable of such observations because they possessed a corps of astronomers working under the authority of the vizier whose job it was to observe the night sky, to note the rising of the stars, especially of Sirius (*Sóthis*), and, above all, to determine the passage of the hours of darkness. These, for the Egyptians, varied in length according to the seasons: night, which was supposed to contain twelve hours, always commenced at sunset and ended at sunrise. Tables have come down to us which indicate that each night hour was marked, month by month, at ten-day intervals, by the appearance of a constellation or a star of the first magnitude. The tables distinguished thirty-six such constellations or stars which constituted *decans*, each one of which inaugurated a ten-day period.

This system dates back at least to the third dynasty (*c.* –2600). Apart from the tables, the priest-astronomer possessed simple observation instruments: a sighting-rod and a square to which a plumb-line was attached and which required a team of two observers. Despite the rudimentary nature of this technique, the observations were precise, as evidenced by the accuracy of the orientations of the pyramids. Certain tombs have paintings representing the sky. The stars are represented in picture form which has made it possible to identify some of the constellations recognized by the Egyptians. Ursa Major is called the Ox Leg; the stars surrounding Arcturus are represented by a crocodile and hippopotamus coupled together; Cygnus is represented by a man with his arms extended; Orion by a person running with his head turned back; Cassiopeia by a figure with outstretched arms; and Draco, Pleiades, Scorpius and Aries by other figures.

To determine the daytime hours, which also varied according to the seasons, the Egyptians used a *gnomon*, a simple rod planted vertically on a graduated board with a plumb-line attached. This instrument served to measure the time spent on the irrigation of the fields, since the water had to be distributed impartially. As well as the *gnomon*, the Egyptians had water clocks which were placed in their temples. These water clocks were borrowed and perfected by the Greeks and are the clepsydras of antiquity. They were made in Egypt as early as –1580.

Architecture

The ancient Egyptians applied their mathematical knowledge to the extraction, transportation and positioning of the huge blocks of stone used in their architectural projects. They had a long tradition in using mudbricks and various kinds of stone from very early times. Their first use of heavy granite was during the beginning of the third millennium before our era. It was used for the flooring of some tombs belonging to the first dynasty at Abydos. In the second dynasty they used limestone in constructing the walls of tombs.

A new phase was started in the third dynasty. This was a vital development in the history of Egyptian architecture, for it was the construction of the first complete building in stone. This is the step pyramid at Sakkara, which forms a part of the huge funerary complex of King Zoser.

Imhotep, who was probably the vizier of King Zoser (c. –2580), was the architect who built the ensemble containing the step pyramid where hewn stone was used for the first time. The blocks were small and looked very much like a limestone imitation of the sun-dried brick used earlier in funerary architecture. Similarly, the imbedded columns and the ceiling joists were stone copies of the bundles of plants and beams used in earlier construction. Thus, there is every indication that Egyptian architecture was amongst the first to use hewn stone in coursed work.

Egypt developed a wide variety of architectural forms, of which the pyramid is, undoubtedly, the most characteristic. The first pyramids were step pyramids and it was not until the fourth dynasty (c. –2300) that they gradually became triangular in form. From that period, the architects gave up the use of the small stones of the third dynasty in favour of large blocks of limestone and granite.

Until the Roman conquest, civil architecture continued to use sun-dried bricks even in the building of royal palaces. The outbuildings of Ramses in Thebes and the great Nubian fortresses provide a very good idea of the versatility of this material. It could be used with the utmost refinement, as can be seen from the Palace of Amenhotep IV at Tell-el-Amarna with its pavements and ceilings decorated with paintings. Another contribution in the field of architecture was the creation of the column. This was at first attached to the wall, but later became free-standing columns.

In developing this architectural skill the ancient Egyptian was much influenced by the local environment. For example, in arriving at the idea of a column, he was inspired by his observation of wild plants such as reeds and papyrus. He cut the capitals of the columns into the shape of lotus flowers, papyrus and other plants, and this was another architectural innovation. The lotus papyrus palm and fluted columns of ancient Egypt were adopted in the architecture of other cultures.

It is likely that the ancient Egyptians invented the vault during the second dynasty (c. –2900). To begin with it was a vault of bricks but by the sixth dynasty the Egyptians were building stone vaults.

The Great Giza Pyramid was one of the seven wonders of the ancient world. A building of such great proportions stands proof of the architectural and administrative ability of the ancient Egyptians. The construction of the ascending corridors, leading to the granite chamber of the king, and the existence of two openings or vents, on both the northern and southern sides of the royal chamber, extending to the outside to provide ventilation, are good examples of their ingenuity.

The exact proportions, measurements and orientation of the chambers and corridors of the pyramids, to say nothing of the cutting and erection of giant obelisks in solid stone, indicate the possession of great technical skills from very early times.

To transport and position the stone blocks, the Egyptians used levers, rollers and wooden cross-bars. Their architectural achievements despite their considerable dimensions were accomplished solely through the strength of human arms, without the use of any mechanical means other than the principle of the lever in its diverse forms.

The technical knowledge acquired by the Egyptians in construction and irrigation as the result of digging canals and building dikes or dams manifested itself in other fields allied to architecture.

By –2550, they had sufficient skill to build a dam of hewn stone in a wadi near Cairo. Somewhat later, their engineers cut navigable channels in the rocks of the First Cataract at Aswan. By all evidence, towards −1740, they seem to have succeeded in erecting a barrage on the Nile itself at Semna, in Nubia, to facilitate navigation to the south. And finally, during the same period, they built a ramp, parallel to the Second Cataract, over which they slid their boats on the fluid mud of the Nile. The ramp extended over several kilometres, a predecessor of the Greek *diolkos* of the Isthmus of Corinth, and ensured that the rapids of the Second Cataract were never a hindrance to navigation.

Garden design and town planning are other aspects of Egyptian architecture. The Egyptians had a great fondness for gardens. Even the poor managed to plant a tree or two in the narrow courtyard of their houses. When they were rich, their gardens rivalled their residences in size and luxury. Under the third dynasty (*c.* −2800), a high official would expect to possess a garden of more than two-and-a-half acres which always contained a pool, which was a distinctive feature of Egyptian gardens. The garden was arranged around the pool or pools, for there could be several of them. They served as fish ponds, as reservoirs for watering and as a source of cooling fresh air for the house nearby. Frequently, the master of the house had a light wooden pavilion built near the pool where he could come for a breath of fresh air in the evening and receive friends for cold drinks.

These artificial pools were occasionally quite large. Snefru's palace lake was large enough for him to sail upon it accompanied by young, lightly clad girls plying the oars, and Amenhotep III had a vast pool built in his Theban palace. This very Egyptian taste for garden parks later passed to Rome.

There are earlier examples of town planning than those attributed to Greek genius. As early as −1895, under the reign of Sesostris II, the city of Kahun was built inside a rectangular wall. The city had both administrative and residential buildings. The workers' houses, nearly 250 of which have been excavated, were built in blocks along streets 4 metres wide which ran into a central thoroughfare 8 metres wide. Each house occupied a ground area of 100 to 125 square metres and contained a dozen rooms on a single level. Located in another quarter of the city were the houses of the leading citizens—town houses which sometimes had as many as seventy rooms, or more modest homes which were, nevertheless, considerably larger than those of the workers. These houses were also built along rectilinear avenues running parallel to the city walls. These avenues had a drain running down the centre.

The large fortresses in Nubia were patterned on the same lines, and the same urban plan was adopted, under the New Kingdom, at Tell-el-Amarna, among other places, where the streets crossed at right angles though the city itself did not have the geometrical severity of Kahun.

It would, of course, be hazardous to suggest that all Egyptian cities were laid out like Kahun or Tell-el-Amarna. Those cities were built at one go under the orders of a sovereign. Cities which grew up over a long period of time must have had a more haphazard appearance. The fact of the matter remains, however, that the geometric plans of the city and the standardized type of houses that were built shed light on the trends of Egyptian town planning. Were they the forerunners of the town planning of the Hellenes? The question is worth asking.

While Egypt unquestionably made a major contribution in the field of architecture, it is nevertheless more difficult to judge the impact it had on the world as a whole in this sphere. Architects in many cultures, to be sure, have used, and are still using, colonnades, pyramids and obelisks which are undeniably of Egyptian origin. But was there not, in addition, an influence that goes back even farther and comes down to us through the intermediary *of* the Greeks? It is difficult not to discern in the clustered columns of Sakkara and the proto-Doric columns at Beni Hasan the remote ancestors of the columns of Greek and, later, Roman classical art. One fact, at least, seems established: the architectural traditions of the Pharaohs made their way into Africa first via Meroe and then Napata, which transmitted forms such as pyramids and pylons, among others, as well as techniques such as building with small, hewn, well-shaped masonry.

CULTURAL CONTRIBUTIONS

This side of the Egyptian Pharaonic legacy is an abstract one. It includes their contributions in the fields of writing, literature, art and religion.

Literature

The Egyptians developed a hieroglyphic writing system in which many of the symbols came from their African environment. For this reason it can be assumed to be their original creation rather than borrowed (see Introduction).

The ancient Egyptian at first expressed himself in pictorial ideograms which were soon formalized into symbols reflecting phonetic sounds which, in their later abbreviated form, could be considered as a step towards an alphabetic script.

Cultural contacts with the Semitic script developed in Sinai, where there appeared distinctive forms of writing which borrowed forms possessing affinities with hieroglyphics, may have contributed to the invention of the true alphabet which was borrowed by the Greeks and had its influence on Europe. Apart from this, the ancient Egyptians invented the tools of writing (which we have already described in the section on crafts). Their discovery of papyrus, handed down to classical antiquity, thanks to its lightweight, flexibility and the almost unlimited dimensions that could be papyrus 'scrolls', certainly played a role in the diffusion of thought and knowledge. There is an extensive literature dating from Pharaonic times covering every aspect of Egyptian life, from religious theories to literature, such as stories, plays, poetry, dialogues and criticism. This literature can be considered as one of the most vital cultural legacies of ancient Egypt. Even though it is impossible to determine what parts of it were taken over by neighbouring African cultures, a modern ethnologist was able to recognize a legend of Egyptian origin, one also found in a text of Herodotus, among the Nilotes of the province of Equatoria in the Sudan.

Some the most impressive examples of Egyptian literature are those written during the First Intermediate Period and during the early Middle Kingdom. One eminent scholar of Egyptology, James Henry Breasted, considered this literature as an early sign of intellectual and social maturity. He described this period as a dawn of conscience when a man could debate with his own soul on metaphysical matters. Another example of the literature of this period was a work written by the Eloquent Peasant which expresses dissatisfaction with the community and with the condition of the land. This could be considered as an early step towards a social revolution and democracy.

A good example of the sentiments expressed in Egyptian literature is seen in the inscription on four wooden coffins found in El-Bersheh in Middle Egypt: 'I created the four winds so every man could breathe … I caused the flood so the poor could benefit as well as the rich … I created every man equal to his neighbour …'.

Lastly, it is conceivable that certain specimens of Egyptian literature have survived to our day thanks to the marvellous stories of Arabic literature. The latter, indeed, seem at times to have their source in Egyptian oral tradition. It has, for example, been possible to establish a parallel between the story of 'Ali Baba and the Forty Thieves' from *The Arabian Nights* and a Pharaonic story, 'The Taking of Joppe', and between 'Sinbad the Sailor' and 'The Shipwrecked Sailor', a Pharaonic tale of the Middle Kingdom.

ART

In the field of art the ancient Egyptians expressed their ideas in a great many techniques including sculpture, painting, reliefs and architecture (see Pls 4–6). They combined worldly affairs and activities with hopes for the after-life, and their art was particularly expressive because it gave representation to beliefs that were deeply held. For them, there was only a semblance of death when all signs of life ceased, for the human being still continued to exist in every way. But to survive they required the support of their body, through mummification or, failing that, through an image. Statues and statuettes, bas-reliefs and tomb paintings are there to perpetuate the life of the individual in the afterworld. This is why the details of the human body are shaped with such precision. To heighten the intensity of his gaze, the eyes of the statues were inlaid, and even the eyebrows were fashioned in copper or silver. The eyeballs were made of white quartz and the pupils were made of resin. Sometimes the Egyptian artists manufactured gold statues or hammered copper ones on a wooden base. This required great skill and experience in the shaping of metal. This skill can be seen in a large number of statues dating from every historical period which have been found in various archaeological sites.

In the field of minor arts, the ancient Egyptians produced a very large number of amulets, scarabs and seals and also ornamental objects and jewellery, which are no less beautiful for their smaller size. It is undoubtedly these small objects which were most widespread and esteemed in Africa, the Near East and even in Europe. It is *often the wide* distribution of these objects that makes it possible to discover the bonds which linked Egypt to other nations long ago.

All artistic objects in ancient Egypt were made, not for the sake of art alone, but above all as an expression of the Egyptian belief that life relating to the living world would be repeated after death.

RELIGION

This can be considered as one of the philosophical contributions of Egypt. For the ancient Egyptians developed a number of theories concerning the creation of life, the role of the natural powers, and the response of the human community towards them; also the world of the gods and their influence on human thought, the divine aspect of kingship, the role of the priesthood in the community and the belief in eternity and life in the netherworld.

It was their profound experience in such abstract thought that influenced the Egyptian community to such an extent that it had a lasting effect on the outside world. Particularly apparent to the historian is the Egyptian religious influence in certain Graeco-Roman religious objects, as can be seen by

the popularity of the goddess Isis and her cult in classical antiquity.

TRANSMISSION OF THE PHARAONIC LEGACY. ROLE OF THE SYRO-PALESTINIAN CORRIDOR

Phoenicia played a special and important role in transmitting the Pharaonic legacy to the rest of the world.

Egypt's influence on Phoenicia can be traced through the economic and cultural contacts between the two areas. Such a relationship became apparent when trade and exploration started to expand during the pre and protodynastic times, in order to fulfil the vast needs of those periods. Even the invention of writing as an essential means of communication developed partly as a result of economic and religious factors. That is to say, the contacts with Phoenicia were indispensable to import vital raw materials like wood, for example, which were necessary for the erection and construction of shrines and religious monuments.

Egyptian traders established a shrine of their own at Byblos, a city with which they had very close trade contacts. Egyptian culture and ideas were spread throughout the Mediterranean basin by the intermediary of the Phoenicians.

The influence of Egyptian culture on biblical wisdom, among other things, is noteworthy (see Chapter 3). With regard to the Levant, commercial and cultural relations existed throughout the second and first millennia before our era, which include the Middle and New Kingdom as well as under the late dynasties. Relations naturally increased following Egyptian political and military expansion, and Egyptian artistic patterns occur in various Syrian and Palestinian sites such as Ras Shamra, Qatna and Megisso, as can be seen from statues, sphinxes and decorative patterns. The exchange of gifts helped in expanding the cultural and commercial relations.

It should be stated that it was the Egyptian artistic influence that affected Syrian local art and this was a direct result of the contacts between Egypt and the Levant. In Mittani, in the north-east of Syria, Egyptian artistic elements can also be observed. For example, the Egyptian goddess Hathor is represented in mural paintings. It seems that Egyptian artistic influence spread from Syria to neighbouring communities; this is indicated by the number of ivory handles and plaques of Egyptian motifs in the decoration of some bronze bowls and especially in attempts to imitate Egyptian dress, the winged scarabs and the falcon-headed sphinxes.

Egyptian artistic influence, which has been observed in Phoenician and Syrian art, is actually combined with local artistic motifs, as well as other foreign elements, both in sculpture in the round and in reliefs. This phenomenon can be observed not only in Syria but also among the Phoenician objects found in Cyprus and Greece, since the Phoenicians played an important cultural and commercial role in the Mediterranean world and carried elements of the Egyptian culture to other areas.

Egyptian hieroglyphic writing has been traced in the Semitic scripts of the Levant. This can be observed by comparing some typical Egyptian hieroglyphs, the proto-Sinaitic signs, and the Phoenician alphabet. The proto-Sinaitic elements were influenced by the Egyptian hieroglyphic ideograms, and they simplified these ideograms in a way which may be considered as a step towards alphabetical signs. Proto-Sinaitic writing could be taken as a step towards the Phoenician alphabet and hence towards the European alphabet.

This vast Pharaonic legacy, disseminated through the ancient civilizations of the Near East, has in turn transmitted to modern Europe a civilization by way of the classical world.

Economic and political contacts between Egypt and the eastern Mediterranean world in historical times resulted in the distribution of objects of the Pharaonic civilization as far as Anatolia and the pre-Hellenic Aegean world. Thus, a cup bearing the name of the solar temple of Userkaf, first Pharaoh of the fifth dynasty, was found on the island of Cythera, while pieces of a gold-plated armchair, carrying Schure's titles, were found at Dorak in Anatolia.

Besides these relations between Pharaonic Egypt and the Mediterranean world, there were also the cultural ties which linked Egypt with the African interior. These relations existed during the earliest stages of pre-history as well as in historical times. Egyptian civilization under the Pharaohs permeated the neighbouring African cultures. Comparative studies prove the existence of common cultural elements between black Africa and Egypt, such as the relationship between royalty and natural forces. This is clear from archaeological findings in the former territory of the land of Kush: royal pyramids were built in El-Kurru, Nuri, Gebel Barkal and Meroe. They bear witness to the significance of Egyptian influence in Africa.

Unfortunately, our ignorance of the Meroitic language, and of the extent of the Meroitic empire, prevents us from judging the impact it had on the cultures of ancient Africa as a whole to the east, west and south of the Meroitic empire.

PERIPLUS OF THE ERYTHRAEAN SEA

By G. S. P. Freeman-Grenville

1. ANONYMOUS

Probably written about 100 C.E. at Alexandria, The Periplus of the Erythraean Sea *was a merchant's guide to the Red Sea and Indian Ocean ports. It is generally accepted as the earliest firsthand account of the East African coast to have survived to the present.*

From Tabai after 400 stades sailing is a promontory towards which the current runs, and the market-town of Opone. ... It produces cinnamon, both the *aroma* and *moto* varieties, as well as the better sort of slaves, which are brought to Egypt in increasing numbers, and much tortoise-shell of better quality than elsewhere.

Voyages from Egypt to all these further market-towns are made in the month of July, that is *Epiphi*. The ships are usually fitted out in the inner [Red Sea] ports of Ariake and Barugaza; and they bring the further market-towns the products of these places: wheat, rice, ghee, sesame oil, cotton cloth (both the *monache* and the *sag-matogene*), girdles, and honey from the reed called *sakchari*. Some make voyages directly to these market-towns, others exchange cargo as they go. The country has no sovereign but each market-town is ruled by its own chief.

After Opone the coast veers more towards the south. First there are the Small and Great Bluffs of Azania and rivers for anchorages for six days' journey southwestwards. Then come the Little and the Great Beach for another six days' journey, and after that in order the Courses of Azania. first that called Sarapion, the next Nikon, and then several rivers and other anchorages one after the other, separately a halt and a day's journey, in all seven, as far as the Pyralaae Islands and the island called Diorux [the Channel].

Beyond this, slightly south of southwest after a voyage of two days and nights along the Ausanitic coast, is the island of Menouthesias some 300 stades from the land. It is flat and wooded. There are many rivers in it. and many kinds of birds and the mountain tortoise. There are no wild animals at all except the crocodile, but they never attack men. In this place there are small sewn boats and dug-outs, which they use for fishing and for catching tortoise. In this island they fish in a peculiar way with wicker baskets, which they fasten across where the tide goes out.

Two days' sail beyond the island lies the last mainland market-town of Azania, which is called Rhapta, a name derived from the small sewn boats. Here there is much ivory and tortoise-shell.

Men of the greatest stature, who are pirates, inhabit the whole coast and at each place have set up chiefs. The Chief of the Ma'afir is the suzerain, according to an ancient right which subordinates it to the kingdom which has become the first in Arabia. The people of

Mouza hold it in tribute under his sovereignty and send there small ships, mostly with Arab captains and crews who trade and intermarry with the mainlanders of all the places and know their language.

Into these market-towns are imported the lances made especially for them at Mouza, hatchets, swords, awls, and many kinds of small glass vessels; and at some places wine and not a little wheat, not for trade but to gain the goodwill of the barbarians. Much ivory is taken away from these places, but it is inferior in quality to that of Adulis, and also rhinoceros horn and tortoise-shell, different from that of India, and a little coconut oil.

And these, I think, are the last of the market-towns of Azania on the mainland lying to the right of Berenice; for after all these places the ocean curves westward and runs along the regions of Ethiopia, Libya, and Africa, stretching out from the south and mingling with the western sea.

NOTES

* From "The Periplus of the Erythraean Sea," in G. S. P. Freeman-Grenville, *The East African Coast, Select Documents from the First to the Earlier Nineteenth Century,* (Oxford: Clarendon Press, 1962), pp.1–2. Reprinted by permission of the Clarendon Press, Oxford.

* From Cosmas Indicopleustes. *The Christian Topography of Cosmas, an Egyptian Monk,* trans, and edited by J. W. McCrindle (London: Hakluyt Society, 1897), pp. 49–54.

1. This would mean the country of the Huns.

2. Nisibis, the capital of Mygdoniia, was after the time of Lucullus, considered the chief bulwark of the Roman Power in the East. It was an ancient, large, and populous city, and was for long the great northern emporium of the commerce of the East and West. It was situated about two days journey from the head waters of the Tigris in the midst of a pleasant and fertile plain at the foot of Mount Masius.

3. Far northern regions (fed).

4. Axomis (Auxume in Ptolemy) is the modern Axum, the capital of Tigre. In the early centuries of our era it was a powerful State, possessing nearly the whole of Abyssinia, a portion of the south-west Red Sea coast and north-western Arabia. It was distant from its seaport, Adule, which was situated near Annesley Bay, about 120 miles, or an eight days' caravan journey. It was the chief centre of the trade with the interior of Africa. The Greek language was understood and spoken, both by the court and the numerous foreigners who had either settled in it or who resorted to it for trading purposes. … Christianity was introduced into Axum in the fourth century by Oedisius and Frumentius. the latter *of* whom was afterwards appointed its first bishop. Sasu, which is next mentioned is near the coast, and only 5° to the north of the equator.

5. A kind of cinnamon (ed.).

6. Reed used as a pen (ed.).

7. The Agau people is the native race spread over the Abyssinian plateau both to the east and west of Lake Tana …

* From J. J. L. Duyvendak, *China's Discovery of Africa* (London: Arthur Probsthain 1949), pp. 12–15, 22–24, Reprinted by permission.

1. A substance used in perfumes (ed.).

2. A piece of close-fitting armor for protecting the breast and back; it was originally made of leather (ed.).

CHRISTIANITY AND ISLAM

BY JOHN ILIFFE

While Bantu-speaking peoples were colonising southern Africa, the north was entering one of its greatest historical periods. Perhaps only in pharaonic times had it been more central to human progress than in the third and fourth centuries AD, when it was the intellectual spearhead of Christianity, and again 800 years later, when it was the pivot of Islam and a commercial network encompassing most of the Old World. This leadership, already threatened, was destroyed during the fourteenth century by the demographic catastrophe of the Black Death, from which the region took 500 years to recover. But in their time of greatness North Africans adapted Christianity and Islam to their own cultures and transmitted both religions to Black Africa, where centuries of internal development had prepared social environments for their reception and further adaptation.

CHRISTIANITY IN NORTH AFRICA

Legend said that St Mark himself brought Christianity to Alexandria in AD 61. In reality the church in Jerusalem probably sent missionaries to Alexandria's large Jewish community. The first firm evidence of Christianity there comes from an early second-century controversy between Jews who had and those who had not accepted the new faith. Shortly afterwards Christianity expanded beyond this Jewish nucleus. By AD 200 there was a Greek-speaking church under a Bishop of Alexandria, with many Christians in Upper as well as Lower Egypt. They saw Christ as a great teacher in the Greek manner; their first major theologian, Origen (c. 185–253/4), believed that man should elevate himself towards God through wisdom and asceticism. Once the first bishops outside Alexandria took office early in the third century, Christianity spread among Egyptians as well as Greeks. By 325 Egypt had fifty-one known bishoprics and the Bible was widely available in the vernacular Coptic language; (Ancient Egyptian written in Greek script). The chief leaders of popular Christianity were monks: first individual hermits like St Antony, who lived in the desert from about 285 to 305, then disciplined communities pioneered inc. 321 by Pachomius. Monasticism may have had models in Ancient Egyptian priestly asceticism, just as the Coptic Church's elaborate charity inherited an ancient tradition of famine relief. Both exemplified the indigenisation of Christianity at a time when Egypt's old religion and culture were disintegrating. In 312 Constantine made Christianity the Roman Empire's official religion. Later in that century the authorities persecuted traditional priests and either closed their temples or converted them into churches or monasteries. By AD 400 perhaps 90 percent of Egyptians were Christians.

Further west, Christianity may have reached the Maghrib through Greek or Roman rather than Jewish networks. The first firm evidence of its existence is the execution of twelve Christians at Carthage in AD 180 for refusing to sacrifice in honour of the emperor. Such early Christians appear to have come from every rank, age, and sex in urban society. Christianity offered fellowship across social divisions in increasingly stratified towns, just as it offered literal bodily resurrection in a purposeless world and spiritual protection in a dangerous world. In place of the multitudinous spiritual forces (*daemones*) and human sorcerers whom pagans feared, Christianity pictured a dualistic conflict between God, who protected the faithful, and the Devil, whose forces included all aspects of paganism. Christianity did not threaten social rank and its teaching generally passed from older to younger people, but it fed upon conflicts of generation and gender in complex, patriarchal households, as it would later in tropical Africa. Among the first North Africans to be martyred, in the arena at Carthage in 203, was a well-born, twenty-year-old wife and mother named Perpetua:

> We walked up to the prisoner's dock. All the others when questioned admitted their guilt. Then, when it came my turn, my father appeared with my son, dragged me from the step, and said: 'Perform the sacrifice—have pity on your baby!'
> Hilarianus the governor ... said to me: 'Have pity on your father's grey head; have pity on your infant son. Offer the sacrifice for the welfare of the emperors.'
> 'I will not,' I retorted.
> 'Are you a Christian?' said Hilarianus.
> And I said: 'Yes, I am.' ...
> Then Hilarianus passed sentence on all of us: we were condemned to the beasts, and we returned to prison in high spirits.[1]

Persecution was sporadic until 249–51, when the Emperor Decius, a soldier who thought Christianity was corrupting the state, launched more thorough repression. Martyrs were especially numerous in prosperous North Africa because the Church was growing most quickly there, with at least 150 bishoprics, concentrated especially in the ancient colonial zone around Carthage but also scattered generously further south in Byzacena and west in Numidia. During the next half-century Christianity spread rapidly in the countryside, especially in Numidia, the inland plains of modern Algeria which were then being planted with olives. In this settler country of estates and Berber villages, Christianity was a religion of protest, infused with Berber traditions or statelessness and honour, which forbade man or woman to betray loyalties from fear of pain or death. When Diocletian launched his Great Persecution in 303 in a desperate attempt to restore the old Roman order, church leaders were required to surrender the scriptures for destruction. Those who complied, the *traditores* (surrenderers), were subsequently denied recognition by zealots who created a schismatic church under the leadership of Donatus, their candidate for the bishopric of Carthage. Where as the Catholics found followers especially among urban notables and in the Romanised farming region near the coast, Donatist leaders, although themselves mostly Latin-speaking urban intellectuals, won support chiefly among the non-Roman lower classes of the towns and, especially, the Berber cultivators and labourers of Numidia. Many Donatist churches there had a local martyr's body beneath the altar. The coincidence of religious and agrarian conflict bred violent zealots, the Circumcellions (those 'around the shrines'), often perhaps seasonal labourers, who defended Donatist institutions and terrorised exploitative landlords and Catholic clergy. Donatism predominated in the Maghrib throughout the fourth century. Its repression was eventually organised by St Augustine of Hippo (in eastern Algeria), who condemned it as narrow, provincial, schismatic, and socially subversive. In AD 411 Donatism became a criminal offence and the Catholic Church, now increasingly integrated with the Roman state, intensified repression. The Vandal invasion of North Africa in 429 interrupted this, but persecution resumed when Byzantine rule was established in 533. Donatism was gradually confined to its Numidian strongholds, but there it survived until the seventh-century Arab invasion.

To this day the Coptic of Egypt dates events not from the Birth of Christ but from 'the era of the martyrs' in AD 284. Yet it forgave its *traditores* and suffered only brief schism. Its crisis came later, following the Council of Chalcedon of 451, which tried to shore up the disintegrating Roman Empire by declaring the primacy of the bishops of Rome and Constantinople (the new imperial capital) at the expense of Alexandria, and by adopting a characterisation of Christ—that He had two distinct but inseparably united natures, divine and human—acceptable to Rome but anathema to Alexandria. Overt schism came in 536, when the Emperor Justinian tried to impose a pro-Chalcedonian hierarchy upon Egyptians who now proclaimed the Monophysite (one-nature) faith. Byzantine persecution of Monophysites prevented united Christian resistance to the Muslim invasion of 639, which destroyed the pro-Chalcedonian hierarchy but left Coptic Christians as protected tributaries concerned ever more exclusively with survival.

CHRISTIANITY IN ETHIOPIA AND SUDAN

The Coptic Church was a missionary church. Its earliest field of expansion was Ethiopia. Following the collapse of D'mt between the fifth and third centuries BC, several small successor states occupied the northern Ethiopian plateau. The growth of Red Sea trade in Ptolemaic times enriched the region and linked it to Mediterranean developments through its chief port at Adulis, famed for its ivory. During the first century AD, at a time of unusually generous rainfall, a kingdom emerged at Aksum which went on to reunite the region, inheriting much South Arabian culture and embellishing its capital with palatial stone buildings, tall stone stelae marking royal graves, and a surrounding belt of rural villas. Two centuries later the kingdom struck coins on Roman models.

The introduction of Christianity to Aksum is traditionally attributed to Frumentius, a young Christian trader kidnapped en route from Tyre to India. He became tutor to the future King Ezana, who officially adopted Christianity in about 333, after Frumentius had been consecrated in Alexandria as Aksum's first bishop. This tradition oversimplifies a complex process, for Christianity was only one of several religions (including Judaism) at Ezana's court; more than a century after his supposed conversion a successor recorded the sacrifice of fifty captives to Mahrem, local god of war. Ezana had probably sought to patronise all religions, including Christianity, whose prominence on his coins suggests that he displayed it especially, but not exclusively, to foreigners. Because Christianity reached Aksum from Alexandria, the Ethiopian Church became Monophysite and was headed by Coptic monks from Alexandria until the mid-twentieth century. Moreover, because Christianity first influenced the court, it became a state religion, gradually extended among the people by priests and monks with royal backing. Between the fifth and seventh centuries the scriptures were translated into Ge'ez (the Semitic *lingua franca* of Aksum, written in a script derived from South Arabian), Christianity and Aksumite authority spread further southwards on the Ethiopian plateau, and pagan temples in Aksum and Adulis became churches. But from the late sixth century Aksum's prosperity declined, first perhaps because warfare between Byzantium and Persia dislocated trade, then owing to Muslim expansion which destroyed Adulis, and finally because increasing reliance on agriculture coincided with declining rainfall. Aksum struck its last coins in the early seventh century. The king who died in 630 was buried not in the capital but further to the south-west, where the merging of Aksumite and indigenous Cushitic cultures was to create the historic church and kingdom of Ethiopia.

Christian origins in Nubia differed from those in Aksum, partly because Nubia immediately adjoined Christian Egypt. After the collapse of Meroe during the fourth century AD, Nubian-speaking rulers created three kingdoms in the Nile Valley: Nobatia in the north with its capital at Faras, Makuria in the centre with its headquarters at Old Dongola, and Alwa in the south based on Soba (close to modern Khartoum). Egyptian traders brought Christianity by at least the fifth century, for archaeologists have uncovered churches of that date at Faras and Qasr Ibrim in Nobatia, while Christians from Aksum apparently visited Alwa. In Nobatia, only commoners' graves contain early Christian objects, suggesting that there, in contrast to Aksum, Christianity grew from the bottom upwards, an impression strengthened by the suppression of the church at Faras and the continuation until 535 of the annual custom of fetching a statue of Isis from Philae in Egypt to bless Nubian crops. When the Byzantine Emperor Justinian banned the ceremony in that year, both the Orthodox (Byzantine) and Monophysite (Coptic) Churches sent missions to Nubia. The Monophysite missionary reached Nobatia first, in 543, 'and immediately with joy they yielded themselves up,' as the chronicler John of Ephesus recorded, 'and utterly abjured the error of their forefathers, and confessed the God of the Christians.'[2] Evidence of village church-building and rapid adoption of Christian burial confirms this account, although pagan temples survived in Nobatia for another two centuries. Alwa was also keen to link itself to the larger world. When the missionary Longinus arrived there from Constantinople in 580, 'he spake unto the king and to all his nobles the word of God, and they opened their understandings, and listened with joy to what he said; and after a few days' instruction, both the king himself was baptized and all his nobles; and subsequently, in process of time, his people also.'[3]

The Nubian kingdoms remained Christian for nearly a thousand years. Nobatia and Alwa were Monophysite from the first; Makuria either was so or soon became so. Nubian bishops appear to have been appointed from Alexandria and the Church dated events by the Coptic era of the martyrs. But the Coptic Church in Egypt soon fell under Muslim rule and Nubian rulers looked increasingly to the Christian Emperor in Constantinople. The beautiful murals in the cathedral at Faras, excavated from the sand during the 1960s, began in Coptic style but gradually changed to Byzantine, although they also displayed distinctive local features. The liturgical language was Greek; only slowly were parts of the liturgy and Bible translated into Nubian, written in the Coptic form of the Greek alphabet. Church architecture suggests that the liturgical role of the laity diminished with time. Kings were in priestly orders and bishops held state offices in the Byzantine manner. Some historians attribute the ultimate disappearance of Nubian Christianity to a failure to adapt as fully to the local culture as did Ethiopian Christianity, which was more isolated from external influence. Nubian paintings, for example, always depicted Christ and the saints with white faces in contrast to Nubians, a distinction not drawn in Ethiopian art. Yet the different fates of the two Churches owed more to different relationships with Islam.

ISLAM IN NORTH AFRICA

The expansion of Arab power and the Islamic religion following the Prophet Muhammad's death in AD 632 was the central process in world history for the next 400 years. During that time Islam became the predominant faith throughout North Africa and established footholds in both West and East Africa. In doing so it not only tied the north permanently to the wider history of the Old World, but it began to reintegrate sub-Saharan Africa into that history for the first time since the desiccation of the Sahara.

Some 4,000 Muslims commanded by Amr ibn al-As invaded Egypt in December 639. Within less than three years they had conquered the Byzantine Empire's richest province. They were helped by deep antagonism between Byzantine rulers and Monophysite subjects, who confined their resistance to defending their villages. But the Muslims' chief strength was the disciplined conviction that characterises the zealots of a new faith. 'We have seen a people who prefer death to life and humility to pride', a later historian imagined the Byzantines saying. 'They sit in the dust, and they take their meals on horseback.

Their commander is one of themselves: there is no distinction of rank among them. They have fixed hours of prayer at which all pray, first washing their hands and feet, and they pray with reverence.'4 In 643 their momentum carried Amr ibn al-As and his horsemen into modern Libya. Four years later they defeated the main Byzantine army near Sufetula (Sbeitla) in modern Tunisia and gained access to the fertile heartland of successive imperialisms in North Africa, more rural then than in Roman times and somewhat depopulated by a great plague in 542, but still rich in grain and olives. At this point, however, the conquest faltered, owing to conflict over succession to the Caliphate. When expansion resumed in 665 the main leader, Ukba ibn Nafi, bypassed North Africa's coastal cities and in c. 670 founded Kairwan in the Tunisian hinterland as the capital of a new Muslim province of Ifriqiya (Africa). Then he drove westwards through the inland plains until he rode his horse into the Atlantic, declaring that he had fought his way to the end of the world in God's name. On his way back, however, his army was annihilated by a Berber coalition led by Kusayla, a chief of the Tlemcen region, who went on to capture Kairwan. This opened a new period in the conquest. For four centuries the Berber peoples of the inland plains and mountains had been regaining strength from Romans, Vandals, and Byzantines. Now they mounted the stiffest resistance the Arabs met during their conquests, restricting Arab power to the colonial heartland of Ifriqiya. When a Muslim army finally conquered western Algeria and Morocco early in the eighth century, it was a largely Berber army, as was the expedition which conquered Spain in 711–12. Islamic predominance in Berber territory meant Berber predominance in Islam.

In North Africa, alone in the continent, Islamisation drew its initial impulse from conquest, but the victors seldom compelled the conquered to accept their faith. Their concern was to establish an Islamic social order, in the confidence that individuals would gradually conform to it. In Egypt, therefore, they offered Christians either client status as Muslim converts or toleration as protected tributaries (*dhimmi*) in return for land and poll taxes, as was initially preferred by most Copts, on whom the Arabs at first relied to administer Egypt's complex society. By the eighth century, however, Arab immigrants had increased and Christians were gradually excluded from office, as one of several social and economic pressures to adopt Islam. By 717–20 so many Copts were becoming Muslims to escape the heavy taxes needed to finance Arab wars that converts were declared still liable to the land tax. At the same period official business finally came to be conducted in Arabic. The Coptic language survived temporarily in the countryside but eventually became purely a liturgical language, while the Coptic Church itself lived on its past as a religion of survival, periodically harried by the authorities and unable to rival the conviction, authority, and modernity of Islam. By the fourteenth century probably fewer than one-tenth of Egyptians were Christians.

The Umayyad Caliphate which lasted until 750 was effectively an Arab kingdom led by the Meccan aristocracy. Egypt in particular was dominated by an Arab garrison. When the Abbasids gained power in 750, however, they relied on non-Arab nationalities and moved their capital eastwards to Baghdad, thereby encouraging North African autonomy. By the late ninth century power in Egypt lay with Turkish military governors and their multiethnic mercenaries, who had supplanted the Arab horsemen of the heroic age. Further west, in the Maghrib, separatist tendencies were even stronger. The Berbers retained their language and, according to the great Tunisian historian Ibn Khaldun, apostasised a dozen times during their first seventy years of Islam. Certainly they displayed the same egalitarianism, puritanism, and particularism as had inspired the Donatist schism. At least one Christian community survived for a thousand years. A group in the Atlantic Plains of Morocco claimed to possess a Koran in the Berber language and maintained its heterodoxy until the eleventh century. But the chief vehicle of Berber aspirations was Kharijism, an extreme wing of Islam born in 657 during the civil war which created the Umayyad Caliphate. It taught the absolute equality of Muslims, the right of any worthy Muslim to be elected Imam of the whole community, and consequently the duty to reject the existing, illegitimate Caliphate. Kharijites escaping persecution in the east left for the Maghrib in c. 714, winning more support among Berbers than anywhere else, especially, it appears, among former Christians. In 740 they launched a revolt in Tangier, led by a former water-carrier, sparking turmoil which eventually overthrew the Umayyads. When the Abbasids proved equally repressive, Kharijites formed several zealous communities in the North African hinterland, especially at Tahert in western Algeria, which from 761–2 became the core of a Kharijite state. In 789–90 a refugee descendant of the Prophet, Idris, created a kingdom based in Fes which became the chief vehicle of Islamisation in northern Morocco. Throughout these disturbances the centre of Abbasid power in the Maghrib and almost the only area of extensive Arab settlement remained Ifriqiya, but there, in 800, an Arab governor established the hereditary Aghlabid dynasty. Thereafter the Maghrib was effectively independent.

During the following five centuries North Africa bred several of Islam's most creative dynasties. The first, the Fatimids, were a Shia family claiming descent from the Prophet through his daughter Fatima. They came to power in Kairwan in 910 on the back of a Berber revolt, incorporated the Aghlabid kingdom, temporarily overran much of Morocco in 958–9, and went on in 969 to take Egypt peacefully from its Turkish military rulers, completing the Berber reconquest of North Africa and building Cairo as a capital fit for a Fatimid Caliph. Despite their heterodox origins, the Fatimids had no radical programme. They had gained power in Ifriqiya at a time of unprecedented prosperity once the Arab conquest was stabilised. The traveller al-Yakubi (d. 891) wondered at Kairwan's wealth, with its flourishing textile industry, growing gold imports from West Africa, surrounding market gardens, and supplies of fruit from the coast, grain from the northern plains, olives from the Sahel, and dates from Saharan oases. Townsmen owned great estates carved out by victorious ancestors and worked by the slaves for which the region was famed, initially Berbers enslaved during the conquest, thereafter white and black slaves imported from Europe and tropical Africa. Cultivation of sorghum and hard wheat expanded southwards, famine was virtually unknown during the tenth century, and population almost certainly increased. Mediterranean trade was largely in Muslim hands, thanks to the Fatimid fleet, which sacked Genoa in 934–5. When this wealth enabled the Fatimid army of Slav mercenaries and Berber auxiliaries to capture Egypt, prosperity shifted to the new capital. The records recovered from the Cairo Geniza—where Jews deposited unwanted papers to avoid destroying any bearing the name of God—show that immigrant Fatimids were followed by merchants from the Maghrib seeking their fortunes in what now became the centre of the Islamic world. 'It was the heyday of the bourgeoisie', their historian has written,[5] a commercial world dominated by family firms of many faiths, operating through partnerships and agencies spread throughout the Mediterranean, profiting from a freedom of movement and religious toleration which caused Jewish merchants to call Fatimid Egypt 'the land of life'. This bourgeoisie dominated a stratified but mobile society with an exceptional level of craft specialisation, many female slaves in domestic service, and numerous paupers. Cairo despised and exploited the countryside, where Arab rule introduced sugar, cotton, and rice, encouraged multicropping, and—after an initial hiatus during the conquest—probably stimulated population growth, which by the fourteenth century was regaining Ptolemaic levels. In the meantime, however, exploitation of the countryside may have contributed to severe famine in 1062–73 which was the first symptom of Fatimid decline. Twenty years later their dominions were confined to Egypt. In 1171 they were overthrown by their Kurdish Vizier, the great Saladin.

In Ifriqiya the shift of power and prosperity to Egypt led the Fatimids' Berber lieutenants, the Zirids, to renounce their allegiance in 1048. Tradition claims that the Fatimids replied not with an army but by encouraging the Banu Hilal and other nomadic Arab tribes who had entered Egypt to move on westwards into Ifriqiya. The Hilal, wrote Ibn Khaldun, 'gained power over the country and ruined it.' In 1057 they sacked Kairwan. The Zirids shifted their capital and their attention to the seaboard, losing control of the interior. Transport was disrupted and gold caravans dispersed to reach the coast at several points, especially further to the west in Morocco. Berber pastoralists retreated westwards. Cultivators withdrew into mountain strongholds. A huge swathe of former Berber plains was permanently Arabised, the nomads' dialect becoming its vernacular Arabic. The effects of this 'Hilalian invasion' have no doubt been exaggerated. It was more an infiltration than an invasion. North Africa's rainfall and cultivated area had probably been contracting since the fifth century AD and would reach their nadir in the fourteenth century.[6] Loss of naval control of the Mediterranean to the Byzantines during the tenth century deprived Ifriqiya of its northern slave supply, which further damaged the rural economy and contributed to repeated famines after 1004. These and the Zirids' political weakness brought commercial decay to Kairwan even before the Banu Hilal sacked it. Their depredations were consequences as well as causes of a collapse from which Ifriqiya never recovered. By the 1090s the former granary of Rome was becoming dependent on imported Sicilian wheat.

Initially the chief beneficiary was the previously fragmented western Maghrib, where nomad ambitions coincided with economic diversification and the full internalisation of Islam among its Berber converts to produce a period of great splendour. It began with the Almoravid movement, which originated among the nomadic Sanhaja Berbers of southern Morocco and the western Sahara, long overshadowed by their more settled Zanata rivals to the north and gradually losing their long-standing control of trade in the western desert. The Sanhaja were largely oral Muslims until the eleventh century, when their leaders sought further instruction from rigorous teachers anxious to root out the Shiite and Kharijite legacies so powerful in the Maghrib. Abdallah ibn Yasin began to teach among the Sanhaja in c. 1039, gathered a following

of zealots and tribesmen, and launched them against Zanata supremacy. In 1070 they created a new capital at Marrakesh. By 1083 they had conquered the whole Maghrib west of Algiers. Three years later they entered Muslim Spain to organise its resistance to Christian expansion. This military supremacy was backed by capturing much of the West African gold trade and by developing the grainlands of Morocco's Atlantic Plains. Prosperity enabled the Almoravids to introduce into Morocco the elegant Islamic culture of southern Spain, which is still resplendent in the architecture of Marrakesh. This attracted puritan criticism, while others resented the regime's ruthlessness in enforcing orthodoxy and its reliance on the tribes who had initially supported Abdallah ibn Yasin.

These criticisms animated the Almohad (Unitarian) movement which was to supplant the Almoravids. It arose not among nomads but among their long-standing enemies, the Berber agriculturalists of the Atlas Mountains. Its leader, Muhammad ibn Tumart, was born there in about 1080 but educated in Baghdad, where he learned to criticise the Almoravids' legalistic rigour and to admire instead the personal spirituality then entering Islam through the mystics known as *sufis*. Returning to his mountain home, he was declared Mahdi by his fellow Masmuda tribesmen and in 1128 led them in a *jihad* against the dominant Sanhaja nomads and all corruptions of the faith. They took Marrakesh in 1147 and Ifriqiya in 1160, checking the expansion of the Banu Hilal and uniting the Maghrib for the first time under a single Berber regime. Almohad rule was rigorously Islamic; Christianity was virtually eradicated from the Maghrib and Jews found Almohads exceptionally intolerant. But they were less legalistic than the Almoravids, enabling *sufi* brotherhoods to establish themselves during the late twelfth century throughout the region, where they were to become the core of popular Islam. The decline of the over-extended Almohad empire began with its defeat by Christian forces in Spain in 1212 and was compounded by its inability to control nomadic tribes, notably the Arab pastoralists whom the regime had deported from Ifriqiya to the Atlantic Plains, thereby initiating further Arabisation of former Berber territory. In 1269 a Zanata tribe already dominant in northern Morocco, the Banu Marin, captured Marrakesh, transferred the capital to Fes, and ruled Morocco for two centuries as the Marinid dynasty.

Marinid rule witnessed general decline in the Maghrib. An Almohad successor dynasty, the Hafsids, ruled Ifriqiya until the Ottomans conquered it in the sixteenth century, while Zayyanids, another Zanata dynasty based in Tlemcen, exercised such central authority as existed in western Algeria. Reliant on mercenary troops rather than their subjects and based in northern cities dependent on maritime commerce controlled by Europeans, these regimes grew away from a countryside increasingly dominated by Arab pastoral tribes and *sufi* brotherhoods. Most important of all, the demographic growth which had underlain the Fatimid and Almoravid regimes was checked during the thirteenth century and dramatically reversed in 1348 when the great plague known in Europe as the Black Death reached the Maghrib from Sicily.

In Egypt, likewise, the Black Death ended nearly four centuries of prosperity and power unequalled since the New Kingdom. The Fatimids had initiated this prosperity. Saladin revitalised the state after he seized power in 1171, making Egypt the champion of Islam against Crusaders and Mongols. In 1250 his Ayyubid dynasty was overthrown by its Mamluk troops. These were slaves purchased as children from the horsemen of the Eurasian steppe, rigorously trained in Islam and the military skills of mounted archers, and then freed to become professional soldiers loyal to one another and to their former masters, forming a caste so exclusive that even their sons were barred from it. This system was designed to combine the virtues of nomadic valour and civilised organisation. Mamluk generals ruled Egypt until 1517. They reorganised its land into fiefs from which officers drew tribute to support themselves and their men. They extended irrigation and cultivation, raised medical skill to new levels, and were Egypt's greatest builders since the Ptolemies.

The expenditure of their great households made early fourteenth century Cairo the 'metropolis of the universe, garden of the world, swarming core of the human species,'[7] as Ibn Khaldun later described it.

Yet this prosperity was already threatened. By the early fourteenth century the international trading system stretching from Flanders to China, with Cairo at its core, was breaking down as the Mongol Empire disintegrated in Central Asia, leaving Egypt as a channel through which oriental goods passed to the increasingly dominant economies of Europe. Christians had enjoyed naval control of the Mediterranean since the tenth century. Italian trading cities such as Genoa and Pisa made commercial treaties with North African rulers from the 1130s. Portuguese and Aragonese (Catalan) mercenaries served the same rulers from the 1220s. Christian friars of the Dominican Order established a house at Tunis in 1250. In 1284–6 Aragon made two islands off the Tunisian coast Europe's first African colonies since Vandal times. By then European traders regularly frequented North African cities, siphoning away the gold trade and damaging Cairo's textile industry by their competition. Europe was outpacing the Islamic world in technology, business organisation, and agricultural production on virgin land no longer available in North Africa.

Relative decline became crisis when the Black Death reached Egypt along the trade routes from the Asiatic steppe. Egypt had suffered sporadic plague since the last great epidemic in the sixth century, but that had been bubonic plague, transmitted by fleas from rats to humans, whereas the Black Death was also the more infectious pneumonic plague, passed aerially from one person to another, making death even more common, rapid, horrible, and certain. Nobody understood the means of transmission and no effective counter measures were taken; all that religious leaders could counsel was prayer, charity, and dignified resignation. In eighteen months the epidemic killed perhaps one-quarter or one-third of Egypt's population.[8] For urban working people the consequence was higher wages, but the immobility of irrigated agriculture enabled Mamluks to respond to rural depopulation by trying to squeeze an undiminished revenue from fewer cultivators, although unsuccessfully in the long term, for shortly after 1517 Egypt's rulers collected less than one-fifth of the land tax paid in 1315. Resilient agriculture and control of trade between Asia and Europe enabled Egypt to survive the Black Death better than the rest of North Africa and the Middle East, but economic decay was nevertheless grave and coincided with recurrent warfare between Mamluk groups and the decline of the whole military class as firearms rendered their skills obsolete. Most devastating of all was that pneumonic plague remained recurrent after the Black Death, as not in Europe. During the next 160 years Egypt suffered twenty-eight plague outbreaks which were probably more destructive cumulatively than the Black Death itself. They continued until the early nineteenth century, when Egypt's population was perhaps between one-half and three-quarters of that of 1346. The Maghrib suffered equally, Tunisia enduring five plague epidemics during the seventeenth century alone. This demographic catastrophe ended North Africa's time of greatness and moved Ibn Khaldun—who lost both parents during the Black Death—to preserve the memory of a vanished world:

> in the middle of the eighth [fourteenth] century, civilization both in the East and the West was visited by a destructive plague which devastated nations and caused populations to vanish … Civilization decreased with the decrease of mankind. Cities and buildings were laid waste, roads and way signs were obliterated, settlements and mansions became empty, dynasties and tribes grew weak. The entire inhabited world changed … Therefore, there is need at this time that someone should systematically set down the situation of the world among all regions and races, as well as the customs and sectarian beliefs that have changed for their adherents.[9]

TRADE AND ISLAM IN WEST AFRICA

The Arab conquest of North Africa led to the transmission of Islam across the Sahara to the West African savanna. Agriculture and iron-using existed here before the Birth of Christ, but the first Muslims who knelt their camels on the northern fringe of the savanna also found towns and a regional trading system which appear to have been predominantly local inventions. Indeed, the chief reason why trans-Saharan trade grew so swiftly in the early Islamic period was probably that it linked two flourishing regional economies.

The best evidence for this comes from archaeological excavations at Old Jenne, a site in modern Mali on the southern edge of the internal Niger delta, where floodplain agriculture met transport routes to both the northern savanna and the southern forest. A settlement existed at Old Jenne by the third century BC and a substantial town with crowded cemeteries from AD 400. Four centuries later the town occupied thirty-three hectares, was surrounded by a two-kilometre wall, and had some sixty-five other settlements within a four kilometre radius. Townsmen worked iron ore brought from at least fifty kilometres away and owned copper objects made no closer than the southern Sahara, although they apparently did not weave cloth—a skill probably introduced by Muslim—traders and in the mid first millennium AD they possessed almost nothing of Mediterranean origin except glass beads. In other words, Old Jenne at that time was part of an extensive but largely self-contained West African trading system.

No other West African site of the early first millennium AD has yet been excavated so thoroughly. Almost nothing is known of agriculture, although from about AD 300 to 1100 rainfall was relatively plentiful. There are more indications of regional trade, especially in metals. Over 30,000 crucibles used in copper-working of around the sixth and seventh centuries AD have been found in the Air region of modern Niger, while an excavated tumulus of the late first millennium at Rao in Senegal has revealed superb gold ornaments. But the most convincing evidence is of towns built in the same sun-dried mud as Old Jenne, a technique whose simplicity may partly explain West Africa's very impressive early urbanisation, as in the ancient Near East. Town sites comparable to Old Jenne and surrounded by similar penumbra of smaller settlements have been found in the middle Niger Valley at Dia, Méma, and especially at Timbuktu, where the environment of the first millennium must have been more favourable for agriculture than it is today.[10] Graves at Old Jenne have not revealed much social differentiation, nor is there evidence of a powerful ruler or major public buildings. The rationale of the Niger Valley towns was apparently purely economic. Elsewhere in West Africa early mud-built towns cluster along the Chari and Logone rivers south of Lake Chad, while eighth-century dates for the earliest settlement at Old Oyo suggest first-millennium origins for Yorubaland's extensive urbanisation.

This pre-Islamic commerce and urbanisation may help to explain one of the mysteries of African history: the discovery at Igbo-Ukwu, in south-eastern Nigeria, of the grave-goods buried with a ninth-century ruler or ritual leader, including bronze artefacts made from local metals, in African style and showing a superb technical skill that was both distinctive and arguably unequalled elsewhere in the world at the time. Their symbolism, especially the use of animal motifs, shows remarkable continuity with that employed by the Igbo people of the area a thousand years later. But Igbo-Ukwu also shows that by the ninth century West Africa was no longer isolated from the outside world, for its grave-goods included over 100,000 glass beads, some probably from Egypt or even India.

By contrast, the two Hellenistic glass beads found in the late pre-Christian deposits at Old Jenne suggest that trade across the Sahara can then have been on only the smallest scale. The Garamantes of the Fezzan (in modern Libya) exported ivory and a few black slaves northwards in Roman times. That was an especially arid period in the Sahara and West African savanna, but by about AD 300 rainfall was increasing and Berbers were exchanging their horses for the camels which enabled them to open

the desert to trade. By AD 296 Roman Carthage was issuing gold coins, probably using metal from the Bambuk goldfield on the upper Senegal—the earliest of West Africa's river-valley goldfields—and bequeathing a standard gold weight (the *solidus* coin) to West African producers, who used it until the late nineteenth century. A growth in desert trade is suggested by Ukba ibn Nafi's actions as he led his men westwards into the Maghrib. In 666–7 he broke off southwards to reconnoitre the road to Fezzan, probably the main source of black slaves. Sixteen years later he made a similar excursion into southern Morocco, possibly to investigate sources of gold, for a subsequent expedition there in the 730s returned with enough gold to excite the Arabs' easily-aroused cupidity. By then they had been minting gold coins at Kairwan for nearly forty years.

On the slave route, a new trading base was established in about AD 700 in the eastern Fezzan at Zawila, a Kharijite Berber settlement which became the major supplier of black slaves to Ifriqiya, Egypt, and the Middle East. It enjoyed a relatively easy desert crossing to the northern environs of Lake Chad. Here the main suppliers of slaves were the Zaghawa, a largely pastoral people, mentioned by an Arab author before 728, who controlled a loose confederation known as Kanem, possibly created as early as the late sixth century. Lacking gold, Kanem and its successor, Borno, were to be the main suppliers of slaves from the West African savanna to the Islamic world for a thousand years, buying in return horses to facilitate further slave-raiding. Many slaves probably went to the Aghlabids who ruled Ifriqiya in the ninth century and relied on black slave soldiers, as did their Fatimid and Zirid successors. Kanem was first mentioned in 872 by al-Yakubi as one of West Africa's three main savanna kingdoms, along with Ghana and Gao to the west.

Ghana, centred in the east of modern Mauritania, was a kingdom of the Soninke people, black speakers of a Niger-Congo language. It was first mentioned in an Arabic source of 788–93 emanating from the Berber Khazijite community at Tahert, who pioneered trans-Saharan trade with the western savanna just as their counterparts in

Zawila developed the trade with Kanem. A trade route ran westwards from Tahert to Sijilmasa in southern Morocco (founded in 757–8) and then southwards to Awdaghust and Ghana, following the easiest desert crossing parallel to the Atlantic coast. This and its strategic position to the north-east of the Bambuk goldfield gave Ghana its importance, although it sought to control gold trade rather than gold production. Ghana's royal town, not yet discovered, was said to be ten kilometres from a traders' town thought to have been identified at Koumbi Saleh, where excavation has shown urban occupation and northern trade from the ninth to the fifteenth century, although on a site which had already been occupied in the mid first millennium AD. Writing in Spain in 1067–8 from travellers' testimonies, the geographer al-Bakri described Ghana's court at its apogee:

> The king has a palace and a number of domed dwellings all surrounded with an enclosure like a city wall … The king adorns himself like a woman round his neck and on his forearms, and he puts on a high cap decorated with gold and wrapped in a turban of fine cotton. He sits in audience or to hear grievances against officials in a domed pavilion around which stand ten horses covered with gold-embroidered materials. Behind the king stand ten pages holding shields and swords decorated with gold, and on his right are the sons of the [vassal] kings of his country wearing splendid garments and their hair plaited with gold.[11]

The king was not a Muslim, although many of his ministers were.

At the time al-Bakri was writing, Ghana was challenged from the west by the Takrur kingdom on the Senegal, which siphoned away Bambuk's gold to feed the newly created Almoravid empire. But Ghana's ancient commercial rival lay to the east at Gao, a town possibly dating back to the fifth century, first mentioned in the early ninth century, and situated on the River Niger where modern Mali and Niger meet. Gao was a city of the Songhay people. Like Ghana's capital, it was a dual town, on both banks of the Niger, whence a desert route led away north through Tadmekka and Wargla to Tahert and the North African coast. Caravans seldom undertook this two-thousand-kilometre crossing as a single journey. Rather, coastal merchants traded their cloth and copper southwards to an entrepôt like Tahert on the northern desert edge. There the trade was taken up by men, chiefly Berbers, who lived in the desert and transported goods across it along a line of oases, gathering their produce of dates, copper, and especially salt—so highly valued at Gao that it was used as currency—until they reached either another entrepôt on the southern desert fringe, such as Tadmekka, or pushed further south to an African town like Gao. A merchant sought partners or agents at each stage of the journey, perhaps men of the same community— Kharijites were ideally organised for this—or even kinsmen. In the thirteenth century two brothers of the Maqqari family lived at Tlemcen (close to the coast of western Algeria), another at Sijilmasa, and two at Walata (on the southern desert edge), cooperating in the family business and investing in wells along the route.

Exports of gold from the western savanna appear to have increased steadily. In the eighth century the only gold mints in North Africa were at Kairwan and Fustat (in Egypt). But gold coins were the mark of a Caliph. When the Fatimids in Ifriqiya, the Umayyads in Spain, and then the Almoravids and Almohads in Morocco aspired to that status, all began to coin gold. In the eleventh century the Almoravids alone had twenty-one gold mints in Spain and the Maghrib and the trade attracted southern European merchants to establish themselves in North African coastal cities. Initially they exported Islamic gold coins to supplement Europe's silver currency. Then Genoa and Florence in 1252, Venice in 1284, and northern European states in the earlier fourteenth century began to coin gold, sparking a late medieval gold rush. Black slaves also appeared in southern European markets during the fourteenth century.

The expansion of the gold trade contributed to a shift of power within West Africa away from Ghana, whose location on the desert edge probably also suffered when a period of desiccation began after about 1100. By then a new goldfield flourished at Bure on the headwaters of the Niger among Malinke-speaking people, who possesed a number of small chiefdoms, some touched by Islam. When non-Islamic Soninke groups sought to dominate them, a hunter and warrior named Sundiata Keita led Malinke resistance and created the kingdom of Mali during the first half of the thirteenth century. Its capital was close to the north eastern edge of the Bure goldfield. Its suzerainty came to extend nearly 2,000 kilometres from the Atlantic coast to the middle Niger, taking four months to cross, according to a long-term resident. Yet Mali was not only a larger and more important state than Ghana. It was centred not at the desert edge but in the agricultural lands of the Upper Niger Valley. It marked a further stage in West Africa's reintegration with the Old World.

Early fourteenth-century Mali was officially an Islamic state and was so recognised in the Islamic world, where its rulers participated conspicuously in the Pilgrimage. In 1352–3 the great traveller Ibn Battuta admired its people's 'assiduity in prayer and their persistence in performing it in congregation and beating their children to make them perform it', but he was less impressed by the coexistence of such non-Islamic practices as masked dancing, public recitation of pagan traditions, self-abasement before the king, eating of unclean foods, and scanty female clothing.[12] Because Islam was not only a religion but a social order, Africans necessarily adopted it only gradually. Whereas conquest had created the conditions for this in North Africa, in the west the initial agency was trade, especially by Berber Kharijites. There was little lasting Kharijite influence in West Africa, except in mosque architecture, but most desert-trading peoples were probably Muslims by the tenth century and traders were probably also among the first to accept the new religion further south, for they had the most contact with foreign Muslims, profited by joining an international community, and were little involved in the agricultural rituals central to indigenous religions. Cultivators, whose circumstances were exactly the opposite, probably resisted Islam most strongly. Rulers, concerned to preserve political unity, generally patronised all their subjects' religious activities in an eclectic manner. That was clearly the case in Mali and also in eleventh-century Gao, whose ruler had been the first in tropical Africa to accept Islam, sometime around AD 1000, followed by Takrur (before 1040) and Kanem (in c. 1067), while Ghana appears to have adopted orthodox Sunni Islam under Almoravid pressure during the 1070s. The eleventh century was a breakthrough period for Islam, as it was on the East African coast, although the extent of conversion varied greatly. In Ghana and Gao Islam seems long to have been confined to traders and the court, but in Takrur and Kanem it spread more quickly to the common people and aroused conflict between Islamic teachers and the practitioners of magic (closely associated with ironworking) who had previously served the throne.

TRADE AND ISLAM IN EAST AFRICA

Whereas Islam reached West Africa across the world's harshest desert, it travelled to East Africa along the easily-navigated trade routes of the Indian Ocean. A mariner's guide shows that during the first century after Christ traders from southern Arabia and the Red Sea penetrated down the East African coast to 'Rhapta', somewhere in modern Kenya or Tanzania, where the main export was ivory. Iranian pottery of the fifth to seventh centuries not only appears at sites on the coast from the Horn of Africa to Chibuene in southern Mozambique, but it has been found nearly fifty kilometres inland of Bagamoyo in Tanzania, suggesting that the Indian Ocean trade was already linked to a regional commerce comparable on a smaller scale to that of the middle Niger. This doubtless underlay the first appearance of Islam in East Africa at Shanga, a settlement in the Lamu Archipelago off the northern coast of Kenya. Excavation here has revealed the post-holes for a wooden mosque, accommodating only about nine worshippers, roughly aligned towards Mecca and associated with eighth-century pottery and radiocarbon dates. This was the first of nine mosques of gradually increasing size (the last three in stone) erected on the site over three centuries. Whether the builders were local people or immigrants is unknown, but their first mosque was at the centre of an agricultural settlement where most pottery was identical to that used by nearby African communities and everywhere on the coast during the following centuries. Shanga also imported small quantities of Iranian pottery and Chinese stoneware, the latter probably coming via the Persian Gulf. From the ninth century Shanga used and probably produced silver coins.[13]

Shanga suggests the establishment within an eighth-century African community of a small nucleus of Muslims—indigenous or alien—who gradually converted their neighbours. On neighbouring Manda Island, by contrast, the small town built in the ninth century appears to have been the work of alien settlers, possibly from Siraf on the Persian Gulf, who employed Middle Eastern building styles, supplemented the local coral stone with burnt bricks imported from Arabia, and were exceptionally well supplied with foreign pottery. From the beginning, therefore, the East African coastal culture showed its enduring tension between indigenous and imported elements. Other settlements of the ninth and tenth centuries were at Gezira (south of Mogadishu), Unguja Ukuu (on Zanzibar Island), and Chibuene. Evidence of trade with the interior is strongest in the south, where a fragment of imported glass has been found at a seventh-century site near Victoria Falls and imported beads of the next two centuries have appeared in southern Zimbabwe, northern Botswana, and eastern Transvaal. The chief export, as al-Masudi found on the coast in 916, was ivory, which went via the Persian Gulf to India and China. Indications of ivory exports of that period have been found in the Limpopo Valley. Mangrove poles were another important commodity for the treeless

Persian Gulf. Whether the coast also exported slaves is uncertain. Al-Masudi did not mention them, but slave revolts in ninth-century Iraq were attributed to 'Zanj', a collective term for black Africans, including a category known as Kunbula, who may have come from 'the island of Kanbalu' which al-Masudi visited, possibly in the Lamu Archipelago. 'The Zanj have an elegant language and men who preach in it', he added,[14] probably referring to Swahili, the one among a cluster of Bantu languages spoken on the Kenya coast which was probably used by those Africans who first participated in overseas trade and was carried southwards with the trade to become the coastal *lingua franca*.

From about AD 1000 the Islamisation and commercial development of the coast accelerated. At least eight coastal settlements built stone mosques during the eleventh and early twelfth centuries. This expansion may have resulted chiefly from the Islamic world's growing prosperity and lust for gold, which al-Masudi first mentioned in 916 as an export from 'Sofala', meaning the Mozambique coast which acted as the outlet for gold produced by ancestors of the Shona peoples of modern Zimbabwe, where archaeological evidence confirms the beginnings of mining at that period. By the late sixteenth century there were probably several hundred Shona Muslims, whose descendants, calling one another 'weaver', were to preserve some Islamic practices into the twentieth century. But the trading system extended beyond even the Islamic world. Between 1050 and 1150 China's imports of African produce increased tenfold.

The most striking evidence of eleventh-century commercial expansion was the foundation of a Muslim dynasty at Kilwa on the southern Tanzanian coast, hitherto a fishing village. Coins bearing the inscription of 'The majestic Sultan Ali bin al-Hasan', remembered in local tradition as the founder of Kilwa, have been discovered in contexts suggesting a date around 1070. They were in the tradition of Shanga and the new dynasty may have come from the Lamu Archipelago. It was overthrown two centuries later by the Mahdali, possibly Yemeni settlers claiming descent from the Prophet. Their rule brought Kilwa to its greatest prosperity in the early fourteenth century, when their governor on the Sofala coast controlled the gold trade and their coins penetrated to Great Zimbabwe. The Mahdali doubled the size of Kilwa's Great Mosque, built a magnificent palace, caravanserai, and slave barracoon known as Husuni Kubwa, and won a reputation for conspicuous largess in a culture whose materialism coexisted with a piety noted by Ibn Battuta when he visited the city in 1331. Yet he remembered Kilwa as a town of wood and thatch, for around a core of stone houses were the simpler huts of the 'Zanj of very black complexion' who comprised most of its estimated 10,000 to 20,000 people. Some were slaves, for Ibn Battuta noted that the Sultan of Kilwa 'frequently makes raids into the Zanj country'.[15] The ruler was probably of mixed race and, like the contemporary Sultan of Mogadishu, knew Arabic but spoke Swahili, which was then still largely free of Arabic loan-words. Kilwa's ruler made pilgrimage to Mecca in 1410–11 and Muslims were probably the great majority of Kilwa's foreign visitors, for the first fleet of Chinese 'treasure ships' did not reach East Africa until 1417–19, only a decade before the Ming government abandoned overseas adventures, while trade with India remained only a background factor until the fifteenth century, when Gujarat's growing prosperity encouraged its merchants to bring their cloth and copper to East African ports. By then Kilwa was in decline. Its rulers abandoned Husuni Kubwa in the later fourteenth century. The reasons are unknown. One could have been the Black Death, but local traditions do not mention it and other coastal towns prospered until Portuguese seamen reached East Africa in 1498.

ISLAM IN SUDAN

The Arabs had barely conquered Egypt when their forces entered Christian Nubia in 641 and met fierce resistance from its famous bowmen. A further costly invasion ten years later deterred the Arabs from again attacking 'those people whose booty is meagre, and whose spite is great'. Instead they made a truce, the *baqt* of 652, with the kingdom of Makuria, which undertook to deliver 360 slaves a year in return for Egyptian products and agreement to respect each other's traders. For the next 500 years slaves, doubtless acquired from the pagan south, were Nubia's chief export. Arabs settled in the Christian kingdoms as traders, miners of gold and precious stones, and, from the tenth century, pastoralists. Egypt's Fatimid rulers from 969 to 1170 relied on black slave soldiers and their rule coincided with the apogee of Christian Nubia. It was a time of high Nile floods when the southern kingdom of Alwa had 'an uninterrupted chain of villages and a continuous strip of cultivated lands',[16] while a vigorous Christianity left remains of churches and a monastery as far west as Darfur.

This prosperity began to crumble when Saladin ousted the Fatimids in 1171 and slaughtered their African slave army, undermining the mutual advantage linking Egypt and Nubia. Nubian forces raided southern Egypt. Saladin replied by attacking northern Nubia. When Arab pastoral tribes in Egypt rebelled in 1253, his successors recalled the use of the Banu Hilal and drove the dissidents into Nubia. Islamic communities in the Christian kingdoms had been expanding slowly for several centuries; now they were swollen by turbulent nomads at a time when river levels were falling, the Christian ruling families were divided, and Nubian society as a whole was increasingly militarised. The crisis began in Makuria in 1268 when an usurper appealed for Mamluk recognition. Repeated dynastic war and Egyptian intervention followed. In about 1317 a Muslim gained Makuria's throne and the cathedral at Old Dongola was converted into a mosque. Eighty years later a King of Makuria is mentioned for the last time. 'No vestige of royal authority has remained in their country,' wrote Ibn Khaldun, 'since the system of Arab nomadism turned them from their own system through utter disorder and unceasing warfare.'[17] Meanwhile the Arabs had gained access to the higher rainfall and better pastures of Alwa. They destroyed the kingdom late in the fifteenth century, only to fall themselves under the suzerainty of the

Funj, Africans of obscure origin who conquered the area in 1504 and rapidly adopted Islam. The next three centuries were a period of poverty and disorder when the Funj ruled as far as the Third Cataract, while the valley further north was dominated by *meks*, robber barons controlling stretches of river from mud-brick castles. But it was also a period of Arabisation and Islamisation, when nomads and Muslim teachers created the basic pattern of the modern northern Sudan. The last report of Christians in Nubia was in 1742, although village women appealed to the Virgin in time of need even in the late twentieth century.

ETHIOPIA

Ethiopian Christianity survived Islamic expansion, chiefly because it was more remote from Islamic power. Underlying Ethiopian history between the ninth and sixteenth centuries was continuing colonisation of former Cushitic-speaking territory in the highlands by Semitic-speaking cultivators. By the ninth century the kingdom's core was no longer in Tigray but further south in modern Wollo, whose indigenous Cushitic people spoke Agaw languages. In 1137 an Agaw prince seized the throne and created the Zagwe dynasty which ruled until 1270, seeking legitimacy through such conspicuously Christian creations as the rock-hewn churches at Lalibela, laid out as a new City of Zion around a stream named Yordanos and a hill named Calvary. Christian settlement was drawn southwards by higher rainfall and the lure of trade through the eastern lowlands to the coast at Zeila, exchanging slaves, gold, and ivory for salt from the lowlands and imported Islamic luxuries. Muslims controlled this trade and the peoples along the route gradually adopted Islam, first the Cushitic speaking Somali peoples of the eastern lowlands, then Semitic-speakers on the south-eastern highland fringes, where small Islamic principalities existed by the twelfth century in eastern Shoa and Ifat.

As Semitic-speakers colonised still further southwards beyond Agaw country into Amhara and Shoa, largely Shoan forces overthrew the Zagwe dynasty in 1270 and installed Yikunno Amlak, who claimed descent from Solomon and the Queen of Sheba. His grandson, Amda Siyon (1314–44), was Ethiopia's greatest warrior king. He conquered Ifat, forcing its Muslim leaders to create a new emirate further east in Harar. He also extended the Christian kingdom's southern and western borders at the expense of non-Christian Cushitic regions and of peoples preserving Aksum's ancient Jewish traditions whose long resistance to royal control consolidated them into the Beta Israel (Falasha) community. The Solomonic kingdom in its classic form was chiefly Amda Siyon's creation.

Thanks to royal chronicles and ecclesiastical documents, Solomonic Ethiopia is the earliest black African society that can be analysed in detail. It was organised chiefly for the control of nature and the colonisation of land, to which Christian merit attached. Settlement concentrated on the relatively warm and moist plateau between about 1,800 and 2,500 metres, avoiding arid lowlands, bleak mountain slopes, and densely wooded valleys. On the plateau the settler surrounded his homestead with concentric rings of gradually less intensive cultivation and defended his fields against the natural forces beyond them. The hagiography of the Shoan abbot St Takla Haymanot (traditional dates 1215–1313) describes his monks carving their fields from the bush, while nearby 'the mountain land was waste and uncultivated'. When animals raided the crops, the saint counselled patience: 'Let them alone, for it is we who have invaded their habitation, and not they who have invaded ours.' But when a huge ape robbed a poor widow, the saint exerted his authority: 'By the Word of God Whom I serve, be ye kept in restraint, O all ye beasts of the desert, for ye have overrun the boundaries which have been appointed to you.'[18] To maintain those boundaries was at the heart of Ethiopian culture. Holy men like St Takla Haymanot often protected people miraculously against wild animals. Satan, when cast out from the sick or sinful, usually appeared as an ape. Only holy men could safely cross the boundary between culture and nature to live as hermits among animals and eat wild produce.

The cultivator had other enemies. Rainfall was probably more generous than it is today, if lake levels are indicative, and famine was less common than it later became, but it was still a constant threat. The Islamic principality in Shoa suffered three famines during the later thirteenth century. In 1520 a Portuguese missionary, Francisco Alvares,

> travelled five days through country entirely depopulated, and through millet stalks as thick as canes for propping vines; it cannot be told how they were all cut and bitten, as if bitten by asses, all done by the locusts ... The people were going away from this country, and we found the roads full of men, women, and children on foot, and some in their arms, with their little bundles on their heads, removing to a country where they might find provisions.[19]

The sources also mention many epidemics, but in terms too general to identify, although they probably included smallpox, which was attributed to an Aksumite army in 569–70. Ethiopia's exceptional range of environments supported a variety of endemic diseases, ranging from leprosy (especially in remote rural areas) and malaria (which Ethiopians associated with mosquito bites) to the intestinal parasites which later European doctors found almost universal. Drastic-folk remedies were supplemented by herbalism, the quasi-magical techniques of the Church's *debtera* (deacons), and miraculous healing at shrines. Dust from St Takla Haymanot's grave 'gave children to barren women, and he gave relief unto women who suffered pain at the time of childbirth, and he gave seed to eunuchs, and he healed the sick, and he destroyed the wild beasts of the desert, and the wild beasts of the belly.'[20]

The cultivator's art was to minimise his vulnerability to disaster. 'We sow so much,' they told Alvares, 'with the hope that even if each of those said plagues locusts and hail should come, some would be spoiled, and some would remain, and if all is spoiled the year before has been so plentiful that we have no scarcity.'[21] Self reliance was vital, for the tropical highland location, avoidance of river valleys, and the absence of even a single bridge prevented anything but local transport of food. Wheat, barley, and *teff* were staples on the plateau, *ensete* (false banana) in the well-watered south. Crops were rotated and fields permanently cultivated with the plough, uniquely in sub-Saharan Africa, but it was a scratch-plough drawn by one or two beasts, so that no manorial structure or serfdom came into being. Only men handled the plough; women did much other agricultural work but had less economic independence that in many African regions. Alvares noted the fertility and populousness of long-settled Tigray. Other highland areas had population concentrations, but much land was still pasture or bush. Families mentioned in Solomonic hagiographies generally had few children, giving point to St Takla Haymanot's grave-dust. It was probably already true, as in the nineteenth century, that not only women but men married young, which was rare in Africa and was probably related to ecclesiastical penalties for polygyny—although great men defied them—and a bilateral kinship system in which young men inherited land rights from both parents and moved away with their brides to establish independent households. Generational conflict was consequently muted in Ethiopia, where Christians had neither corporate lineages nor even family names. Small hamlets existed in some regions, but elsewhere elementary families formed dispersed homesteads whose chief institutional nexus was the parish and its church.

Scattered through this mobile, colonising society were noble households, which over time gained greater permanence. Their wealth came from estates cleared by ancestral pioneers and from royal grants of the right to collect tribute in kind and labour from surrounding peasants. Such grants were revocable in theory but often hereditary in practice, so that royal power depended on constant territorial expansion in order to reward followers. Holders of tribute-collecting rights were charged to maintain law and order and supply fighting men, who at this period were not normally peasants but their enemies:

> Whose face have you not disfigured?
> Whose wife and child have you not captured?[22]

War-horses were probably more important than ploughs in enabling the ruling class to extract up to an estimated 30 per cent of the peasant's crop. But the peasant (*gabbar*, tribute-payer) was no serf, for his multiple land rights enabled him to quit an unpopular lord. The nobleman, too, was a Big Man (*tellek saw*) whose status was earned by talent and favour in a fluid and competitive military society whose strongly localised rulers had little corporate identity or distinctive culture. They displayed their rank by a surfeit of servants and by ostentatious largess to the incapacitated poor who thronged public places. Popular insurrection on class lines appeared only in the seventeenth century, and then under leaders claiming to be messiahs or rightful kings.

The government of this dispersed and mobile society was necessarily loose and personalised. Yikunno Amlak and his successors ruled partly by right of Solomonic blood but chiefly by force of arms. They were generally succeeded by their sons, usually their eldest sons, but only after conflict among them. The king ruled an agglomeration of principalities whose chiefs valued his recognition but resented his control, which depended on appointed regional governors with garrisons of royal troops from elsewhere in the kingdom. To exert their authority, Solomonic kings abandoned permanent capitals until the mid-fifteenth century in favour of huge itinerant camps. 'They have no written Laws,' a seventeenth-century European wrote, 'Justice and Right is determined by Custom, and the Example of their Ancestors: and most differences are ended by the Will of the Judge.'[23] Punishments were usually physical and brutal, as in other societies where offenders were seldom caught. Unflinching endurance of pain was a point of honour for all classes, while noblemen observed a heroic code personified by Amda Siyon:

> Some among them said to the king, 'Let us go inside the defences of the camp and fight there.' But the king said, 'No, I will not die in my wife's embrace, but I will die the death of a man in battle.' … So saying, he bounded like a leopard and leapt like a lion, and mounted his horse whose name was Harab Asfare … They surrounded him with their swords and he, his face set hard like stone and his spirit undaunted by death, clove the ranks of the rebels and struck so hard that he transfixed two men as one with a blow of his spear, through the strength of God. There upon the rebels scattered and took to flight, being unable to hold their ground in his presence.

Amda Siyon's conquests created a vast mission field for the Ethiopian Church. Its evangelists were the spiritual counterparts of military heroes: holy men like St Takla Haymanot, usually of gentle birth, who created pioneer monasteries in non-Christian areas, practised extreme self-mortification, waged epic struggles against indigenous nature religions, and attracted the people to Christianity by their power, their sanctity, their miracles, and the services they could perform in the new Christian order. Monasticism had existed in Tigray since the fifth century, according to tradition. Iyasus Mo'a extended it southwards to Amhara in c. 1248. His pupil, St Takla Haymanot, created the great monastery of Debra Libanos in Shoa in c. 1286. Its monks built scores of daughter-houses throughout the south during the next two centuries, while Tigrayan monasticism was revitalised by Ewostatewos (c. 1273–1352), both monastic movements expressing regional hostility to royal centralisation. Indigenous Cushitic religion centred on nature spirits which could possess and speak through their priests or ordinary people. Christian holy men accepted the reality of nature spirits but identified them as demons or manifestations of Satan and waged personal warfare against them. On one missionary journey, for example, St Takla Haymanot had the people cut down the tree housing the spirit they venerated, 'and that tree was by itself sufficient to provide all the wood which was required in the church.[25] In retaliation the indigenous priests had the holy man flogged and tortured, while the pagan king twice hurled him from a precipice, only for St Michael to save him. But other local rulers allied with holy men and were the first to accept Christianity, perhaps to free themselves from indigenous priestly control. This could bring violent persecution of the old religion, but more frequently the conquered peoples appear to have added aspects of Christianity to indigenous practices in an eclectic way, worshipping at the church built from the sacred tree, celebrating the Maskal feast of the Cross supplanting the festival at the end of the rains, and perhaps even becoming-possessed by St Michael or St Gabriel. Indigenous, Christian, and Islamic spirits gradually fused into a possession (zar) cult providing psychological relief for the marginal and unfortunate.

Missionary adaptations reinforced the distinctiveness of Ethiopian Christianity. The kingdom's retreat southwards into the highlands, together with the simultaneous expansion of Islam, had accentuated Ethiopia's partial isolation from the Eurasian core of Christianity. The Bible—as much the Old Testament as the New—therefore came to dominate Christian imaginations. Ethiopia was Zion, a nation defined by religion, a second Israel defending its faith against surrounding enemies. That faith stressed the majesty of Jehovah and the divinity rather than the humanity of Christ. Judaic practices—dietary restrictions, ritual dancing, use of the tabot or holy ark—were emphasised, while polygyny was hard to eradicate and eschatology and mysticism were less prominent than in European Christianity. But New Testament practices also shaped behaviour, as in the emphasis on charity, miracles, and spiritual healing. The only bishop, sent irregularly from Alexandria, concentrated on ordaining numerous priests, often barely literate and very young, lest the kingdom should long be without a bishop. These secular clergy were almost a hereditary caste, married and engaged in agriculture. Monks generally had more education, but few noblemen could read. The result was a colourful, symbolic, largely oral, village Christianity with little hierarchical structure but a clear distinction between the laity and a spiritual elite—a pattern remarkably akin to secular society. Ethiopian Christianity expressed a heroic culture: the spectacular 'contendings' of holy men, the self-mortification of fasting, the symbolic role of St George and the Archangels, all headed by a South Arabian priest-king renowned for his violence in war, notorious for his polygyny, claiming in the Byzantine manner to preside over declarations of doctrine.

The king who filled this role most completely was Zara Yaqob (1434–68). He gave order to the church during its outburst of monastic evangelisation, codified its distinctive practices, strengthened the parochial system, and strove to uproot eclecticism and impose orthodoxy. In secular affairs, similarly, Zara Yaqob sought to consolidate his predecessors' conquests into a stable kingdom, creating a fixed capital at Debra Berhan in Shoa and reviving the ancient custom of coronation at Aksum. Yet he only partially succeeded and acted with such authoritarian brutality that his death was followed by particularistic reactions in all directions. The new capital was abandoned, centralisation was relaxed. Between 1478 and 1527 the average age of kings at their accession was eleven.

The beneficiary was the Sultanate of Harar, where zealous Muslims had taken refuge from Amda Siyon. Reinforced by the Islamisation of the neighbouring Somali and by Turkish and Arab adventurers, Harar's forces invaded the Christian highlands in 1529 under the leadership of the Imam Ahmad ibn Ibrahim. His astounding success was not only because Christian forces were divided and ill-led but because newly conquered, Cushitic-speaking subjects joined the invaders in hope of regaining independence. Muslim forces devastated the highlands for fourteen years, destroying Debra Libanos and leaving damage still visible on the rock churches at Lalibela. The Imam appointed governors in each province, but in 1543 he was killed in battle with a Christian army which included a body of Portuguese musketeers. His forces dissolved back to Harar, leaving the Ethiopian Church, alone in Africa, to survive in independence into the modern world.

THE WESTERN SUDAN IN THE SIXTEENTH CENTURY, 1526

By Leo Africanus

A DESCRIPTION OF THE KINGDOME OF GUALATA [WALATA]

This region in regarde of others is very small: for it containeth only three great villages, with certaine granges and fields of dates. From Nun it is distant southward about three hundred, from Tombuto [Timbuktu] northward fiue hundred, and from the Ocean sea about two hundred miles. In this region the people of Libya, while they were lords of the land of Negros, ordained their chiefe princely seate: and then great store of Barbarie-merchants frequented Gualata: but afterward in the raigne of the mighty and rich prince *Heli*, the said merchants leauing Gualata, began to resort vnto Tombuto and Gago, [Gao] which was the occasion that the region of Gualata grew extreme beggerly. The language of this region is called Sungai, [Songhai] and the inhabitants are blacke people, and most friendly vnto strangers. In my time this region was conquered by the king of Tombuto, and the prince thereof fled into the deserts, whereof the king of Tombuto hauing intelligence, and fearing least the prince would returne with all the people of the deserts, graunted him peace, conditionally that he should pay a great yeerely tribute vnto him, and so the said prince hath remained tiributarie to the king of Tombuto vntill this present. The people agree in manners and fashions with the inhabitants of the next desert.

Here groweth some quantitie of Mil-seed, and great store of a round & white kind of pulse, the like whereof I neuer saw in Europe; but flesh is extreme scarce among them. Both the men & the women do so couer their heads, that al their countenance is almost hidden. Here is no forme of a common wealth, nor yet any gouernours or iudges, but the people lead a most miserable life.

OF THE KINGDOME OF MELLI [MALI]

This region extending it selfe almost three hundred miles along the side of a riuer which falleth into Niger, bordereth northward vpon the region last described, southward vpon certaine deserts and drie mountaines, westward vpon huge woods and forrests stretching to the Ocean sea shore, and eastward vpon the territorie of Gago. In this kingdome there is a large and ample village containing to the number of six thousand or mo families, and called Melli, whereof the whole kingdome is so named. And here the king hath his place of residence. The region it selfe yeeldeth great abundance of corne, flesh, and cotton. Heere are many artificers and merchants in all places: and yet the king honourably entertaineth all strangers. The inhabitants are rich, and haue plentie of wares. Heere are great store of temples, priests, and professours, which professours read their lectures only in the temples, bicause they haue

Leo Africanus, Selections from *The History and Description of Africa and the Notable Things Therein Contained*, ed. Robert Brown; trans. John Pory, pp. 821, 823–827, 829–830, 832–834. Copyright in the public domain.

no colleges at all. The people of this region excell all other Negros in witte, ciuilitie, and industry; and were the first that embraced the law of Mahumet, [Muhammad] at the same time when the vncle of *Ioseph* the king of Maroco [Yusuf ibn Tashufin] was their prince, and the gouernment remained for a while vnto his posterity: at length *Izchia* [Askiya Muhammad, 1493–1538] subdued the prince of this region, and made him his tributarie, and so oppressed him with greeuous exactions, that he was scarce able to maintaine his family.

OF THE KINGDOME OF TOMBUTO [TIMBUKTU]

This name was in our times (as some thinke) imposed vpon this kingdome from the name of a certain towne so called, which (they say) king *Mense Suleiman* [Mansa Sulayman, ed.] founded in the yeere of the Hegeira 610, [1213–1214] and it is situate within twelue miles of a certaine branch of Niger, all the houses whereof are now changed into cottages built of chalke, and couered with thatch. Howbeit there is a most stately temple to be seene, the wals whereof are made of stone and lime; and a princely palace also built by a most excellent workeman of Granada. Here are many shops of artificers, and merchants, and especially of such as weaue linnen and cotton cloth. And hither do the Barbarie merchants bring cloth of Europe. All the women of this region except maid-seruants go with their faces couered, and sell all necessarie victuals. The inhabitants, & especially strangers there residing, are exceeding rich, insomuch, that the king that now [in 1526] is, married both his daughters vnto two rich merchants.

Here are many wels, containing most sweete water; and so often as the riuer Niger ouerfloweth, they conueigh the water thereof by certaine sluces into the towne. Come, cattle, milke, and butter this region yeeldeth in great abundance: but salt is verie scarce heere; for it is brought hither by land from Tegaza, which is fiue hundred miles distant. When I my selfe was here, I saw one camels loade of salt sold for 80 ducates. The rich king of Tombuto hath many plates and scepters of gold, some whereof

weigh 1300. poundes: and he keepes a magnificent and well furnished court. When he trauelleth any whither he rideth vpon a camell, which is lead by some of his noblemen; and so he doth likewise when hee goeth to warfar, and all his souldiers ride vpon horses. Whosoeuer will speake vnto this king must first fall downe before his feete, & then taking vp earth must sprinkle it vpon his owne head & shoulders: which custom is ordinarily obserued by them that neuer saluted the king before, or come as ambassadors from other princes. He hath alwaies three thousand horsemen, and a great number of footmen that shoot poysoned arrowes, attending vpon him. They haue often skirmishes with those that refuse to pay tribute, and so many as they take, they sell vnto the merchants of Tombuto. Here are verie few horses bred, and the merchants and courtiers keepe certaine little nags which they vse to trauell vpon: but their best horses are brought out of Barbarie. And the king so soone as he heareth that any merchants are come to towne with horses, he commandeth a certaine number to be brought before him, and chusing the best horse for himselfe, he payeth a most liberall price for him. He so deadly hateth all lewes, [Jews] that he will not admit any into his citie: and whatsoeuer Barbarie merchants he vnderstandeth haue any dealings with the lewes, he presently causeth their goods to be confiscate. Here are great store of doctors, iudges, priests, and other learned men, that are bountifully maintained at the kings cost and charges. And hither are brought diuers manuscripts or written bookes out of Barbarie, which are sold for more money than any other merchandize. The coine of tombuto is of gold without any stampe or superscription: but in matters of smal value they vse certaine shels brought hither out of the kingdome of Persia, fower hundred of which shels are worth a ducate: and six peeces of their golden coine with two third parts weigh an ounce. The inhabitants are people of a gentle and chereful disposition, and spend a great part of the night in singing and dancing through all the streets of the citie: they keep great store of men and women slaues, and their towne is much in danger of fire: at my second being there halfe the town almost was burnt in fiue howers space. Without the suburbs there are no gardens nor orchards at all.

OF THE TOWNE AND KINGDOME OF GAGO [GAO]

The great towne of Gago being vnwalled also, is distant southward of Tombuto almost fower hundred miles, and enclineth somewhat to the southeast. The houses thereof are but meane, except those wherein the king and his courtiers remaine. Here are exceeding rich merchants: and hither continually resort great store of Negros which buy cloth here brought out of Barbarie and Europe. This towne aboundeth with corne and flesh, but is much destitute of wine, trees, and fruits. Howbeit here is plentie of melons, citrons, and rice: here are many welles also containing most sweete and holesome water. Here is likewise a certaine place where slaues are to be sold, especially vpon such daies as the merchants vse to assemble; and a yoong slaue of fifteene yeeres age is sold for six ducates, and so are children sold also. The king of this region hath a certaine priuate palace wherein he maintaineth a great number of concubines and slaues, which are kept by eunuches: and for the guard of his owne person he keepeth a sufficient troupe of horsemen and footmen. Betweene the first gate of the palace and the inner part thereof, there is a place walled round about wherein the king himselfe decideth all his subiects controuersies: and albeit the king be in this function most diligent, and performeth all things thereto appertayning, yet hath he about him his counsellors & other officers, as namely his secretaries, treasurers, factors, and auditors. It is a woonder to see what plentie of Merchandize is dayly brought hither, and how costly and sumptuous all things be. Horses bought in Europe for ten ducates, are here sold againe for fortie and sometimes for fiftie ducates a piece. There is not any cloth of Europe so course, which will not here be sold for fower ducates an elle: and if it be anything fine they will giue fifteene ducates for an ell: and an ell of the scarlet of Venice or of Turkie-cloath is here worth thirtie ducates. A sword is here valued at three or fower crownes, and so likewise are spurs, bridles, with other like commodities, and spices also are sold at an high rate: but of al other commodities salt is most extremelie deere. The residue of this kingdome containeth nought but villages and hamlets inhabited by husbandmen and shepherds, who in winter couer their bodies with beasts skins; but in sommer they goe all naked saue their priuie members: and sometimes they weare vpon their feet certaine shooes made of camels leather. They are ignorant and rude people, and you shall scarce finde one learned man in the space of an hundred miles. They are continually burthened with grieuous exactions, so that they haue scarce any thing remaining to liue vpon.

OF THE PROUINCE OF CANO [KANO]

The great prouince of Cano stadeth eastward of the riuer Niger almost fiue hundred miles. The greatest part of the inhabitants dwelling in villages are some of them herdsmen and others husbandmen. Heere groweth abundance of come, of rice, and of cotton. Also here are many deserts and wilde woodie mountaines containing many springs of water. In these woods growe plentie of wilde citrons and limons, which differ not much in taste from the best of all. In the midst of this prouince standeth a towne called by the same name, the walles and houses whereof are built for the most part of a kinde of chalke. The inhabitants are rich merchants and most ciuill people. Their king was in times past of great puissance, and had mighty troupes of horsemen at his command; but he hath since beene constrained to pay tribute vnto the kings of Zegzeg and Casena [Katsina, ed.]. Afterwarde *Ischia* the king of Tombuto faining friendship vnto the two foresaid kings trecherously slew them both. And then he waged warre against the king of Cano, whom after a long siege he tooke, and compelled him to marie one of his daughters, restoring him againe to his kingdome, conditionally that he should pay vnto him the third part of all his tribute: and the said king of Tombuto hath some of his courtiers perpetually residing at Cano for the receit thereof.

OF THE KINGDOME OF BORNO [BORNU]

The large prouince of Borno bordering westward vpon the prouince of Guangara [Wangara] and from thence extending eastward fiue hundred miles, is distant from the fountaine of Niger almost an hundred and fiftie miles, the south part thereof adioining vnto the desert of Set, and the north part vnto that desert which lieth towards Barca. The situation of this kingdome is very vneuen, some part thereof being mountainous, and the residue plaine. Vpon the plaines are sundry villages inhabited by rich merchants, and abounding with come. The king of this region and all his followers dwell in a certain large village. The mountaines being inhabited by herdesmen and shepherds doe bring foorth mill and other graine altogether vnknowen to vs. The inhabitants in summer goe all naked saue their priuie members which they couer with a peece of leather: but al winter they are clad in skins, and haue beds of skins also. They embrace no religion at all, being neither Christians, Mahumetans, nor Iewes, nor of any other profession, but liuing after a brutish manner, and hauing wiues and children in common: and (as I vnderstood of a certaine merchant that abode a long time among them) they haue no proper names at all, but euery one is nicknamed according to his length, his fatnes, or some other qualitie. They haue a most puissant prince, being lineally descended from the Libyan people called Bardoa. Horsemen he hath in a continuall readiness to the number of three thousand, & an huge number of footmen; for al his subiects are so seruiceable and obedient vnto him, that whensoeuer he commandeth them, they wil arme themselues and follow him whither he pleaseth to conduct them. They paye vnto him none other tribute but the tithes of all their corne: neither hath this king any reuenues to maintaine his estate, but onely such spoiles as he getteth from his next enimes by often inuasions and assaults. He is at perpetuall emnitie with a certaine people inhabiting beyond the desert of Seu; who in times past marching with an huge armie of footemen ouer the said desert, wasted a great part of the kingdome of Borno. Whereupon the king of Borno sent for the merchants of Barbary, and willed them to bring him great store of horses: for in this countrey they vse to exchange horses for slaues, and to giue fifteene, and sometime twentie slaues for one horse. And by this meanes there were abundance of horses brought: howbeit the merchants were constrained to stay for their slaues till the king returned home conquerour with a great number of captiues, and satisfied his creditors for their horses. And oftentimes it falleth out that the merchants must stay three months togither, before the king returneth from the warres, but they are all that while maintained at the kings charges. Sometimes he bringeth not home slaues enough to satisfie the merchants: and otherwhiles they are constrained to awaite there a whole yeere togither; for the king maketh inuasions but euery yeere once, & that at one set and appointed time of the yeere. Yea I my selfe met with sundrie merchants heere, who despairing of the kings paiment, bicause they had trusted him an whole yeere, determined neuer to come thither with horses againe. And yet the king seemeth to be marueilous rich; for his spurres, his bridles, platters, dishes, pots, and other vessels wherein his meate and drinke are brought to the table, are all of pure golde: yea, and the chaines of his dogs and hounds are of golde also. Howbeit this king is extreamely couetous, for he had much rather pay his debts in slaues than in gold. In this kingdome are great multitudes of Negros and of other people, the names of whom (bicause I tarried heere but one moneth) I could not well note.

THE ADVENTURES OF IBN BATTUTA: MALI

By Ross E. Dunn

13: Mali [para. 686–736]

> The people of Mali outnumbered the peoples of the Sudan in their neighborhood and dominated the whole region … Their authority became mighty and all the peoples of the Sudan stood in awe of them. [₁]
>
> Ibn Khaldun

[Page 290]

When Ibn Battuta visited Cairo in 1326 on his way to his first *hajj*, the population was undoubtedly still talking about the extraordinary pilgrim who had passed through the city two years earlier. Mansa Musa, ruler of the West African empire of Mali, had arrived at the Nile in the summer of 1324 after having crossed the Sahara Desert with a retinue of officials, wives, soldiers, and slaves numbering in the thousands and a train of one hundred camels loaded with unworked gold. A handsome young king of piety and noble bearing, he had created a minor sensation among Cairo's protocol-conscious officials by refusing to kiss the ground before the Mamluk sultan, al-Nasir Muhammad. Yet he "flooded Cairo with his benefactions," writes the historian al-Umari, and "performed many acts of charity and kindness." [2]

Having come so far from their distant grassland kingdom, the emperor and his gold-heavy entourage spent freely and indiscriminately in the Cairo bazaars, like prosperous and naive tourists from some American prairie state. "The Cairenes," says al-Umari, "made incalculable profits out of him and his suite in buying and selling and giving and taking. They exchanged gold until they depressed its value in Egypt and caused its price to fall." [3]

Musa was not the first *mansa* (king, sultan) of Mali to go on pilgrimage to Mecca, but none before had made such a dazzling display of pomp and riches. Well into the next century Egyptian chroniclers wrote about the event and its disturbing short-term effects on the Cairene gold market. In the history of medieval West Africa no single incident has been more celebrated. Indeed the *hajj* of Mansa Musa sums up Mali's important place among the kingdoms of Africa and Asia in Ibn Battuta's time.

[Page 291] The unworked gold which the *mansa* showered on Cairo came from three major alluvial deposits in West Africa. The mines of the *bilad al-sudan*, or simply the Sudan, as the Arab geographers called the steppe and savanna region south of the Sahara, had been known to the Mediterranean world since Phoenician times. But it was only the introduction of the dromedary to North Africa about the second century A.D. that made feasible in terms of costs and risks regular caravan trade from one rim of the Western Sahara to the other. The one-humped camel is a difficult and disagreeable animal, but he could carry a load of 125–150 kilograms, go without water ten days or more, and travel faster than any other available beast of burden. When Islam reached the Western Maghrib in the seventh century, Berber-speaking merchants were already running camel caravans to commercial settlements on the far side of the desert.

The founding of the Arab Empire and later the High Caliphate created an ever-growing demand in the Islamic heartland for West African gold to make coins and finery. This demand impelled Muslim merchants and cameliers of the Maghrib and the North Sahara to organize trans-desert business and transport operations to an unprecedented level of sophistication. About the same time, the Kingdom of Ghana emerged in the steppe region of West Africa known as the Sahel (Sahal), the transitional climatic zone between the southern desert and the savanna lands. The appearance of Ghana as an imperial state was undoubtedly linked to the gold trade, which encouraged the rise of military leaders aggressive enough to seize monopolistic authority over the commercial routes and settlements leading from the gold fields deep in the Sudan to the "ports" at the edge of the desert where the North African caravans arrived. The empire declined in the eleventh century, perhaps in connection with a prolonged drought, and eventually withered away.

Yet the pattern of imperial state-building in the Sudan continued with the rise of Mali early in the thirteenth century. The founders of this kingdom were Malinke-speaking people whose homeland was the region between the upper valleys of the Senegal and the Niger Rivers. This region was in the heart of the savanna and much nearer to the two gold-bearing areas, known as Bambuk and Bure, than the center of Ghana had been. The early kings of Mali, members of a chiefly clan of the Malinke known as the Keita, succeeded in taking control of territory between the gold [**Page 292**] fields and the Sahel, thereby positioning themselves to exact tribute in gold from the producing populations. In this way the cycle of expansion began. The gold revenues of the *mansas* permitted heavier expenditures on the army, which was comprised mainly of infantry bowmen and armored cavalry. As the royal forces were deployed across the fertile grasslands both east and west, greater numbers of farming and herding folk were subdued and taxed, expanding the wealth and military energies of the state even more.

In the course of the thirteenth and early fourteenth centuries, the *mansas* extended their domains westward to the Atlantic coast, eastward past the great bend of the Niger, and northward to the commercial towns scattered along the Saharan fringe, building an empire that incorporated many non-Malinke peoples. By achieving political domination over a band of steppe and savanna some 1,200 miles long at the peak of the empire, they effectively controlled and taxed the north–south flow of commerce across the Western Sudan.

Indeed, Mali's high age from the mid thirteenth to the mid fourteenth century corresponded to the period when Europe was exchanging silver for gold as its principal currency, prompting Italian and Catalan merchants to offer higher and higher prices for the little bags of dust and nuggets that were transported across the Sahara and over the Atlas Mountains to Ceuta and other North African ports. The rising European demand for gold, added to the perennial market in the Islamic states, stimulated more gold production in the Sudan, to the enormous fiscal advantage of Mali. In the later medieval period overall, West Africa may have been producing almost two-thirds of the world's gold supply. [4]

In addition to gold, north-bound caravans carried numerous products originating either in the grasslands or the tropical forests—ivory, ostrich feathers, kola nuts, gum resins, hides, and slaves. In return for these goods the southbound trade brought many products from North Africa and the Mediterranean basin: textiles, copper, silver, books, paper, swords, iron ware, perfumes, jewelry, spices, wheat, and dried fruits. Horses, which did not prosper in the deep savanna country owing to the lethal bite of the tsetse fly, were imported from the Maghrib to meet the needs of the Malian cavalry.

Cowrie shells were used as a form of currency in the Sudan, as they were in India. As Ibn Battuta attests, they were harvested exclusively in the Maldive Islands, then exported [Page 293] to West Africa by way of Egypt and the Maghrib ports. The single most precious commodity imported to the Sudan was salt, a food essential to the human body that West Africa was unable to produce in sufficient quantity to meet demand. Salt came from mines in the Sahara and was transported southward in the form of giant slabs, two to a camel.

In the fourteenth century that section of the West Africa-to-Europe commercial exchange system extending from the northern edge of the rain forest to the Mediterranean coast was entirely in the hands of Muslims. Indeed from a global perspective the trans-Saharan trade routes were north-south branch lines of the hemispheric Muslim network that extended right across northern Africa and Asia to the ports of the South China Sea. As early as the ninth century, Berber-speaking merchants settled in commercial centers in the Sahel belt, where they acted as hosts and business agents for fellow Muslims who organized caravans in the corresponding entrepôts along the northern rim of the desert. In the time of Ghana, Muslim towns rose up alongside older Sahelian centers. In these new towns merchants of North African Berber or Arab origin were permitted by royal authority to govern their internal affairs according to the standards of the Sacred Law, just as they were beginning to do among non-Muslim peoples in the Indian Ocean basin.

These expatriate merchants did not organize the trade directly to the gold fields or to the towns deep in the savanna. That stretch of the network remained under the control of professional Sudanese traders. Most of them were of the Soninke and, later, Malinke culture groups. These men were among the first West Africans to convert to Islam, thereby linking themselves into the brotherhood of shared norms and trust that encouraged order and routine along the trans-Saharan system.

As in India and Southeast Asia, the founding of new Muslim trading communities created an immediate demand for literate cadres to organize and superintend Islamic worship, education, and law. From the beginning of Islamic expansion into West Africa, Maghribi men of learning were accompanying the merchant caravans across the desert to settle in the towns of the Sahel. These centers supported Islamic education south of the Sahara, and over the course of time gave rise to a class of Muslims grounded in the "normative" traditions of piety and scholarship as preached and practiced in North Africa. In the [Page 294] period of the Mali empire the communities of 'ulama in the Sahelian towns included families of both Arabo-Berber and Sudanese origin, the latter mainly Malinke or Soninke. Deeper in the Sudan, learned families of purely West African origin predominated.

Sudanese chiefs and petty kings are known to have converted to Islam as early as the tenth or eleventh centuries. Whatever purely religious feelings may have motivated such men individually, conversion enhanced their esteem among Muslim merchants, the economically most powerful group in the land, and potentially tied them into a much wider commercial and diplomatic world than they had known before. The origins of Islam among the Malinke are obscure. In their tradition the founder of the empire was Sunjata (or Mari-Jaata), a larger-than-life homeric figure of the early thirteenth century who rose from physical adversity and exile to rid his homeland of an alien tyrant, then rebuilt the Malinke capital and ruled from it for 25 years. The reign of Sunjata is only vaguely associated with Islam, but at some point in the thirteenth century his successors made it the official religion of state, an act certainly linked to the growing importance of the Muslim mercantile communities which inhabited the main towns along the trans-savanna routes.

Yet the military and political success of the *mansas* also depended on the continuing allegiance and cooperation of the mass of their subjects—farming, fishing, and herding people who for the most part adhered to ancient animistic beliefs and rituals, not Islam. Unlike the sultans of Delhi, the *mansas* had not come to power as foreign invaders, prepared to organize a state as formally Islamic as they pleased. The legitimacy of their authority rested to a large extent on satisfying traditional Malinke expectations in their public conventions and ceremonies. Consequently, they were obliged to walk a narrow line between their urban Muslim subjects, who wanted them to behave up to the public standards of their Marinid or Mamluk counterparts, and the vast majority of the tax- and tribute-paying population, which took no notice of Maliki law or proper procedures at Friday prayer.

The character of official ritual and administration as more or less Islamic probably depended on the ruler's perception of the relative importance of his Muslim and non-Muslim subjects from one period to the next. Mansa Musa was naturally a great favorite of Muslim opinion, both in Mali and the wider Islamic world. His [Page 295] prestige resulted not only from his sensational pilgrimage, but also, writes al-Umari, because

> he built ordinary and cathedral mosques and minarets, and established the Friday observances, and prayers in congregation, and the muezzin's call. He brought jurists of the Malikite school to his country and there continued as sultan of the Muslims and became a student of religious sciences. [5]

Yet Mansa Musa also reigned during a period when relations with the Muslim merchants and with the states of North Africa were particularly important owing to the strong market for gold.

This expansive period in the trans-Saharan trade continued into the reign of Musa's brother Sulayman, who came to the throne about 1341. Sulayman came close to matching his brother's reputation for Islamic leadership and piety. Moreover, he ruled Mali in prosperity and peace. He was the sort of king from whom Ibn Battuta had come to expect an honorable and large-hearted reception.

In the autumn of 1351 the relentless traveler set out from Fez to visit Mali. He says nothing in the *Rihla* to explain why he felt impelled to cross the Sahara Desert. We may suppose he had the usual private plans to seek favor from yet another Muslim court. Obsessive traveler that he was, he may even have been urged on by the knowledge that the Sudan was the one important corner of the Dar al-Islam he had not yet seen. [6]

Some modern historians have suggested that Sultan Abu 'Inan appointed him as a state envoy to the emperor. Both Mansa Musa and Mansa Sulayman had initiated diplomatic exchanges with Abu l'Hasan, Abu 'Inan's father. Because of the Marinid campaign to conquer all of North Africa and thereby control the northern termini of the trans-Saharan trade from the Atlantic to Ifriqiya, the rulers of Mali had abundant reason to cultivate good relations with their northern neighbor. Abu 'Inan certainly knew that Ibn Battuta was making the journey and expected him to report in detail upon his return to Fez. Yet there is no convincing evidence that this Tangierian *faqih*, who was little known in Morocco's official circles, had anything like the ambassadorial status he had enjoyed (with such disastrous results) under Muhammad Tughluq. [7]

[Page 296] Traveling due south from Fez across the ranges of the Middle and High Atlas Mountains, he arrived in Sijilmasa, the preeminent desert port of the Western Maghrib, after a journey of eight or nine days. Sijilmasa lay in the midst of an immense oasis called Tafilalt, the last important outpost of sedentary life at the northern edge of the void. Today nothing remains of the city except an agglomeration of unremarkable ruins strewn among the palm groves. In the fourteenth century it was, according to alUmari, a place "of imposing palaces, high buildings, and tall gates." [8] Tafilalt's rich agriculture, fed by a river flowing down out of the Atlas 50 miles to the north, supported the urban population, including a large resident community of Berber and Arab merchants. From the perspective of Mali, Sijilmasa was the chief northern terminus of the trans-Saharan gold caravans. Here the products of the savanna and forest were off-loaded, stored in warehouses, and finally carried by camel, mule and donkey trains over the mountains to Fez, Marrakesh, Tlemcen, and the Mediterranean ports.

Ibn Battuta spent about four months in Sijilmasa, waiting for the winter season, when the big caravans set out for Walata, their destination at the far side of the desert. During this time he purchased camels of his own and fattened them up. When he was in Ceuta some months earlier, he may have become acquainted with the al-Bushri family, whose kinsman he had met in China. For he lodged during his entire stay in Sijilmasa with one Muhammad alBushri, a legal scholar and brother of the al-Bushri of Qanjanfu. "How far apart they are," he remarks blandly in the *Rihla*.

In February 1352 (beginning of Muharram 753) he set out from Tafilalt with a caravan of "merchants of Sijilmasa and others." The leader was a fellow of the Masufa Berbers, a herding people of the Western Sahara who appear to have had something close to a monopoly on the supply of guards, guides, and drivers on the entire route between Tafilalt and the Sahel. The twelfth-century geographer al-Idrisi describes the normal routines for traveling safely across "the empty waste" that yawned for a thousand miles south of Sijilmasa:

> They load their camels at late dawn, and march until the sun has risen, its light has become bright in the air, and the heat on the ground has become severe. Then they put their loads down, hobble their camels, unfasten their baggage and stretch awnings [**Page 297**] to give some shade from the scorching heat and the hot winds of midday … When the sun begins to decline and sink in the west, they set off. They march for the rest of the day, and keep going until nightfall, when they encamp at whatever place they have reached … Thus the traveling of the merchants who enter the country of the Sudan is according to this pattern. They do not deviate from it, because the sun kills with its heat those who run the risk of marching at midday. [9]

Twenty-five days out of Sijilmasa the caravan reached the settlement of Taghaza, the main salt-mining center of the Western Sahara. The paradox of Taghaza was the grim, treeless desolation of the place set against its extreme importance to the entire interregional commercial system. All the south-bound caravans took on loads of slab salt, since no product was in greater demand in the Sudan. "This is a village with nothing good about it," Ibn Battuta complains. "It is the most fly-ridden of places." Then he goes on to speak of the enormous amounts of gold that changed hands there.

The caravan stayed in the village for ten days, giving him an opportunity to watch wretched slaves belonging to Masufa proprietors dig slabs out of the open mine and tie them against the sides of the dromedaries. He also had the curious experience of sleeping in a house and praying in a mosque made entirely of salt blocks, except for the camel-skin roofs. The water of Taghaza was brackish, and every bit of food for the laborers, except for camel meat, had to be brought in from either Morocco or Mali. More than a century and a half later the Granada-born traveler Leo Africanus would visit Taghaza and find conditions little changed:

> Neither have the said diggers of salt any victuals but such as the merchants bring unto them: for they are distant from all inhabited places, almost twenty days journey, insomuch that oftentimes they perish for lack of food, whenas the merchants come not in due time unto them: Moreover the southeast wind doth so often blind them, that they cannot live here without great peril. [10]

Between Taghaza and Walata lay the most dangerous stretch of the journey, almost 500 miles of sand desert where the average annual rainfall is a scant five to ten millimeters and where only one watering point exists, a place called Bir al-Ksaib (Tasarahla). [11] If [**Page 298**] rain fell at all in the region, it usually came in late winter. [12] Ibn Battuta and his fellows were, according to his chronology, traveling south from Taghaza sometime in March. Fortunately, the rain had come that year, leaving pools of water here and there along the track, enough in fact for the caravaners to wash out their clothes. Yet there was danger enough in this wilderness for all that:

> In those days we used to go on ahead of the caravan and whenever we found a place suitable for grazing we pastured the beasts there. This we continued to do till a man named Ibn Ziri became lost in the desert. After that we neither went on ahead nor lagged behind. Strife and the exchange of insults had taken place between Ibn Ziri and his maternal cousin, named Ibn 'Adi, so that he fell behind the caravan and lost the way, and when the people encamped there was no news of him.

Arriving safely at Bir al-Ksaib minus Ibn Ziri, the caravan stopped for three days to rest and to repair and fill the water skins before navigating the trek across the vast sand desert called Mreyye, the final and most dangerous stage of the trip. Keeping to the usual procedure, the company hired a Masufa scout called the *takshif*, whose job it was to go on ahead of the caravan to Walata. If he did not lose his way among the dunes, or run out of water, or fall prey to the demons which Ibn Battuta tells us haunted those wastes, he would alert the people of the town to the caravan's approach. A group of Walatans would then be sent four days' journey north to meet the caravan with fresh water.

The Masufa *takshif* earned the 100 mithqals of gold the caravaners paid him, for on the seventh night out of Bir al-Ksaib they saw the lights of the Walata relief party. A few days later, sometime in the latter part of April 1352 (beginning of Rabi' I 753), they reached the sweltering little town. Its mud brick houses lay along the slope of a barren hill, a scattering of palm trees in a little wadi below. The site was bleak, but as the main southern terminus of the camel trains the town nonetheless supported a population of two or three thousand. [13] It ranked as a provincial capital of Mali and had an important community of educated men of Berber and Sudanese origin.

By a letter entrusted to the *takshif* Ibn Battuta had arranged to rent a house through the good offices of a "respectable" Moroccan **[Page 299]** trader named Ibn Badda', who resided in the town. Yet as soon as he arrived, he found cause to regret having come at all. Walata was the most northerly center under the jurisdiction of the *mansa*. Following custom, the members of the caravan went immediately to pay their respects to the *farba*, or governor. They found him seated on a carpet under a portico, surrounded by lancers, bowmen, and warriors of the Masufa. Though he sat very close to the visitors, he addressed them not directly but through a spokesman. In Mali this was proper ceremonial procedure symbolizing the sacred character of the *mansa*, in whose name the *farba* held his authority. Ibn Battuta, however, thought the governor's behavior a shocking display of bad manners, misinterpreting it as a show of contempt for the visiting "white men." [14] Later, the newcomers all went to receive hospitality from one of the governor's officials. The welcome turned out to be a bowl of millet with a little honey and yogurt.

> I said to them: "Was it to this that the black man invited us?" They said: "Yes, for them this is a great banquet." Then I knew for certain that no good was to be expected from them and I wished to depart.

He soon got the better of his urge to retreat back to Morocco, but the inclination of the Sudanese to combine Islamic practice with regional custom was no end of irritation to him. His prejudice, if he were to try to explain it, had nothing directly to do with race. It was a matter of the failure of the Malians to conduct themselves according to the normative standards that pious Muslims from North African cities might expect of virtuous officers of state. Such standards did not include rulers speaking to fellow believers through ritual heralds or entertaining visiting '*ulama* with small dishes of porridge.

The incident, unfortunately, was to be only the first of many occasions when Ibn Battuta, the sophisticated Maliki jurist, would find the Sudanese coming up short in their attention to moral and legal niceties. He admits that the scholars of Walata treated him warmly during his sojourn in the town, but he found their failure to subscribe to what he regarded as the civilized rules of sexual segregation even worse than the practices of the Central Asian Turks. On one occasion he appeared at the house of the *qadi* to find him seated in casual conversation with a young and beautiful [Page 300] woman. That a woman should be present in the reception room of a Muslim's house when a male guest arrived was bad enough. But the judge's explanation, that it was all right to come in because the woman was his "friend," made the visitor recoil in shock. On another occasion Ibn Battuta paid a call to a Masufa scholar and found this worthy's wife chatting with a strange man in the courtyard. When he expressed profound disapproval of such goings-on, the scholar replied insouciantly that "the association of women with men is agreeable to us and a part of good conduct, to which no suspicion attaches. They are not like the women of your country." Unpersuaded, Ibn Battuta left the house at once and never came back." He invited me several times," he tells us, "but I did not accept."

He stayed in Walata several weeks, then started out for the capital of Mali in the company of three companions and a Masufa guide. He remarks that he did not need to travel in a caravan because "neither traveler there nor dweller has anything to fear from thief or usurper" owing to Mansa Sulayman's firm government. Nor did he have to carry a large stock of supplies. As he moved southward from the Sahelian steppe into the grassy plains, giant baobab trees rising stalk-like on the horizon, he encountered village after village of Sudanese farming folk. In them he and his comrades offered glass beads and pieces of Taghaza salt in return for millet, rice, milk, chickens, and other local staples. After two weeks or more on the road by way of Zaghari (which may be identified with the Sokolo area in modern Mali), he reached the left bank of the Niger River at a place

he names Karsakhu. [15] He calls the river the Nile (Nil), following the mistaken notion of medieval Muslim geographers that that great river was a branch of the Egyptian Nile. Whatever his error, the crocodiles here were as dangerous as the ones he had seen in Egypt:

> One day I had gone to the Nil to accomplish a need when one of the Sudan came and stood between me and the river. I was amazed at his ill manners and lack of modesty and mentioned this to somebody, who said: "He did that only because he feared for you on account of the crocodile, so he placed himself between you and it."

The traveler's precise route from Walata to the Malian capital is a puzzle because we do not know for certain where the town was.

[Page 301] The *Rihla* gives neither a name to the place nor a very useful topographical description of it. The chief seat of royal power may have changed location from one period to another, indeed more than one "capital" may have existed at the same time. Some modern scholars identify the site, at least at that time in Mali's history, with the village of Niani, located south of the Niger in the modern Republic of Guinea. But the town may also have lain north of the river somewhere east of Bamako. [16] About ten miles from his destination Ibn Battuta crossed what he calls the Sansara River on a ferry (he never mentions crossing the Niger). If the capital is to be identified with Niani, that river would have been the Sankarani, a southern tributary of the Niger.

The seat of Mansa Sulayman was a sprawling, unwalled town set in a "verdant and hilly" country. [17] The sultan had several enclosed palaces there. Mansa Musa had built one under the direction of Abu Ishaq al-Sahili, an Andalusian architect and poet who had accompanied him home from the *hajj*. Al-Sahili surfaced the building with plaster, an innovation in the Sudan, and "covered it with colored patterns so that it turned out to be the most elegant of buildings." [18] Surrounding the palaces and mosques were the residences of the citizenry, mud-walled houses roofed with domes of timber and reed. [19]

Ibn Battuta arrived in the town on 28 July 1352 (14 Jumada I 753) and went immediately to the quarter where the resident merchants and scholars of Maghribi origin lived. He had written to the community in advance of his arrival, probably from Walata, and was relieved to learn that his letter had been received and a house made ready for him to occupy. Within a day, he made the acquaintance of the *qadi*, a Sudanese, as well as the other members of the Muslim notability. He was also introduced to the *mansa's* "interpreter," or *griot*, a man named Dugha. This official was a Sudanese of special social caste who performed a multiplicity of important state functions: master of state ceremonies, royal bard and praise singer, herald, confidant, counsellor, and keeper of the oral traditions of the Keita dynasty.

Ibn Battuta no doubt expected to see the king promptly, but ten days after his arrival he fell grievously sick after eating some yams or similar root that may not have been cooked long enough to remove the poison from its skin. [20] He fainted away during the dawn prayer, and one of the five men who had shared the meal with him subsequently died. Ibn Battuta drank a purgative concoction [**Page 302**] to induce vomiting, but he remained so ill for two months that he could not rouse himself to make an appearance at court. He finally recovered just in time to attend a public memorial feast for the deposed and deceased Moroccan sultan Abu l'Hasan, with whom Mali had had amicable diplomatic relations. The ceremonies of the *mansa's* public sitting were not unlike the pageants the traveler had witnessed in dozens of Muslim courts, but elements of traditional Malinke chieftaincy were in evidence to be sure:

> [The sultan] has a lofty pavilion, of which the door is inside his house, where he sits for most of the time ... There came forth from the gate of the palace about 300 slaves, some carrying in their hands bows and others having in their hands short

lances and shields ... Then two saddled and bridled horses are brought, with two rams which, they say, are effective against the evil eye ... Dugha the interpreter stands at the gate of the council-place wearing fine garments of silk brocade and other materials, and on his head a turban with fringes which they have a novel way of winding ... The troops, governors, young men, slaves, the Masufa, and others sit outside the council-place in a broad street where there are trees ... Inside the council-place beneath the arches a man is standing. Anyone who wishes to address the sultan addresses Dugha and Dugha addresses that man standing and that man standing addresses the sultan.
> If one of them addresses the sultan and the latter replies he uncovers the clothes from his back and sprinkles dust on his head and back, like one washing himself with water. I used to marvel how their eyes did not become blinded.

The *qadi* and other scholars brought Ibn Battuta forward and presented him to the gold-turbaned monarch seated on his dais under a silken dome. There was nothing particularly special about a Moroccan *faqih* passing through the kingdom and this first meeting was perfunctory. Later, when Ibn Battuta had returned to his house, one of the scholars called to tell him that the sultan had sent along the requisite welcoming gift.

> I got up, thinking that it would be robes of honor and money, but behold! it was three loaves of bread and a piece of beef fried in *gharti* [shea butter] and a gourd containing yoghurt. When I [**Page 303**] saw it I laughed, and was long astonished at their feeble intellect and their respect for mean things.

To make matters worse he spent almost another two months attending court before the sultan paid any further attention to him. Finally, on the advice of Dugha, he made an appeal to Sulayman, brashly raising the issue of the *mansa's* prestige among the Muslim rulers of the world:

> I have journeyed to the countries of the world and met their kings. I have been four months in your country without your giving me a reception gift or anything else. What shall I say of you in the presence of other sultans?

In all probability Sulayman could not have cared less what this wandering jurist said of him. At first he sublimely disavowed having even known that Ibn Battuta was in the town. But when his notables reminded him that he had received the Moroccan a few months earlier and "sent him some food," the *mansa* offered him a house and an allowance in gold. Notwithstanding the sultan's desultory effort to put things right, Ibn Battuta never got over the indifferent treatment he received, concluding in the *Rihla* that Sulayman "is a miserly king from whom no great donation is to be expected" and that Mansa Musa by contrast had been "generous and virtuous." Ibn Battuta ended a sojourn of a little more than eight months in the capital in a state of ambivalence over the qualities of Malian culture. On the one hand he respected Sulayman's just and stable government and the earnest devotion of the Muslim population to their mosque prayers and Qur'anic studies. "They place fetters on their children if there appears on their part a failure to memorize the Qur'an," he reports approvingly, "and they are not undone until they memorize it." On the other hand he reproached the Sudanese severely for practices obviously based in Malinke tradition but, from his point of view, either profane or ridiculous when set against the model of the rightly guided Islamic state: female slaves and servants who went stark naked into the court for all to see; subjects who groveled before the sultan, beating the ground with their elbows and throwing dust and ashes over their heads; royal poets who romped about in feathers and bird masks. Ibn Battuta seems indeed to be

harsher on the Malians than he [**Page 304**] does on other societies of the Islamic periphery where behavior rooted in local tradition, but contrary to his scriptural and legal standards, colored religious and social practice. We may sense in his reportage a certain embarrassment that a kingdom whose Islam was so profoundly influenced by his own homeland and its Maliki doctors was not doing a better job keeping to the straight and narrow.

Ibn Battuta left Sulayman's court on 27 February 1353 (22 Muharram 754), traveling by camel in the company of a merchant. Since the location of the capital is uncertain, his itinerary away from it is equally problematic. If he had a general plan of travel, it seems to have been to explore the provinces of Mali further down the Niger. He mentions that in the ensuing days he crossed, not the great river itself, but a tributary channel, which might be identified with the "canal du Sahel," a northerly flood branch located east of the modern Malian town of Ségou. [21] From there he followed a northeasterly route, keeping well to the west of the river, then rejoining it again somewhere not far upstream from Timbuktu.

In the *Rihla* Ibn Battuta expresses no particular wonder at that legendary "city of gold." In fact the rise of Timbuktu as a trans-Saharan terminus and capital of Islamic learning came mainly in the fifteenth and sixteenth centuries. In the mid fourteenth century, when Ibn Battuta passed through, the town was only beginning to flower. It had a population of about 10,000 and a Malian governor, who had been installed when Mansa Musa visited the town on his return from the Hijaz. [22] It almost certainly had a sizable community of Maghribi and Sudanese scholars. According to tradition, Mansa Musa had commissioned an impressive grand mosque. [23] Yet until later in the century Timbuktu was junior to Walata as a trade and intellectual center. Ibn Battuta found nothing there to detain him for long and was soon on his way down the Niger.

At Kabara, Timbuktu's "port" on the river four miles south of the city, he abandoned his dromedary and boarded a small boat, a type of canoe ("carved out of a single piece of wood") that is still used in the region today. [24] From Kabara the Niger flows due eastward for about 180 miles through the flat Sahelian steppe. "Each night," he reports, "we stayed in a village and bought what we were in need of in the way of wheat and butter for salt, spices [**Page 305**] and glass trinkets." At one village he celebrated the Prophet's Birthday (12 Rabi' I 754 or 17 April 1353) in the company of the local commander, whose generosity the *Rihla* praises so effusively that the tacit negative comparison to Mansa Sulayman is not lost on the reader. The officer not only entertained his visitor warmly but even gave him a slave boy as a gift. The lad accompanied Ibn Battuta back across the Sahara and remained with him for some years.

Continuing down river, the traveler spent about a month in Gao (Kawkaw), a thriving commercial city at the eastern extremity of Mali's political orbit. Then, having by this time crossed a large part of the empire from west to east and visited most of the towns with important Muslim populations, he decided to make for home. Gao paralleled Walata and Timbuktu as a terminus of trans-Saharan trade, but with relatively more important route connections to Ifriqiya and Egypt. Ibn Battuta found "a big caravan" departing from Gao for Ghadamès (Ghadamis), a major stop in the northern desert about 450 miles due south of Tunis. He had no plans to go to Ghadamès, but it made sense for him to accompany the convoy as far east as the oasis of Takedda (Azelik), which lay to the southwest of the Saharan highland region called Air. [25] From there he could expect to intercept a caravan *en route* to Sijilmasa from the central Sudan (the region corresponding to the northern part of modern Nigeria).

His journey to Takedda was disagreeable. In Gao he purchased a riding camel, as well as a she-camel to carry his provisions. But the sweltering desert summer was approaching, and after only one stage on the trail the she-camel collapsed. Other travelers among the company agreed to help transport Ibn Battuta's belongings, but further on he fell sick, this time "because of the extreme heat and a surplus of bile." Stumbling on to Takedda, he found a house in which to recuperate as well as a welcoming community of resident Moroccans.

Like Taghaza, Takedda was a grim spot in the desert important for its mine, in this case copper. Unlike Taghaza, the town was also a junction of trade routes and consequently a place of some slight urbanity. Ibn Battuta reports:

> The people of Takedda have no occupation but trade. They travel each year to Egypt and import some of everything which is there in the way of fine cloth and other things. Its people are [**Page 306**] comfortable and well off and are proud of the number of male and female slaves which they have.

Recovering from his illness, he thought of buying "an educated slave girl" for himself. The effort brought nothing but trouble, not least for the unfortunate young women involved. First, the *qadi* of the town got one of the other notables to sell the traveler a girl of his own for a quantity of gold. Then the man decided he had made a mistake and asked to buy her back. Ibn Battuta agreed on condition that a replacement be found. Another Moroccan in the caravan, a man named 'Ali 'Aghyul, had a woman he was ready to sell. But Ibn Battuta and this fellow had already had a personal row. On the journey to Takedda, 'Ali 'Aghyul had not only refused to help carry the load from Ibn Battuta's dead camel but even denied a drink of water to his countryman's slave boy. Nevertheless Ibn Battuta went through with the deal, this girl "being better than the first one." But then

> this Moroccan regretted having sold the slave and wished to revoke the bargain. He importuned me to do so, but I declined to do anything but reward him for his evil acts. He almost went mad and died of grief. But I let him off afterwards.

Some time following this shabby incident, a slave messenger arrived in a caravan from Sijilmasa carrying an order from Sultan Abu 'Inan that the *faqih* should return immediately to Fez. Ibn Battuta offers no explanation why the sultan should have kept such close track of his movements south of the Sahara. It seems likely that Abu 'Inan was anxious to have a report from him on political and commercial conditions in Mali, matters so important to the health of the Marinid state. [26]

Ibn Battuta left Takadda on 11 September 1353 (11 Sha'ban 754) in the company of a large caravan transporting 600 black female slaves to Morocco. These unfortunates had probably started out from the savanna lands southeast of Takedda, regions which, in the absence of gold deposits, engaged more extensively in slave commerce than did Mali. [27] Once arrived in Sijilmasa or Fez, the women would be sold into service as domestics, concubines, or servants of the royal court.

The caravan trekked northward through 18 days of "wilderness without habitation" to a point north of Air (possibly Assiou or In [Page 307] Azaoua, [28] where the route leading to Ghadamès forked off from the road to Sijilmasa. From there the convoy skirted the western side of the Ahaggar (Hoggar, or Hukkar) Mountains of the central desert. Here they passed through the territory of veiled Berber nomads who, Ibn Battuta informs us, were "good for nothing ... We encountered one of their chief men who held up the caravan until he was paid an impost of cloth and other things."

Now veering gradually to the northwest, the company eventually reached the great north Saharan oasis complex of Tuwat (Touat). Ibn Battuta mentions only one stopping place in this region (Buda), then tells us simply that they continued on to Sijilmasa. He stayed there no more than about two weeks, then continued on over the High Atlas in the dead of winter. "I have seen difficult roads and much snow in Bukhara, Samarkand, Khurasan and the land of the Turks, but I never saw a road more difficult than that." Somewhere along that frigid highway he halted to celebrate the Feast of Sacrifice, 6 January 1354.

> Then I departed and reached the capital Fez, capital of our Lord the Commander of the Faithful, may God support him, and kissed his noble hand, and deemed myself fortunate to see his blessed face. I remained in the shelter of his beneficence after my long travels, may God ... thank him for the great benefits which he bestowed on me and his ample benignity.

Indeed Abu 'Inan could afford to be amply benign, for his reign had just about reached its high point when Ibn Battuta returned to the capital. Morocco was generally at peace, and the sultan was even planning for the day when he would best his father at conquering Ifriqiya and unifying North Africa once and for all. If the Black Death had temporarily deflated Fez's productiveness in craft and industry, the city was still the center of the intellectual universe west of Cairo. Among the stars of saintliness and erudition gathered there, Ibn Battuta might expect to shine for a moment or two on the strength of the stories he had to tell.

NOTES

13. Mali

1. Abu Zayd 'Abd al-Rahman Ibn Khaldun, *Kitab al-'Ibar*, in L&H, pp. 333–34.
2. Ibn Fadl Allah al-Umari, *Masalik al-absar fi mamalik al-amsar*, in L&H, pp. 269–70.
3. [Page 308] Al-Umari, L&H, pp. 270–71.
4. Andrew M. Watson, "Back to Gold and Silver," *Economic History Review* 20 (1967): 30–31; Nehemia Levtzion, *Ancient Ghana and Mali* (London, 1973), pp. 131–33.
5. Al-Umari, L&H, p. 261.
6. The *Rihla* is the only existing eye-witness testimony on the Mali empire and therefore a precious historical source.
7. The commentaries are divided on the question of IB's purpose in going to the Sudan. The issue hinges on the translation of the phrase *bi-rasm al-safar* in the Arabic text. One version has it: "I took leave of our Master (may God uphold him). I departed *with orders to accomplish a journey* to the land of the Sudan." R. Mauny *et al., Textes et documents relatifs à l'histoire de*

l'Afrique: extraits tirés des voyages d'Ibn Battuta (Dakar, 1966), p. 35. Levtzion and Hopkins (L&H, p. 414), however, believe that this translation "seems to read too much into the text." They prefer "and set off *with the purpose of traveling* to the land of the Sudan." Both D&S (vol. 4, p. 376) and H&K (p. 22) give similar meaning to their translation of the phrase. Levtzion (*Ghana and Mali*, p. 216) states that IB was "on a private visit to the Sudan" but that Abu 'Inan knew of his movements. When IB was at Takadda in the southern Sahara, the sultan sent a messenger telling him to return to Fez. I agree with Levtzion. If IB were on an official mission to Mali, we might expect him to make a good deal of it in the *Rihla* or at least refer to it in connection with his appearance at the Mali court.

8. Al-Umari, L&H, p. 275.

9. Abu 'Abd Allah al-Idrisi, *Nuzhat al-mushtaq fi ikhtiraq al-afaq*, L&H, p. 118.

10. Leo Africanus, *The History and Description of Africa*, trans. Robert Pory, ed. Robert Brown, 3 vols. (New York, 1896), vol. 3, pp. 800–01. Modern spelling mine.

11. Mauny *et al. (Textes et Documents*, p. 38) identify IB's Tasarahla with Bir alKsaib.

12. Mauny *et al., Textes et documents*, p. 37.

13. Raymond Mauny, *Tableau géographique de l'Ouest Africain au Moyen Âge d'après les sources écrites, la tradition et l'archéologie* (Amsterdam, 1967), p. 485.

14. H&K, p. 70n.

15. J. O. Hunwick identifies Zaghari with the Sokolo region and Karsakhu with a point on the Niger south of there. "The Mid-Fourteenth century capital of Mali," *Journal of African History* 14 (1973): 199–200. Other hypotheses on this stretch of IB's itinerary are offered by Claude Meillassoux, "L'itinéraire d'Ibn Battuta de Walata à Malli," *Journal of African History* 13 (1972): 389–95; and Mauny *et al., Textes et documents*, pp. 46–47.

16. Textual, linguistic, and archaeological evidence have all been marshalled to find the fourteenth century capital of Mali. Recent discussions, which also review the earlier literature on the problem, are Wladyslaw Filipowiak, *Études archéologiques sur la capitate médiévale du Mali*, trans. Zofia Slawskaj (Szczecin, 1979); Hunwick, "Mid-Fourteenth Century Capital," pp. 195–206; and Meillassoux, "L'itinéraire d'Ibn Battuta," pp. 389–95. Hunwick hypothesizes that IB did not visit Niani but a place north of the Niger, pointing out that the traveler never mentions crossing the river.

17. Al-Umari, L&H, p. 263.

18. Ibn Khaldun, L&H, p. 335.

19. Al-Umari, L&H, pp. 262–63.

20. H&K, p.72n.

21. Hunwick, "Mid-Fourteenth Century Capital," p. 203.

22. Elias N. Saad, *Social History of Timbuktu: the Role of Muslim Scholars and Notables, 1400–1900* (Cambridge, England, 1983), pp. 11, 27.

23. Levtzion, *Ghana and Mali*, p. 201; Mauny, *Tableau géographique*, pp. 114–15; and Saad, *Social History of Timbuktu*, pp. 36–37.

24. Mauny *et al., Textes et documents*, p. 71.

25. [**Page 309**] Mauny (*Tableau geógraphique*, pp. 139–40) identifies IB's Takadda with Azelik. Most other commentators agree.

26. Jean Devisse presumes that IB was on a mission for Abu 'Inan and speculates that the sultan wanted up-to-date intelligence out of fear that the gold trade was being increasingly diverted towards Egypt. "Routes de commerce et échanges en Afrique Occidentale en relation avec la Méditerranée," *Revue d'Histoire Économique et Sociale* 50 (1972): 373.

27. Levtzion, *Ghana and Mali*, pp. 174–76.

28. Mauny *et al. (Textes et documents*, p. 79) identify IB's watering place with one or the other of these points. L&H (p. 418n) are doubtful but offer no alternative.

BIBLIOGRAPHY

Chapter 13: Mali

Bovill, E. W. *The Golden Trade of the Moors.* London, 1968

Chapelle, F. de la. "Esquisse d'une histoire du Soudan Occidental." *Hespéris* 11 (1930): 35–95

Conrad, David, and Fisher, Humphrey. "The Conquest that Never Was: Ghana and the Almoravids, 1076." *History in Africa* 9 (1982): 21–59; 10 (1983): 53–78

Delafosse, Maurice. *Haut-Senegal-Niger.* 3 vols. Paris, 1919; reprint edn., 1972

Conrad, David, and Fisher, Humphrey. "Le Gana et le Mali et l'emplacement de leurs capitales." *Bulletin du Comité d'Études Historiques et Scientifiques de l'A.O.F.* 9 (1924): 479–542

Conrad, David, and Fisher, Humphrey. "Le Les relations du Maroc avec le Soudan à travers les âges." *Hespéris* (1924): 153–74

Devisse, J. "Routes de commerce et èchanges en Afrique Occidentale en relation avec la Méditerranée." *Revue d'Histoire Économique et Social* 50 (1972): 357–97

Filipowiak, Wladyslaw. "Contribution aux recherches sur la capitale du royaume de Mali à lépoque du haut Moyen-Âge." *Archaeologia Polona* 10 (1968): 217–32

Filipowiak, Wladyslaw. Études archeologiques sur la capitale mediévale du Mali. Translated by Zofia Slawskaj. Szczecin, 1979

Hiskett, M. *The Development of Islam in West Africa.* London, 1982

Hopkins, A. G. *An Economic History of West Africa.* New York, 1973

Hunwick, J. O. "The Mid-Fourteenth Century Capital of Mali." *Journal of African History* 14 (1973): 195–208

Leo Africanus. *The History and Description of Africa.* Translated by Robert Pory and edited by Robert Brown. 3 vols. New York, 1896

Levtzion, Nehemia. Ancient *Ghana and Mali.* London, 1973

Levtzion, Nehemia. and Hopkins, J. F. P. (trans, and eds.). *Corpus of Early Arabic Sources for West African History.* New York, 1981

Lewis, I. M. *Islam in Tropical Africa.* 2nd edn. Bloomington, Ind., 1980

Lhote, H. "Recherches sur Takedda, ville décrite par le voyageur arabe Ibn Battouta et située en Air." *Bulletin d l'IFAN* 34 (1972): 429–70

[Page 342] McIntosh, Roderick J. and Susan Keech. "The Inland Niger Delta before the Empire of Mali: Evidence from Jenne-Jeno." *Journal of African History* 22 (1981): 1–22

McIntosh, Susan Keech. "A Reconsideration of Wangara/Palolus, Island of Gold." *Journal of African History* 22 (1981): 145–58

Malowist, M. "Sur l'or du Soudan: quelques observations sur le commerce de l'or dans le Soudan Occidental au Moyen Âge." *Annales E.S.C.* 25 (1970): 1630–36

Mauny, Raymond. *Tableau geographique de l'Ouest Africain au Moyen Âge d'après les sources ècrites, la tradition et l'archéologie.* Amsterdam, 1967

Monteil, Charles. *Les Empires du Mali.* Paris, 1968

Niani, D. T. *Sundiata: An Epic of Old Mali.* Translated by G. D. Pickett, London, 1965

Peres, Henri. "Relations entre le Tafilelt et le Soudan à travers le Sahara du XIIe au XIVe siècle." In *Mélange de géographie et d'orientalisme offerts à E.-F. Gautier.* Tours, 1937, pp. 410–14

Saad, Elias N. *Social History of Timbuktu: The Role of Muslim Scholars and Notables, 1400–1900.* Cambridge, England, 1983

Sa'di, 'Abd al-Rahman ibn 'Abd Allah al-,. *Tarikh es-Soudan.* Translated by O. Houdas. Paris, 1964

Terrasse, Henri. "Note sur les ruines de Sijilmasa." *Revue Africaine* 368–69 (1936): 581–89

Trimingham, J. Spencer. *A History of Islam in West Africa.* Oxford, 1962

Wansbrough, John. "Africa and the Arab Geographers." In *Language and History in Africa.* Edited by D. Dalby. London, 1970, pp. 89–101

Watson, Andrew M. "Back to Gold and Silver." *Economic History Review,* 2nd ser., 20 (1967): 1–34

Willis, John R. (ed.). *Studies in West African Islamic History.* 3 vols. *Vol. 1: The Cultivators of Islam.* London, 1979

THE RISE AND FALL OF ZIMBABWE

By T. N. Huffman

RANDALL-MacIver developed the theory that Zimbabwe was 'essentially African' over sixty years ago.[1] It has been reaffirmed with every Iron Age excavation in Rhodesia and never seriously scientifically questioned. To say 'essentially African', however, gives only the barest outline of a very complex situation.

Approximately 150 ruins are similar to Zimbabwe in Rhodesia, Mocambique, Botswana and the Transvaal. According to our present knowledge, Zimbabwe is the earliest, and, therefore, the place of origin of this culture. For the present, the Zimbabwe culture is probably best considered as an incipient state organization. Certainly, it was not a civilization, since no evidence exists for the organization that makes possible writing, specialized crafts and city status. Most of the other ruins are irrelevant to the origin of this culture, and the present discussion will be limited to Great Zimbabwe.

Two opposing schools of thought exist within the framework of the 'essentially African' theory: a religious and a trade hypothesis. The religious hypothesis proposes that Bantu-speaking migrants with a special religious superiority established a kingdom prior to any external trade connections. Only later did Arabs on the coast hear of a wealthy nation and develop commercial contacts with it.[2] Alternatively, the trade hypothesis maintains that

Zimbabwe was a result of surplus wealth from the East African gold trade.[3]

Presentations of these two explanations are limited and occasionally inconsistent. Liberty has been taken here to formalize them and emphasize their major components to present a better understanding of their implications about state formation.

THE 'ESSENTIALLY AFRICAN' THEORY

Any theory concerning Zimbabwe's origin must be based on its stratigraphy and the known Iron Age sequence of the area. The Acropolis contains the only complete sequence at Zimbabwe, and both Caton-Thompson's[4] and Robinson's[5] excavations are in general agreement. The reader is referred to Robinson's report for details about the stratigraphy, which is only summarized here.

Bedrock was covered by an ochrous hill-earth containing Class 1 pottery. Overlaying the hill earth were Class 2 pottery, Type A huts (pole and daga) and cattle figurines, covered in turn by Type A huts with Class 3 pottery. Class 3 pottery continued, but now with Type B huts (solid daga walls and floors). The first stone wall was then built on top of a solid daga structure. Class 4 pottery was found above this, associated with a hut with radiating stone walls. Overlying all of the previous material were thin deposits of Class 5 pottery. Classes 1, 2 and 5 were not associated with stone walls. Other than obvious imports, all the material from the excavations was African in character, both under, above and within the stone walls.[6] This evidence is the foundation of the 'essentially African' theory.

In the 1958 excavation report this stratigraphy was divided into five periods and interpreted as a different people for each period.[7] Period I represented an Early Iron Age occupation with Class I pottery, ending about A.D. 400. Period II began soon after with a new population and lasted until A.D. 1100. It was characterized by Type A huts, clay figurines and Class 2 pottery. Period III started immediately afterwards and lasted till the 15th century. During this period the south wall of the Western Enclosure was begun, and towards the end of the period the valley was inhabited and the Great Enclosure constructed. Class 3 pottery and Type B huts characterized this time. During Period IV all the major buildings were built in Q style, and gold imports were numerous. This period was thought to have ended with the sacking of Zimbabwe by Nguni speakers in the 1800s.

Subsequent evidence has altered the above interpretation and has produced a shorter chronology. Firstly, the upper end of the sequence was revised because of the absence of Portuguese Period imports. Periods III and IV were merged and the end of the sequence placed at about A.D. 1500, 300 years earlier than previously thought.[8]

This revision has not been totally accepted,[9] because it could be argued that the crucial evidence was removed by Hall and other early excavators. It could also be argued that the Monomatapa in northern Mashonaland cut off the trade channels to the south, so there would not have been sixteenth-century porcelain anyway.[10] Recent salvage excavations at Zimbabwe by the author substantiate Garlake's conclusion, since no later material overlay the Period III/IV deposits in an undisturbed area.

This abandonment of Zimbabwe is also compatible with oral tradition. Whereas to the north such chiefdoms as Manyika, Barwe, Teve and Danda were well established by the mid-sixteenth century,[11] the polities around Zimbabwe for about fifty miles are

of recent origin, dating from the late seventeenth century or later. This applies to the Bonda, Ngowa, Rufura, Govera, Manwa, Nini, southern Hera, Mhari and Duma peoples. References to chiefdoms predating these people, such as Gwadzi and Dewe, do not suggest large polities, although obviously later traditions would tend to underestimate their size. Traditions from Zimuto and Gurajena, just north of Fort Victoria, stress the emptiness of the land.

Around Zimbabwe itself the *shumba*-totem Nemanwa chiefdom supplanted that of Gwadzi at the end of the seventeenth century,[12] and entered into a close relationship with the Mwari-cult officers who continued to offer sacrifices on the Acropolis until *c.* 1820–30.[13] Nemanwa's control of the Zimbabwe area ended at about this time, but this was due to a westward move by Mugabe's *moyo*-totem Duma, not to the Nguni.[14] There is no reliable oral evidence that Zwangendaba approached Zimbabwe before he crossed the Zambezi in 1835. Shortly before this, Ngwana Maseko ('Masesenyana') passed nearby on his way from Urozvi (the Rozvi area in modern Matabeleland) to the Manyika country.[15] He fought in the Jena country south of Zimbabwe,[16] until Mugabe drove him from the area,[17] but there is no evidence that he or any other Nguni leader did any damage to Zimbabwe itself.

Secondly, the lower end of the 1958 chronology was revised when the beginning of Period II was placed in the eighth century because of eighth and ninth century dates for Leopard's Kopje II.[18] Leopard's Kopje II and Zimbabwe Period II represent the first Later Iron Age cultures in Matabeleland and southern Mashonaland. Nowhere in Rhodesia does the Later Iron Age begin until after at least two phases of the Early Iron Age, and since Leopard's Kopje II, Bambandyanalo and Zimbabwe Period II ceramics are similar, it is postulated that they should be contemporaneous. By the same logic Woolandale, Mapungubwe and Zimbabwe III/IV should also be contemporaneous. Recent excavations at Leopard's Kopje Main Kraal place Zhizo (a second phase of the Early Iron Age) in the ninth century and Leopard's Kopje II (the beginning of the Later Iron Age) in the tenth and eleventh centuries.[19] This eleventh-century beginning for Leopard's Kopje II is supported by similar dates for Bambandyanalo and Mwala Hill.[20] The eleventh-century date from Zimbabwe, previously used to mark the end of Period II, is probably best considered now as a general indication of Period II occupation.

Zhizo pottery, or any other late stamped-ware pottery is absent at Zimbabwe; thus, there must have been an appreciable gap between Periods I and II. Taking the rest of the Later Iron Age into consideration, Period II could not have started until at least A.D. 1000. Zimbabwe's rise, florescence and decline, therefore, probably occurred within a maximum of 400 years.

The shorter chronology also affects the interpretation of the ceramics. The 'one-class one-people' interpretation appears to be based on an *a priori* assumption that ceramic change must be initiated by outside influences, and that change over time is not a normal process. The converse assumption, that change is normal, is equally plausible.

The 1958 interpretation has been criticized for its subjectivity, and the small sample on which it was based, and a continuum hypothesis for Classes 3 and 4, has been suggested as an alternative.[21] The ceramics from the salvage excavation support this continuum and extend it to include Khami band-and-panel ware. Figure 1 illustrates this seriation. There is a gradual lengthening of jar necks and complication of design in Classes 3 and 4, and during the Khami phase, bands and panels are added to the neck. The development from Zimbabwe Class 3 to Khami band-and-panel ware can be seen as a gradual evolution in one ceramic tradition.

The change from Class 2 to Class 3 is not only one of degree. All Iron Age ceramic traditions in Rhodesia, other than the Ruins Tradition, are characterized by a multiplicity of shapes. One of the most conspicuous differences between Classes 2 and 3 is the absence of bowls in 3. This difference cannot be easily explained by a new population, for it is more likely to represent a social or economic change. Since there is no evidence of an economic

difference between Periods II and III, the most plausible explanation is a social change. If Period III represents a new population, then the social change was made elsewhere. But the gradual replacement of Type A huts by Type B huts and, later, the building of stone walls suggest that the social transition took place at Zimbabwe, and it is unnecessary to postulate a new population to explain Period III.

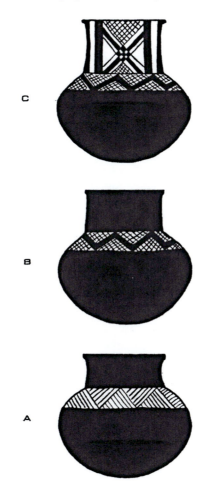

Fig. 1. Diagrammatic seriation of Zimbabwe pottery to Khami band-and-panel ware: A = Zimbabwe Class 3; B = Class 4; C = Khami.

The two hypotheses are really concerned with explaining the transition from Period II to III. The time of this transition is not known, even though it is generally accepted to have taken place in the eleventh century.[22] If the eleventh century date is interpreted as a general indication of Period II, as suggested here, then a seventy-year gap exists between the standard deviations of the Period II and III/IV radiocarbon dates. This seventy year gap centres around A.D. 1250.

Other Zimbabwe-phase ruins in Rhodesia, such as Zaka,[23] Lekkerwater, Harleigh Farm[24] and Little Mapela[25] date from the fourteenth to the sixteenth centuries. Mapungubwe, Woolandale and Ingombe Ilede are peasant sites typologically contemporary with Zimbabwe III/IV, and they date from the fourteenth to the sixteenth centuries.[26] If all these Later Iron Age dates are plotted together (Table 1), a chronological gap also appears about A.D. 1250,

Table 1. *Later Iron Age dates*

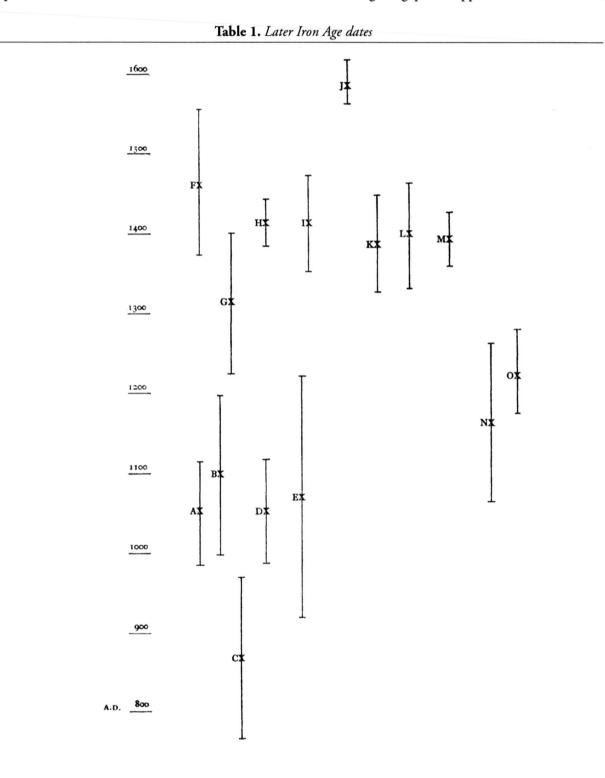

confirming the impression from Zimbabwe that the transition from Period II to III occurred in the thirteenth century at the earliest.

Figure 2 summarizes the Iron Age sequence for Matabeleland and southern Mashonaland. Zimbabwe Period II begins about A.D. 1000 and develops into III/IV in the thirteenth century. Zimbabwe is virtually abandoned by A.D. 1500, and the centre of the Ruins Tradition shifts to Matabeleland.

All samples (see Table 1 opposite) representing a single component have been combined with the formula:

$$\text{mean} \pm \sqrt{\frac{S_1^2 + S_2^2 + S_3^2}{9}} \dots$$

A = Mambo level at Leopard's Kopje Main Kraal: (SR-224) 845 + 85, (N-772) 900±100, (SR-216) 1000±50, (SR-217) 1070 + 65, (SR-218) 1070 + 80 and (SR-219) 1410±75 combined to 1050±65; B = Mwala Hill (SR-134); C = Taba Zika Mambo (SR-68); D = Bambandyanalo (Y-135-17); E = Zimbabwe Period II (M–914); F = Little Mapela (SR-120); G = Woolandale (SR-44); H = Mapungubwe (Y-135-14) 1380±50 and (Y-135-9) 1420±60 combined to 1400±65; I = Zimbabwe III/IV (SR-47) 1380±90 and (M-915) 1440±150 combined to 1410±60; J = Zaka (SR-196) 1485 ± 50 and (SR-196) 1695 ± 55 combined to 1590±25; K = Harleigh Farm (SR-25) 1300+120, (SR-70) 1340±90 and (SR-71) 1510±90 combined to 1385 ± 60; L = Lekkerwater (SR-109) 1300±120, (SR-108) 1390±120 and (SR-124) 1510±90 combined to 1400±65; M = Ingombe Ilede (GX-1368) 1340±85 and (GX-1369) 1445 ± 85 combined to 1395 ± 30; N = Geelong Mine (SR-143); and O = Aboyne Mine (SR-53) 1170±110 and (SR-58) 1300 ±110 combined to 1235 ± 50.

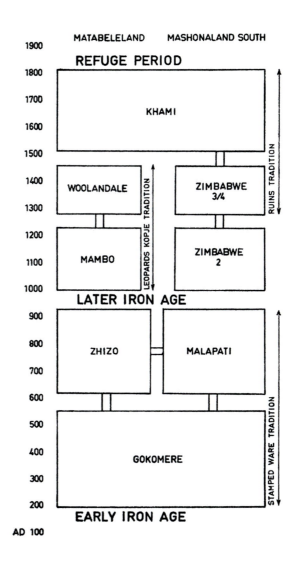

FIG. 2. Iron Age sequence for Matabeleland and southern Mashonaland. Double bonds represent genetic affinities between phases.

RELIGION VERSUS TRADE

To evaluate both hypotheses it is necessary to consider their implications about state formation. One variant of the religious hypothesis introduces the religious minority with a new population,[27] and another develops it from a local Leopard's Kopje base.[28] But both versions imply that Zimbabwe was a primary incipient state. The archaeological evidence indicates that all Iron Age societies before A.D. 1250 in Rhodesia were based on mixed farming at a subsistence level. It is equally clear that no known primary state has ever developed from such a foundation.[29] In all areas of primary civilization the centralized political authority developed from a reasonably large population based on intensive agriculture. It is also highly unlikely that a horticultural society would value gold to the extent assumed by the religious hypothesis. Furthermore, primary states did not originate in extensively open country like that around Zimbabwe, but rather in isolated areas of high productivity that provided an incentive for people to stay, even when they were confronted with escalating population and military pressures.[30] The first large population anywhere in Rhodesia did not develop until Period III/IV, and then it was limited to Zimbabwe.

These points should be sufficient to make the religious hypothesis highly improbable, but perhaps a review of the evidence for trade would be more convincing.

PORTUGUESE DOCUMENTS

When the Portuguese first entered the Indian Ocean they found an extensive trade network between Arabs and Shona-speaking peoples in the interior. Gold and ivory were the major exports from Rhodesia, while cloth, beads and glazed ceramics were the imports. Sofala was only a clearing house, for the trade goods that were brought from India and China were taxed at Kilwa before they were allowed to continue.[31]

ARABIC DOCUMENTS

The earliest reference to a trade through Sofala in Arab documents is the tenth century writing of Masudi.[32] A Sofala area is mentioned thereafter by Bozora (c. A.D. 950), al-Biruni (c. 1030), al-Idrisi (c. 1154), Yakut al Rumi (c. 1225), Ibn Sa'id (1214–74), Abu al-Fida (1273–1331), al Dimshki (c. 1325), Ibn Battuta (c. 1331), al Wardi (c. 1340) and Ibn Khaldun (c. 137s).[33] Both Ibn Sa'id and al-Fida place the principal town of thirteenth century Sofala at 2° south of the equator and its southern boundary at 12° south.[34] Modern Sofala is 20° south, 512 miles away. Consequently, the location of early Sofala is

in some doubt, although a trade with its hinterland and probably Rhodesia, can be assumed to have begun at an early date.

Confirmation of the documentary evidence has been found in the salvage excavations at Zimbabwe in the form of an Arab coin. This coin has the signature of al-Hasan bin Sulaiman on the obverse[35] (Plate 1), and a phrase on the reverse which probably starts with the word 'trusts'. There were two Sultans at Kilwa known as al-Hasan bin Sulaiman, but only the second one (c. 1320–33) is thought to have minted any coins. If this view is correct, his inscription is one of the most common on all Kilwa coins. By a remarkable coincidence, al Hasan bin Sulaiman II was Sultan when Ibn Battuta visited Kilwa in A.D. 1331.

Ibn Battuta referred to Yufi in the land of the Limis, one month's march from Sofala, as the source of gold for the Sofalan trade.[36] If thirteenth-century Sofala was near the modern one, then the land of the Limis was probably the Rhodesian plateau. If this is true and Yufi was a settlement, then Yufi could only have been Zimbabwe, for no other place at that time could compare in size and importance. It seems remarkable that the only coin ever recovered from Zimbabwe in a scientific context was minted at the same time as the only known possible Arab reference to Zimbabwe was recorded.

IMPORTS

It is difficult to establish precisely when Arab trading began in Rhodesia. Kilwa is thought to have taken over the Sofalan gold trade from Mogadishu about A.D. 1300, when there was a marked increase in the prosperity at Kilwa.[37] The comparable time at Zimbabwe, Period III/IV, also shows an increase in trade activities and wealth. Beads are found in profusion in these deposits, besides other imports, such as fourteenth-century Syrian glass, fourteenth-century Persian faience and fourteenth- to sixteenth-century Chinese celadon.[38] Although cloth itself is rarely found, spindle-whorls are common in Period III/IV deposits and at other Zimbabwe-phase sites. They probably represent the introduction of weaving by Arabs.[39] Clearly, trade with the East Coast was well established by the fourteenth century.

Plate I. Kilwa coin found at Zimbabwe. Obverse reads al-Hasan (bin) Sulaiman. Scale in centimetres.

Period III/IV, however, was not the first time that trade occurred at Zimbabwe. Glass beads were found throughout the Period II deposits,[40] and they are common in all Later Iron Age sites.[41] Because only a few are known from the first Phase of the Early Iron Age, and many Early Iron Age sites contain only shell beads, these earliest glass beads could easily have been the result of small scale village-to-village barter. They are considerably more common in tenth-century Phase II sites, such as the Zhizo level at Leopard's Kopje Main Kraal, Makuru near Shabani and the Three-Mile-Water site near Que Que.[42] This increase in beads may not indicate direct trade contact with Arabs, but it does indicate an increase in trading activities.

EXPORTS

Gold mining can be proved for Period III/IV, since gold has been found in the Leopard's Kopje III levels at Taba Zika Mambo,[43] at Mapungubwe,[44] Ingombe Ilede[45] and several Zimbabwe-phase sites.[46] The crucial question is whether the mining of gold can be substantiated before Period III/IV. Ancient gold mining is said to have begun by A.D. 600,[47] but the

evidence is circumstantial: (a) similarities in simple digging techniques between India and Rhodesia do not necessarily imply an historical connexion; (b) the early dates for trade at Ingombe Ilede have been rejected;[48] and (c), only one ancient working, Golden Shower, actually has pottery in the stopes. All other Early Iron Age evidence for gold mining consists of ancient workings with Iron Age sites nearby. But Late Stone Age, Middle Stone Age and Later Iron Age sites are also in the neighbourhood and could just as easily be associated with the ancient workings. If the Golden Shower pottery was actually made by the miners, then it would be a strong case for extensive early gold mining. But until proof has been found for gold mining or smelting in the associated village, then the logical possibility remains that an earlier village's refuse was used to fill a later mine stope. Considering that Golden Shower is the only site which might contain evidence for gold mining before A.D. 1000, it should be held in reserve.

Only six radiocarbon dates are available for ancient mining in Rhodesia. The earliest three range from the twelfth to the fourteenth centuries.[49] Even though the sample size is small, it appears significant that these three dates bridge the time gap between Periods II and III/IV (Table 1).

By correlating the independent evidence from Arab documents, glass beads and ancient mining, one can suggest that trade contacts between the East Coast and Rhodesia were well established before Period III/IV, possibly by A.D. 1000. There should be little doubt, then, that Zimbabwe's origin is due in some way to trade. This is not to deny the importance of religion. Indeed, if the association at Golden Shower is reliable, a difference in the political influences of religions might explain why Later Iron Age people were able to develop a state and Early Iron Age people were not. Rather, the emphasis here has been on the hypothesis that Zimbabwe could not have developed without the stimulus from the Arab gold trade.

THE RISE OF ZIMBABWE THROUGH TRADE

A trade stimulus is a well-known mechanism for the formation of secondary states in Africa,[50] as well as in other parts of the world.[51] The evolution of such a state can be summarized as follows:

Given a tribal society with some social stratification, the chief is the most wealthy person. Because he entertains visiting dignitaries, donates to weddings and funeral feasts of his people and supports other functions, his wealth is constantly re-cycled within his tribe. Once trade contacts with an existing state organization are established, the chief invariably monopolizes the tribal end of it. Since the new wealth is far in excess of that which is normally generated within the system, it cannot be redistributed, and wealth and political authority become increasingly concentrated. People can then be hired to perform a duty instead of cooperating through a system based on kinship ties. An army, or police force, can be established to collect taxes to support the government, and the functions of a state emerge.

This generalization also provides a plausible explanation for the construction of Zimbabwe's monumental architecture. As the paramount chief's wealth increased, the population of the royal settlement would swell, partly because of the prestige of living in the settlement and the chance that some of the wealth might find its way through the normal redistributive channels. Even though it might not have been conceptualized in this manner, this increased population has to be controlled. Armies and public work projects are two alternatives which come readily to mind. The availability of construction material at Zimbabwe makes the latter a logical course to take, especially considering that building in stone was probably a common feature among other Later Iron Age cultures.[52] The stone walls at Zimbabwe can then be seen as a typical step in the formation of a state. Not only were they an ostentatious display of wealth, but they were also a method for organizing an existing labour force.

Once the Ruins Culture reached a certain level, other areas would have been absorbed by this state.

No logical necessity arises, then, to postulate independent origins for any other Zimbabwe- or Khami-phase ruin. Other Zimbabwe-phase ruins appear to have been built during Zimbabwe's peak (c. 1350-1450), and probably represent an extension of political authority. They can be visualized as local administrative centres, while Khami-phase ruins probably represent the geographical shift of a political centre within the same culture group.

DECLINE OF ZIMBABWE

An ecological explanation has been suggested for the decline of Zimbabwe which is virtually indisputable.[53] The large Period III/IV population at Zimbabwe must have taxed the environment heavily. The constant demand for firewood over several decades and the gradual exhaustion of the soil must have made it increasingly difficult to live there without a more efficient agricultural system. Irrigation might have been one alternative, but it does not appear to have been practised.

Attention has been drawn to the coincidence between the decline of Zimbabwe and the beginning of the Mwene Mutapa dynasty.[54] According to oral tradition, the move was made because the king was tired of eating salt made from goats' dung.[55] The African strategy of abandoning the land once it is exhausted is well known, and the reference to salt sounds like a social rationalization of this strategy.

Archaeologically speaking, it does not matter if the first Mwene Mutapa was the last king at Zimbabwe,[56] or just a dissatisfied person who broke off with a small following. Nor does it matter if Changamire was originally a vassal of the Mwene Mutapa,[57] or another member of the royal household who established an independent dynasty on the break-up of Zimbabwe. The significance of the ecological explanation is that the fragmentation of Zimbabwe was ultimately due to the deterioration of the environment.

SUMMARY

Two hypotheses are available for the origin of the Zimbabwe culture. A religious hypothesis attributes its development to an African society in isolation, placing it in the class of a primary state. In contrast, the trade hypothesis maintains that it was a secondary state resulting from the gold trade.

If the religious hypothesis is correct, then Zimbabwe would be an exception to all other known cases of primary state formation. The archaeological evidence points to a horticultural subsistence throughout the Iron Age sequence in the area and a small population until Period III/IV. On the other hand, all known primary states were based on large populations and intensive agriculture. It is more likely that Zimbabwe is a typical case of secondary state formation.

The stratigraphy on the Acropolis indicates that a social transition from Period II to III probably occurred at Zimbabwe and was not the result of an immigrant group, and the short chronology places this transition around A.D. 1250. The evidence available from Arab documents, trade imports and ancient mining demonstrates that trade existed well before then. Consequently, the evolution of the Zimbabwe culture was almost certainly due to the Arab gold trade.[58]

NOTES

1. D. Randall-MacIver, *Mediaeval Rhodesia* (London: MacMillan and Co., 1906), 85.
2. D. P. Abraham, 'The early political history of the Kingdom of Mwena Mutapa (850–1589)', in *Historians in Tropical Africa, Proceedings of the Leverhulme Inter-Collegiate History Conference* (Salisbury, 1962), 61–92. B. M. Fagan, *Southern Africa during the Iron Age* (London: Thames and Hudson, 1965), 120–1.
3. G. Caton-Thompson, *The Zimbabwe Culture, Ruins and Reactions* (Oxford: Clarendon Press, 1931), 196 * A. J. E. Jaffey, 'A reappraisal of the history of the Rhodesian Iron Age up to the fifteenth century', *J. Afr. Hist.* VII, 2 (1966), 193–4.
4. Caton-Thompson, *Zimbabwe Culture*, 69–85.
5. K. R. Robinson, 'Excavations on the Acropolis Hill', in R. Summers, K. R. Robinson and A. Whitty, 'Zimbabwe excavations; 1958', *Occ. Papers Natn. Mus. Sth Rhod.* III, 3A (1961), 159–92.
6. Randall-MacIver, *Mediaeval Rhodesia*; Caton-Thompson, *Zimbabwe Culture*; Summers, *et. al.*, 'Zimbabwe excavations' *op cit.*
7. Summers, ibid, 326–30.
8. P. S. Garlake, 'The value of imported ceramics in the dating and interpretation of the Rhodesian Iron Age', *J. Afr. Hist. Ix, I* (1968), 13–33.
9. E.g., Summers, *Ancient Mining*, 126. Although a sixteenth century date is accepted for the end of the sequence, separate classes and periods are kept. In 'Forty years progress in Iron Age studies in Rhodesia, 1929–69', *S. Afr. archaeol. Bull.* xxv (1970), 95–103, Garlake's work is entirely omitted.
10. P. S. Garlake, 'Rhodesian ruins—a preliminary assessment of their styles and chronology', *J. Afr. Hist.* XI, 4 (1970), 508.
11. D. P. Abraham, 'The early political history of the kingdom of Mwene Mutapa', 67.
12. Sr. Mary Aquina, O.P. (Dr A. K. H. Weinrich), 'The Tribes in Victoria Reserve', *NADA*, IX, 2 (1965), 8.
13. *The Journals of Carl Mauch, 1869–1872*, E. E. Burke (ed.) (Salisbury, 1969), 215–18.
14. Aquina, 'Tribes in Victoria Reserve', 8–9.
15. M. Read, *The Ngoni of Nyasaland* (London), 8–9.
16. H. von Sicard, 'The Dumbuseya', *NADA*, Ix, 5 (1968), 22–3, describes this, but wrongly assumes Zwangendaba to be the 'Swazi' leader. A much more accurate account by W. M. Thomas in 1906 (National Archives of Rhodesia, A 3/18/28, N. C. Insize to C.N.C. Bulawayo, 16 May 1906) identified 'Masesenyana', who was in turn identified as Ngwana Maseko * G. J. Liesegang, 'Nguni migration between Delagoa

R. Summers, 'Ancient Mining in Rhodesia', *Natn. Mus. Rhod. Mem. 3* (1969), 218.

Bay and the Zambezi, 1821–1839', *African Historical Studies,* III, 2 (1970), 319.

17. *Mauch,* 186. This information regarding oral tradition has been supplied by D. N. Beach.

18. Summers, *Ancient Mining,* 126.

19. T. N. Huffman, 'Excavations at Leopard's Kopje Main Kraal: A preliminary report', *S. Afr. Archaeol. Bull.* xxvI (1971), 495–513.

20. Y-135–17, a.d. 1050±65 (Bambandyanalo) and SR-134, a.d. 1090±95 (Mawala Hill).

21. Garlake, 'Rhodesian ruins', 504.

22. M–914, a.d. 1085 ± 150, Robinson, op. cit. 191.

23. P. S. Garlake, 'New Rhodesian Iron Age radio-carbon dates', *Khodesian Prehistory,* 111 (1969), 8.

24. Summers, op. cit. 126.

25. P. S. Garlake, 'Test excavations at Mapela Hill, near the Shashi River, Rhodesia', *Arnoldia, Rhod.* III, 34 (1968), 1–29.

26. Summers, *Ancient Mining,* 124 → D. W. Phillipson and B. M. Fagan 'The date of the Ingombe Ilede burials', *J. Afr. Hist.* x, 2 (1969), 199–204.

27. Abraham, 'History of Mwene Mutapa', 61–2.

28. Garlake, 'Rhodesian ruins', 507. All of the Later Iron Age ceramic traditions share many attributes, and it is possible that they had a common ancestor. But it is a complete misunderstanding of ceramic typology to consider Zimbabwe Class 2 as part of the Leopard's Kopje tradition or to have derived from it.

29. M. C. Webb, 'Carneiro's hypothesis of limited land resources and the origins of the state; a Latin Americanist's approach to an old problem', *S East. Latin Amst.* xII, 3 (1968), 1–8.

30. R. L. Carneiro, 'Slash-and-burn cultivation among the Kuikuru and its implications for cultural developments in the Amazon basin', in Y. A. Cohen (ed.), *Man in Adaptation: The Cultural Present* (Chicago: Aldine, 1968), 131–45. Webb, 'Carneiro's hypothesis'.

31. 'Description of the situations, customs and produce of some places of Africa (*c.* 1518)', in *Documents on the Portuguese in Mozambique and Central Africa* (Lisbon: National Archives of Rhodesia and Centro de Estudos Historicos Ultramarinos, 1966), v, 373–81. 'Notes made by Gasper Veloso, clerk of the factory of Mozambique and to the King (*c.* 1512)', in *Documents,* III (1964), 181–9.

32. G. S. P. Freeman-Grenville, *The East African Coast—select documents from the first to the early 19th century* (Oxford: Clarendon Press, 1962), 14–17.

33. E. E. Burke, 'Some aspects of Arab contact with Southern Africa', in *Historians in Tropical Africa* (1962), 93–166.

34. Freeman-Grenville, 'Select documents', 23–4. Burke, 'Arab contact', 101.

35. Kindly identified by N. Chittick.

36. Freeman-Grenville, op. cit. 31.

37. N. Chittick, 'A new look at the history of Pate', *J. Afr. Hist.* x, 3 (1969), 375–91. 'Discoveries in the Lamu Archipelago', *Azania.* III (1069), 37–67.

38. Summers, *Ancient Mining,* 197–8.

39. T. N. Huffman, 'Cloth from the Iron Age in Rhodesia', *Arnoldia, Rhod.* v, 14 (1971), 15.

40. Robinson, 'Excavations on the Acropolis'.

41. J. F. Schofield, 'Southern African beads and their relation to the beads of Inyanga', in R. Summers, *Inyanga; Prehistoric Settlement in Southern Rhodesia* (Cambridge: University Press, 1959), Appendix 10, 180–229.

42. T. N. Huffman, unpublished field notes.

43. K. R. Robinson, 'Archaeology of the Rozvi', in E. Stokes and R. Brown (eds), *The Zambesian Past: Studies in Central African History* (Manchester: University Press, 1966), 3–27.

44. L. Fouché, *Mapungubwe, ancient Bantu civilization on the Limpopo* (Cambridge: University Press, 1937); G. A. Gardner, *Mapungubwe, Vol. 2* (Pretoria: Van Schaik, 1963).

45. B. M. Fagan, *Iron Age cultures in Zambia, Vol. 1* (London: Chatto & Windus, 1967).

46. Summers, *Ancient Mining,* 184–94.

47. Ibid. 119.

48. D. W. Phillipson and B. M. Fagan, 'The date of the Ingombe Ilede burials', 199–204.

49. Summers, op. cit. 134.

50. M. Gluckman, 'Economy of the Central Barotze plain', *Rhodes Livingstone Papers No. 7*; A. Smith, 'The trade of Delagoa Bay as a factor in Nguni politics, 1750–1835', in L. Thompson (ed.) *African Societies in Southern Africa* (New York: Praeger, 1969), 171–89.

51. Webb, 'Carneiro's hypothesis'.

52. E.g., Leopard's Kopje. K. R. Robinson, 'The Leopard's Kopje culture its position in the Iron Age of Southern Rhodesia,' *S. Afr. Archaeol. Bull.* XXI, 81 (1966), 26.

53. Garlake, 'Rhodesian ruins', 507–8.

54. Ibid. 507.

55. Abraham, 'History of the Mwene Mutapa', 62.

56. Ibid. 62.

57. D. P. Abraham, 'The Monomotapa dynasty', *NADA,* xxvi (1959), 59–84.

58. Previous drafts of this paper have benefited by comments from Dr D. N. Beach, Mr G. Bell-Cross, Mr C. K. Cooke, Miss P. Hobley, Mr M. A. Raath, and Mrs R. White.

VILLAGE PEOPLES OF THE GUINEA FOREST: THE IBO AND IBIBIO

By G. T. Stride and Caroline Ifeka

We now turn to the peoples who were the source of so many slaves for delta middlemen—the Ibo and Ibibio of the forest hinterland. Like the delta peoples the Ibo and Ibibio are organized into villages, and many of their institutions are similar to those of peoples in the low-lying swamps. But the inhabitants of the Guinea forest were spared the immediate impact which the overseas slave trade had on delta political organization. There, more centralized government was an important adaptation to internal changes stimulated by external forces. In the forest hinterland, however, the Ibo and Ibibio remained tenaciously attached to their village democracies, resisting any potential innovation which might deprive citizens of their right to share in decision-making. The political system of these communities is an outstanding example of participational democracy: every adult man has an inalienable right to voice his opinion on public affairs at the village assembly.

We know nothing of able leaders among the Ibo; we do not know of any great battles or political crises. The past of any people is often significant for reasons which distinguish that people from its neighbours. And so we consider the Ibo and Ibibio to be important for three reasons.

In the first place the way in which these forest dwellers orgnized their political life provides a fascinating point of comparison with the political organization of centralized states and empires. Secondly, the Ibo in particular had a complex network of trading routes which linked the separate settlements in which they lived. These trade routes and commercial contacts created bonds between settlements which might otherwise have lived in a state of semi-isolation. Thirdly, the remarkable role of the Arochuku group in the political, religious and economic life of the Ibo and Ibibio deserves detailed consideration. It was the Aro people of the middle Cross river who monopolized the slave-carrying trade to the city-states of the central and eastern Niger delta.

THE ORIGIN OF THE IBO AND IBIBIO

The Ibo have no weighty traditions of origin. Nevertheless, oral evidence and settlement patterns suggest that in about A.D. 1300 to 1400 Ibo began to move south and east from the region of Awka and Orlu. Later there seems to have been a second wave of migration to the eastern Isu Ama area around Orlu, and from there parties of migrants went to Aba, the Arochuku ridge, and other places.

The Ibibio believe either that they come from a place called Ibom, or that their ancestor is called Ibom. Early on Ibibio appear to have settled in the lands between Arochuku to the north, Ika to the west and Oron to the south. A second dispersal then took place from a centre around Abak and Uyo when the Ibibio separated into the Anang (western) and Ibibio (eastern) peoples. It is likely that the people who eventually became the Efik of Old Calabar originated in this second wave of migration.

POLITICAL ORGANIZATION

The Ibo and Ibibio were organized in a vast number of relatively small and independent villages. On account of their larger size, Ibo villages were often arranged into a group: that is, they formed a village group. So there were often two levels of political organization in Iboland: that of the village, and that of the village group.

The most characteristic part of Ibo country lies towards the centre around Orlu, Okigwi, Aba and Owerri. Here, among the southern Ibo, several villages were often joined together into a group by a mythical charter of common descent from a founding ancestor, whose sons were believed to have established the constituent villages of the group. In other words, territorial divisions were thought of as kinship units. All the lineages in a village were believed to have descended from one ancestor; it is this common descent which justified and validated the existence of the village. Kinship links were sometimes invoked to create special relationships with neighbouring village groups or villages. Owing to their close kinship ties the men of a village had to go outside to find their wives.

In southern Iboland, government was based on village and village group councils. The councils were composed of descent group heads each holding the *ofo* stick (the symbol of their descent group's ancestors), and other wealthy or influential men. One man who held the senior *ofo* of the village or village group was regarded as a titular 'father'. But he had no political powers other than those given to any elder.

The wider community

The village groups were, as we have seen, politically independent. But we need not jump to the conclusion that there were no links between different village groups. On the contrary, Ibo were loosely tied into a wider community than that of the village group and the various links between settlements were important for two reasons. Firstly, they show that the principal objective of government—the maintenance of law and order—can be achieved by other methods than those open to a centralized authority. Secondly, the loose ties between some groups help us to understand why it was that in the absence of centralized government Ibo country was not in a perpetual state of warfare, skirmishes, raids and the like.

One kind of link between villages and village groups arose out of the rule that men were obliged to marry outside their village. (Sometimes, as in the case of Owerri village group or town, men had to marry outside the group). Ibo men looked for wives from other villages in the group, and often from outside their village group. And so villages in a group, as well as neighbouring village groups, were linked by the bonds arising out of marriage alliances.

The second kind of link between Ibo groups arises out of the economic system. Because Ibo country lies inland, the people had to import salt and protein food like fish from the delta. Certain areas in north-eastern Iboland around Abakiliki produced a surplus of yams, which were exported to more populated regions in the vicinity of Awka, Orlu and Okigwi. It is very likely that this system of re-distributing food has been in operation for many centuries. Markets, large and small, sprang up to facilitate the re-distribution of goods. Different Ibo groups specialized in certain craft work, ritual services and the like so that itinerant traders, native doctors and priests covered many miles on their journeys. In this way traders and ritual specialists put village groups in touch with each other and created a wider community than that of the local settlement. Thus, economic organization was well developed before the hey-day of the slave trade in the eighteenth century. In fact local trade routes were used for the slave carrying trade, which probably developed speedily because there was already an established pattern of trading.

The third link is provided by the network of oracles: some of them were only of local significance, but some were nationally famous. Famous oracles were served by traders acting in the capacity of agents, who brought clients to the oracle from far-off village groups. And so a belief in the efficacy of supernatural judgements and sanctions was used to create an extensive religious community of priests and clients who hailed from different village groups.

ORACLES AMONG THE IBO

Oracles are shrines at which appeals can be made to a god. A priest, who acts as the god's mouthpiece, issues the god's judgement or opinion after offerings are made by clients. Ibo oracles secured the blessings of fertility to barren women and pronounced judgement on disputes.

Four oracles in Iboland became nationally renowned for their 'impartial' verdicts. They were the Agballa oracle at Awka, the Igweke Ala oracle at Umunora, the Amadioha oracle at Ozuzu and—most famous of all—the Ibini Okpabe or 'Long Juju' oracle at Arochuku.

It was believed that the farther away the oracle was from the disputants, the more chance there was of an impartial verdict. However, as G. I. Jones, an authority on the Ibo, Efik and Ijo, has pointed out, the effectiveness and therefore the fame of an oracle lay in its apparent ability to kill by supernatural means those disobeying its verdict. Generally such supernaturally caused deaths took the form of a lingering illness which was putdown to disobedience against the oracle.

The other way in which an oracle was effective was when it 'killed' disputants who invoked it falsely: a litigant who invoked an oracle falsely was believed to be the guilty party. Such offenders were said to be killed at once by the oracle, because they were never seen again. People saw trails of blood flowing out of the grove and this was taken to prove that the guilty party was dead. However, old informants told early British district officers that the Ibini Okpabe oracle priests at Arochuku used to sacrifice an animal whose blood was then seen flowing out from the grove. The litigant was hidden for a few days and later sold into slavery. It was in such a manner that 'justice' was done. Nevertheless, it is likely that on the whole litigants were so convinced of a famous oracle's powers that they would tell the truth. And so the final result may have been that innocence and guilt were correctly apportioned.

The Ibini Okpabe oracle at Arochuku

The Aro live on the west bank of the Cross river, near Itu. Tradition says that the Aro village group included people of non-Ibo descent. Aro tradition tells us that an Ibo settler rose up in revolt against his Ibibio landlord. The settler consulted an Ibo doctor friend, who arranged to invite some raiders of the Akpa (a tribe on the east bank of the Cross river) to fight the Ibibio residents. They were successful, but as one of the Akpa warriors was killed the Ibo settler was held responsible and he had to flee. However, the doctor made peace between the Akpa and the Ibo and, after swearing a covenant, they all lived happily ever after.

This myth is told by Aro to explain how it is that of the present nineteen villages in the group, seven claim descent from the Ibo doctor's son, six villages claim to be descended from the Akpa warriors and five derive from the Ibo settler. There are also some Ibibio elements in the village group. Today the senior living descendant of the Ibo doctor holds the title of Eze-Aro or chief of Aro.

Effective political power in the village group was in the hands of the elders who tried to keep the secrets of the oracle from being public knowledge. In this way the oracle helped the Aro to develop a greater sense of political direction and unity than existed elsewhere in Iboland.

The oracle at Arochuku (which means 'the voice of God') became the most famous of all Ibo oracles for several reasons. To begin with, Ibini Okpabe had the most efficient and prosperous network of agents known in Ibo country—the Aro middlemen who monopolized the slave trade and dealt in other valuable commodities. Secondly, whereas other oracles did not administer immediate 'justice', that at Arochuku did. Only one party survived. And so people respected and feared the oracle of the Aro's deity Chuku to the extent that kings of delta city-states brought cases to the oracle. Some historians, repeating the Aro myth, have alleged that the oracle's power lay in its ability to mobilize armed mercenaries from the Abam, Ada and Ohaffia groups near Arochuku. According to G. I. Jones this is not correct: Ibini Okpabe's fame and prestige lay in the deity's ability to apparently administer instant punishment by 'killing' the guilty party. The oracle was feared because people then believed that its supernatural sanctions were indeed a reality, and not because of its alleged power to organize mercenaries to crush the villages of disobedient clients. Armed with apparently effective supernatural powers to kill the guilty, the oracle had no need to mobilize mercenaries.

The third reason for Ibini Okpabe's fame was that the commercial and ritual activities of the Aro had a mutually reinforcing effect. Traders spread the name of the oracle to an increasing number of clients. It is said that, by the late eighteenth century, the Aro had prospered so much from commerce and the fees their middlemen received for providing safe passage to the deity that most people did not need to farm.

THE EXTENT OF THE ARO TRADING SYSTEM

We know all too little about the exact organization of trade in precolonial days. Nevertheless we do know that Iboland seems to have been carved up into spheres of commercial and religious influence. One village group would develop a monopoly of religious or commercial services over a wide but delimited area. Sometimes the same village group increased its dominance by possessing a well known oracle or priestcult, in which case economic influence was reinforced by religious authority. The Aro were the most famous Ibo religious and commercial traders of the hinterland. But there were other village groups too which made a lesser name for themselves.

A village group would specialize in one or two activities, its men travelling widely over a specific territory selling their services. In this way links were created between settlements. Priests from Nri, and blacksmiths from Awka, travelled between northern Ibo country and the river Niger; traders and blacksmiths from Nkwerri journeyed south as far as Ogoni; wood carvers and native doctors from Abiriba near Ibibio country worked in the Cross river area. The Aro trading system stretched as far west as Nri Awka and penetrated south over much of the central and eastern delta.

It does seem, though, that the Aro trading system penetrated little into other areas outside their sphere of influence. The Aro traded and inter-married with Ozo title holders at Awka, for example, but this seems to have been as far as they got in a westerly direction. Perhaps Aro and other groups made informal agreements to divide up their spheres of influence. Or, and perhaps this is more likely, Aro were prevented by sheer distance and problematical communications in the absence of navigable rivers from trading extensively in the Niger area.

Another area where the Aro did not come to monopolize commercial activities was that dominated by the kingdom of Aboh, which is situated where the Niger enters its delta. Aboh had become an important political unit by 1800 because of her strategic position on the Niger: she was able to control access to the more westerly parts of the slave-producing hinterland, and to the coastal ports of Nembe and Kalahari.

Before the slave trade provided the Aro with the chance of dominating the economy of the hinterland, there were rural markets and long-distance trading. Men travelled far to obtain horses and cows from the savanna, and salt and fish from the delta. With the growth of the overseas slave trade such markets as Uburu, Uzuakoli, Oguta and Bende rose to prominence as slave marts.

These markets served as a distribution centre for slaves, which were transported there by a variety of routes. For instance, slaves from northern Ibo country could be taken to Uburu market near Afikpo; from there they would be taken to Uzuakoli, which linked up with Bende to the south-east. At Bende, purveyors would hand slaves over to Aro middlemen, who then sold them to traders from Old Calabar and Bonny. The slaves were of northern origin or of Ibo stock; some Ibo slaves were captured during village raids, and others were sold into slavery to meet pressing indebtedness.

REASONS FOR ARO DOMINANCE IN THE HINTERLAND

How was it that the Aro, lacking centralized government and without a standing army (they just hired raiding parties from the Abam, Ada and Ohaffia), had managed by the nineteenth century to dominate the hinterland both religiously and economically? It is impossible to give a precise answer owing to insufficient factual information. But the following factors appear to be relevant in explaining why the Aro achieved such influence.

The Aro were favourably situated on the Cross river so they had a ready-made communications system. Given a readiness to exploit the demand by coastal city-states for slaves, the Aro could control their immediate section of the Cross river. However, this factor alone does not explain their economic dominance because other peoples on the Cross river also had this geographical advantage.

A second factor of much more significance is that the Aro had cultural and ethnic links with sections of the Ibibio, Ibeku Ibo, the Akpa people of the Cross river, and the Enyong Ibibio. Endowed with a natural talent for salesmanship, possessing an oracle that dealt with judicial and fertility difficulties, and encouraged by the development of the overseas slave trade in the eighteenth century, the Aro exploited these links with other peoples to further their commercial interests. According to G. I. Jones, the Aro used their links with the Ibeku Ibo of the Umuahia area to penetrate south to Ndokki country, where the New Calabar and Imo rivers link the hinterland with the city-states of Bonny and Kalahari. The Ibibio elements in Aro helped her traders to travel in southern Ibibio country, while the Akpa element provided contacts in Obubra and the Cross river area. The Enyong people, who border Arochuku and were a part of the Ibibio group that became the Efik people of Old Calabar, enabled Aro middlemen to trade with this city-state.

Armed with these vital contacts, which provided safe trade routes, the Aro were able to offer slaves for sale to whichever state offered the highest prices. The Aro played off Kalahari traders against merchants from Old Calabar, and even managed to obtain higher prices for slaves in the Nri-Awka markets than other traders. And so during the eighteenth century the Aro obtained a monopoly on supplying slaves by applying their shrewd business sense to exploit their contacts with other peoples.

However, a third factor also contributed to Aro dominance. Acting as commercial intermediaries, they purchased the services of eager warriors from their neighbours—the Ada, Abam and Ohaffia peoples—from time to time. Aro used these warriors to get hold of more slaves, and to defend waterways or nearby trading routes if the need arose.

Fourthly, such activities were bound to have cumulative results. Although the Aro trading system appears to have emerged later than that of, for example, Nri Awka, Aro people seem to have accumulated wealth quite rapidly. Once middlemen had obtained enough capital from their trading and religious activities, some of them engaged in other enterprises which extended Aro influence yet again. Some Aro settled down at key villages on trading routes. These new settlements became politically independent of Arochuku, but they increased Aro contacts with the local population through intermarriage. Aro settlers also booked orders from local people who wanted commercial goods or religious services, and passed them on to itinerant traders from Arochuku. Such new settlements as Ujalli or Ndizorgu helped to increase and strengthen the Aro trading network. If a local man needed a loan, an Aro settler would arrange for it to be provided by one of his relatives. The debtor could repay in kind by providing his Aro creditor with an unwanted kinsman to be sold as a slave.

Finally, the Aro's hold over trade between the coast and the hinterland became so strong that they virtually monopolized the supply of guns and shot in the interior. Aro used this highly convenient monopoly to supply raiders from Abam, Ada and Ohaffia with weapons. Warriors from these groups were then better equipped for slave raiding on behalf of the Aro, who paid them for doing this job, and for conducting raids on villages that clients wanted to punish. If a village wanted to humiliate another, representatives would approach an Aro agent. The agent then arranged, for a fee, to purchase a raiding party of Abam or Ohaffia warriors to do the job. Aro agents guided the warriors to the chosen village; when it was sacked, the same agents led the party of raiders back to Abam or Ohaffia country.

These, then, are the factors which could explain the economic and religious influence of Aro in the hinterland by the nineteenth century. But as Aro dominance during this period was much increased as a result of opportunities presented by the slave trade, it seems appropriate to end with a quotation from a book which tells us about the terrible shock and personal disaster experienced by people unfortunate enough to be enslaved.

Olaudah Equiano, an Ibo from near Onitsha, was born in about 1745. He told the story of how he was kidnapped by three strangers in his book, *The Interesting Narrative of the Life of Olaudah Equiano or Gustavus the African*. He wrote: 'My father, besides many slaves, had a numerous family of which seven lived to grow up, including myself and a sister. … One day, when all our people were gone to their works as usual and only I and my dear sister were left to mind the house, two men and a woman got over our walls, and in a moment seized us both, and without giving us time to cry out or make resistance they stopped our mouths and ran off with us into the nearest wood'.

QUESTIONS

1. Write short notes on the Ibo and Ibibio traditions of origin. Why do we know so little about the history of the Ibo people?

2. Examine the political organization of villages and village groups among the southern Ibo and explain how Ibo villages were linked to other village groups.

3. What was the role of oracles in Ibo society and why were they politically important? Discuss the reasons for the pre-eminent position of the Arochuku oracle.

4. Give an account of the Aro trading system. What is the 'Aromyth' and why is it important in Aro history?

5. Examine the factors which you think explain the economic and religious dominance of the Aro in the hinterland by the nineteenth century.

6. Write briefly on each of the following: (a) the organization of trade and markets among the Ibo: (b) democracy among the southern Ibo.

SOCIAL INSTITUTIONS: KINSHIP SYSTEMS

BY AUSTIN M. AHANOTU

DEFINITIONS

Many scholars of African social life,[1] in their formal analysis of kinship systems, have assumed the primacy of kinship as an organizing principle in preindustrial African societies. This corpus of information on African kinship generally agrees that kinship is a set of relations existing at a given moment in time which link together a number of people. Certain things emerge in the context of these relations between individuals. Social actions come out of kinship ideology, cultural behavior also comes out of kinship ideology, and, in political terms, hierarchy and political esteem are among the projects of kinship construction. Societies act in pursuit of ends, a process that involves allocation of resources within the scheme of value judgements.

During the last fifty years, the study of structures and of kinship structures in particular has been most rewarding. As African historians, we have a greater need to borrow and incorporate the findings of other disciplines and little preoccupation with maintaining sacred and impermeable interdisciplinary boundaries. Yet, as historians, we have to insist that structure and history account for each other. To neglect either one is perilous. We must keep both in sight.

All kinship is based ultimately upon relationships of consanguinity and affinity (blood and marriage), or so the argument goes (see Fig. 3–1). But each African society has stressed some genealogical links and ignored others. This process of selection gives each kinship system a distinctive shape or form. All the differentiations must be related pragmatically to the historical development of the society. African kinship concepts, then, have not stood alone, but have to be understood

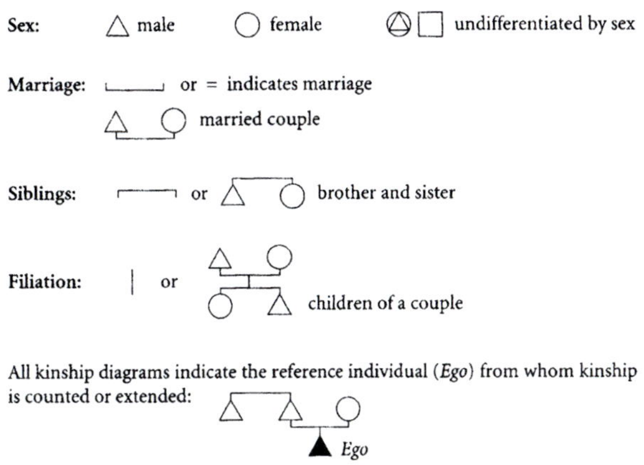

Figure 3–1. Kinship Signs

in their multitudinous relations with class and other bases of social differentiation. We can safely say that in African societies before outside interventions, kinship was often the most embracing or privileged mode of social relationship. The history of each lineage was grounded in common ancestry and this became the glue that held them together. The basic objective of the kinship ideology was to enhance the survivability of the kinship group and its physical residence. Igor Kopykoff's assertion reflects the inner core of kinship ideology:

> Traditionally, African kin groups had an almost insatiable demand for people and jealously guarded those they already had. Socially, this meant the existence of corporate groups of kinsmen, collectively holding resources, carefully enforcing their rights in membership ... every newborn was legally spoken for and eagerly appropriated at birth by one or another autonomous kin group ... similarly, the reproductive capacity of every woman was a resource to be appropriated at birth ... Culturally, all this had produced a variety of elaborations of systems of rights in person, so that these appropriations could be accomplished unambiguously, flexibly and with minimum of conflict.[2]

Kinship gave the individual full personhood. This is best reflected in a Yoruba proverb that says: "Ebi eni l'aso eni (your extended family members act as your closest apparel)." Scarification (ila) in Yorubaland was thus kinship protection which said if an individual ever got lost they would find him. Other social networks, for example, age groups, secret societies, and guilds, which were in abundance in African history, in certain cases supplemented kinship.

Various circumstances triggered different forms of family and kinship systems. Family and kinship ideologies were influenced by group history. Shared ancestry—the common beginning and separate histories of kin and family—was affected by economic forces, migrations, and internal tensions. There were attempts by individuals or the group to recreate and manipulate family and kinship ties to promote social order. We need to ask why African lineages responded to family matters in the way they did. History was largely the story of family relationships. Families interacted with each other. To cope with such interactions, various methods were used.

Rights and duties defined boundaries within which family members were expected to confine their behavior. A great deal of social learning in African societies was about one's duties to others and the situations in which these duties were owed.

Two questions need to be addressed as we explore the idea of kinship: Who are my relatives—how is it that an African comes to be a kinsman or kinswoman? What do my relatives and I have to do with each other? Each African group came up with answers from its own historical experience. Thus, there were great variations in who qualified as a relative, in the things relatives were expected to do, and in the relatives that a given individual or group felt closest to. Kinship is a social convention. It is biological, but the biology is filtered through value systems and social usage.

KINSHIP CLASSIFICATION: PATRILINEAL AND MATRILINEAL DESCENT

Kinship can be classified into different categories (see Fig. 3–2). A descent group (i.e., lineage) emerges when the membership of a kinship group has grown beyond one generation. The type of descent varies from one society to another. Many African societies reckoned descent through the male-father line, a system known as patrilineal. Others reckoned relationships through the female line, a system that is described as uterine or matrilineal. In a few others, stress is put on neither patrilineal nor matrilineal; both are given equal importance. This arrangement is known as bilateral. For societies such as the San, Twi, and Kanuri, the double unilineal descent (in which access to high office was based on blood lineage) was preferred.

African societies that reckoned descent unilineally had a marked preference for patrilineal descent. Matrilineal descent occurred in societies such as the Asante, Bemba, Tonga, and Tuareg. In Asante, for example, the abusua—the matrilineage—traced relationships in the female line. The abusua united by common blood (mogya) which was passed from women to their children. The village where the abusua members lived was headed by a senior man or elder (*abusua panin*) and a senior woman (*obaa panin*).

The location of women after marriage was very important. So long as women left their families (and often their communities as well) to marry, they were considered lost to other descent groups in many systems where residence was patrilocal.

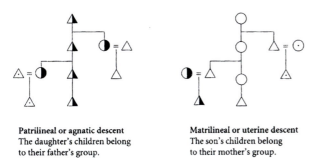

Patrilineal or agnatic descent
The daughter's children belong
to their father's group.

Matrilineal or uterine descent
The son's children belong
to their mother's group.

Figure 3–2. Unilineal Descent

In a matrilineal system, avunculocal residence (i.e., the bride and groom moved to settle with the bride's mother's brother—the maternal uncle) was the common practice. In the case of the Asante, residence was duolocal/natolocal, that is, the bride could stay with her matrilineal relatives and the groom with his matrilineal relatives.

KINSHIP OBLIGATIONS

The hunting and gathering period in Africa was a very challenging time.[4] Survival in the precarious environment of this period required cooperation. Forms of solidarity approximating to kinship developed. Prehistoric artists showed us this sense of solidarity in their rock paintings. In these paintings we see man the hunter, parents, families, and woman the gatherer, but more importantly, the band and community. With the emergence of agriculture came a more differentiated and complex human organization and a recognized inventory of rights and obligations. The basis for this was human relationships with others through *birth, marriage,* or *fictional* kinship. In each of these categories, the obligations of kinship were formalized.

The emotional side of kinship was reflected in individual's ties of affection, creating a feeling of belonging to a group in which membership was unquestioned. Studies of the kinship ideology of different African societies have shown that the sentimental attachment to families and kinsmen came out of the reinforcement of *love, respect, protection,* and *identity.* Even though kinship relationships were in creative tension, a heavy emphasis on family pedigree persisted. The kinship group had certain natural limits, such as the limitations of remembered history. Class formation was not in competition with kinship. Large kinship groupings usually went along with wealth and power.

Keeping track of kinship relations and connections was essential. To know the names and relationships of many people was no mean feat. Africans knew that kinship relations had a real existence only if the relationship was reinforced by continued contact. This led to the following: (a) *visitations*—such as social calls, home visits, and market-day meetings to discuss issues of common concern; (b) *festivities*—important social occasions like naming ceremonies, weddings, and funerals; and (c) *obligations* to help a kinsman. When seen as an issue of obligations and expectations, kinsmen were naturally divided into two categories of persons: beneficiaries and providers, that is to say, takers and givers. The obligations of kinship in most cases were formalized. There were those who benefited from kinship and those who were expected to make sacrifices for others. This tended to define the arena of tension in kinship ideology. Disposal of property, for example, was rarely simple. Claims and duties were summed up in the property relations internal to the family and kinship ideology, and at marriage certain rights were exchanged. The dynamics of property shaped the range of relationships. A hierarchy of power distribution appeared and, in most cases, it favored the African male. Thus patriarchal authority was the norm in the majority of African societies. Family and kinship structures became carriers of patriarchy. The hierarchical model of social order was heavily implicated in questions of marriage, domestic life, sexuality, and work.

There were dominants and dependents in the social ideology of kinship relations. Kinship ideology helped to produce patriarchy. It was the contrivance of the elders, who benefited from it. The particular cultural traits of eldership were mediated by local considerations and regional inclinations. In some areas eldership was diluted, but the social structure remained exploitative. Many African activities, values, attitudes, and beliefs were anchored to eldership. The institution of the "elders" was one form of political contract and social arrangement.

THE NUCLEAR FAMILY AND THE ROLE OF ELDERS

The primary institution at the core of the labor force was the nuclear family. The nuclear family (i.e., a family incorporating a husband, his wife, and their children) was the basic building block for kinship systems. The matricentric unit (i.e., a mother and her children—the Igbo *umunne otu afo* [children of the same womb]), a farming and eating unit, could also be central in the labor force. But the *umunna* patricentric unit was crucial. Membership in this extended family, which the Igbo called *umunna* (children of the same father, and in a historical and political sense, descended from a common ancestor), was not optional but compulsory. The elder was crucial both in the nuclear family and in the extended family. He is the eldest living male descendant of the eldest son of the original founder of the lineage. The Igbo called him *Opara* or *Okpara*. He performed all rituals demanded by custom. It was he who held the staff *ofo* that personified truth and justice. He was at the center of family contractual arrangements. He was expected to provide structure, permanence, and continuity in family social life. The elder male thus provided the environment in which nuclear and extended families obeyed the precepts of the elders and behaved with relative decorum. Everything stemmed from the elder. In principle all powers of decision and all material resources belonged to him. He had a religious duty to ensure the survival of the kinship system. He officiated at the family shrine, and when he died he became an ancestor.

The eldest man in the patrilineal nuclear family instructed the members in the ways of loyalty and obedience. He was held responsible for his family and he was expected to keep its members within bounds, to insist upon conforming to customs, laws, and traditional observances of the kin group. He controlled the means of production and access to women, and hence political power within the kin group was in part based on gerontocracy. It was he who administered the family oath which was based on the vital potency of the ancestors. He assigned living quarters within the compound and made sacrifices to the founding ancestor of the compound. In brief, he maintained peace. The Yoruba word *bale* does not just mean "father" but "father of the house." The *bale* was the transmitter of kinship solidarity, and his job was to lead and instruct. He was distinguished by his wisdom. He was expected to be versed in folk lore, ancestral theology, and the veneration of family and kinship relics.

Although the elder held a special status, it was not a status of unqualified superiority. In some ways, he might be overruled by the council of elders, or the chief, or the king. To help the elder, other authority figures such as senior wives and oldest first daughters were put in place.[5] Senior wives were also important in the affairs of the women in the kin group, thus the *Iyale*, the senior wife in Yoruba communities, was addressed as "the mother of the house." For the Igbo, the oldest first daughters (*umuada*) who had married out of the kin group played important roles in peacemaking in their original kin group when needed. The point, then, is that the ideology of eldership was not the total picture but just part of the total system of taking care of the "children of the compound" or "house."

For a long time, Africans believed in the idea of the extended family as reflecting the continuity that bound various generations and nuclear families through lineal or horizontal networks of affinity (see Fig. 3–3). It was a cultural trait marked by geographic propinquity and the authority of the presiding elders over the component nuclear families. It was given resources and territory, power, status, and prestige. To facilitate the functions intended for extended families, African cultural innovators such as elders, titled men and women, and ritual leaders, intended the members of the extended family to have rights with respect to one another; at any given time depending on the political, economic, and social conditions of the time, these reciprocal rights could be active or dormant. Each person and each nuclear family became an actor playing roles in the network of relationships dictated by the moral sanctions of the extended family. The codes governing extended family relationships could not be avoided, ignored or forgotten without repercussions.

The moral pretexts of extended family ideology were not static. They were constantly reinterpreted, extended into the realm of the symbolic, and constituted a kind of discourse held by members of a nuclear family. There was a dialectic between practice and ideology. The way the idea of the extended family was

articulated or translated into practice was a negotiated process. This, at times, could even contradict the idea of the extended family itself. The extended family offered a wide network of security, but it also imposed the burden of extensive obligations. Victor Uchendu declared that "Ezin'ulo" (the Igbo extended family ideology) "is not just a bundle of material cultural traits, it is a people united by a bond of kin network and interlocking functions and reciprocities."[6]

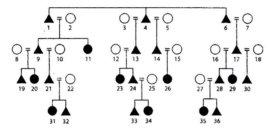

Extended families showing division into lineage members (dark) and wives who come from other lineages (uncolored)

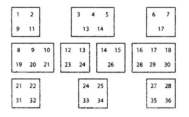

Extended family divided into separate conjugal families

▲ male member of the patrilineal core of the extended family
● female member of the patrilineal core of the extended family
○ "Wives of the Compound" (wives who marry in from other lineages)

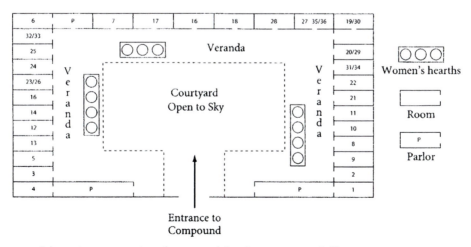

Entrance to Compound

Schematic representation of compound showing rooms occupied by members of extended family shown in kinship diagram above

Figure 3–3. Family Compound

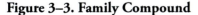

The notion of ancestral lineage singles out marriage as critical in one's life. The kinship groups constituted, formulated, and accounted for the continuance of the lineage. All African adults were expected to marry. Marriage built meaningful and enduring ties between families and kin groups. Marriage, in this sense, increased the "social capital" of the joined lineages. In African parlance, marriage created networks with social linkages and implied societal responsibilities. Since marriages were expected to strengthen families as corporate units, such issues as love, monogamy, plural marriages—polygyny and "female husbands" (literally a female master who contracted a form of marriage in which if she was barren and could afford it paid a dowry for another woman for her husband and any children from this arrangement would be regarded as the children of the barren woman for the purpose of representation in respect to estates and inheritances)—sex roles, and divorce, family and gender expectations should be seen within the context of the vested interest of the corporate group. In practical terms, for Africans, it was well-nigh impossible to get along without being married. Marriage made it possible to do the work that had to be done every day, and at least in theory only married people had a legitimate right to sexual relations.

African marriages seem to have taken varied forms: child betrothal or marriage by promise; marriage by abduction or consensual union; leviratic marriages in which a dead husband's wife or wives would be inherited by his younger brother or another family member; bride service marriage in which a wife was acquired by the prospective husband through his labor for his in-laws; marriage by exchange in which if you give someone your sister, one gives his sister in return; marriage by reimbursement in which a kinship group was expected to give a woman after taking one from another group; and finally bridewealth marriage. This means marriages for which the families arranged beforehand the amount, the composition, and payment schedule for what some call the "price of the fiancée." But it should be stressed that bridewealth carries no connotation of sale. The bridewealth paid was strongly regarded as a reflection of the honor, beauty, and righteousness of the bride, and the reputation of her natal family. Bridewealth partially determined the survivability of a marriage. Divorce, for example, was more likely to occur when fewer yams or cattle were paid. Bridewealth marriages were the most common form of marriage.

The paying and collection of bridewealth and its handing over to the bride's family was a group responsibility. This helped maintain interrelationships among lineage members. But a European observer of Igbo bridewealth in the 1920s noted the social and economic consequences of the practice:

> Young men find it extremely difficult to raise the ever-increasing prices now demanded, and they must either postpone marriage until well advanced in years, or contract loans. Grave evils arise from the latter course, for a man may be burdened by the incubus of debts incurred in connection with his marriage which will cripple him financially through his life … on the other hand, girls will not wait an indefinite period. Faced with almost insurmountable obstacles, the young people are much more readily disposed to cohabit without marriage.[7]

Basden, the observer, was stating the impact of capitalism on Igbo marriages when the practice of sharing the responsibility of paying the bridewealth was diminishing as well as the inability of the men in paying the bridewealth.

It is true that marriage starts a family, but a lot has to happen before marriage occurs. The members of kin groups knew that once the marriage topic was on the table it became the concern of all the kinsmen. The fortunes of the kinship group were at stake. The kin group found wives for the young men, and disposed of the girls in marriage to the advantage of the family and the kin group. Parental approval was imperative before a girl was given out for marriage, although go-betweens or marriage brokers could be used. These go-betweens were usually women because they were familiar with the behavior of the maidens. The behavior of the maiden was essential to the family of the groom. The go-betweens were those who knew the types of behavior that produce good or bad marriages. Although it was assumed that all marriages were arranged for reasons of family advantage and custom, marriage was not a cold transaction devoid of love and romance. Everyone looked out for "good" marriages. African social life, however, provided many social occasions for unmarried people to socialize and get to know each other. Public events like festivals and village market days provided such occasions, but most of the time older people were present. These occasions were opportunities to look, talk, and touch, but all were aware that the loss of virginity was considered a disaster. Mothers of girls understood that the reputation of their family was deeply involved in their daughters' premarital chastity. They did everything to maintain their daughters' chastity and to avoid scandals.

Premarital virginity was important, but good behavior and hard work were also required. With regards to premarital virginity and sexuality, customs ranged from those of the Azande of the Sudan, who permitted sexual intercourse for unmarried boys and girls (to them the attainment of physical maturity was assumed to depend upon an active sexual life), to those of the Ethiopian Kafa who, if a male had sexual intercourse with an unmarried female, might have his head or hands cut off. He was also required to pay a fine of two cows to the young woman's father and to the emperor. The girl was not punished, although she might subsequently have trouble finding a man who would marry her.[8]

It also appears that women who were voluptuous were greatly admired. The Igbo referred to *ahunwa*—a body full of children. It was no wonder, therefore, that marriage invariably carried with it the expectation of children. Childless marriages were likely to have grave repercussions, as we shall see in the section subtitled *Children*. The background of the proposed spouse was properly investigated to ensure that the rule of endogamy, and the rule which separated people (for example among the Igbo, the *osu*, ritual

slaves, from the *diala*, freeborn were not broken; and that no incestuous relationship was entered into.

Marriage was a serious business, and arranging marriages was an important and time-consuming activity. Parents of the couples to-be were expected to inform you and notify the elders of the lineage about the forthcoming initiation of the marriage transaction. These elders were attentive to, and major witnesses to, all the steps in the process. The presence of these elders and their participation would subsequently legitimize the marriage. The prospective husband was expected to satisfy the demands of the women from the bride's kin group, but more importantly to satisfy the demands of the mother of the bride. The corporate significance of marriage was reflected in the fact that, whatever the details of kinship, most traditional African marriages were contracted as agreements between lineages. Yet the parental role was very important. In the eighteenth century, the traveller Mungo Park wrote about the Mande of present-day Mali:

> … [i]f the parents agree to the [match] and eat a few kola nuts, which are presented by the suitor as an earnest of the bargain, the young lady must either have the man of their choice, or continue unmarried for she cannot afterwards be given to another.[9]

Various rites and ceremonies were used to establish the legality of marriage. Drinks and kolanuts are mentioned in many accounts of the marriage process. Victor Uchendu, the Igbo cultural scholar writing in 1965, stated:

> Before the father takes the bride wealth, he gives his daughter a cup of palm liquor and asks her to show her husband to the audience by giving him the liquor. The shy girl walks with faltering steps to her husband, sips the liquor and as she gives it to him, tells her shouting audience: "this is my husband. Father may take the bride-wealth."[10]

Describing the same situation among the Asante of Ghana, Meyer Fortes observed:

> The decisive formality for the establishment of a legal marriage is the giving of the "tirinsa" the head wine which Ashanti describe as a thanking gift (aseda) most commonly this consists of two bottles of gin or an agreed equivalent in cash. It is handed over on behalf of the husband by the head of his lineage to the head of the bride's lineage through her legal guardian in the presence of the representatives of both groups ... the payment of tirinsa gives the husband exclusive sexual rights over his wifeand the legal paternity of all children born to her while the marriage lasts ... tiri nsa may be paid before or at any time after the couple begin to cohabit.[11]

In these observations, drinks and kolanuts were mentioned. Drinks, especially palm wine, were poured on the ground as a libation or as a "blessing ceremony," during which elders from both the bride's and the groom's sides would pray to their ancestors. In many West African societies, such as Igbo, kolanuts symbolized unity, blessing, peace, and long life. The symbolic significance of palm-wine and kolanuts as markers to indicate the date of celebration of marriage could be revealed in the question: "In what month and year did your husband give the drink or the kola for the marriage?" This symbolism of kolanut and palm-wine rites appears to distinguish marriage that the kin groups recognize as legitimate from those that are not.[12]

Marriages were expected to be permanent and wives were expected to be faithful. The rituals of the Gusii in Kenya tended to reinforce these expectations. Here, the women underwent an elaborate wedding ritual (*enyangi*). This was a life-long bond to the husband who gave bridewealth for her. Iron ankle rings were then given to the married woman after another ritual (*ebitinge*) was performed.[13]

The process of contracting marriages involved meetings of whole delegations of kin groups, preceded by exploratory contacts made by family go-betweens, in formal and public circumstances. Gifts were exchanged. The quantity and quality of the gifts depended on the items valued in a given kinship group. Cattle could be held in trust by the family for the marriages of their sons. The main bride wealth payment in such societies vary according to the wealth in cattle at any given time. Among the pastoral peoples of Africa:

> the man-cattle cycle is uninterrupted. Girls marry and bring more cattle into the family. When boys marry, the family loses cattle, but these sons' wives will eventually have more girls who will bring more cattle into the family again ... the more wives a person has, the more cattle—thus wealth—it is assumed he also has.[14]

Cattle were widely distributed through the bridewealth system. This same bridewealth custom of cattle exchange was so hedged about with rules and prejudice that the Tutsi in Ruanda made intermarriage difficult and prevented Bairu and Bahatu from becoming cattle owners. Among the forest peoples of Nigeria, yams and livestock were exchanged. Gift-giving was one of the most important modes of social exchange in Africa. One was obligated to give and take gifts. It was believed that gift-giving created and strengthened social kinship bonds. The cultural rules that governed gift-giving were extended to weddings and marriages, burials and funerals, ancestral rites, child naming, childbirth, mutual visitation between relatives, coronations, and agricultural ritual festivities. Market days were times of gift exchanges. Grandmothers, although aged, took time to visit their grandchildren on market days with gifts of foodstuffs. Reciprocity was regarded as a way to distinguish kin from non-kin. African gift-giving was also designed to maintain the social equilibrium between potentially conflicting kin groups. Prestige items such as cattle, metal bars, and bags of cowries or money currency were also exchanged as gifts. It is important to emphasize this culture of gift-giving and exchange in Africa because it was that which bound the kinship together, whether in marriages, personal relations or family-lineage, social and political life.

Far from being a market situation or "bride purchase," the payment of bridewealth was a form of compensation to the bride's kin group for the "loss" of a daughter and her procreative capacities. The marriage contract involved gift giving that at times might continue even after the bridewealth had been paid. Symbolic acts demonstrated that one was always indebted to one's in-laws. Elaborate reciprocal exchanges of visits and services between the families of the groom and the bride continued even after the marriage had been sealed. Felicia Ekejuba has reminded us that bridewealth was a symbolic compensation for the transfer of the sexual and other services of the bride from her family to that of the groom. "These payments," she continues, "also legitimatized the marriage and defined the membership of the offspring in the patrilineal of the groom."[15]

POLYGYNY

Successful African farmers, traders and political leaders tended to enter into polygynous marriages. Their continued success, they believed, was dependent on the number of wives they had. Agricultural societies such as those in Africa encouraged the practice of polygyny. The number of units of agricultural production would increase as more wives were brought into the household. Wives, then, acted as a safeguard for more labor. In some parts of West Africa, polygyny was an element of social prestige, but in some areas of South Africa there was no particular barrier to a commoner becoming wealthy in stock and wives, so that the margin favoring the prominent person was not always wide. Writing about the Xhosa, a missionary observed that they had chiefs who took four or five wives.[16]

Polygyny served as a socially accepted alternative to post-partum abstinence. In some societies, for example, it was viewed as an abomination for the

wife to meet her husband sexually during the long period (3–4 years) of lactation. We can assume that polygyny was an accepted, honorable and respected form of marriage. G.T. Basden, a missionary in Igboland in the 1920s, observed that:

> A man who is able to multiply his wives rises automatically to social scale. They largely constitute his working capital. Every fresh outlay for the prevision of an additional wife is looked upon as a shrewd investment ... polygyny to pristine Ibo is a worthy institution.[17]

Yet, another observer in the early twentieth century speculated that only about twenty-five percent of Igbo men were polygynous.[18] In general, however, it appeared that polygyny was a desirable form of marriage. Through polygyny, among patrilineal peoples, it was reasoned that a man could produce many sons to avoid the extinction of his name. Daughters from such marriages would also enrich the man through the acquisition of bridewealth. This would then enable him to pay bridewealth for his sons and even acquire more wives himself. The additional wives and children would further elevate his social status.

Though marriage was encouraged, in some societies sources of tension and potential cleavage appeared between the governing elders and the young men. In these societies the elders maintained tight, even oppressive, control over the younger men, monopolizing both women and cattle and thus delaying marriage and economic independence for the young. In such cases the young men occasionally migrated to escape their frustrations.[19]

CHILDREN

Marriage was only the beginning, not the whole story. The wife or wives were expected to have children. There was an abhorrence of childlessness. It was this abhorrence that encouraged the practice of a sororate system, whereby a barren woman's sister was given in marriage to the husband to procreate "on her behalf." Parenthood was always respected. Childbearing for both men and women created lifelong ties, linking kin groups into networks that were important to social and political life. An African proverb has it that: "The clan that is great in number is also great in strength." In songs and folklore, to be barren was lamented. Bethwell Ogot, an East African historian, reflected this in his reproduction of a Padhola song:

Eee one child is not enough, One child is inadequate, Eee, when the war drum sounds "tindi! tindi!" Who will come to your rescue—one child?[20]

Through her fertility, a married woman contributed to the growth of her husband's kin group. The Dinka position in these matters is aptly presented:

A Dinka man's desire for more wives and more children is predicated upon knowledge that many children will not reach adulthood, so a large number are required to assure perpetuation of the family line (a major concern based partially on beliefs that it is possible to communicate with spirits of their ancestors). Also since grown children are expected to take care of the parents in old age, children are the only "pension scheme" available. In the interval children ensure the labor force essential to care for the cattle and other livestock.[21]

All daughters hoped to get married and, more importantly, become mothers. Daughters and wives became defined by motherhood. Men and husbands were proud of their wife or wives when childbirth occurred. Those from patrilineal systems expected their wives to produce especially male children. The value of sons tended to center on their obligations to the kin group and nuclear and extended families. A woman left her natal home and was only truly accepted in her new family upon the production of

a male child. The ritual significance of sons to the family and to women was immense. Efforts at promoting fertility, rather than limiting it, dominated people's thoughts. It was not unusual for wars to be fought for the purpose of capturing women as booty so that they would in turn give birth to children to increase the size of the kin group.[22] The notion of continuity through children became a central theme in life. The ancestral geneology had to be continued. Fertility rites, ritual intercourse, and the use of fertility charms and folklore and other artistic expressions were crafted into the ideology of family procreation. African families were aware of the grim facts—stillbirths and deaths due to parturition, disease, famine, and warfare (this last especially during the wars that produced Africans for the Atlantic slave trade). All these took their toll. Infant mortality was high.

Childbirth in Africa was reserved to the world of women. Fathers were seldom participants in childbirth. But they were known to help if husband and wife were alone on the farm and the wife delivered a child. A male diviner might be called in to assist in difficult births. Both women largely depended on other women for advice about conception, pregnancy, and birth. The African midwife ritually and practically asked for a safe delivery. Mothers-in-law played a very crucial role in delivery and in what the Igbo called *omugwo* (the period of celebration of the new birth). African child mortality rates were high, so survival was a major concern during the early years. Thus, African women's high fertility may well have been based on the assumption that one could never have too many children. African husbands and wives voiced no concern over being burdened with too many children, though many complained when they had all girls or twins. African societies such as the Yoruba honor twins, but to some Africans, such as the Igbo and Efik, twin children were considered an aberration. They were thrown into the forest where they were left to starve or be ravaged by wild animals. A mother of twin children, in this case, had to go through a cleansing ritual to drive off the evil that had possessed her body. But other African groups honored twin children. In general, children were a source of labor, represented social continuity, provided risk insurance, and provided a large sibling group in which children socialized with each other. In practical terms children had three obligations to their parents: they must give them grandchildren, support them in old age, and perform ritual respect to them after death.

The productivity of children, whether actual or ritual, guaranteed that after death parents would be properly commemorated. The Nuer and Zulu believed that the kinship group owed an obligation to dead kinsmen who did not have children. A kinsman of the deceased married the dead man's betrothed and bore children in the dead man's name. In some African societies, one had to be married with children to qualify as an ancestor. Everyone in this environment aspired, therefore, not to just marry at an appropriate time, but also to have an heir. This was seen as a major reason for the institution of ghost marriages among the Nuer and the Zulu. Due to this institution, even after death, a male kinsman was not deprived of the opportunity of becoming an ancestor.[23]

The African mother-child household grew its own food. The mother depended on her children to help in cultivation, food processing, and household tasks (including child care. Children were important to the household economy, as they were required to participate in the domestic labor force.

African families and kinship groups formulated socio-religious and economic discourses which emphasized the value of children. Women were honored for having many children. In Igbo society, those women who had ten or more living children were honored with a ceremony which they performed by "sacrificing a goat on their hips." This was a mark of achievement. The husband had to buy expensive elephant tusks (*odu*) for the wife's wrist and ankles.[24] This recognition ceremony for such women encouraged other women's aspirations for ten or more children. It appears that early marriages for the women made this feat possible. In the past, Igbo girls for example, married early, usually between fifteen and nineteen years of age.

The naming of a child was an important occasion. Its ritual significance dictated that the oldest man in the family, with the support of other male elders of the kinship group, should preside at this occasion. This naming ceremony was observed with feasting and joy. The Asante, though their kinship descent was matrilineal, believed in a form of patrilineally inherited non-physical link. The Asante called this *ntoro* (a kind of spiritual influence). It was due to this notion that an Asante male acknowledged paternity by naming his child on the eighth day after birth. This ritual infused the father's *ntro* (paternal spirit) into the child. For the Igbo of Nigeria, the naming took place seven traditional weeks (that is, twenty-eight days) after the birth of the child. Names given to the child could reflect the family's experience with life, human aspirations, requests of the spiritual world, and kinship ideals and goals. These names were highly meaningful to the child as he/she grew and developed.

EDUCATION

The learning process was a cultural activity. Kin groups devised ways to enable them to pass down their store of accumulated knowledge from one generation to another. Child-training in kin groups projected the values that the groups cherished and admired, and would like to protect and propagate. At the center of this child-training was the father. He was the center of authority and emulation, especially for sons. The father of the nuclear family disciplined the children. But the term "father" might also apply to all males of the father's generation in the lineage. These "fathers" were culturally authorized to discipline all persons called "children." Mothers were also critically important in the education of the children—especially the education of the girls. They taught them how to cook and perform domestic work. Good cooking was a recognized means for a wife to become a husband's favorite. Thus the apt observation that "the kitchen became a refuge and food then is a strong weapon in the hands of women in a culture that disparages "eating out" … women hold on jealously to their kitchen power."[25] Teaching about cooking and procreation seemed to have dominated the domestic training of girls.

Oldest siblings were also involved in the training of their younger siblings. For example, among Fulani pastoralists the eldest brother taught the younger ones how to herd cattle and obey their seniors.

The education of the child in the ways of the kinship group was a collective affair. The task of socializing the child was the responsibility not only of the parents but of the extended family and the kinship group. That a child was always watched and guided by so many relatives made one scholar categorically state that: "the training of children is everybody's responsibility and every person is expected to correct a child whether they are related or not. 'Nwa bu nwa oha'—a child is the child of all."[26] Character formation was central in children's socialization. It was believed that good character was the very stuff which made family life a joy, because it was pleasing to the gods. It was also believed that a well formed character was an asset during matrimony. Child rearing was a serious communal duty: thus the dictum, "it takes a village to raise a child." The African child was made to feel deeply the debt he/she owed to the extended family, kinship group, and parents. Babs Fafunwa, the Nigerian historian of education, observed that "[t]he parent's siblings and other members of the community participate in the education of the child. Everyone wants him to be sociable, honest, courageous, humble, persevering and of good report all the time."[27] These were attributes the child had to acquire and exhibit.

The Kaguru people of Central Tanzania in East Africa had an initiation ceremony of rites of passage for girls:

> During a girl's confinement she is thought to undergo a gradual process of change produced by intense care from the women attending her. They feed or nurture the child like a novice ... making her more fit to become a wife and mother. A well initiated girl should emerge fat, pale, soft and well schooled in both sexual and household matters. At the end of this period, the girl is brought out from the initiation house and into the village square to be recognized as a newly constituted woman ready to be wed and bear children.[28]

In certain areas of Africa the ceremony where girls undergo extensive and painful tattooing or genital operations such as clitoridectomy and the removal of the labia minora was performed. The circumcision of the youth in certain areas was seen as a rite of passage. The Kukuyu, for example, say that to make a boy into a man, the "feminine" prepuce must be removed. Clitoridectomy was performed according to the men to satisfy their male sexual fantasies, enjoyment and desires. African children, both girls and boys, had to be groomed to become men and women. Manhood and womanhood are not naturally occurring conditions but ones that must be created.[29]

WOMEN

Much about African women in the context of African social institutions remains to be explored. At present, however, the discussion of women's lives in African social life fall into two contested terrains. On the one hand, scholars argue that many African societies provided opportunities for exceptional women to lead very productive lives;[30] on the other hand, another group of scholars[31] argues that African patrilineal ideology prevented women from achieving autonomy. African males, they argue, sought to control the conditions under which women interacted with African males. Both arguments dig deep into African social institutions, beliefs and rituals, and history to support their contentions.

It is true that most African women were preoccupied with the home economy, and were unable to accumulate wealth outside the domestic terrain. It is also true that in hunting and gathering societies, women's domestic sphere was critical for the survival of the group. The household depended on them for their expertise in foraging and the collection of food. The interdependence of men and women was remarkable.

A queen mother often had a role in the choice of a new king. The office of the king's mother existed in many African political organizations and it was very influential in Buganda, Mwenemutapa, and Asante, and among the Ankole and Shilluk. In the kingdom of Kush, the queen mother was called "Mistress of Kush." Some queen mothers became famous and assumed political power. In Greco-Roman times, Meroe was ruled by a line of "Candaces" or queen regents. If there were no male heirs in the Egyptian ruling family, a woman could inherit the throne. Four Egyptian women became Pharaohs: Nitokris, Sebeknefru, Hatshepsut and Tanosre. In other parts of Africa one could also list women who projected their political and social presence: the queen mothers of the Asante, the Empress Menetewab of Ethiopia (1720–1771), the mother or Kabaka Mutesa of Buganda Muganzirwazza (1817–1882), Queen Nzinga of Ndongo (1582–1663), Queen Aisa Kili Ngirmaramma of the Kanuri kingdom of Borno (1563–1570) and Mamy Yako (1849–1906) of the Mende Confederacy.

After the visit of Mansa Musa, the king of Mali, to the Islamic lands of the Arabs, the domestic life of women in the Savannah Kingdoms was transformed. On his return he introduced the purdah system of secluding married women. The custom spread all over the Islamic West African Savannah Kingdoms. This innovation was institutionalized and influenced the status of women in Hausa-speaking communities.[32] Yet Hausaland produced women of influence. Queen Amina of Zaria was one of these and the history of Kano is signposted by the names of celebrated princesses. For example, madarki (queen mother) Auwa intervened energetically to save Abdullahi (1499–1509) from the hands of rebels.[33] The sarki's sister, for example, played a leading political role, although she did so through the traditional form of worship. The Bori religion provided Hausa women with ritual authority which supported and legitimized the rulers of pre-Islamic Hausaland. The jihad (holy war) of Usman Dan Fodio and its aftermath at the beginning of the nineteenth century reduced the political and ritual power of the Bori religion. But there is plenty of evidence that Bori continued to be practiced as a re-ligion although the men had appropriated women's titles.

The women of Dahomey took an active part in politics. Every officer of the state had a woman counterpart who acted as a spy, reporting to the king all the doings of the male officers. Women were recruited into the army and made up a strong fighting unit in Dahomey's military establishment; and like their counterparts in Ndenye (in present day Ivory Coast), they even acted as custodians of the history of the people. The transmission of collective memory in Africa was usually in the form of praise songs. Qualified old women such as those in Yorubaland were allowed to be the transmitters of the oriki (praise songs).

The commercial initiatives of African women have been well documented.[34] Through various means within kinship contexts, women were able to accumulate capital to enable them to start their career as traders—such was the origin of Yoruba women traders. The participation of Igbo women in the palm-oil, palm-kernel, and casava trade increased their usefulness and autonomy within the Igbo household. Again, G.T. Basden observed:

Marketing is the central feature in the life of every Ibo woman and to be successful in trade is the signal for generous congratulations. By this a woman's value is calculated, it affects her position and comfort, a man considers it in the choice of a wife, and the husband's favor is bestowed or withheld largely, according to the degree of his wife's success in the market.[35]

The accumulation of wealth enabled certain Igbo women to take coveted titles. This was so in the case of Madam Nwagboka who was crowned as queen of Onitsha in 1884 by the Obi of Onitsha, Anazonwa I. Other Igbo business women also rose to fame. The life of Omu Okwei (1872–1943), the merchant queen of Ossamari, was a case in point. Women had the opportunity to become wealthy and could, therefore, acquire the things that wealth could buy.[36]

African women were also accorded politico-ritual potency. Their ritual status in kinship was so well established that, though this was an exaggeration, Nilotic women were said to be prime movers in all things except wars. In Zulu communities there existed great prophetesses, and, among the Mende, women had their own secret societies which they could manipulate to gain some political influence. The Bori religion of the Habe-Hausa accorded women great power, and in Kenya the great seer Syokimau (1840–1880) was a woman. Syokimau's ability to foretell events, to heal, and to give protection against epidemic diseases were highly regarded. She was a military adviser both to the Kamba and to the Masai warriors.[37] The politics of women's spirituality in Africa was deep rooted. Religious innovators, ritual functionaries, and religious resisters abounded. Nehauda Nyakasikana of Mwenemutapa-Zimbabawe (1862–1898) and Kimpa Vita Dona Beatrice of the Kongo kingdom (1682–1705) were cases in point. Scholars who argue the dynamic role of African women in social institutions argue that gender in African societies essentially ran along parallel, different, and contrasting rather than along hierarchical lines. Africans thereby gave, in general terms, equal value to male and female parallel autonomy. Notions of gender relations, according to this school of thought, varied depending on the lineage ideology, the group, and the economic and political circumstances of the historical period and the moment.

African women projected their ambitions in their roles as daughters, as wives, as mothers, as queens, as priestesses, as goddesses, and even as "husbands." Some of them found prestige, honor, and power but some scholars contend that these examples were exceptions. These scholars conclude that the triumph of male ideology in African history initiated the controlling influence of patriarchy in African male–female interactions. They contend that African men employed African kinship networks, secret societies, and the appropriation of history to actualize the triumph of patriarchal values. Thus many African societies, these scholars argue, came to be organized by gender, and tasks were divided and standards set according to patriarchal values. These values were provided the social environment in which each sex was evaluated. Initiation into gendered adulthood became the political and socio-economic hegemonic theme that has dominated the history of African social systems. Yet Jack Goody's caution is apt:

> Male domination in the political or economic sphere may not simply be reflected in the family. Among the Asante of West Africa, the political system is staffed by males. The role of the Queen Mother alone reflects politically the fact that this is a matrilineal society in which women—and their brothers as distinct from their husbands—play an important part in determining the residence of men. Male authority at the political level is consistent with quite a different distribution of power in the domestic domain.[38]

DIVINE KINGSHIP

Matriliny and patriliny were used in African social organization to adjust to the agrarian revolution that required a flexible mechanism for mobilizing and incorporating vast numbers of unfree laborers into an expanding agricultural society. The subsequent emergence of African state formations and increased social differentiation based on wealth and political power led the kings to appropriate certain aspects of patriliny and matriliny to consolidate kingship.

In the patrilineal kinship social system that has been examined in this chapter, it was believed that usurpation would normally not occur or be contemplated. The rules of succession to a patrilineage were usually indisputably clear and strictly adhered to, and were regulated on the basis of lineage seniority. The rules were sustained by supernatural sanctions. The ideology of kinship implied that seniority can only be claimed by one lineage at a time. This would normally rule out the possibility of competing claims. But the appearance of a "political chief" grew out of "kinship chiefs." The increased revenues in the hands of a lineage group reinforced chiefly authority, and the absorption of other lineages through the imposition of authority by force of arms attracted a growing clientele of lineages who depended on the chief for spiritual and material sustenance.

A hegemonic culture of kingship was initiated in which multiple processes of cultural and ritual renegotiation occurred and the remanipulation of mythical-political rituals, ceremonies and organized beliefs led to a new form of political and social organization—divine kingship. Once this was achieved, as in Nilotic Societies, Ogot reminded us:

> Instead of groupings based entirely on kinship relations, territorial groupings began to emerge ... yet both leadership and politics were conceived largely in kinship terms ... the lineages coincided with the territorial boundaries ... both kinship and chiefship principles began to be applied to political organization.[39]

Two things happened. At one level, this process betrayed the inefficiency of the political system based upon kinship ties, and at another level, it portrayed the emergence of a powerful, cohesive kin group that presented a united front and well organized ideology—factors that assisted the kin group to impose its rule over other kinship groups.

Examples abound in African history to confirm this progress. The ancient Swahili custom of reckoning kinship evolved into the title and office of *mfalme* which defined the functions of property, marriage, and the transfer of ritual power. But as class formation evolved, various Swahili ethnic groups started claiming Arab or Shirazi ancestry despite their indubitably African origin—thus linking Islam to the ideology of power. Luba royalty was founded on the principle of *bulopwe* or "sacredness" inherent in the royal blood, which the Luba called *mpifo*. They insisted on "purity of blood" within the patrilineal kinship. In the kingdom of Zimbabwe, royal usurpation was based on some form of unifying Luth in the powers of the divine Mwari religious catalyst

that reached out to every family. It was the Ntemi in Nyamwezi who claimed the political-religious authority. The Nandi, a section of the Kalenjin, crafted and adopted a spiritual leader whom they called the orkoiyot, and by the end of the nineteenth century, this spiritual leader had transformed the Nandi polity into a theocracy with himself as the sovereign. The Maasai laibons (ritual leaders) were also beginning to claim greater political authority than their predecessors had envisaged. In Ruanda, on account of numerous taboos, certain lineage groups crafted the *buhake*—protection guaranteed to a family in exchange for increased obligations. This was used especially by the Tutsi to subjugate influential Hutu lineages. The Asante accepted the "Golden Stool" myth developed by Anokye, the chief priest, and Osei Tutu, the Asantehene. The myth of "Oduduwa" gave the Yoruba kings their rights. In Kalabari, the title of amanyanabo, "the owner of the land," emerged.

The Igbo, for a period of their history, looked towards the Nri mythology to formulate kingly culture, but some Igbo did not continue with that experiment and resorted to village-lineage gerontocracy. In Hausaland there was the sarki, whose ancestors had seized political power. In the city-states of Kano, Katsina and Zamfara, power had been wrested from the hands of a high priest, while in Kebbi it was a magaji (warrior) who rose to the rank of sarki. The warrior tradition crafted by Shaka of the Zulu also transformed Zulu kinship ideology. But, it should be noted, for centuries the incessant wrangles within dominant Xhosa clans and Nguni societies were undoubtedly encouraged by thoughtful commoners who sought to paralyze the central authority by turning it against itself. These constraints on the evolution of a despotic style of administration were not broken until the end of the 1700s when strong confederacies were formed and ultimately led to the formation of the Zulu state.

In all the examples cited the royal family or king's men used kinship ideology to consolidate their positions. The manipulation of marriage links and gifts made other clans indebted to the king. Furthermore, the ability to bestow wives, gifts, and land depended ultimately on the royal household's ability to out-produce other households and clans. Thus, members of the royal lineage usually had more wives, hence more units of production than others. But in the Great Lakes region the Kintu complex of clans and the Kimera complex of clans worked out a compromise. Each clan wanted to participate in the monarchy, and therefore there arose in Buganda the custom of clans presenting wives to the kabaka, giving each clan the opportunity to provide a successor. Thus, unlike other Great Lake states, Buganda had no royal clan, each prince belonging to the clan of his mother, although the general population followed the rules of patriliny. Any clan in Buganda had a chance to provide the monarch, but the system also encouraged each clan to give a wife to a new *kabaka* with the consequent rapid proliferation of potential royal heirs. The kings of Buganda were therefore forced to be more extravagantly polygamous than many other rulers. This contrasted with the Acholi system where, upon coronation, the king was given a wife by the elders, the heir to come from the sons of this wife only.

CONCLUSION

The African experience confirms the notion that kinship is itself part of the mode of production. This is significant because much of the social change in Africa since the nineteenth century has occurred in the context of radical changes in production modes: land was being gradually privatized, and cash crops, entrepreneurial enterprises, and wage labor introduced. Kinship production has been challenged by capitalist production. Given the structural links between lineage organization and economic organization, the intrusion of capitalist forms has inevitably altered the means (and the effectiveness of these means) by which kinship was used to exert social control. Kinship descent, however, continued to be the major system that permitted the Africans to govern themselves with a minimum administrative burden and tedium. Kinship relations continued to be one of the main relations of production, of juro-political and

ritual significance. Kinship, thus, governed the way African communities organized and used the resources of the environment, notably the land, and spatial interaction between societal members.[40] The Vai proverb, "What belongs to me is destroyable by water or fire; what belongs to us is destroyable neither by water or fire," succinctly expresses the abiding strength of kinship in Africa. Kinship provided the anchor for people's membership, the anchor for people's identification, and the safety of effortless, secure belonging. Kinship added meaning to people's actions, which became not only acts of individual accomplishment but also part of continuous creative efforts whereby culture was made and remade. It promoted solidarity, trust, and valuable intergenerational bonds, although it also created tension. It enabled the African individual to transcend individual mortality by linking each one to an institution whose existence seemed to extend back into time immemorial and forward into the indefinite future. The endurance of kinship is explained by what it did.

REVIEW QUESTIONS

1. How is it that an African came to be a kinsman or kinswoman? Discuss.
2. In what ways did Africans activate kinship ties? Explain.
3. Explain how African men and women came to define themselves within the kinship ideology. Were women constrained by kinship ideology? Elucidate.
4. What functions did African kinship ideology perform?
5. African kingship was an assault on the conventions of kinship. Do you agree? Explain.

ADDITIONAL READINGS

Coquery-Vidrovitch, Catherine. *African Women: A Modern History*. Boulder: Westview, 1995.

DAS, Man Singh, ed. *The Family in Africa*. New Delhi: M.D. Publications, 1993. Kavongo-Male, Diane and

Philista Onyango, *Sociology of the African Family.* London: Longman, 1984.

Special Issue on the History of the Family in Africa, *Journal of African History* 24. 2 (1983).

Southhall, A. *Lineage Formation Among the Luo.* London: International African Institute, Oxford University Press, Memorandum 26, 1952.

Vuyk, Trudeke. *Children of One Womb: Descent, Marriage and Gender in Central African Societies.* Leiden, Netherlands: E.J. Brill, 1991.

NOTES

1. A.R. Radcliffe-Brown and D. Forde, eds., African Systems of Kinship and Marriage Oxford University Press, 1950, re-edited by International African Institute, London, 1987) which is a formalistic analysis of kinship system as a category. See also Claude Lévi-Strauss, Les Structures élementaires de le parenté (Paris: Mouton, 1967). This massive opus made a strong plea for what he called "structure" as against the "study of events." For a rethinking at kinship systems see Rodney Needham, ed., Rethinking Kinship and Marriage (London: Livestock, 1971); and Schneider, "What Is Kinship All About?" in Priscilla Reining, ed., Kinship Studies (Washington, D.C.: The Morgan Centennial Year, 1972).

2. Igor Kopytoff, ed., *The African Frontier* (Indiana University Press, 1989), 43.

3. —————

4. Peter Garlake, *The Hunters Vision: The Pre-Historic Art of Zimbabwe* (Seattle: University of Washington Press, 1996). See also T. Price and Ann Gebauer, eds., *Last Hunters-First Farmers: New Perspectives on the Prehistoric Transition to Agriculture* (Santa Fe: School of American Research Press, 1995).

5. For Yoruba example see Bolanle Awe, "The Iyalode in the Traditional Yoruba Political System," in Alice Schlegel, ed., *Sexual Stratification: A Cross-Cultural View* (New York: Columbia University Press, 1977), and for the Igbo see Mary Anochie, *The Igbo Woman and Consecrated Life* (Onitsha: Effective Key Publishers Limited, 1994), 14–15.

6. Victor Uchendu, "Ezi Na Ulo: The Extended Family in Igbo Civilization," 1995 Ahijoku Lectures, Owerri, Ministry of Information and Social Development (1995), 40.

7. G.T. Basden, *Among the Ibos of Nigeria* (London: Frank Cass, 1966, first edition 1921), 218.

8. See Gwen J. Bronde and Sarah J. Greene, "Cross-Cultural Codes on Twenty Sexual Attitudes and Practices," *Ethnology, 15* (1976): 409–29; and Alice Schlegel, "Status, Property and the Value of Virginity," *American Ethnologist, 18* (1991): 719–34.

9. M. Park, *Travels in the Interior District of Africa in the Years 1795, 1796 and 1797,* 1799 facsimile reprint (New York: Arno Press, 1971), 266.

10. V.C. Uchendu, The Igbo of South Eastern Nigeria (New York: Holt, Rinehart and Winston, 1965), 51–52.

11. M. Fortes, "Kinship and Marriage Among the Ashanti," in Radcliffe Brown and Forde, eds., *African Systems of Kinship* and Marriage, 279–80.

12. For more accounts of marriage in Africa, see Caroline Bledsoe and Gilles Pison, *Nuptiality in Sub-Saharan Africa* (Oxford: Clarendon Press, 1994).

13. Though we have an excellent work on widows in Africa, Betty Potash, *Widows in African Societies: Choices and Constraints* (Stanford: Stanford University Press, 1986), we still need an authoritative work on African traditional marital dissolutions.

14. Aggrey Majok and Calvin W. Schwabe, *Development Among Africa's Migratory Pastoralists* (Westport, Conn: Bergin and Garvey, 1996), 51–52. See also A. Kuper, *Wives for Cattle: Bridewealth and Marriage in Southern Africa* (London: Routledge & Keegan Paul, 1982).

15. Felicia Ekejiuba, "Currency Instability and Social Payments Among the Igbo of Eastern Nigeria 1890–1990," in Jane I. Guyer, ed., *Money Matters: Instability, Values and Social Payments in the Modern History of West African*

Communities (London: James Currey, 1995), 149. Cf. C. Mba, *Matrimonial Consort in Igbo Marriages* (Rome: Press, 1974).

16. J.T. Vanderkemp, "An Account of … Caffaria," in *Transaction of the [London] Missionary Society, 1* (1795–1802): 439.

17. G.T. Basden, *Among the Ibos of Nigeria* (New York: Barnes and Nobles, 1966), 228.

18. J.P. Jordan, *Bishop Shanahan of Southern Nigeria* (Dublin: Elo Press, 1971 edition), 15.

19. See Elliot Skinner, "International Conflict among the Massai: Father and Son," *Journal of Conflict Resolution*, vol. 5, no. 1 (1961): 55–60.

20. B.A. Ogot, *History of the Southern Luo*, vol. 1 (Nairobi: East African Publishing House, 1967), 99.

21. Majok and Schwabe, *Development Among Africa's Migratory Pastoralists*, 51.

22. Especially in the Khoisan wars in South Africa. See H.B. Thorn ed., *Journal of Jan Van Riebeeck, 3 vols., vol. 2* (Capetown: Published for the Van Riebleck Society by A.A. Bolkema, 1952–58), 172.

23. Ghost marriages are fictive marriages by which a kinsman of a man or boy who died before he had any legal heirs could marry a woman in the name of a deceased relative. E.E. Evans-Pritchard, *Kinship and Marriage Among the Nuer* (New York: Oxford University Press, 1951).

24. This ceremony is still practiced in Igboland. Cf. Anochie, *The Igbo Women*, 18.

25. Mercy Amba Oduyoye, *Daughters of Anonwa: African Women and Patriarchy* (New York: Orbis Books, 1995), especially the section, "The Power of the Kitchen," 53.

26. F.C. Ogbalu, *Igbo Institutions and Customs* (Onitsha, Nigeria: University Publishing Co., 1973), 19.

27. A. Babs Fafundwa, *History of Education in Nigeria* (George Allen and Unwin: London, 1974), 21.

28. T.O. Berdelman, "Containing Time: Rites of Passage and Moral Space of Bachelorhood Among the Kaguru 1957–1966," *Anthropos*, 86 (1996): 453.

29. For the Kikuyu, see Carol Worthman and John Whiting, "Social Change in Adolescent Sexual Behavior, Mate Selection and Premarital Pregnancy Rates in a Kikuyu Community," *Ethos*, 15 (1987): 145–65. For an Igbo community, see Ifi Amadiume, *Male Daughters, Female Husbands: Gender and Sex in an African Society* (London: Zed Press, 1994), especially sections on "How They Made Them Men" and "Coming into Womanhood," 93–98.

30. See Kamene Okonjo, "The Dual-Sex Political System in Operation: Igbo Women and Community Politics in Mid-Western Nigeria," in Nancy J. Hafkin and Edna G. Bay, eds., *Women in Africa: Studies in Social and Economic Change* (Stanford, California: Stanford University Press, 1976); Amadiume, *Male Daughters, Female Husbands*; O. Muchena, "The Changing Position of African Women in Rural Zimbabwe," *Zimbabwe Journal of Economics*, 1, 1 (1979): 50–63; S. Afonja, "Changing Modes of Production and Sexual Division of Labor Among the Yoruba," in E. Leacock and H. Safa, eds., *Women's Work. Development and the Division of Labor* By Gender (South Hardley: M.A. Bergin and Garney, 1986); K.O. Poewe, *Matrilineal Ideology* (New York: Academic Press, 1981); E.C. Mandala, *Work and Control in a Peasant Economy: A History of the Lower Tchri Valley in Malawi* (Madison: University of Wisconsin Press, 1990); R.S. Oboler, *Women, Power and Economic Change: The Nindi of Kenya* (Stanford, California: Stanford University Press, 1985); Filomena Chioma Steady, "African Feminism: A Worldview Perspective," in Rosalyn Terborg-Penn and Andrea Benton Rushing, eds., *Women in Africa and the African Diaspora: A Reader* (Washington, D.C.: Howard University Press, 1996), 3–21; and Niara Sudarkasa, "The Status of Women in Indigenous African Societies," in Rosalyn Terborg-Penn and Andrea Benton Rushing, eds., 73–87.

31. Catherine Coquery-Vidrovitch, *African Women: A Modern History?* trans. Beth Gillian

Raps (Colorado: Westview, 1997); and Onaiwu Ogbomo, *When Men and Women Mattered: A History of Gender Relations Among the Owan of Nigeria* (Rochester, New York: University of Rochester Press, 1997). For a general discussion of African women in pre-colonial Africa see: Mary E. Madupe Kolawole, *Womanism and African Consciousness* (Trenton, N.J.: Africa World Press Inc., 1997), 43–50, and Catherine Obianuju Acholonu, *Motherism: The Afriocentric Alternative to Feminism* (Oweri: Afa Publ., 1995), 24–51.

32. Cf. Beverly B. Mack, "Harem Domesticity in Kano, Nigeria," in Karen Tranberg Hansen, ed., *African Encounters with Domesticity* (New Jersey: Rutgers University Press, 1992).

33. For women in Kano history see Bawuro Barkindo, ed., *Studies in the History of Kano* (Ibadan, Nigeria: Published for the Department of History, Bayeko University, Kano, by Heinemann Education Books Nigeria, 1983) and Beverly B. Mack, "Hajya Ma'deki: A Royal Hausa Woman" in Patricia W. Romero, ed., *Life Histories of African Women* (Atlantic Highfields, N.J.: Ashfield Press, 1988), 47–77.

34. Bessie House-Midamba and Felix Ekechi, eds., *African Market Women and Economic Power: The Role of Women in African Economic Development* (Westport, CT.: Greenwood Press, 1995).

35. Basden, *Among the Ibos of Nigeria*, 194.

36. Richard N. Henderson, *The King in Everyman: Evolutionary Trends in Onitsha Igbo Society and Culture* (New Haven: Yale University Press, 1972), 464; and Felicia Ekejiuba, "Omu Okwei, The Merchant Queen of Ossomari: A Biographical Sketch," *Journal of the Historical Society of Nigeria*, 2/4 (June 1967).

37. Rebeka Njau and Gideon Mulaki, *Kenya Women Heroes and Their Mystical Power*, vol. 1 (Rick Publication, Nairobi, 1984), 55–59. For Bori and women, see M. Onuluejeogwu, "The Cult of Bori Spirits among the Hausa," M. Douglas and P.M. Kabry, eds., *Man in Africa* (London: Tavistock Press, 1969).

38. Jack Goody, "Women, Class and Family," *New Left Review*, 219 (Sept./Oct. 1996):

39. Bethwell A. Ogot, *History of the Southern Luo V.I.: Migration and Settlement 1500–1900* (Nairobi: East African Publishing House, 1967), 169–171. For matriliny and state formation see I. Wilks, "Founding the Political Kingdom: The Nature of the Akan State," in I. Wilks, ed., *Forests of Gold: Essays on the Akan and the Kingdom of the Asante* (Athens, Oluo: Ohio University Press, 1993), 91–126.

40. Renée Ilene Pittin, "Households and Families: Sub-Saharan Africa," in *Women Studies Encyclopedia* (Hemel Hempstead, England: Harvester Wheatsheaf Press, Ltd., Paramount Publishing International, 1996).

AFRICAN HISTORY

PART THREE

EUROPEANS IN AFRICA

THE ATLANTIC SLAVE TRADE, SIXTEENTH TO EIGHTEENTH CENTURIES

By Kevin Shillington

THE ORIGINS OF EUROPEAN MARITIME TRADE WITH WEST AFRICA

The aims of Portuguese Initiatives

When the Portuguese first sailed out on their voyages of exploration along the west African coast, the desire to reach India was a distant objective. Of more immediate concern was their attempt to bypass Muslim north Africa and gain direct access to the gold-producing regions of west Africa. This would provide the poorly-endowed state of Portugal with a major source of national wealth, for sub-Saharan west Africa was known to be the main source of gold for the coinage of western Europe (see the fourteenth-century European map of Africa illustrated on page 100, showing Mali as a major source of gold). Once access to this had been achieved, the wealth it provided could finance further exploration round the southern tip of Africa and so towards India. Ultimately, by reaching India via a southern route the Portuguese would be bypassing the Muslim-controlled trading routes of western Asia. In doing so they hoped to reap rich rewards from the Indian trade in spices, perfumes, silks and other luxuries. These could then be carried to western Europe in Portuguese ships and sold at considerable profit for the Portuguese.

Early Portuguese trade on the west African coast

Portuguese sailing ships first reached the west African coast south of the Akan goldfields in the 1470s. They built a fort there, known as Elmina ('the mine'), to protect their trading post from rival European shipping. At first the Portuguese traded copper, brass and European cloth in exchange for gold. They thus offered the forest peoples goods which they had previously got from Songhay and the trans-Saharan trade. The Portuguese also sold them a certain number of slaves bought from the forest kingdom of Benin near the Niger delta. It appears that for some time slave labour had been used to run the gold mines of the Akan forest region (see p. 194). In the early 1500s the Portuguese added cowrie shells and luxury cloths from the Indian Ocean trade to the range of goods they offered in exchange for west African gold. It was not long before half the produce of the Akan goldfields was being diverted southwards, away from Songhay and the trans-Saharan trade, and towards the European trading forts along the coast.

Origins of European-controlled plantation slavery

Meanwhile in the 1480s, the Portuguese had discovered the uninhabited equatorial islands of Principe and São Tomé. In the years that followed, Portuguese settlers developed thriving sugar plantations in the rich volcanic soils of these islands. They manned their plantations with slave labour drawn from the African mainland.

The plantation system for growing sugar cane had originally been developed in various Mediterranean islands and in southern Spain and Portugal during the fourteenth and early fifteenth centuries. The slave labour for these plantations was drawn not only from north Africa but also from among the Slavs of southern Russia. Indeed the European word 'slave' comes from the use of Slavs for this kind of unpaid labour. As the Portuguese captured Atlantic islands from Madeira southwards to São Tomé, they extended to the tropics their plantation system for growing sugar.

In the early sixteenth century São Tomé became the largest single producer of sugar for the European market. Ultimately, the São Tomé plantation system, owned and run by European overseers and manned by African slave labour, was to become the model for plantation slavery in the Americas and the Caribbean.

Origins and development of the trans-Atlantic trade in slaves

From early on in the Portuguese presence along the coast of tropical west Africa captives were bought from local chiefdoms for sale into slavery. Initially, in the fifteenth and early sixteenth century, they came largely from the Senegal and Gambia region and were transported to the farms and plantations of southern Spain and Portugal. Those taken from the Niger delta and the Zaire river region went mostly to the island of São Tomé.

Meanwhile, as Portuguese venturers traded with west Africans and sought an eastern route to India, their neighbours, the Spaniards, were opening up the trans-Atlantic route to the Americas and the Caribbean. European colonisation and exploitation of this tropical 'New World' followed swiftly upon Columbus's voyage of 'discovery' of 1492.

The colonisers soon felt the need for a large imported labour force to work the gold and silver mines of the mainland and their tobacco plantations on the islands. The local indigenous Amerindian population quickly succumbed to the harsh treatment of the colonisers and unfamiliar European diseases. By the end of the first century of European contact ninety per cent or more of the Amerindian population of the Caribbean islands had been wiped out—victims of European violence or disease. Criminals and outcasts from Europe were transported to the Americas in the early sixteenth century, but their numbers were limited. Those that were sent did not long survive attacks of tropical disease. Faced with these problems the European colonisers of central and south America turned to Africa for their slave labour force.

Africans had developed a certain level of immunity to some tropical diseases. They were known to have experience and skills in metal-working, mining and tropical agriculture. Portuguese experience had already shown that there was always somewhere along the west African coast when African rulers were prepared to sell their war captives and criminals. And the example of São Tomé had shown the possibilities of using African slave labour on plantations.

The first African captives to be taken directly across the Atlantic and sold into slavery were transported in 1532. Thereafter a steady trans Atlantic trade in human cargo developed though annual numbers remained relatively small for the first one hundred years. But from the 1630s, as first the Dutch and then the French and English became involved, there was a rapid expansion of sugar plantations in Brazil and the Caribbean. Demand for slave labour increased and the scale of the trade in captives from west Africa reached enormous proportions. There developed over the next two-hundred years the largest-scale forced transportation of captive people ever devised in human history.

The question of scale

Over recent years there has been considerable dispute among historians about the numbers involved in the trans-Atlantic trade. Recorded statistics show that at least ten million Africans were landed alive and sold into slavery in the Americas and the Caribbean in the three hundred years that followed 1532. Allowing for a further two million that died on the trans Atlantic voyage, a total of at least twelve million people were taken captive out of Africa. Numbers which were only a few thousand a year in the sixteenth century rose to an average of 20000 a year in the seventeenth and further rocketed to between 50000 and 100000 a year for much of the eighteenth century. Numbers tailed off during the nineteenth century, but the trade did not altogether cease until the 1870s and 1880s. Some historians argue that a huge amount of traffic went unrecorded and that the real scale of the trade was double the amount indicated here.

The African dimension

Though numbers taken out of Africa were clearly huge, they varied very widely from one region to another. Senegal was an important early source of slaves, in the sixteenth century. The Angolan coastline was unusual in that it remained a major slave-exporting region for most of the period, from the sixteenth to the nineteenth century. The effects of this on the peoples of Angola will be discussed further in Chapter 14 (pp. 198–201). With the rise of Caribbean sugar plantations from the mid-seventeenth century, Dutch, French, English, Danes and other Europeans became more actively involved in the carrying trade. Then the so-called 'Slave Coast' (the western coast of modern Nigeria) became a major source of slaves. With the rapid expansion of slave exports in the eighteenth century virtually every part of the Atlantic coastline from Senegal to southern Angola became involved in the human traffic. The greatest concentration of European trading forts was along the so-called 'Gold Coast', the coastline of the modern state of Ghana. Slaves continued to be taken from the 'Slave Coast' and Angola until well into the nineteenth century when many other regions had ceased their trade in people.

On the whole European slave traders were not active in the business of capturing their victims. European traders did not have the military power to go on their own extensive raiding expeditions. In any case, why go on expensive raiding expeditions when captives could be bought more cheaply and with less risk at the coast? When they did enter the interior, as in Angola, European armies either suffered military defeat or were weakened by disease. Nevertheless in the Angolan case they stirred up warfare between the kingdoms of Kongo and Ndongo which provided ample numbers of captives for sale at the coast. European activity in the trade in Africans was usually restricted to their trading forts along the coast. And they sought permission to build these from local African rulers to whom they were obliged to pay tribute. In general it was African rulers who provided the captives, and specialist African and Afro-European slave dealers who conveyed them to the coast for sale.

The main source of people for sale into slavery was those captured in warfare. Previously war-captives would either have been ransomed back to the people that they came from or integrated into the captor's society. In the latter case they were often forced to work as slaves, but they were at least considered a definite part of that society, even if at a subordinate level. It was not unknown for them to gain their freedom, marry into their captor's society and rise in economic and social status. With their sale into European slavery, war-captives were totally removed from African society, with a short life-expectancy in harsh conditions and no hope of return.

It used to be assumed that most captives offered for sale at the coast were the product of wars deliberately waged for this purpose. This undoubtedly did happen on occasion, especially in the eighteenth century when prices offered by Europeans were rising. But recent research has revealed that there was considerably more local African initiative involved than was previously assumed to be the case.

A number of careful regional studies have revealed that the supply of captives at the coast was usually the result of specific local wars being waged in the interior. And the prime motive of these wars was the formation and expansion of states rather than simply a free-for-all in which the losers ended in slavery. Thus the forest state of Benin sold captives to the Portuguese in the late fifteenth century while they were undergoing a period of military expansion. Significantly, in the sixteenth century they refused to trade in people. The export of captives from Benin was only renewed in the eighteenth century as the formerly powerful kingdom went into decline. During the first half of the sixteenth century the Mane, a branch of the Mande-speaking peoples, colonised the highlands of Sierra Leone, making local people captive and selling them at the coast. In the early eighteenth century the coastline of modern Guinea reached a peak of slave exports when the Muslim Fulbe of Futa Jalon created a new state and waged holy war against their neighbours. The result was a large number of captives for sale into slavery. Similarly wars waged by the expanding states of Oyo (pp. 191–2), Dahomey (pp. 192–3) and Asante (pp. 193–6) in the seventeenth and eighteenth centuries produced specific local peaks in the supply of captives for sale to European slavers at the coast.

Basically, powerful African rulers provided captives when it suited them, and some of them became very rich in the process. But they rarely sold people from their own society, except unwanted criminals and outcasts. On the other hand, small societies, the weak states and 'stateless' village communities, the neighbours of the large expanding states, undoubtedly suffered greatly. Some disappeared altogether, their lands taken over by other, more powerful neighbours.

Wars in the west African interior may not have generally been waged deliberately just to produce captives for sale. But the presence of Europeans on the coast offering what appeared to be high prices for captives undoubtably stimulated warfare. This was especially so in the eighteenth century when Europeans offered guns as their major trading item. It made warfare more profitable, at least in the short term. Whereas previously war might have stopped at the levying of tribute and the taking of some captives, now it became 'total'—the total destruction of weaker societies.

As a result of the slave trade, there was not only an increased level of general warfare in the west African interior. In purely economic terms, there was also a serious loss to the productive potential of the region. Previously war had produced tribute from the vanquished, and captives to work for the victors. But now the increased level of warfare produced a 'surplus' of captives. These were no longer kept, even as forced labour, within the African society that had captured them. They were no longer ransomed back to the society that had lost them. Instead they were sold right out of Africa, and sold for goods which were worth a fraction of what those people might have produced within their own lifetime. In addition, those sold were the young, most productive sector of the population, mostly aged between fourteen and thirty-five. It varied from one region to another, but all areas of western sub-Saharan Africa were seriously affected at some time or other during the seventeenth and eighteenth centuries.

The trans-Atlantic trade

Whatever its effect in terms of depopulating or distorting the development of the continent, the greatest evil of the trans-Atlantic trade in people was the extent of human suffering involved, and the callous disregard for human life and dignity displayed by those who dealt in slaves. When a person was captured in the interior and dispatched to the coast for sale, it marked the beginning of a short remaining life of appalling degradation and suffering. Captives were no longer treated as fellow human beings but rather as property, like domestic livestock, to be herded together, examined and bartered over.

Captives were chained together and marched to the coast where they were locked up in wooden cages to await the arrival of the next European trading ship. They were then stripped naked, men and women together, and examined minutely to see if they were fit, strong and healthy. Once a deal had been struck between African middleman and European slave merchant the most terrible part of their voyage began. On board ship they were chained together in rows and forced to lie on specially constructed 'decks' which were arranged like shelves barely half a metre one above the other (see illustration). This made it impossible for a person to sit up straight or to move freely. They lay like this for weeks on end, suffering in the stench of their own excreta and urine and given barely enough food and water to keep them alive. Those that died were simply thrown overboard. On average between fifteen and thirty per cent could be expected to die from disease, maltreatment or exhaustion during the three to six weeks of the trans-Atlantic crossing. Ships' captains allowed for this loss by packing in more people. In this way enough could be expected to survive the crossing for sale in America to make a handsome profit for the merchant who financed the voyage. On occasion disease would spread so rapidly in the terrible conditions below decks that it wiped out a whole shipload of captives. But this kind of misfortune was rare and on the whole the trade in human cargo was a highly profitable concern for the shipping merchants. If it had not been, the trade would not have continued on such an ever-increasing scale.

In this manner tens of thousands of Africa's fittest young men and women were removed from the continent every year, all in the name of profit for European merchants and plantation owners.

Plantations in the Americas and their demand for slave labour

The main plantations were for growing sugar and coffee in Brazil, sugar in the Caribbean islands and tobacco and cotton in the southern part of north America. The largest number of slaves were taken to the Caribbean islands. For most of the seventeenth and eighteenth centuries the number and size of plantations was constantly expanding. This meant an ever-greater demand for new slaves. Even on the long-established estates there was a persistent demand for replacements. Life on the plantations of the New World was hard and short. Some never survived the trauma and depression of leaving Africa and the trans-Atlantic voyage. A third died within the first three years and few survived beyond ten years. The main causes of death were underfeeding and overwork.

The economics of the plantation system was such that until the end of the eighteenth century it was cheaper to import fresh slaves from Africa than it was to allow them to rear their own children. A woman in childbirth could no longer labour effectively on the plantation, and a child had to be fed for a number of years before it could be forced to work on the land. Thus in the British colony of Jamaica, for example, three-quarters of a million slave workers were imported from Africa over a period of some two hundred years; and yet, at the time of emancipation in 1834 the population of Jamaica was only a third of a million.

There is not room here to consider the further history of those Africans sent to the Americas. Suffice it to say that the productive wealth of the New World rested very heavily on the shoulders of African labour. And those who profited most from this wealth were the merchants of Europe who financed the whole system.

PROFIT FROM THE SLAVE TRADE: THE EUROPEAN DIMENSION

The 'triangular trade'

To European merchants involved in the slave trade the export of Africans across the Atlantic was only one part of a wider trading system. A single ship setting out from Europe completed three main stages in its voyage, each with its own separate cargo, before finally returning to its home port in Europe. At each stage of this three-sided or 'triangular' trade there was profit for the European merchant who financed the voyage. The first stage carried manufactured goods from Europe to Africa.

Significantly, the original Portuguese imports into Africa had included raw materials such as copper and other metals in exchange for gold. By the seventeenth and eighteenth centuries this early pattern of trade had changed. Now the principal European imports into Africa were cheap manufactured goods—mainly cotton cloth and metal hardware, especially guns—in exchange for slaves. Indeed in the late eighteenth century the special manufacture of cheap, substandard guns for the African market became an important source of profit for the new British industrial city of Birmingham. As dependence upon European manufactured imports increased, further development of African craft industries declined. At the same time, as we have seen, the import of European guns made African warfare more effective and increased the supply of slaves. This ensured that the price of slaves exported from Africa remained fairly static for most of the seventeenth and early eighteenth century. It was not until the 1780s that increasing European competition along the west African coast finally drove up the price of slaves. It was only then that European merchants began to question the trade's continued profitability (see below, pp. 233–4).

Across the Atlantic, slaves were sold for two or three times what they had cost on the African coast. Sometimes they were sold for cash which was then used to buy plantation crops. At times, especially on the sugar-producing islands, slaves were directly bartered in exchange for sugar, which was then sold in Europe.

Though risks were involved, as ships could be lost at sea, profits to the European merchants were generally huge. Profits from the 'triangular trade' largely accounted for the rising wealth of a number of major European port cities, such as Bristol and Liverpool in Britain, Bordeaux and Nantes in France, and Amsterdam in Holland. Merchants moved into banking and ultimately helped finance the capitalist factory system of European industrial revolution. And as European merchants were well aware at the time, the key to their source of Atlantic trading profits was the systematic exploitation of African slave labour.

Slavery and the origins of racism

It has been argued that the roots of European racism are to be found in the European exploitation of Africans through the trans-Atlantic trade and the plantation slavery of the New World. The deep roots of racism are probably more complex than this, though European enslavement of Africans undoubtably played its part. For some three hundred years Africans were viewed by Europeans almost exclusively as slaves, as though this was their natural state. Europeans argued that in taking Africans out of their native continent, they were 'rescuing' them from a 'primitive' and 'barbaric' existence. It was a short step from this to arguing that Africans were naturally inferior. And when Europeans sought to colonise the African continent in the late nineteenth century, they used arguments such as these to justify their actions in the name of spreading Christianity and 'civilisation'.

EARLY TRAVELS OF OLADUAH EQUIANO

By Olaudah Equiano

I hope the reader will not think I have trespassed on his patience in introducing myself to him with some account of the manners and customs of my country. They had been implanted in me with great care, and made an impression on my mind, which time could not erase, and which all the adversity and variety of fortune I have since experienced served only to rivet and record; for, whether the love of one's country be real or imaginary, or a lesson of reason, or an instinct of nature, I still look back with pleasure on the first scenes of my life, through that pleasure has been for the most part mingled with sorrow.

I have already acquainted the reader with the time and place of my birth. My father, besides many slaves, had a numerous family, of which seven lived to grow up, including myself and a sister, who was the only daughter. As I was the youngest of the sons, I became, of course, the greatest favourite with my mother, and was always with her; and she used to take particular pains to form my mind. I was trained up from my earliest years in the arts of agriculture and war: my daily exercise was shooting and throwing javelins; and my mother adorned me with emblems, after the manner of our greatest warriors. In this way I grew up till I was turned the age of eleven, when an end was put to my happiness in the following manner:—Generally, when the grown people in the neighbourhood were gone far in the fields to labour, the childen assembled together in some of the neighbour's premises to play; and commonly some of us used to get up a tree to look out for any assailant, or kidnapper, that might come upon us; for they sometimes took those opportunities of our parents' absence, to attack and carry off as many as they could seize. One day, as I was watching at the top of a tree in our yard, I saw one of those people come into the yard of our next neighbour but one, to kidnap, there being many stout young people in it. Immediately, on this, I gave the alarm of the rogue, and he was surrounded by the stoutest of them, who entangled him with cords, so that he could not escape till some of the grown people came and secured him. But alas! ere long, it was my fate to be thus attacked, and to be carried off, when none of the grown people were nigh. One day, when all our people were gone out to their works as usual, and only I and my dear sister were left to mind the house, two men and a woman got over our walls, and in a moment seized us both; and, without giving us time to cry out, or make resistance, they stopped our mouths, and ran off with us into the nearest wood. Here they tied our hands, and continued to carry us as far as they could, till night came on, when we reached a small house, where the robbers halted for refreshment, and spent the night. We were then unbound; but were unable to take any food; and, being quite overpowered by fatigue and grief, our only relief was some sleep, which allayed our misfortune for a short time. The next morning we left the house, and continued travelling all the day. For a long time we had kept to the woods, but at last we came into a road which I believed I knew. I had now some hopes of being delivered; for we had advanced but a little way before I discovered some people at a distance, on which I began to cry out for their assistance; but my cries had no other effect than to make them tie me faster and stop my mouth, and then they put me into a large sack. They also stopped my sister's mouth, and tied her hands; and in this manner we proceeded till we were out of the sight of these people. When we went to rest the following night they offered us some victuals; but we refused them; and the only comfort we had was in being in one another's arms all that night, and bathing each other with our tears. But alas! we were soon deprived of even the smallest comfort of weeping together. The next day proved a day of greater sorrow than I had yet experienced; for my sister and I were then separated, while we lay clasped in each other's arms: it was in vain that we besought them not to part us: she was torn from me, and immediately carried away, while I was left in a state of distraction not to be described. I cried and grieved continually; and for several days did not eat any thing but what they forced into my mouth. At length, after many days travelling, during which I had often changed masters, I got into the hands of a chieftain, in a very pleasant country. This man had two wives and some children, and they all used me extremely well, and did all they could to comfort me; particularly the first wife, who was something like my mother. Although I was a great many days journey from my father's house, yet these people spoke exactly the same language with us. This first master of mine, as I may call him, was a smith; and my principal employment was working his bellows, which were the same kind as I had seen in my vicinity. They were in some respects not unlike the stoves here in gentlemen's kitchens; and were covered over with leather; and in the middle of that leather a stick was fixed, and a person stood up, and worked it, in the same manner as is done to pump water out of a cask with a hand pump. I believe it was gold he worked, for it was of a lovely bright yellow colour, and was worn by the women on their wrists and ankles. I was there I suppose about a month, and they at least used to trust me some little distance from the house. This liberty I used in embracing every opportunity to inquire the way to my own home: and I also sometimes, for the same purpose, went with the maidens, in the cool of the evenings, to bring pitchers of water from the springs for the use of the house. I had also remarked where the sun rose in the morning, and set in the evening, as I had travelled along; and I had observed that my father's house was towards the rising of the sun. I therefore determined to seize the first opportunity of making my escape, and to shape my course for that quarter; for I was quite oppressed and weighed down by grief after my mother and friends; and my love of liberty, ever great, was strengthened by the mortifying circumstance of not daring to eat with the free-born children, although I was mostly their companion. While I was projecting my escape one day, an unluckey event happened, which quite disconcerted my plan, and put an end to my hopes. I used to be sometimes employed in assisting an elderly woman slave to cook and take care of the poultry; and one morning, while I was feeding some chickens, I happened to toss a small pebble at one of them, which hit it on the middle, and directly killed it. The old slave, having soon after missed the chicken, inquired after it; and on my relating the accident (for I told her the truth, because my mother would never suffer me to tell a lie), she flew into a violent passion, threatening that I should suffer for it; and, my master being out, she immediately went and told her mistress what I had done. This alarmed me very much, and I expected an instant flogging, which to me was uncommonly dreadful; for I had seldom been beaten at home. I therefore resolved to fly; and accordingly I ran into a thicket that was hard by, and hid myself in the bushes. Soon afterwards my mistress and the slave returned, and not seeing me, they searched all the house, but not finding me, and I not making answer when they called to me, they thought I had run away, and the whole neighbourhood was raised in the pursuit of me. In that part of the country (as well as ours) the houses and villages were skirted with woods or shrubberies, and the bushes were so thick, that a man could readily conceal himself in them, so as to elude the strictest search. The neighbours continued the whole day looking for me, and several times many of them came within a few yards of the place where I lay hid. I expected every moment, when I heard a rustling among the trees, to be found out, and punished by my master; but they never discovered me, though they were often so near that I even heard their conjectures as they were looking about to me; and I now learned from them that any attempt to return home would be hopeless. Most of them supposed I had fled towards home, but the distance was so great, and the way so intricate, that they thought I could never reach it, and that I should be left in the woods. When I heard this I was seized with a violent panic, and abandoned myself to despair. Night too began to approach, and aggravated all my fears. I had before entertained hopes of getting home, and had determined when it should be dark to make the attempt; but I was now convinced it was fruitless, and began to consider that, if possibly I could escape all other animals, I could not those of the human kind; and that, not knowing the way, I must perish in the woods. Thus was I like the hunted deer:

"Ev'ry leaf, and ev'ry whisp'ring breath
Convey'd a foe, and ev'ry foe a death."

I heard frequent rustlings among the leaves; and being pretty sure they were snakes, I expected every instant to be stung by them. This increased my anguish; and the horror of my situation became now quite insupportable. I at length quitted the thicket, very faint and hungry, for I had not eaten or drank any thing all the day, and crept to my master's kitchen, from whence I set out at first, and which was an open shed, and laid myself down in the ashes with an anxious wish for death to relieve me from all my pains. I was scarcely awake in the morning, when the old woman slave who was the first up, came to light the fire, and saw me in the fire place.

She was very much surprised to see me, and could scarcely believe her own eyes. She now promised to intercede for me, and went for her master, who soon after came, and, having slightly reprimanded me, ordered me to be taken care of, and not ill treated. Soon after this my master's only daughter and child by his first wife sickened and died, which affected him so much that for some time he was almost frantic, and really would have killed himself, had he not been watched and prevented. However, in a small time afterwards he recovered; and I was again sold. I was now carried to the left of the sun's rising, though many dreary wastes and dismal woods, amidst the hideous roarings of wild beasts. The people I was sold to used to carry me very often, when I was tired, either on their shoulders or on their backs. I saw many convenient well-built sheds along the roads, at proper distances, to accommodate the merchants and travellers, who lay in those buildings along with their wives, who often accompany them; and they always go well armed.

From the time I left my own nation I always found somebody that understood me till I came to the sea coast. The languages of different nations did not totally differ, nor were they so copious as those of the Europeans, particularly the English. They were therefore easily learned; and, while I was journeying thus through Africa, I acquired two or three different tongues. In this manner I had been travelling for a considerable time, when one evening, to my great surprise, whom should I see brought to the house where I was but my dear sister? As soon as she saw me she gave a loud shriek, and ran into my arms—I was quite overpowered: neither of us could speak, but, for a considerable time, clung to each other in mutual embraces, unable to do any thing but weep. Our meeting affected all who saw us; and indeed I must acknowledge, in honour of those sable destroyers of human rights, that I never met with any ill treatment, or saw any offered to their slaves, except tying them, when necessary, to keep them from running away. When these people knew we were brother and sister, they indulged us to be together; and the man, to whom I supposed we belonged, lay with us, he in the middle, while she and I held one another by the hands across his breast all night; and thus for a while we forgot our misfortunes in the joy of being together; but even this small comfort was soon to have an end; for scarcely had the fatal morning appeared, when she was again torn from me forever! I was now more miserable, if possible, than before. The small relief which her presence gave me from pain was gone, and the wretchedness of my situation was redoubled by my anxiety after her fate, and my apprehensions lest her sufferings should be greater than mine, when I could not be with her to alleviate them. Yes, thou dear partner of all my childish sports! thou sharer of my joys and sorrows! happy should I have ever esteemed myself to encounter every misery for you, and to procure your freedom by the sacrifice of my own! Though you were early forced from my arms, your image has been always riveted in my heart, from which neither time nor fortune have been able to remove it: so that, while the thoughts of your sufferings have damped my prosperity, they have mingled with adversity, and increased its bitterness. To that Heaven which protects the weak from the strong, I commit the care of your innocence and virtues, if they have not already received their full reward; and if your youth and delicacy have not long since fallen victims to the violence of the African trader, the pestilential stench of a Guinea ship, the seasoning in the European colonies, or the lash and lust of a brutal and unrelenting overseer.

I did not long remain after my sister. I was again sold, and carried through a number of places, till, after travelling a considerable time, I came to a town called Timnah, in the most beautiful country I had yet seen in Africa. It was extremely rich, and there were many rivulets which flowed through it, and supplied a large pond in the centre of the town, where the people washed. Here I first saw and tasted cocoa nuts, which I thought superior to any nuts I had ever tasted before; and the trees, which were loaded, were also interspersed amongst the houses, which had commodious shades adjoining, and were in the same manner as ours, the insides being neatly plastered and white washed. Here I also saw and tasted for the first time sugar-cane. Their money

consisted of little white shells, the size of the fingernail: they were known in this country by the name of core. I was sold here for one hundred and seventy-two of them by a merchant who lived and brought me there. I had been about two or three days at his house, when a wealthy widow, a neighbour of his, came there one evening, and brought with her an only son, a young gentleman about my own age and size. Here they saw me; and, having taken a fancy to me, I was bought of the merchant, and went home with them. Her house and premises were situated close to one of those rivulets I have mentioned, and were the finest I ever saw in Africa: they were very extensive, and she had a number of slaves to attend her. The next day I was washed and perfumed, and when meal-time came, I was led into the presence of my mistress, and eat and drank before her with her son. This filled me with astonishment; and I could scarce help expressing my surprise that the young gentleman should suffer me, who was bound, to eat with him who was free; and not only so, but that he would not at any time either eat or drink till I had taken first, because I was the eldest, which was agreeable to our custom. Indeed every thing here, and all their treatment of me, made me forget that I was a slave. The language of these people resembled ours so nearly, that we understood each other perfectly. They had also the very same customs as we. There were likewise slaves daily to attend us, while my young master and I, with other boys, sported with our darts and bows and arrows, as I had been used to do at home. In this resemblance to my former happy state, I passed about two months, and I now began to think I was to be adopted into the family, and was beginning to be reconciled to my situation, and to forget by degrees my misfortunes, when all at once the delusion vanished; for, without the least previous knowledge, one morning early, while my dear master and companion was still asleep, I was awakened out of my reverie to fresh sorrow, and hurried away even amongst the uncircumcised.

Thus, at the very moment I dreamed of the greatest happiness, I found myself most miserable; and it seemed as if fortune wished to give me this taste of joy only to render the reverse more poignant. The change I now experienced was as painful as it was sudden and unexpected. It was a change indeed from a state of bliss to a scene which is inexpressible by me, as it discovered to me an element I had never before beheld, and till then had no idea of, and wherein such instances of hardship and fatigue continually occurred as I can never reflect on but with horror.

All the nations and people I had hither to passed through resembled our own in their manners, customs, and language; but I came at length to a country, the inhabitants of which differed from us in all those particulars. I was very much struck with this difference, especially when I came among a people who did not circumcise, and eat without washing their hands. They cooked also in iron pots, and had European cutlasses and cross bows, which were unknown to us, and fought with their fists among themselves. Their women were not so modest as ours, for they eat, and drank, and slept with their men. But, above all, I was amazed to see no sacrifices or offerings among them. In some of those places the people ornamented themselves with scars, and likewise filed their teeth very sharp. They wanted sometimes to ornament me in the same manner, but I would not suffer them; hoping that I might some time be among a people who did not thus disfigure themselves, as I thought they did. At last, I came to the banks of a large river, which was covered with canoes, in which the people appeared to live with their household utensils and provisions of all kinds. I was beyond measure astonished at this, as I had never before seen any water larger than a pond or a rivulet; and my surprise was mingled with no small fear, when I was put into one of these canoes, and we began to paddle and move along the river.We continued going on thus till night; and, when we came to land, and made fires on the banks, each family by themselves, some dragged their canoes on shore, others stayed and cooked in theirs, and lay in them all night. Those on the land had mats, of which they made tents, some in the shape of little houses: In these we slept; and, after the morning meal, we embarked again, and proceeded as before. I was often very much astonished to see

some of the women, as well as the men, jump into the water, dive to the bottom, come up again, and swim about. Thus I continued to travel, sometimes by land, sometimes by water, through different countries, and various nations, till, at the end of six or seven months after I had been kidnapped I arrived at the sea-coast. It would be tedious and uninteresting to relate all the incidents which befel me during this journey, and which I have not yet forgotten; of the various lands I passed through, and the manners and customs of all the different people among whom I lived: I shall therefore only observe, that, in all the places where I was, the soil was exceedingly rich; the pomkins, eadas, plantains, yams, etc., were in great abundance and of incredible size. There were also large quantities of different gums though not used for any purpose; and every where a great deal of tobacco. The cotton even grew quite wild; and there was plenty of redwood. I saw no mechanics whatever in all the way, except such as I have mentioned. The chief employment in all these countries was agriculture, and both the males and females, as with us, were brought up to it, and trained in the arts of war.

The first object which saluted my eyes when I arrived on the coast was the sea, and a slaveship, which was then riding at anchor, and waiting for its cargo. These filled me with astonishment, which was soon converted into terror, which I am yet at a loss to describe, nor the then feelings of my mind. When I was carried on board I was immediately handled, and tossed up, to see if I were sound, by some of the crew; and I was now persuaded that I had got into a world of bad spirits, and that they were going to kill me. Their complexions too differing so much from ours, their long hair, and the language they spoke, which was very different from any I had ever heard, united confirm me in this belief. Indeed, such were the horrors of my views and fears at the moment, that, if ten thousand worlds had been my own, I would have freely parted with them all to have exchanged my condition with that of the meanest slave in my own country. When I looked round the ship too, and saw a large furnace or copper boiling, and a multitude of black people of every description chained together, every one of their countenances expressing dejection and sorrow, I no longer doubted of my fate; and, quite over-powered with horror and anguish, I fell motionless on the deck and fainted. When I recovered a little, I found some black people about me, who I believed were some of those who brought me on board, and had been receiving their pay; they talked to me in order to cheer me, but all in vain. I asked them if we were not to be eaten by those white men with horrible looks, red faces, and long hair. They told me I was not; and one of the crew brought me a small portion of spirituous liquor in a wine-glass; but, being afraid of him, I would not take it out of his hand. One of the blacks therefore took it from him, and gave it to me, and I took a little down my palate, which, instead of reviving me, as they thought it would, threw me into the greatest consternation at the strange feeling it produced having never tasted any such liquor before. Soon after this, the blacks who brought me on board went off, and left me abandoned to despair. I now saw myself deprived of all chance of returning to my native country, or even the least glimpse of hope of gaining the shore, which I now considered as friendly; and I even wished for my former slavery, in preference to my present situation, which was filled with horrors of every kind, still heightened by my ignorance of what I was to undergo. I was not long suffered to indulge my grief; I was soon put down under the decks, and there I received such a salutation in my nostrils as I had never experienced in my life; so that, with the loathsomeness of the stench, and crying together, I became so sick and low that I was not able to eat, nor had I the least desire to taste any thing. I now wished for the last friend, death, to relieve me; but soon, to my grief, two of the white men offered me eatables; and, on my refusing to eat, one of them held me fast by the hands, and laid me across, I think, the windlass, and tied my feet while the other flogged me severely. I had never experienced any thing of this kind before; and, although not being used to the water, I naturally feared that element the first time I saw it; yet, nevertheless, could I have got over the nettings, I would have jumped over the side; but I could not; and, besides, the crew used to watch us very closely who were not chained down to the decks, lest we should leap into the water: and I have seen some of these poor African prisoners most severely cut for attempting to do so, and hourly whipped for not eating. This indeed was often the case with myself. In a little time after, amongst the poor chained men, I found some of my own nation, which in a small degree gave ease to my mind. I inquired of them what was to be done with us? they gave me to understand we were to be carried to these white people's country to work for them. I then was a little revived, and thought, if it were no worse than working, my situation was not so desperate: but still I feared I should be put to death, the white people looked and acted, as I thought, in so savage a manner; for I had never seen among any people such instances of brutal cruelty; and this not only shown towards us blacks, but also to some of the whites themselves. One white man in particular I saw, when we were permitted to be on deck, flogged so unmercifully with a large rope near the foremast, that he died in consequence of it; and they tossed him over the side as they would have done a brute. This made me fear these people the more; and I expected nothing less than to be treated in the same manner. I could not help expressing my fears and apprehensions to some of my countrymen: I asked them if these people had no country, but lived in this hollow place the ship? they told me they did not, but came from a distant one. "Then," said I, "how comes it in all our country we never heard of them?" They told me, because they lived so very far off. I then asked, where were their women? had they any like themselves? I was told they had. "And why," said I, "do we not see them?" they answered, because they were left behind. I asked how the vessel could go? they told me they could not tell; but that there were cloth put upon the masts by the help of the ropes I saw, and then the vessel went on; and the white men had some spell or magic they put in the water when they liked in order to stop the vessel. I was exceedingly amazed at this account, and really thought they were spirits. I therefore wished much to be from amongst them, for I expected they would sacrifice me: but my wishes were in vain; for we were so quartered that it was impossible for any of us to make our escape. While we staid on the coast I was mostly on deck; and one day, to my great astonishment, I saw one of these vessels coming in with the sails up. As soon as the whites saw it, they gave a great shout, at which we were amazed: and the more so as the vessel appeared larger by approaching nearer. At last she came to an anchor in my sight, and when the anchor was let go, I and my countrymen who saw it were lost in astonishment to observe the vessel stop; and were now convinced it was done by magic. Soon after this the other ship got her boats out, and they came on board of us, and the people of both ships seemed very glad to see each other. Several of the strangers also shook hands with us black people, and made motions with their hands, signifying, I suppose, we were to go to their country; but we did not understand them. At last, when the ship we were in had got in all her cargo, they made ready with many fearful noises, and we were all put under deck, so that we could not see how they managed the vessel. But this disappointment was the least of my sorrow. The stench of the hold while we were on the coast was so intolerably loathsome, that it was dangerous to remain there for any time, and some of us had been permitted to stay on the deck for the fresh air; but now that the whole ship's cargo were confined together, it became absolutely pestilential. The closeness of the place, and the heat of the climate, added to the number in the ship, which was so crowded that each had scarcely room to turn himself, almost suffocated us. This produced copious perspirations, so that the air soon became unfit for respiration, from a variety of loathsome smells, and brought on a sickness amongst the slaves, of which many died, thus falling victims to the improvident avarice, as I may call it, of their purchasers. This wretched situation was again aggravated by the galling of the chains, now become insupportable; and the filth of the necessary tubs, into which the children often fell, and were almost suffocated. The shreaks of the women, and the groans of the dying, rendered the whole a scene of horror almost inconceivable. Happily perhaps for myself I was soon reduced so low here that it was thought necessary to keep me almost always on deck; and from my extreme youth I was not put in fetters. In this situation I expected every hour to share the fate of my companions, some of whom were almost daily brought upon deck at the point of death, which I began to hope would soon put an end to my miseries. Often did I think many of the inhabitants of the deep much more happy than myself; I envied them the freedom they enjoyed, and as often wished I could change my condition for theirs. Every circumstance I met with served only to render my state more painful, and heighten my apprehensions and my opinion of the cruelty of the whites. One day they had taken a number of fishes; and when they had killed and satisfied themselves with many as they thought fit, to our astonishment who were on the deck, rather than give any of them to us to eat, as we expected, they tossed the remaining fish into the sea again, although we begged and prayed for some as well as we could, but in vain; and some of my countrymen, being pressed by hunger, took an opportunity, when they thought no one saw them, of trying to get a little privately; but they were discovered, and the attempt procured them some very severe floggings.

One day, when we had a smooth sea, and moderate wind, two of my wearied countrymen, who were chained together (I was near them at the time), preferring death to such a life of misery, somehow made through the nettings, and jumped into the sea; immediately another quite dejected fellow, who, on account of his illness, was suffered to be out of irons, also followed their example; and I believe many more would very soon have done the same, if they had not been prevented by the ship's crew, who were instantly alarmed. Those of us that were the most active were in a moment put down under the deck; and there was such a noise and confusion amongst the people of the ship as I never heard before, to stop her, and get the boat out to go after the slaves. However, two of the wretches were drowned, but they got the other, and afterwards flogged him unmercifully, for thus attempting to prefer death to slavery. In this manner we continued to undergo more hardships than I can now relate; hardships which are inseparable from this accursed trade. Many a time we were near suffocation, from the want of fresh air, which we were often without for whole days together. This, and the stench of the necessary tubs, carried off many. During our passage I first saw flying fishes, which surprised me very much: they used frequently to fly across the ship, and many of them fell on the deck. I also now first saw the use of the quadrant. I had often with astonishment seen the mariners make observations with it, and I could not think what it meant. They at last took notice of my surprise; and one of them, willing to increase it, as well as to gratify my curiosity, made me one day look through it. The clouds appeared to me to be land, which disappeared as they passed along. This heightened my wonder: and I was now more persuaded than ever that I was in another world, and that every thing about me was magic. At last, we came in sight of the island of Barbadoes, at which the whites on board gave a great shout, and made many signs of joy to us. We did not know what to think of this; but, as the vessel drew nearer, we plainly saw the harbour, and other ships of different kinds and sizes: and we soon anchored amongst them off Bridge Town. Many merchants and planters now come on board, though it was in the evening. They put us in separate parcels, and examined us attentively. They also made us jump, and pointed to the land, signifying we were to go there. We thought by this we should be eaten by these ugly men, as they appeared to us; and when, soon after we were all put down under the deck again, there was much dread and trembling among us, and nothing but bitter cries to be heard all the night from these apprehensions, insomuch that at last the white people got some old slaves from the land to pacify us. They told us we were not to be eaten, but to work, and were soon to go on land where we should see many of our country people. This report eased us much; and sure enough, soon after we landed, there came to us Africans of all languages. We were conducted immediately to the merchant's yard, where we were all pent up together like so many sheep in a fold, without regard to sex or age. As every object was new to me, everything I saw filled me with surprise. What struck me first was, that the houses were built with bricks, in stories, and in every other respect different from those I have seen in Africa: but I was still more astonished on seeing people on horseback. I did not know what this could mean; and indeed I thought these people were full of nothing but magical arts. While I was in this astonishment, one of my fellow prisoners spoke to a countryman of his about the horses, who said they were the same kind they had in their country. I understood them, though they were from a distant part of Africa, and I thought it odd I had not seen any horses there; but afterwards, when I came to converse with different Africans, I found they had many horses amongst them, and much larger than those I then saw. We were not many days in the merchant's custody, before we were sold after their usual manner, which is this: on a signal given (as the beat of a drum), the buyers rush at once into the yard where the slaves are confined, and make choice of that parcel they like best. The noise and clamour with which this is attended, and the eagerness visible in the countenances of the buyers, serve not a little to increase the apprehension of the terrified Africans, who may well be supposed to consider them as the ministers of that destruction to which they think themselves devoted. In this manner, without scruple, are relations and friends separated, most of them never to see each other again. I remember in the vessel in which I was brought over, in the men's apartment, there were several brothers who, in the sale, were sold in different lots; and it was very moving on this occasion to see and hear their cries at parting. O, ye nominal Christians! might not an African ask you, learned you this from your God? who says unto you, Do unto all men as you would men should do unto you. Is it not enough that we are torn from our country and friends to toil for your luxury and lust of gain? Must every tender feeling be likewise sacrificed to your avarice? Are the dearest friends and relations, now rendered more dear by their separation from their kindred, still to be parted from each other, and thus preventing from cheering the gloom of slavery with the small comfort of being together, and mingling their sufferings and sorrows? Why are parents to love their children, brothers their sisters, or husbands their wives? Surely this is a new refinement in cruelty, which, while it has no advantage to atone for it, thus aggravates distress, and adds fresh horrors even to the wretchedness of slavery.

AFRICAN CHRISTIANITY: AN OVERVIEW

By Ogbu U. Kalu

INTRODUCTION

Since the conversion of Emperor Constantine, the story of Christianity has increasingly appeared to be the story of a western religion. Appearances can be deceptive precisely because there are communities in Africa that could claim an involvement in the Jesus movement from its inception till today. When Christianity abandoned its Palestinian roots, its new home in the Graeco-Roman world included North Africa (Maghrib), which was the breadbasket of Rome, and shared extensive commercial and cultural relations with Palestine and the Levant. Before the story of Judich, the treasurer to Candace (Queen Mother) of the Nubian kingdom of Meroe, who met Philip en-route from a pilgrimage to Rome, geographical contiguity had made it possible for the infant Jesus to take refuge in Africa. The Coptic Orthodox church celebrates this event annually. Later, Christianity shifted its center of gravity yet again into barbarian Europe where every effort was made to domesticate and repackage it in western imagery. Recently, commentators have observed another shift from the northern hemisphere into the south. David Barrett's annual statistics in his *World Encyclopedia* (1982, 2000) reads as follows:

He shows that the number of Christians in Africa grew from 8.75 million in 1900 to 117 million in 1970 to 335.1 million by mid-2000, and projects a figure of 360 million for mid-2003 and 600.5 million for 2005.[1] Thus by 1999 most Christians in the world lived in Latin America, Africa and Asia in that order; that out of 1.87 billion Christians in the world, 1.11 billion are non-white. Africa looms large again. Out of 210.6 million Evangelicals, Africa tops the list with 69.5 million; out of 423.7 million Pentecostals/Charismatic Christians in the world, 126 million live in Africa.

Year	World Pop.	Christian	Christian	Non-West	West
1900	1,620m	558m	34%	14%	86%
1950	2,510m	856m	34%	36%	64%
1970	3,696m	1,236m	34%	44%	56%
1990	5,266m	1,747m	33%	56%	44%
2000	6,055m	2,000m	32%	60%	40%

Given the growth rate, these figures are much larger now. There are more Anglicans in Nigeria (with a Christian population of 49 million) than in England and Europe put together. The significance of Africa's role in the formation of Christianity was remembered in 1971 when the All African Council of Churches convened an emergency session to reflect on an indigenous confession of faith in Alexandria, because the Alexandrian School was prominent in the task of consolidating Christian theology and identity amidst the constraints of Roman imperial culture. When the doctrines, polity, liturgy and ethics of Christianity were still being formulated, African voices were powerful. Alexandria and Antioch constituted the dominant and competing schools in Christian apologetics. St. Augustine and Tertullian were not Italians! The Islamic scourge in the seventh century gradually dismantled certain aspects of African Christianity as it retreated into Coptic villages as a symbol of nationalism and as it struggled in Nubia (till the fifteenth century) and in Ethiopia to witness amidst the harassments by various Muslim dynasties. Ken Sawyer and Youhana Youssef argue strongly that this story is a part of Africa's history just as Akin Akinade urges that Islam is also important in Africa's religious journey and must not be perceived as hostile religions dividing the communities.

In the fifteenth century, Europe abandoned the crusades and initiated a more creative response to Islamic economic, cultural and political challenges. In this attempt to use sea routes to circumvent the Muslims, new efforts were made to evangelize Africa but both the slave trade and colonization combined to stunt the vigor of evangelization. Christian presence in Africa retreated into the *feitoras*, trading forts, of various European nations until the large-scale missionary enterprise commencing in the nineteenth century created a resurgence into the hinterlands of the communities that lived south of the Sahara Desert. This enterprise laid the roots of the numerical explosion and maturity of the modern period. The poignancy of this is buttressed by the fact that at the World Missionary Conference, Edinburgh, 1910, no African was present; Asia

including Japan occupied more of the interest of the conferees. Significantly, contemporary Africa is the laboratory of Christianity in the twenty-first century. Its story could be told in four sequences.

I. THE FIRST TIME: EARLY CHRISTIANITY IN NORTH AFRICA

There is little certainty about the date of entry of Christianity into Egypt and much of the regions to the west such as Cyrenia, Numidia, Africa and Mauretania. The story of the Pentecost event indicates clearly that people from this region were present at the crucial launching of the church; they were both diasporic Jews and non-Jewish proselytes. Indeed, the Coptic Orthodox Church claims that both Thomas and Mark were in Egypt during the persecution of the Jesus movement; that Thomas moved from here to India and that Mark was the first of the over 100 *abunas* of the church. The pattern of vertical expansion of Christianity indicates that there was an insignificant Christian presence in Egypt in about 239AD, and that from 274AD the percentage of Christians in the population grew at a significant rate, more than the percentage growth rare for the rest of the Graeco-Roman world.

A number of reasons have been adduced; the first relates to the political and social forces that shaped the movement, especially the shift of the class structure of membership as upper class women joined and provided facilities for the predominantly lower class votaries. Equally crucial was the conversion of some Jews; their social and commercial prominence protected the fledging movement in its early days because Judaism was the only non-Roman *licita religio* in the sprawling empire. The measures of suppression and repression against the new religion ironically benefited the new subversive religion; the intermittent persecutions, such as the Decian, Severian, Valerian and especially the long-drawn Diocletian, strengthened rather than weakened the confessors, and as they escaped the onslaught they spread their belief. From this perspective, those debates about purity and against *traditores* betrays the degree of commitment by ordinary believers who served as everyday evangelists. Committed agency was the core of Christian survival and martyrdom became a means of witnessing. The power of the message of Christianity was important but the indigenous worldview was equally crucial as traditional Egyptian religion contained much that resonated with the new: notions of salvation, eschatology, ethics and liturgy could find parallels in the Osiri-Horus myth; so did the intellectual environment that comprised gnostic thought forms—preserved in papyrus manufactured in ancient Egypt. Alexandria was the intellectual capital of the Mediterranean and paraded Egyptian contributions in writing, philosophy, art and architecture. The catechetical school in Alexandria under famous leaders such as Pantaneus, Origen and Dionysius used both allegorization and creative syncretism, known as "spoiling the Egyptians" to interpret the Christian faith to a less educated populace and for the consolidation of the new religion amidst competing prescriptions about the way to heaven.

In this fluid period of the Jesus movement, theological debates were rife about the nature of God, Jesus and the character of the Holy Spirit. It was often argued whether Jesus was truly human or only appeared to be so; had one nature; two natures (human and divine); or two natures in one person; whether the Holy Spirit issued *from the Father* or *from the Father and the Son;* and how both were related to God. Such theological issues have not been resolved until this day. Whoever had the power to uphold their views, would declare the opponents as heretics. The canon did not have clear boundaries as many manuscripts circulated with the semblance of authenticity. These same manuscripts are fuelling the denial of the speech of God and repudiation of canonicity in Western Christian traditions such as in contemporary feminism and the Jesus Seminar. Power politics in the church became the tradition partly because Constantine's conversion that removed persecution thrust Christianity into the center of the public space and created more opportunities for ecclesiastic politics, debates and conciliarist posture that was bereft of consensus. The councils held at Nicaea and Chalcedon created more warring parties. Constantine's conversion may have weakened the tensile strength of the Jesus movement. Yet the period yielded many doctrinal confessions that have stood the test of time and brought Africa into the center of World Christianity.

For some, the indigenization of the message was achieved through the vernacular translations of the Bible into Coptic languages such as Sahidic (Upper Nile), Boharic (Nile Delta) and Bashmuric (Middle Nile). The use of the Coptic language in the liturgy and Bible domesticated the message and aided personal witnessing, which was the most powerful form of evangelism in this period. Evidence of deep religious consciousness was betrayed by the proliferation of Christian art especially the distinctly embellished genre of icons. Indeed, the indigenous culture was reshaped as evident in the funerary artifacts found in a tomb excavated at Antinoe in Upper Egypt; however, mummification persisted as indigenous religion proved resilient. Another lasting contribution of this region was the eremitic tradition as hermits of various types and numbers built their retreats in the deserts and mountains. The Pachomian regulation was adopted by many hermitages in due course. These enclaves contributed in nurturing Christian spirituality, sense of mission, and served as havens for the persecuted or for those who got tired of the virulent politics of the day. In later years, as the gilded Christianity in metropolitan Alexandria was emasculated, monasteries would prove to be the surviving centers of the Jesus movement. It should be stressed that Christianity in Egypt flourished amidst resilient ancient mystery religions that would later enjoy a renaissance.

At some point in time, the movement flowed west and exhibited a character typical of those who are far from urban centers and its flaunt of learning and scholarship. Two types of Christianity developed in Africa and Numidia: one was the ascetic tradition typified by the Donatists. They mixed Christianity with nationalism and saw the Romans, whether clerics or merchants in agricultural goods, as exploiters. By this time, this region had replaced Egypt as the granary of Italy. A particular group, the Circumcellion, became pirates who terrorized the upper classes. The socio-economic and class dimensions were as important as the insistence that those who did not stand faithful during the persecutions had no business in leadership roles in the church; after all, translation ensured that the lower classes understood the Scriptures. Similarly, the conflict between Gospel and culture troubled the Montanists who emphasized the pneumatic tradition in Christian life and despised the tango with Roman idolatrous culture in the philosophical theology of the Alexandrian school. Yelling that they had Jesus and did not need the schools, they rejected the "spoiling of the Egyptians", a method that sought to express the fundamentals of Christian faith in the idiom of Rome's imperial religion. The vitality of this Christian movement breathed through the ardent apologetics in Tertullian's *Ad Uxorem* as well as his treatise on baptism. As fishes they lived in the water of the new birth. They enlarged the space for women and challenged the patriarchal tradition of the period. Needless to add, many of these issues dominate contemporary theology on the continent.

The tendency has been to argue that the virulent debates, arid philosophy and the lack of a vibrant evangelism among the indigenous Berber, Tuareg and Kworaraffa people embedded a weak Christianity that could not survive the fiery test of Islamic onslaught. The story is more complicated. Christianity in Africa was only gradually becoming African Christianity. The Maghrib passed through many foreign rules; each left its imprint on the language, racial composition and sense of community. As the Roman Empire declined, Byzantine rule was riddled with heavy taxation, doctrinal controversies, competing claims between Rome and Constantinople over supremacy, before the period of rule under the Vandals privileged Arianism and more financial burden. The re-conquest of Africa by the Byzantines was carrion-comfort relief and naturally the populace mistook the arrival of Islam as a welcome. Quite important is the fact that the early Muslim dynasties did not try to wipe out Christianity. Their victory over the Christian territories was so rapid and extensive that they lacked the human resources for governance and needed Christian bishops of all doctrinal persuasions to serve as civil officials. The early Caliphs themselves were not secure; assassinations boiled their political pots; and they were still close to the tolerant teaching of the prophet towards "the people of the book". Christianity enjoyed growth until the period of the fourth Caliph when new leadership and new political conditions compelled and intensified the program of Arabization.

William B. Anderson, who worked for many years in Sudan, has contributed an aspect of the research on Sudanese Christianity that he did with Wheeler and Werner. The cultural flows between Egypt and its southern neighbor included the spread of the gospel. South of the first cataract was the region that Egyptians called the Kush Kingdom, a reference that included both Nubia and Abyssinia or Ethiopia. It covered the region between Egypt and central Africa and its mineral resources and commercial potentials allured the Egyptians. The relationship remained rife with ambiguities as the warlike Blemmyes (the ancestors of the Beja people) constantly raided the Egyptian towns around Thebes; yet the Nubians pilgrimaged to the cultic center at Philae. Egypt occupied parts of Nubia at certain points in time; for instance, in retaliation against Nubian attacks they sacked the ancient Kush capital of Napata and Nubians retreated to the second cataract and founded the rich kingdom of Meroe, whose court is referred to in the pages of the Bible. This fact and other archeological evidence shows that Christianity had moved down to this region before Empress Theodora of Byzantium subverted her husband by dispatching a Monophysite priest, Julianos in 543AD.

First, vast commercial and cultural contacts introduced Christianity to the Kush; second, Judich's story suggests familiarity with the Septuagint within a few years after the resurrection; third, archeological evidence shows that a church existed at Farah in the fourth century; fourth, Jewish communities at Elephantine and the evangelistic bishops of Philae must have introduced the Hebrew Bible and Christianity into Nubia; and fifth, many who escaped from the various persecutions took their

Christianity down the Nile, Julian's enterprise in the sixth century reflects on the new political context when the Nobadian rulers who benefited from dismantling the Meroe kingdom, sought political alliance with Emperor Justinian. The fall of Meroe was brought about through a combination of raids by the king of Ethiopia and the incursion of Kush communities from the interior into the Nile basin. Both Julianos and Longinus, who came later, actually evangelized the Nobadian court and initiated the spread of the gospel further down the Nile to the Alowa though the other Nubian community, Makuria had a Melkite (pro-Chalcedonian) version of the gospel.

The spread of Christianity gradually moved from the courts as churches took over the temples of indigenous gods; Episcopal sees with cathedrals were built in Faras, Ibrim, Sai, Dongola and other places. Egyptian influence continued to hold sway as the Patriarch of Alexandria supplied the leadership and personnel with monks from Egypt, Syria and a muscular corps of indigenes. Eremitic tradition planted the gospel into the soil such that Christianity in Nubia survived Islamic onslaught until the fifteenth century. The unification of the northern kingdoms of Nobades and Makuria after the seventh century meant that the whole of Nubia acted in concert as a Christian kingdom. But state-driven Christianity tends to privilege an institutional character and archeology does not leave much evidence of the level of the conversion of the people or the appropriation of the charismatic resources of the gospel for everyday life.

Further down the fourth cataract, Ethiopian (Abyssinian) Christianity has survived from the early period to the present. Ogbu Kalu tells the story from two perspectives: the insider and outsider versions of the history. Court influence was equally the key to the survival. The reference, Ethiopia, only became the designation for the entire region when the translators of the Septuagint in 300BC mistakenly translated the Hebrew "Kush" into Greek *Aithiopia*, a word that the Greek used for any country south of their known world, and derived from their word for "black face", *aithiops*. Inscriptions confirm that King Ezana converted as a child and imaged himself as a Constantine whose victories over the straw houses of the Nobia and the stone-built cities of the Kush came from God. Two young Syrian Monophysites, who were captured on the Red Sea port of Adulis, became creative evangelists in the Aksum court located a hundred miles inland. They were brought to the court when it was under a regency. Frumentius not only reared the young king but was enthroned as the first bishop. This stamped the power of the state on the character of the church as various kings sustained the church: Digna-Jan in the ninth century, Dilna'od in the tenth, and Amda-Siyan who restructured the church extensively in the fourteenth century. Yohannes IV (1872–1889) and Menelik II (1889–1913) left indelible imprints on the modern face of Ethiopian Orthodox Church. The kings built many churches and monasteries while Egypt supplied the *abuna*.

The Nine saints or *Sadaqan* (Syrian Monophysite exiles) not only extended rural evangelization, but established monasteries that became important in rooting the gospel and an identifiable spirituality. Soon rival abbots of monastic houses, standing on the precedence of their foundations, turned church politics around the tripod of king, *abuna* and abbots. When the power of Aksum declined and the center of Ethiopia shifted south from the Tigre, the story remains one of inculturation of the gospel within the vernacular: retention of Jewish traditions of the early church; liturgical innovations that utilized ingredients of traditional culture; and virulent debates on Sabbath observation and other finer points of theology. Ethiopian contributions to Christian art, architecture, music, literacy and liturgy have remained enduring. The Ethiopian church, with its large number of aesthetic crosses, remained in splendid isolation and served as an ingredient of the national culture, until Europe rediscovered it in the fifteenth century in the quest for the mythical kingdom of Prester John. This contact saved it from the jihadist attacks of the imam, Ahmed Gran (the left-handed), but it exposed it to disruptive foreign influences especially efforts to annex it to Rome. A combination of soft state and foreign influences created more internal debates that weakened the church by the nineteenth century.

The story of Islam and Ethiopia is a long one, because just as Jesus was sheltered in Egypt so also was the prophet Mohammed in Ethiopia, when the king refused to repatriate him in spite of all blandishment from his enemies in Mecca. He instructed a tolerance that his followers reneged. The survival of Christianity once again was linked to the recovery of the state due to two able monarchs, Yohannes IV and Menelik II, who dealt with the problem of foreign influence, held off the Mahdists from Sudan (1899), defeated Italian colonial endeavor in 1896, and recovered the impetus from the Muslims who had gained high political positions as supporters of Gran. Yohannes revitalized the church through four Coptic bishops and evangelized the Galla who had clung tenaciously to traditional religion through the years. Menelik established the structures of modern Ethiopia which was inherited and developed by Emperor Haile Selassie. This story will be important for reconstructing the anti-structural agency of those dubbed as "Ethiopians" in the nineteenth century.

II. THE SECOND CHANCE: IBERIAN CATHOLICISM

Two scholars, David Kpobi and Paul Gundani deal with the extensive Iberian presence started when a new style of the European response to the challenges of Islam was signaled by the recapture of Ceuta in 1415. Imaged as a crusade, its immense significance included the recovery and retention of the source of grain supply from Muslims' clutch; the information about the extent of Arab trans-Saharan commerce in salt and gold that extended into western and central Sudan or the Senegalese Futa Jallon region. Psychologically, it released a daring temper and maritime exploits. Prince Henry's nautical school at Sagres experimented with sails, keels, compasses and astrolabes. The Portuguese could dare sail the Atlantic in the quest for a sea route to the source of the spices, encircle, circumvent and cut into the Arab trans-Saharan gold trade from the south.

Couched in Christian idiom, they sought to reconnect with the empire of Prester John and convert the heathens. In the combined motives for gold, glory and God, the Christian motif fitted into the rhetoric of the period while the commercial drive remained privileged. Papal bulls offered the *padroado* rights to the Portuguese monarch to appoint clerical orders for evangelization and to fend off competing European interests.

Iberian Catholic presence in Africa from the sixteenth through to the eighteenth centuries was characterized by certain facts: Portugal was a small country and did not possess the manpower to control and evangelize the large territory that was "discovered" between the years 1460 and 1520, and stretched from Cape Blanco to Sumatra and Java. They chose to stay on the islands and coastal regions of their shoe-string empire. Iberian Catholicism was a social ornament, a religion of ceremonies and outward show; thus in the islands and a few areas where they established Christian presence on the mainland, adherence supplanted strong spiritual commitment. Court-alliance used religion as an instrument of diplomatic and commercial relationship. A missionary impact that insisted upon transplantation of European models remained fleeting, superficial and ill-conceived. In the islands of Cape Verde and Sao Thome, the Portuguese built prototypes of Lisbon and established churches and cathedrals that also formed the pastors for interior ministry. In the Gold Coast of the Atlantic Ocean and at Kilwa in the Indian Ocean, they built their first forts, but the only serious evangelization was among the *mestizo* children of the traders. The incursion into the Kingdoms of Benin and Warri soon failed as the Portuguese found more pepper in India. The enduring presence only occurred in the Kongo-Soyo kingdoms until the eighteenth century. Here they priested some indigenes, especially the children of Portuguese traders and gentlemen and some of the servants of white priests, but the force of the ministry weakened with the changing pattern of trade, internal politics and the disbanding of the Jesuits.

Celebrated cases, such as the conversion of the *Monomotapa* of Mashonaland, central Africa, soon faded in disasters, while the Iberian presence in *Estado da India* or East African coast was riddled with competition against Indians and Arabs. The thirteen ethnic groups of Madagascar warred relentlessly against the Portuguese while the Arabs of Oman re-conquered the northern sector of the eastern coast. Finally, other European countries challenged them for a share of the lucrative trade, which then turned primarily into slave trading. Iberian hegemony collapsed; broken statues in certain parts of Africa betrayed the missionary exploits of yesteryears. In the Gold Coast, a syncretistic religion that uses crosses and candles is aptly named *Nana Antoni*, perhaps in faded memory of St Anthony. By the end of the eighteenth century, twenty-one forts dotted the coast of West Africa; some had chaplains and many did not. These were poorly paid in compromising trade goods. The Dutch and Danish experiments that employed indigenous chaplains equally failed. The fleeting encounter with Christian presence in South Saharan Africa after the debacle on the Maghrib collapsed as the gospel bearers concentrated on enslaving prospective converts.

III. RESILIENT VISION: ABOLITIONISM AND EVANGELICAL REVIVAL

In the twilight of the eighteenth century, two forces combined to regenerate the evangelization of south Saharan Africa: abolitionism and evangelical revival. Spiritual awakenings occurred in many nations from the mid-eighteenth century into the nineteenth century. Its register included an emphasis on the Bible, the cross-event, conversion experience and a pro-active expression of ones faith. Their connection with abolitionism was through the social activist component of evangelicalism that proposed to stop slave trade by involving the chiefs who controlled the supply side. Through the establishment of legitimate trade, a new administrative structure secured, with agreements and the use of Christianity as a civilizing agent, an enabling environment. This was established for combating slave traders. A network of philanthropists and religious groups prosecuted the abolitionist agitation across

the Atlantic Ocean. As Jehu Handles argues, the crucial dimension in the story is the role of African Americans, including liberated slaves, Africans in diaspora such as Cuguano and Equiano (who wrote vividly about their experiences), and entrepreneurs such as Paul Cuffee, who spent his resources in creating a commercial enterprise between Africa, Britain and America. Motives varied: religion; politics; commerce; rational humanism; and local exigencies.

In England, the Committee of the Black Poor complained about the increasing social and financial problem caused by the number of poor liberated slaves. In America, an educated African American elite became concerned over the welfare of the race and drew up plans for equipping the young with education and skills for survival. Meanwhile, those slaves who took the dangerous option to desert their masters and fight on behalf of the British forces in the War of Revolution complained about their excruciating conditions. They had perceived the revolutionary war as an opportunity for their liberation; absorbed the liberal constitutional ideology and struggled against odds in Nova Scotia and the West Indies to create a space for the practice of their ideals. Anglican patriots had emigrated out of America with their racism intact. Indeed, the next century would witness many rebellions in the West Indies over liberation from slavery. The liberated slaves also created a link between abolitionism and mission by weaving the intriguing link between de Tocqueville's liberal philosophy and Henry Alline's New Life Evangelicalism; between Enlightenment ideas and Christianity. They shared the same ideals of individual enterprise, personal responsibility, equality before the law, and freedom to practice one's religion, as the Republicans against whom they fought.

As Jehu Hanciles shows, when the British philanthropists chose Sierra Leone as a haven for liberated slaves in 1787, the experiment nearly foundered because of the attacks from local chiefs and the lack of adequate provisions for the new settlers. At this point, the Nova Scotians and West Indian maroons were dispatched to Sierra Leone. From their own perspective, they went out on a mission to Sierra Leone in 1792, before any British missionary society was founded and with a clear vision to build a new society under the mandate of the gospel, and one that avoided the indigenous chiefs who had been compromised through the slave trade. Indeed, they advocated a separation of church and state so as to de-link the missionary enterprise of redeeming Africa through religion from the patronage of the Governors of trading companies. They set the cultural tone of industry and religion that nurtured thousands of recaptives in Sierra Leone between 1807 and 1864. These freed slaves became agents of missionary enterprise throughout the West Coast. The liberated slaves who returned to Yoruba land served variously as educators, interpreters, counselors to indigenous communities, negotiators with the new change agents, preachers, traders and leaders of public opinion in many West African communities. Adjai Crowther, who was made a bishop in 1864, signified their achievement. Furthermore, the Colonization Society recruited enough African Americans to found Liberia in 1822 and from this period until the 1920s, African Americans were a significant factor in the missionary enterprise in Africa. Specifically, their Methodist and Baptist spirituality created a form of appropriation of the gospel that endured.

But other crucial factors determined the patterns of Christian presence in nineteenth century Africa. The resurgence of the missionary enterprise enlarged in the scale of number of missionary bodies, individuals, theologies, motives and vocations, and modes of funding and training. In spite of wide acceptance by denominations, the significance was its popular appeal as all classes of society in various countries voluntarily sustained the enterprise. By mid-century, the faith movements encouraged individuals to foray into mission fields without institutional support. Many women used the opportunity. Biblical roots and the general optimism of the century set the tone, perhaps to the chagrin of Western Europeans who had started missions in the eighteenth century before England and America became engaged. Education, Translation of the

Scriptures into indigenous languages and charitable institutions such as medical/health care delivery and artisan workshops domesticated the message and equally changed the character of Christian presence. These bred loyalists.

Evangelicalism accomplished certain functions in the resurgence: it reconciled the developed consciousness of individual responsibility to the Christian faith; by developing a close fellowship of believers, it served as antidote to atomistic individualism; and its distinction of nominal/formal Christians from real Christianity yielded a corps of committed personnel that could be mobilized and deployed into mission. Through its network, an organization emerged that could recruit, train, fund and network with global centers. Logistics, access to indigenous people and organization changed the face of Christianity. The bands of evangelicals of various hues were able to extend the campaign for a life of holiness from the boundaries of the individual to family and society; radical discipleship and personal decision meant responding to a call to save the heathens. As America warmed to foreign missions, it brought enormous energy, optimism and vigor and human resources. It was felt that the development of technology and the strength of North Atlantic powers created a viable environment for missions; that there was civil and religious liberty at home and that popery was diminishing. Other racial theories, such as chosen people, covenant, burden, responsibility, civilization, manifest destiny, and other Rudyard Kipling ideas, came later and linked missions to the imperial idea. It is important to understand the development of these ideas as well as their impact on the character of Christianity in Africa. Emphasis changed through time and each phase compelled different rationalizations.

The Roman Catholics revamped their organization and fund raising strategies for missions such that the rivalry with Protestants influenced the pace and direction of the spread of the gospel. However, these changes coincided with new geopolitical factors. Competing forms of European nationalism changed the character of the contact with Africa from informal commercial relations into formal colonial hegemony by mid-nineteenth century. The Berlin Conference of 1884/5 partitioned Africa and insisted on formal occupation. It introduced a new spirit that overawed indigenous institutions and sought to transplant European institutions and cultures. Collusion with the civilizing project diminished the spiritual vigor of missionary presence and turned it into cultural and power encounters. This explains the predominant strategy of enslavement in the missionary presence in southern Africa. Holy Ghost Fathers, at Bagamoyo, off the coast of Zanzibar, turned their plantation into a lucrative exploitation of young people. The white settler communities in East Africa established a tight control of ministry that spurned the cultural genius of the people. Quite typical was the change in the attitude towards the Bombay Africans, who had been repatriated from Bombay where they had acquired education and whose resources sustained the CMS activities in Mombasa as the mission moved further inland. Their enormous contributions were spurned in a welter of hostile antagonism. The Catholic missionary presence in the Congo colluded with the brutality of Leopold, until the international outcry of 1908 forced him to sell the colony to Belgium. The abusive Portuguese presence in Angola, Mozambique, Guinea Bissau and Cape Verde Islands would later elicit anti-clerical and Marxist response after the forced decolonization.

Indeed, the dominant aspect of the story became the forms of African Christian initiatives, hidden scripts and resistance to the system of control that sought to make the agent legible. In one place after another, indigenous prophetic figures inspired a charismatic response to the gospel and through their efforts Christianity grew. "Native" agency became the instrument of growth. Some Africans gave voice to the indigenous feeling against Western Cultural iconoclasm and control of decision-making in the colonial churches. Using the promise in the Psalms that Ethiopia shall raise its hands to God, "Ethiopianism" became a movement of cultural and religious protest. As a form of cultural appreciation, it indulged in social and historical excavation, a recovery and re-contextualization of black traditions of emancipation hidden from consciousness of black people by colonial hegemony. In its religious guise, it breathed with hope that Africans would bear the burden to evangelize and build an autonomous church devoid of denominations and shirk European control of the church. They wove a network of educated Africans across West Africa to evangelize, inculturate, and create African Christianity. Typical of their ideology was *Ethiopia Unbound* by the Gold Coast lawyer, Casely Hayford and *The Return of the Exiles* by Wilmot Blyden of Liberia, Mojola Agbebi and others changed their English names, wore African clothes and decided to exit from the colonial religious establishment by founding African churches without foreign aid. Products of missionary enclaves in southern and central Africa did the same.

In southern Africa, the movement gained strength by its alliance with the American African Methodist Episcopal Church and its black ideology. Its leaders used the ideology to reintegrate their dispersed communities. Meanwhile, a strong charismatic religious force emerged. As racism divided whites and blacks in the Pentecostal impulse that came from Zion City, Indiana, the latter claimed the Zion and Apostolic rubrics and integrated symbols from indigenous religions to reformat the polity, liturgy and ethics of Western Christianity. Through mine workers, the movement percolated through the region. Between 1913 and 1990, the number of African Indigenous Churches in South Africa grew from 30 to more than 6,000. By the late 1920s, and in the midst of the second wave of the influenza that came with the First World War, visions and dreams and prayer led some to tap the pneumatic resources of the gospel, emphasize healing and use of African symbolism, musical instruments and leadership. The space for women enlarged as it did with the Montanists of the early years. African Indigenous/Initiated Churches (AICs), differently referred to as *Zionists* in southern Africa, *Aladura* in West Africa and *Roho* in East Africa, changed the face of Christianity in the twentieth century in Africa. Graham Duncan and Ogbu Kalu image the varied forms of revivalism that characterized the period as patterns of indigenous appropriation of the gospel message. But specifically, the AICs are paid closer attention by Afe Adogame and Lizio Jafta, because these churches constitute an important African contribution to world Christianity.

However, a number of AICs separated from the classical forms and mutated into the genres that had tenuous roots with the original impulse; for instance, in Nigeria, the Zionist type, Cherubim and Seraphim, split into 51 groups between 1925 and 1975. Other genres emerged such as the *vitalistic* (who in the quest for miraculous power resort to occult resources as in the Sixth and Seventh Book of Moses), and *nativistic* healing homes that clothe indigenous religion with a veneer of Christian symbolism. The fastest growing groups among them are the *messianic* forms in which the leader claims to be one or the other of the Trinity. These have shifted from the centrality of the Bible. Sabbatharian forms emerged that did not confess that Jesus is Lord. Some have incautiously romanticized the AICs because they wish to be inclusive and non-judgmental. This is a dilemma that church history must face and a call must be made. H.W. Turner, who pioneered this field, pointed to the need for a typology, however difficult, imprecise or lacking in political correctness. An eye to typology aids analysis as the movement has widened beyond the pale of Christianity. Some *revivalist* groups are nationalistic apologists who feel that Africa knew and worshipped God; they repackage indigenous religion with Christian format such as statements of belief, Christian architecture and the resonance between the Bible stories and African religions. One group calls itself, *Godianism*, another, *Orunmila* and yet another, *Afrikania*.

The story of Christianity in Africa has always been linked to the Muslim factor. Islam benefited from colonialism and expanded south of the Sahara, not just because of jihads that led to state formations but because Europe shifted from an idea that Islam was a form of superstition to the acceptance that since it acknowledged one God, it was superior to African religions. Bosworth Smith provided the arsenal that combined evolutionary theory with

observations in India to argue that it was a religion suited for primitive races; that a religion that prohibited the use of alcohol was best for the 'natives'. For other political reasons enshrined in the Indirect Rule strategy, the official policy protected Islam that used improved modes of communication to trade and spread. The battle with Christian "Soudan" parties merely modified protectionist structures to "one, one emirate". The power of Islam has continued to challenge Christianity even when the state adopts a secular ideology because Islam perceives the state as an instrument for promoting religion. Thus, Moslems grab the center of power in every state. Akintunde Akinade explores these challenges.

The significant aspects of the nineteenth century are that—as missionaries sowed the seed of the gospel—Africans appropriated it from a primal, charismatic worldview and read the translated Scriptures from that hermeneutic. Indigenous agency subverted control through voice and exit; recovered the pneumatic resources of the Gospel and challenged missionary Christianity to be fully biblical. This set the stage for the decolonization process that followed the world wars. New forces such as the implosion of the state challenged the heritage of African Christianity; the collapse of the dictatorial states and attendant poverty probed the tensile strength of the church's stewardship. Inexplicably, charismatic and Pentecostal spirituality resurfaced to provide the energy for growth and sustainability in the midst of untoward circumstances.

IV. NEW DIMENSIONS IN AFRICAN CHRISTIANITY: POWER, POVERTY AND PRAYER

Ogbu Kalu examines the vast changes that occurred in African Christianity between the world wars and that catalyzed decolonization. Between the First World War and the emergence of political independence, several denominations sought to consolidate their enterprises just as many religious entrepreneurs hatched various "Christianities" out of a vibrant religious culture. The two world wars and economic depression created so much disquiet that the pace of revivalism and religious innovation increased. Wade Harris, for instance, trekked across Liberia, Ivory Coast to the Gold Coast, preaching and healing. His ministry benefited the mainline churches and inspired charismatic movements. In the Congo, Simon Kimbangu prophesied that the global disorder signaled that God was changing the baton from whites to blacks. His imprisonment did not deter the growth of his movement. In the 1930s the Balokole Movement spread from Rwanda through the Congo into Uganda, Kenya, Tanganyika and into the Sudan. It urged repentance, holiness ethics and a closer relationship to Jesus.

Examples could be multiplied to show that, just as the wars increased African confidence and shifted the vision of cultural nationalists to the quest for political independence, so were the efforts of missionaries to consolidate denominationalism confronted by intensified, subversive, indigenous initiatives. Missionary response to nationalism was informed by a number of factors—including individual predilection, the negative racial image of Africans, some liberal support, and regional variations as those in the settler communities—and responded with fright and built bulwarks with apartheid laws. As the wind of change gusted more brutally, it became clear that the missions had weak roots: few indigenous clergy; a dependency ideology; undeveloped theology; poor infrastructure; and above all, little confidence in their votaries. From the 1950s, the Roman Catholics led in the hurried attempt to train indigenous priests. Missions conceived opportunities to waltz with nationalists because the educated elites were products of various missions and their control of power could aid their denominations in the virulent rivalry for turf. This strategy implicated Christianity in the politics of Independence.

Matters went awry when the elite grabbed the politics of modernization, mobilized the states into dictatorial one-party structures, castigated missionaries for under-developing Africa, promoted neo-Marxist rejection of dependency syndrome, and seized the instruments of missionary propaganda such as schools, hospitals and social welfare agencies. J.W. Hofmeyr analyses the impact of the implosion of the state that challenged the churches. But the failure of the states produced the rash of military coups and regimes, abuse of Human Rights and economic collapse. Poverty ravaged many African countries. Militarization of the society intensified inter-ethnic conflicts and civil wars. The religion of displaced people in refugee camps is a key aspect of contemporary African Christianity. Natural disasters such as drought in the Horn of Africa worsened matters. A part of the problem could be traced to weak leadership; a part to external forces that used the continent as fodder in the Cold War; patronized dictators exploited the mineral resources and manipulated huge debts that have burdened and crippled many nations permanently. Meanwhile, the structure of the countries changed dramatically, as each country became more pluralistic in comparison to the beginning of the century. In many countries, Islamic rulers dominated and Christianity fought for space in the public square. A good example of the new dispensation is the Christian Association of Nigeria, which was formed in 1975 and brought many forms of embattled Christianity together to explore new models of presence that could serve as balm of Gilead in the untoward circumstances. As civil society was decimated, Christianity remained as the survivor. This explains why, at the end of the Cold War and the renaissance of Western interest in democratic structure, Christian leaders were chosen in one country after another to serve as presidents of consultative assemblies that sought to renew hope and banish the pessimism that imaged African problems as incurable.

A number of factors explain the survival of Christianity: the first, as Sam Maluleke shows, is that the development of African Christian theologies from the mid 1970s enabled a critique of inherited traditions and theologies. In southern Africa, the emphasis shifted from cultural theologizing to black consciousness; this sustained a black revolution against apartheid in South Africa, Namibia and Zimbabwe. The second is the rise of youthful charismatism and Pentecostalism. Kwaben Asamoah-Gydau provides a readable historical understanding of this subject matter, which has attracted a wild number and versions of sociological analyses. One commentator observed that in one country after another, young puritans emerged as if from the wormwoods in urban settings from 1970 onwards. With a message of repentance and holiness ethics, secondary school and university students transformed dowdy organizations such as Scripture Union and Students Christian Movement into emotionally expressive charismatic movements. Mainline churches struck back with disciplinary rebuttals that forced them out into organizations that changed the face of Christianity. The classic Pentecostal and Holiness groups that had entered Africa between 1906 and the 1940s suddenly came alive during the 1970s, benefiting from the youthful revivals. Women featured prominently in these organizations and churches were compelled to create a space for charismatism or otherwise lose their members to new-fangled Pentecostalism.

This form of Christianity has changed shape in every decade, absorbing American prosperity preaching in the 1980s and reverting to holiness and intercessory traditions in the 1990s. Pentecostal-charismatic influence is generating rapid growth in Africa. Reasons include the cultural "fit", because they bring the resources of the Gospel as answers to questions raised within the primal worldviews. Healing and deliverance feature prominently. As an instrumentalist response, they provide coping mechanisms in the midst of economic collapse. The religious dimension is the inexplicable power of the Holy Spirit in Africa that has set the missionary message to work. The movement has flowed from urban centers into rural Africa.

Nyambura Njoroge and Philomena Mwaura explore a third feature of the times, namely, the rise of Christian feminist theology challenging the churches to become less patriarchal. Through many publications and programs, churches are compelled to ordain women and increase their participation in decision-making processes. Two challenges stare visibly, whether the churches will mobilize their resources and use the new opportunities to combat poverty in pluralistic environments and what the resurgence of Christianity in Africa could contribute to world Christianity. A fourth feature has two prongs: the explosion of African Christianity in the Western World; as well as the emergence of charlatans in the religious landscape. Afe Adogame has done much research on the African churches that are proliferating in Europe. The largest Pentecostal Church in Kiev, Russia was founded by Sunday Adelaja. In America, the Nigerian-based Redeemed Christian Church of God and the Ghanaian-based Church of the Pentecost are highly visible. African churches have woven linkages with both western and southern Asia. Quite interesting is the social relevance of charismatic religiosity: many people boldly use biblical names for their businesses, and political leaders declare themselves to be born again. Charismatic and evangelical bodies are founding crèches, Bible schools and universities and regaining a Christian hold on the family through education. Beyond quantitative growth there is much evidence of the deepening of the Gospel in the lives of people who would have been lost to secularism. Contemporary Africa looks like a replay of early Christianity in the Maghrib.

NOTES

1. Barrett. D.B., Kurian, G.T. & Johnson, T.M. (eds), *World Christian Encyclopedia: A Comparative Survey of Churches and Religions in the Modern World* (New York: Oxford University Press, 2001), 25.

IMPACT OF CHRISTIANITY ON AFRICA

By Emory Ross

AFRICANS south of the Sahara in our day face a challenge not before put to so large a group of people. This challenge is for an unprecedentedly complex triple change:

1. Horizontal change, across the whole range of concepts and practices of life—in thought, language, religion, political and social organization, land, marriage, inheritance, occupations, economics, housing, disease causation and cure, recreation, communications of all kinds, and in nearly every other aspect of life.

2. Vertical change, from the most primal large society remaining on earth, the animistic communal primitivism of 160 million Africans, to something approaching the West's present society, the most individualistic, specialized, and technological society which the world has yet seen.

3. Speedy change, both horizontally and vertically, at a pace not before attempted by any such mass—change attempted by many thousands of Africans in two or three generations instead of in the three or four milleniums "normally" taken by Western society.

UNORTHODOX NATURE OF CHANGE

Such triple change cannot be effected in any orthodox or perhaps in any orderly fashion. There is no established order for it in past experience with such mass. It is in essence unorthodox.

Because it is thus unprecedented, this speedy change from animistic communalism to some pattern of an individualistic democracy based in considerable measure on the Hebraic-Christian religion suffers from the ignorance and inexperience both of the West and of Africa.

FORCES IN CHANGE

The West did not intentionally initiate such inclusive and speedy change in Africa. It began with merely incidental touching of Africa four or five hundred years ago as a way station on the journey in the search for the fabulous Indies. It later scratched spots on the fringes of Africa to seize slaves destined to bring change and progress in the West's own New World, not in Africa. Then, a century or so ago, it ventured exploration here and there in Africa, and finally produced a Livingstone.

Livingstone stimulated a Stanley and other venturesome penetrators of Africa. King Leopold II of the Belgians sparked a Western political acquisitiveness aimed at Africa. British, French, and German rivalries began to heat over several fires. Africa was involved and was "partitioned" in a fashion unprecedented in any other like land mass.

Two power crises then took their names from Africa, Fashoda and Agadir, the latter in 1911. Three years later the Western world went to war. Africa had no initiative in the war but was engulfed in it. It suffered greatly, and its whole fabric was rent. Thereafter, its raw materials were dug and taken with ever increasing speed to repair the West's self-ravages and to prepare for further struggle.

World War II

This came in 1939 without Africa's volition, but with even more involvement than in 1914. Rommel hit Egypt, pounded Suez, and a thousand African communities, some of them thousands of miles away, were shaken. Troops, artillery, bulldozers, airfields, harbors, bridge gangs, pipelines, tank depots, naval stores, munition dumps, roads—in two years Africa was penetrated by the "fall out" of World War II from the Mediterranean to Table Bay, from Monrovia to Mackinnon Road.

Six or seven hundred thousand Africans were drawn into military combat and labor services in distant places. Many hundred thousand others were used nearer home in these strange new works of global war.

Billions of dollars poured through millions of man-hours to spread throughout Africa elements of almost the total product of the scientific, technological, war-waging West. The multiple effects on Africa can never be assessed or measured with certainty. One only knows that they were immense.

In the interest of the West

This whole long onslaught has not been primarily for Africa's sake but for that of the West. It is unlikely that anyone would have had the temerity, or would have put up the money or mobilized the outside manpower, to risk so untried and unpromising an experiment in such swift human change for the sake of Africa itself. It was rather the mounting expansion and crisis of the West in these past two or three generations—its hungry maw reaching for raw materials in greater and greater volume than ever before demanded or even imagined; its need for political, economic, and strategic bases overseas to support its own internal struggle and to arm for its own crises—which originally contributed most heavily to European action in Africa.

Africans were initially prodded, pushed, and in some cases even compelled by forced labor and then military enlistment into a speed and type of change they had not dreamed of, and which many did not want. Pressures built up, speed stepped up. And now a mass is in movement. It probably will not stop, cannot be stopped. The desire is for change. Africa's triple change-across the board, up the scale, unprecedented and unpredictable in speed—is under way.

AFRICAN CONCEPTIONS OF CHRISTIANITY

In considering the impact of Christianity in Africa south of the Sahara, it is essential that we keep clearly in mind that the African animistic communal society links its religion tightly with the whole of its life. There are great variations in belief and practice within the approximately eight hundred tribes in Africa. But long association and friendship with Africans through the years evoke the conviction that Africans, in their tribal societies, generally regard life as the product and within the control of their religion. The whole of their life and society is the expression of their religion.

This being so it is natural that in their new contact with a new type of life and society possessing a religion new to the African, they should regard this new life and society as the expression of that new religion.

What then is more logical to the African than that the West should be regarded as the product of Christianity, its society as a Christian society, its people as Christians—in short, the West and all its products as Christian?

The early tendency of the Africans to so classify the West was perhaps reinforced by the not infrequent past references in the West—less frequent in later years—to the "Christian West," to our "Christian civilization."

When therefore the African point of view is considered in terms of the part played by the Christian religion in Africa in the past century or so, it is not sufficient to confine attention only to Christian missionaries, missions, and churches, to Christian schools and hospitals. The Africans early tended to regard all Westerners as representatives of Christianity, all these Westerners' political, economic, social, racial, personal patterns and actions as representing Christianity in life. It was in essence doing only what perhaps most Westerners were doing with respect to African people and society: regarding that society and all its works as representative of an animistic religion.

It is probable that today some Africans educated in Western patterns are prepared intellectually to accept the idea that important segments of our Western life and action are not Christian, and even that numbers of professing Western Christians do not expect or work towards the Christianization of all these segments. But that does not mean that these Africans all admire that philosophy. Indeed it probably means in numbers of cases that Africans are disappointed, uncertain, and confused. They see that the Christianity which they thought had undergirded, stimulated, and controlled the great new Western accomplishments which they now desire was in important ways not even as powerful as their old animism in controlling a whole life and society. Christianity probably seems an insecure base on which to build a whole new life.

The slave trade

It is with some such background as this that we should try to evaluate Christianity in Africa. In such an evaluation it is essential to remember that the "Christian" West's first large-scale approach to Africa was for slaves. Slavery had long existed in Africa, as in almost all primitive societies: a domestic slavery, largely, with all the attendant abuses and cruelties. It was the West, however, which, touching the coast in many places and stimulating coastal Africans to raiding the interior for slaves, internationally commercialized the slave trade, established

transoceanic transport for it, made it "big business" in its day. Accompanying this was a certain amount of talk of the Christianizing advantages which pagan Africans had in being captured, shipped, sold, and worked in the Christian West.

This doubtless appears now to most Westerners as what it was: pious humbug, a negation of Christianity. But there are here and there in Africa today some of Western descent who appear to Africans to be invoking their Christianity and the value to Africans of their Western science and productivity as reasons for their minority, and almost exclusive and complete, domination of the social, economic, and political scene throughout large African areas and over large numbers of Africans.

The parallel between this and the earlier Christian apologetic for slavery is of course not exact, but it is suggestive enough to Africans who remember the religious sanctions set forth for the "Christian" West's first large-scale relations with Africa—slavery.

Race prejudice

The common racial and cultural prejudices are likewise important factors in parts of Africa in making Africans critical of the Christianity with which those prejudices seem to enter Africa. Of course, it can be and is pointed out that Christ's teachings and constant examples while on earth were all against racial and cultural prejudices and exclusions, and that therefore Christianity cannot be held responsible for the prejudice now found. That attitude doubtless seems unrealistic or even hypocritical to a good many Africans. They believe they can see Western "Christians" putting numerous disabilities on other races and cultures in the West, in the East, and in Africa.

IMPACT OF CHRISTIANITY

It seems clear then that the impact of Christianity in Africa has by no means come only through Christian missions. These impacts have come through many different national cultural, economic, and political channels from the West. Even within the different Christian missions those national forces have not infrequently produced quite different attitudes, methods, and results.

The theme of this paper therefore is that religion, in this case Christianity, is not something in a separate compartment of life called church or missions or worship. It is an integral, inextricable part of life, all life. It is a major element of that holism of which Jan Smuts, Haldane, Whitehead, and others have written. Its impact upon that wholeness of life represented within a tribe by Africa's animistic communal society comes through the whole of the life poured in upon Africa in these later years from the so-called Christian West. The impact is from many sources; it is direct and indirect. Its effect is total in character.

Generally, despite weaknesses and errors already named and later to be named, it seems correct to say that the impact of Christianity from the West upon African life has been thus far the strongest element in change and progress in the past three generations. The following points support this conclusion.

Individual choice

First, Christianity has been the chief influence in introducing and spreading the concept—revolutionary in Africa's communal society—of individual choice, initiative, and power, coupled with sobering individual responsibility for one's fellows and one's society. This has been a power of Christianity in all lands and in all generations since Christ. It has entered Africa not only through teaching and example in Christian missions but also in many political and economic contexts, in social customs, and in the historic bases of the Western peoples entering Africa who had themselves gained it through the influences of Christianity in their own lands.

The whole man

Second, Christianity has been, everywhere in Africa south of the Sahara, the introducer of Western-type education of the whole man: head, hand, and heart. Christian missions still carry the bulk of the load of this broad education, sometimes without, but increasingly with, the aid of public funds.

Medical and health gains

Third, Christian missions have been almost everywhere the introducer of Western medical, surgical, and public health methods, and the pioneer trainer of Africans in these skills.

Self-help

Fourth, Christianity has pioneered in self-help programs, in agricultural improvements, in training for trades and professions, and it was in many cases earliest in giving Africans practice and responsibility in these. It was the pioneer in aiding Africans to travel and study in the outside world.

Displacement of animism

Fifth, through Christian spiritual illuminations and through slowly convincing demonstrations in medicine, surgery, science, agriculture, and general education, all in a Christian atmosphere, it has given many Africans most powerful aid in the essential displacement of animistic superstitions, fears, and oppressions. The continuance of those animistic inhibitions in full strength would render quite impossible African advance in modern science, economics, technology, and political forms, and in new optimum social forms and toward a new spiritual community embracing all.

African Christians

Sixth, although statistics are never wholly revealing in matters of the heart and mind, and most African statistics have special weaknesses, the best available figures indicate that there are 21 million or more professing African Christians. The same source indicates that in all the rest of the so-called non-Christian world, with about fifteen times the population of Africa, there are some 20 million Christians. As of now, Christianity has drawn more Africans together than any other power entering Africa in modern times.

These elements are of great importance in the building of a new society in Africa. But human weaknesses among Christians in the West and among such Westerners in Africa are so numerous and so great that Christianity cannot yet develop its fullest re-creative power in Africa. As there are splits in human personalities and societies, so are there splits in the Christianity brought in from the West to Africa, sharply reducing its effectiveness.

Let me suggest four splits in the spiritual and cultural forces in the West and in Africa which now exist, which in some places appear to widen, and which, if they continue unrepaired and uncontrolled in the future, may bring crisis mounting to explosion and despair in the spiritual and cultural experiences of Africa and the West and remove or greatly reduce the most powerful of all forces guiding economic, political, and social development.

Split between Protestants and Roman Catholics

The first of these four splits in the Christian world is the split between Protestants and Roman Catholics. We in the West know something of the historical, national, and political reasons behind this split. We are still somewhat emotionally sensitive to it all. But those historic and current conditionings of ours are for the most part quite hidden as yet from the Africans. Probably for most Africans this is one of the incomprehensible and bewildering aspects of the Christian religion as imported from the West. This is a split of the first magnitude in Christianity in Africa.

Its gravity is, of course, also recognized in the West, but oftentimes with a kind of fatalistic sense of inevitability. It does not at first appear as inevitable to the African as he hears both groups preaching from what appears to him as the same book, the Book of Books, and teaching the Fatherhood of God, the brotherhood of man, and the unity with our Maker within the church.

It would seem that whatever may be possible to be done for the healing or the narrowing of this first split I mention, and for the development of better functional understandings and relationships in many parts of Africa between Roman Catholics and Protestants, would make a contribution of the first magnitude in our spiritual and cultural fellowship and cooperation with Africa.

Splits among the Protestants

The second of the four splits is among Protestants themselves. Protestants' Western denominational divisions are nearly all represented in Africa, at least all of those having missionary interests. There are fifteen Christian councils in as many political divisions in Africa south of the Sahara, and most of them represent some solid co-operative Protestant planning and action. But none of them has within its membership all of the Protestant forces within its area. In public education matters the co-operation among most members within a given Christian council is generally good. This is also true with regard to government relationships and in the production of general Christian literature and other good reading materials. Co-operation in leprosy work and in some places in other medical undertakings is to be found.

But the fact remains that in what is the most important single training task which Christians alone must do in Africa—the training of the Christian ministry and the church's lay leadership—there is only limited interdenominational and international co-operation here and there throughout the continent. There is not, for example, in the whole of Africa a single union Protestant theological seminary of full rank. There are, indeed, very few spots where any solid co-operation exists between denominations for the training of the Protestant ministry.

This example of Protestant divisions is not lost upon African Christians. In some places it operates to divide members of the same or related tribes along theological lines, although it must be said that for the most part the Western denominational loyalties appear to be rather less rigid among large numbers of Africans than they are in the Westerners' homelands. This is hopeful for the future.

But where political, economic, educational, cultural, and other disabilities put upon Africans are most pronounced and severe, as currently for example in the Union of South Africa, there the Western religious denominational pattern is not only followed but widened. There are more than 1,100 separatist African denominations registered in the Union. Using the split pattern of Western Christianity, as between Protestants and Roman Catholics and among Protestants themselves, the underprivileged majority has run denominational riot in the Union. This is in considerable measure an effort to escape white domination in at least one sector of life. But the adoption of the Western Christians' split pattern is demonstrably not the way to gain spiritual solidarity in Africa any more than it has been in Europe and the Americas.

Split between Negro and white

The third of these four splits within the church and our society is that between colors, between black and white. Segregation on grounds of color in our home churches and society, and barriers, tangible and sometimes rather intangible, on color grounds in Africa is for Africans—as it should be for us—a negation of the basic Christian Gospel of God's Fatherhood, of love and brotherhood, and sharing of the "oneness" there is in Christ.

What seems to Africans as color discrimination exists in almost all parts of Africa, brought chiefly by the Christian West. It may not be in reality discrimination based wholly on grounds of color. There has been historically discrimination of various types in Liberia and Ethiopia by members of the ruling group in relation to some or most of the people making up the mass of the population. This is now diminishing and was obviously not color discrimination. But when such discrimination occurs between white and Negro the general tendency of the Negro is to assign it almost wholly to color. Reasoning and argument

about such assignment is often of little avail, for emotions and feelings and not the more rational processes of the mind are in control. And, besides, obvious and avowed color discrimination does exist in many parts of the West and in Africa, and Africans know it.

Nowhere in the West is color discrimination more evident than in the United States. And no groups seem slower to root it out than thousands of individual Christian congregations in this country. More interracial progress has been made in political, industrial, labor, academic, sport, theatrical, musical, and other groups, than in tens of thousands of churches. Africans are coming to know this also. For there are more than a thousand African students in America now, and scores of other Africans come each year here on government or private business.

And when, in addition, they see the excesses regarding race in the Union of South Africa, and the place of the dominant church in them, and the segregation within and without the church in many other places in Africa, it is small wonder that this split between black and white assumes major proportions as they think of Christianity and of continuing Western dominance in most of Africa.

The progress toward better racial attitudes in the United States both before and after the Supreme Court decision of May 1954 holds great promise in our international relations. But there is much lost ground to be made up by Christians in Africa, ground indispensable for the foundations of a world Christian society.

Split between spiritual and secular elements

The fourth of these four splits is the one in the West between the elements we call "spiritual" and those we classify as "secular." It is difficult, confusing, and often painful for the African to learn that Christians seem to regard some things as spiritual and some others as "secular," separated fairly sharply from the spiritual. To African traditional thought and action such a division does not make sense. It is a negation of the facts of life as he and his fathers have observed and lived it for generations. Life to him is a unity guided and almost always controlled by the spirit.

To accept a religion with all the power, beauty, and promise of Christianity and then gradually to find that this Gospel as practiced so largely in the West is expected to control only a part of life and not to enter, except rather superficially, into what is called "secular" aspects of life—that is a disillusionment of great dimensions.

One doubts that any other one split in spiritual and cultural concepts in the West is more important in our relations with the Africa of today and tomorrow than is this Western split between religion and great sectors of human life.

This split seems to Africans to manifest itself, for example, in our reluctance, sometimes refusal, to try to deal with political problems where Africans feel their interests are jeopardized. In industrial, labor, economic, and related matters they feel their basic rights are often acutely involved. It is hard for them to understand Western Christians' attitude that these somehow are things with which spiritual forces do not seek directly to deal. We need not be surprised, in these circumstances, if they rather suspect that our reluctance stems from our feeling of group identification, racially and culturally, with the ruling white political and economic powers, and from our hesitancy to do things which might weaken white solidarity and white supremacy. That may seem to them a more likely explanation than that this new and powerful Christian Gospel cannot tackle effectively these urgent problems of life.

This split manifests itself, too, in our not bringing from the West a clear, viable Christian philosophy of man's spiritual relationship to the all-giving and all-powerful Mother Earth. We from the West can produce more crops from the land, sometimes. We often urge Africans to use "better" methods of agriculture. We on occasion seem to agree when governments or plantation owners (with government sanction) force Africans to adopt new commercial crops or new methods of cultivation.

But where, Africans can naturally ask, in all this Western emphasis on land and the new uses of it is there a clear Christian replacement of the old and tried animistic spiritual attitude and practice regarding land? This right relationship to land is one of the most important things in the African's life. His life and all life depend on it. It is a matter that must be spiritually based, and soundly. It must be spiritually, as well as "physically" (there is little difference to the animistic African), good for the whole "tribe," that is, society. What is the Christian West's spiritual attitude and control regarding land, the African wonders?

The fact is that in the West a spiritual conception of the land has disappeared. Our real approach is technological, not spiritual. Yet we should have been able to gain the former without losing the latter. That combination of the two is what masses of Africans instinctively want. That is what nearly all of the so-called "underdeveloped" peoples of the world want. They have a deep inner reluctance to become as highly developed technologically as we are if at the same time they must become as underdeveloped spiritually as we appear to them to be. They cannot yet believe that is truly necessary. Even primitive Africans instinctively resist such "progress."

The African's spiritual linkage to his tribal land is one of the most powerful forces in his life. It is embittering to be put off his land by foreign whites, as in some places he is. Or to be concentrated on "locations" that are a stench. Or to be assigned "reserves" within his own ancestral lands by foreigners who, when they came, "had the Bible and we had the land. Now we have the Bible and they have the land."

It is hard for him to accept the separation, in a religion as powerful as Christianity, of things spiritual from things physical like land; of things spiritual from things "secular," as in industry, labor, and politics. It is not illogical that he should begin to suspect that Christianity is not as powerful as he had thought it to be, and that some of its practices developed in the West may not be as pure as its pulpit presentations.

These four splits and others growing out of them in the Christian life in the West are great handicaps to the Christian Gospel in Africa. The oneness, the wholeness, of the hoped-for Christian life and community are broken. The fullness of life which Christianity promised in Africa seems to them not yet widely produced. They freely aver that Christianity has helped them do many things in Africa. But they wonder if Western Christianity is really concerned with the whole of life in Africa.

CONCLUSION

If the foregoing be accepted as a generally valid sketch of some of the effects of Western Christianity in Africa, two conclusions may be drawn:

1. Christianity, in direct and indirect ways, has had probably the most fundamental, widespread, and creative effect of any element entering Africa south of the Sahara in modern time.
2. Christianity, handicapped by its Western human distortions from the original teachings Christ gave in a society not so far removed from its own animistic communal origins, has failed to give everything it might to Africa's rapidly changing people.

This failure presents grave dangers. It may so discourage and embitter the African that he will in the end fanatically combat the West on all fronts. It may lead him to develop his own distortions of Christianity on the ground that if the West can warp that powerful religion to its own selfish national and cultural ends, so can Africa. Finally, it may leave him as defenseless prey to other outside philosophies and ideologies which at this stage are not yet established among Africans and thus are not required to produce anything at all in African society. They have now only to promise. And they cleverly promise among their most attractive wares what seem to Africans to be some of the same values offered by Christianity, and partially produced, but then frustratingly refused completion by the "Christian" West.

Such dangers are serious; and they pose a critical challenge to Christianity and the peoples and governments of the West.

Emory Ross, D.D., New York City, was a missionary in Africa from 1912 to 1933, serving four years in Liberia, and about eighteen years in the Belgian Congo as missionary and secretary of the Congo Protestant Council. From 1934 to 1953, he was secretary of the Africa Committee of the Canadian and North American Mission Boards for Africa South of the Sahara. He is the author of several books, including Out of Africa *(1936) and* African Heritage *(1953). He gave the Lugard Lecture in 1953 and the Hoernle Lecture in 1954. He is president of the Phelps-Stokes Fund and president of the American Leprosy Missions.*

EUROPEAN SCRAMBLE
AND COLONIAL
CONQUEST

THE EUROPEAN CONQUEST OF AFRICA

By Robert O. Collins and James M. Burns

After 400 years during which Europe had displayed little or no interest in Africa beyond its coastline, suddenly—in the twenty years between 1878 and 1898—the European states partitioned and conquered virtually the entire continent. To observers in the last quarter of the nineteenth century this sudden conquest was a frantic, often unseemly, and largely unexpected scramble for territory in a continent about which the Europeans knew little and for which most cared nothing. Their sentiments were encapsulated in the famous remark by the English imperial historian John H. Seeley, that his generation had conquered half of the world "in a fit of absence of mind." Today, however, with the advantage of hindsight historians have perceived several fundamental causes and events which combined to upset 400 years of equilibrium between Africa and Europe and precipitate the European conquest and colonial rule of virtually the entire continent. The Industrial Revolution in several European nations resulted in a need for raw material from Africa, while at the same time the Africans represented a large, new market for European manufactured goods. More over, the new technologies produced by the Industrial Revolution provided the instruments that upset the long standing balance of power between Africa and Europe. Popular nationalism was transformed into imperial rivalry, as imperial strategy and the defense of empire became of great concern to European statesmen. Changing terms of trade required European merchants to seek political stability in Africa, where for centuries they had profited from the instability that had fostered the slave trade. Christianity was also changing in the nineteenth century, as the new and powerful Evangelical movement inspired aggressive missionary activity, which in the past had been fragmentary and largely confined to the African coast, throughout the continent.

This "scramble for Africa," however, should be perceived as but another chapter in the larger story of nineteenth-century global imperialism by the West. While Western statesmen were asserting claims to large portions of African territory, they were also staking out spheres of influence in China, prying open Japanese trade with gunboats, and dispatching armies to conquer much of Southeast Asia. The progress of the European conquest in Africa was in many ways determined by the actions of the inhabitants, and differed according to region, state, or even village. Some communities fought ferociously against European encroachment; there were those who successfully forestalled or mitigated European influence, while others profited little from their defiance. Numerous Africans welcomed the European imperial powers as potential allies against their enemies. Some in the more remote and isolated regions of the continent remained oblivious for years to the fact that they had become a part of one or the other European empire.

The conquest of Africa was a manifestation of the European Industrial Revolution, and the principal instrument for its accomplishment was the steam engine. Steam was the driving force of those industries that produced railroads and steamships to conquer land and sea. This revolution in transportation had particular significance in Africa, for unlike the other continents it possessed no great navigable rivers that could provide a passage from the oceans into the heart of the continent—no Amazon, Mississippi, Rhine, Ganges, or Yangtze.

Except for the Gambia all the great rivers of Africa were obstructed by cataracts and falls at the lip of the African Plateau, whose waters tumble down onto the short coastal plain and over the shoals of their estuaries. Once above the falls, however, the African rivers—the Congo, Niger, Nile, Zambezi—were navigable for hundreds of miles. On these broad and placid reaches European steamers and gunboats dominated the vigorous and profitable flow of commerce on the rivers and could intimidate African authorities to obtain favorable terms of trade in their markets.

The nineteenth century was also the great age of the steam locomotive and its railways that spanned continents. It was the railway that enabled the imperialists to avoid the rapids and gain supremacy of the navigable rivers. These rail lines were built primarily to carry and support sufficient military forces to conquer Africa, but after the subjugation of the Africans was complete, the railways become the means to spread colonial administration and the transport of colonial commerce. Railway building was a long, expensive, and arduous process. In 1879 the French government appropriated funds for the Senegal Railway to link the Senegal River with the Niger, the construction of which was not completed until 1905. In the 1890s Henry Morton Stanley cut a passage around thirty-two cataracts for a railway from the port of Matadi on the Congo Estuary to Stanley (Malebo) Pool on the navigable Congo that enabled King Leopold of the Belgians to conquer the vast interior beyond the banks of the river and its tributaries. Between 1896 and 1898 the British constructed a railway across the Nubian Desert to bypass five cataracts to the navigable Nile in order to conquer the Sudan; this was later extended, for administrative and commercial needs, to the capital, Khartoum. In Uganda the British constructed a railway from Mombasa to Lake Victoria to forestall French encroachment at Fashoda on the Upper Nile, but it was not completed until 1902, and the cost of its construction could only be justified by the British commercial exploitation of East Africa.

In southern Africa the railway was instrumental in the growth of the mining industry, whose riches fueled imperial expansion. After the discovery of diamonds at Kimberley in 1867, railways from the southern ports of Cape Town, Port Elizabeth, East London, and Durban were constructed to supply the miners, bring out the diamonds, and insure that the mines became part of the British empire. When gold was discovered on the Witwatersrand in the Transvaal in 1885, it was the extension of the rail line to Johannesburg in the independent Republic of the Transvaal that symbolized the advance of British power into southern Africa, contributing to the outbreak of the South African (Anglo-Boer) War in 1899. North of the Transvaal the conquest of the Ndebele kingdom of Lobengula, which became part of Southern Rhodesia, was accomplished by a mercenary army, mostly of British subjects, which entered Mashonaland in 1890. It was no coincidence, however, that the first train to arrive at Bulawayo seven years later carried sufficient arms and ammunition to suppress the Ndebele-Shona revolt of 1896–1897 against the British occupation of their country, in which 10 percent of the settler population had been killed.

African railways were built for the most part by forced labor (called by the French the *corvee*), and conditions of railway construction were dangerous, with a high rate of mortality. Although apologists for colonialism later argued that railways were a beneficent legacy of imperial rule, they were built by African labor, mostly for the benefit of the Europeans. Railway construction was very hard, debilitating work, of little or no interest to African farmers and pastoralists. In some areas, such as British East Africa, it proved impossible to coerce them into construction work, so the Ugandan railway was built in large part by South Asian laborers, indentured servants, from British India, who after its completion remained to form the nucleus of the Asian community in British East Africa.

Each of these European innovations presented different challenges for the Africans, but the most devastating technological disparity to emerge in the nineteenth century was the revolution in firearms. For over 300 years the musket had been an inefficient weapon, and its short range and inaccuracy against individual moving targets was not much superior to the spear, arrow, knife, and second-hand muskets used by Africans, particularly in the coastal rainforests, where it frequently misfired from moisture-saturated powder. In the 1860s the muzzle-loading musket of the Napoleonic era was replaced by the single breech-loader, and, by the 1880s, the magazine repeating rifle. The change from musket to rifle dramatically upset the balance of African warfare. The repeating rifle with its bullets, rather than powder and ball, was easy to load for rapid fire, and was reliable. It was very accurate at long range against massed or mobile targets, with speed improved by the smooth ejection of the used cartridge. In 1885 Hiram S. Maxim (1840–1916) took the logic of the repeating rifle one step further by binding several rifle barrels into a revolving column, the Maxim gun, the prototype of the modern machine gun. Although the trade in firearms remained as vigorous as ever on the African coast, African leaders found it increasingly difficult to equip their armies with these new weapons. The European imperial nations, determined to maintain their superiority in firearms, were increasingly reluctant to export modern weapons to African leaders who resorted to purchasing rifles from unreliable and often untrustworthy arms merchants. Moreover, unlike the eighteenth-century muskets, these new rifles were mass-produced by machine tools and could not be repaired by African blacksmiths using their traditional technology.

Artillery was used infrequently in Africa. In Europe, particularly during the Napoleonic wars, it had often been the decisive factor in battle. In Africa artillery only became significant in the late nineteenth century when light mobile field guns were introduced to breach the walled cities of the Western Sudan. Moreover, combat on the savanna and sahel was dominated by cavalry and light infantry whose maneuverability limited the value of heavy artillery, which would have to be carried long distances across difficult terrain. However, artillery had not been unknown in Africa before the nineteenth century. The fortifications of the slave trading forts of the West African coast all had cannons—pointing seaward to defend them against European rivals—and one of the most sumptuous gifts for a West African chief in the elaborate negotiations accompanying the slave trade was a cannon for him to fire on ceremonial occasions.

All of these instruments of empire building would have remained useless so long as disease threatened to strike down European invaders. There were numerous diseases—yellow fever, sleeping sickness, yaws, leprosy—but the greatest killer for Europeans in the nineteenth century, as well as Africans then and now, was malaria, which is endemic throughout Africa, except in the cooler and less humid uplands. Until the mid-nineteenth century the average annual death rate of British garrisons on the coast and the Royal Naval Squadron at sea was 77 percent, overwhelmingly from malaria. Another 21 percent became invalids, and only 2 percent remained fit for further service. Explorers, missionaries, and merchants suffered similarly, and empires could not be established or expanded at such human cost. European missionaries in West Africa rarely ventured from their coastal stations, leaving Christian evangelism in the interior to freed slaves converted to the faith at the British colony of Sierra Leone. Malaria as well as the other endemic diseases also kept European traders and explorers from venturing far into the interior, leaving large blank spaces on European maps. In 1854 the Scottish doctor W. B. Baikie successfully demonstrated that by taking the prophylactic quinine, an extract taken from the bark of a tree native to Brazil, the men of his ship were able to reach the pestilential confluence of the Niger and Benue Rivers without loss. By the 1860s and 1870s quinine was in regular use by European missionaries, merchants, and soldiers and even more than steam, telegraphy, and firearms made possible the new imperialism.

The imperialism of the nineteenth century was also accompanied by a new self-confidence, which cannot be measured like ships, guns, or quinine. The unprecedented productivity of European industrialization gave the Victorians a sense of superiority and invincibility that drove them to use their new technologies to control continents, command millions, and harness knowledge for prosperity, progress, and prestige. Was it not their duty, the Victorians insisted–indeed, moral obligation—to promote the advancement of European civilization in Africa? Were they not ordained to bring light to those living in darkness and to march with the civilized vanguard of humanity motivated by a supreme calling, what the Anglo-Indian writer Rudyard Kipling called the "White Man's Burden"? The Victorians invoked this humanitarian crusade to justify the imposition upon the Africans of a new—and presumably better-way of living by the extension of empire, even if it required the slaughter of those who refused to accept an alien culture and its civilization. The conquest of Africa could not have been accomplished without this sincere faith in their mission. Although in retrospect the fervor of their convictions today appears naive, if not hypocritical, many of the Victorians firmly believed in the ultimate beneficence of their actions.

The scramble for Africa was also spurred by the rise of popular nationalism in late nineteenth-century Europe. Before the rise of the new nations of Germany and Italy, the older imperial powers expressed little interest in African expansion. While the local agents of France, Britain, and Portugal in Africa had from time to time encouraged an expansion of their small African holdings, their governments had consistently refused to support them. African colonies were rightly perceived as expensive, and tolerated more to stop the trade in slaves than to make a profit. Unlike the eighteenth century, when European governments sought to control commerce, the old and the new nations of the nineteenth century were committed to the principles of "free trade" whereby commerce along the African coast was regulated by the current market price, safeguarded by the occasional display of gunboat diplomacy.

The creation of the new nations of Italy in 1866 and Germany in 1870 threatened the European balance of power, which had governed international relations since the age of Napoleon. European nationalists came to see African colonization as a prerequisite for great power status, and they envied the extensive and established empires of Great Britain and France. Their jealousy, however, was to some extent an illusion, for the colonies of France brought her considerable expense and little profit, and the British thought so little of their insignificant holdings in West Africa that in 1868 Parliament seriously considered abandoning all of them. Perceptions, however, were more appealing and powerful than the costs and realities of empire, and the voters in Germany and Italy supported the imperial ambitions of their leaders to challenge the older empires of Britain and France.

The first European to take the initiative to acquire an African empire was, surprisingly, King Leopold of tiny Belgium. He created the facade of a supposedly scientific Committee for the Study of the Upper Congo, but his agents were instructed to obtain large tracts of territory rather than pursue any scientific investigations. They coerced African chiefs to sign treaties by which they unwittingly granted to Leopold more than a million square miles of the vast Congo Basin as his own personal colony. The king's astonishing success immediately motivated France to secure the territory north of the Congo River, and even the German chancellor, Otto von Bismarck (1815–1898), who at first resisted any colonial ambitions in Africa, sought to placate the increasingly vocal groups of merchants, missionaries, and nationalists who insisted that the German empire in Europe must now expand into Africa. Eventually, a reluctant Bismarck perceived that he could use an African empire as diplomatic leverage with his European rivals—particularly France and Great Britain, who were suddenly and to their surprise confronted with German colonies in Togo, Kamerun, South West Africa, and German East Africa (Tanganyika).

Like the Germans, the Italians, seeking to convince themselves they were a great power, used the growing power of Italian nationalism to justify their colonial ambitions. Although Italian imperial designs in Tunisia were checked by the French occupation in 1881, the Italians eventually conquered the vast, arid territory of Libya in order to claim both shores of the Mediterranean as their *mare nostra*, but in fact their principal designs were in Ethiopia, although these were crushed by the victory of Emperor Menelik II (1844–1913) over the Italian army at the battle of Adua in 1896. The Italians fared better in the Horn of Africa, where they established a colony in the sands of Somaliland.

Faced with these developments the older imperial powers could no longer remain idle. Portugal, a nation whose fortunes had declined precipitously since the days of Henry the Navigator, rallied to consolidate its African empire in the belief that this would secure its future status in Europe. Portuguese expeditions sought to expand the colonies of Mozambique and Angola from the coasts deep into the interior. French governments, which had long tried to restrain the enthusiasm for expansion by their men in Senegal, the infamous *officiers soudannais*, now became ardent advocates of a forward policy in what would become the French Soudan. British politicians, who in the past had been stalwart "Little Englanders," now found themselves reluctant imperialists, acquiescing to new conquests or supporting the expansion of allies in order to preserve free trade for British merchants and to placate the vociferous demands of the missionaries for the government to protect and support their missions.

European imperialism was not simply a nationalistic urge, as many Europeans had concluded that the tropical commodities of Africa were essential to the industrial growth of Britain, France, Belgium,

Germany, and Italy, all with rapidly growing urban populations. When merchants sought to protect their profits on the West African coast or missionaries insisted on the expansion of their endeavors in southern Africa, the politicians and statesmen began to listen to their arguments and to believe that imperial conquest would open African markets for European manufactured goods, there by protecting the jobs of workers at home, while enabling missionaries to bring their civilizing mission to the African peoples. These were powerful and persuasive interests who converted their nationalist leaders into global imperialists in which the promise of new colonies in Africa would contribute to the prosperity of the nation and thwart the ambitions of rival states, all in the name of civilization, commerce, and Christianity. In the end these promises were to prove illusory, a testament to the profound European ignorance of Africa and the Africans.

While Africa was not to be a new India for European economies, it did nevertheless produce a variety of tropical products that were in demand by manufacturers in the new industrial cities. Indeed, the abrupt partition of the continent exposed Africa's growing vulnerability to dramatic changes in global commerce ushered in by the Industrial Revolution. The demand for East African ivory in Europe and America for piano keys and billiard balls was only exceeded by the insatiable demand from Asia for the highly prized ivory ornamentation and carvings. The need for soap to cleanse the body from the industrial dirt of machines and mines strengthened the demands by European merchants for the British government to insure political stability for the palm oil markets of the Niger Delta. The invention of the pneumatic tire and the subsequent mania for cycling among the middle classes of Europe and America in the 1880s suddenly made the wild rubber trees of the Central African rainforest an essential commodity. In an increasingly competitive marketplace, European merchants frequently sought to lower their costs by cutting out traditional African middlemen—who, not surprisingly, resisted, which in turn provoked European military punitive expeditions. Merchants also hoped that imperial rule would guarantee supplies of tropical products that could not be acquired elsewhere, and upon which industrial manufacturing depended. Rivalries among commercial firms in London, North Germany, and Paris led to demands for imperial conquest in East Africa and the Niger Delta.

A justification for empire equal in importance to commerce or Christianity was the strategic and diplomatic consideration of consolidating and defending existing empires. Indeed, some historians have viewed the advent of the "scramble" as the defensive reflex of European politicians anxious to protect their imperial possessions. Many of these statesmen were from the European aristocracy, who frequently regarded merchants and manufacturers with disdain and evangelists with contempt. Bismarck was surrounded by his circle of Prussian nobility, Lord Salisbury by Tory ministers and conservative civil servants. They were deeply imbued with the responsibility of defending the empire by diplomacy and military might, and were not sympathetic to the activities of European adventurers, traders, or missionaries in Africa if they did not coincide with their own views and needs for imperial defense and expansion. These were the men who constituted the official mind of the Victorians, and who were directly responsible for the imperial decisions and diplomacy of empire.

Most of Africa was partitioned in Europe's corridors of power by men totally ignorant of Africa drawing lines on maps of territory about which they knew little or nothing. It was empire on the cheap, for it was easily acquired by the stroke of a pen. All that was required by the European statesmen was a map of Africa and a fistful of treaties—usually obtained by false promises or veiled threats. To actually occupy and assert European authority over these new possessions, however, was quite another matter, which frequently required the military subjugation of formidable African opposition. The African armies that confronted the European imperialists were either those that had sought to adopt European weaponry and military tactics—the Asante of modern Ghana, the armies of the Tukulor in modern Mali, and the Dyula leader Samori Ture (1830–1900), whose sprawling empire encompassed much of modern Guinea and Cote d'Ivoire, and the Ethiopians—or those who relied upon their traditional weapons and ways of waging war—the Sokoto caliphate of northern Nigeria and the Zulu kingdom of South Africa. Each in their own way proved to be impressive opponents to the African armies led and equipped by Europeans. The Asante army numbered some 40,000 infantry equipped with obsolete but serviceable muskets and led by an effective command structure centered on the *asantehene*. The Tukulor army and that of Samori Ture were composed of *sofas*, infantry armed with muskets and later repeating rifles purchased from the English, cavalry with traditional weapons, and artillery captured from the French. The Ethiopians had first experienced the power of modern breech-loading rifles during a brief punitive campaign in 1867 when a British column assaulted the royal residence at Magdala to free the British ambassador from captivity. After Menelik II succeeded the emperor Yohannes IV to the Ethiopian throne in 1889, he assiduously acquired modern European weapons that enabled him to mobilize an army of 70,000 repeating rifles and quick-firing artillery against the Italians in 1896. The army of Sokoto, however, remained dominated by the ideal of the Hausa warrior and relied on its aristocratic cavalry equipped with lance, sword, and bows with arrows. The more disciplined Zulu army with its age-set regiments (*impis*), warriors in superb physical condition who could perform complex tactical maneuvers, and led by officers, the *indunas*, would advance against the enemy behind their walls of great shields to destroy them at close quarters with their short stabbing assegai, an eighteen-inch broad-bladed spear (*iklwa*). The Zulu armies had long familiarity with European firearms, and some warriors carried rifles into battle, but they never integrated firearms into their *impis*, relying on their traditional tactics which had served them well for a generation and inflicted a devastating defeat on a British army at the battle of Isandlwana in 1879.

Not every colonial acquisition was preceded by violence. Many African leaders willingly, if unwittingly, signed treaties that effectively placed their territory under the protection of a European patron. Some believed that a voluntary submission to European colonial rule was an opportunity to acquire a powerful ally—and perhaps firearms—that would consolidate their personal power and insure the continuation of the indigenous political system, with themselves as the local ruling authority. Others, like the king of the Tio, whose agreement with the French explorer Savorgnan de Brazza (1852–1905) placed much of the modern Congo Republic under French rule, had little concept of what their treaties entailed. Others, such as the Ndebele king Lobengula (c. 1836–1894), bartered away the autonomy of their neighbors in order to retain the integrity of their own kingdoms. Most African rulers were painfully aware during these negotiations of the possibility that the Europeans would use their superior weaponry, if their demands were not met.

The swift defeat of African armies by European forces has produced among the public and historians alike the false impression that those who did resist gained little, but upon closer examination this does not prove to be the case. Shona and Ndebele resistance to the British South Africa Company forced Cecil Rhodes to grant important concessions in a negotiated peace. Although the bloody uprising against German rule in Tanganyika, known as Maji-Maji, claimed over 100,000 African lives, fear of another uprising ultimately forced the German government to temper some of the demands it made on the survivors as well as agreeing to a host of administrative reforms. In Asante and Zululand those rulers who resisted were initially exiled after their defeat, but eventually their dynasties were restored. Despite their ultimate defeat, armed resistance by Africans against European-led armies later was to become the focus of important and symbolic remembrance, providing a rallying point for independence movements after the Second World War. In the Sudan the family of the Muhammad Ahmad al-Mahdi, the religious founder of the Mahdist state (1885–1898), became an important political force

in nationalist politics. In Zimbabwe the struggle against white rule which emerged during the 1970s, came to be called the Second Chimurenga, a name that harkened back to the Chimurenga or war of liberation fought against the agents of Cecil Rhodes in 1896. In Guinea during the 1950s the nationalist Sekou Ture drew legitimacy from his claim to be the grandson of the great warrior Samori Ture (c. 1830–1900).

Although the conquest of Africa took place during the last twenty years of the nineteenth century, the coastal roots of European expansion had been inexorably spreading into the interior of Africa since the 1850s. The foundations for a French empire, later known as the French Soudan, had been established as early as 1860 in the valley of the Upper Niger River where in the remote garrison of the forgotten French colony of Senegal ambitious French officers initiated an aggressive military policy—to further their own careers as much as to extend the French empire. Their ambition placed them in the path of the expanding power of the Tukulor empire of al-Haj Umar (c. 1794–1864). Al-Haj Umar was always wary of the French and reluctant to make war against them, as his jihad (holy war) was not with the Christian French, with whom he carried on a vigorous trade in arms, but the non-Muslim Africans, the kafirin (infidels) of the savanna. From April to July 1857 his army of 15,000 had besieged the advanced French fort at Medine, the end of navigation on the Senegal. After losing 2,000 of his talibes (Arabic, "student"; the name applied to his disciples) Umar withdrew eastward into the vast hinterland of the Western Sudan. His Tukulor talibes, inspired by his appeals to jihad, did not lack courage—only the artillery to breach the walls of French forts and sink their gunboats on the Niger. Having lost Medine, al-Haj Umar negotiated a strategic armistice with the exhausted French in 1860 that checked their conquest of the Western Sudan for another ten years.

After 1870 the advance of the French into the hinterland of the Western Sudan was revived, but its pace was painfully slow. Under a succession of French commanders, the *officiers soudanais*—who frequently ignored orders from Paris to seize large tracts of territory for France and win medals and promotion for themselves—the struggling columns of their African troops, the *tirailleurs sénégalais*, equipped with repeating rifles and artillery, marched eastward into the heartland of the Sudanic kingdoms. Segu did not fall until 1889, but its capture opened the navigable Niger to French gunboats, which bombarded and secured the surrender of Timbuktu in December 1893. The *seku* Ahmadu Tal (1836–1902), son and successor to al-Hajj Umar, implacably opposed the French advance until he was forced to flee for safety to the caliphate of Sokoto, where he died in 1902. He left his empire in the hands of a few French officers, who did not know what to do with the vast territory they had finally occupied.

The French had even more difficulty establishing control over the empire of Samori Turé. Samori was a Dyula trader who became one of the most famous soldiers in pre-colonial Africa due to a combination of political acumen and military genius. He forged a multi-ethnic empire from his capital at Bissandugu, which was divided into administrative districts and controlled by a 5,000-man army of *sofas* loyal only to him and equipped with muskets and, by 1890, rifles. He learned early to avoid the French in set-piece battles, preferring to have his highly mobile columns of *sofas* harass the French lines of communication and attack their isolated units. He employed scorched-earth tactics, but after the British refused to supply him with rifles from Sierra Leone, he could no longer sustain his forces in the field and in 1898 surrendered to the French, who sent him into exile in Gabon. Despite the collapse of his empire, he remains for many one of the first African modernizers in trade, politics, and war.

The French-led African armies had won for France a vast empire across the Western Sudan which consisted for the most part, however, of sandy "light soil," as the British prime minister Lord Salisbury commented undiplomatically, but the enormous geographical sweep of their new African empire restored French national pride, which had

been badly tarnished by the French defeat at Sedan at the hands of Prussia in 1870.

In Central Africa, Leopold, king of the Belgians, sought to exploit the natural wealth of the Congo Basin by raising a private army of mercenaries, who collected wild rubber and ivory using intimidation, torture, and mutilation to build a vast private estate for the monarch. During the first decade of the twentieth century the scandal of his gross exploitation of the Africans was fully exposed by the reformer E. D. Morel (1873–1924), Christian missionaries, and the British consul, Roger Casement (1864–1916). This compelled the Belgian parliament in 1908 to demand that the king relinquish his personal control to a reluctant Belgian government to become the Belgian Congo—but not before he had spent many of his ill-gotten gains on the beautification of Brussels at an estimated cost of some 3 to 10 million African lives, before he died the following year. Events far to the North on the Nile Valley also drew Europeans more deeply into the affairs of African states. In 1869 the khedive of Egypt, Ismail Pasha (1830–1895), opened the Suez Canal with panache and splendor. There were four days of massive festivities, and armies of servants and cooks to entertain the guests from every royal house in Europe. Giuseppe Verdi was commissioned to compose the opera *Aida*. Religious patriarchs from Islam, Christianity of every persuasion, and even a Hindu priest blessed the waters. This grand event in one stroke dramatically changed the global defensive strategy of the British empire. Suddenly, the Suez Canal—and with it all of Egypt and the Nile Valley stretching all the way to the Great Lakes in the interior—became the linchpin of Great Britain's vast South Asian empire.

Although the British had long been fascinated with Egypt, their interests were largely concerned with its long history, dynastic monuments, and its strategic location in the eastern Mediterranean. Since 1801 the country had been ruled by a dynasty founded by an astute and ruthless Rumelian Turk, Muhammad Ali (1796–1849), who had come to Egypt in command of a Macedonian detachment of the Ottoman army to fight the French and had seized power in 1805. He and his successors sought to modernize the agricultural economy of Egypt, a policy that culminated in the 1860s when Egypt became the principal source of long-staple cotton for the textile mills of Lancashire during and after the American Civil War. The enormous profits from the Egyptian cotton crop enabled Ismail Pasha to embark upon the modernization of Egypt. He built palaces, an opera house, railways, and irrigation canals, but his greatest achievement was the Suez Canal. When Egyptian revenues could no longer service the interest on its debt, Britain and France imposed a European commission, the Caisse de la Dette Publique, in 1879 that effectively took over control of the Egyptian government by ruthlessly reducing expenditure, particularly in the army. When Ismail objected, he was forced to abdicate by Britain and France in place of his son, Muhammad Tawfiq Pasha (1852–1892), who was disdainfully dismissed by the Egyptian nationalists as a European puppet.

The political situation in Egypt rapidly deteriorated as the various classes of the Egyptian establishment—the liberal Western-oriented professionals, the conservative Muslim clerics, and the powerful landlords—rallied around the leader of Egyptian nationalism, Colonel Ahmad Arabi Pasha (1839–1896). Neither the British nor the French had any desire to occupy Egypt in order to continue their financial reform program, but when British and French citizens were killed in anti-European riots and Arabi threatened to seize the Suez Canal, a British expeditionary force landed at Ismailia and on September 13, 1882 destroyed the Egyptian army at Tel el-Kebir to occupy Egypt. Prime Minister William Ewart Gladstone (1809–1898) announced that the British troops would be withdrawn from Egypt as soon as law and order were established. They were to remain for another seventy-five years.

The British occupation of Egypt insured control of the Suez Canal, but its security depended on a constant flow of water from the Nile. Without the Nile Egypt would be nothing but sand and rock and wind. The desire to protect the Nile water obliged the British to go thousands of miles up the river to secure it from any encroachment by potential rivals.

By 1889, twenty years after the opening of the Suez Canal, the British were completely committed to employ all their considerable military, diplomatic, and economic power to exclude any European or African state from the Nile waters in order to secure Egypt and Suez. Although the Germans and Italians were restrained from any Nilotic adventures by British diplomacy, the French sought to challenge British control in Egypt by seizing the Upper White Nile at Fashoda, which precipitated the Anglo-Egyptian invasion of the Sudan, the conquest of the Mahdist state, and the humiliation of France when it was compelled to recall its filibusterin expedition under Captain Jean-Baptiste Marchand (1863–1934) from Fashoda in 1898; this marked the end of the European scramble for Africa.

Often overlooked in the conquest of this vast continent was the crucial role played by Africans in the process. Despite the technological sophistication of the imperial armies, black African soldiers recruited by Europeans did most of the fighting. They were less susceptible to tropical diseases than their European allies, and much cheaper. The French employed the largest number of African troops, the famous Senegalese light infantry, the *tirailleurs sénéalais*, who subsequently conquered all of French West Africa. In 1900, at the end of their conquest of West, East, and Central Africa, British African troops numbered 11,500 African soldiers, commanded by no more than 300 British officers and NCOs. In the west there was the British West African Frontier Force, composed of men of numerous African ethnicities, but in which the language of command was Hausa. In the east Nilotes and Luo dominated the battalions of the King's African Rifles and the Sudanese battalions of the Anglo–Egyptian army. The German East African *Schutztruppe* relied heavily on its African askaris, led by a handful of white German officers. The Italians also had askaris, who won victories over the Sudanese Mahdists at Agordat in 1893 and the Ethiopians at Coatit in 1895; and even during their disastrous defeat by the Ethiopian host of Emperor Menelik II at Adua in 1896 the Italian troops were supported by over 10,000 askaris and Tigrayan irregulars. Portugal, the oldest European colonial power in Africa, had used African troops for centuries. In one of their last colonial campaigns, in 1902, against the kingdom of Barue in the Zambezi Valley of Mozambique, only 477 of its 15,000 men were Portuguese. Although not officially a colony even the Congo Free State recruited its *force publique* to conquer the vast expanse of the Congo for King Leopold. An ethnic conglomeration of 6,000 African mercenaries infamous for their brutality, they ultimately defeated the Arabs in the Upper Congo, the Zande kingdoms in the north, the Yaka of the western Congo, and the headwaters of the Lualaba River.

The composition and motivations of these African troopers were strikingly similar. They were often marginalized members of their societies, or bound by personal and ethnic friendship to accept the pay, prestige, and security of the battalion in return for their submission to European discipline, demands, and their lives in combat against other Africans. Many learned skills for later civilian employment after demobilization. Others established family traditions for sons to follow fathers in the colonial and, after independence, the national armed forces.

The European conquest of Africa was shrouded in misconceptions by all of its participants. European statesmen knew little about African geography or the natural resources of its interior. What information they did receive came from explorers, merchants, and missionaries, who invariably embellished the truth to further their own ends. Lamenting the dearth of reliable information at his disposal, Lord Salisbury once remarked that he knew more about the moon than the interior of Africa, because at least he could see the moon. Ignorance bred mystery, and mystery led Europeans to harbor unrealistic expectations of the wealth that African imperialism might offer. African ignorance of European culture played an equally important role in the scramble. European notions of international law and freehold property were nonsensical to many of the Africans—accustomed to their communal control of land—who were signatories of the treaties that gave a patina of legitimacy to the European seizure of their land. It was only after the conquest that the reality of European imperialism in Africa became increasingly apparent. The European powers found that their new colonies were likely to require greater expense in men and money than they were worth, and the African communities discovered that the treaties signed by their hapless leaders legalized European rule. By the beginning of the twentieth century the popular enthusiasm for empire began to fade, symbolically, with the death of Queen Victoria in 1901. The European public soon lost interest in Africa. It would pay little attention to the affairs of the continent for the next fifty years.

FURTHER READING

Headrick, Daniel R., *The Tools of Empire: Technology and European Imperialism in the Nineteenth Century*, New York: Oxford University Press, 1981

Pakenham, Thomas, *The Scramble for Africa, 1876–1912*, New York: Random House, 1991

Robinson, Ronald and John Gallagher with Alice Denny, *Africa and the Victorians: The Official Mind of Imperialism*, London: Macmillan, 1961

Vandervost, Bruce, *Wars of Imperial Conquest in Africa, 1830–1914*, Bloomington: Indiana University Press, 1998

THE ECONOMIC BASIS OF IMPERIALISM

By A. G. Hopkins

Once the European powers had decided to abolish the external slave trade, West Africa was faced with the problem of developing alternative exports. The outcome was a period of transition and experimentation, which is customarily referred to as the era of 'legitimate' commerce in order to distinguish it from the illegal trade in slaves. This chapter will try to establish two conclusions about West African history in the nineteenth century. First, it will be argued that the structure of legitimate commerce marked an important break with the past and signified a new phase in the growth of the market, a phase which can be seen as the start of the modern economic history of West Africa. This argument contrasts with the traditional view, which stresses continuities with the past and the ease of the transfer to legitimate trade. Second, it will be suggested that the strains involved in creating this economy, combined with fluctuations in its performance, are central to an understanding of the partition of West Africa in the last quarter of the nineteenth century. This proposition, too, is intended to be set against current interpretations, most of which hold that imperialism was the product of political motives stemming from Europe. For these two reasons the analysis of legitimate commerce and partition has been combined in one chapter.

These are large claims, and they require some initial elaboration before the historical evidence is presented. The main structural features of the new commerce will be outlined first of all. The foreign trade statistics will then be used to support the theoretical argument, and to indicate the relationship between commercial fluctuations and the economic and political history of West Africa in the nineteenth century. Finally, the development of legitimate commerce will be considered with reference to specific African and European interests in order to demonstrate how the interaction of these groups produced the partition of West Africa. Two points need to be borne in mind in evaluating the argument of this chapter. First, the economic theme is emphasised, here partly because this book is concerned with economic history. It is argued that economic motives are a central and neglected feature of partition, not that they provide a complete explanation of it. Second, in relating the economic theme to the timing of partition, it is important to remember that though the tensions caused by structural change were felt in West Africa from the early nineteenth century, they became acute only in the last quarter of the century, when they were aggravated by a serious downturn in the terms of trade.

A. G. Hopkins, "The Economic Basis of Imperialism," *An Economic History of West Africa*, pp. 124-135, 137-162, 164-166. Copyright © 1973 by Columbia University Press. Reprinted with permission.

THE ECONOMY OF 'LEGITIMATE' COMMERCE

There is no novelty in saying that slaves and palm oil are commodities with obvious physical differences. What has not been appreciated fully is that these differences had far-reaching consequences for the structure of the export economy. The main features of the new economy can be analysed by making use of staple theory, which has been developed specifically to explain the particular type of growth stemming from diversification around a well-defined export base.[1] Staple theory has grown up and been applied chiefly in North America and Australia.[2] These are countries of recent, European settlement, which at critical stages of their economic growth have relied on primary exports, such as fur, wheat and wool, to stimulate the expansion of the domestic market. The aspects of the theory which are especially relevant to the West African case are those which stress the economic consequences of the physical properties of the staple and the type of linkages which it establishes with the rest of the economy.

The physical properties of the staple are important because they influence the factor combination and the nature of returns to scale. In the case of West Africa the basic point is a simple one, which may explain why it has not engaged much interest: the vegetable oils which became staple exports in the nineteenth century could be produced efficiently and on a small scale by households possessing little capital, employing family labour, and using traditional tools. Palm products and groundnuts, unlike slaves, were divisible into very small units, each of which was of low value per unit of weight, yet was still marketable and yielded a return in the same season. Land, moreover, was cheap and readily available. Admittedly, the new exports could also be produced on sizeable estates, but the few farmers who did so simply increased their inputs of land and labour without securing any of the economies of large scale production because there was little scope for substituting machinery for labour, and few advantages to centralised management. Large producers were not particularly inefficient, but they no longer had a monopoly of the export market.

This change in the structure of export-producing firms was a key event in African history. The capital and labour requirements of slave raiding and trading had encouraged the rise of a relatively small group of large entrepreneurs, many of whom became the rulers or senior officials of great states in the Western Sudan and in the forest. Producing and selling palm oil and groundnuts, on the other hand, were occupations in which there were few barriers to entry. Legitimate commerce therefore enabled small-scale farmers and traders to play an important part in the overseas exchange economy for the first time. In so far as firms of this type and size are the basis of the export economies of most West African states today, it can be said that modernity dates not from the imposition of colonial rule, as used to be thought, but from the early nineteenth century.

The character of the staple also influences the nature and strength of the linkages between export activities and the domestic economy. In an underdeveloped economy dominated by an indigenous society linkages tend to be weaker than in an area of recent settlement, such as North America, where there were special advantages of capital and modern skills in the nineteenth century. Nevertheless, the linkages created by legitimate commerce were much stronger than those set up previously by Saharan and Atlantic commerce.[3]

The new export trade saw a marked increase in the commercialisation of labour and land in Africa, instead of, as in the eighteenth century, the export of one factor of production (labour) and the comparative neglect of another (land), except for domestic needs. Support for this contention can be found in the migration of peoples from the Western Sudan to the 'groundnut coast' of Senegambia, and in the influx of newcomers into the forest in search of the wealth which could be won from the palm tree. An idea of the scale of the new, legitimate enterprise is provided by an estimate that in 1892 no less than 15 million palm trees were in production for the export market in Yoruba country alone.[4] The expansion of legitimate commerce also provided additional employment opportunities in export-processing, even though the methods in use remained technically simple.[5] Admittedly, it was not until the coming of railways and roads that areas in the interior could participate in export production. Nevertheless, a start had been made: after 1900 the colonial rulers simply carried further a process which was already underway.

The import trade still consisted of manufactured consumer goods. However, as a result of the industrial revolution, the consumer imports of the nineteenth century were mainly cheap, mass-produced goods, which offered large numbers of inconspicuous Africans opportunities of material improvement and of emulating the superior, inherited status enjoyed by a minority of their compatriots. To the extent that the revolution of rising expectations is an identifiable phenomenon, then it can be said to have started in West Africa early in the nineteenth century. Furthermore, it is worth observing at this point that imports of cheap manufactures provide a more favourable base for the introduction of modern industries than imports which contain a high proportion of luxuries. If the market for imports grows, then there may well come a time when it is feasible and profitable to manufacture some of these goods on the spot instead of buying them from other countries. This time came in parts of West Africa after 1945.

The change in the quality of consumer imports was made possible not only by cost reductions on the supply side, but also by a shift in the distribution of incomes in Africa. As a general proposition, it can be said that the more equal the distribution of incomes, the smaller the demand for luxury items and the greater the demand for cheap, mass-produced goods.[6] Down to the nineteenth century the distribution of incomes from foreign trade had been very uneven, and purchasing power had been concentrated in a relatively few, large units. With the development of exports of vegetable oils, earnings from overseas commerce began to be spread over many small units of consumption, and incomes achieved greater equality.[7] The evidence for the nineteenth century suggests that imports were being distributed more widely, socially as well as geographically. Furthermore, and again

in contrast to the period before the nineteenth century, the size of export proceeds increased as a result of the growth of demand for tropical raw materials and of West Africa's ability to meet that demand. Goods other than slaves were exported before the nineteenth century, but were unable to generate much additional income because the demand for them was still limited. The expansion in the volume and value of trade in the nineteenth century also gave a further stimulus to service industries, especially those providing transport and accommodation, and it led to the development of market gardening to supply foodstuffs to the larger commercial centres.

It is necessary now to show that the statistics of overseas trade are consistent with the argument advanced so far. In particular, the value and volume of trade should show an upward trend; the character of staple exports should conform in detail to the specifications which have been outlined in brief; and the dominant European powers on the West Coast should be those best fitted to supply manufactured goods and to process tropical raw materials.

Although the details of the transition to legitimate commerce are not yet known, it would seem that on the whole West Africa did not experience a prolonged period of economic crisis, principally because many areas were able to export legitimate goods and slaves side by side down to about the middle of the nineteenth century. It is clear that there was a remarkable expansion in the value of overseas trade in the second quarter of the century. Newbury, who has carried out some much-needed research on West African trade in the nineteenth century, has estimated that the total value of the overseas commerce of the region in legitimate goods alone amounted to a minimum of £3½ million a year in the early 1850s.[8] This figure may be compared with Fage's estimate that at the end of the eighteenth century, at the height of the Atlantic slave trade, West Africa's overseas commerce was worth about £4 million a year.[9] In the second half of the century trade expanded roughly four times, and by 1901–1905 amounted to about £15 million a year. The rate of growth was not even throughout this period, and it was to be dwarfed by the expansion which occurred during the colonial era. Nevertheless, it was great enough to support the proposition that the new economy was also a much bigger economy. It is worth emphasising that European commercial involvement in West Africa was expanding rather than diminishing, as this is a factor which has not been taken into account by historians who have argued that economic motives were of little significance in the partition of West Africa.

No useful comparison of volumes can be made between legitimate commerce and the slave trade. However, the main point to note with regard to the volume of trade in the nineteenth century is that West African societies had to adjust in a relatively short time to the immense physical task of transporting huge quantities of low value, bulky commodities. Imports of palm oil into the United Kingdom from West Africa reached 1,000 tons in 1810, 10,000 tons in 1830, over 20,000 tons in 1842, over 30,000 tons in 1853, and over 40,000 tons in 1855. Even this expansion was dwarfed in the second half of the century, when there was a rapid growth in shipments of groundnuts, and a still more dramatic rise in overseas trade in palm kernels. Two examples will illustrate the size of the increase. Exports of groundnuts from Senegal rose from virtually nothing in the 1840s to an average of 29,000 tons a year in the period 1886–1890, while exports of palm kernels from Lagos, one of the great slave ports in the 1840s and 1850s, reached an average of 37,000 tons in the same period. The palm oil trade failed to maintain its early rate of progress, but exports still averaged about 50,000 tons a year between 1860 and 1900. The organisation required for moving, let alone producing, tonnages of this magnitude provides some indication of the skill and adaptability of African entrepreneurs.[10] The return trade in imported goods also involved transporting much greater quantities than ever before. For instance, the quantity of cotton goods (measured by the yard) exported from the United Kingdom to West Africa increased thirty times in the short period between 1816–1820 and 1846–1850.[11] The

increase was partly a reflection of the rise in the value of trade, but was mainly an outcome of the industrial revolution in Europe and of the shift in the social composition of demand in Africa arising out of the structure of the new export economy. It is safe to conclude that the volume of exports and imports expanded considerably as a result of the rise of legitimate commerce and the decline of the external slave trade.

Vegetable oils, as noted already, became the staples of legitimate commerce. Palm oil was the pioneer export early in the nineteenth century, and it was joined by palm kernels and groundnuts in the second half of the century. The fact that these products already grew in West Africa, where they were traded and consumed as foodstuffs, helps to explain why the end of the Atlantic slave trade did not cause a complete disruption of overseas commerce, though it does not mean that the transition was entirely smooth. The expansion of exports of palm products and groundnuts was a response to industrial growth in Europe, which led to a rise in the demand for oils and fats. Palm oil was used in the production of soap, lubricants and candles. Soap was required for cleansing the population in the growing urban centres; lubricants were needed to oil the new machinery, especially the railways; and candles were in demand for lighting the expanding towns and factories. Manufacturers, happily uniting material and moral motives, urged the public to 'buy our candles and help stop the slave trade'.[12] Palm kernels, though jointly produced with palm oil, were not exported at first, and a large proportion were not used at all, even in West Africa.[13] This was not because the African producer was fickle, or because his wants could be satisfied from the sale of palm oil alone, but because there was little demand in Europe for palm kernel oil, which had a different chemical composition from the oil extracted from the outer part of the fruit. Only in the late nineteenth century was it found possible to employ kernel oil in the manufacture of margarine, then a new product, and to process the residue for cattle food. Groundnuts were used mainly in the manufacture of cooking oil and soap. Other commodities, many of which had been shipped abroad before the nineteenth century, continued to be exported after abolition. The most important of these were gum from Senegal, gold from the Gold Coast, and timber, ivory and cotton from various parts of the forest zone.

Four items accounted for about three-quarters of the value of all imports into West Africa. These were textiles (a classification covering a wide range of cotton and woollen goods), spirits (especially rum and gin), salt and iron. Other prominent items were hardware, tobacco, guns and gun powder.[14] Textiles remained the leading commodity, as in the eighteenth century. In Senegal, for example, one popular variety alone (known as 'guinea' cloth) accounted for no less than 25 per cent of the value of total imports during the third quarter of the nineteenth century. At Lagos (about 1,800 miles away) textiles of all kinds averaged 44 per cent of total imports in the period 1880–1892. Similarities between the types of goods imported before and after the end of the external slave trade should not be allowed to disguise some important differences: by the middle of the nineteenth century the quantity had increased greatly, and (as will be pointed out) the price per unit had declined.

On the European side of the trade, Britain and France continued to be the most important foreign powers on the West Coast, as they had been in the eighteenth century. Liverpool dominated the new trade, just as it had the old, and was by far the largest importer of palm oil in Europe. Nantes under went a decline in the nineteenth century, but Bordeaux and Marseilles, the ports which took its place, both had long standing connections with Africa. Most of West Africa's groundnut exports were shipped to France, where they enjoyed tariff advantages over certain other vegetable oils, including palm oil. The most striking aspect of the national distribution of trade was the pre-eminence of Britain.[15] In 1868 a French consul estimated that Britain and France shared four-fifths of Europe's trade with West Africa, and that two-thirds to three-quarters of this total was in the hands of Great Britain. Furthermore, as much as 70 per cent of Britain's

trade in the period 1860–1880 was conducted with areas outside her few, small colonies. France's trade, by contrast, was centred on her traditional base and colony of Senegal, which accounted for between half and three-quarters of her total trade with West Africa during the same period. A new feature of the second half of the century was the rapid growth of German commerce. By the 1880s Hamburg was said to handle nearly one third of all West Africa's overseas trade.[16] This expansion was the result of three factors: the rise of the palm kernel market, which was dominated by Hamburg because German farmers were the main buyers of cattle cake, and because the Dutch were the largest manufacturers of margarine; the ability of Hamburg to supply cheap liquor; and the development of steamship services between Germany and West Africa.

The abolition of the Atlantic slave trade and the rise of legitimate commerce were events which undoubtedly favoured Britain, the first industrial nation. She, above all others, was in a position to cater for the mass market which was beginning to emerge in West Africa, though her supremacy was being challenged in the late nineteenth century by new competitors. No other foreign powers were of any account in West Africa apart from Britain, France and Germany. The Danes sold their Gold Coast forts to the British in 1850, and the Dutch followed suit in 1872. The Portuguese, once the great innovators of European enterprise in Africa, had difficulty in maintaining even one tiny colony (Portuguese Guinea). All three countries had been overtaken by a world in which industrialisation had become the basis of commercial and political power.[17]

The rapid expansion of overseas commerce has tended to overshadow the history of West Africa's external trade across the Sahara. It is commonly supposed that by the nineteenth century this trade was only a fraction of the value it had attained in the golden age of the sixteenth century. Professor Boahen, for example, has suggested that total trade on the trans-Saharan routes amounted to no more than about £125,000 a year in the first half of the nineteenth century.[18] However, the deficiencies in the evidence for both the sixteenth century and the early nineteenth century are so great as to make calculations and comparisons a matter of guesswork. Recent research indicates that the old caravan routes still had a surprising amount of life left in them in the second half of the nineteenth century. To begin with, it is now apparent that trans-Saharan trade was *not* seriously affected by competition from goods brought by sea until the very end of the century. Indeed, Manchester textiles were carried across the Sahara and achieved a wide distribution. As late as 1869, for example, the town of florin was said to be commercially nearer the Mediterranean (some 2,000 miles to the north) than it was to the Bight of Benin, even though the port of Lagos was only about 150 miles away.[19] Secondly, in the most detailed examination of the trade figures yet attempted, Newbury has shown that the total value of trans-Saharan trade actually increased from the 1840s, and reached a peak in 1875, when it was worth around £1,500,000.[20] It was only after this date that a slow and final decline set in. Thus the Sahara developed its own brand of 'legitimate' commerce. Because of transport limitations, however, the overland routes failed to develop a sizeable export trade in bulky, low value goods, and the boom in the third quarter of the century was based partly on the ephemeral demand of the Victorian world for ostrich feathers.[21] Even with this boost to the trade, trans-Saharan commerce was worth only a fifth of the value of the West Coast's seaborne trade in 1875.

Economic development by way of staple exports can be a precarious and lengthy process. Changes in supply and demand can set back the progress of the staple, retard the development of the economy as a whole, and have serious social and political repercussions. West Africa's raw material exports entered a wide range of manufacturing processes, and the price paid for them and the volume required tended to vary in accordance with the level of business activity in industrial Europe. West African producers had to accept the world price as given because they were unable to control the volume of palm produce and groundnuts placed on the market, and because the industrial countries could buy alternative, competing products from other underdeveloped regions. By the mid nineteenth century the days when West Africa enjoyed a monopoly as the sole supplier of labour to the plantations of the Americas were over, and the silent imperialism of the steamship was beginning to bring vegetable oils and substitute products from other continents besides Africa.

The identification of fluctuations in West Africa's external trade is a matter of considerable historical importance. The progress of the new economy of legitimate commerce is best charted by changes in the terms of trade of West African export producers: the net barter terms provide an index of the import-purchasing power of a unit of exports, and the income terms measure the import-purchasing power of total exports.[22] Insufficient data are available at present to enable precise calculations to be made, but the general trends are clear enough, and are confirmed by the evaluation of contemporary observers. It is hoped that others will find this subject important enough to carry out the research needed to improve the provisional and approximate analysis presented here.[23]

Information on the early nineteenth century is particularly sparse. However, as far as the main staple, palm oil, was concerned, prices on the West Coast and in Europe appear to have pursued an upward trend, with the exception of falls in 1844–1846 and 1851–1852, reaching a peak in 1854–1861, when the Liverpool price stood at around £45 per ton. At the same time, the prices of manufactured goods imported into West Africa fell dramatically as a result of the industrial revolution. By 1850 staple items cost half and in some cases only a quarter of what they had at the start of the century. Consequently, the barter terms of trade moved in favour of primary producers. Since the volume of exports was rising during the first half of the century, the income terms also improved. The result was a period of prosperity for West African trade. Indeed, since 1800 West Africa has experienced only three periods when both barter and income terms have moved sharply in favour of producers for at least ten years. The first period played an important part in establishing the new commerce; the second, from 1900–1913, helped to install the colonial rulers; and the third, from 1945–1955, was a phase of expanding expectations and economic diversification which was associated with the end of the colonial era.

In all situations of historical change there are elements of continuity. During the first half of the nineteenth century, when legitimate commerce was in its infancy and was also comparatively prosperous, producers and traders were encouraged to believe that the transition from the slave trade would be an easy one. Initially, various features of commerce on the West Coast were simply carried over from the eighteenth century. For example, a number of established European traders and African producers managed to adapt from the old trade to the new; some of the minor exports of legitimate commerce continued to be shipped after abolition just as they had been before; the credit or trust 'system' survived and expanded, in spite of repeated complaints from those who thought that it was morally reprehensible and economically risky; sailing ships remained in use on routes between Europe and Africa; and business was still transacted by means of barter and 'transitional' currencies, such as cowries and manillas. Above all, the effort to stop the slave trade and to establish legitimate commerce, though it led to voyages of exploration, to missionary enterprise, and to a slightly greater degree of official activity on the West Coast, did not bring about any major alterations to the political map. Because an adjustment was made to the economy without causing an immediate and total upheaval, traders and officials felt confident that casual and limited political commitments could be maintained, much as they had been in the eighteenth century. The European frontier did not extend inland; it did not even cover all parts of the coast. There was no partition of Africa in 1807 or 1833.

The position changed considerably in the second half of the century. The boom came to an end in 1861, and there was a depression between 1862 and 1866, when the European price for palm oil fell to around £32 per ton. Although prices revived in 1866–1867, they never again reached the peaks of 1854–1861. On the contrary, they underwent a serious decline from an average of £37 per ton in 1861–1865 to £20 a ton in 1886–1890, the lowest on record since the early days of the trade. Thus in twenty-five years prices were cut by nearly 50 percent. There was a very slight improvement in the 1890s, but it was not until 1906 that prices regained the levels achieved in the 1850s. Palm kernel prices fell by about a third from roughly £15 per ton in the 1860s to just over £10 in the period 1886–1890. Groundnut prices at Rufisque in Senegal also fell by roughly a third from 25 to 27½ francs per 100 kilos in the period 1857–1867 to around 15 francs in the period 1877–1900. In both cases, there was no recovery until after the turn of the century. There were two main causes of this fall, though there were several contributory factors, such as reduced ocean freight rates. First, there was an increase in the supply of mineral and vegetable oils following the discovery of petroleum resources in the United States in the 1860s, and the entry into the market of Indian groundnuts and Australian tallow after the opening of the Suez Canal in 1869. Second, European demand for a wide range of raw materials, including oils and fats, was checked in the last quarter of the nineteenth century with the advent of the so called Great Depression.[24]

There is little systematic information available about the local prices of goods imported into West Africa in the second half of the nineteenth century. The trend was probably a downward one, reflecting the fail in freight rates, an increase in competition on the West Coast, and continuing improvements in industrial efficiency. However, it is certain that the substantial price reductions of the early nineteenth century were not repeated, and that any decline which occurred was relatively slight and also gradual.[25] In the third quarter of the nineteenth century, when export prices fell particularly sharply, the barter terms of trade moved decisively against primary producers.

The question now arises as to what extent and in what sense an increase in the volume of exports can be said to have compensated for this adverse movement in the barter terms of trade. The broad trend, as noted earlier, was a rising one, but with few exceptions expansion levelled off in the late 1870s and in the 1880s, and in some cases the volume of exports actually declined. A few examples will illustrate how widespread this experience was: in the Niger Delta palm produce exports showed no clear upward movement in the 1870s and 1880s, and there was a decrease at Opobo during the period 1887–1893; at Lagos, one of the major centres of legitimate commerce, there was a slight, but indecisive, trend towards expansion in the 1870s and 1880s; on the Gold Coast oil and kernel exports were almost static from 1886–1900; on the Ivory Coast palm oil exports fell sharply in the mid-1880s; and in Sierra Leone the picture was much the same. The position with regard to groundnuts was very similar; shipments from Gambia declined in the 1870s and 1880s; and in Senegal exports reached a plateau in the late 1870s which was not substantially exceeded until about the turn of the century. Even in cases where the volume of exports rose to the extent that total earnings were maintained, producers were still not as well off in the 1880s as they had been earlier. In the absence of technical improvements in agriculture or in internal transport during the second half of the century, a rise in the volume of exports could be achieved only in one of two ways: first, by existing producers deciding to increase their labour inputs, thus reducing net incomes by cutting down on leisure or other activities, or by paying for additional labour services; and second by expanding the total number of independent producers, thus causing the average per capita incomes of export producers to fall.

It seems likely that the income terms of trade either declined or maintained a precarious stability during the last quarter of the century. Even in the latter case there is a strong probability that the real income of the average export producer was reduced.

The foregoing analysis has referred to the major staples of overseas trade. How ever, it is important to realise that the late nineteenth century was also a time of crisis for minor staples and for trans-Saharan trade. The Senegalese gum trade declined in the second half of the century as a result of the development of chemical substitutes and the growth of competition from Egyptian gum. Gold exports from the Gold Coast were static, cocoa exports were negligible, and rubber exports did not expand until the 1890s. The Western Sudan was affected in the nineteenth century by a series of political upheavals stemming from the *jihads* (holy wars), which were launched by the protagonists of a revived Islam. The nature of these revivalist movements is still a subject of dispute.[26] Their economic influence appears to have been conservative, except, possibly in the case of Senegal. At best they preserved traditional agricultural and trading activities; at worst they perpetuated archaic economies based on plunder, tribute and slavery. To these troubles was added another, namely the decay of trans-Saharan trade, which declined after 1875, and was reduced to a trickle by 1900. Initially, this slump was the result of slackening demand in Europe, but by the end of the century the desert trade had also been seriously affected by the disintegration of the slave system which supported the oases, and by competition from ocean routes, which could deliver manufactured goods more cheaply.

The evidence indicates that West Africa's external trade experienced a crisis in the last quarter of the nineteenth century. Export producers had become caught in a staple trap: the barter terms of trade had turned against them, and attempts to increase the volume of exports had either failed or, where successful, had contributed to a further decline in the terms of trade, with the result that growth had become self-defeating. Within a relatively short space of time primary producers and traders came under severe pressure to develop alternative exports and to adopt cost-reducing innovations. This 'general crisis' of the late nineteenth century led to strains, misunderstandings and conflicts between all those, Europeans as well as Africans, who in varying degrees had become dependent on legitimate commerce for their livelihood. The expansion in the volume of overseas commerce in the second half of the nineteenth century, combined with the adverse movement in the terms of trade, led to the modification or abolition of many of the early features of legitimate commerce that had been inherited from the time of the external slave trade, and also caused the European powers to discard the assumptions governing their traditional policy of limited intervention in West Africa. Just as pronounced booms have had a marked effect on the course of West African history, so, too, have serious slumps. Since the beginning of legitimate commerce there have been two periods of ten years or more when the barter terms of trade have moved against export producers and when the income terms have either fallen or remained static. The first period of depression was in the last quarter of the nineteenth century, and helped to bring the Europeans into Africa. The second period, covering the years 1930–1945, helped create the movement which was to expel them.

ECONOMIC MOTIVES IN PARTITION

Imperialism is seen here as a process of interaction and, ultimately, conflict between the industrialised nations and the underdeveloped world. To analyse this process parallel analyses are required, the first dealing with intra-group relations, that is among African producers, traders and politicians on the one hand, and among European manufacturers, traders and politicians on the other; the second covering inter-group strategy, that is between Africans and Europeans at what, broadly, can be called the national level. The principal difficulty, apart from the problem that there is considerable controversy about the role of the Europeans, is that so little is known about the part played by Africans both in assisting and in opposing the invasion of their continent. The argument presented here is by no means complete, but it does try to establish and explore a framework of analysis which it is hoped will lead to further, more detailed research.[27] This framework is in three different sections, all of which are concerned with the implications of the economic structure created by legitimate commerce: the first will consider problems of supply and their effect on intra-group relations on the African side of the frontier; the second will focus on problems of demand and their effect on intra-group relations on the European side of the frontier; and the third section will examine how the economic crisis of the late nineteenth century affected inter-group relations at the national level, and led to the decisions to move the established frontier inland, that is to partition West Africa.

It was by no means easy to develop satisfactory substitutes for the Atlantic slave trade, even though some of the staples of legitimate commerce were already grown in West Africa, and the terms of trade favoured primary producers in the second quarter of the nineteenth century. With the benefit of hindsight, historians have been able to point, justly, to the success of palm produce and groundnuts. For contemporaries, however, legitimate commerce was a long, precarious experiment, an era of fluctuating fortunes which held out no guarantees for the future. This explains why European interests, official and private, thought it necessary to tangle with a series of risky ventures in tropical agriculture. In the 1820s, for example, the French undertook an ambitious agricultural project in Senegal.[28] The main idea behind this scheme was to grow in Africa, and with African labour, the crops which had been produced on slave plantations in the Americas. A model farm was established, several crops, including cotton and indigo, were tried out, and new techniques of irrigation and ploughing were introduced. The experiment was abandoned in 1831 as a result of mismanagement, lack of capital, and ignorance of tropical conditions. In the 1840s British commercial interests established a model farm at Lokoja on the Niger, but this, too, was a failure.

The next important wave of experiments occurred just after the middle of the century, and was prompted by a cotton famine in Europe arising out of the American Civil War. Attempts were made to grow cotton at various points on the West Coast, such as Senegal, southern Nigeria and the Gold Coast.[29] In the 1860s the French still thought that Senegal was destined to become a leading exporter of cotton. Again they were disappointed. Many previous errors were repeated, and American production recovered far more quickly than had been anticipated. Above all, the Senegalese farmer, envisaging a rather different future for his country, preferred groundnuts to cotton because they were more profitable. A greater degree of success was achieved at Abeokuta in south-west Nigeria, though there, too, cotton exports dwindled in the 1870s.[30] The promoters found that they were unable to compete in international markets, partly, it is interesting to note, because of the high cost of free African labour. The final phase of experiments came in the 1880s as a result of declining profits in the palm produce trade. Many proposals were put forward to remedy the problem, and several of the more feasible were tried out. Arthur Verdier, a prominent French merchant, began coffee plantations in the Ivory Coast; the Royal Niger Company started plantations of cocoa, coffee and rubber in the Niger Valley; and the colonial administration established botanic stations at Lagos (1887) and on the Gold Coast (1889).

These experiments have implications which extend beyond the local details given above. As a record of early European endeavours in tropical agriculture, they are important for geographers and botanists, as well as for historians. They also represent an interesting stage in the development of economic policy, for they stand mid way between the mercantilist concept of colonies serving the needs of the mother country, and the realisation of this ideal in the different circumstances of the twentieth century. Furthermore, these nineteenth-century debates over the means of achieving agricultural progress anticipate the controversy which arose in the colonial period between the protagonists of peasant and plantation crops. For historians the schemes are especially noteworthy because they expressed the realisation that the external slave trade would not simply die of its own accord, and that a positive effort was required to find substitute exports. Many of those engaged in this search were energetic and commercially-minded Christians, who were intent on converting the soul of Africa as well as its economy. These men, the militant arm of the abolitionist movement, saw it as their mission to carry the moral convictions and economic optimism of the industrial world into the Dark Continent.

The most important and successful experiments, however, were those undertaken by Africans themelves, without European supervision, indeed frequently without expatriate officials and traders knowing what was happening. It is not always realised just how varied the export economy was in some parts of West Africa during the era of legitimate commerce. At Freetown, for instance, timber accounted for about 70 percent of all exports by 1829; by 1860 timber exports had almost disappeared, and the main items of overseas trade were gold, palm oil and groundnuts, each of which accounted for about 20 percent of total exports; by the 1880s these three products had also declined, and palm kernels had become the dominant export.[31] It was in the 1880s, too, and as a direct result of the economic problems of the period, that Africans began cocoa farming in the Gold Coast and southern Nigeria, achieving results which none of the European 'experts' could emulate. These examples illustrate that African responses to changing returns on their exports were flexible and rapid, given the natural resources at their disposal and the technical constraints operating in the nineteenth century, notably in internal transport.

Palm oil, palm kernels and groundnuts, the main staples of legitimate commerce, were produced and delivered to the coast entirely through indigenous enterprise. Yet because of the widespread assumption that the transition to legitimate commerce was easy and uneventful, some basic questions about the historical development of these crops have still to be asked. For example, few historians have appreciated that palm oil was not a homogeneous commodity. Some regions, such as south-west Nigeria, produced a soft quality oil which fetched a high price; others, such as the Gold Coast, supplied a harder oil which was less in demand. These distinctions deserve further consideration, for they are likely to supply much-needed information about the resource base of the various export regions, about differences in methods of preparation, and about the motives for developing alternative exports, such as why the Gold

Coast expanded cocoa production at an earlier date than did Nigeria. Similarly, not enough attention has been paid to the fact that palm kernels did not simply join palm oil as an additional export, but were developed largely to compensate for the decline of the latter in the second half of the nineteenth century. Yet some regions exported a much greater proportion of kernels to oil than did others, though both products were in joint supply. This, too, is a difference which needs exploring further, for it may provide a clue to important problems, such as the extent of internal trade in palm oil, and the ability of various parts of the coast to adjust to the decline of staple exports in the late nineteenth century. Finally, more thought needs to be given to the remarkable 'do it yourself' character of staple export production, in which each man became an entrepreneur in his own right, albeit on a modest scale. Traditional economic frontiers were broken down through the initiative of African migrants and settlers, who colonised and developed previously underused land, and in doing so brought about changes in settlement patterns, farming practices, land tenure, and in the role, status and size of the labour force engaged in export production.[32] This is a theme of epic proportions, which still awaits epic treatment.

European demand for vegetable oils had far-reaching economic, social and political consequences in West Africa, though it is important to stress that these were not identical in all parts of the region. Ultimately, it should be possible to define and classify the various areas of West Africa according to the precise type of adaptive challenge which confronted them, and the nature of their responses to it. At present it is hard to do more than sketch the outlines of a complex regional map. Three categories will be suggested here by way of preliminary analysis.

First, there were areas which experienced a decline in the staple export, slaves, without securing adequate compensation in the form of new products. This was particularly true of those parts of West Africa which were either unsuitable for growing palm trees and groundnuts, or were too far from the coast for export production to be remunerative. The Western Sudan, with its famous trans-Saharan commerce in decline after 1875, was a case in point, for palm produce and groundnuts were bulky items with a low value to weight ratio, unlike slaves, which could be traded profitably over long distances. Second, there were areas which had not been involved in the external slave trade to any great extent, and which were presented with new openings in the export sector. This was the case along parts of the coast between Senegal and the Ivory Coast, which began to export vegetable products in the nineteenth century. Third, there were areas in which the change to legitimate commerce meant a shift from the production of slaves (at least as an export commodity) to the production of vegetable oils. This applied to Senegambia and to most of the forest from the Gold Coast eastwards. There is considerable justification for concentrating on the third category, apart from the convenient fact that it happens to be the best documented. Not only was this extensive region by far the most important supplier of legitimate exports, despite its close involvement with the Atlantic slave trade,[33] but it was also from points within this area that the Europeans launched their invasion of the interior at the close of the century.[34]

Three aspects of the economic history of this region will be considered here. First, its general development as an export centre will be outlined; next, the position of export producers will be investigated with particular reference to the fortunes of the large entrepreneurs who had dominated production during the time of the Atlantic slave trade; finally, the situation of the coastal wholesalers will be examined, using the Niger Delta as a case study.

The supply of West African palm produce came from an area which stretched from Guinea to the Cameroons, though the most important source lay in the eastern section from the Gold Coast to Old Calabar. The prominence of this sub-division was the result of the abundance of its oil palms, which occurred naturally in a broad belt lying close to the coast,[35] and of the network of lagoons and inland waterways stretching from Porto Novo to Old Calabar, which made it possible to transport produce relatively cheaply. In the period immediately after 1807 the leading centre of production in West Africa was Old Calabar, which shipped well over half the total palm oil imports entering Great Britain. In the 1830s Old Calabar was joined, and for a while overtaken, by Bonny, further west in the mouth of the Niger Delta. In the 1840s exports from the Delta as a whole averaged 15–20,000 tons per annum, which was equivalent to about three-quarters of total oil imports into the United Kingdom. Bonny's supremacy lasted until the 1870s, when its suppliers and outlets were captured by the nearby port of Opobo following a political coup. After the middle of the century other centres sprang up, and the Niger Delta, though still very important, no longer completely dominated the West African oil trade. The geographical and quantitative expansion of legitimate commerce was closely associated with the decline of the Atlantic slave trade, for until about the 1860s slaves still competed successfully with palm oil at several points along the coast, especially at Whydah and Lagos. By the third quarter of the century palm produce was the leading overseas export along a broad stretch of the West Coast. During the last twenty years of the century oil and kernels accounted for over 70 percent of the value of total exports from the Gold Coast, over 80 percent at Lagos and over 90 percent in Dahomey and the Niger Delta. A remarkable transformation of the export economy had been achieved in a comparatively short space of time.

Groundnuts, an annual crop, were grown for export in a region which extended from Senegal to Sierra Leone, though as they prefer sandy soils and a long, reliable dry season, Senegambia became by far the most prominent area of production. Transport costs made it uneconomic to grow the crop for export very far inland, so the main areas of production, as in the case of palm oil, lay near the coast. The small British colony of Gambia was the earliest focal point of the trade, partly, it is interesting to note, as a result of purchases made by American traders.[36] In the 1820s about 90 percent of Gambia's exports consisted of beeswax and hides. Groundnuts were exported for the first time in the 1830s, and by the middle of the century they accounted for two-thirds of all exports. A proportion of the groundnuts shipped from Gambia were grown in areas which would have made use of ports in neighbouring French territory, except for the fact that an export duty was levied on agricultural exports from Senegal until 1855. With the removal of this duty, exports from Senegal greatly increased. By the last quarter of the century the export trade of Senegambia was as dependent on groundnuts as that of the forest was on palm produce. The main areas of production were Casamance south of Gambia, and Cayor to the north. (However, further north still, around St Louis, the export trade relied principally on gum, as it had in the days of Atlantic commerce.) The groundnut trade, like the palm oil trade, saw the conversion of former slave ports into centres of legitimate commerce. Kaolack, for example, became a large centre for the groundnut trade from the 1860s onwards.[37] A great deal of additional historical research needs to be carried out on most aspects of legitimate commerce, but especially on the development of groundnut production. Fouquet, Pelissier, and others have made substantial contributions to the study of Senegalese groundnuts in the modern context, but the economic history of the crop remains to be written.

In some parts of the underdeveloped world the requirements of the industrial nations were consistent with the maintenance of the established social and political order. Britain's demand for Argentinian beef, for example, strengthened the position of an already existing class of large landowners in that area, since cattle rearing was most efficient on sizeable units of land.[38] Peaceful economic integration was also associated with a policy of political neutrality in Latin America, though it was not the only reason for it. In West Africa, on the other hand, the accidents of geography and history which enabled small farmers and traders to participate efficiently in overseas commerce posed acute problems of adaptation for the traditional warrior entrepreneurs who had co-operated so profitably with European slavers during the days of the Atlantic trade. African rulers experimented with a number of modes of adaptation to their new situation, and these can be classified according to their negative or positive character. Four of the most important, which were adopted singly or in conjunction, will be dealt with here.

The first negative response was to continue exporting slaves in defiance of the ban imposed by the European nations. Little is known at present about the relative profits of slaving and legitimate commerce, but it seems that few African slave exporters turned willingly to the new trade, even though the terms of trade were more favourable in the second quarter of the century than they were to become later on. This reluctance may be taken as an indication that for established exporters the costs of legitimate commerce (in terms of diminished political power as well as of cash income) outweighed the returns. The predicament of Ghezo, the ruler of Abomey, was duplicated in other parts of the West Coast:

> The state which he maintained was great; his army was expensive; the ceremonies and customs to be observed annually, which had been handed down to him from his forefathers, entailed upon him a vast outlay of money. These could not be abolished. The form of his government could not be suddenly changed, without causing such a revolution as would deprive him of his throne, and precipitate his kingdom into a state of anarchy.[39]

As for the palm oil trade, that was 'a slow method of making money, and brought only a very small amount of duties into his coffers'. Ghezo's support of the slave trade ceased only with his death in 1858. After the withdrawal of European nations from the Atlantic trade, the shipment of slaves was handled mainly by Brazilian merchants, such as Domingo Martinez, who operated in the Bight of Benin between 1833 and 1864.[40] The Brazilians were

eventually eliminated by the naval squadron, by the closure of foreign slave markets, and by their own inability to procure the necessary European trade goods. By the end of the 1860s the overseas slave trade had been reduced to a trickle. Responding to the new trade by trying to perpetuate the old was no longer possible.

Next, African rulers attempted to bolster their fortunes by means which were familiar to pre-industrial governments throughout the world, namely by employing armed strength to plunder and to exact tribute from their neighbours. The kings of Senegambia used this tactic as an outlet for the energies of their hard drinking, hard fighting warrior élite (*tyeddo*); Ashanti mixed force with diplomacy in order to control, or secure access to, the wealth of the coastal peoples; the kings of Dahomey made annual incursions into Yoruba country; and the Yoruba states themselves fought a series of wars in which economic goals were prominent. Military operations, and, perhaps more important, the constant threat of them, led to the abandonment of fertile land, and to the creation of broad areas of neutral territory between hostile states. They perpetuated conditions which were inimical to the growth of the petty capitalism that had been fostered by legitimate commerce. They dramatised what may be called the crisis of the aristocracy in nineteenth-century West Africa, a social and political crisis stemming from a contradiction between past and present relations of production. They were a last resort, and, as such, represented the ultimate failure of the *ancien régime* to adapt peacefully and efficiently to the demands of the industrial world.

The first of the two positive modes of adaptation was for former slave suppliers to develop an export trade in legitimate goods. Some of them became employers rather than exporters of slaves, and they used servile labour to harvest palm trees, to grow groundnuts and to transport produce to markets. The rise of legitimate commerce, far from bringing about the abolition of domestic slavery, increased the demand for cheap labour in Africa itself, and so perpetuated a service industry (the supply of slaves) which was detrimental to the long term development of the natural resources of the region. The result was the growth of a small group of large export producers in areas which were near enough to the coast for the transport of bulky goods to be a feasible proposition. In Dahomey and some of the Yoruba states, for example, the rulers and important chiefs established large palm oil estates worked by slave labour. However, these men now had to face competition at their palace gates from a multiplicity of small, efficient farmers who were only partly committed to the overseas market, but who supplied the greater part of the produce shipped to Europe in the second half of the nineteenth century. The large producers found that they were unable to influence local export prices simply by controlling production, as they had done previously, yet at the same time they themselves were highly vulnerable to changes in the prices paid for produce by European merchants on the coast, since a sizeable part of their total incomes was derived from export earnings.

States which were not situated close to the coast had great difficulty in making constructive adjustments to legitimate commerce. Ashanti, however, is an interesting example of a partially exceptional case.[41] Faced with a severe crisis early in the nineteenth century, the rulers of Ashanti responded by expanding their export trade to the north, selling kola nuts and buying cattle and slaves. Demand in the Hausa states had grown following the *jihads* of the early nineteenth century because kola was an approved stimulant in Muslim communities, which were denied alcohol. Supplies were increased partly by gathering kola nuts from wild trees, but mainly, it appears, through the establishment of plantations worked by slave labour.[42] Good fortune, commercial skill and a highly efficient system of government helped Ashanti to adjust to the central economic problem which it faced in the nineteenth century. Yet some important questions still have to be answered before the response of Ashanti can be counted as an unqualified success. In the first place, not enough is known about the total value and the rate of profit of the northern trade to say whether its expansion in the nineteenth century

fully compensated for the diminution of exports to the south. It has to be remembered that the size of the internal market was still severely limited by transport costs, and that the decline of trans-Saharan trade after 1875 might well have affected purchasing power in the north. Secondly, Ashanti still depended on the coast for supplies of munitions, salt and cotton goods, which came through satellites, such as the Fante states. These states now produced palm oil and kernels for export, and no longer relied on Ashanti for supplies of slaves for shipment overseas. Thus it is likely that there was, from the Ashanti point of view, an unfavourable shift in the balance of economic power. What is certain is that the attempt to reassert control over the Fante in the second half of the century brought Ashanti closer to conflict with the British. Finally, more research is needed into the potentially disintegrative elements within the Ashanti state: the implications for her long-term economic welfare and political stability of the existence of marked inequalities of wealth, the growth of the slave labour force, and the frustration of the merchant class, whose development was deliberately restrained, lest private enterprise should harm the national interest, as conceived by the king.[43]

The second positive mode of adaptation was for traditional rulers to recognise the small producers as a serious new force, and to give them an increased stake in a reformed political system. For example, Lat Dior, the ruler of Cayor in Senegal, tried to forge an alliance with the groundnut farmers of his state in the 1870s in an attempt to counter-balance the power of the traditional military estate. However, support could not always be relied on, and aspirations, once encouraged, tended to multiply. The small producers used their new wealth to purchase, among other items, guns, and with these they could threaten the rulers who sought their co-operation;[44] The new generation of export producers in West Africa had every reason to be wary of encouragement from their superiors, for rulers who allowed independent producers to develop did so in the hope of taxing their wealth. Not surprisingly, this aim became a cause of friction, particularly in the last quarter of the century, when profits from the export trade were reduced to a minimum. Furthermore, taxing small producers posed serious practical problems. Collecting tolls from a convoy of slaves travelling on an established route was easy enough, but, as the Aro of south-east Nigeria found, levying duties on palm oil was an entirely different matter, for oil was produced and traded in small quantities at many diverse points. Thus the attempt to accommodate the new capitalist class and secure the incomes of traditional rulers was a difficult operation.

The negative responses may have helped to prevent a sudden decline in incomes, but were ultimately self-defeating. The positive responses achieved better results, but were still not wholly successful. The difficulties of the progressive rulers arose first from an internal conflict of interest stemming from a basic change in the structure of export-producing firms, and second from the fact that they were unable or unwilling to make the necessary adjustments in the time allowed by impatient and often unsympathetic foreigners. For a while it seemed that there was a chance of stabilising the existing frontier between Europeans and Africans on the West Coast, but in the last quarter of the century the indigenous rulers were called on to make concessions over such matters as railways, internal tolls and slavery, which they judged, quite rightly, would undermine their political independence. At that point the dialogue over peaceful coexistence came to an end. Possessing fewer internal assets, and experiencing at the same time greater external pressures, the modernising aristocracies of West Africa were less able to control their future than were their revolutionary counter parts in Japan after 1868.[45]

As a general proposition, it can be said that the traditional unit of trade was less affected by the structural changes brought about by legitimate commerce than was the traditional unit of production. This was because large wholesalers were still necessary, whether the commodities to be handled were slaves or palm oil, whereas large producers were not. Many established entrepôts, such as Whydah, Lagos, Bonny and Old Calabar,

substituted palm oil for slaves and survived as major ports right down to partition, and in some cases beyond. Their rulers continued to levy traditional taxes on visiting ships, and their leading merchants received credit and goods on a larger scale than ever before. Even the old trading premises survived: after abolition, the barracoons (warehouses where slaves were kept pending shipment) were used to store the new, legitimate exports. Although the entrepôts were not affected in precisely the same way as producers in the hinterland, it does not follow that they were not affected at all by the development of legitimate commerce, or that they found it any easier to establish a lasting and satisfactory relationship with their European customers. On the contrary, African rulers had to struggle in the nineteenth century to control destabilising forces which threatened the cohesion of the entrepôts, and sometimes their very existence. Some indication of the nature of these forces is necessary for an understanding of the degrees of solidarity and disunity exhibited by the middlemen states when faced with increased European pressure towards the close of the century. The best illustration of their problems is provided by the history of the area centring on the Niger Delta, which has been the subject of some important research in recent years.[46]

Legitimate commerce presented opportunities to a new generation of traders, as well as producers, because it gave employment to a greater number of intermediaries, who were needed to collect export crops and to distribute manufactured goods. Entry into small scale trade was easy because there were few barriers of capital or skill. The result was that existing wholesalers faced more competition than they had in the past, though this is not to imply that such rivalry was unimportant during the time of the Atlantic slave trade. The new traders won their most striking success in the Niger Delta. Virtually all the 'city states', as Dike has called them, experienced serious political unrest between 1850 and 1875, as slaves and ex-slaves challenged the authority of the established wholesalers and rulers. This movement was personified by Ja Ja, the former slave who rose to a position of economic importance in Bonny in the 1860s, but whose social origins prevented him from attaining the highest political office. In 1869 Ja Ja founded his own state at nearby Opobo, thus conferring on himself the political power which he felt his commercial success deserved. The career of Nana Olomu, the leading figure in Itsekiri trade and politics in the 1880s, provides another striking example of how advancement was becoming based on commercial achievement rather than on inherited status, though Nana's social origins were less humble than Ja Ja's, and he was able to further his political ambitions in his home territory.[47] Ability put a man in a strong position; ability and acceptable family connections made him almost unassailable.

Indigenous commercial institutions in the Delta states were not entirely immune from change, and were affected by the alterations in personnel. At Bonny and Kalahari, for example, the rise of men whose success was a result of trading ability rather than of ascribed social position had repercussions on the traditional canoe 'house' (a compact and well organised trading and fighting corporation capable of maintaining a war canoe) because increased social mobility led to a greater turnover of commercial and political authority. Jones has analysed the history of these states in the nineteenth century in terms of a developmental cycle, which started with the expansion of a canoe house, moved on to a phase of political accretion, in which several houses coalesced, and culminated in varying degrees of disintegration, as unity broke down. For present purposes it might also be useful to think of the economic aspects of this cycle in terms of the theory of the firm, whereby a successful company expands, takes over its rivals, and achieves a local monopoly, only to find that its dominance is undermined from within, as managers leave to start their own businesses, and challenged from outside, as new competitors move in to try and secure a share of the monopoly profit.

Certain qualifications to the foregoing analysis have to be made, even at the risk of complicating the story. In the first place it should be noted that legitimate commerce speeded social change in the trading states, but did not initiate it, for social 'upstarts' had also found scope for their talents during the days of the Atlantic slave trade.[48] Secondly, some states escaped slave revolts, and in others slave risings were not always movements of the downtrodden against their masters. In Kalahari, for example, class conflict was minimised by integrating mechanisms which helped to assimilate slaves into society.[49] In Old Calabar slave risings were partly demonstrations in support of established, rival political factions, and so served a functional purpose in reinforcing the status quo. Finally, care must be taken not to romanticise the careers of the famous Delta traders. Some scholars, understandably anxious to write African rather than Imperial history, have seen in these men the forerunners of the nationalist movements which developed in the colonial period. This interpretation bestows on the actors a motive and sense of purpose which they themselves would have had difficulty in recognising. The leaders of the Delta states were great traders, and they certainly fought hard to maintain their independence, but their world view did not extend much beyond their local commercial interests, their vision of social justice did not include the emancipation of their own slaves, and they resisted African as well as European rivals with the true impartiality of *homoeconomicus*.

Besides the problem of internally-generated instability, the entrepôts faced an additional complication which did not affect the producers directly, namely the physical presence of commercial agents from the Western world. In the second half of the nineteenth century the growth of a bulk trade, combined with the advent of the steamship, led the European merchants to set up many more shore bases. With the merchants came missionaries and educated African ex-slaves. This development was a serious threat to the position of the ruling oligarchy in the entrepôts. In contrast to the era of the slave trade, when European visitors tended to be sailors first and traders second, the newcomers were permanent and competitive wholesalers. Furthermore, the presence of an expatriate community, however small, had important political consequences. It acted as a magnet for the disaffected, from slaves seeking freedom to disgruntled members of the local oligarchy looking for external support for battles which they could not win on their own. Since the European merchants were the main suppliers of credit, whatever action they took, whether Machiavellian or innocent in intent, was bound to have repercussions on the internal political situation, either confirming the power of the existing rulers or building up the claims of rivals.

Potentially the most serious destabilising influence was the possibility of a serious trade depression, an event which would have affected the large wholesalers in much the same way as the large producers because both depended on foreign trade for their livelihood. Indeed, it could be argued that the middlemen were even more vulnerable than the producers since some of the entrepôts relied on local imports for their basic supplies of food, and they nearly all lacked an alternative means of maintaining their incomes. A crisis in foreign trade would intensify internal rivalries by fostering disputes over the allocation of shares in the export trade, over the prices to be asked and given, and over the distribution of reduced profits. It would also increase external pressures. On the one hand, European traders would try to pay less for produce and charge more for manufactured goods; they would become more closely concerned as creditors of faltering and bankrupt African wholesalers; and they would be tempted to give support to families and houses which appeared more capable of safeguarding their interests than did the existing rulers. On the other hand, the wholesalers would run into difficulties with their hinterland customers, as they tried to pass on the price changes which they themselves had been forced to accept. While trade remained prosperous these tendencies, though present, were held in check. In the last quarter of the century, however, there was a radical change in the situation.

African producers and wholesalers were not alone in facing problems of adaptation in the nineteenth century. Commercial interests on the European side of the frontier were also profoundly affected by the expansion of overseas trade and by the change in its character following the rise of legitimate exports. Two developments in particular helped to bring about a fundamental reorganisation of West African trade after 1850, resulting in a greater degree of competition, the final liquidation of eighteenth-century commercial practices, and the beginnings of a recognisably modern organisational structure for the expatriate firms. The first development, in terms of chronology, concerned ocean transport, and the second involved alterations to the media of exchange used on the West Coast. Just as there were reactionary, as well as progressive, elements on the African side of the frontier, so, too, contrary to what might be supposed, there were those among the European community who did their best to convince themselves and their customers that the industrial revolution had never occurred.

In the first half of the nineteenth century, the products of legitimate commerce were carried to Europe by sailing ships, and the leading trading firms all possessed ocean-going vessels. The Bordeaux firm of Maurel et Prom kept a sizeable fleet of three-masted ships in service on the route to Senegal between the 1830s and the 1880s, and other large merchants, such as the London firm of F. & A. Swanzy, which traded to the Gold Coast, followed this practice. However, shortly after the middle of the century the technical development of the steamship reached a point where it could begin to compete successfully with sail.[50] The African Steam Ship Company was formed in England in 1851 and began a regular service to the West Coast in the following year. This firm was joined by another, the British & African Steam Navigation Company in 1868, first as a rival and then as an associate. The British Lines were the most important serving West Africa, but other European interests were also represented. In France a consortium of Bordeaux and Marseilles firms ran steamships to parts of West Africa in the 1870s before the formation of the Fabre-Fraissinet line in 1889, and in Germany the merchant house of Woermann began to run steamers to the West Coast in the 1870s, before the establishment of the

Woermann-Line in 1886. During the third quarter of the century the West African carrying trade was converted to steam, and by the 1870s the sailing ship was playing a secondary and diminishing role. In 1880 the number of sailing vessels entering Lagos harbour, for example, was about a third of the number of steamers and represented only one sixth of the tonnage of the latter.

The second change centred on the decline of the main transitional currencies, and on an increase in the circulation of modern money (especially British and French silver coins) in the key exporting areas.[51] In the present state of knowledge it is hard to make firm generalisations about this process, but three points can be established. First, the change was underway *before* the advent of colonial rule, though the timing varied at different points along the West Coast. In the second half of the nineteenth century Iron and copper currencies and cowries underwent a serious depreciation, and by the close of the century had ceased to play an important part in external trade. Francs were used extensively in the groundnut trade as early as the 1850s, and florins and shillings became the main media of exchange for palm produce during the last quarter of the century. Second, it seems clear that the decline of these currencies was closely associated with a fall in the cost of supplying them to West Africa. In Europe technical advances made it possible to manufacture manillas and iron currencies more cheaply, and in Africa new resources of cowrie shells were discovered on the East Coast around the middle of the century. Improvements in ocean transport made it possible to deliver all these currencies at reduced cost. European merchants, competing with each other for the purchase of produce, began to flood the West African export market with transitional monies. Over-issue undermined confidence and led to a fall in exchange rates with other currencies. By the 1880s traders in some centres needed porters to headload their small change, in much the same way as workers in Germany needed suitcases to carry home their weekly earnings following the depreciation of the mark in the 1920s. Third, the collapse of transitional currencies undermined the

barter system, which was closely associated with it, and the mythical ounce and bar trade too, though again little is known at the moment about this aspect of African monetary history.[52]

In the long run the advent of the steamship and the introduction of modern money brought advantages to those engaged in overseas trade, principally because they assisted the expansion of the market. Without these innovations West Africa would certainly have become uncompetitive in International trade. The steamship was cheaper per ton/mile than sail, and this was a vital consideration at a time when the West African export trade had become centred on bulky vegetable products, which, as noted earlier, were of low value per unit of weight compared with slaves. The steamer was also faster than sail; in the middle of the century sailing ships took about thirty-five days to reach West Africa, but by 1900 the steamer had reduced this time by half. The speed of the steamship made it possible to transport a wider range of perishable goods, and it enabled traders to complete their transactions more quickly, thus helping them to economise on capital. Finally, the steamship, being less dependent on natural conditions than was sail, could guarantee regularity of service. Fore-knowledge of the steamer's arrival enabled traders to purchase and prepare goods for shipment. Greater readiness reduced the time spent in port, and so lowered running costs.

Modern money helped to increase the number and variety of possible transactions. British and French silver coins were almost perfect substitutes, that is to say they were acceptable for virtually all goods and services. Africans who were paid in silver coin for their produce received units of general purchasing power instead of a packet of goods and transitional currencies. Export earnings could be diverted more easily to domestic uses, or could be spent on imported goods supplied by a variety of firms. African producers and traders had more freedom of choice: they were no longer tied to the firm which bought their produce, and they enjoyed greater Independence from rulers who previously had exercised a degree of central control over export sales and over the distribution of foreign trade earnings. It was no coincidence that francs and shillings spread in areas where legitimate exports were developing most quickly, and it was no coincidence either that low denomination coins were in great demand, for they were an indication of the growing importance of small producers and traders in the new export economy. These men were not innocents who had a modern money economy thrust upon them by rapacious expatriate firms; they embraced the new system willingly because it gave them the means of striking a better bargain.

In the short run, however, the steamship and modern money had a profoundly unsettling effect on West African trade. Essentially, they can be regarded as external economies which made it easier for newcomers to enter West Coast commerce. The result was a marked increase in competition in the second half of the nineteenth century. With the arrival of the steamship, the trader whose resources were very limited could hire a small amount of cargo space for a short period of time. Merchants trading to West Africa did not need to buy a ship of their own, nor did they have to join a consortium to charter one. Few of the established firms, apart from Woermann, were able to convert to steam, partly because the initial capital investment needed to build an ocean-going steamer was much greater than that required for a sailing vessel, and partly because more working capital was needed to finance the expansion of legitimate commerce.[53] The result was that trading and carrying became separate activities, and the established firms were less able to keep control of new entrants than in the days when they also monopolised shipping space. Moreover, and this is a feature which is often overlooked, the steamer also concentrated competition at the ports of call, in contrast to the days of sail, when ships could adapt their schedules to meet varying market conditions. Evidence of increasing concentration was to be seen in the expansion of a few favoured centres, such as Dakar, Freetown and Lagos, and, ultimately, in the decline of well-known trading stations, such as St Louis, Cape Coast, and Opobo.

The commercial effect of the steamship has been commented on by McPhee and subsequent writers, but the consequences of monetary change have not been fully appreciated. The steamer brought new traders to the coast, but it could not help them to trade once they had arrived. As long as barter and transitional currencies remained firmly entrenched, newcomers were at a severe disadvantage, for they had to master the complexities of a pre-industrial monetary system, itself a serious barrier to entry; they had to acquire these strange currencies, in some cases from the established firms; and they had to be prepared to engage both in importing and in exporting. For example, a new trader hoping to sell cotton goods would have to take produce in exchange, since transitional currencies were not an acceptable means of payment in Europe. Cash payments made it possible to separate the two trades, and enabled firms to specialise in one or other if they wished. This specialisation reduced the capital required for entering West African trade and encouraged competition. No wonder the old-established European firms, far from trying to 'entangle Africans in the web of a money economy' strove to maintain the barter system for as long as possible. In this respect some of the 'natives' of Liverpool and Marseilles were far more conservative than those in the hinterlands of Dakar and Lagos!

Evidence of increasing competition can be seen in the appearance of two new groups of traders in the second half of the century. First, there were progressive European merchants who had little or no previous connection with West Africa, but who established themselves by taking advantage of the steamer and of cash transactions. For example, Cheri Peyrissac began as a clerk at St Louis (Senegal) in 1862, and later built up a large independent import and export business based on manufactured goods and groundnuts; the Hamburg industrial concern of G. L. Gaiser expanded into West African trade in 1869 in order to secure supplies of palm produce for its oil mills, and was one of the first firms to develop a cash trade; the Manchester firm of John Walkden & Company started to trade with West Africa in 1868 as a mail order business, supplying manufactured goods on commission; and John Holt, a Liverpool merchant, broke into the Niger Delta trade in the 1870s, and later established branches in other parts of what was to become Nigeria.[54] Many of the older firms tried to adapt to legitimate commerce, but very few lasted until the end of the century. They had every incentive to adjust to the new conditions because they had sunk capital into African trade, they had spent years building up connections, and many of them were creditors of African suppliers. Thus John Tobin, a Liverpool slave trader, pioneered the palm oil trade in the Niger Delta early in the century. However, firms of this type were nearly all eliminated by the steamship and by the collapse of barter. Perhaps the most spectacular rearguard action was that fought by F. & A. Swanzy, which, with Forster & Smith, dominated the overseas trade of the Gold Coast in the early 1850s. Swanzy's reaction to the advent of the steamer was not to modernise their business, but to try to establish a local monopoly of palm oil supplies. Unfortunately for them, the producers retaliated by successfully boycotting the firm between 1858 and 1866.[55] Swanzy's managed to survive, but the firm declined in importance. The steamer, it could be said, had taken all the wind out of their sails.

The second new group of merchants were Africans, consisting mainly of liberated slaves and their descendants, men who grew up in settlements such as Freetown and Libreville, where they were converted to Christianity, took European names, and received some education from expatriate missionaries. These merchants, in sharp contrast to their slave-trading predecessors, were noted for their Victorian dress, bourgeois values and commitment to legitimate commerce. It was intended that they should form the nucleus of an African middle class, which would develop the continent's economy and uplift its spiritual life. Although numerically a small group, these liberated Africans had considerable importance in the second half of the nineteenth century. Many of them returned to their homelands, and so made their presence felt in most of the main urban centres on the West Coast. Furthermore, since they became lawyers, civil servants and missionaries,

as well as merchants, their influence spread over a wide occupational front. Essentially, their role was that of cultural intermediaries, men who straddled the frontier between Europe and Africa, interpreting, in the broadest sense of the word, one to the other. Europeans often referred to them, contemptuously, as 'trousered Africans', and Africans have criticised them for behaving as Uncle Toms. However, thanks to the painstaking work of Christopher Fyfe and others, it is now appreciated (or at least it should now be appreciated) that these were men of genuine dignity and considerable historical significance.[56] They performed an important function in introducing the Western world to Africa, yet they were by no means as alienated from their indigenous culture as has been alleged. They demonstrated to sceptical Europeans that Africans were not barbarians, and they were among the first to proclaim that Africa had a history of its own.

Helped by the steamer and by the transition to cash payments, these merchants mostly became low-cost, import specialists, acting either as independent wholesalers and retailers, or as agents selling goods on commission for manufacturing firms in Europe. Some were involved in the export trade, but the import business was preferred because it required less capital and also spread investments over a wider range of goods than the produce trade, which in addition experienced considerable short-run price fluctuations. Before 1900, when trading conditions once again began to favour large firms, a number of African merchants owned businesses which were as large as some of the European firms, though of course the latter were much smaller than they were to become in the twentieth century. Business profits tended to be attracted into property and education, two assets which continued to appreciate during the nineteenth and twentieth centuries irrespective of political changes.

One of the most outstanding of this new generation of Africans was Richard Blaize (1845–1904), who left Freetown in 1862 and made his business career in Lagos.[57] Blaize reckoned that he had earned the greater part of his fortune during the 1860s and 1870s, and was appalled by the narrow profit margins which ruled towards the end of the century. In the 1880s he built a new house and shop, which still stand on the Marina, and he also acquired 'a landau and pair of greys with which he drives out occasionally—footman and coachman on the box'. In 1896 a European official estimated that Blaize was worth about £150,000, which is a large sum even today, when the value of the pound sterling is far less than it was in the nineteenth century. Blaize's business, like that of most of his African contemporaries, died with him. However, the Blaize Memorial Institute, which was founded soon after his death with money left by him for that purpose, still flourishes, and contributes to what are now regarded as important functions, namely encouraging local manufacturing activities and providing Africans with technical training.

These two groups of merchants will be considered in more detail in Chapter 6. The main point to record in the present context is that there, were pronounced economic rivalries among firms on the European side of the frontier, just as there were among African suppliers. Competition between European firms was characterised by bouts of co-operation and conflict which bore some resemblance to the accretion-fission cycle experienced by the canoe houses of the Niger Delta. Typically, a newcomer trying to become established in one of the West African markets would begin by fixing his prices at levels which were more attractive than those of the established firms. These firms retaliated, and a price war followed. If this failed to drive out the new entrant, a compromise was eventually reached which allowed him to trade in the area on the understanding that competition was kept within 'reasonable' bounds. However, usually it was not long before the equilibrium was upset once again, either by the defection of an existing firm, or by the arrival of another outsider.

The trend was undoubtedly towards greater efficiency. In order to survive, firms had to adjust to the advent of the steamship, and to the development of cash transactions, and they also had to make internal improvements, as did John Holt, by employing better staff and by buying manufactures

in bulk where possible. By the last quarter of the century evidence from the Gold Coast, Dahomey, Lagos, the Niger Delta and Old Calabar indicates that profit margins had been greatly reduced. The commercial practices of the eighteenth century had finally disappeared, and the merchants, though not all of them realised it, were, in terms of business history, on the brink of the twentieth century, when wholesalers became accustomed to relying on narrower margins and on a much larger turnover. In 1875, however, the import and export market was still confined to a few coastal enclaves, and no additional cost-reducing innovations were possible within the existing political framework.

The adverse movement in the terms of trade in the last quarter of the nineteenth century had a serious effect on those engaged in the difficult process of adapting to legitimate commerce. Normal, non-violent commercial relationships started to break down, and the 'moral community' of traders, already under some strain, began to dissolve. The trade depression intensified rivalries within the various interest groups and between African producers on the one hand, and European firms on the other. Essentially, the dispute was over the distribution of reduced profits. The decline in the barter terms of trade affected the European firms in West Africa as well as primary producers. Initially, it was these firms which received lower prices for produce in Europe, and it was up to them to try and pass on reductions to their African suppliers. The extent to which they were successful depended on the balance of commercial power in individual West African markets. Not surprisingly, there was a fierce struggle in the late nineteenth century as each party sought to control the local market and to dictate terms to the other.

Evidence from various parts of the West Coast suggests that there were five main aspects of this struggle. None was entirely new, but each became more pronounced during the last quarter of the century. First, there were malpractices, such as diluting palm oil and misrepresenting the quality and length of cloth, which both sides adopted in an attempt to secure a better bargain than could be contrived by legitimate means. Second, there were demarcation disputes over functions and areas of influence. For example, some European firms, such as the Royal Niger Company, tried to move inland in the hope of buying export crops more cheaply from the producers than from the coastal wholesalers.[58] These moves often provoked retaliation, as when traders from Brass destroyed the Niger Company's base at Akassa in 1894. Similarly, some Africans tried to sell their oil direct to Europe. It was Ja Ja's threat to bypass the European middlemen in this way that was largely responsible for his expulsion from Opobo in 1887. Third, there were serious disputes, common everywhere at times of depression, and aggravated in the African case by the depreciation in the value of transitional currencies, about the repayment of the advances which European firms had made to African suppliers. Fourth, there were deliberate interruptions to the supply of produce. The Moors withheld supplies of gum in 1885–1886, the Yoruba closed their export markets at one time or another during the 1880s, and the Itsekiri held up palm oil exports in 1886–1887. The aim in all cases was to force European merchants to accept the suppliers' terms of sale, a policy which was to be repeated in the 1930s, when West Africa's foreign trade underwent its next great crisis. Finally, there were arguments about escaped slaves, many of whom sought refuge in the European colonies on the coast. Large scale African producers and traders resented the loss of their human capital, especially at a time when trade conditions dictated that slave labour should be fully exploited.

The outcome was a compromise which affected both parties adversely, and so satisfied neither. Africans were hit at a time when they were unable to achieve economies in production and transportation, and Europeans were hit at a time when their profit margins had already been reduced by increased competition. In these unprecedented circumstances the merchants, though traditionally suspicious of moves to expand the role of government, which they associated with increased regulations and additional taxes, began to press for a more active policy.[59] What is more,

they also displayed an unaccustomed willingness to accept higher taxation to pay for action taken on their behalf. In making this decision, the merchants were undoubtedly influenced by the fact that the cost of coercion had been greatly reduced in the late nineteenth century by the invention of two daunting pieces of military equipment, the Gatling gun and the Maxim gun.

The merchants' call for action was backed, and Indeed, often led, by colonial administrators.[60] Ambitious officials were well aware that posts in West Africa were rarely springboards to fame even at the best of times, and that a trade depression was scarcely the ideal setting for a distinguished career. They were charged with the task of protecting trade, yet when diplomacy failed, as it frequently did, they were unable to influence the policies of the African states which were the main trading partners of the European colonies. The administration's difficulties were increased at a time of depression because the colonies had overheads (in the shape of public debts and staff) which were fixed, and incomes which, because they were dependent on customs revenues, were either static or declining. In their own career interests and in the cause of duty, local officials decided that a radical change of policy was required. The missionaries, too, acting on their traditional postulate about the relationship between commercial prosperity and the progress of Christianity in Africa, urged the metropolitan governments to adopt more positive policies. Their views were of some significance in the nineteenth century, though ironically the missions were to be overtaken by the rush of events which they had helped to encourage. In the colonial period the missionaries found themselves pushed to one side, and they became, in political terms, mere clerical notes in the margins of empire.

There was some confusion about what was meant by an active policy, and there was a certain lack of realism about what it was expected to achieve. In broad terms, however, the merchants and officials made five main demands, though the stress laid on each varied at different parts of the West Coast. First, there was a call for the imposition of law and order in places such as Senegal, the Gold Coast, Yorubaland and the Niger Delta, where interstate conflict was thought to be interrupting the supply of produce and the distribution of manufactured goods. Second, there were widespread complaints against the coastal middlemen, who were blamed (in much the same way as Africans were later to blame the expatriate firms) for using their monopolistic powers to impose one-sided trading contracts. Some European firms wanted to end the 'unproductive middleman system'; others were prepared to make use of a reformed trading organisation providing internal free trade was established. Third, there was pressure for the abolition of the tolls levied by African states. This issue was important because the European merchants were concerned not simply to increase the volume of produce on offer, but to see that export crops were delivered to the coast as cheaply as possible.

The last two demands were more positive. The fourth request, for example, was for the construction of railways. The railway, the White Hope of the nineteenth century, was thought to be capable of transforming the economies of West Africa, just as it had those of Europe. In 1879 the French adopted an ambitious scheme for building a railway line from Senegal into the interior, and in the 1890s the British made similar plans for their colonies. Finally, there was a realisation that the time had come to advance the frontier of expatriate trading influence by creating a much larger market for European goods than had ever existed before. Some expatriate firms, as Gertzel has pointed out, were still content to remain on the coast, either because they were willing to work through a reformed middleman system, or because they lacked the capital to set up branches inland.[61] Others, however, and especially the large firms, were now prepared to move inland once the government had cleared the way. A bigger turnover was needed if profits were to grow; firm political boundaries were required to prevent trade from falling into the hands of other European rivals; and new products had to be found to re-establish the prosperity of the export trade. France and Britain hoped that there was more than fool's gold

in the interior, and that some of the fabled wealth of the Western Sudan would rub off on them.

It is now necessary to take a closer look at the policies of the three main European nations with interests in West Africa, because ultimately it was decisions made by them which led to the partition of the continent. As far as Great Britain was concerned, her trading success appeared to support the anti-colonial arguments of Adam Smith and his followers, and it was certainly hard to see what Britain could gain by creating colonies in West Africa when she already dominated trade without them. In contrast to a once popular view, Britain's policy makers were not itching to establish colonies throughout the world.[62] Britain's chief aim in West Africa was to maintain free trade without political involvement, and to persuade France and Germany to do the same. Free trade, though sometimes presented as a high-minded principle capable of bringing prosperity with honour to the comity of nations, was in reality a passport to British supremacy. In conditions of 'equal' competition Britain was likely to dominate most world markets because she could produce and transport manufactured goods more cheaply than could any of her rivals. Given this advantage, it is understandable that Britain was unlikely to initiate a forward policy.

At the same time, it is important to remember that the maintenance of the status quo in West Africa depended on factors which were largely beyond Britain's control. If Britain's European rivals decided not to co-operate in upholding her supremacy, or if there was a serious threat to trade as a result of developments on the African side of the frontier, then Britain might be forced to change her traditional policy, for she had a moral obligation to support her traders in international markets. The obligation was not binding in all cases, and it had to be judged in relation to the wider, national interest, but it was a factor to be considered in the formulation of policy. In 1865 a Parliamentary Committee had recommended withdrawing from several parts of the West Coast, but by the 1880s it was realised in the metropolis that Britain's commitments were too large for disengagement to be possible.

Superficially, French policy appeared to have much in common with that of Great Britain. France, like Britain, wanted to develop a flourishing and peaceful trade with West Africa, and she was willing to work through indigenous authorities where possible.[63] From the 1830s she began to move towards a liberal tariff regime on the West Coast, and she also exercised a degree of political restraint which, broadly speaking, kept her in step with Britain. Yet it is now recognised that France took the initiative in the 'scramble'[5] for West Africa. Gallagher and Robinson have argued that it was a political crisis in Egypt in 1882, a rebuff for France, which caused her to adopt a more aggressive policy in West Africa, but so far this view, stimulating though it is, has not been confirmed by the research it has helped to inspire. Brunschwig has explained French expansion in terms of a search for national prestige, but this interpretation is not quite as helpful as it seems at first sight, since without close definition the phrase 'national prestige' becomes a vague and all-embracing concept. It will be suggested here that there was an important economic motive in French imperialism, and that France altered her policy not because her basic aims had changed, but because she came to realise that different means were required if they were ever going to be achieved. This conclusion did not come as a sudden flash of insight. It was a gradual acknowledgement of long-standing facts, namely that with the passage of time the disparity between French and British economic progress and global influence had increased rather than diminished, and that France was also being overtaken in Europe by German industrial and military power.

France had long-standing, global commercial ambitions, but few of these had been realised. Where she laboured, it seemed, Great Britain collected the rewards. India and Canada were lost to Britain in the eighteenth century, and France herself was defeated in Europe in 1815 after a series of wars which played a large part in retarding her economic development in the nineteenth century.[64] Britain, by contrast, emerged from the Napoleonic Wars with her industrial revolution already underway. Since the victors of Waterloo then pressed the French into declaring the slave trade illegal, it is not surprising that France viewed abolition as the final move in a British plot to destroy what was left of her Atlantic commerce. Any illusions that France had recovered her former power by the middle of the nineteenth century, at least in Europe, were shattered by the defeat which she suffered at the hands of Germany in 1870.

France was anxious to emulate Britain's industrial progress, which, according to some observers, was closely related to the growth of her trading and political influence overseas. Africa was regarded as a hopeful starting point for a French recovery because it was reasonably close to Europe, it had long-standing connections with France, and, above all, it was still largely unclaimed—except, of course, by Africans. Senegal was re-occupied in 1817, and some fortified posts were established at Assinie, Grand Bassam and Gabon in the 1840s. These moves, together with the conquest of Algeria in the 1830s, gave some momentum to the notion that France had an Imperial destiny in Africa: the idea of linking West and North Africa was current in Paris long before the British began talking of joining the Cape to Cairo. Yet France gained no spectacular successes. The fortified posts, as Schnapper has shown, achieved very little, and the expansion of legitimate commerce benefited Britain more than any other European power. Only in Senegal was there some basis for optimism. French commercial interests there had been saved by the fortuitous development of the groundnut trade, and also by the adoption of measures which limited the entry of foreign traders. Even in the mid-nineteenth century France had not allowed herself to be mesmerised completely by Britain's advocacy of the free trade cause. During the last quarter of the nineteenth century she was to move even closer to protectionist policies, and in doing so was to undermine the basis of Britain's position in West Africa.

France, unlike Britain, had an incentive to upset the status quo in West Africa. She did not want to provoke Britain by a direct challenge, but she still had plenty of room for manoeuvre, for it was the weakness as well as the strength of the British position that her commercial supremacy had not been accompanied by the large scale annexation of territory. French imperial policy in the late nineteenth century was driven by a potent combination of forces: on the one hand by a fear that British economic expansion, spearheaded by Manchester textiles and backed by the world's strongest navy, would frustrate her ambitions once again; and on the other by an optimism about the wealth of Africa which had not been equalled since the Moroccans trekked hopefully across the desert in 1591.

German interests in West Africa will be noted briefly in order to explain their influence on the policies of the two major powers.[85] The German presence became a factor of some weight in the deliberations of London and Paris during the last quarter of the century, when, as has been pointed out, Hamburg merchants were rapidly expanding their share of West African trade. German firms were concentrated at some sensitive points: in Liberia, which was flanked by British interests in Sierra Leone and French interests in the Ivory Coast; in what was to become Togoland, a thin wedge of territory between the Gold Coast and Dahomey, centres of British and French activity respectively; in Dahomey itself, where they had succeeded in capturing the greater part of the region's overseas trade by the 1880s; and in what were to become Southern Nigeria and the Cameroons, which coincided with; Britain's major trading interests in Lagos, the Niger Delta, and Old Calabar. In the 1880s the German government made an increasing show of protecting its traders on the West Coast, partly as a result of direct mercantile pressures, and partly as an offshoot of a campaign for tariff protection started by industrialists in response to the onset of the Great Depression.[66] Britain and France regarded the German presence as a serious threat to their own West African interests, and feared that a forward move by her might result in the exclusion of their trading firms from the unclaimed markets of Africa. For France, already worried about British commercial dominance, this new danger appeared to justify a more decisive, forward policy; for Britain, slowly waking up to the fact that the era of *laissez-faire* might not last indefinitely, it meant that she had to consider defensive action against two ambitious rivals, not just one.

The demands made by British and French merchants were very similar, but rivalry between the European powers meant that they did not co-ordinate their policies to produce a joint invasion of Africa, though gentlemen's agreements were occasionally made with regard to specific areas. On the contrary, the economic crisis between 1875 and 1900 intensified the antagonism between Britain and France, and led to competition for African territory. There were two main features of this rivalry. The first was characterised by a more aggressive element in the relationship between British and French firms. The foundation of the Compagnie Française de l'Afrique Équatoriale in 1880 and the Compagnie du Sénégal in the following year marked a new phase in French efforts to break into richer and predominantly British markets in West Africa.[67] These firms started trading in the Niger Delta, quickly established branches as far as the River Benue, and threatened to expand further still into what is now northern Nigeria. This enterprising exercise of the rights of free trade caused Britain some initial embarrassment. However, the French could not compete for long against the might of the National African Company, which bought out the French firms in 1884.[68] This episode demonstrated that British supremacy could not be challenged successfully by purely commercial means, at least by France. The French did not give up their hopes of penetrating the interior from the Guinea coast, but future efforts were to be launched from bases in their own colonies of Dahomey and the Ivory Coast, and were to be directed by soldiers rather than by traders.

The second feature of Anglo–French commercial rivalry was growing friction over areas of customs jurisdiction and levels of tariffs. The economic crisis of the late nineteenth century intensified the search for revenue, and led officials to extend the boundaries of their colonies, sometimes with, but usually without, instructions from the metropolis. These moves caused serious disputes, as rival administrations, expanding laterally along the coast, met each other, as they did for example in the area of Sierra Leone, on the Gold Coast, and at the frontier between Dahomey and Lagos. At the Same time France began to adopt differential tariffs in West Africa as a means of increasing revenue and assisting her trade. The shift to a more protectionist policy was mainly a result of pressure from French metallurgical, textile and chemical industries, which had difficulty in competing with British products in world markets.[69] Many of the traders in centres such as Nantes, Bordeaux and Marseilles were opposed to protection to begin with, but were won over in the 1880s. Differential tariffs were imposed in Senegal in 1877 and in the Ivory Coast in 1889. Britain, of course, protested that these actions were contrary to the principles of free trade. The French replied that tariffs in British colonies already had a differential effect because they were high on certain goods, such as brandy and wine, which were mainly French, and low on textiles, which were mainly British. By the 1880 the concept of free trade in West Africa was coming under attack, and the weak spots in Britain's empire of informal rule were being revealed.

In Britain, France and Germany West African affairs were taken up by specialised organisations, such as chambers of commerce, and by an assortment of more broadly-based imperial movements which were developing rapidly in the last quarter of the nineteenth century.[70] The chambers of commerce in Liverpool, Manchester, Bordeaux, Marseilles and Hamburg publicised African problems in the press, lobbied local members of parliament, and made direct contact with leading figures in the government. Outside the chambers of commerce African questions were drawn into a variety of campaigns: some dominated by economic interest groups which, without necessarily having any specific involvement in Africa, were agitating in France for protectionist measures, and in Britain for what, more circumspectly, was called 'fair' trade;[71] others led by politicians who saw Imperialism as a means of saving Europe from socialism; and others still, headed by geographers, journalists, intellectuals and sundry eccentrics, who were beginning to talk in somewhat mystical terms about the relationship between empire and national greatness. Of course, the imperial movement was by no means united. Some industrialists wanted colonies in order to create guaranteed markets for their exports, but others were indifferent to colonial expansion because in the late nineteenth century, with the terms of trade moving against primary producers, they were able to buy raw materials cheaply.

It is clear that further research is needed to identify all the channels of communication which existed between the men on the spot in Africa and those who formally announced decisions in London and Paris, and to evaluate the extent to which politicians were susceptible to pressures from pro-imperial interest groups representing what might be called the 'unofficial mind' of imperialism.[72] At present it can be said that governments were subjected to considerable and increasing pressures in the later nineteenth century, and that these pressures were more effective in France than in Britain because French businessmen were less divided by entrenched commitments to free trade, and were more inclined to put their faith, if not always their investments, in Imperial expansion.

What seems beyond dispute is that those in power in France were more inclined to take notice of imperial pressure groups than were those in Britain. Under the Third Republic the political influence of provincial businessmen increased, and a group of leaders emerged, such as Freycinet, Jauréguiberry and Rouvier, who were prepared not merely to be influenced by others, but actually to direct the movement for colonial expansion.[73] In Britain, by contrast, policy-makers in both parties were reluctant to admit that circumstances had altered, and that attitudes would have to change too. In the 1880s British policy was still based on two established notions: first, an unrealistic optimism about the possibility of equalising tariffs and preserving free trade, an optimism which France was happy to encourage while her troops advanced inland; and second, a belief in the value of appeasement, that is the distribution of other peoples' territories in the hope of stabilising an inherently unstable situation. Since the facts refused to change, no matter how long British politicians kept their eyes closed, it was the politicians themselves who eventually had to modify their traditional attitudes towards empire. By the 1890s both Liberals and Conservatives were beginning to recognise that a more active policy was required if any of Britain's traditional spheres of influence in West Africa were to be preserved. It would be a mistake to think that Joseph Chamberlain came, like a bolt from the blue, and created, single-handed, a new attitude towards imperial affairs. Nevertheless, it was not until he became Colonial Secretary in 1895 that Britain had a Rouvier of her own.

By the time Britain had decided that a more positive policy was needed, the partition of West Africa was well underway. In 1879 the French began to advance across the Western Sudan from Senegal, reaching Bamako (six hundred miles inland) in 1883, Timbuctu in 1893, and Lake Chad (two thousand miles from Dakar) in 1900. At the same time, the invasion forces branched south, striking deep into the Fouta Djallon (later part of French Guinea), the Ivory Coast and Dahomey, and meeting the northwards advance of French troops from the Guinea coast. As a result of this strategy, tight boundaries were drawn around the coastal settlements of Gambia, Sierra Leone and Liberia. In the mid-1880s Germany made two relatively unambitious forward moves, one into Togo (between the Gold Coast and Dahomey), and one into the Cameroons (on the eastern flank of the Niger Delta). By the mid—1890s France had successfully claimed the greater part of West Africa, and Britain was left with the task of defending her two most important interests; the Gold Coast and what was to become Nigeria. The former, as Dumett has shown, was saved for Britain mainly as a result of mercantile pressure.[74] Kumasi, the Ashanti capital, was captured in 1896, and expansion further north gave Britain a sizeable colony. In the case of Nigeria, it was again successful mercantile agitation

in the 1890s that kept the French out of Yorubaland and the Lower Niger.[75] Conspicuous in the latter area was the Royal Niger Company, which, in the classical manner of chartered companies, used administrative as well as commercial weapons to drive out its competitors, English as well as French. By 1900 the partition of West Africa was over.

AN EXPLANATION OF IMPERIALISM IN WEST AFRICA

The invasion of West Africa occurred in such a short space of time, and marked such a radical break with past policy, that historians have been tempted to fasten on specific military or diplomatic events as causes. Some writers have emphasised the importance of the Egyptian crisis of 1882, or of the Berlin Conference of 1884–1885. Others have drawn attention to the rise of particular military and political figures, men who were keen to do more than merely chalk hopeful arrows on departmental maps. A number of names come to mind: the French Prime Minister, Freycinet; his Minister of Marine, Admiral Jauréguiberry; the British Secretary of State for the Colonies, Joseph Chamberlain; and men on the spot, such as Archinard, Gallieni, Goldie and Lugard. These events and these men undoubtedly played a part, and in some cases a very important part, in determining the timing and the nature of the partition of West Africa, but their responsibility for causing it was of much the same order as that of the unfortunate Archduke Franz Ferdinand, whose assassination sparked off the First World War. The central problem is to clarify the circumstances which enabled these prominent politicians and soldiers to make a mark on history where others before them, men of similar ambitions, such as Faidherbe and Glover, had been frustrated.

This chapter has tried to show that the solution to this problem lies in the economic history of the nineteenth century. Economic motives do not constitute a complete analysis of imperialism, but there is considerable justification for concentrating on them here because on the whole they have been neglected in the past. This neglect is understandable in view of the current dominance of political and diplomatic interpretations of imperialism, but it has the fundamental disadvantage of abstracting from West African realities. Trade first brought the Europeans to Africa in the fifteenth century, and trade remained the basis of their relations with the continent from then onwards. It is the economic historian's task to see whether, and, if so, in what ways, commercial ties were related to the scramble for Africa.

What happened to Africa was part of a global confrontation between the developing and the underdeveloped countries in the nineteenth century, though the nature of the interaction between them, and its outcome, varied in different parts of the world. The economic expansion of Europe in the nineteenth century had a profound and destabilising effect on West Africa because it changed the structure of export production and involved the region in the trade cycle of the new, industrial economy. The Afro-European alliance which had made the external slave trade possible and profitable started to dissolve early in the nineteenth century. A new generation of African producers and traders began to develop outside the limits of the old, foreign trade enclaves, but was unable to establish a completely satisfactory partnership with merchants on the European side of the frontier. In some cases difficulties arose because of obstruction from traditional rulers, but even where the indigenous authorities were willing to co-operate, and achieved a measure of success in doing so, there were limits to the concessions which they were prepared to make. In the event, time was also against them. During the early, prosperous phase of 'legitimate' commerce, each side could afford to tolerate the economic imperfections (real and alleged) of the other, and it seemed possible that economic integration could be achieved by informal means. But the serious decline in the terms of trade in the last quarter of the nineteenth century upset the precarious balance which maintained the frontier between Europe and West Africa. Those on the European side of the frontier had no further scope for improving their efficiency, and they now feared that West Africa, with its pre-industrial

transport system and its numerous tolls, was in danger of becoming, by international standards, a high-cost producer. Those on the African side of the frontier decided that if modernisation meant railways, the end of internal customs duties and the abolition, for whatever reasons, of slavery, then it also meant the end of their political independence. At that point they decided to resist and to defend their sovereignty, though there were some who, for reasons which have been indicated, were less than wholehearted in their opposition to European demands.

The economic depression transmitted by the industrial nations caused England, France and Germany to come into conflict with each other, as well as with African states. Their rivalry was partly a reflection of shifts in the balance of economic and political power in Europe following industrialisation, and partly the outcome of particular problems which arose during the Great Depression. These problems affected interest groups in the leading industrial states, as well as merchants trading to the West Coast. The extent to which interest groups succeeded in generating a forward policy depended on the strength of the pressure they exerted and on the responsiveness of those in power at the time. Reasons have been advanced under both headings to explain why, in the case of West Africa, it was France rather than Britain which took the initiative. The resolution of the problems which led to partition, can be seen in the creation of colonial economies in the first half of the twentieth century.

It is for future research to elaborate and improve the analysis advanced here, and also to modify it, where necessary. The aim of this chapter has been to establish a framework of analysis which contains the main variables, but not, it must be stressed, to rank them in a fixed order of importance applicable to every point on the West Coast. At one extreme it is possible to conceive of areas where the transition from the slave trade was made successfully, where incomes were maintained, and where internal tensions were controlled. In these cases an explanation of partition will need to emphasise external pressures, such as mercantile demands and Anglo–French rivalries. At the other extreme it is possible to envisage cases where the indigenous rulers adopted reactionary attitudes, where attempts were made to maintain incomes by predatory means, and where internal conflicts were pronounced. In these cases an explanation of imperialism will need to place more weight on disintegrative forces on the African side of the frontier, though without neglecting external factors. Current contributions to the study of nineteenth-century imperialism frequently fail either to take adequate account of interests and attitudes on the indigenous side of the frontier with the Western world, or to organise local case studies in such a way as to permit systematic comparisons with other parts of other continents. The typology established here, based on the identification and interaction of interest groups, may prove useful in understanding the decisions which regulated the frontier between the industrial powers and the Third World in the nineteenth century.

NOTES

1. A good introduction to staple theory can be found in Melville H. Watkins, 'A Staple Theory of Economic Growth', *Canadian Journal of Economics and Political Science*, 29, 1963, pp. 141–58.
2. It should be added that staple theory is generally thought to be inapplicable in cases where export growth occurs in indigenous, subsistence economies. However, the reasons given in support of this view rest on assumptions about 'traditional' societies which have been criticised earlier in this study (Chapter 2).
3. The discussion which follows should be compared with the conclusions reached in the previous chapter, pp. 119–23.
4. *Kew Bulletin*, 1892, p. 208.
5. Female labour appears to have been particularly important in preparing groundnuts and palm produce for export. The division of labour between the sexes is a subject which merits further research.
6. R. E. Baldwin, 'Patterns of Development in Newly Settled Regions', *Manchester School of Economic and Social Studies*, 24, 1956, pp. 161–79.
7. This change is analogous to the distinction between the cotton economy of the American south, where plantations were dominant in the nineteenth century, and the wheat belt of the west, where the typical unit was the small, family farm. See Douglass C. North, 'Agriculture and Regional Economic Growth', *Journal of Farm Economics*, 41, 1959, pp. 943—51.
8. C. W. Newbury, 'Trade and Authority in West Africa from 1850 to 1880', in *Colonialism in Africa, 1870-1960*, ed. L. H. Gann and Peter Duignan, I, *The History and Politics of Colonialism, 1870-11) 14*, Cambridge 1969, pp. 76–9.
9. Page, *A History of West Africa*, pp. 91–2.
10. The subject of internal transport in the pre-colonial period still awaits investigation.
11. Calculated from C. W. Newbury, 'Credit in Early Nineteenth-Century West African Trade', *Journal of African History*, 13, 1972, pp. 83–4.
12. Quoted in Allan McPhee, *The Economic Revolution in British West Africa*, 1926, p. 31, n. 2.
13. Though some were used in Africa for fuel.
14. Rum and tobacco imports dwindled in the last quarter of the nineteenth century following the decline of trade with America and Brazil, the two principal suppliers.
15. Newbury, 'Trade and Authority in West Africa from 1850 to 1880' in *Colonialism in Africa, 1870-1960*, ed. L. H. Gann and Peter Duignan, I, *The History and Politics of Colonialism, 1870-1914*, Cambridge 1969, pp. 79–80.
16. K. Vignes, 'Étude sur la rivalité d'influence entre les puissances européennes en Afrique équatoriale et occidentale depuis l'acte général de Berlin jusqu'au seuil du XXᵉ siècle', *Revue Française d'Histoire d'Outre-Mer*, 48, 1961, p. 14.
17. Shortage of space has caused this rather cavalier treatment of minority expatriate interests, each

of which is worthy of study in some detail. There was also an interesting trade between North America and West Africa which has been investigated and, indeed, virtually discovered by George E. Brooks, *Yankee Traders, Old Coasters and African Middlemen*, Boston 1970.

18. A. Adu Boahen, *Britain, the Sahara, and the Western Sudan, 1788-1861*, Oxford, 1961, p. 131.

19. A. Millson, 'Yoruba', *Manchester Geographical Society Journal*, 7, 1891, p. 92.

20. C. W. Newbury, 'North African and Western Sudan Trade in the Nineteenth Century: a Re-evaluation', *Journal of African History*, 7, 1966, pp. 233–46.

21. These decorated the hats of Victorian ladies in much the same way as they had adorned the ostriches themselves. African traders may well have wondered at the strange values of the white man, who was prepared to sell manufactured cloth for such an item, and for such a purpose!

22. These terms are introduced here briefly, and are dealt with at greater length in Chapter 5, where the data available are sufficient to justify more extended treatment.

23. Mention should be made of Patrick Manning's excellent special study, *An Economic History of Southern Dahomey, 1880-1914*, University of Wisconsin Ph.D. thesis 1969, which contains a thorough investigation of the overseas trade of that particular region.

24. The best recent analysis of what in some respects was a non-event, is S. B. Saul's *The Myth of the Great Depression, 1873-1896*, 1969, though this study analyses the problem from a British, rather than from a European, point of view.

25. See Lars G. Sandberg, 'Movements in the Quality of British Cotton Textile Exports, 1815-1913', *Journal of Economic History*, 28, 1968, p. 19.

26. The Russian scholar, D. A. Ol'derogge, has argued that the *jihad* in northern Nigeria was primarily a protest of Hausa and Fulani commoners against oppression by the ruling class. So far, this view has not made much impression, at least on British scholars. However, Ol'derogge's interpretation deserves attention, not least because testing his theory involves writing the history of ordinary Africans, as opposed to that of prominent religious and political figures, and this is surely highly desirable. On the *jihad* in Senegambia see Martin A. Klein, *Islam and Imperialism in Senegal.*, Edinburgh 1968.

27. In this respect the analysis is a response to the plea made by J. D. Hargreaves in an important article written more than ten years ago, 'Towards a History of the Partition of Africa', *Journal of African History*, 1, 1960, pp. 97–109. For the most recent statement of Professor Hargreaves's own view see his contribution 'West African States and the European Conquest', in *Colonialism in Africa, 1870-1960*, ed. L. H. Gann and Peter Duignan, I, *The History and Politics of Colonialism, 1870-1914*, Cambridge 1969, pp. 199–219. I should like to acknowledge my debt to Dr Martin Klein, Dr Patrick Manning and Dr C. W. Newbury, who (though they may not be fully aware of it) have caused me to re-think my ideas on this subject over the past few years.

28. Roger Pasquier, 'En marge de la guerre de sécession: les essais de culture du coton au Sénégal', *Annales Africaines*, 1955, pp. 185–202.

29. Plantation agriculture on the Gold Coast, where experiments sponsored by the Basel Mission were of great importance, has been studied by Kwamina B. Dickson, *A Historical Geography of Ghana*, Cambridge 1969, pp. 120–32.

30. J. B. Webster, 'The Bible and the Plough', *Journal of the Historical Society of Nigeria*, 2, 1963, pp. 418–34.

31. P. K. Mitchell, 'Trade Routes of the Early Sierra Leone Protectorate', *Sierra Leone Studies*, 16, 1962, pp. 204–17.

32. On migration see Marion Johnson, 'Migrants' Progress', *Bulletin of the Ghana Geographical Association*, 9, 1964, pp. 4–27, and 10, 1965, pp. 13–40; and R. K. Udo, 'The Migrant Tenant Farmer of Eastern Nigeria', *Africa*, 34, 1964, pp. 326–39. On land tenure see

Akin L. Mabogunje, 'Some Comments on Land Tenure in Egba Division, Western Nigeria', *Africa*, 31, 1961, pp. 258–69, The expansion of 'peasant' exports in the twentieth century is dealt with in Chapter 6.

33. In some cases (Old Calabar and Whydah are two obvious examples) it is clear that the overseas slave trade developed entrepreneurial skills and commercial institutions which greatly assisted the rise of legitimate trade. However, it would be wrong to infer that the slave trade was in any sense necessary to the successful expansion of legitimate commerce. Everything that is known about African enterprise in internal trade in the pre-colonial period strongly suggests that indigenous societies would have produced the required number of wholesalers and traders, and in a short space of time, even if the Atlantic slave trade had never existed.

34. At the same time, it is worth while pointing out that areas in the second category also experienced some of the difficulties of economic transition. See E. A. Ijagbemi, 'The Freetown Colony and the Development of "Legitimate" Commerce in the Adjoining Territories', *Journal of the Historical Society of Nigeria*, 5, 1970, pp. 252–6.

35. Many palm trees were also planted deliberately.

36. Brooks, *Yankee Traders, Old Coasters and African Middlemen*, pp. 184–9.

37. A. Dessertine, 'Naissance d'un port: Kaolack, des origines à 1900', *Annales Africaines*, 1960, pp. 225–59.

38. H. S. Ferns, 'Latin America and Industrial Capitalism—The First Phase', *Sociological Review Monograph*, II, 1967, pp. 18–20.

39. Brodie Cruickshank's report of 1848, quoted in C. W. Newbury, *The Western Slave Coast and its Rulers*, Oxford 1961, p. 51.

40. David A. Ross, 'The Career of Domingo Martinez in the Bight of Benin, 1833–64', *Journal of African History*, 6, 1965, pp. 79–90.

41. Very few historians of Africa can match Ivor Wilks's achievement in reconstructing the history of Ashanti. See, for example, 'Ashanti Government', in *West African Kingdoms in the Nineteenth Century*, ed. Daryll Forde and P. M. Kaberry, 1967, pp. 206–38, and his study of the 'war' and 'peace' parties in *Political Bipolarity in Nineteenth-Century Asante*, Centre of African Studies, Edinburgh 1971.

42. Ivor Wilks, 'Asante Policy Towards the Hausa Trade in the Nineteenth Century', in *The Development of Indigenous Trade and Markets in West Africa*, ed. Claude Meillassoux, 1971, pp. 124–41.

43. Some important work on these topics is being undertaken by K. Arhin. See, for example, 'The Structure of Greater Ashanti', *Journal of African History*, 8, 1967, pp. 65–85, and 'Aspects of Ashanti Northern Trade in the Nineteenth Century', *Africa*, 40, 1970, pp. 363–73.

44. These developments are discussed by Martin Klein in 'Slavery, the Slave Trade, and Legitimate Commerce in Late Nineteenth-Century Africa', *Études d'Histoire Africaine*, 2, 1971, pp. 22–4.

45. A brief survey of this aspect of Japanese history is given in Thomas C. Smith, 'Japan's Aristocratic Revolution', *Yale Review*, 5, 1960–1, pp. 370–83.

46. The major studies are K. O. Dike, *Trade and Politics in the Niger Delta, 1830–1885*, Oxford 1956; G. I. Jones, *The Trading States of the Oil Rivers*, Oxford 1963; Obaro Ikime, *Merchant Prince of the Niger Delta*, 1968; and A. J. H. Latham, *Old Calabar, 1600–1861: the Economic Impact of the West upon a Traditional Society*, University of Birmingham Ph.D. thesis, 1970.

47. On the problems of economic transition among the Itsekiri see P. C. Lloyd, 'The Itsekiri in the Nineteenth Century: an Outline Social History', *Journal of African History*, 4, 1963, pp. 307–31.

48. See, for example, Kwame Y. Daaku, *Trade and Politics on the Gold Coast, 1600–1720*, Oxford 1970, ch. 5.

49. Robin Horton, 'From Fishing Village to City State: a Social History of New Calabar', in *Man in Africa*, ed. Mary Douglas and Phyllis M. Kaberry, 1969, pp. 37–58.

50. Technical supremacy, however, did not come until the 1880s. See Gerald S. Graham, 'The

Ascendancy of the Sailing Ship, 1850-85', *Economic History Review*, 9, 1956, pp. 74–88. Further information about the beginnings of steamship services to West Africa can be found in P. N. Davies, 'The African Steam Ship Company', in *Liverpool and Merseyside*, ed. J. R. Harris, 1969, pp. 212–38, and in a neglected article by Emile Baillet, 'Le rôle de la marine de commerce dans l'implantation de la France en A.O.F.', *Revue Maritime*, 135, 1957, pp. 832–40.

51. For further details see A. G. Hopkins, 'The Currency Revolution in South-West Nigeria in the Late Nineteenth Century', *Journal of the Historical Society of Nigeria*, 3, 1966, pp. 471–83, and a more comprehensive article by Marion Johnson, 'The Cowrie Currencies of West Africa', *Journal of African History*, 11, 1970, pp. 331–53.

52. Further work is also needed to clarify the consequences of the decline of transitional currencies for African societies, particularly for fixed income groups and those wealthy enough to hold stocks of money. It would also be interesting to know whether a depreciating exchange rate assisted exports in the 1860s and 1870s.

53. C. W. Newbury, 'Credit in Early Nineteenth-Century West African Trade', *Journal of African History*, 13, 1972, pp. 81–95.

54. On Gaiser and Holt see Ernst Hieke, *G. L. Gaiser: Hamburg—Westafrica*, Hamburg 1949; and Cherry J. Gertzel, *John Holt: a British Merchant in West Africa in the Era of Imperialism*, University of Oxford D. Phil, thesis, 1959.

55. Freda Wolfson, 'A Price Agreement on the Gold Coast—The Krobo Oil Boycott, 1858-1866', *Economic History Review*, 6, 1953, pp. 68–77.

56. Christopher Fyfe, *A History of Sierra Leone*, Oxford 1962. See also Arthur T. Porter, *Creoledom*, Oxford 1963, and Margaret Priestley, *West African Trade and Coast Society*, 1969.

57. A. G. Hopkins, 'Richard Beale Blaize, 1854–1904: Merchant Prince of West Africa', *Tarikh*, 1, 1966, pp. 70–9.

58. See J. E. Flint's important study, *Sir George Goldie and the Making of Nigeria*, 1960.

59. Information about mercantile pressures can be found in many of the items listed in the bibliography: see especially Aderibigbe, Dike, Dumett, Flint, Hopkins (1968), Latham, and Newbury (1959, 1968, 1969 and 1972).

60. C. W. Newbury and A. S. Kanya-Forstner, 'French Policy and the Origins of the Scramble for West Africa', *Journal of African History*, 10, 1969, pp. 253–76.

61. Cherry J. Gertzel, 'Relations between African and European Traders in the Niger Delta, 1880-1896', *Journal of African History*, 3, 1962, pp. 361–6.

62. Two of the best studies of British policy towards Africa are Ronald Robinson and John Gallagher with Alice Denny, *Africa and the Victorians*, 1961, and John D. Hargreaves, *Prelude to the Partition of West Africa*, 1963. For a global perspective see D. C. M. Platt, *Finance, Trade and Politics in British Foreign Policy, 1815–1914*, Oxford 1968.

63. On French policy see Henri Brunschwig, *French Colonialism, 1871-1914: Myths and Realities*, 1966, and, for more detail on West Africa, Bernard Schnapper, *La politique et le commerce français dans le Golfe de Guinée de 1838 à 1871*, Paris 1961.

64. See two essays by F. Crouzet, 'England and France in the Eighteenth Century: a Comparative Analysis of Two Economic Growths', in *The Causes of the Industrial Revolution in England*, ed. R. M. Hartwell, 1967, pp. 139–74, and 'Wars, Blockade and Economic Change in Europe, 1792-1815', *Journal of Economic History*, 24, 1964, pp. 567–88, which between them revise many of the standard views about the French economy in the late eighteenth and early nineteenth centuries.

65. For further information see *Britain and Germany in Africa: Imperial Rivalry and*

Colonial Rule, ed. Prosser Gifford and William Roger Louis, New Haven 1967.

66. Hartmut Pogge von Strandmann, 'Germany's Colonial Expansion under Bismarck', *Past & Present,* 42, 1969, pp. 140–59; and Hans-Ulrich Wehler, 'Bismarck's Imperialism 1862–1890', *Past & Present,* 48, 1970, pp. 131–9.

67. C. W. Newbury, 'The Development of French Policy on the Lower and Upper Niger, 1880–98', *Journal of Modern History,* 31, 1959, pp. 16–26.

68. This firm began life as the United African Company in 1879, became the National African Company in 1882, and finally turned itself into the Royal Niger Company in 1886.

69. C. W. Newbury, 'The Protectionist Revival in French Colonial Trade: the Case of Senegal', *Economic History Review,* 21, 1968, pp. 337–48.

70. Bernard Semmel, *Imperialism and Social Reform,* 1960.

71. The best general study is still B. H. Brown, *The Tariff Reform Movement in Great Britain, 1881–95,* New York 1943. For a case study of one area see R. J. Ward, *The Tariff Reform Movement in Birmingham, 1877–1906,* University of London M.A. thesis, 1971.

72. Two interesting local studies are John F. Laffey, 'The Roots of French Imperialism in the Nineteenth Century: the Case of Lyon', *French Historical Studies,* 6, 1969, pp. 78–92, and W. Thompson, *Glasgow and Africa: Connexions and Attitudes, 1870–1900,* University of Strathclyde Ph.D. thesis, 1970.

73. C. M. Andrew and A. S. Kanya-Forstner, 'The French "Colonial Party:" its Composition, Aims and Influence, 1885–1914', *The Historical Journal,* 14, 1971, pp. 99–128.

74. R. A. Dutnett, *British Official Attitudes to Economic Development on the Gold Coast, 1874–1905,* University of London Ph.D. thesis, 1966, pp. 149–80.

75. A. G. Hopkins, 'Economic Imperialism in West Africa: Lagos, 1880–92', *Economic History Review,* 21, 1968, pp. 580–606, and Flint, *Sir George Goldie,* chs 10, 11 and 12.

KINJIKITILE AND THE IDEOLOGY OF MAJI MAJI

By G. C. K. Gwassa

INTRODUCTION: MAJI MAJI AND IDEOLOGY

Maji Maji was a mass movement waged by Africans against German colonial rule in what was then German East Africa. It lasted from July 1905 to August 1907 and covered over 100,000 square miles of the southern third of what is now mainland Tanzania. It involved over twenty differing ethnic groups. In its organisational scale and its ethnic variety Maji Maji was a movement both different from and more complex than earlier reactions and resistances to the imposition of colonial rule, for the latter had usually been confined within ethnic boundaries. By comparison with the past Maji Maji was a revolutionary movement creating fundamental changes in traditional organisational scale. The problem is to show how this revolutionary development came about when and where it did.

One explanation often advanced is to stress German brutality which gave the varying peoples involved in Maji Maji a common grievance. Another is to stress the realisation by these southern Tanzanian peoples that such brutality was the consequence of alien over-rule and so to stress their desire for independence. Maji Maji *was* a protest against German oppression and it was also in a real sense a war for independence. But these cannot be total explanations. Other parts of the country were oppressed; other parts of the country desired independence from the Germans. But they did not revolt. Thus we must ask not only *why* people wished to rise up against the Germans but *how* they were able to do so. How were so many people brought out in arms against the Germans in southern Tanzania?

The answer to this question must be sought mainly in terms of ideology. The peoples of southern Tanzania wished to rise up in arms but they did not believe that they could do so effectively: 'Thus they waited for a long time because there was no plan or knowledge. Truly his (the German's) practices were bad. But while there were no superior weapons should the people not fear? Everywhere elders were busy thinking, "What should we do?"'[1]

A crisis of resentment against German rule and of frustrated desire to rise up against it had become widespread by 1903–4. The crisis was resolved by the emergence of an ideology which offered solutions to the problems of unity and morale. This ideology was couched in religious terms. It was revolutionary and it was created at that specific time for a specific purpose. Yet it drew upon pre-existing religious beliefs, combining them into new patterns. In order to understand how it did this we must examine briefly the peoples of southern Tanzania.

THE PEOPLES OF SOUTHERN TANZANIA

Most of the peoples of the Maji Maji area were organised on a small scale, usually into clans which constituted political units. The Ngoni of Songea provide a rare example of a centralised political system but even they were divided into two sometimes conflicting kingdoms. Yet despite this apparent diversity and even extreme disunity, the effects of the slave trade and of the raids of the Ngoni and Yao and the constant movements of peoples had produced so complex an ethnic ad mixture that it became impossible to draw meaningful ethnic boundaries. Thus Crosse-Upcott in his study of the Ngindo, who played an important role in Maji Maji, urges that Ngindo were scattered over the whole area between the Rufiji and the Ruvuma rivers and between the coast and Lake Nyasa.[2] In 1875 Thomson, travelling among the Mbunga, found that 'their language is identical with that of the Wagindo ... One of our porters who had been brought up in Gindo, spoke the M'henge (Mbunga) idiom quite easily although he had never been in the country before.'[3] In the Rufiji valley Beardall found Wamahoro and Wamamboka who spoke the same language 'as that spoken by the Wangindo and the Wamatumbi.'[4]

These wide linguistic and cultural connections help to explain the present feeling of common origin among Ngindo, Kichi, Ikemba and the peoples of the Rufiji valley. There is evidence, too, which shows intermarriage between Ngoni and Ngindo, and between the latter and the Mwera. In all this intermixture was the basis of a cultural affinity.

Thus the old view that the southern Tanzanian peoples had had little in common, that they were perpetually at each other's throats, that they were so divided and weak that it was impossible for them to combine, falls away. Instead it has been shown that a complex web of cultural inter-mixture, and of wide-ranging social and marital relationships had been woven by events taking place before and during the nineteenth century. By the time Maji Maji broke out, southern Tanzania possessed the potentiality for some semblance of unity because ideological communication was possible and could be made both meaningful and effective. In other words most or all the Maji prescriptions and practices could be understood and accepted by the majority of the peoples of the Maji Maji area because the Maji ideology drew upon their commonly shared beliefs.

THE MAJI MAJI IDEOLOGY AND THE GENERAL CONCEPT OF THE HIERARCHY OF FORCE

The essence of the Maji ideology, as it was pronounced by Kinjikitile Ngwale of Ngarambe, can be simply stated. For a people politically divided and used to fighting limited defensive wars it was necessary to unite and take the fullest advantage of numerical superiority if victory over the Germans was to be assured. The teachings of Kinjikitile Ngwale were that all Africans were one, that they were free men, and that those who partook of the *maji* (water) would be immune from European bullets. The dead ancestors would assist them in a war which had been commanded by God.

We can perhaps best understand what is involved in this message in its most general terms by transposing Father Tempel's concept of 'vital force' into the southern Tanzanian context. All southern Tanzanian peoples believed in a hierarchy of forces. At its head is the Creator, the Supreme Being, who is himself the source of all power and who can therefore increase it in men. Below the Creator come the ancestors, the first founders of clans or ethnic groups who are believed to have received 'vital force' from the Creator and who are held to powerfully influence posterity. Among the Matumbi, for instance, each clan performs the *Mbekia* ceremony to propitiate such ancestors every year in August after the harvest. This explains why in August and September some Maji Maji fighters were seen drunk. They had come to fight the Germans from the *Mbekia* ceremonies.[5] Next in this hierarchy of forces come the dead members of a particular family who have immediate influence on their offspring. Lastly, it is believed that the oldest living members of society are endowed with more 'vital force' than the younger ones and the clan head is considered to have more 'vital force' than any other man.

This hierarchy of forces has relevance to the Maji ideology in two ways. In one sense Kinjikitile's message combined the 'vital force' of the Creator, who had commanded the war; of the ancestors, who were to return to assist the living warriors; and of the living war leaders who were accepted by their followers at the ceremonies at Kinjikitile's pool.

In another sense Kinjikitile's exercise of his own powers fits into this hierarchial pattern. Kinjikitile as man could exercise influence on those below him in the hierarchy of force—on trees or animals. Thus he is said to have made lions and snakes tame. Then it is believed that a man can influence the *being* of other men if he can obtain recourse to a vital external power and particularly through the intervention of God. Kinjikitile was believed to be endowed with force by God, who had entered and possessed him, and through this force it was believed that he could strengthen Africans against Germans.

Thus Kinjikitile was acceptable to the societies among whom he worked because his *being* and teaching conformed to known metaphysics. At Ngarambe pool, where he preached the message, he provided a unitary ideology which cut across clan and ethnic boundaries and which in fact discouraged these boundaries. *Maji* as a war medicine was not to be of or for any single group, clan or ethnic identity, but of and for all people; his was a universal medicine having a universal appeal. Therefore the *Maji* ideology became the basis of a revolutionary commitment to mass action against German colonial rule. In addition, Kinjikitile, based in Ngarambe, and later his ambassadors to the various areas, provided means of contact between potential leaders from various localities, and in so doing gave opportunity for establishing ties and inter-group communications which became increasingly necessary in the mass movement.

THE MAJI IDEOLOGY AND THE CULT OF POSSESSION

The idea of the hierarchy of 'vital force' only explains Kinjikitile's teaching and its acceptability in the most general way. In order to grasp more exactly the ways in which he was accepted and in which his ideology was effective it is necessary to examine in more detail other related but more precise religious ideas, and particularly the immediate antecedents to Kinjikitile's meteoric rise to charismatic leadership. First it is necessary to grasp the nature of the cult of possession extant among Kinjikitile's client societies.

Among the Matumbi-Ngindo group possession is believed to give a man access to certain supernatural powers. He is said to have *Lilungu* and to be the symbolic representation of the spirit of *Lilungu* that has possessed him. He is above society, for he can walk naked and not be punished. Although he is not a prophet, but a medium through which God or a given spirit operates, his 'vital force' is greater than the greatest possible force in normal human beings. And because of this the man with *Lilungu* is held to have powers over all other beings inferior to him, not only ordinary men but also man-eating lions as well, so that he can sleep in the open without being harmed by them. Ordinarily he does not eat and yet he cannot die from hunger. Above all, he is pure from sin. When in the company of witches he hunts them down until he kills them all for it is said they stink before him. All field authorities agree that Kinjikitile had *Lilungu* and it was therefore natural that he should order all his clients to renounce witchcraft, failing which death would attend them. One informant put the powers of a man with *Lilungu* quite clearly:

> People who have *Lilungu* were feared very much since the days of old. They can do anything. And if a man with *Lilungu* killed a person where could you go to charge (him)? The *Lukumbi* (inter-clan court)? Never at all! His affairs are god-like. A man with Lilungu does not fear anything. He can even go naked. Those things that are forbidden or are too dangerous to eat, he eats.[6]

But Kinjikitile was more powerful than an ordinary man who has an ordinary *Lilungu*. Kinjikitile was possessed by the Hongo spirit, which was in itself very powerful, and it was believed that the Hongo spirit had been sent to Kinjikitile by the superior divinity, Bokero. At Ngarambe, which was Kinjikitile's headquarters, one informant explained that 'Hongo was to Bokero as Jesus is to God, or as Prophet Mohamed is to God.'[7] This hierarchical relationship between Bokero, Hongo and Kinjikitile was later extended to define the relationship between Kinjikitile and his assistants and messengers. Particularly outside the outbreak area of Maji Maji the title of Bokero came to be applied to Kinjikitile himself while the title of Hongo was reserved for those who carried and dispensed the *maji* and supervised drilling in the various areas of the war zone.

KINJIKITILE AND THE BOKERO CULT AT KIBESA

What was the significance of this claimed relationship with Bokero? Clearly Kinjikitile used the Bokero/Hongo concept to innovate. But the concept of the influence and power of the Bokero spirit long pre-dated Maji Maji. So also did the idea of Bokero's close link with water as a medicine. One of the main centres of the Bokero cult was situated in the Rufiji valley, outside the outbreak area of Maji Maji, but well known to the peoples who initiated the uprising. This cult centre had been located, for very many years before Maji Maji, at a place called Kibesa, above the Mpanga Falls on the Rufiji river; the place was sometimes known as Rufiji Ruhingo, i.e. the upper reaches of the Rufiji. The riverine ecology of the Rufiji made that river affect the lives of the people there as the Nile affects the Egyptian's, though on a much smaller scale. When the floods were too high the Rufiji people lived in houses raised several yards above the ground and all movement from place to place had to be done in canoes. When the waters were too low and rain scarce famine threatened the people of the valley. Thus too low or too high waters could cause disaster to the population.

The Bokero cult in Rufiji had developed out of this situation. The people of Rufiji addressed Bokero, and his fellow divinities, Ulilo and Nyamguni,

seeking from them enough but not excessive rain, the fertility of their soil, and so on. Originally it seems that Bokero, Ulilo and Nyamguni were all three propitiated at the Kibesa centre. At some time in the past the propitiation of Ulilo shifted to Mgende, which is still today a famous centre of *Uganga*. At any rate at the time of Maji Maji Bokero was certainly still being propitiated at Kibesa.[8] The peoples of Rufiji travelled annually to his cult centre to pray for rain. The rock shrine of Bokero was controlled by one Kologelo, which may have been the hereditary clan name of the medium of the divinity.

It appears from oral authorities that 1904–5 was a period of drought. Towards the end of 1904 people went to Kibesa to ask for rain. Jumbe Mbanga Mbite and another clan head, Mapende Mburu, went to consult the divinities at Kologelo's: 'All went with salt and *kaniki* cloth (blue calico). They went there, they prayed for rain and water. They were successful.'[9] The medium-priest Kologelo gave to these, as well as to other applicants, water from the Kibesa pool, telling them to sprinkle it on their land and to use it in general as a panacea.[10]

It seems plain that there were close connections between this long-established cult and the practices of the cult centre which Kinjikitile set up at Ngarambe immediately preceding Maji Maji. There seems no doubt that Kinjikitile borrowed the idea of water, *maji*, as the panacea from the Bokero cult centre at Kibesa, though he developed it into a war medicine by combining the possession cult with ancestor observances and immunity beliefs. Kinjikitile himself acknowledged the seniority of the Kibesa or Rufiji Ruhingo shrine. After he had addressed his clients at Ngarambe and given them his message in a manner resembling a political rally, he would say, 'If there be anybody amongst you who does not believe me, let him go to prove this from Bokero in Rufiji Ruhingo.'[11]

Moreover, there were striking similarities of ritual procedure. Kinjikitile lived near to the shrine of the divinity as did Kologelo. All oral authorities agree that both mediums went under the water to consult the spirits before they addressed their clients. Both Kologelo's clients and the Maji Maji people dressed in *kaniki*. And today people at Ngarambe, the site of Kinjikitile's cult centre, still speak of the Bokero centre on the Rufiji and of Bokero's great powers.

'There at Bokero's there is a huge rock,' says Mzee Nimewako. 'Up to now motor-boats have failed to go beyond that rock of Bokero. The rock of Bokero has four windows and it is there at Ruhingo. The Germans tried to use a powder magazine to break it. They failed. They wanted recently to close those windows in order to get hydro-electricity; they failed … You cannot cross the river there … If you try you fall off and die. But there is nearby a guardian (or medium) of the rock of Bokero. This is the propitiator and the spirits of Bokero have possessed him. If you want to go across the rock you must first call on him, whereupon he will propitiate the spirits on your behalf. The following day you can cross safely.'[12]

KINJIKITILE AND OTHER CENTRES OF THE BOKERO CULT

Obviously Kinjikitile borrowed a great deal from the Kibesa cult centre of Bokero. The question now arises whether he had any connections with other centres of Bokero observance. The Bokero cult—or as it is most often called in the evidence, the Kolelo cult, from a condensation of the name Kologelo—is widespread. It extends to the Ndengereko, the Zaramo and the Luguru peoples as well as to the Rufiji. In addition to the Kibesa shrine on the Rufiji there was at least one other major centre of the cult situated in Uluguru.

The earliest known written reference to this centre comes from Burton:

> They (the Luguru) have a place visited even by distant Wazaramo Pilgrims. It is described as a cave where a P'hepo or the disembodied spirit of man, in fact a ghost, produces a terrible subterraneous sound, called by the people Kurero or Bokero; it arises probably from the flow of water underground … men sacrifice sheep and goats to obtain fruitful seasons and success in war.[13]

The existence of this cult centre in the Luguru mountains was subsequently confirmed by Martin Klamroth, a missionary at Maneromango. According to him, Kolelo was a great snake god, a point that is reminiscent of Hongo at Ngarambe, since the Hongo spirit was also supposed to embody itself on occasions in a snake. Like Hongo also, Kolelo in Klamroth's version was said to have come as a messenger of the great Creator to remove corruption. Kolelo was said to have marital connections with the Mlali clan, whom he commanded: 'You people of the Mlali clan shall be my people and serve me here forever in this cave in the Luguru mountains.' The Mlali clan guarded an area called Kolelo in the Matombo district of Morogoro to which representatives from various areas of Uzaramo brought offerings. As at the Kibesa shrine on the Rufiji, Bokero/Kolelo of Uluguru had a medium who interpreted the message of the divinity to clients.

It seems certain that the cult centre of the Uluguru mountains was part of a common system of belief and practice with that on the Rufiji river. But the question is whether it was also connected to the Maji Maji rising. Klamroth certainly believed that it was. According to him, Kolelo/Bokero of Uluguru had customarily concerned himself only with problems of fertility and rain. But in 1905:

> Kolelo also concerned himself with politics. Kolelo had forbidden the further payment of taxes to the white foreigners; in mid-July a great flood would come and destroy all whites and their followers. Later it was said the earth would open and swallow them, that no bullets but only water would come from the soldiers' guns, seven lions would come and destroy the enemy; 'be not afraid, Kolelo spares his black children.'[14]

According to Klamroth the power of Kolelo/Bokero proved inadequate, so 'God himself now appeared' and people began talking about the 'resurrection of the dead.' Klamroth maintains that Kibasila, leader of Maji Maji in southern Uzaramo, was won over to the movement by being shown the resurrected ancestors.

Klamroth's account, though admittedly garbled, seems at first sight to describe the same sort of deployment of the hierarchy of force that comes out of the oral descriptions of Kinjikitile's teaching at Ngarambe. It is tempting to see the Maji ideology as the product of a general development out of the Bokero cult. And yet there is no further sound evidence that Kolelo/Bokero of Uluguru contributed to the Maji Maji ideology. Lloyd Swantz, who has made an ethnographic study of the Zaramo, has found no connection between their participation in Maji Maji and the Kolelo cult centre in Uluguru.[15] Oral authorities in Uzaramo are adamant that no connection existed. 'This Kolelo is in Uluguru mountains and has *no* relationship whatever with the Maji Maji war. Since the days of our ancestors (Wahenga) there were always his (Kolelo's) special servants.'[16] Or again: 'As for Kolelo this is an established tradition … For in times of drought and illness—life and rain—people receive these from Kolelo … Kolelo had nothing to do with Maji Maji for the work of Kolelo is good, it is to ensure affluence.'[17]

The case seems clearer still with yet another centre of Kolelo/Bokero propitiation. This concerns the Wadoe people. According to Mtoto bin Mwenyi Bakari, the Wadoe address prayers for rain to Kolelo, as prayers are addressed to Bokero in Rufiji. Kolelo is said to be the name of a place in Nguu country and the spirit living there is said to be that of a headman of Ukami who, being a great *mganga* and invulnerable to weapons, met a miraculous death, for his body vanished. 'All the elders and *Pazi* and the headmen of Kingalu's family revere this spirit.'[18] But the Wadoe did not participate in Maji Maji and no authority, archival or oral, has sought to associate the Kolelo shrine in Nguu with the uprising.

In short it seems that Kinjikitile had been associated with the Bokero shrine at Kibesa on the upper Rufiji river and that when he went south to open his own shrine at Ngarambe he developed the Bokero ritual and teaching as one of the bases of the Maji ideology. But it also seems that the Bokero network as a whole did not participate in or give spiritual support to the uprising.

KINJIKITILE AND THE SPIRITS OF THE DEAD

We have seen, then, the importance of the idea of possession in general and of the Bokero cult in particular to the making and acceptability of Kinjikitile's message. Further related beliefs were also very important. One of the commonest religious beliefs in the Maji Maji districts is the belief in the importance of *Mahoka* (singular *lihoka*), the spirits of the dead. The term is widespread in Mtwara, Ruvuma, Coast and perhaps Morogoro regions. In the outbreak area nearly every homestead has a *Kijumba-Nungu*, the House of God. Each head of a family makes offerings to the *Kijumba-Nungu* for his ancestors' *Mahoka* who are then seen as *Nungu* or *Mulungu*. Now, Kinjikitile built at Ngarambe a very large *Kijumba-Nungu* at which he insisted that all clients should make offerings of rice, millet, salt or money before even greeting him as the great *Mganga*. In yet another sense, then, Kinjikitile was creating a unitary ideology for his was a *Kijumba-Nungu* not for individual families but for all Africans—Pogoro, Matumbi, Ngindo and so on. In a sense, the offerings were directed to the ancestors of all blackmen.

In order to appreciate the force of this idea it is necessary to remind ourselves of what Bishop Komba has written of the place of *Mahoka* in Ngoni metaphysics:

> *Mahoka* … resembles *Mulungu* (God) in certain respects … According to Bantu thought that state of *Mahoka* resembling *Mulungu* makes *Mahoka* become the symbol of *Mulungu*. And the philosophy of Bantu symbolism identifies symbol with the object symbolised—*Mahoka* to become *Mulungu* or *Mulungu* to become *Mahoka*.[19]

Thus when Kinjikitile announced that all dead ancestors were at Ngarambe and that anybody who came there would see them, he was stressing not so much the idea of resurrection as the fact that *Mulungu* in the symbol *of Mahoka*, in the symbol of the totality of the ancestral spirits, was there to help Africans. So every morning the pilgrims to Ngarambe, astonished that their offerings to the *Kijumba-Nungu* had vanished, were told by Kinjikitile's assistant: 'Do you see? The gods are pleased. They have taken all your good offerings.'[20]

Further, it was customary for all the people of the Maji Maji area, from the Matumbi to the Ngoni, to pray to their *Mahoka* before going to war. Offering at a 'national' *Kijumba-Nungu* at Ngarambe before going to war with the Germans was therefore both consistent with tradition and with a 'national' commitment, for there it was done on a wider and unitary scale.

KINJIKITILE AS MGANGA

Kinjikitile had *Lilungu*. He was possessed by Hongo, emissary of Bokero. At his cult centre offerings were made to the totality of the ancestors. He also enjoyed the prestige of the *Mganga*. The Matumbi and Ngindo regard the *Mganga* as an expert (*Pundi*), who enjoys high respect. *Pundis* used to walk about the country holding large fly whisks. Kinjikitile did not walk about, but he had a fly whisk as did his ambassadors. One authority tells us: '*Pundis* used to be feared very much. They were also honoured and respected a lot … if a *Pundi* said something we agreed. Today if a Bwana Doctor says a thing do we not believe?'[21]

Evidence from the field does not suggest that ordinary *Pundis* or *Waganga* were also possessed. So having *Lilungu* Kinjikitile was regarded as more powerful than any of the *waganga*. 'Kinjikitile excelled them all (aliwapiku). He was too powerful and too full of wisdom for them. They (Waganga) did not know how to go about him.'[22] Yet in some ways Kinjikitile performed as a characteristic *Mganga*. 'He could tell matters secret to the people and yet he was a mere newcomer there at Ngarambe. His instructions were good. He

had said, 'Adultery is bad for it puts the body out of joint and God does not want it. Witchcraft is also bad and God hates it.' Then people said, 'Ayi, this man is truly from God for he forbids even witchcraft.'[23]

There is evidence also that some of Kinjikitile's ambassadors to the peoples beyond Ngarambe's direct area of influence—the so-called *Hongo* or *Mpokosi*—had formerly been traditional *Waganga*. It is certain that the woman who administered the *maji* medicine to the warriors of Matumbi was an *Mganga*.

In Nandete the *jemadar* of the war was Sikwato Mbonde. And his wife, Nantabila Naupunda, my aunt, administered *maji* to the warriors and she lay across their path and they stepped over her. And if you ask why a woman was selected, it is because women are extremely expert at *Uganga* and they were thereby weakening that one (the Germans) so that he becomes like a woman.[24]

KINJIKITILE AND THE MAJI AS WAR MEDICINE

It remains to examine one last element in the syncretist ideology created by Kinjikitile—the belief that the *map* would bestow invulnerability to bullets. Once again the idea of a war medicine was not new. As an informant testified:

The reason why many people believed that bullets would turn into water or that they would not enter the body, was simply because that was our established tradition. Since our ancestors … these matters were extant in Umatumbi. All hunters had *dawa* (medicine) and even today these still exist. They used amulets for their safety and so that they could be more accurate … First, there is *Kirughe*. If you use this medicine neither bullet nor spear … can enter your body.[25]

Each group had its own trusted war medicines. An informant at Kibata listed the most famous medicines of the Matumbi and Ngindo:

> There are war medicines as well. There are two types. First there is *ndyengu*, which if used causes weapons, spears, arrows or bullets to be deflected away from the man who is the target. On the other hand, another medicine, *Kalunde*, prevents bullets, spears, knives or arrows from entering the body of the person who has taken it.[26]

Kinjikitile did not introduce the idea of a medicine that would make a man weapon proof. What he did was to universalise the idea. Traditional medicines were used within clan boundaries. Kinjikitile's *maji* was a 'national' medicine, promising 'national' victory. Ironically, Africans who fought on the side of the Germans against the Maji Maji warriors often made use of their own particularistic medicines—and boasted that they were more efficient in giving protection than the *maji*!

A NARRATIVE OF THE CAREER OF KINJIKITILE

It is necessary now to turn to the career of the remarkable man who brought together all these traditional elements to create his revolutionary ideology. Kinjikitile is known to have been a recent immigrant into Ngarambe, arriving some three years before 1905. As a man he was very eloquent, brave and wise—a born leader. (These qualities are quite apparent today in his brother who is now the Chairman of the Village Development Committee of Ngarambe.) An elderly lady who saw Kinjikitile, one Nambulyo Mwiru, described him as follows:

> He was a middle aged man, an *Mpindo* of wisdom. But he was very tall and very strong … He wore white robes (*Kanzu*) down to his feet … His hair was not long and not white.[27]

It may be that people in the Matumbi-Ngindo areas were waiting for the arrival of such a leader to resolve their frustrated desire to fight; 'since olden times if there was an impending war some person came out and taught something, as Nguvumali later did. And so Kinjikitile himself.'[28] But Kinjikitile the man still had to be legitimised as Kinjikitile the leader.

A man who now resides in Kinjikitile's former homestead, and who claims to have been fifteen when Maji Maji broke out, has given the following account of Kinjikitile's emergence as leader which has been well corroborated by other Ngarambe authorities. A huge snake of a size and type never seen before, and having the head of a small black monkey, paid a visit to the house of one Mzee Machuya Nnundu of Lihenga near Ngarambe. The occupants of the house moved out in favour of the visitor. The snake was too big for the house so that its coils overflowed outside while it kept its head above the coils at the entrance into the house. It had large red glowing eyes and looked at people, who came to see the unwelcome visitor over the next three days, in a fearsome manner. It was coloured like the rainbow—one of the commonest attributes of the divinity, Hongo. On the third day the huge snake disappeared miraculously. Two women who had been harvesting sorghum that afternoon suddenly beheld a man dressed in a dazzlingly white *kanzu*—it was too white to look at in the afternoon sun. Before they could run away in fear the man disappeared and he and the snake were never seen again. Subsequent examination by the villagers revealed that the trail of the snake disappeared at the point where the man in the white *kanzu* was seen and was renewed where he had disappeared. From there the trail led to the Ngarambe river into which the huge snake was believed to have vanished.

The day following this incident, Kinjikitile, who lived three hundred yards from the river, was taken. He was taken by a spirit one day in the morning at about nine o'clock. Everyone saw it, and his children and wives as well. They were basking outside when they saw him go on his belly, his hands stretched out before him. They tried to get hold of his legs and pull him but it was impossible, and he cried out that he did not want (to be pulled back), and that they were hurting him. Then he disappeared in the pool of water. He slept in there and his relatives slept by the pool overnight waiting for him. Those who knew how to swim dived down into the pool but they did not see anything. Then they said, 'If he is dead we will see his body; if he has been taken by a spirit of the waters we shall see him returned dead or alive.' So they waited and the following morning, at about nine o'clock again, he emerged unhurt with his clothes dry and as he had tucked them the previous day. After returning from there he began talking of prophetic matters. He said, 'All dead ancestors will come back; they are at Bokero's in Rufiji Ruhingo. No lion or leopard will eat men.'[29]

Kinjikitile taught other things too. He claimed to possess a medicine which would give invulnerability against white weapons. He mocked the whites with names like *utupi nkere*, red potter's clay, or *liyomba lya masi*, ugly fish of the sea, and stressed their weakness. He taught a new song, derived from the days of the power of the Sultan of Zanzibar, Seyyid Said, and meaning that all Africans were freemen, not slaves.

> Twe mkina seyyid Said twate
> Twe mkina seyyid twenga.
> (We are all members of Seyyid Said's clan.
> We are all freemen, all by ourselves).[30]

Report of Kinjikitile's experience and of his teaching spread through a movement called variously *Njwiywila*, *Jujila*, *Njwito* or *Mtemela*. Literally *Njwiywila* was a whispering campaign spreading the message of Kinjikitile.

> *Njwiywila* meant a secret communication such as at a secret meeting. At the time if you listened to *Njwiywila* you paid one *pice*.[31]

Another authority put it more aptly:

> Then through the whole country it sprang. A man met another, stopped him

and said, 'I have a message, a special word to tell you. But first you must give me one *pice*.' Then on receiving the *pice* he said, 'Bring your ear closer,' and said he should not tell anybody, it was secret. We all continued whispering behind their (the German's) backs.[32]

Njwiywila was not meant to reach German ears or those of their representatives. It had started by the middle of 1904 for Kinjikitile must have been possessed by June/July of that year and pilgrimages to Ngarambe seem to have begun by July/August. The message was from the first specifically about war:

> The message in *Njwiywila* was like this: 'This year is a year of war, for there is a man at Ngarambe who has been possessed. He has *Lilungu*. Why? Because we are suffering like this and because ... we are oppressed by the *akidas*. We work without payment. There is an expert at Ngarambe to help us. How? There is *Jumbe* Hongo ...' In the message of *Nijwiywila* was also the information that those who went to Ngarambe would see their dead ancestors. Then people began going to Ngarambe to see for themselves.[33]

The second phase of the movement, after *Njwiywila*, was the phase of the 'pilgrimages' to Ngarambe. These began in late July or early August 1904. Mzee Ambrose Ngombale tells us that 'it was about the month of July or August 1904 when people began going to partake of *maji*, for it all developed very gradually until 1905 when war broke out.'[34] Pilgrims went to Ngarambe in their respective clans led by their own military veterans. They described themselves not by religious but by military terms. Thus each clan group became a *litapo* (detachment). Merit was the criterion for the choice of *litapo* leaders:

> A leader of a *litapo* was chosen at home. He was the one who was extremely brave, a strongly built and fierce looking man,

one with muscles bulging out. He was very well known. Then on arriving there he (Kinjikitile) asked, 'Where do you come from?' 'We come from such a place.' 'Who is your leader?' 'It is so and so.' Then Kinjikitile took that same leader and confirmed him leader of war in that area. He received very many and much ... better medicine so that he could secure himself better. He received a very large amulet.[35]

The *litapo* groups began to drill during the night they spent at Ngarambe:

Every company came with its own leader chosen from their home. If asked, 'Where are you going?' 'To Kinjikitile's,' they answered. It was like a wedding ceremony, I tell you. People sang, danced and ululated throughout. On arriving they were asked, 'Who is your leader?' ... When they arrived at Ngarambe they slept there. They did *likinda* (military drilling) everyone in his own *litapo*. The following morning they received *dawa* and returned home.[36]

According to a German military officer who conducted operations in Matumbiland and the Kichi hills, the pilgrims went in 'great crowds of people—some of as many as 300 adults.'[37] But as the rains increased it became more and more difficult to travel to Ngarambe and the third and last phase of Kinjikitile's movement began.

In the last phase Kinjikitile 'regionalised' the *maji* movement. He sent out his ambassadors to various centres in the outbreak area. The title of those posted in Kichi and Matumbiland, as well as Ngarambe itself, was *Mpokosi*. Elsewhere they went by their personal names or by the more common title of *jumbe Hongo*, which strictly speaking, belonged to Kinjikitile himself. An informant at Ngarambe outlined the place of these assistants:

Mpokosi or *Wampokosi* were leaders chosen by him himself (Kinjikitile). His

younger brother Njugwemaina was an *Mpokosi* here at Ngarambe and the other one was an Mpogoro called Ling'ang'a. These were not *Wapindo* (clan heads) necessarily.[38]

'These *Wampokosi* were his assistants,' says a Matumbiland authority, 'He despatched them in all directions to spread his teaching ...' He had said, 'But War is not yet. It will come from inland (*bara*) to the coast and from the coast to *bara*. The reason he said that was that he wanted his *Wampokosi* to teach everywhere about the coming war.'[39]

THE OUTBREAK OF THE MAJI MAJI WAR

Thus Kinjikitile had carefully prepared the peoples of the outbreak area for war. His syncretic cult had provided an ideology which met their problems of morale and organisation. But he ordered them not to declare war before he commanded it:

'The Germans will leave,' he said. 'There will definitely be war. But for the time being go and work for him. If he orders you to cultivate cotton or to dig his road or to carry his load do as he requires. Go and remain quiet. When I am ready I will declare the war.'[40]

Kinjikitile presumably hoped to be able to extend his message further afield. But at this point we can see the inadequacies of his movement as well as its strengths. The movement had brought together war bands and their leaders, thereby improving communication and co-ordination. But it had not been able to replace the existing very fragmented military structures with anything more coherent or more directly under Kinjikitile's control. Military initiative lay firmly with the secular war leaders. Moreover, Kinjikitile's movement had greatly improved morale—but in some ways it had improved it too much. The Matumbi were confident, and thus they were impatient. They said to themselves:

> This *Mganga* said he would declare war … Why then is he delaying? When will the Europeans go? After all we have already received the *dawa* and we are brave men. Why should we wait? And yet we continue to dig and clean his roads, carry his loads, grow his cotton and carry bales to Kilwa. And always he continues lashing at us with his *kiboko* on our behind … And yet he was not one of us … he was not our ruler.[41]

In Nandete itself the bitterness ran deep:

> We became full of bitterness. German rule was no rule. It was impossible to wait and live under such torturous rule.[42]

Thus the Matumbi mobilised and declared war against Kinjikitile's instructions. They decided to uproot cotton as a symbol of defiance. It is interesting to note that the three people who uprooted cotton were Ngulumbalyo Mandai and Lindimyo Machela, both celebrated local *waganga*, and the woman over whom each soldier jumped, Nantabila Naupunda. There is no evidence that they were appointed to office by Kinjikitile. In this way, in the last week of July 1905, Maji Maji broke out.

War having broken out, Kinjikitile became the first Maji Maji victim on the German gallows. He was hanged, together with his assistant, on 5 August, 1905. But before he died Kinjikitile declared that his teaching had already spread far. German sources are silent on the circumstances of his capture. From oral authorities we get the following picture. All Ngarambe informants say that Juma Ndembo and Athuman Ndete, both of Mohoro, went to steal offerings made at the *Kijumba-Nungu*. Having cleared the *Kijumba-Nungu* of everything, the two returned to Mohoro where they reported having gone to the residence of 'the man of troubles,' the *mganga*. Then Juma Ndembo guided German agents to the

unsuspecting Kinjikitile. After his arrest and death, his brother, Njugwemaina, assumed command of the administration of *maji* under the title of *Nyamguni*, one of the three divinities at Kibesa.

It is evident that Kinjikitile was in no sense a leader of the war once it had broken out. The Nandete leaders acted independently even of his ambassador in their area. Thus there were two main patterns of leadership in Maji Maji. One pattern was ideological and the other military. Kinjikitile's contribution was to the ideological pattern. He was the source of inspiration for the great uprisings which raged for so many months after his death.

CONCLUSION

Kinjikitile's career was obviously as remarkable as it was short. We may close with an assessment of its essential significance. This did not lie, as we have seen, in an *invention* of the idea of the commands of the divinities mediated through a possessed man, or of the idea of the influence of the ancestors, or of the idea of a war medicine. It lay in his demonstration that these ideas could be combined and above all universalised. It has often been said that the weakness of African traditional religious systems in the face of European pressure was that each was so limited in its area of application. Kinjikitile's importance lies in the attempt he made to overcome this weakness.

This attempt depended in general upon the essential similarities which underlay the different religious systems of southern Tanzania—upon the common notions of 'vital force.' In particular it depended upon the interaction of the specific religious ideas of the outbreak area. Merely to describe Kinjikitile's movement as 'superstitious' misses altogether the significance of his 'universalisation' of these religious ideas.

In the end Kinjikitile's movement went down in the defeat of Maji Maji. The future did not lie with a universalised traditional religion. But his message could be re-interpreted in secular terms. The theme of his teaching was 'unity to regain independence.' The echoes of 'Unity and Freedom' in Tanzania's coat of arms were implicit in Kinjikitile's teaching, and perhaps therein lies the legacy of the *maji* ideology to Tanzanians.[43]

NOTES

1. Cited in G. C. K. Gwassa and John Iliffe *Records of the Maji Maji Rising* (Nairobi 1968) pp. 8–9.

2. A. R. W. Crosse-Upcott, 'The Social Structure of the Ki-Ngindo Speaking Peoples,' unpublished Ph.D. Thesis for the University of Cape Town, 1955, p. 5.

3. Joseph Thomson, 'Notes on the Route taken by the Royal Geographical Society's last East African Expedition from Dar es Salaam to Uhehe, May 19th to August 29th 1879' *Proceedings of the Royal Geographical Society* II (1880) pp. 102–22.

4. William Beardell, 'Exploration of the Rufiji under the Orders of the Sultan of Zanzibar' *PRGS* III (1881) pp. 641–2.

5. Senior-Lieutenant Paasche saw drunken warriors in an engagement at Kipo on the northern bank of the Rufiji. Telegram, Back to Admiral, Berlin, 25 August, 1905 (Deutsches Zentralarchiv, Potsdam: Reichskolonialamt 722/21).

6. Interview with Mzee Ndundule Mangaya, 10 September, 1967, Kipatimu Mission, Matumbi, Kilwa District.

7. Interview with Mzee Mohamed Nganoga Nimekwako, 31 August, 1968, Ngarambe, Kilwa/Utete boundary.

8. Subsequent to Maji Maji, so it is said, the Bokero spirit moved downstream to Kibesa towards the estuary of the Rufiji, where he became Islamicised under the title of Mgambo, and was accounted one of the coastal divinities. There is evidence that a Mgambo shrine was destroyed by a Muslim sheikh on the lower reaches of the Rufiji in 1954. Information from Mr R. A. J. Lwanda, University College, Dar es Salaam, October 1969.

9. Interview with Mzee Omari bin Said Bumbo, 25 October, 1967, Kilingongo, Utete.

10. Clients always declared that they were going to Kolelo's, *kwa Kolelo*, meaning that they were going to approach the divinities at Kibesa through their guardian and medium, Kologelo. In the same way people who went to Ngarambe to receive the message of the spirit Hongo spoke of going to Kinjikitile's. The Rufiji, Matumbi and Ngindo pronounced their 'g' rather faintly so that to an untutored ear it may be taken for a 'w.' Thus Kologelo may have become Kolowelo and eventually Kolelo.

11. Interview with Mzee Mohamed Nganoga Nimekwako (see note 7).

12. Interview with Mzee Mohamed Nganoga Nimekwako (see note 7).

13. Richard Burton *The Lake Regions of Central Africa* (London 1860, reprinted New York 1961) vol. 1, pp. 88–9.

14. Martin Klamroth, 'Beiträge zum Verstädnis der religiösen Vorstellungen der Saramo im Bezirk Dar es Salaam' *Zeitschrift für Kolonialsprachen* I, 1910—11.

15. L. Swantz, 'The Zaramo of Tanzania: An Ethnographic Study,' M.A. Thesis, Syracuse University, 1956, p. 60.

16. Interview with Mzee Juya Dyanhutu, 17 January, 1968, Ruvu, Kisarawe.

17. Interview with Mzee Shuruti, 17 January, 1968, Ruvu, Kisarawe.

18. Carl Velten (ed) *Safari za Wasuaheli* (Göttingen 1901) pp. 172–90; also German translation of above *Schilderungen der Suaheli* (Göttingen 1901) pp. 138–97.

19. Bishop James Komba, 'Uisharisho wa Kingoni,' paper presented to the Swahili Writers' History Workshop, Dar es Salaam, December 1969.

20. Interview with Mzee Mohamed Nganoga Nimekwako.

21. Interview with Mzee Ndundule Mangaya (see note 6).

22. Interview with Mzee Mangaya.

23. Interview with Mzee Mangaya.

24. Interview with Mzee Elisei Simbanimoto Upunda, 4 September, 1967, Nandete, Matumbi.

25. Interview with Abdulrahman Lipunjo Mandwanga, 19 August, 1967, Kibata, Matumbi.

26. Interview with Mzee Ambrose Ngombale Mwiru, 8 August, 1967, Kipatimu Mission, Matumbi. Mzee Mwiru fought on the German side in Maji Maji. He spent over six months in the German stockade at Kibata. He recalls seeing other African supporters of the Germans, who had applied traditional protective medicines, saved by them from death. 'When we were in Kibata I saw two people being shot at and bullets dropping down off their bodies. One of these was *Jumbe* Matenga of Kibata, at whom the Maji Maji soldiers shot twelve bullets but all dropped off him. Another was Nakauka. This one received eight bullets and they all dropped down.'

27. Interview with Bi. Nabulyo Mwiru, 31 August, 1967, Ngarambe.

28. Interview with Mzee Ndundule Mangaya.

29. Cited in Gwassa and Iliffe *op. cit.* p. 9.

30. Interview with Mzee Said Mwingi, 31 August, 1967, Kiboko, Kichi, Utete.

31. Cited in Gwassa and Iliffe *op. cit.* p. 9.

32. Interview with Mzee Nassoro Hassan Kipungo, 14 October, 1967, Makata, Liwale.

33. Cited in Gwassa and Iliffe *op. cit.* pp. 9–10.

34. Interview with Mzee Ambrose Ngombale. This view was confirmed by Mzee Ngapatu Mkupali, 21 September, 1967, Mipoto Chumo, Matumbi. This evidence shows that Bell and other authorities on Maji Maji are mistaken in thinking that people only began to go to Ngarambe in 1905.

35. Interview with Mzee Ndundule Mangaya.

36. Interview with Mzee Mohamed Nganoga Nimekwako.

37. Moritz Werjer, 'Uber die Aufstandsbewegung in Deutsch-Ostafrika' *Militä r-Wochenblatt* 91 (1906) 1922–3.

38. Interview with Mzee Nimekwako.

39. Interview with Mzee Mangaya. Oral evidence tells us much of the activity of the *Mpokosi*. Bwana Sebastian Upundu, whose father fought in Maji Maji, tells how the *Mpokosi* at Kitumbi Hill taught military drill and strict discipline. In some areas these representatives of Kinjikitile came to enjoy much prestige on their own account. In Liwale, for instance, the *Mpokosi* Ngameya is often confused with Kinjikitile himself. Stories are told about Ngameya which involve a descent into a pool and other events based on Kinjikitile's career. But it is plain that Ngameya was an ambassador of Kinjikitile rather than a distinct religious leader.

40. Cited in Gwassa and Iliffe *op. cit.* p. 12. This account shows that those authorities who argue that the Maji Maji revolt broke out more or less spontaneously in 1905 are incorrect. The rising had been carefully prepared for many months before the outbreak.

41. Cited in Gwassa and Iliffe *op. cit.* p. 12.

42. Interview with Mzee Kibilange Upundu, 22 October, 1968, Nandete, Matumbi. Also with Mzee Nduli Njimbwi, 23 October, 1967, Kipatimu, Matumbi.

43. This study is based on four years of research on 'The Outbreak and Development of the Maji Maji War, 1905–1907,' the results of which will be submitted in 1971 for the doctoral degree of the University of Dar es Salaam. Much of the information used comes from oral interviews in the outbreak area. There has been no attempt made here to present a narrative of Maji Maji or to discuss the many other issues raised by an examination of the rising. These matters are fully discussed in my doctoral dissertation. Meanwhile readers are recommended to consult: Graf von Götzen *Deutsch-Ostafrika in Aufstand 1905/06* (Berlin 1909); R. M. Bell, 'The Maji Maji Rebellion in Liwale District' *Tanganyika Notes and Records* 28 January, 1950; John Iliffe, 'The Organisation of the Maji Maji Rebellion' *Journal of African History* VIII, 3, 1967; and G. C. W. Gwassa and John Iliffe *op. cit.* The writer is deeply indebted to Bishop James Komba for a valuable discussion on Bantu symbolism.

CONSOLIDATION OF COLONIAL RULE

THE CONSOLIDATION OF EUROPEAN RULE, 1885–1914

By Felix K. Ekechi

The European scramble to colonize Africa culminated in the Berlin West African Conference of 1884–85. This conference, which was called by the German leader, Bismarck, set up the parameters for the partition of Africa. The Berlin Conference was summoned to discuss the issue of free navigation along the Niger and Congo rivers, as well as to settle new claims to the African coasts. In the end, the European Powers signed the Berlin Act (Treaty), which set the rules for the European occupation of African territories. It stated, among other things, that a European's claim to any part of Africa would only be recognized if it was "effectively occupied." In essence, the Berlin Conference set the stage for the European military invasion and conquest of the African continent. Thus, in the critical years, 1885–1914, Africa experienced the trauma of invasion, conquest, and European colonial domination. With the exception of Ethiopia (in the northeast) and Liberia (in the west), the entire continent came under European colonial rule. The major powers were Britain, France, Germany, Belgium, Italy and Portugal. For all practical purposes, the story of Africa from the Berlin Conference to c. 1914, revolves around these five major themes: the establishment of European colonies, the consolidation of political authority, the development of the colonial estate through forced labor, the cultural and economic transformation of Africa, and African resistance. Basil Davidson, a popular British writer on Africa, has aptly described the colonial period as "a prolonged interlude of destructive subjection and foreign occupation [of Africa], whose main achievement was not to carry Africa into a new world [of progress] but merely to complete the dismantlement of the old [order]."[1] The dismantling of the old order included, of course, the loss of political independence and sovereignty, the radical transformation of the traditional economy, as well as the society. The colonial period marks, therefore, a revolutionary era in which African institutions and cultural practices were fundamentally altered and undermined.

* * *

EUROPEAN PENETRATION AND AFRICAN RESISTANCE

To begin, it should be noted that the "effective occupation" clause in the Berlin Treaty (1885) gave Europe a blank check to use military force to occupy African territories. Thus the years 1885–1914 were years of European conquests and amalgamations of pre-colonial states and societies into new states. However, the European imperialists continued to pursue earlier treaty making processes, whereby African territories became European protectorates.

In other words, there was a "loaded pause" before the eventual European military occupation of Africa. Because these protectorate treaties posed serious challenges to African independence, most African rulers naturally rejected them. In West Africa, for instance, Asantehene Prempe II, the King of Asante, was firmly resolved not to submit to British protection. Instead, he maintained the integrity of Asante "as of old." When pressured in 1891 to sign a protection treaty, which implied British control of Asante, Prempe firmly and confidently rejected the idea, stating to the British envoy:

> The suggestion that Asante in its present state should come and enjoy the protection of Her Majesty the Queen and Empress of India, is a matter of very serious consideration, and ... I am happy to say we have arrived at this conclusion, that my Kingdom of Asante will never commit itself to any such policy. Asante must remain [independent] as of old[2]...

Similarly, in modern Tanzania, King Machemba rejected German entreaties to bring his kingdom under German control. His self-confidence is clearly reflected in his defiant reply to the German envoy Hermann von Wissemann in 1890, "I have listened to your words but can find no reason why I should obey you—I would rather die first. ... If it should be friendship that you desire, then I am ready for it, today and always; but to be your subject, that I cannot be. ... If it should be war you desire, then I am ... ready, but never to be your subject. ..."[3] Also in Namibia, the Nama leader Hendrick Witbooi, warned his Herero antagonist Chief Maherero against forging an alliance with the Germans. To Chief Maherero, he wrote:

> You think you will retain your independent Chieftainship after I have been destroyed ... but my dear Kaptein you will eternally regret your action in having handed over to the White man the right to govern your country. ... But this thing you have done, to surrender yourself to the Government of the White man, will be a burden that you will carry on your shoulders. You call yourself Supreme Chief, but when you are under another's control you are merely a subordinate Chief.[4]

Clearly, African rulers adopted a negative stance towards European attempts to occupy their states and kingdoms. Their strategies to forestall European occupation included recourse to diplomacy, alliance and, above all, military confrontation. Where alliances were struck between the African leaders and the imperialist powers, as in the above quotation, it should be emphasized that the Africans did so in an attempt to enhance their commercial and/or diplomatic advantages. Thus, for instance, the king of Daboya in northern Ghana (West Africa), who signed a treaty of friendship with the British in 1892, did so with the hope of attracting British trade. "Tell my friend, the Governor of Accra," Daboya told the British representative, "I like my country to be quiet and secure; I want to keep off all my enemies and none to be able to stand before me. ... Let plenty guns, flint, powder and cloth, and every kind of cost goods be sent here for sale."[5] In essence, the king did not sign away his independence.

In Nigeria, King Jaja of Opobo resorted to diplomacy as a means of resistance to European intrusive imperialism. A former slave of Igbo origin, Jaja was elected as the king of the Anna Pepple House in Bonny, in the Niger Delta, in 1863. This election followed the death of his master, Alali, in 1861. But struggle for power between the Anna Pepple House and the Manilla Pepple House, under the leadership of Oko Jumbo, led to the outbreak of civil war in Bonny in 1869. The civil war resulted in King Jaja's migration and the founding of an inland kingdom of Opobo, which lay in the palm oil producing hinterland. Jaja, an avowed nationalist, was determined to control the trade in his political domain. He was also determined to prevent European incursions into the interior, which would invariably disrupt the economic organization on the Niger Delta. Essentially, his ambition was to maintain full control of the palm oil trade. More specifically, Jaja wanted to ensure that Opobo oil markets remained outside the sphere of foreign traders. To this end, he signed a trade treaty with the British Government in 1873. Part of the treaty reads as follows:

> After April 5, 1873, the King of Opobo shall allow no trade establishment or hulk in or off Opobo Town, or any trading vessels to come higher up the river than the whiteman's beach opposite Hippopotamus Creek. If any trading ship or steamer proceeds further up the river than the creek above mentioned, after having been fully warned to the contrary, the said trading ship or steamer may be seized by King Jaja, and detained until a fine of 100 puncheons [of palm oil] be paid by the owners to King Jaja.[6]

By this treaty, the British formally acknowledged Jaja as the king of Opobo, and also as the dominant middleman in the Niger Delta trade. However, the ensuing Scramble of the 1880s upset this understanding, as British merchants and officials were no longer in the mood to respect Jaja's preeminence in the Niger Delta hinterland. Instead, by penetrating the hinterland they sought to open free trade in Opobo and elsewhere, making confrontation with Jaja inevitable.

King Jaja's response to the British about-face was unequivocal. He was not only determined to control the hinterland trade, but he also sought to export palm oil directly to Europe. In the process, he sought to bypass the African Merchants Association, a British commercial organization that monopolized the palm oil export trade in the Niger Delta. To this end, Jaja appointed a Scottish merchant, Alexander Miller, as his agent. Through him the palm oil would be sold directly in Europe. But this was not to be. For just as Jaja was determined to maintain control of palm oil trade, as well as to preserve the political integrity of his kingdom of Opobo, so also were the British determined to trade directly in the interior. Indeed, as a matter of policy, the British supported their nationals in matters of

trade. Said the British consul Wylde: "Wherever there is money to be made, our merchants will be certain to intrude themselves, and … public opinion in this country practically compels us to protect them."[7] Consequently, as British merchants aggressively intruded into King Jaja's political domain, conflict ensued. Ultimately, King Jaja was ruined. In 1887, the British consul Harry Johnston cunningly enticed Jaja to a British gunboat for discussions but then exiled him to the West Indies, where Jaja died, in 1891. But even at death, Jaja continued to be remembered. A monument erected in his honor at Opobo reads, in part:

> A King in title and in deed
> Always just and ever generous
> Respected and revered in life
> Lamented and mourned by all when dead.[8]

Obviously Jaja's diplomatic resistance failed. Yet other African rulers adopted other strategies, largely military confrontation, to resist European encroachments. In West Africa, rulers like Samori Toure of the Mandinka, in modern Guinea, fought the French for about sixteen years (1882–1898) before he was finally defeated and exiled. Samori was an Islamic reformer, a nationalist to the core, and an outstanding African military leader and strategist. He used both guerilla warfare and scorch-earth policy to harass the French. Besides, he had his own well-trained, professional cavalry (sofas), an ammunitions industry, as well as an abundant supply of gold with which he was able to buy arms and ammunition. Sadly, in 1898, Samori was captured by the French and exiled to Gabon, where he died. To contemporary West Africans, Samori was the quintessential African nationalist and one of the most illustrious military leaders of the age. Many even saw him as "the Napoleon of West Africa." Nationalist newspaper editorials held him in high regard, no matter what opinion the outside world held of him. The Nigerian *Lagos Weekly Record* stated: "no matter how much effort may be put forth to detract from the renown which belongs to him, the intelligent African will always regard Chief

Samadu [Samori] as one of the ablest of Negro generals and rulers [in modern history]."[9] And there were, of course, other resistors. For example, King Behanzin of Dahomey, who prided himself as the "shark of sharks," courageously fought the French for four years (1890–94). Dahomey was, without question, the strongest state in West Africa in the nineteenth century. But it constituted an obstacle to the French economic interests in the hinterland. For the French, Dahomey was the gateway to the rich palm oil hinterland. Egged on by the nationalist press, the French committed huge military and financial resources to the Dahomean military campaign. By the end of the war, France had spent about 27 million francs and committed over 4,000 men to the military expedition. Indeed, between 1890 and 1894 war raged, and Dahomey was ultimately defeated. King Behanzin was captured and exiled to Martinique, West Indies. He died in exile at Blinda, in 1906, but his remains were brought back to Dahomey in 1928. With the fall of Dahomey, the French then colonized the palm oil rich Dahomean hinterland as well.[10]

While the focus so far has been on centralized states, decentralized societies, where there were no paramount rulers, equally resisted European penetration. Indeed, both the British and the French found segmentary or decentralized societies particularly difficult to subdue. The Baule of the Ivory Coast and the Tiv and the Igbo of Nigeria were among the African peoples that most stiffly resisted colonial occupation. The Baule, for example, fought the French from 1891 to 1911 and beyond, while the Tiv fought the British from about 1900–1930s. The Igbo resistance to British imperial pretensions, as in the case of the Baule and the Tiv, was particularly widespread and prolonged. Because of the nature of their society, which is characteristically egalitarian in its social ethos and republican in political structure, the British found it extremely difficult to subjugate them. In fact, the British had literally to fight its way from Igbo village to village and from town to town before it could finally declare its imperial authority over the people. Even then, British authority remained precarious well into the Nigerian independence in 1960.

The Igbo were hostile to British imperial encroachments from the start, as was clearly revealed in their refusal even to parley with British officials. The elders challenged British imperial pretensions and even invited the British to "come and fight": "If you want war, come, we are ready."[11] The British, of course, came and war raged from about 1898 to after 1910. The Anglo-Igbo confrontation can be separated into the western phase (1898–1905) and the eastern phase (1901–1910).

The war on the "western front" (i.e. west of the River Niger), directly involved a secret society known as the Ekumeku Society. This nocturnal society attacked the Roman Catholic missions, which had been established in the area since the early 1880s, and also waged a guerilla war against the British colonial forces. Of the numerous military encounters, the battle of Ubulu-Ukwu in 1905, seems to have been the fiercest. Because of Ubulu Ukwu's strategic location, the British considered its capture particularly crucial. Of this war, Don Ohadike writes:

> The Ekumeku warriors assembled at Ubulu-Ukwu [and] began to make war preparations. ... There were hot exchanges on all fronts as the [British] soldiers fought to gain entrance into the town. Ekumeku riflemen occupied the natural and artificial trenches they had dug on the eastern approaches of Ubulu-Ukwu, from where they kept up a brisk fire and were able to move rapidly through the bush from one point to another. ... The colonial forces were strained to their limit not only because of the skill of the military operations of the Ekumeku, but also because of logistics. [In large measure,] the colonial troops were disturbed by the fact that they fought an enemy they could not see, [given that the Ekumeku warriors fought a brilliant guerilla war].[12]

Despite Ekumeku successes, British colonial forces ultimately triumphed, resulting in the suppression of the Ekumeku movement and the consolidation of British power and authority in Western Igboland. As punishment, "All the towns that took part in the uprising were made to pay heavy fines and to surrender their guns. Many were compelled to rebuild the mission and government houses that had been destroyed during the war."[13]

On the eastern front, that is, eastern Nigeria, the British also fought a most determined people, who, like their western Igbo counterparts, sought to maintain their independence and to preserve their traditional way of life. The British sought to take control of the rich eastern Nigerian hinterland, the richest region of palm oil production in Nigeria. Before they could gain access to this rich hinterland, however, they had first to deal with the Aro of Arochukwu. Through their manipulation of the most powerful Igbo oracle known as *Chukwu*, the Aro had established considerable commercial and religious influence in the region. However, the British objective was to eliminate the Arochukwu Oracle, known to the Europeans as the "Long-Juju" of Arochukwu, so they could operate freely in the region. Even the Christian missionaries, as elsewhere, supported the military invasion, ostensibly in the name of "Christian civilization." In the words of the Roman Catholic Superior, "This war is necessary. It is necessary to abolish slavery, human sacrifices, twin murder … and to destroy the Long Juju of Aro Chuku. … Were it not the duty of European powers to prevent even by force such murders?"[14] Accordingly, the famous Arochukwu expedition was launched on December 1, 1901 and ended on March 24, 1902.

Armed with rifles and a variety of guns, the Igbo and their neighbors stoutly resisted British attempts to take over their country. As the British officers ruefully acknowledged, "the enemy, who occupied strategic positions in the bush and in trenches, attacked from all sides." But in spite of the stiff resistance, the British ultimately triumphed. The Arochukwu Oracle was destroyed and many of its priests were either executed or sent to prison. Indeed, the British conquest of the Aro was cause for jubilation among the Christian missions because the expedition resulted in throwing open the hitherto closed doors of the Igbo hinterland to missionary enterprise. The expedition, also "opened up" eastern Nigeria to British imperialism. What followed was colonial resistance.

In East and Central Africa, the story was similar: conquest and resistance predominated. In Southern Rhodesia (now Zimbabwe), it was the British South African Company, under the control of the imperialist megalomaniac Cecil Rhodes, that waged war against King Lobengula, ruler of the Ndebele kingdom. Rhodes' forces, known as the "Pioneer Column", invaded the kingdom in 1890. From that time on, white settlers gained dominance, politically and economically. The colonial exploitation and extortion, which followed, gave rise to the famous Ndebele and Shona Rebellion (Chimarunga War) of 1896–97. Virtually everywhere, Africans were subjugated, largely because of the European possession of superior firearms, such as the Maxim gun. Even the Africans acknowledged the superiority of European technology. "He who possesses the Maxim wins the war," conceded the King of Dahomey. A Senegalese elder concurred: The French "got their power from their cannon, [which] enabled them to dominate the people here."[15]

But the Ethiopian defeat of Italy provides a classic example of a successful African resistance to European imperialism. Like other Europeans during the Scramble, the Italians sought to stake out territories in Ethiopia by making treaties with Ethiopian rulers. They claimed, in 1891, that Emperor Menelik II had ceded a part of Ethiopian territory to them by the Treaty of Wuchale, signed on May 2, 1889. But this was contested. Reminded by his wife, Empress Taytu, of the supreme price that his predecessors had paid in defense of Ethiopian land, Emperor Menelik firmly intimated to the Italians that "[This] country is mine and no other nation can have it." He accordingly annulled the Treaty and with some trepidation braced himself for war. "Not only do I dread this war, but the thought of shedding Christian blood also saddens me."[16] The Ethiopian-Italian war, which broke out in 1895, resulted in the defeat of the Italian forces at the historic battle of Adowa in 1896, signifying a momentous event for the African resistance. "The victory was a tremendous life for the Ethiopians. Fear of the white man's invincibility was [forever] laid to rest."[17] But virtually everywhere else, as already indicated, the Europeans were triumphant.

COLONIAL RULE AND SOCIO-POLITICAL CHANGE

In establishing of colonial rule with its far-reaching changes, Africa was radically and fundamentally transformed. In some places such as Algeria, Kenya, Southern Rhodesia (Zimbabwe), European settlers occupied the best lands and hoarded the indigenous inhabitants into unproductive reserves. In Algeria, the settlers (*colons*), who called themselves *pieds noirs*, dominated both the politics and the economy. In Kenya, too, the white settlers claimed title to the "White Man's Country," appropriating the best land, the Kenya Highlands, as theirs. By the 1950s, the "stolen land" question led to the famous Mau Mau Rebellion. The introduction of new administrative systems almost certainly obliterated indigenous African systems of government.

Demographically, "[p]eoples and groups were [arbitrarily] partitioned by competing European countries. New countries were formed, with new boundaries to replace the pre-colonial states."[18] Almost everywhere, European conquest heralded the fusion of pre-colonial states and societies into new colonial states, such as Nigeria, Kenya, Ghana, Zimbabwe, to name but a few. Because of the arbitrary redrawing of pre-colonial boundaries, ethnic groups such as the Ewe of modern Ghana were disrupted, resulting in the location of the same ethnic group in different colonial states. Today, the Ewe are found in Ghana and Togo in West Africa. The same is true of the Somali in northeast Africa, whose inhabitants are today located in Somalia, Kenya, and Ethiopia. Indeed, European colonial presence marked a revolutionary period in African historical experience. The forced unity, brought about by the artificial creation of colonial states, has been the bane of modern African politics. In short, the persistent "nationality" problems in contemporary African societies stem from colonial state structures. Oliver and Atmore put it succinctly:

> The very basis of nationality, to which all states laid claim [at independence], was nothing but a colonial superstructure hastily erected over very diverse populations still speaking many different languages, in which only a small minority of the best-educated people had any strong sense of an allegiance wider than the ethnic group.[19]

Economically, pre-colonial Africa was fundamentally restructured to suit European interests, whose major focus was on the exploitation of human and natural resources. Indeed, forced labor and human degradation became the essential components for developing the colonial estate.

Practically all colonial administrations operated under the colonial hierarchy dominated by colonial Governors (*Commandant de Cercle* in the French colonies), Residents (as in British colonies), and District Commissioners (DCs). Because the number of Europeans was so small, the colonial regimes actually found it much cheaper to employ Africans rather than Europeans. In fact, the African presence allowed the administrative systems to function. Africans, for example, served as soldiers, police officers, court messengers and clerks, as well as chiefs, interpreters and so on. African armies were not only involved in the colonial conquests, but they also generally "provided the coercive force that made European rule in Africa possible."[20] In most cases, they were used for the maintenance of "law and order." In addition, the rank and file of the European regiments, such as the British King's African Rifles (KAR) in East Africa, the Royal West African Frontier Force (RWAFF) in West Africa, the French *Tirailleurs Senegalais* (Senegalese Army), or the Belgian *Force Publique* in the Congo, were essentially Africans. In the era of almost interminable military operations, euphemistically called "pacification," African soldiers were routinely sent to "pacify" recalcitrant towns and villages.

Indeed, all colonial administrative systems gave orders through some African intermediaries, including the colonial chiefs. These chiefs recruited labor and collected taxes. They also heard cases in the native courts, set up by the colonial administrations. Chiefs, therefore, played important roles in the working of the new colonial society. But because most of them were corrupt and exploitative, as well as tyrannical, they were almost uniformly resented and hated. The colonial regimes' aim was to "control the African populations, either directly through their appointed officials or indirectly through the existing African authorities."[21] This system of administration, known as indirect rule, was popularized by the British but adopted by almost all the colonial administrations. Hence, the ubiquitous colonial chiefs through whom government orders filtered down to the local people.

FORCED LABOR

The establishment of colonial rule heralded the era of forced labor. Practically everywhere, Africans were forced to work. Failure to comply with labor requirements generally resulted in severe punishments, such as being flogged publicly, or being incarcerated in prison for any length of time. Many Africans died in colonial prisons. As a matter of fact, being sent to prison in the early colonial times was almost tantamount to being condemned to death. In desperation, Africans at times killed the colonial oppressors, as was the case of one Crewe Read and Dr. Stewart, both officers in Nigeria. Indeed, other than taxation, no colonial exaction proved as vexing as forced labor. From the onset of European colonial administration, up to the Second World War, Africans were faced with endless demands for labor. Colonial labor laws made it possible for officials to force Africans to work, even without pay. For instance, the Rivers and Roads Proclamation (Ordinance)

empowered District Commissioners (DCs) to compel able-bodied men and women to work. These Africans were compelled to build roads and railways, clear rivers for ship and boat transportation, construct government houses, military and police barracks, and so on. To insure an ample labor force, the European officials held African elders to ransom. A missionary's eyewitness account of German practices states, "An assistant district officer summoned a large meeting of elders. Eight hundred attended. After business an order was issued that none would go unless a young man came in [the] place [of each elder] ready to start for the coast plantations."[22] Under the compulsory labor regulations, those who resisted recruitment or who deserted were severely punished. Roadwork, a hard and backbreaking labor, was particularly hated, essentially because it denied Africans their basic freedoms. Besides, it left an enduring mark on "the laboring poor Africans," who grew old prematurely because of extremely hard work. Indeed, to most Africans, forced labor was pure "hell" on earth.

Africans were also forced to produce and deliver commodities such as palm oil, cotton, groundnuts (peanuts), tea, rubber, and so on to the European commercial stations. In the white settler areas like Algeria, Kenya, Northern and Southern Rhodesia (Zambia and Zimbabwe respectively), as well as South Africa, Angola and Mozambique, the Compulsory Service laws or regulations empowered the colonial authorities to compel Africans to work in the European settler plantations and mines. In fact, imperial decisions to allow forced labor continued well into the World War II and beyond, with African chiefs entrusted with the recruitment of labor. In many instances, these chiefs had to meet assigned quotas, or face severe punishments, including removal from office. Men, women, and children in the Belgian Congo were forced to collect rubber from the wild rubber trees of the forest. And even though they were not paid for this, those who failed to comply had their hands cut off to teach them and others "a sharp lesson"! Many were also massacred, as contemporary and historical accounts reveal. In *The Crime of the Congo*, for example, the British writer and creator of Sherlock Holmes stories, Sir Arthur Conan Doyle (1859–1930), provides this ugly portrait of the Belgians:

> There are many of us in England who consider the crime which has been wrought in the Congo lands by King Leopold of Belgium and his followers to be the greatest which has ever been known in human annals. ... There have been massacres of populations [elsewhere]. ... But never before has there been such a mixture of wholesale expropriation and wholesale massacre all done under an odious guise of philanthropy and with the lowest commercial motives as a reason. It is this sordid cause and the unctuous hypocrisy which makes this crime unparalleled in its horror.[23]

To add to the ordeal, Africans were compelled to carry loads for government officials, the military, as well as for the Christian missionaries. Africans even had to carry District Commissioners (DC) and missionaries in hammocks during their travels! It was commonplace for Africans to carry heavy loads to far away places, and thereby expose themselves to the dangers of life and limb. To the colonial administration, however, the carrier or porterage system seemed inevitable. As a British governor in Nigeria argued, "Where there are no other means of transportation, the natives must be utilized for the purpose of transport." He went on: "It must never be overlooked that the Government cannot go on without it, the people cannot even be fed without it. It is the basis of the whole life of the country."[24] African experiences with the carrier system may be appreciated from the poignant words of a Nigerian elder, who himself was a victim of forced labor:

> The loads were heavy. And we traveled for many, many miles without food or rest. On many occasions we, the carriers,

decided to stop and rest or to find something to eat. Often, however, this brought instant harassment from the soldiers or the DC, or the overseer. My son, remember we traveled through unfamiliar places and many of us were deeply concerned about our safety. So, apart from the bad treatment from the officers, fear of losing our lives weighed heavily on our minds. This is why we often dropped the loads, escaped into the bush and returned home. But if you were caught, that was the end of your life.[25]

In the European settler areas, Africans had to work for the government as well as for the settlers. In the Portuguese colonies of Angola and Mozambique, Africans were subjected to forced labor as a matter of policy. In the words of a Portuguese official, "The rendering of work in Africa cannot continue to depend upon the whim of the Negro, who is, by temperament and natural circumstances, inclined to spend only the minimum effort necessary to meet his basic needs." Therefore, whenever a private European farmer or labor recruiter, or even a company needed African labor, all they had to do was simply contact the colonial administrators, and the request was promptly met. Similarly, in Kenya:

> ... a settler who wanted labour for his farm would write to the DC saying he required thirty young men, women or girls for work on his farm. The DC [thereupon] sent a letter to a chief or headman to supply such and such a number, and the chief in turn had his ... retainers to carry out the business. They would simply go to the people's houses—very often where there were beautiful women and daughters—and point out which were to come to work. Sometimes they had to work a distance from home, and the number of girls who got pregnant in this way was very great.[26]

A Protestant missionary in Kenya further commented on the ordeal of forced labor:

> I was in a village a few weeks back, when a poor man just dragged himself in and threw himself down exhausted. I could see he was ill, and gave him some medicine. He had stopped there to rest, and was just off ten days' work ... some miles away from home, and ill possibly part of the time without enough to eat, as when they are on the work of that kind. ... The poor man did not recover; in five days he was dead. ... When I asked the other man with him: "Why did not the sick man tell the overseer of the road he was sick?" the reply was: "If we say we are sick, they say we are telling lies [or are lazy], and beat us back to work; it is better to go as long as we can."[27]

Accounts of the horrors of forced labor abound. In Mozambique and Angola, the Portuguese were particularly exploitative. They not only forced Africans to cultivate cotton, rice, sugar, and other cash crops, but they also claimed lands belonging to the Africans. Land alienation meant limited amount of lands available to the indigenous to grow staple food crops. Hence the frequent famines in the colonies. Equally disturbing is the brutality that accompanied forced labor. A Mozambican elder recounted his experience to an American scholar as follows:

> I was in my village at Nawana quite ill. The *sipais* [labor recruiters] entered my hut and beat me because I had not completed planting my cotton field. One raped my wife. Then I was bound and taken with other villagers to Nangoro [sisal plantation] where I was given a strip of land to work each day. Because I was still sick I could not finish, so the overseers beat me. At Nakoro we only received food once a day and only if we completed our task. ... On occasion they gave us corn with a bit

of dried fish but it was never enough to go round. Many workers died.[28]

To this day, memories of forced labor continue to linger in people's minds, most of which are now expressed in popular songs.

TAXATION, FORCED LABOR, AND REVOLTS

Taxation and forced labor were inextricably linked because taxation was an important instrument for the recruitment of labor. Listen to this policy statement by the governor of Kenya: "We consider that taxation is the only possible method of compelling the native to leave his reserve for the purpose of seeking work ... and it is on this that the supply of labour and price of labor depends."[29] Accordingly, whenever the Africans showed any reluctance to turn up for work on the settler farms, taxes were not only imposed, they were often increased to force Africans to work. The constant raising of taxes, as well as the imposition of pass laws, which meant Africans had to carry identity cards (*kipande*), led to the nationalist protests spearheaded by Harry Thuku, in the 1920s. Predictably, his protests led to his arrest and incarceration in a Nairobi prison in 1922. Attempts by Kikuyu women to rescue him proved futile. Sadly, British forces fired at the unarmed women, fatally shooting some. Among them was Mary Nyanjiru, who has now become a symbol of nationalist resistance to British colonial rule in Kenya.

Taxation served many functions, in addition to raising revenue. It was used as an instrument of political control. As a British official in Nigeria conceded, "to pay tax is to admit the overlordship of the person to whom it is paid." In that regard, he considered taxation to be "a most useful means of asserting and augmenting [our] authority" over colonized peoples. "Where it is absent," he insisted, "the people have that much more excuse for attempting to flout the Government."[30] In essence, taxation was an expeditious means of consolidating European power in Africa. While it was hated virtually everywhere by Africans, colonial governors had no qualms about imposing it. Frederick Lugard (later Lord), the former Governor General of Nigeria (1914–22), justified the imposition of direct taxes on the people of the Southern Provinces on grounds of revenue derivation. In 1914, he explained it to the Colonial Office in London:

> Recent events in Europe have completely altered the outlook [of the economy] and it may be that the institution of direct taxation will be necessary … to enforce revenue. [Furthermore] I anticipate a very serious shortage of imports and exports for some time to come which will decrease the revenue both from customs and railway freights. In the circumstances it may be imperative to augment the revenue by direct taxes.

Initially, the Colonial Office demurred, largely because of fear of possible revolts in time of war. Therefore, Lugard was instructed to shelve his "ridiculous suggestion," at least "for the present time."[31]

Years later, direct taxes were introduced in Southeastern Nigeria. The imposition was explained in terms of laying the foundation for "the political education of the people," but this exploitative mechanism invariably led to "worries of the heart." Indeed, said a Dahomean elder ruefully, "I can't sleep for thinking of the taxes; if I am put in prison [for non-payment] what will happen to my children?

> [The French] force us to make roads and don't pay us; they don't give us any time to make up; what can I do?"[32] Hatred of colonial taxation was so widespread that it was often greeted with revolts. Perhaps the most celebrated tax revolt of the twentieth century was the women's revolt in eastern Nigeria, known popularly as the Women's War. This revolt, which occurred in 1929, was triggered by the rumor that the British administration was about to

tax women just as the men. So at Aba, in eastern Nigeria, women revolted *en masse* against Chief Okugo, who was entrusted with the compilation of the tax rolls. They attacked British facilities, including government houses, native courts, prisons, factories and so on. As the revolt spread, the British administration responded by sending soldiers to quell the disturbances. In the ensuing conflict, British soldiers killed over 50 women and wounded several others. By 1930, the revolt was all over, but a new era of reforms dawned. Eventually, the women's war forced the British to reexamine the indirect rule system, leading to its collapse in Eastern Nigeria and beyond.

THE INTRODUCTION OF EUROPEAN CURRENCY

Taxes were paid in European currencies. This introduction of foreign currencies served as a practical method of consolidating European power and control, and implied the elimination of African currencies. Prior to the 1900s, Africans traded with a variety of currencies, notably cowrie shells, nzimbu shells, nji, manillas, iron rods, copper, and so on. With the advent of colonialism, all these currencies were replaced with European currencies. In effect, only the new European coins and paper money became the accepted legal tender.

For purposes of illustration of the way the currency revolution transformed African economy and African economic life, let me provide a brief history of the currency revolution in Eastern Nigeria. Although the currency revolution had begun in Western Nigeria as far back as the late nineteenth century, it was not until the Arochukwu expedition (1901–02) that both silver coins and currency notes were first introduced in Eastern Nigeria. The commander of the expedition explained how silver coins were first introduced:

[During the war] every column carried cash with it; and all towns who were not hostile and who were called upon to supply food to the troops, were paid for the same in cash. By this means quite a considerable amount of money was distributed throughout the country. ... On the termination of the operations the permanent garrisons ... had about four months pay to them, which they received in cash; consequently after the next few weeks there will be quite a large amount of cash in circulation in the new territories.[33]

The new coins, as well as the currency notes that came later were unpopular. African market women, in particular, would not touch them. Instead of advancing trade, the new currency actually hindered it, in the beginning. In fact, both British merchants and colonial administrators lamented the rejection of the new currency notes: "Currency Notes will not be received by the average native attending the market," reported the District Officer of Owerri District. Agents of the United African Company (UAC) also lamented the decline of trade resulting from the unpopularity of the currency notes.

It was not until the early 1920s that both the silver coins and the currency notes were finally accepted, but only because of the use of force. "By the Currency Ordinance of 1918 Africans who resisted the new notes were liable for prosecution."[34] At any event, economic historians seem to agree eventually that the currency revolution marked a progressive step towards modern commercial expansion because it facilitated trade and led to a remarkable increase in "the number and variety of possible transactions," including modern banking transactions.[35]

SPIRIT MEDIUMS, RESISTANCE TO COLONIAL RULE, AND PACIFICATION

African resistance to European imperialism was widespread and prolonged. Indeed, "primary resistance" movements dotted the African landscape from the onset of colonial rule, unleashing a new wave of European violence, euphemistically termed "pacification." Colonial forces were generally mobilized to maintain law and order. In almost every case, the soldiers became armies of occupation, resulting in predictable bloodshed and loss of life. In fact, military occupation became standard practice, and was considered by the Belgians as "one of the best ways of preventing any idea of revolt, [or] of making the natives carry out their legal duties, and of keeping up habits of work among them." The British adopted a similar tactic. "Where a town refuses to submit to Government control or supervision," declared the governor, "it is our policy ... to occupy it ... until the chiefs and people have been made thoroughly to understand that Government laws must be obeyed."[36] Joseph Chamberlain, the British Colonial Secretary, while admitting that military force entailed the loss of "native life" and the destruction of property, nevertheless endorsed its use as a means of attaining colonial objectives. As he bluntly stated, "you cannot have omelettes without breaking eggs."[37] Thus control through coercion became a characteristic feature of European rule in Africa.

Africans, of course, adopted several methods of resistance against forced labor and other forms of colonial oppression. Often spirit mediums played an important role in the African resistance movements. In many places, resistance was mediated through oracular powers or through the use of medicines believed to work magic. In their desperate efforts to drive out the hated imperialists from the land, Africans occasionally resorted to supernatural forces or divine intervention. In the case of Southern Rhodesia (Zimbabwe), for instance, spirit mediums played a crucial role during the Chamuranga War of 1896–97. Also, in Tanzania, spirit mediums featured prominently in the revolt against the Germans. Here, the Maji Maji Rebellion (1905–1907) was directed against German oppressive forced labor policy. In preparation for war, a priestess concocted a medicinal potion, which the warriors drank. This medicine, believed to render the warriors immune to bullets, was supposed to turn the German bullets into water. But sadly, German guns pulverized the local population. By 1907, therefore, the Germans had succeeded in brutally and ruthlessly suppressing the rebellion. Yet, the war was not a total failure, for the Germans were forced to introduce reforms.[38]

Similarly in German Southwest Africa (Namibia), the Herero were up in arms. As in the Tanzanian case, the Herero-German war (1904–07) arose from labor recruitment problems. In this case, Prophet Stuurman, claiming to have been sent by God to drive out all whites from Africa, spread the millenarian message that the time had come for the Herero to fight a war of liberation. He said that, God had taken power from white men throughout the world, and that blacks would "inherit the land" after the war. The Germans, who remained, would become servants, a reversal of roles. But the revolt failed to dislodge the Germans. On the contrary, the war resulted in unspeakable horror and brutality. "Herero society, as it had existed prior to 1904, had been completely destroyed" and many were either killed or lynched. The majority of those who survived were women and children who were incarcerated in prison camps and made to work as forced laborers for the German military and settlers. Worse still, "German authorities set up concentration camps in which they placed their prisoners. … The inmates of these camps were distributed, as forced labourers, among various settlers, businesses and military units." In addition, Herero women were raped with reckless abandon.[39] A missionary provided this eyewitness account:

> When … [I] arrived in Swakopmund [one of the prison camps] in 1905 there were very few Herero present. Shortly thereafter, vast transports of prisoners of war arrived. They were placed behind double rows of barbed wire fencing, which surrounded all the buildings of the harbour department quarters … and housed in pathetic … structures … in such a manner that in one structure 30 to 50 people were forced to stay without distinction as to age and sex.

> From every morning until late at night, on weekends as well as on Sundays, they had to work under the clubs of raw overseers … until they broke down. Added to this the food was extremely scarce: rice without any necessary additions was not enough to support their bodies, weakened by life in the field. … Like cattle, hundreds were driven to death and like cattle they were buried.[40]

In West Africa, as well, Africans had recourse to religious symbols as weapons of colonial resistance. In Nigeria, the Igbos consulted the Ogbunorie Oracle, believed to have the power to "drive out the white man" from the country. Of this oracle, the DC of Owerri Division reported ominously: "There is reported to be a big *juju* called Obonorie which, as far as I can gather, is at Nsu. … This *juju* is becoming a serious danger to this district, as people from all parts are visiting it and professing that it enables them to disregard the white man, and their chiefs, and the courts. … [Furthermore] there have been open manifestations of it, even in the most friendly towns."[41] Consultants were said to have sworn an oath with the water from the lake that surrounded the shrine of the oracle. This oath, which symbolized unity and resolve, apparently emboldened the people to fight and "kill anyone associated with the government." When government troops were dispatched to "pacify" the recalcitrant towns, the officers found to their dismay that the "enemy was waiting in large numbers." From "everywhere," reported the military commander of the operation, "we were fired upon." Indeed, war raged from 1909 until 1911. In the end, the British were triumphant, largely because it was a war of attrition. As an elder said of the war, "the destruction was too much." To completely eradicate the "baneful influence" of the Ogbunorie Oracle, its shrine was "bombarded for weeks" and finally set on fire. Captain Ambrose, who commanded the colonial troops, was jubilant: "We accomplished the work of destruction by cutting down all the trees around the water, and adding the skull altar to the bonfire."[42]

Punitive measures, to be sure, entailed the infliction of both physical and psychological terror on the Africans. As was common practice, colonial forces "burnt down whole villages, wantonly destroyed farms and other property, seized goats and cattle, took hostages, and demanded heavy ransom."[43] Terrorism and plunder thus characterized European imperialism. In the words of a Belgian official, "when an immediate chastisement became necessary, when it had to be proved on the spot who is master: I believe that burning [of homesteads] should be used [systematically] in such cases." Other colonial regimes, of course, adopted similar measures, as illustrated in the case of the Portuguese in Mozambique.

> In 1910 a Portuguese force of more than 4,600 men, supported by heavy artillery, simultaneously attacked the positions of Angoche and its Makua allies. The unprecedented commitment of manpower and the deployment of the most sophisticated weapons in the colonial arsenal clearly indicated Lisbon's commitment to impose its rule. ... By the end of the year the Makua had surrendered. Spurred on by this success, Portuguese troops attacked Quitanghona, and within a year they established their hegemony over this region as well. The defeat of the Makua, Angoche, and Quitanghona ensured Portuguese control over the northern coastal region. ...[44]

Clearly, the consolidation of colonial authority in Africa was a thoroughly bloody affair. Colonial armies and administrators were feared because of their brutality, harshness and their overbearing attitude towards Africans. The British District Commissioner H. M. Douglas, who served in Eastern Nigeria in the early colonial period, clearly illustrates all that was rotten with European imperialism. Douglas had a pathological addiction for violence, as manifested in his constant beating of young men as well as the elders. His imperious behavior drew this poignant rebuke from a Protestant bishop:

> Adopt a kinder and more generous attitude towards a subject people. ... From what I heard from the people as I passed through your district ... your system of administration appears to be nigh unbearable. The people complained bitterly of your harsh treatment of them, while those who accompanied me (through your district) do not cease to speak in the strongest terms of your overbearing manner towards them.[45]

Similarly in Senegal, French officials treated African life with levity, as reflected in this account by a Senegalese *griot*: "One Sunday, at a house next to ours—which was a commercial house—a 'Tubab' [Frenchman] was on the balcony with his wife. A Senegalese was walking by wearing a tarboosh on one side of his head. ... And the Tubab said to his wife, 'I can shoot the hat [off his head] with my hunting rifle.'" He fired, but missed the hat and fatally shot the man on his forehead![46]

CHRISTIAN MISSIONS

No account of European colonialism in Africa is complete without at least a brief mention of the role of the Christian missionaries who paved the way for European imperialism. By all accounts, missionary activity made it easier for Europe to consolidate its hold in Africa. Years before the European Scramble and conquests, American and European missionaries had established mission stations in various parts of Africa. In the first half of the nineteenth century, for example, it was the missionaries who, by and large, called upon their home countries to take control of the regions of missionary propaganda. David Livingstone, of the London Missionary Society, for instance, implored the British government to colonize the Zambezi region so that Christian civilization might flourish. Arguably the most articulate proponent of European colonization of Africa, for the so-called advancement of trade and Christian civilization, was Bishop Ajayi Crowther, a freed Yoruba slave, who was educated in Sierra Leone and ordained a bishop in 1864. He pioneered the British

Church Missionary Society's enterprise in the Niger Delta, in Nigeria. As early as the 1860s, Bishop Crowther had called upon the British to "pacify" the Niger Delta city-states and their neighbors, so that missionary and European commercial enterprise might flourish. Unless "the hostile" Delta-city states were "humbled," Crowther insinuated, mission stations in the interior would collapse for lack of regular supervision. He explained, "As long as the [River] Nun is left unoccupied [by force of arms] the passage through the Delta left unsafe and closed up to legitimate commerce, slave ships will never cease entering and screning [sic] themselves behind the mangrove network like creeks between the Nun and Brass." Accordingly, Crowther strongly urged the British to occupy the Niger Delta and its hinterland, otherwise the French would do so. To H.S. Freeman, Governor of Lagos, Nigeria, Crowther wrote:

> I know you are very much interested in the opening of increased commerce to European markets, as well as in the civilization and evangelization of the teeming population on the banks of that noble river [Niger] and its tributary the Tshadda [Benue]. ... The natives know no other European nation in that river but the English. ... I have heard with some solicitude by a letter from England, that the French had an eye to the Niger, which I am inclined to believe; and if decided steps are not taken by the English Government to occupy the Niger I am afraid the French will step in on a sudden and occupy it in the same or like ways as they have done Porto Novo [in Dahomey].[47]

In Crowther's mind, the pacification of the Niger Delta would not only foster the spread of Christianity into the hinterland, but it would also advance legitimate trade. With respect to the latter, he strongly appealed to British merchants to come to the Niger because "there is plenty of cargo" to be had. He even promised to help: "I will gaurantee to send 200 tons of [palm] oil home monthly. *There is work for ten steamers*" here. [Italics in the original] To the Liverpool cotton barons, Crowther also promised to help, noting that the Lower Niger "[is] a place in West Africa capable of supplying a very large quantity of raw cotton for Manchester."[48] By the 1880s and 1890s, to be sure, the Niger Delta and its hinterland had become regions of effective missionary work as well as arenas of British commercial activity. By 1900, the region had been colonized by the British, thanks, in part, to the missionary pioneers, whose missionary intrusion prepared the ground for the ultimate British conquest of Nigeria.

Elsewhere, as in central Africa, missionaries also played critical roles in European colonization. For example, it was the Roman Catholic missionary Francois Coillard, of the Paris Missionary Society, who facilitated the British South African Company occupation of the Lozi kingdom under King Lewanika. By 1888, the BSAC had signed a treaty with King Lewanika. Father Coillard was the interpreter for the king during the treaty negotiations with the BSAC. By deliberately and cunningly mistranslating the terms of the treaty to the Lozi king, he contributed to the company's occupation of Northern Rhodesia (Zambia). Ultimately, as missionary Christianity gained ground, and especially in the colonial period, African institutions, customs, and value systems crumbled. Most of the damage was done through missionary education.

Admittedly Western education resulted in the rise of the educated African elite, and provided new avenues for social and economic mobility. Yet missionary schools became the veritable centers of indoctrination and denationalization. Through missionary education, African schoolboys and girls were systematically wooed away from their cultural heritage. They were taught that Africa was uncivilized and primitive; and that whatever is African was bad and pagan. Catechisms reinforced this image, being replete with caricatures of African religion and life: "native ways are silly, repulsive and unrefined." Customs are superstitions. To be judged as being "civilized," Africans had to use the European language, dress, and habits. The colonial mentality was in this way thoroughly instilled in African minds. In schools, conceded a Portuguese priest, "we teach the native [our civilization and] the grandeur of the nation which protects him." To this, a Mozambican girl protested that colonialists, "wanted to form in us a passive mentality, to make us resigned to their domination. We couldn't [then] react openly, but we were aware of their lie; we knew that what they said was false; that we were Mozambicans and we could never be Portuguese."[49]

Missionaries, of course, firmly believed in the superiority of their own civilization, holding that it was in the Africans' best interests to change completely every aspect of their lives, including their social, economic, and political organizations, religious beliefs, clothes, food, cosmology, and so on. Accordingly, as school children and converts embraced missionary teaching, propaganda, and indoctrination, respect for traditional institutions, customs and practices almost vanished. Indeed, missionaries prided themselves as revolutionaries. Their spokesman, H. Kraemer, of the International Missionary Council, for instance, defended the radical stance of missionaries. "The missionary is a revolutionary and he has to be so, for to preach and plant Christianity means to make a frontal attack on the beliefs, the customs, the apprehensions of life ... on the social structures and bases of primitive society." Indeed, Kraemer went on, "missionary enterprise need not be ashamed of this, because [to] transplant and transfer [the people's] life-foundations into a totally different spiritual soil, [missionaries] must be revolutionary."[50] Not surprisingly, missionaries tended to condemn African culture and society with reckless abandon. Of these missionaries the American critic James Coleman writes:

> The early missionaries were inclined to feel that the African was in the grip of a cruel and irrational system from which he ought to be liberated. ... [Thus] they included among the preconditions for entry into the Christian fold the abandonment of such customs as initiation ceremonies ... dancing (a vital part of the aesthetic and recreational life of the African), marriage payment ... polygamy ... African names, and traditional funeral ceremonies. Renunciation of the old order of things was a prerequisite to acceptance of the new.[51]

By undermining or destroying African religious and social rituals and beliefs, the missionaries unwittingly destroyed all that gave coherence and meaning to the religious and social fabric of society. As already noted, church and school became the chief "agencies of conformity and coercion." They were, indeed, the effective centers of acculturation, as Africans assimilated European culture and values through them. What seems even more sinister, and certainly disturbing, is this: missionary teachings tended to predispose Africans to accept and even to admire the colonial system. In this, and in many other ways, missionary activity created "loyal citizens" and enabled Europe to consolidate its hold in Africa. As one missionary critic put it pointedly, "The interpretation of the Bible in mission lands tended to emphasize the themes that upheld subjugation and subservience, and passages which threatened European control and comfort were carefully screened out. Great Biblical themes of freedom and justice, which liberation theologians in former colonial lands are hammering upon today, were almost ignored."[52]

Missionaries themselves took some pride in that they, in one form or another, made the consolidation of European rule possible. In the words of the superintendent of the London Missionary Society: "Missionary stations are the most efficient agents which can be employed to promote the internal strength of our colonies, and the cheapest and best military posts a government can employ."[53] Is it any wonder, therefore, that colonial administrations valued the work of the missions? As a matter of fact, colonial governments supported the missions, despite occasional disagreements between church and state. After all, both shared a common universe—the transformation of the African into a submissive Black European. But African intellectuals and nationalists were not amused. First, they saw the missionaries' "logic of domination" as arrogant and abhorrent. Second, they argued, and rightly so, that missionary work corrupted African traditions, and was essentially injurious to Africa. Finally, they contended that, because the missionaries' "program" was part and parcel of the assertion of European sovereignty in Africa, the "colonial stereotype" or claim of European humanitarianism must, therefore, be rejected. "Suppose we had come to Europe in the twelfth century and claimed we were sent," an inquisitive African student once asked a missionary, "what would you have thought of us?"[54] Let me close this discourse with the trenchant words of V.Y. Mudimbe, the distinguished African scholar and philosopher:

> The more carefully one studies the history of mission in Africa, the more difficult it becomes not to identify it with cultural propaganda, patriotic motivations, and commercial interests; since the missions' programme is indeed more complex than the simple transmission of Christian faith. … Missionaries were part of the political process of creating and extending the right of European sovereignty over newly "discovered" lands.[55]

CHARTERED COMPANIES

Like the missions, European companies played a vital role in the colonization and consolidation of European rule in Africa. First and foremost, it should be recognized that European expatriates, largely private or chartered companies, dominated the economy. In places like Nigeria, Zimbabwe, Zambia, Congo, and South Africa, to name only but a few, private companies dominated the scene. Some, in fact, not only conquered but they also ruled the areas until their charters were revoked. Examples include the Royal Niger Company in Nigeria and the British South African Company in Southern Rhodesia (Zimbabwe). As Kevin Shillington notes, "European governments used concessionary companies to colonize their new-found empires. By this system private, European companies were granted vast stretches of African territories to exploit and colonise at their own expense in the name of the European country concerned. It was an attempt by Europe to colonise 'on the cheap.'"[56]

Finally, let me briefly look at the patterns of European domination of the economy, with particular reference to the Elder Dempster Company in West Africa. In West Africa, British and French companies dominated the export and import trade. Companies like the British United African Company (UAC), the Elder Dempster Company (ED), or the French Societe Commerciale de l'Ouet Africain (SCOA) and Compagnie Française de l'Afrique Occidentale (CFAO) were the prominent companies that actually dominated the commercial life of West Africa. For convenience, I shall examine, in summary form, the imperial character of the Elder Dempster Company, which was founded by the British businessman Alfred Jones. His commercial empire stretched throughout the British and French West African colonies. In fact, the ED established and dominated the most profitable shipping line in West Africa. The shipping business included the export of palm oil, cocoa, cotton, coal, etc. from West Africa to Europe. In fact, it was the company's control of the palm oil trade that enabled it to garner huge profits.[57]

Additionally, the company controlled considerable banking operations in British West Africa. It virtually controlled the British Bank of West Africa (BBWA), through which much of the financial transactions of the region were effected. As it turned out, the company's activities put African entrepreneurs at a great disadvantage. Not only did the banks deny Africans loans and credits, but the Elder Dempster also made it impossible for the Africans to ship their goods directly to Europe. As the American critic of European imperialism Leslie Buell noted in 1928, "some native traders have attempted to ship directly to England and the United States, but they have found it almost impossible to obtain shipping and credit." In practical terms, "Africans' power to compete with European firms in any aspect of trade and production was almost obliterated by policies of the banks."[58] The denial of access to capital proved to be most injurious to African business initiatives. First, the lack of capital tended to retard the development of indigenous businesses. Second, the absence of capital/credits significantly contributed, as Sherwood has shown, to the collapse or destruction of many African businesses, including the tin-plating industry, which required substantial capital outlay.[59] Equally serious, the Elder Dempster Company often fixed the price of produce. In the process, it deprived African producers and merchants of a fair balance of trade.

Moreover, although the ED employed Africans in its various enterprises, it would not let them rise above the menial or lowest ranks, nor did it allow them to unionize. In fact, those who belonged to unions were summarily dismissed. By all accounts, the company's treatment of African employees was manifestly unfair.

> Clerks, who had to have the Senior Cambridge Certificate, had to work a probationary period of three to twelve months without pay, as apprentices. Their starting salary was between 10 and 20 shillings (50 pence to £1); the maximum pay was £6 per month, *after about 10 years experience*. Clerks were not given annual leave, paid or unpaid. A European clerk [on the other hand] was paid ca. £400 p.a."[60]

Significantly, it was over European economic dominance and discriminatory shipping and banking policies that spurred, for instance, the National Congress of British West Africa's 1920 response. It proposed, among other things, the founding of African banks, which would provide loans to African entrepreneurs. Moreover, the Congress adopted an action plan to provide "shipping facilities" to Africans. Such facilities, it was hoped, would enable African business enterprises to flourish. Furthermore, they would

help Africans compete effectively with their European counterparts.[61] In short, European domination of the economy provoked African nationalist movements, such as the activities of the National Congress of British West Africa and those of Marcus Garvey, the Pan-Africanist from the West Indies. Garvey's "Africa for the Africans" movement and his programs for the economic emancipation of Africa from European economic strangulation resonated widely in colonial Africa. Indeed, the abundant literature on foreign companies in Africa clearly suggests that the Elder Dempster Company, as well as others, not only exploited Africans, but also contributed to the underdevelopment of Africa.[62]

CONCLUSION

Throughout this chapter, we have sought to highlight some of the major issues relating to the European consolidation of power in Africa. Special emphasis has been given to forced labor and African responses. On the whole, it has been argued that European colonialism was a curse to Africa. It is further argued that explanations for many of Africa's persistent troubles—political, social, and economic—can be found in the legacies of European colonialism. Certainly, much of the general underdevelopment of Africa may be traced to European imperialism.

REVIEW QUESTIONS

1. What was the Berlin Conference?
2. Why did the Europeans establish colonies in Africa?
3. What factors enabled Europeans to conquer Africans?
4. Carefully explain the nature of European rule in Africa and the patterns of African resistance.
5. "The European colonization of Africa was an unmitigated disaster." Discuss.

Additional Reading

Shillington, Kevin. *History of Africa*, revised edition. New York: St. Martin's Press, 1995.

Iliffe, John. "The Maji Maji Rebellion," Chapter 2 in *Tanganyika under German Rule, 1905–1912*. Cambridge: Cambridge University Press, 1969.

Ohadike, Don. *The Ekumeku Movement: Western Igbo Resistance to the British Conquest of Nigeria, 1883–1914*. Athens, OH: Ohio University Press, 1991.

Ekechi, F.K. "The Pacification of Igboland, 1900–1910," Chapter 6 in *Missionary Enterprise and Rivalry in Igboland, 1857–1914*. London: Frank Cass & Co., 1972.

Obichere, Boniface I. *West African States and European Expansion: The Dahomey-Niger Hinterland, 1885–1898*. New Haven, CT: Yale University Press, 1971.

NOTES

1. Quoted in Lewis H. Gann and Peter Duignan, *Africa and the World* (San Francisco: Chandler Publishing Company, 1972), 484.

2. Quoted in A. Adu Boahen, *African Perspectives on Colonialism* (Baltimore: The Johns Hopkins University Press, 1987), 24.

3. Ibid., 23.

4. Quoted in Kevin Shillington, *History of Africa*, revised edition (New York: St. Martin's Press, 1995), 328.

5. Boahen, *African Perspectives*, 37.

6. S. J. S. Cookey, *King Jaja of the Niger Delta: His Life and Times 1821–1891* (New York: NOK Publishers, 1974), 77.

7. K. Onwuka Dike, *Trade and Politics in the Niger Delta 1830–1885* (Oxford: The Clarendon Press, 1956), xx.

8. Cookey, *King Jaja*, 168.

9. *Lagos Weekly Record*, 31 Dec. 1898, cited in Georgia McGarry (ed.), *Reaction and Protest in West African Press* (Cambridge: African Studies Center, 1978), 146.

10. Boniface I. Obichere, *West African States and European Expansion: The Dahomey-Niger Hinterland, 1885–1898* (New Haven: Yale University Press, 1971).

11. CMS Archives (London): G3/A3/0, "Report of a Journey into the Hinterland of Iboland" by Bishop James Johnson, 24 February–8 April 1903. See also Felix K. Ekechi, *Tradition and Transformation in Eastern Nigeria: A Sociopolitical History* of Owerri and its Hinterland, 1902–1947 (Kent, OH: Kent State University Press, 1989), 29–30.

12. Don C. Ohadike, *The Ekumeku Movement: Western Igbo Resistance to the British Conquest of Nigeria, 1883–1914* (Athens, OH: Ohio University Press, 1991), 121–22.

13. Ibid., 124.

14. See F.K. Ekechi, *Missionary Enterprise & Rivalry in Igboland, 1857–1914* (London: Frank Cass, 1972), 122.

15. Joe Lunn, *Memoirs of the Maelstrom: A Senegalese Oral History of the First World War* (Portsmouth, NH: Heinemann, 1999), 23.

16. Quoted in Chris Prouty, Empress Taytu and Menelik II: Ethiopia 1883–1910 (London: Ravens Educational and Development Services, 1986), 90.

17. Ibid.

18. Toyin Falola, "*Africa in Perspective*," in Stephen Ellis (ed.), *Africa Now: People, Policies & Institutions* (London: James Currey, 1996), 10.

19. Roland Oliver and Anthony Atmore, *Africa Since 1800, New Edition* (Cambridge: Cambridge University Press, 1995), 267.

20. Timothy Parsons, *The African Rank and File: Social Implications of Colonial Military Service in the Kings African Rifles, 1902–1964* (Portsmouth, NH: Heinemann, 1999).

21. Philip Curtin et al., *African History* (Boston: Little, Brown and Co., 1978), 473.

22. *Church Missionary Review* (1918): 457.

23. Quoted in Bruce Fetter (ed.), *Colonial Rule in Africa: Readings from Primary Sources* (Madison, WI: The University of Madison Press, 1979), 87. See also Adam Hochschild, *King Leopold's Ghost* (London: Macmillian, 1999).

24. Ekechi, *Tradition and Transformation*, 40.

25. Ibid., 39–40.

26. Quoted in Audrey Wipper, "Kikuyu Women and the Harry Thuku Disturbances: Some Uniformities in Female Militancy," *Africa* Vol. 59, No. 3 (1989): 323.

27. E. Mayor, "Report on Forced Labour in Kenya," *Church Missionary Review,* Vol. 72 (1921): 89.

28. Allen Isaacman and Barbara Isaacman, *Mozambique: From Colonialism to Revolution, 1900-1982* (Boulder, CO: Westview Press, 1983), 42.

29. B.A. Ogot & W.R. Ochieng', *Decolonization & Independence in Kenya, 1940-93* (Athens, OH: Ohio University Press, 1995), 7.

30. Ekechi, *Tradition and Transformation,* 165.

31. Ibid.

32. Fetter, *Colonial Rule in Africa,* 111.

33. F.K. Ekechi, "Aspects of Palm Oil Trade at Oguta (Eastern Nigeria), 1900-1950," *African Economic History* No. 10 (1981): 47.

34. Ibid., 49, 50.

35. A.G. Hopkins, *An Economic History of West Africa* (New York: Columbia University Press, 1973), 150; R.O. Ekundare, *An Economic History of Nigeria, 1860-1960* (London: Methuen & Co., 1973), 197. For more on the new currencies in Eastern Nigeria see Ekechi, "Aspects of Palm Oil Trade," 48-49.

36. Basil Davidson, *Modern Africa: A Social and Political History, Third Edition* (London: Longman, 1994), 23; Ekechi, *Tradition and Transformation,* 40.

37. Quoted in T.N. Tamuno, *The Evolution of the Nigerian State: The Southern Phase, 1898-1914* (New York: Humanities Press, 1972), 48.

38. For these rebellions see T.O. Ranger, *Revolt in Southern Rhodesia 1896-7* (New York: Heinemann, 1967); John Iliffe, *Tanganyika Under German Rule, 1905-1912* (Cambridge: The University Press, 1969), Chapter 2.

39. Jan-Bart Gewald, "The Road of the Man Called Love and the Sack of Sero: The Herero-German War and the Export of Herero Labour to the South African Rand," *Journal of African History* Vol. 40, No. 1 (1999): 21, 27.

40. Quoted in ibid., 27-28.

41. Ekechi, *Tradition and Transformation,* 29.

42. Ibid., 29-32.

43. Isaac M. Okonjo, *British Administration in Nigeria, 1900-1950: A Nigerian View* (New York: NOK Publishers, 1974), 57.

44. Jean Suret-Canal, French *Colonialism in Tropical Africa, 1900-1945* (New York: Pica Press, 1971), 27; Isaacman, *Mozambique,* 22.

45. Ekechi, *Tradition and Transformation,* 19-20.

46. Lunn, Memoirs, 17.

47. Church Missionary Society Archives, London: CA3/04(a), Crowther to Venn, 6 Sep. 1860; Crowther to H.S. Freeman, 2 March 1863.

48. Ibid., Crowther to H.G. Foote, 3 May 1861; Crowther to Venn, 9 July, 1862.

49. Africa Research Group, *Race to Power: The Struggle for Southern Africa* (New York: Anchor Press/Doubleday, 1974), 52, 51.

50. Angola under the Portuguese, 153; Hendrik Kraemer, *The Christian Message in a Non-Christian World* (London: The Edinburgh House Press, 1938), 342.

51. James S. Coleman, *Nigeria: Background to Nationalism* (Berkeley: University of California Press, 1958), 97.

52. Kofi Asare Opoku, "The West Through African Eyes," *The International Journal of Africana Studies (The Journal of the National Council of Black Studies, Inc.)* Vol. 4, Nos. 1 & 2 (December 1996): 91.

53. Ibid., 85; Suret-Canale, *French Colonialism,* 366.

54. Opoku, "The West through African Eyes," 85.

55. Quoted in ibid.

56. Shillington, *History of Africa,* 333.

57. Marika Sherwood, "Elder Dempster and West Africa, 1891-c. 1940: The Genesis of Underdevelopment? *The International Journal of African Historical Studies* Vol. 30, No. 2 (1997): 260-264.

58. Ibid., 261, 274.

59. Ibid., 259.

60. Ibid., 265-6.

61. Ibid. For more on African reactions see Akintola J.G. Wyse, *Bankola-Bright and Politics in Colonial*

Sierra Leone, 1919–1958 (Cambridge: Cambridge University Press, 1990).

62. See, for example, Walter Rodney, *How Europe Underdeveloped Africa* (London: Bogle-L'Ouverture Publications, 1972); Robin Palmer and Neil Parsons (eds.), *The Roots of Rural Poverty in Central and Southern Africa* (Berkeley: University of California Press, 1977).

BLACK AND WHITE: THE 'PERILS OF SEX' IN COLONIAL ZIMBABWE

By John Pape

Black peril incidents of alleged sexual violence by black men against white women, was at times a fully hysterical obsession amongst the white population of colonial Zimbabwe. Fear of 'black peril' spawned a wide range of legislation, including the prohibition of sexual relations between white women and black men. In addition, dozens of blacks were executed, both legally and extra-legally, for supposed 'black peril' violations. Yet for the most part, 'black peril' was a manufactured phenomenon, with the number of such cases being extremely small.

In contrast, 'white peril', or sexual abuse of black women by white men, was far more frequent. These incidents rarely appear in either contemporary newspaper reports or colonial history. However, on many occasions white women and black men protested against the ignoring of the 'white peril'. Despite these protestations there was never any law passed to prohibit white men from having sexual relations with black women.

The main reason for the differing official response to the 'black' and 'white perils' was the nature of race, class and gender relations in the colony. The 'perils' were necessary in order to solidify racial and gender differences and thereby to construct a white and male supremacist social order.

Continual association with European women is dangerous for adult male natives. Some mistresses forget that the average male native has strong sexual passions and act carelessly in his presence. It is undoubtedly true that in most 'Black Peril' cases, and in nearly all cases of *crimina injuriae*, the culprit is or has been, a domestic servant. (W. Bazeley, Native Commissioner. 1930[1])

The true position about this problem has been that most white women, as most men in Rhodesia, especially if they were the employers, could have sexual intercourse on demand with their African servants. (Lawrence Vambe[2])

O black people! You my esteemed people! You my despised, pauperised and down trodden people! How many more years shall you sleep under a white man's foot?

Wake up and rub your eyes and see what he is doing to your daughters. Let us defend our girls and die defending them. A white man has taken our country and has deprived us of all our rights, must he take our girls also? God forbid. A white man's flesh is not of iron, nor is his sinew of wire.

Wake up and protect your women and girls ere we are submerged by a wave of half castes. (Gabriel Mabeta, *Whitemen and Blackwomen*[3])

INTRODUCTION

Sexual relations rarely earn a mention in history books. Within our daily experience we often see people's lives enormously altered because of their choice of sexual partners. Individuals can change their work, place of residence, class position, and cultural environment to accommodate or avoid intimacy with a certain person. In the political world, a leader's career can rise with the selection of an appropriate spouse or fall because of publicity surrounding some sexual indiscretion.

At the societal level sexual relations can play an equally important role. Class and ethnic divisions are generally reinforced by sanctions against sex between members of different classes or ethnic groups. Sexual customs are integral in deciding the relative power of men and women in a given society. Attitudes toward sex affect the quality of life of the population either providing them the opportunity for satisfaction of their needs or forcing them into alternatives of repression or closet affairs. Yet, when most histories of a given nation or period are written, these critical factors receive barely a footnote. The sexual life of the people is subsumed under the headings of more determinant factors such as the economic base or disappears into the shadows of the intellectual inspiration of great men.

The history of southern Africa during the early colonial period presents a classic example of how sexual relations both influence and reinforce the values of a ruling class, race, and gender. Zimbabwe, the focus of this paper, is representative of the dynamics of sex between blacks and whites in the region. The phenomena that the settlers called the 'black' and 'white perils' were an essential factor in building and maintaining a white and male supremacist society. As the history of the 'perils' will show, the roots of racism can be found not only in the demands of the economic forces of the day, but in sexual relations between the races as well.

The question of 'black peril' alleged sexual violence by black men on white women was at times a fully hysterical obsession within colonial Zimbabwe's white settler community. Van Onselen has detailed how 'black peril' scares 'embittered race relations' in South Africa during the years before the First World War.[4] In Southern Rhodesia, the situation was even more traumatic, since the 'black peril' scare of the early 1900s came in the wake of the 1896 war of resistance. Resultant embitterment lingered to the extent that throughout the first decades of colonialism there were periodic campaigns to control the supposedly excessive fundamental urges of African men. Much more clandestine, but far more of a reality was the rarely noted 'white peril', a wide range of sexual abuse of black women (and occasionally men) by settler males.

Before detailing the history of these 'perils' it is necessary to look briefly at the political economy from which they emerged. Numerous writers have described Southern Rhodesia as a 'labour coercive' economy.[5] Two aspects of this labour coercion are especially important for the 'perils'. First, while the major component of African labour was mobilised for the mines and farms, a large number of black men were also channelled into domestic service. In fact, throughout the first half century of colonialism domestic service ranked third as a source of African employment. Even as early as 1904, there were 6,991 African domestic workers, more than one for every two white people in the colony. Some 90 per cent of these domestics were male. The ratios of both servants to whites and males to females in domestic service remained relatively constant until 1940.[6] Hence, the white household economy depended to a large extent on black domestic labour. From this arrangement, which often meant that white women spent most of their days alone with black male servants, the complex paranoia called the 'black peril' was manufactured.

Secondly, in the early years settler society was overwhelmingly male. For the first two years after occupation white women were not even allowed in the colony. In fact, the first white woman to enter Southern Rhodesia came in disguised as a man.[7] As late as the 1911 census white men outnumbered white women by nearly two to one. It was not until 1921 that females reached 40 per cent of the settler population and census takers could boast that 'the population has now attained a settled character comparable with that of much older countries'.[8] Along the road to that settled character white males in Rhodesia often soothed their feelings of isolation by sexual relations with black women. These sexual encounters were not usually based on mutual attraction but on coercion. As two observers have noted they were 'similar to those between masters and slaves, feudal lords and serfs, conquerors and conquered in other countries'.[9] This side of the interracial sexual coin was the 'white peril', a term which rarely appeared in Rhodesian annals.[10]

The combination of a household economy heavily reliant on black male labour and a 'Pioneer' society numerically dominated by men was the foundation upon which much of colonial racial/sexual relations were developed. As many analysts have noted[11] the interaction between white employers and black domestic workers was the most 'intimate' contact between the races in colonial Zimbabwe. From their domestic workers whites painted their picture of 'the African'. By observing by their employers' behaviour, domestic workers were able to provide the rest of the black population with detailed information about the ways of the whites. The 'black' and 'white perils' were deeply intertwined with and, in fact, largely grew out of this most intimate of relationships.

However, the 'perils' did not develop in a vacuum of the household political economy. They were also reflective of the complex dynamics of the construction of the social order of colonial society. As Curtin and others have shown, the European 'image of Africa was largely created in Europe to suit European needs sometimes material needs, more often intellectual needs'.[12] While one might query Curtin's giving priority to intellectual needs in the age of imperialism, nonetheless the construction of a sexually dangerous black male was no mere chance occurrence. As Hansen has demonstrated in her pathbreaking study of domestic workers in Zambia, the race/sexual dynamic in the household was part of creating the 'difference' necessary to solidify a class structure where whites were primarily rulers and blacks comprised the subordinate classes.[13] The manufacture of black men unable to control 'primitive urges' was an added, but crucial,

touch of 'difference'. Furthermore, attributing an ungovernable libido to black men corresponded well with the tenets of Social Darwinism which formed such a crucial ideological underpinning to colonial conquest.[14] A black male prey to unrestrained sexuality could easily fit into the categories of the likes of Professor Henry Drummond who succinctly expressed the Social Darwinist view of Africans: 'To the ignorant these men are animals; but the eye of evolution looks on them with a kindlier and more instructed sense. They are what we were once; possibly they may become what we are now'.[15]

THE 'BLACK PERIL': HISTORY AND REPERCUSSIONS

The 'black peril' became a public issue in the settler community just after the turn of the century. The rise of alleged sexual attacks on white women around 1902 was, according to settler consensus due to an influx into Southern Rhodesia of a number of prostitutes who were racially undiscerning in choosing their customers. A government report of 1914 presented this historical analysis:

> On the question of prostitution by white women with natives it is pertinent to state that the prevalence of 'black peril' during the years 1902 and 1903 in Bulawayo was mainly attributed by the general public to the presence and operation of the women referred to in the instances quoted under the heading of 'white peril'.[16]

Among these women of ill repute were Maud Cotter who 'was known to live with natives and commit such acts of immorality which are too impossible to describe' and Ann Guiney 'guilty of unmentionable practices'.[17] The white population was quick to unleash their wrath upon any white women who were not prepared to toe the racial line in their business affairs. A concerted campaign was mounted to drive women like Cotter and Guiney out of the colony. Those not inclined to moderation on such issues took stronger action. In December, 1902 Louisa

Newman, to whom the settlers 'attributed the responsibility for a number of 'black peril' cases which occurred at this period' was tarred and feathered in downtown Bulawayo.[18] Perhaps frightened by the rise of both non-discriminating white women and vigilanteeism, the Legislative Assembly took its own action passing the Immorality Suppression Ordinance in September 1903. According to this law a man could face the death penalty for anything which constituted 'attempted rape'. The legislation also affected maximum sentences of two years imprisonment for white women and five years for black men who engaged in interracial sex. Even these penalties were not sufficient to please all the whites. One Rusape missionary, a Dr Arthur Dunley thought castration without an anaesthetic was a preferable punishment for convicted black sexual offenders.[19] Legislative Council member Mr Frames suggested other preventative medicine: 'The attitude of the native of this country to the white women should be that of a servant or that of an inferior creature: when he passes her in the street he should walk with his hand over his face'.[20]

While neither Dunley's nor Frames' suggestions were put into action, the 1903 ordinance did silence 'black peril' panic for a few years. The next wave of white worry came in 1910. In that year an alleged 'black peril' case in Umtali sent repercussions throughout the empire provoking editorials in the *London Times* and the *Cape Herald*). The incident involved 'Alukuleta',[21] a former domestic worker at the house of the eventual victim. On 2 October the accused was sacked by the victim's husband. A few nights later, when the husband had gone out of town, 'Alukuleta' became drunk and broke into the house. Surprisingly, he began to search for food. After spending a few minutes in the pantry he supposedly went into the woman's room grabbed her by the throat and raped her. The woman was not killed.

On 27 October 'Alukuleta' was found guilty of rape and sentenced to death. However, Gladstone, then Governor-General in the Colonial Office, commuted the sentence to life imprisonment. In his view the crime was not premeditated since the accused had gone first to the pantry. In supporting his decision he was clear as to his position on the 'black peril' question:

I am in full agreement with the principle of dealing firmly and whenever necessary in an exemplary manner in putting down criminal assaults by natives on white women. *Such cases cannot be said to have been frequent in Southern Rhodesia in recent years, nor are there signs of any tendency on their part to increase.*[22]

With regard to the Umtali case and 'black peril' in general, Gladstone's relative caution was well-founded. Two years earlier a jury in Umtali had sentenced another black man, 'Singana', to death for attempted rape. Gladstone's commutation in that instance saved an innocent man. Later findings revealed a case of mistaken identity and 'Singana' was released. Though the court records have been lost, the hysterical tone of the voluminous newspaper reports of the Alukuleta case, makes ascertaining the details of the alleged rape almost impossible. A subsequent government study of all incidents of 'black peril' in Southern Rhodesia supported Gladstone. The compiler noted: 'I may state that I have personal reason to believe there were certain circumstances in connection with the case which undoubtedly had a very direct bearing on His Excellency's decision'.[23]

Majority white opinion was insensitive to such mitigating circumstances. Gladstone's intervention brought a tumultuous response from the settler community. In Umtali within a few hours of the announcement of Gladstone's decision, a mass meeting took place to protest the commutation. The assembled white citizens resolved:

With reference to the heinous crime of rape recently committed on a white woman of this town, we the undersigned inhabitants of Umtali and districts, strongly deplore the action of His Majesty's High Commissioner for South Africa in commuting the death sentence passed on the native culprit named Alukuleta, alias, Valeta.[24]

Reaction to Gladstone's conclusion given above was not confined to Umtali. Other 'indignation meetings' took place throughout the colony. In small towns such as Hartley and Gatooma, settlers came together to condemn the Governor-General. The Salisbury Municipal Council passed a resolution objecting to Gladstone's decision to 'interfere with the course of justice'.[25] The reverberations did not stop there. As far away as Johannesburg an estimated 5,000 people gathered both to protest Gladstone's actions and to pass a resolution urging that the 'gradual elimination of the male native as a domestic servant was most essential'.[26] The editorial in the *Cape Times* called Gladstone's judgement 'washy sentimentalism'. Even the executive of the Rhodesian Chamber of Mines got into the act by passing a motion condemning Gladstone.[27]

The publicity generated by the 'Umtali case' fuelled mounting white irrationality. Predictably several 'black peril' cases occurred in the ensuing period. In Avondale (Salisbury) in February, 1912 a woman shot her domestic servant in the leg for an alleged sexual assault. When the case came to trial the court concluded that 'it turned out to be a very paltry affair ... and it became evident that as the case proceeded that in her nervous excitement consequent upon an assault, she had exaggerated the extent of the native's delinquency'.[28]

While the actual details of the case were not revealed in the *Chronicle* account, the apparent excessive 'nervous excitement' of the woman did not totally absolve the sixteen-year-old accused. He was convicted of common assault and given fifteen cuts with a cane. As it turned out, during the short interval between the date of the incident and the trial, the woman complainant had also shot another African in the leg.[29]

But it was the case of Sam Lewis that was to have the most extensive international impact. In May 1911 an African newspaper delivery man, 'Titus', supposedly made overtures to Lewis' two young daughters. According to Lewis' testimony in the case, 'Titus' had asked my daughters 'to commit an immoral act'.[30] When Lewis heard of the incident he took his daughters to the offices of the *Chronicle* with the hope of identifying the culprit. When the girls pointed out 'Titus', Lewis ordered him outside into an alleyway. Lewis then shot the delivery man through the head, killing him instantly.

Lewis had two trials. The first resulted in a hung jury. In the second, the jury deliberated only ten minutes before declaring Lewis innocent. Lewis never denied the act. His line of defence was summarised by his lawyer:

> Is it not absolutely abhorrent and does it not make your blood boil to think that any man should approach girls of such an age and suggest to them things which girls of that age should know nothing whatever about? ... but when beyond that, when this result, the degradation comes from a native, one of the race, which rightly or wrongly, for generations past, white people have considered absolutely below them in the human ladder ... I submit absolutely that human nature has its limits.[31]

For Lewis and the jury, racial grounds constituted sufficient basis to justify murder.

The Lewis case prompted widespread discussion in the British papers. Excitement was magnified by a concurrent 'black peril' scare in South Africa.[32] The *Daily Express* ran the story under the headline 'White Girls' Honour'. Articles on the Lewis affair appeared in the English *Morning Leader*, *Daily News*, and *Stamford and Rutland Guardian*. Debate over Lewis entered the British Houses of Parliament on 18 August just after the *Manchester Guardian* had considered the judgement in the case in its editorial.

> Nearly all white opinion was sympathetic to Lewis. The majority seemed to agree with the general view of the South African press that he should have been found guilty and 'extreme mercy' recommended.[33] Regardless of viewpoint, the intensity of

the discussion verified the *Westminster Gazette*'s opinion that the 'black peril' was 'a subject of great importance'.[34]

Within Rhodesia itself, perhaps the *Herald* editorial of 17 August most accurately echoed white sentiments: 'The feeling here undoubtedly is that Lewis' action checked a wave of lawlessness that was spreading over the country as a result of the deplorable weakness of the High Commissioner in the Umtali case'.[35]

While many blamed 'black peril' on Gladstone's 'weakness', others sought to reorganise Rhodesian society so as to prevent the situation which might precipitate sexual assaults. John White, a missionary often considered an advocate of African rights by the most racist Rhodesians, castigated especially those whites who he believed complicit in the 'black peril': 'The other day a white man was fined £300 and sent to prison for six months for selling certain photographs of white women to natives. No right-thinking person thinks it was a pound too much or a day too long'.[36]

White's concern related directly to Lewis' case since among 'Titus' possessions had been some pornographic photos. However, White went on to counsel further vigilance on the part of the white community: 'Every arrangement of our households, all our relations with natives living there ought to be such that even the suspicion of indelicate familiarity will be impossible'.[37]

For White, the *Herald*, and the white population in general the central issue in the Lewis controversy was the control of the libidinous black male. Indeed the vast bulk of white public commentary somehow managed to make Titus more culpable than his murderer. However, a close scrutiny of the Lewis case and incidents of 'black peril' of the period show that the over-sexed black male was simply a product of a racist imagination.

To many whites, Lewis appeared to be a man who reacted with perhaps excess emotion to a horrid situation. An investigation into his personal history shows that he was a conscious advocate of racist vigilanteeism. As early as 1902, Sam Lewis had organised anti-'black peril' meetings in Bulawayo. Always a supporter of the most extreme positions, in December 1902 he brought together some 200 whites to form a Vigilance Committee 'so that the inhabitants should take into their own hands and carry out by killing any native who raped or attempted to rape a white woman'.[38] In true Ku Klux Klan fashion Lewis wanted such a committee to be constituted as a secret society. While his dream did not materialise in 1902, he got his chance nine years later. A more predictable murderer of an innocent black man could not have existed.

While Lewis and others considered 'black peril' to be a 'wave of lawlessness', statistics portrayed an entirely different picture. A government study of all the reported 'black peril' incidents from 1898 to 1912 found eighty-seven cases in Salisbury and seventy-five in Bulawayo. At first glance this may seem a rather high figure.[39] But a careful examination shows that referring to this as a 'peril' at all was a complete misnomer. First, there is the above-mentioned matter of questionable evidence which was brought against many of the defendants. The 1908 Umtali case was but one instance of a rush to judgement of an innocent black man.

Even some Rhodesians noted this problem. Mr McChlery, an MP in the early 1920s recalled a 'black peril' case in which he had been a juror in 1901. The charges were brought six weeks after the event. The girl 'gave no satisfactory evidence'. The step-father told the story and 'no attempt was made to cross examine'. McChlery's conclusion was that 'there was no evidence to convict the boy at all'. The accused was convicted and sentenced to fifteen years and twenty-five lashes. McChlery also noted he could give 'many more examples of 'black peril' trials' where due process was doubtful.[40]

One of these trials would have been that of Mampela and Manxwena charged with attempted rape of a six-year-old girl in Bulawayo in 1902. Though the court records have been preserved from this case, they are written in an illegible script.[41] At the end of the file though a typed comment from the Solicitor-General notes: 'There is a great deal that requires cleaning up in this case. I myself interviewed Mrs Sandham (mother of the victim) on several occasions and I regret to state her evidence does not agree with my recollection of what she told Mr Bradford and myself'.[42] He went on to list six points where Mrs Sandham's evidence contradicted her earlier statements. Despite these elements of doubt the two men were sentenced to ten years' hard labour and twenty-five lashes each.

Even in rare cases where defendants admitted guilt, the charge and sentence was frequently inappropriate. A domestic worker, 'Bonali' confessed his intentions when he attacked a white woman neighbour in Salisbury in 1911: 'I don't know why I should have gone to that house. Satan must have told me to do so'.[43] Despite such diabolical inspiration, 'Bonali' failed in his mission. He only got as far as breaking a window next to where the woman was standing. When he grabbed her, the intended victim succeeded in scratching and clawing him and made her escape. For this incident, Bonali was convicted of assault with attempt to commit rape and sentenced to death.

Such cases support the contention of Philip Mason: 'There can be little doubt that if some of the cases tried in Rhodesia on the capital charge of attempted rape had been reported to the police in another country … the charge would have been for some offence with a lesser penalty'.[44] For the purposes of government statistics, 'black peril' included not only rape and attempted rape, but *crimina injuriae* and being in the 'madam's' bedroom without explanation. Under the former heading, any slight sexual suggestion could result in a criminal charge. While court records of most of these early cases have been lost, we do have detailed evidence from a 1938 case which demonstrates the menial nature of many of these offences.

In August 1938 'Dambi' was newly in the employ of Mr and Mrs Etches as a child minder at 12s.6d. per month. In his second week of service, he was walking through the yard with the couple's two young daughters. According to a white man who lived in one of the outbuildings 'Dambi' shouted in Shona to another domestic worker: *Mombe. Mombe. Yangu ndiyemukuru, yako ndiye mudikwana* meaning (according to the white man) 'you can have the smaller girl and I will take the bigger'.[45] The white man, a Mr Liedenberg, understood Shona and reported the comment to the Etches who went to the police and accused Dambi of *crimina injuriae*. There was considerable conflict in the testimony of the various witnesses. For his part 'Dambi' proclaimed his innocence:

> Why should I refer to such small children in that manner? I am not mad. The children are far too young to be spoken of in that way and besides there were Europeans all around. I state most positively that I did not make that statement. I know it is very wrong to say anything of this kind and even if I was mad I would not do so'.[46]

Apparently the judge in the case thought 'Dambi' must have been, 'mad'. He was found guilty and sentenced to four months' hard labour. In addition he was restricted to the Victoria reserve for two years. In other words his utterances (assuming he was guilty) in front of two girls who did not understand Shona were included among cases falling under the sinister 'black peril' category.

Despite all the above-mentioned sources of distortion, even taking government figures literally, the occurrence of sexual offences was extremely rare. By 1912 there were more than 4,000 domestic workers in Salisbury and Bulawayo.[47] Since domestic workers were contract workers and well-known for desertion and changing employers, an estimate of 10,000 domestic workers in the two cities during the 14 year period of the report would be minimal. Therefore, 162 sexual assault cases out of 10,000 male domestic workers (not even counting the rest of the black male population) is minuscule. But there are other factors which must be considered. Black domestic workers lived in a situation of extreme sexual deprivation. Most lived in *kias*, small rooms built at the back of their employers' plots. Few men were allowed to have their wife or any woman living with them in the *kia*. The work week, which typically ranged from eighty to ninety hours left little time for any social life. A 9 p.m. curfew for Africans further limited chances to establish relationships. Even for those men free to move about town, chances of finding African women were slim. The 1911 census enumerated 271 African women in Salisbury as compared to more than 6,300 men![48]

To this sexual isolation must be added the constant degradation to which male domestic workers were subjected by their employers. Sheila MacDonald was the most detailed chronicler of the Rhodesian household economy. Her attitude was typical of the day: 'I don't hate the negro. I quite like him as a servant, an animal, a beast of burden ...'[49] These 'beasts of burden' were subjected to a range of physical and psychological intimidation. Sjambokking was routine.[50] Criminal prosecution of a domestic worker was possible on grounds of refusing to obey 'any reasonable command of his master' or for being 'abusive or insulting, either by language or conduct to his master, his master's wife or children'.[51] This whole range of oppression of domestic workers within such an extensive system of labour coercion makes sexual attack on the 'madam' seem like one of the few possible outlets for exacting justifiable revenge.

Viewed in the broader context of hysterical legal proceedings, sexual deprivation of black workers, and labouring conditions of constant degradation, black males emerge as virtual paragons of sexual restraint. The 'black peril' then becomes a non-event a product of a racist Rhodesian mind which could not conceive of the 'native' in any human terms.

The reasons for this manufacture of the 'black peril' are manifold. Mason has stressed psychological factors:

> All the world over, both men and women, though perhaps more often and more violently women, who have been kept in stricter bonds, attribute to some dark and shadowy figure which they fear

and hate the desires they disapprove of most strongly in themselves. And for Rhodesians that dark and shadowy figure was ready made in the person of 'the native', at the same time scapegoat and shadow, while those cellars of the mind where rejected desires were stowed were also the repository for fears, fears that remembered the rebellions in Matabeleland and Mashonaland. And when desire emerged, fear was not far away. So it was that almost every white Rhodesian spoke with horror of the African's lustful immorality, his utter lack of restraint. And he took elaborate precautions to safeguard his women against these tendencies.[52]

But causation goes deeper. The creation of a sexually uncontrollable black male inhibited the development of any intimacy between African men and white women who often spent the vast majority of their waking hours together. The promotion of 'black peril' fear was an effective tool for white males to protect their women from directing their affection elsewhere.

Equally crucial was the diversionary aspect. By encouraging white rage against black sexual offenders, settler men were able to hide their own far more widespread and often violent sexual relations with black women. This was the real sexual 'peril' in colonial society, but it can only be discovered by reading between the lines of the tirades against the 'Alukuletas' and 'Dambis'.

THE 'WHITE PERIL'

The vast majority of the white population remained undeterred from their obsession with the African's 'lustful immorality'. But in the wake of Sam Lewis' murder of 'Titus', Salisbury's Reverend Simpson did manage to bring the other 'peril' to the attention of his congregation, albeit within the framework of white supremacy:

Looming behind this unhappy case is the 'black peril' a grave and loathsome peril indeed, to be dealt with effectively yet justly every case on its own merits. We may not forget, however, that from the side of the native there is the 'White Peril'. It is common knowledge that in these parts native women are not immune from the attentions of men whose skins may be white, but who are white in no other sense. The shame of this ... we should feel as keenly as the dread danger of the other peril.[53]

A letter to the *Manchester Guardian* took the analysis even further: 'There would be no danger to white women in Africa if the white men behaved as gentlemen ... if people in England only knew what goes on in Africa they would not be surprised at anything the black man does. At his worst he is a mild copy of his "masters"'.[54]

While only a few dared to publicly expose the violence of white men, behind closed doors the severity of the 'white peril' began to receive official attention after 1912. Law enforcement agencies concentrated their efforts on so-called 'miscegenation' through white fathers. By 1916, the Criminal Investigation Division (CID) was instructing district offices to compile confidential reports of all local white men having sexual relations with black women. In a memo to all district CIDs (labelled 'Strictly Confidential') the CID chief stated:

It is well known that illicit intercourse between European males and native and coloured females is commonly practised in the Territory and grave consequences result therefrom.

It is therefore desirable that the persons who practise this form of immorality should be known to this Department, as well as the conditions under which such exists.

From the date of receipt of these instructions all members of this Department will, in the ordinary course of their duty, obtain all information in this connection.

The names, occupations and nationalities of all persons concerned, also places of residence, must be clearly stated; in addition to which it should be mentioned whether such illicit intercourse consists of continuous cohabitation or promiscuous sexual relationship with various females ... Separate reports concerning such Europeans are to be submitted and these instructions are to be filed with others and kept *strictly confidential*.[55] (emphasis in original)

Local CID officers enthusiastically embraced their superintendents' instructions. Mountains of detailed reports on errant white men flowed into the files at headquarters. While it is unlikely investigators found every practicioner of 'immorality', by 1920 the Bulawayo CID could inform that the 'number of Europeans who are reported to live or habitually have sexual intercourse with native females between 1916 and 30 June 1920 is 77'.[56] Other districts brought to the CID's attention the likes of Gatooma's George

Blackburn said to be 'addicted to intercourse with native females, his modus operandi being either clandestine visits to women at Gatooma Native Location or taking women out into the veld in a motor car'.[57] Further CID curtain peeping caught Joseph Holden in Umtali with a 'certain Selina as a concubine' for whom he had 'provided a hut in the centre of the Railway Compound'.[58] Even mail was intercepted to incriminate the culprits. Letters such as Frank Green's to his fifteen-year-old lover 'a native half caste female, Martha' revealed that perhaps more than simple lust was behind their relationship:

My dearest Martha
Please darling do not be cross with me. I am very very sorry true. Dear I love you. I love you. I will be yours always. Come tonight dear I will be very good to you.
Please write to me now and give Nyonyo your answer and tell me that you

are not cross. 1000 kisses and best love to you my best girl.

Your loving boy
Frank[59]

But the systematic recording of 'immorality' revealed more than the addictions of Blackburn or the infatuations of Frank Green. First, while the police investigators were loath to admit it, a few white men and black women did engage in 'continuous cohabitation' for lengthy periods of time and raised children of their own. Thus, a report from the CID in Umtali in 1925 revealed that there were 'a very few men who live openly with Native women, not more than half a dozen'.[60] Typically, the report gives no further mention of these half a dozen. Perhaps one reason why investigators gave little space to such long-term relationships was that they often involved colonial officials. The frequency of Native Commissioners and other administrators cohabiting with black women is occasionally noted in official correspondence.[61] The case of Native Commissioner Scott of Melsetter is one such example. Scott was married to a black woman and they had two children together in the early 1900s. Scott died sometime before 1910 but left his wife and children a farm. However, according to a daughter of Scott's wife, the white community acknowledged the so-called 'coloured' children as legitimate. Scott's brother even went so far as to try to take them away from their mother so that he could look after them. A few years later, when Scott's wife had a child by a black man, she was arrested 'for producing a black man's children when she had been a white man's wife'.[62] In the twisted racial/sexual politics of Southern Rhodesia, this evidence does indicate that in some cases interracial marriages were not based solely on coercion and could even be recognised by the white population.

However, far more common than relationships like that of the Scotts were those which could be considered 'white peril'. One common form of such activities fell under the colonial legal terms of procurement and incitement. Colonial laws forbade any white to 'incite a native' to 'procure

a female for immoral purposes'. In practice such violations usually took place when a white man asked his domestic worker to go to the location or farm compound to find a woman for him. In many instances such arrangements amounted to rape. In rural areas parents who were employed by a white farmer were often threatened with sacking if they didn't surrender their daughter to the master's desires.

Possibly the most notorious case of a procurement ring on record was that of John Thornett, a mine manager in the Battlefields area in the 1920s. Thornett used his 'police boy', 'Sandy' to make his arrangements for him. A married man, Thornett dodged his wife's view by setting aside a special hut for his affairs in the workers' compound. Several of these liaisons finished up in the court-room. An employee of Thornett and the father of one of his victims, Sereta, testified that the manager used to sleep with two young girls intermittently, generally taking his daughter Raika one night and a Mwanatima, the next. He said that 'Sandy' used to lock the two girls in Thornett's hut 'like a jail'. In the end, Sereta quit his job and Raika ran away from Thornett's compound.[63]

Subsequently, Thornett was prosecuted for both rape and inciting to procure. Several other young girls aside from Mwanatima and Raika were also complainants against the mine manager. Mwanatima's testimony revealed the predicament of young girls on Thornett's mine: 'I have wanted to live with my mother for a long time but Thornett would not let me. I don't want to live with Thornett … I think Thornett was going to keep Jane Jasula until she was big enough to have connections with'.[64]

Ultimately Thornett was acquitted on all rape charges. In Mwanatima's case, a doctor exonerated Thornett by testifying that the rupture of her hymen 'was not recent'. So if she had already had sex with anyone before Thornett, he could not have raped her. For his conviction for inciting to procure Thornett was sentenced to six months imprisonment with hard labour. 'Sandy' was given four months.

Thornett was far from alone in running procurement rackets. Shopowner John Kazazis' procuring was so habitual that he was eventually deported back to Greece in 1925, despite the fact that ninety-five residents of Bindura, Mazowe Valley, and Salisbury signed a petition to block his deportation.[65]

Many white sexual victimisers were businessmen like Kazazis who offered young women the wares of their shop in exchange for sex. A CID report in the late 1920s revealed the habits of some of these men: 'Cohabitation between white and black concerns generally a certain type of white man either storekeeper or farmer, who, when he has tired of the native woman returns her to her kraal with the coloured children … who are no more recognised by the white man'.[66]

By the 1930s the problem of rural shopkeepers having sex with black women had reached such proportions that the Commissioner of Police was urging the denial of a business licence to any man known to 'cohabit with native women'. He insisted such licencees must have an 'unblemished character'.[67]

Those white men who would have failed such character tests in colonial Zimbabwe did not confine their offences to black women. Even young boys were known to be forced into sex with their 'masters'. Though such cases were rare in the criminal records, in 1911 Frederick Morrison was charged with having a 'venereal affair' with one of his workers, 'Morenyu'. The victim, a sixteen-year-old farmworker was summoned out of his hut late one night and ordered to cook 'skoff' for Morrison. When Morrison had finished his supper he turned his appetites to the young boy. 'Morenyu' testified that the accused: 'took hold of me and placed me upon the bed. I was lying face downwards and the accused then got on top of me and had connection with me … I attempted to get away but the accused held me fast; he was holding me by the neck with both hands'.[68]

'Morenyu' shared his hut with four other men. All of them testified at a hearing that they remembered him returning on the night in question, carrying his clothes in his hand and being very upset. He informed them of the events and they all examined the wet semen on his legs. Yet, the attorney-general declined to prosecute. Such was the license of white men in colonial Rhodesia. Regardless of sexual preference, if the victim was black, the risk for white sexual offenders was almost non-existent.

Even in the realm of inciting to procure usually the black procurer rather than the white inciter was prosecuted. The case of 'Jongwe' is instructive. He was convicted of procuring and given a six month sentence at hard labour in Gwelo in 1921. 'Jongwe' refused to name the white man who had 'incited' him. Subsequent investigations uncovered a Mr Bailey but the Sub-Inspector of the CID issued an order to all his employees: 'Do not divulge the name of the white man concerned in this case to anyone'. His superintendent concurred stating it would be 'impolitic to inform the man Bailey of his alleged connection with the case'.[69] The interpretation of colonial law apparently meant that an incitee could force a procured female on an innocent inciter!

THE 'PERILS': THE RESPONSE OF WHITE WOMEN

While the 'black peril' produced newspaper headlines and international white panic, the far more widespread and pernicious 'white peril' began to take its emotional toll even on settler women by the post World War I years. Despite the quiet outrage of white women, changes in the laws in 1916 failed to include any sanction against white men should they engage in 'illicit' activity. The new legislation merely extended the areas of punishment for black men and white women to cover 'acts of indecency'. Such acts included 'the raising or opening of any window, blind or screen of a room, or the trap door or flap of any privy, for the purposes of observing any woman or girl who may be in such a room in a nude or semi-nude state, or may be using such privy for the necessary purposes of nature. Under this ordinance an arrest could be affected 'by any other person having reasonable and probable grounds for believing that such an offence was committed'.[70] In essence this statute meant that any white could arrest a black man for being in the vicinity of a window, door or toilet. While further clamping down on already hamstrung black workers, this was not a law destined to satisfy the colony's white women at the time.

The exemption of white men under the 1916 Ordinance led indignant white women to take the situation into their own hands. Far from worrying over the supposed daily threat to their womanhood from black domestic workers, white women's anger over sexual matters pin-pointed their own men. By 1921 they were circulating a petition to the white female population of the colony stating: 'the conditions of the country imperatively call for legislation making the cohabitation between white men and Native women a criminal offence, as by statute it is criminal for white women to cohabit with Native men'.[71] The response from white women was astonishing. Over 1,600 signed, more than half the white adult females in Southern Rhodesia.[72]

This was not the end of white female lobbying. Formal women's organisations also joined the campaign. In 1924 the Rhodesian Women's League made a passionate plea for new laws:

> European prestige is lowered in the eyes of even the uneducated natives, not so much in the commission of the offence as in the sanction given to it ... the natives know that white women resent the cohabitation between white men and native women. It should not be necessary anywhere in this age, least of all in an English-speaking Colony, for white women to have to battle for their own protection ... From one objector again we hear that the 1916 Ordinance which penalises women guilty of intercourse with natives, far from being a reflection on white women, is a tribute to their superior purity, and that therefore, instead of clamouring for a similar law to be passed as regards white men, we should rest satisfied proud of our distinction. Thus, pursuant of this logic, the law, say of larceny, is a tribute to the extreme nobility of would-be thieves ... what

happens at present is that the offender gets off free, while the innocent his wife, children, neighbours, his country pay the dear penalty.[73]

In 1927 the League joined forces with the Women's Christian Temperance Union and the Women's Federation of Southern Rhodesia to once again petition the Legislative Assembly:

> We therefore pray that laws should be framed to protect both white and Native women in Southern Rhodesia, and while the severest punishment should continue to be inflicted upon the native, commensurate punishment should most certainly be meted out to the white man for immorality with Native women.[74]

Perhaps the women's only organised source of support came from the Rhodesian Coloured Society, formed in 1928. An association 'open only to the children of white men by native women' the RCS's 23 founding members resolved in 1929: 'if possible to prohibit white and black from living together'.[75] The Coloured Society claimed that white fathers often failed to acknowledge their black children. If they were recognised, the RCS said 'their white father often causes them to work without pay'.[76]

Colonial officials, fanatical monitors of 'miscegenation' reinforced the Society's assertions. By 1930 the government enumerated 1,138 'coloured' children from white fathers. Of these 379 were acknowledged and provided for; 139 were acknowledged but not provided for; 297 known but not acknowledged, and the rest did not know their father.[77]

While the RCS was the most organised voice backing the Women's League, some echoes of agreement did come from both white and African men. In legislative debates on the topic Labour spokesperson Mr Davies said his party supported the bill to punish white men having sex with black women. Labour's motives, he noted, would be based on maintaining racial purity not promoting equality of the sexes.[78]

Less backhanded support came from other MPs. Mr McChlery chastised fellow male members of Parliament and stated that 'until they legislated equally between white men and white women, they had no right to legislate at all'.[79] MP Hadfield parallelled McChlery's position by calling for a 'moral sanitary service'.[80] Hadfield also cited what he believed to be widespread African support for the white women's position. He even quoted one black man who after the 1916 Ordinance was passed had told him: 'We hear that in the House this was especially aimed at alien Natives. Yet you have done nothing to stop your own white men having intercourse with our Native women. Have you forgotten that you are alien to us Natives?'[81]

In fact Hadfield's remarks touched on a subject that had apparently been troubling black males for some time. The few times where the African voice was audible on this question reflect the sentiment of Hadfield's informant. In 1924, John Kwembe, a police constable from Mutoko, wrote to the Native Commissioner to complain of a white policeman, Mr Hutchinson, who was living with a black woman in the camp. Kwembe felt doubly victimised by the law. First he said that two friends from his early days in Rhodesia in 1897 had been hanged 'because of having been coveted or falsely loved by white women'.[82] Then he himself had been fined £5 for keeping an unregistered wife at the Mutoko Police Camp the very same thing Hutchinson was doing without being bothered.

Kwembe's remarks were mild as compared to others who had previously spoken out. As early as 1911 a government inquiry into Native Affairs had touched on the question. Black witnesses had commented: 'it is very bad, whites ought to take whites and blacks ought to take blacks'; 'it is very evil and we resent it very much in our hearts'.[83] Many traditional leaders were more militant. In 1912 an Ndebele chief had told a colonial official: 'There will never be peace between the black man and the white man ... until you give our women the protection you demand for your own'.[84]

Yet despite outcries from white women and other quarters of the population white men remained untouched by penal sanctions of immorality legislation throughout the colonial period. Having sensed the futility of their struggle, after several years white women in Rhodesia gave up the quest to bring their men's sexual indiscretions under legal control. Instead, as the men would have it, attention went back to the old obsession the 'black peril', particularly as personified by the black male domestic worker.

Southern Rhodesia's first female MP, Elizabeth Tawse-Jollie threw down the gauntlet for a new phase of racist women's rights campaigning: the elimination of black males as domestic servants. Her comments in 1925 foretold another futile decade-long attempt by Rhodesia's white women to preserve their supposed virtue and the innocence of their children:

> There is only one remedy for the evil as it exists, and that is the employment of women as house servants ... Rhodesia has not, fortunately, the large supply of coloured women who are now filling the domestic service ranks (in South Africa) and it is presumably out of the question to suppose that the many women of education who find life so hard in England will be prepared to take posts as children's nurses or mothers' help in Rhodesia.[85]

While Tawse-Jollie believed that Rhodesia had a 'good record as to 'black peril' cases' she was convinced that 'there is no doubt that as the native becomes more sophisticated the danger increases'.[86]

So Tawse-Jollie, along with other noted white women of Rhodesia, began to push for the hiring of black women in place of men as workers within the house. This campaign produced a lively and typically racist debate within two commissions investigating the plausibility of recruiting women: the Standing Committee of the Federation of Women's Institutes of Southern Rhodesia (1930) and the government Departmental Committee on Native Female Domestic Labour (1932).

Each of these commissions called a large number of citizens to give evidence on this issue. Only a minority opposed the transition to black females. Typical of their views was Mrs Williams, a witness for the Governmental Committee: 'Native girls in this country are really not suitable for domestic service. They have not got the moral character. I consider they are immoral and I feel I could not trust them ... I do think that at present the native girl is definitely inferior to the native boy'.[87]

While some witnesses specifically opposed women as domestic workers, others used the controversy to protest against any blacks in household labour. Mrs Bullock told the government committee:

There is no necessity for the employment of native labour in households and because we do employ native labour we are content with homes that no other people would be content with today houses absolutely lacking in nearly all modern labour-saving devices which make European labour possible ... a point that should be stressed and pointed out to the Europeans in this country is that they must cease to regard domestic servants as slaves. If the women of this country stopped doing that, there would be an opening for the vast number of women in this country who are without service. It is economically and socially possible to employ Europeans in domestic service.[88]

In addition, Mrs Bullock and other witnesses wanted European servants in order to protect their children. In this regard she maintained 'it must be admitted that close association with an inferior race is bound to have reactions'.[89]

Despite the testimony of the likes of Mrs Bullock, in the end both inquiries showed strong sympathies for changeover from black males to females, though neither body fully backed female domestic workers. Nonetheless, the government's concluding remarks were representative of general sentiments of the Commissions:

The evidence which has been obtained points to the conclusion that ... the girl responds readily and becomes in course of time a valuable servant ... [many witnesses said] girls exhibit more fully than boys very desirable qualities especially those of cleanliness, conscientiousness, and tractability.[90]

And just to make sure that the original purpose of the report was not lost, Native Commissioner C.L. Carbutt reminded the committee that the document should be 'regarded from one point of view only, i.e., the safety of our womenfolk, an aspect admittedly of paramount importance'.[91]

Throughout the dozens of witnesses called before both commissions, the voices of Africans were only faintly heard. Less than five were called all of them women in the domestic employ of a white witness. 'Sophie', worker for a Mrs Jowitt, typified the African testimony: 'I can say that the girls like working here and are quite happy. More of them want to come'.[92]

In the background to these efforts of social reformers and protectors of white womanhood, the greater forces of the national and regional political economy were at work. The dependency of settler capital on black males as a cheap source of labour blocked the introduction of women as domestic workers. Mining and agricultural employers minimised labour costs by paying wage levels which were only adequate to sustain the individual worker.[93] As a result, few black men who worked for wages lived with their families. Wives and children remained behind in the rural areas. Women's agricultural production was then a necessary complement to the earnings of the male in order for the family to survive. If women were brought to town in large numbers to work as domestics, the rural economy would have suffered. Employers would then have been pressured to pay not only wages for a head of household, but also to supply housing and other amenities to accommodate workers who had broken all ties with the land. By the 1930s the Rhodesian economy was not yet ready for that level of industrialisation and proletarianisation. Consequently, despite the moral arguments raised by the commissions and the bulk of the colony's white women, domestic service remained a male domain. Even as late as 1948, 88 per cent of domestic workers were men.[94]

So while Tawse-Jollie and other dedicated moralist-racists continued to proselytise for the employment of black women as domestic workers, their demands fell on deaf, profit-maximising ears. The best white male officialdom was prepared to tolerate was a few black women in town as a calming force on the black male libido. Van Onselen has shown how upstanding mineowners were prepared to turn a blind eye to black prostitutes who sneaked into the compounds.[95] A quiescent work force was more important than upholding morals on the mines. Municipal authorities had the same attitude. A 1929 memo from the Ministry of Health was quite overt in stating that in Salisbury 'prostitutes at the Location were a necessity, as a safe-guard for the white women'.[96] For these men, half or even quarter measures then were preferable to any adherence to notions of morality or other issues of 'paramount importance'.

CONCLUSION

The machinations of the 'perils' served to solidify whites' racial stereotypes. The black man, as personified by the domestic worker was mythologised into an uncontrollable sexual animal who had to be blocked at every opportunity from satisfying his primitive urges. Few whites, of either gender, deviated from that manufactured concept of the black male during the first half century of colonialism.

While the 'black peril' created an hysteria which sent thirty men to the gallows, white men faced only mild reprimand at worst for the same crimes.[97] Not one white man was ever executed for a sexual crime against a black woman. The vast files on immorality reveal white men's sexual interaction with and abuse of black women far exceeded the sexual contact between black men and white women.

Yet the intricacies of the 'perils' also reveal the male supremacy endemic to Rhodesian society. White women could go about organising their social clubs, tyrannising their domestic servants, and occasionally helping out with more productive tasks. However, in the political realm, especially with regard to sexual politics, white men guarded and nurtured their power. These men were not prepared to yield even to the petitions and pleadings of their own women, let alone those of the black majority. Only the bullets of black guerillas could pull them down from their throne. But even military conquest has not quickly erased whites' virulent racism. The sexual dynamics described here as the 'perils' were an essential part of the development of that racism. Not surprisingly, the legacy of the 'perils' remains evident in race relations in independent Zimbabwe where whites continue to try to maintain their own segregated social environment and thereby protect themselves and their daughters from any perilous contact with black Zimbabweans.

NOTES

1. National Archives of Zimbabwe (NAZ) File S 235/475, *Report of the Departmental Committee on Native Female Domestic Labour, 1932*, p. 43.
2. Lawrence Vambe, *From Rhodesia to Zimbabwe* (London, 1976), p. 109.
3. Gabriel Mabeta, *Whitemen and Blackwomen* (Johannesburg, 1925), p. 8.
4. Charles Van Onselen, *Studies in the Social and Economic History of the Witwatersrand, 1886–1914*, Volume 2; *New Nineveh* (London, 1982), pp. 45–6.
5. Among these are Charles Van Onselen: *Chibaro*, (London, 1976); and in I. Phimister and C. Van Onselen (eds), *Studies in the History of African Mine Labour*, (Gweru, 1978); and Tsuneo Yoshikuni, 'Strike Action and Self-Help Associations: The Emergence of an African Working Class in Zimbabwe, 1918–21', Seminar Paper, History Department, University of Zimbabwe, 13 May, 1987.
6. NAZ, SRG 4, CE 6, *Census Reports 1901–36*.

7. G.H. Tanser, *A Scantling of Time* (Salisbury, 1965), p. 45.

8. NAZ, SRG 4, CE 6, *Census Reports 1901–36*.

9. C.A. Rogers and C. Frantz, *Racial Themes in Rhodesia* (New Haven 1962), p. 284.

10. While a few writers used *White Peril* in the sense in which I have used it here, the official study undertaken in 1914 only included the activities of white women, namely 'white females who prostitute themselves with natives,' the 'indiscreet and careless attitude adopted by white females in their personal relations with their native servants,' and 'nymphomania'; NAZ S 1227 *Immorality Reports*. This file, like two other major sources for this paper, S 1222 and S 144/4–5 contains assembled papers with no page numbers, so references will be made simply to the file number.

11. These include Philip Mason, *Birth of a Dilemma* (Oxford, 1958); B.W. Gussman, *African Life in An Urban Area* (Federation of African Welfare Societies, Bulawayo, 1952); A.K.H. Weinrich, *Mucheke: Race Status and Politics in a Rhodesian Community* (UNESCO, Paris, 1979).

12. Philip Curtin, *Image of Africa: British Ideas and Action 1780–1850* (Madison, 1964), p. 480.

13. Karen Hansen, *Distant Companions: Servants and Employers in Zambia, 1900-85* (Ithaca, 1989), especially Chapters 1 and 2.

14. For a broad sampling of British colonial ideology including Social Darwinism see H.A. Cairns, *Prelude to Imperialism: British Reactions to Central African Society 1840–1890* (London, 1965).

15. Henry Drummond, *Tropical Africa* (London, 1908), p. 4.

16. NAZ, S 1222.

17. Ibid.

18. Ibid.

19. *Bulawayo Chronicle*, 29 November 1902, p. 4.

20. Ibid.

21. I have elected to put names of most Africans in inverted commas here since they were usually chosen or spelled arbitrarily by both colonial employers and court recorders. The inverted commas merely indicate that the name used in court was unlikely to be the individual's given name.

22. NAZ, S 144/4–5 (Emphasis added; this is a file of newspaper clippings. Where possible the date and title of the paper will be given.).

23. NAZ, S 1227.

24. NAZ, S 144/4–5, *Rhodesia Herald*, 13 January 1911.

25. Ibid.

26. Ibid.

27. Ibid.

28. Ibid., *Bulawayo Chronicle*, 17 February 1911.

29. Ibid.

30. Ibid., *Bulawayo Chronicle*, 15 August 1911.

31. Ibid., *Cape Times Weekly*, 23 August 1911.

32. For a detailed discussion of the South African *Black Peril* situation in the pre-World War 1 years, see Van Onselen, *New Nineveh*, pp. 45–54.

33. Ibid.

34. Ibid., *Westminster Gazette*, 25 August 1911.

35. Ibid.

36. Ibid.

37. Ibid.

38. *Bulawayo Chronicle*, 13 December 1902.

39. NAZ, S 1227.

40. *Legislative Assembly Debates*, Government Printer, Salisbury, 26 May 1921.

41. NAZ, D 3/6/28, Bulawayo District Court, Criminal Cases, 2 January 1903.

42. Ibid.

43. NAZ, D 3/5/27, Salisbury District Court, Criminal Cases, 31 January 1911. The big one is mine, the little one is yours'.

44. Mason, *Birth of a Dilemma*, p. 246.

45. The phrase means literally: 'One cow, one cow.'

46. NAZ, S 1046, Case 483, 1938.

47. Data extrapolated from 1911 Census in SRG 4 CE 6.

48. Ibid.

49. Sheila Macdonald, *Sally In Rhodesia* (Sydney, 1932), p. 7.

50. Sheila Ndlovu, 'A History of Domestic Workers in Bulawayo 1930 50', Dissertation Paper,

History Department, University of Zimbabwe, 4 July 1986.

51. Claire Palley, *The Constitutional History and Law of Southern Rhodesia* (Oxford, 1966), p. 594.

52. Mason, *Birth of a Dilemma*, p. 244.

53. NAZ, S 144/4–5, *Rhodesia Herald*, 25 August 1911.

54. Ibid., 22 August 1911.

55. NAZ, S 1222.

56. Ibid.

57. Ibid.

58. Ibid.

59. Ibid.

60. NAZ, S 1227.

61. For example, see NAZ, MF 351 which contains numerous letters between Native Affairs and CID officials concerning Black Peril during this period.

62. T. Barnes and E. Win, unpublished interview with Mrs Bertha Charlie, 21 February 1989.

63. NAZ, S 1222.

64. Ibid.

65. Ibid.

66. NAZ, S 1227.

67. Ibid.

68. NAZ, D 3/5/28, Salisbury District Court, Criminal Cases, 30 September 1911.

69. NAZ, S 1222.

70. NAZ, A 3/21/28, Vol. 1.

71. *Bulawayo Chronicle*, 29 January 1921.

72. *Legislative Assembly Debates.*

73. *Bulawayo Chronicle*, 6 November 1924.

74. NAZ, S 1227.

75. Ibid.

76. Ibid.

77. Ibid.

78. *Legislative Assembly Debates.*

79. Ibid.

80. Ibid.

81. Ibid.

82. NAZ, S 1222.

83. *Legislative Assembly Debates.*

84. Quoted in Mason, *Birth of a Dilemma*, p. 242.

85. Elizabeth Tawse-Jollie, *The Real Rhodesia* (Bulawayo, 1971), p. 284.

86. Ibid.

87. NAZ, S 235/475, p. 128.

88. Ibid., p. 143.

89. Ibid., p. 142.

90. Ibid., p. 5–6.

91. Ibid.

92. Ibid., p. 136.

93. For a summary of this dynamic see Giovanni Arrighi 'Labour Supplies in Historical Perspective' in G. Arrighi and J. Saul, *Essays on the Political Economy of Africa* (New York, 1973) and Lloyd Sachikonye, *Capital, Proletarians and Peasants in Southern Africa*, Zimbabwe Institute of Development Studies Paper Number 19, Harare, 1984.

94. Duncan Clarke, *Domestic Workers in Rhodesia* (Gwelo, 1974), p. 48.

95. Van Onselen, *New Nineveh*, p. 181.

96. NAZ, S 1542/S12, 'CNC to Town Clerk', Salisbury, 5 September 1936.

97. Vambe, *From Rhodesia to Zimbabwe*, p. 107.

IGBO WOMEN FROM 1929–1960

By John N. Oriji

The Aba Women's Revolt was one of the most significant events that occurred in Nigerian history during colonialism.[1] It was for example, the first major revolt of its type that was organized and led by rural women of Owerri and Calabar Provinces which contained a population of two million people, located in a total land mass of about 6,000 square miles (Van Allen 1981, 60). Like other major events of its magnitude, the revolt has continued to attract much scholarly inquiry and discourse, unparalleled in Igbo history until the Nigeria-Biafra war.

The historiography of the revolt itself is revealing in terms of the methodological problems it has raised, and the conflicting interpretations scholars and feminists have offered to explain its underlying roots, the organization of women, and their overall achievements.[2] While some of these themes will be covered in this essay, I hope to address different aspects of the revolt that have received little attention by attempting to answer the following questions: What type of women led the revolt, and how did their leadership enhance their social status during and after the revolt? What legacies did the revolt leave in Igbo society before Nigerian independence in 1960, and how have the legacies helped women to attain a better social standing in modern Igbo society?

METHODOLOGICAL PROBLEMS: SOURCES

Most of the primary sources used in studying the revolt were compiled by colonial officers who were largely concerned with finding its causes to establish a more functional and practical way of implementing the policy of indirect rule in southeastern Nigeria. The orientation of the colonial officers which, in the first instance, was meant to justify colonialism, affected the reports they compiled in varying ways. For example, the Women's Revolt was known in official circles as the Women's riots, to create the impression that they were "disturbances" caused by inarticulate, irrational, and disorderly women who woke up one morning on the wrong sides of their beds. But modern historiography has shown that the women were well organized, and had leaders who clearly articulated their grievances during what they saw as "Ogu Ndem" (Women's War). That's why their movement is captioned in this paper as a revolt instead of "riots."

One can also raise issues about the linguistic difficulties some of the colonial officers who did not speak Igbo encountered. Their reports, which were compiled through interpreters who were barely literate in English, are subject to misinterpretations and distortions. The Igbo dialect is complex, and to an outsider, it could be perplexing. It is then not surprising that when Captain John Cook, a District

Officer who had mastered the Onitsha dialect was transferred to Bende District during the genesis of the Women's revolt, he confessed that he did not understand the Igbo language spoken in his new area of jurisdiction.[3]

The major primary source for studying the revolt is the Report of the Aba Commission of Inquiry (1930). The report itself is problematic since all those who testified, took an oath, and the hearings were regarded as formal court proceedings. Women in many communities retained lawyers who briefed them on what to say, and what to withhold. Under the circumstance, it is unlikely that some of the testimonies represented the actual feelings and views of the women.[4]

My own field experience shows that people were still afraid of being interviewed by colonial officers many years after the Women's revolt. In 1933 for example, J. G. C. Allen who wrote monumental intelligence reports on the Ngwa clan, visited the Amavo community to interview its elders on their local history and culture. Those who saw him simply took to the bush, fearing that he came to ask them implicating questions about the Women's revolt. Allen frustratingly left Amavo without saying much about its history in his report.

The primary sources, however, are valuable, especially if they are compared and used along with the numerous works written on the Women's revolt by professional anthropologists, historians, feminists and others. The historiography of the Women's revolt will also be enriched when the findings of some of the recent research projects are published. As discussed below, all the sources constitute one of the major legacies the Women's revolt has left in Igbo studies.

ACHIEVEMENTS OF THE WOMEN'S REVOLT

Renaissance in Igbo Studies

Igbo studies experienced a remarkable renaissance as a result of the women's revolt. The colonial administration, which was taken by surprise by the revolt, realized that it knew little about the Igbo whom it had ruled for almost three decades. The administration then took various measures that helped in promoting Igbo studies. It, for example, asked District Officers (DO) to submit "intelligence reports" on the history and culture of Igbo societies. The administration also set up a Commission of Inquiry in 1930 to determine the causes of the revolt, and commissioned in the 1930s, anthropologists like M. Green and S. Leith-Ross to study Igbo culture, paying particular attention to the varying roles of women in their societies. These and other works which constitute the primary sources for studying Igbo history and culture, have enabled modern researchers and feminists to embark on more detailed and scholarly analyses of the Women's revolt. The women's revolt, no doubt, provided an incredible stimulus to Igbo studies, comparable to the Nigeria-Biafran war of the 1960s.

ENRICHMENT OF IGBO FOLKLORE AND RITUALS

Igbo folkloric songs, and dance were greatly enriched during the women's revolt. Women composed songs embodying their grievances, as they danced, and "sat" on the Warrant Chiefs, or marched to the District Officer to present their petitions. In Aba-Ngwa area, women chanted traditional war songs sang by male warriors while marching to battle entitled: "Nzogbu, Enyimba Enyi" (literary meaning: We are like elephants, marching to battle, crushing obstacles on our way). Some even sang saying that women were as strong as the elephant, "Ndem mbu Enyi, Enyi, Ndem Mbu Enyi." Interestingly, these songs were quite popular in Biafra, revealing the extent to which the folkloric songs of the women's revolt influenced Igbo "martial songs and music" during the Nigerian civil war.[5]

As for the rituals, my recent trip to Nigeria was quite insightful. During the trip, I happened to have gone to Union Bank, Aba, for some transactions on August 12, 1999. During my discussion with the accountant, the Senior Manager whom I had not met before was passing by, and the accountant introduced him to me. The Manager politely invited me to his office, looking quite excited. While in his office, he told me of an event that would take place shortly, and appealed to me as an educated Ngwa man living in the U.S., to spend a few minutes and watch it with him and other bank officers. The Manager then gave me a gist of what was happening: there was a large tree, which posed a threat to the bank building, and the yardmen refused to trim its branches because they believed it was a sacred tree where 25 women killed in Aba during the Women's revolt were buried. According to the yardmen, any time one of them trimmed the branches, the individual got mysteriously sick, and in one instance, they remembered one of their crew members died after cutting the branches. The only remedy, the yardmen claimed, was to invite the Traditional Ruler of the town to pour libations and perform rituals around the tree before anybody could touch it. That was why the Manager wanted me to wait, and happily, within a few minutes, the Traditional Ruler arrived with some elders, and in a solemn mood, he paid tribute to the "unknown soldiers" buried under the tree, and performed the rituals necessary for cutting its branches. This rare event reminded me about the significance of the Women's revolt in traditional Igbo religious values and ideas, and the important place it continues to occupy in their rituals practices.[6]

THE EMERGENCE OF POWERFUL AND HEROIC LEADERS

It is a well-known adage in history that heroes and heroines are born during a crisis. The Aba Women's revolt produced many heroines who emerged as distinguished and courageous leaders of the movement in their communities. Interestingly, while the names, and varying roles of these heroines were recorded in the Collective Punishment Inquiry, and the Commission of Inquiry held in 1930, oral traditions conducted recently in parts of Igboland have revealed the towering influence some of them acquired during and after the revolt. A broad

analysis of the heroines beginning with the community where the revolt started is insightful:

Nwanyeruwa and the Crisis that Sparked off the Revolt in Bende District

The Women's revolt of 1929 was sparked off by a scuffle between Nwanyeruwa, a woman of Ngwa ancestry married in Oloko, and an enumerator, Mark Emereuwa who was asked by Okugo, the Warrant of the town, to help in obtaining an accurate census of his people as mandated by the District Officer. In Oloko and others parts of Igboland, census was associated with taxation, especially, as the colonial administration had taken a similar census in 1926 without revealing the fact that it would be used in imposing tax on men in 1928. In addition, there was widespread rumor that fueled the fears of women claiming that both men and their wives would be taxed after the next enumeration. Thus, before the counting began, women had decided in their meetings to wait and see who would tax them during the hyperinflation of the 1920s when family incomes were declining rapidly (Oriji 1997, 90–97).

Emeruwa never expected that task he was asked to perform would trigger a massive revolt of Igbo women when on that fateful day, November 18, 1929, he went to late Ojim's compound, his first place of call, and asked his widow, Nwanyeruwa, to "count her goats, sheep and people." In anger, the woman retorted, "was your [late] mother counted?" In order words, why do you want me to pay tax? Don't you know that women don't pay tax in traditional Igbo society? The violent encounter and verbal exchanges between the two, infuriated Nwanyeruwa who then rushed to the town square to report the incident to women who were incidentally holding a meeting that day to discuss how they would respond to the "tax problem."[7]

Oloko women, after hearing Nwanyeruwa's account, went into action, believing that women would be taxed. They sent leaves of palm-oil tree (a symbol of invitation) to women in other parts of Bende District, nearby Umuahia and Ngwa areas and other places, and within a few days, about 10,000 women were said to have assembled in Oloko, "sitting" on Warrant Chief Okugo, and demanding his trial and resignation.[8]

Nwanyeruwa: An Apostle of Non-Violence and the Heroine of Heroines

Nwanyeruwa played a major role not only in precipitating the revolt, but emerged as a leading advocate of non-violence during the protest marches. As an elderly woman, her words of wisdom were often heeded by more youthful women in her community who led the revolt and started "sitting" on Warrant Chiefs, singing, and dancing around their houses until they surrendered their insignia of office and resigned. Although Nwanyeruwa's influence was largely confined to her community, it's noteworthy that the revolt in many parts of Igboland took a similar pattern, as women first massed in their village squares, and then moved to sit on their Warrant Chiefs. Perhaps, without the influence of Nwanyeruwa, and others to be discussed, the revolt would have led to more bloodshed, and casualties.[9]

Women from Oloko, Umuahia, and northern Ngwaland in the then Bende District, as well as other parts of Igboland, saw Nwanyeruwa as their heroine who courageously fought for their cause, and "prevented women from paying tax." It's noteworthy that when the revolt spread, leaders of the revolt from various places came to Nwanyeruwa, requesting her to put in writing, the assurances she had received from the District Officer (DO) that women would not be taxed. She complied, and a letter written on her behalf stated that the District Officer "said women will not pay tax till the world ends [and] Chiefs were not to exist any more" (Ibid. cited by Mba 1982, 82).

It is also significant that women from Bende, Ngwa and other places rallied round Nwanyeruwa during the revolt, and gave her donations of ten shillings per village. The money was used partly to entertain the large number of women who visited Oloko, and partly to defray the transport expenses of Oloko women who travelled to Umuahia, Nbawsi and Port Harcourt to cool the tempers of women

in those towns, and reassure them that they would not pay tax.[10] Members of the Aba Commission of Inquiry were then right when they noted that:

Nwanyeruwa became and still remains a name to conjure with … [and the Oloko trio] cleverly used her as the symbol of womanhood rising against oppression (The Aba Commission of Inquiry (1930), 9).

"Emissaries of Peace, and Apostles on Non-Violence": The Oloko Trio: Ikonnia, Mwannedia and Nwugo

The influence of Nwanyeruwa on the Oloko trio is yet to be studied. But as their elder, the trio who probably listened to her appeal for non-violence, are celebrated today as the most outstanding "emissaries of peace" during the revolt. The Oloko trio was selected as the spokespersons of Oloko women due to their youthful vigor, intelligence and oratory. The District Officer (DO), Captain John Hills who paid tribute to their leadership qualities, often sent them to "hot spots" during the revolt, to ensure that the protests did not escalate and lead to violence. In Oloko for example, tempers ran high among women on November 30, 1929, when the DO who assumed duty that day, refused to accede to their demand for the immediate trial of Warrant Chief Okugo who had been arrested for allegedly assaulting some of them during the revolt. The women continued to follow the DO wherever he went from morning till evening, kind of "sitting on him" until his wife got in touch with the trio and reached an agreement with them. The trio promised to get the women out of the DO's way if he granted their request. Although the DO doubted the ability of the trio in controlling the women who had become increasingly restless, he was surprised that as soon as he announced that Okugo would be tried the next day, the women quietly dispersed. The women, however, returned on the day of the trial, and when Okugo was found guilty and jailed two years, they all jubilated (Ibid.).

The DO, realizing how powerful the trio was, used them to prevent violence in other areas. In Umuahia for example, women had massed in the town to begin protest against the Warrant Chiefs.

As the DO feared that the protest might get out of control and endanger European factories and government establishments, he quickly contacted the trio to dissuade the women from embarking on their protest. The trio addressed the women, and to the amazement of the DO, the protest march did not take place (Mba 1982, 82).

It is noteworthy that the DO was also greatly concerned about the situation in Aba where women had started to burn government offices and European factories after two of them were killed in a car accident by a reckless British driver. The DO invited the trio to send a telegram to Aba women to eschew violence, and carry out their protests peacefully. The telegram did not, however, appear to have had any significant effect since arson and looting continued in Aba until the police and army was dispatched to the town (Ibid.).

Heroine of the Revolt in Aba-Ngwa Area: The Power of Literacy

One of the most outstanding leaders of the revolt in Aba-Ngwa area was Madam Mary Okezie (1906–99), the first Ngwa woman to gain Western education. She started to attend the Anglican Mission school at Opobo in 1915, and after her graduation, she became a teacher in her alma mater, and other mission schools in Umuahia, and Aba. Madam Okezie continued teaching till 1938 when she went to a nursing school at Aba and England, and later served as a Health Visitor in the Ministry of Health until 1964.[11]

Madam Okezie was teaching at the Anglican Mission school in Umuocham Aba in 1929 when the women's revolt broke out. Although she did not as a civil servant participate in the revolt, Madam Okezie was very sympathetic to the women's cause. It is not surprising that when some Ngwa women requested her to write a memo on their behalf to be submitted to the Commission of Inquiry in 1930, she willingly granted their request without charging them any money. Her memo is significant not simply because it was the

only one written by a woman, but due to the fact that it clearly articulated the grievances of the women, and gave some insight into the course and consequences of the revolt in Aba-Ngwa area where the most violent protests took place in Igboland (Ibid.).

Madam Okezie clearly emerged as the most famous leader of Ngwa women after the revolt. She became a leading exponent of women's rights, calling for better health facilities for women, and their involvement in governance. Her influence towered in 1948 when she founded the Ngwa Women's Association to promote the education and welfare of women. Madam Okezie was continuously elected the president of the Association for over two decades, and her achievements have continued to be a source of inspiration for the younger generation of Ngwa women (Ibid.).

Women Chieftains of Mbaise, and Royalty Accorded to Them
a) Mary of Ogu Ndem, "Mary of the Women's War"

Research in Mbaise folk tradition has shed some light on the towering height leaders of the women's revolt attained in their communities.[12] Among the women called "Eze Ndi-Iyom" (chief of women), was one Mary, the overall leader of the women's revolt in Onicha Ezinihitte, who was popularly known as "Mary Ogu Ndem" (Mary of the Women's war). According to an informant, Mary:

Was treated as a V.I.P, and caused tremendous stir of excitement whenever she visited any village. Not only were all the village roads swept and weeded, but valuable sheep and goats would be killed for festive eating. All the women would stand along the road to watch and wait for [her]. She would come shaded by an umbrella and her deputy leaders would process behind her. She was the great mistress who laid down the rules (Ibid. 13–14).

b) The Heroic Warrior: Ihejilemebi Ibe of Umuokirika Village

Similarly, the fame the next woman, Ihejilemebi Ibe of Umuokirika, attained was very remarkable. She was a woman known for her incredible bravery and strength of character before and during the women's revolt. Ihejilemebi (meaning: may good things not end when it's my turn), had before the revolt, served as the head of women's spy team during local wars, and a member of the war council. It is not surprising that when the women's revolt broke out, she naturally emerged as a "warrior" who led women to "sit" on the Warrant Chiefs in various communities, burning the houses of those who refused to resign, and hand over their insignia office to her. Ihejilemebi took personal custody of the caps of the Warrant Chiefs who abdicated their office and probably displayed them as a symbol of women's power. She was so much feared by Warrant Chiefs that in one instance, a Warrant Chief of Obohia, Eze Anyanwuagwu is said to have secretly negotiated a truce with her by agreeing to resign, and offer her two big goats and a huge sum of money to save his life (Ibid. 14–16).

Some women, who felt that they were violently abused by their husbands, brought their cases before the "warrior" for arbitration. The men found guilty were disgraced by the "warrior" who selected younger women to beat them up, and carry them shoulder-high around the village as a lesson to others (Ibid. 18).

Ihejilemebi was accorded the privileges powerful men enjoyed in her society. She dressed like a warrior during funeral ceremonies, slung a gun over her shoulder, and joined men of bravery in participating in dances, and rituals reserved for them. Little wonder when Ihejilemebi died, the Ese and Nkwa Ike music, meant exclusively for titled men and warriors respectively, were played in her honor during an elaborate funeral ceremony (Ibid. 14).

Abolition of the Warrant Chief System, and Involvement of Women in the Appointment of New Court Members

Some critiques have attempted to underrate the achievements of women in the political arena, especially in terms of the various demands they made. But bearing in mind the hurdles they faced, and the political climate during and after the revolt, some of their achievements are quite impressive. As an example, in virtually all the communities, women complained about the oppressive and corrupt rule of the Warrant Chiefs whom they described as usurpers, and called upon the administration to abolish the Warrant Chief system, and involve them in governance. The administration acceded to these demands, and in many localities, women helped the government to identify the Ezeala or sacred authority holders of their communities. Some of the Ezeala were appointed to replace the Warrant Chiefs in Native Courts of the 1930s called "massed benches."[13]

Appointment of Women to Native Courts

The administration for the first time in its history, also appointed a few influential leaders of the women's revolt to serve as Native Court members, including Chinwe, the only female member out of the 13 members of the Nguru Mbaise Native Court. Similarly, in Umuapko Native Court area, three out of 30 members were women, while one out of 9 members of the Okpuala Native Court was a woman (Mba 1982, 96).

Ahebi Ugabe of Enugu-Ezike: "The Female Leopard" as a Native Court Member

Perhaps, the most prominent female member of the Native Courts during colonialism was Ahebi Ugabe of Enugu-Ezike in Nsukka area. Ahebi who was appointed a Native Court member in 1930, was reputed for her spiritual prowess, and popularly called "Agamega" or "Female Leopard." Like the Warrant Chiefs, Ahebi was carried to the Native Court in a hammock, and the road she passed to the Native Court in Ogrute village is still called "Akpata Ahebi" (Ahebi's road). Because of her fame and spiritual prowess, Ahebi is the only woman known in remembered history who was permitted by the elders to watch the powerful Omabe masquerade, and build an Omabe shrine in her compound (Meek 1930, 136-139).

c) Continuation of the Legacy of Revolts During the 1930s & 1950s

It is tempting to speculate that due to the high-handed manner in which the Aba Women's revolt was suppressed, Igbo women were cowed down, and many retreated to their safe and peaceful village enclaves where they continued to live as second class citizens. The fictional images of Igbo women, which portray them as marginalized, and passive do not reflect objective reality. Surely, policemen and soldiers were mobilized to suppress the revolt in the "disaffected areas," and Igboland was occupied by the military, to intimidate the people, and prevent further "disturbances." But these severe measures did not stop women from revolting in future whenever they felt that their collective interests were threatened. The 1929 example showed women what could be achieved when they mobilize, and it served as an inspiration to them in organizing the revolts of the 1930s–1950s.

i) The Tax Protests of 1938

Unlike 1929, the tax protests of 1938 were confined largely to Okigwe and Bende Divisions of Owerri Province covering a total area of about 500 square miles. The protests, which in some places became violent, spread like wild fire from Isiukwuato, Uturu, Nneato, Isuochi, Umuchieze, Otanzu, and Otanchara communities of Okigwe Division to Alayi, Item, and Umuimenyi communities of Bende Division (Mba 1982, 98).

As in 1929, the tax protests of 1938 were caused by a variety of factors like inefficient and corrupt tax collectors, and the rumor that the colonial administration had during the Women's revolt, promised to stop collecting tax from people after seven years. The global depression of the 1930s that led to a sharp decrease in the price of palm produce also contributed to the revolt. Men resented paying tax at a time when their annual income could hardly

sustain their families. The grim economic situation in Okigwe Division partly explains why women got involved in the tax protests. Women throughout the Division were economically hard-hit when in December 1938, troops of the Royal West African Frontier Force who had become the major consumers of their foodstuffs, were relocated from Okigwe town to Enugu (Ibid. 99).

Interestingly, the protests started in Okigwe Division where the police arrested some men who failed to pay their tax due in November 1938. Concerned about the situation, women began massive anti-tax protests in Okigwe Division from December 5–15, and in some places like Isuochi, they destroyed the Native Court house, and released prisoners. The administration forcefully suppressed the disturbances, and failed to appoint a Commission of Inquiry to investigate its origins. In addition, the administration did not accede to any of the requests made by the women, including the demand that some of them be appointed tax collectors (Ibid. 100–101).

ii) Oil Mill Protests of the 1940s in Owerri and Calabar Provinces: The Example of Nsulu in Northern Ngwaland (1948)

Rural women continued their legacy of protests in the 1940s whenever they felt their economic and social interests were undermined. As an example, in 1949, the colonial government decided without consulting women, to set up agencies that would supervise the installation of oil mills to enhance the production of palm produce in the eastern region. Women correctly smelt a rat in the proposed oil mill project, and quickly mobilized themselves to protest against it for varying reasons. They were for example, concerned that women could not afford to buy the oil mills costing 2,500 pounds each. In addition, women argued that the rich men who owned the oil mills, bought palm fruits directly from their husbands, and thereby, deprived them of the income they derived from palm kernels (Ibid. 107).

Even though the oil mill protests were quite widespread in parts of Owerri and Calabar Provinces, the Nsulu example is quite illustrative. Women of Ubaha village of Nsulu were infuriated when on January 3, 1948, a woman in tears, reported to them that her cassava farm had been destroyed to make room for the installation of an oil mill purchased by the president of the Nsulu Group Council, Chief J. N. Wachuku. Within two days, hundreds of women from neighboring villages of Umuosu, and those from Oloko in Bende bordering the Nsulu community, embarked on a massive protest. They drove away the workers sent to install the oil mill, and then moved to nearby Nbawsi town to burn down the Nsulu Native Court and free all the prisoners (Ibid. 109).

Altogether 36 women were arrested, and later fined five pounds each. But the Nsulu protests and others convinced the colonial government that it was necessary to take measures to allay the fears of women. The government, for example, instructed members of Group Councils to consult women and other people before oil mills were installed in any community within their jurisdiction. Interestingly, Nsulu people turned out in large numbers during a meeting of their Group Council summoned in January 12, 1948, to determine the fate of the oil mill. 90% or 3,000 out of the 4,000 people present voted against the oil mill project (Ibid.).

iii) Women and the Urban Revolts of the 1950s & 1960s: The Tax Revolt in Aba and Onitsha in 1956

Unlike earlier revolts, urban women dominated the protest movements of the 1950s–1960s. The tax revolt of 1956 occurred in Aba and Onitsha, the leading commercial centers of eastern Nigeria where a large number of women were engaged in occupations such as teaching, nursing, retail trading and sewing. To raise money from the growing number of urban women professionals, the government of Eastern Region led by its premier, Dr. Nnamdi Azikiwe (Zik), passed in April 1956, a finance law which for the first time, imposed an income tax on urban and rural women whose total income exceeded 100 pounds per annum (Ibid. 102).

The finance law was fiercely resisted by Aba and Onitsha women. In Aba for example, more than a thousand market women marched to the Tax Authority to protest against the taxation of women. They then formed the Aba Women's Association to articulate their grievances, threatening to withdraw support for Zik and his party, the National Council of Nigeria and the Cameroon (NCNC) during the next election. Onitsha women took similar measures, and in consequence, the tax law was amended to the satisfaction of women.[14]

iv) Women in Party Politics, 1950s–1960s

Women participated actively in the struggle for Nigerian independence, and some of them attended the constitutional conferences held in London to work out the modalities of governing the country. Their influence was very much felt in the Women's Wing of the major political parties, which they used in articulating their interests. But unlike the earlier movements that were concerned with the localized interests of women, urban and educated women led the women's wing of the NCNC. They used their position to address national issues that were of common interest to women.

Among the leading women of the NCNC was Mrs. Margaret Ekpo, an Efik who in 1936, settled in the town of Aba which she adopted as her home. Mrs. Ekpo was in 1953, elected to the National Executive Council or decision-making organ of the NCNC. She also served as a special member of the Eastern House of Chiefs in 1959 and the vice-president of the NCNC Women's Wing of Eastern Nigeria, which had over 200 branches. Similarly, Mrs. Janet Mokelu of Enugu, the secretary of the Eastern Region NCNC Women's Association, was appointed a special member of the House of Chiefs. She and Mrs. Ekpo were elected to the Eastern House of Assembly in 1961.[15] These and other women, laid the foundation for the modern Igbo women engaged at the present time in a variety of professional activities as lawyers, high court judges and magistrates, medical doctors, and educationists. It is also noteworthy that some Igbo women are holding key cabinet positions at the Federal and State levels, and a few serve as advisers and special assistants to heads of governments.[16]

CONCLUSION

The various revolts, and women's movements discussed in this paper can be divided into two main categories. The first category, beginning with the Aba women's revolt, till the 1950s, was organized and led by rural women. The second category, which took place from 1950–1960, was associated with educated urban women. The Aba women's revolt, however, served as an inspiration to those who organized subsequent revolts, and women's movements. The achievements of the Aba women's revolt and the legacies it left are noteworthy. The revolt helped women to mobilize themselves, and change the existing political order during colonialism. It also enabled some of their leaders who emerged as heroines, to attain a privileged status in Igbo society comparable to those of titled men and warriors. The revolt contributed to the emergence of modern Igbo women who are currently engaged in diverse occupations. It ranks as one of the most outstanding primary resistance movements in Nigerian history.

REFERENCES

Afigbo, A. E. *The Warrant Chiefs: Indirect Rule in South-Eastern Nigeria, 1891–1929* (London: Longman, 1972).

Gailey, H. A. *The Road to Aba: A Study of British Administrative Policy in Eastern Nigeria* (New York: New York University Press, 1970).

Green, M. M. *Igbo Village Affairs*, (London: Frank Cass and Co. Ltd., 1964).

Ifeka-Moller, Caroline. "Female Militancy and Colonial Revolt: The Women's War of 1929, Eastern Nigeria" in Shirley Ardener (ed.), *Perceiving Women* (New York: John Wiley & Sons, 1975), 128–132.

Leith-Ross, Sylvia. *African Women*, (London: Routledge & Kegan Paul Ltd., 1965).

Mba, Nina. "Heroines of the Women's War" in B. Awe (ed.), *Nigerian Women in Historical Perspective*, (Ibadan: Sankore/Bookcrat 1992), 75–88.

—————. *Nigerian Women Mobilized: Women's Political Activity in Southern Nigeria, 1900–1965*, (Berkeley: Institute of International Studies, University of California, 1982).

Meek, C. K. *Ethnographical Report on the Peoples of Nsukka Division of Onitsha Province*, (Lagos, 1930), 136–139.

Nwoga, Ezi-Nwanyi Patricia "Proud Confidence: An Approach to the Heroine Concept in the Folk Tradition of Mbaise."

Okonjo, Kamene. "Women's Political Participation in Nigeria" in E. C. Steady (ed.), *The Black Woman Cross-Culturally*, (Cambridge, Mass: Schenkman Publication Co, 1981), 97–103.

Oriji, J. N. "The Aba women's Revolt" in J. N. Oriji, *Ngwa History* (New York: P. Lang, 1997).

Sklar, R. L. *Nigerian Political Parties*, (Princeton: Princeton University Press, 1963), 402–403.

Van Allen, Judith. "'Aba Riots' or Igbo 'Women's War'? Ideology, Stratification, and Invisibility of Women," in F.C. Steady (ed.), *The Black Woman Cross-Culturally* (Cambridge, Mass: Schenkman Publication Co, 1981), 60.

—————. "Sitting on a Man: Colonialism and the Lost Political Institutions of the Igbo," *Canadian Journal of African Studies*, 6, 11 (1972): 178. © Copyright 2000 Africa Resource Center, Inc. Citation Format

Oriji, John N. (2000). IGBO WOMEN FROM 1929–1960. *West Africa Review*: 2, 1. [iuicode: http://www.icaap.org/iuicode?101.2.1.14].

EXPLOITATION AND UNDERDEVELOPMENT

By L. H. Gann, peter Duignan, D. K. Fieldhouse, Michael Crowder, Walter Rodney and Bade Onimode

THE BURDEN OF EMPIRE

By L.H. GANN and PETER DUIGNAN[1]

The history of Africa, the argument goes, is obviously the history of Africans, not that of its conquerors, and against the vast time span of Africa's past, the imperial period is but a brief interlude. Western conquest in Africa, starting in the 1870s and 1880s, therefore formed but an episode. The "new imperialism" arose from the inner needs of an overripe capitalist system which called for protected markets and even more for new opportunities for Western investors' growing stock of capital. Relying on their temporary military superiority, the whites conquered Africa and introduced new techniques of government and economic exploitation. Under the imperial aegis Africa nevertheless remained poor. Its economy, where not deliberately distorted to suit the victor's purse, was stagnant. African living standards were stationary or declined.

Western man, the argument continues, used the peoples of Africa and their natural riches for his own selfish purpose. His activities therefore help to account for Africa's present backwardness. Empires in Africa greatly contributed to the accumulation of Western capital resources and present-day Western prosperity. One continent's loss was another's gain. But Africa, at long last, revolted against the white

conqueror and has achieved its political liberation, with the exception of a few remaining bastions of Western rule. This victory forms only one of the many struggles in the emancipation of underprivileged classes and races all over the world. African political independence, however, is meaningless without economic independence. Economic, or even cultural, colonialism continues to threaten emergent Africa, and the battle must continue until the levers of financial, commercial, and industrial power pass into black hands and until the last remnants of Western colonialism are liquidated.

We believe that many of these views are wrong and that others stand in need of modification. We are critical of what seems an unduly philanthropic approach to world affairs, of an outlook which springs from a justifiable attempt at cultural self-criticism—commendable within limits—but which nevertheless is as much a distortion as the old-fashioned flag-waving view of history.

We hold that cultures differ objectively in the number of choices which their members can make and in their ability to develop man's potentialities. Matabele society, for instance, possessed some admirable features. Warriors belonging to the ruling stratum were trained to display courage, fortitude, and self-respect. But the number of effective alternatives open to a Matabele fighting man ... was very limited. He might earn renown in battle. He could accumulate wealth in the shape of horned beasts. He could marry many wives and, if successful, gather a large following of kinsmen and captives. But these achievements exhausted the limits of his choice. This is hardly surprising; the resources of Matabele society were small. Drought might destroy the crops, disease might strike down the cattle, and war and pestilence might wipe out a whole community. The margin of survival remained small even at the best of times, and there was relatively little room for innovation or experiment. It is our contention that imperial rule helped to bring about major social, economic, and ideological changes which in turn vastly extended social opportunity. The Matabele warriors' modern descendant can make a living as a teacher, a trader, a bus owner, a civil servant, a farmer, or a tailor. This advance was not only relative, but absolute. It was made possible by a great cultural transfusion in which the West took the leading part and which was not limited to technical factors alone.

In the race for development, the Union of South Africa had many advantages. The country contained more people of European ancestry than all the rest of the continent together; the young dominion therefore commanded the greatest reservoir of human skills and capital existing in Africa. South Africa had a developed transport system. There was an efficient public service and, by African standards, a fairly productive agriculture; there were some excellent ports; there was a developed system of trade and finances. South Africa moreover possessed great mineral riches; the country's gold resources kept their value during periods of depression, when the price of commodities such as copper, maize, or peanuts rapidly dropped. Not surprisingly, South Africa attracted more than twice as much money as all the rest of British Africa. From the mid-1920s to the mid-1930s, South Africa thus nearly doubled the value of its gold output. Mining supplied the government with an enormous amount of revenue and also provided funds for development of other industries.

Copper production in the Belgian Congo made similar progress. Development began in a small way during the first decade of the 1900s. Organized mineral production was incompatible with a "robber economy" based on the export of ivory and wild rubber. The original abuses practiced under the Congo Free State administration disappeared, and after 1908 a more orderly Belgian colonial administration enforced a more sensible policy of economic development. In 1910 a southern railway reached Elisabethville, provided the mines with an outlet for their products to Beira in Portuguese East Africa and enabled the Belgian mines to import coal from Southern Rhodesia and stores and mining equipment from South Africa. World War I stimulated activities, and in 1918 over 20,000 tons of copper were turned out. The slump occasioned a serious setback, but world capitalism surmounted the crisis. In 1936 output reached well over 100,000 tons, and by 1958 copper output amounted to 237,000 tons. The Congo also became the world's greatest producer of industrial diamonds and one of Africa's largest suppliers of hydroelectric power. Mining development went with improved social legislation; the Belgians proved intelligent employers, and after thorough investigation during the late 1920s, the Belgian administration came out with model labor laws for its territory.

South and South Central Africa thus developed into major mineral exporters. Mining dominated the local economy, and minerals from the southern portion of the continent accounted for most of sub-Saharan Africa's foreign trade. In addition, other territories as well made advances. The proclamation of imperial rule over the Gold Coast encouraged an influx of European capital. Foreign entrepreneurs imagined that deep-level mining might also create a second Rand on the West Coast. British and South African investors, however, suffered many disappointments. The gold-bearing strata proved insufficiently rich, and the African people were too numerous and tenacious to give up long-established rights. Gold mining nevertheless made some advance; by 1935 about 41 percent of the country's exports consisted of minerals, mainly gold and diamonds. Gold mining, together with the need to secure a firm hold over the Ashanti, also caused the government to embark on railway building. The opening of the forest by railways and later by motor roads in turn gave great stimulus to the production of cocoa on the part of individual peasant owners.

All Marxist and many non-Marxist economists believe that a country which makes a living by selling raw materials to foreigners necessarily stays poor. Prosperity supposedly cannot be gained without factories, especially steel mills and machine-tool manufactures. There is, however, no justification for this belief. The doctrine rests in the highly ethnocentric assumption that the chronological pattern of the British industrial revolution must prevail all over the world. ... The question of priority also needs to be considered. Modern Zambia may well make money in manufactures, but this does not mean that Northern Rhodesia would have done better in the 1920s and 1930s, at an early stage in its development, by directing funds into factories. Thirty years ago the country lacked an economic infrastructure; manufacturing would have been expensive in social as well as economic terms and might merely have led to a dead end.

The next point concerns the general relationship between colonial capitalism and secondary industry. Marxist arguments notwithstanding, a capitalist economy does not necessarily preclude industrial development in colonial or ex-colonial territories. South Africa and Southern Rhodesia both started as mining and farming countries. In time they built up factories and steelworks with money made in primary industries, an economic policy which they shared with countries as diverse as Australia and the United States.

Large-scale mining, moreover, was not confined to purely extractive processes, but also set off development in what might be called the "nonmetallic" sectors of the economy. Here a distinction must be made between simpler forms of enterprise, such as alluvial gold washing, and complex ventures, such as the deep-level excavation of copper, vanadium, or gold. The technology of alluvial gold production is comparatively simple and requires little capital. Many African communities in countries as widely separated as Ghana and the ancient kingdom of Zimbabwe knew the art of washing the yellow metal and worked this natural resource. That does not mean that mining of this type, needing little capital and often stopping short of processing the extracted raw material, did not contribute to economic wellbeing. In East and Central Africa, indigenous miners sold their gold to Arab or Portuguese traders and thereby acquired more consumer goods than they would otherwise have enjoyed. Large-scale mining, however, made for much greater changes. The mines created markets for more agricultural produce. The flow of investment was not confined just to sinking shafts and driving tunnels. Smelters and electrolytic plants went up in the bush. Mining gave rise to railway development, to road construction, and to the provision of port facilities. Money went into workshops, electric power plants, waterworks, and cement factories. The concentrations of population created a demand for permanent housing. The emergence of townships, large and small, required public utilities and public services. Development in turn attracted a multitude of people eager to meet the growing demand for building material, food, fuel, clothing, and all kinds of services. Banks and trading stores opened their doors. White and black farmers alike found new opportunities for selling their grain and cattle, and "the basis was thus laid for a multiplier-accelerator process of economic growth."

[Some scholars] express indignation over the figures devoted to African wages. [They] point out that only £2 million in money and rations went to Africans working on the mines, out of a gross value of output amounting to £36,742,000. The mineowners, however, also had a case. The mines ... paid £3,600,000 into the public coffers. The government spent some of this on projects benefiting Africans on the Copper Belt, a contribution to African living standards ignored by the conventional Marxist argument. Wages for unskilled men were small because the supply of such labor was large and its competence was low. But African copper miners went to work because they wanted to; in Northern Rhodesia there was no compulsory labor of the type practiced under the fully collectivist system that then prevailed in the Soviet Union. The Central African mines, with their high level of technology and their paternalistic outlook, also eschewed the kind of underground labor on the part of women and children that was utilized during the early industrial revolution in Great Britain. The African proletariat in some ways, therefore, paid a lower price for incipient industrialization than did the British workers in the eighteenth century. African mine workers on the Copper Belt enjoyed a higher standard of living than they did in their native villages; they received better housing and food than at home, so much so that their average physical well-being consistently improved in employment.

For many decades mining dominated the cash economy of sub-Saharan Africa. From the first decade of the 1900s, however, agricultural exports began to rise sharply, and agriculture rapidly increased in relative importance. Much of this development centered on South Africa, by far the most advanced country and the most important pioneer on the African continent. Yet economic growth in many other parts of Africa also went forward at a rapid pace. There is, accordingly, no justification at all for the view, fashionable among critics of the colonial system in the 1920s and 1930s, which saw Africa as nothing but a stagnant pool, whose people, under the imperial aegis, either stood still or were retrogressing. Africa's agricultural progress was all the more surprising in view of the many natural obstacles faced by cultivators black and white alike. Many parts of Africa suffer from alternating cycles of drought, followed by heavy tropical downpours which leach the soils. Erosion forms an everpresent threat to inexpert farmers. The peoples of Africa faced all kinds of human, plant, and animal diseases peculiar to tropical areas. Development was desperately hampered until Western research found means of coping with afflictions such as malaria, sleeping sickness, and parasites attacking cattle. The lack of transportation facilities further impeded development. Most parts of Africa lacked good riverine communications; because of the great distances, inland producers in the past could rarely market their crops. The imperial impact vastly changed this situation. The period from 1880 to 1920 was the great age of railway building in Africa. By the end of the 1930s about 32,000 miles of railroad track were in operation, about two-thirds of which served South Africa, the Rhodesias, the Congo, and the Portuguese colonies.

The steam locomotive helped bring about a social revolution. An ordinary freight train used nowadays in Africa will do the work of 15,000 to 20,000 carriers for one-fifth to one-tenth the cost. The steam engine thus relieved the sweating African porter from his age old labors; for the first time in the continent's history farmers could produce economic crops away from coastal and river ports. Africa's scarce manpower could at last be used in pursuits more profitable to the economy than head porterage. In the 1920s and 1930s motortrucks and bicycles also began to make their appearance in the bush. The new means of locomotion might in some ways be called "markets on tires," providing backward farmers with new incentives for turning out more and better crops.

Agricultural development in twentieth-century Africa stood, so to speak, on three legs. There was cultivation by African peasants; there was farming by European settlers; there were some large-scale plantations run by big concessionary companies. Of all these, African enterprise was by far the most important, but it was also the form of enterprise that varied most extensively in methods, technical skill, and output. African peasants faced many obstacles. They had to contend not only with the difficulties of nature, but also with lack of physical and social capital. Throughout most of Africa their work continued to depend on hoes and axes and on the unaided power of the human muscle. In most parts of Africa tribesmen lacked incentives for intensive cultivation. Land was plentiful; whenever cultivators had exhausted the fertility of their gardens, they moved on, allowing nature to restore the fertility of the soil. As long as the supply of land seemed unlimited and storage facilities and markets few or nonexistent, African cultivators would only have wasted time and effort by producing more specialized crops. Where conditions became favorable, however, African farmers did make use of new opportunities and in some areas made astonishing progress.

One of the best-known success stories concerns the development of cocoa in the Gold Coast (now Ghana). The Gold Coast had an ancient tradition of overseas trade. The commerce in palm oil and other commodities had created a certain amount of capital. Long-standing links with the Western world and improved railway and port facilities created under British aegis put bush farmers in touch with metropolitan customers. Contacts with other countries also introduced new cultivable plants, including the cacao tree. The colony's agricultural department provided valuable help [for cocoa production], and by 1935–1936 output amounted to 285,351 tons, that is, nearly half the world's supply. Cocoa enabled the Gold Coast to pay for substantial imports of cement, machinery, flour, and so forth, commodities unknown to the country in the 1890s. Carriers and canoes gradually gave way to steam locomotives, trucks, and bicycles, and conditions of life underwent a major transformation.

African society at the same time experienced a new kind of social differentiation. The old pattern of a small family farm, run entirely by the labor of the peasant's own kinsfolk, gradually disintegrated. The majority of growers came to rely on hired labor; some accumulated great wealth, but others fell into poverty. West Africa as a whole now had to face the problem of migrant labor, with the additional disadvantage that small proprietors could not afford welfare facilities remotely comparable to those provided by big European-owned mining companies. The growers also believed that foreign buyers combined to keep down cocoa prices. In 1937 most of the big European firms entered into an agreement to restrict competition and to prevent local prices from rising above the world market level. The African growers, to their good fortune, were not then tied down by any official distribution monopoly, and they retaliated by refusing to sell to the buyers' combine. Some European firms, moreover, remained aloof from the restriction scheme, and in the end the two

parties to the dispute concluded a truce which once again allowed cocoa to be sold abroad. There were many other difficulties, but by and large African agricultural enterprise made considerable progress, especially on the West Coast; the black farmer became what he had never been before in the history of his continent—a factor of some importance in the world economy.

In relation to the enormous size of the African landmass, white agricultural enterprise remained restricted in extent, being confined to a few relatively limited areas. … [In its early days] South Africa never experienced any large-scale white immigration, and economic progress remained relatively slow. Cape farmers turned out limited quantities of grain, fruit, vegetables, wine, and livestock for local consumption and for ships plying the Indian trade. But the settlers who pushed inland had to rely largely on grazing of a simple type, requiring many acres. Territorial expansion in most parts of South Africa thus owed its primary impetus to cattlemen rather than to capitalists with land as the prize of victory. Technically backward as the settlers might have been, their economic and military potential nevertheless remained far superior to that of the Bantu. The black tribesmen thus lost control over most of the available land, and South Africa became the only region on the continent where the overwhelmingly greater part of the available acreage passed into white ownership.

After about the middle of the nineteenth century, moreover, European farmers at the Cape strengthened their economic potential and found a modest kind of prosperity. Growing ports and expanding mining compounds furnished farmers with additional markets. Engineers put up roads, bridges, railways, and dockyards. The growth of shipping and banking helped to put the country in touch with new customers overseas. Some farmers began to work out more intensive methods, and various technological improvements made their appearance in the countryside. Landowners experimented with new products such as mohair and ostrich feathers, while South African Merino wool acquired a recognized place on the world markets.

In the twentieth century, technological change acquired increasing momentum. Agricultural mechanization and progress in agricultural processing industries such as fruit canning, tobacco manufacture, and meat refrigeration vastly added to the country's wealth. Farmers developed better methods of plant selection, stockbreeding, and soil management. Veterinary surgeons learned how to cope with various kinds of animal diseases. Despite large remaining islands of backwardness, South Africa developed into the most skilled and most versatile of Africa's agricultural exporters.

[Another] instrument of progress was company enterprise. Big business preferred to put its resources into mines and railways and, in South Africa, into factories. There were, however, some notable exceptions. Unilever in the Congo and the Cameroons Development Corporation in West Africa promoted extensive agricultural enterprises. Liberia also owed much of its development to similar foreign initiative. In 1926 the Finance Corporation, a Firestone subsidiary, concluded an agreement with the Liberian government and advanced money to the small, financially unstable republic. ... The Liberians secured sufficient cash to satisfy some of their creditors and attained the unusual distinction of being one of the few nations to repay their war debts to the United States in full. Firestone received extensive land and tax concessions and in turn initiated the world's largest rubber undertaking. Furthermore, the company acquired a good reputation as an employer. It paid its workmen much more adequately than the government and other local entrepreneurs and also subsidized wages by bonuses for increased output and by selling low-priced food to its employees. Plantation labourers could work their own plots in spare-time hours; debt peonage was strictly avoided. The company put up hospitals, built roads, and established a public radio service and other undertakings. Firestone had sufficient perception to encourage independent rubber production in Liberia, proving thereby that company enterprise need not necessarily conflict with private initiative. The company provided free rubber seeds to independent growers, as well as high-yielding clones, or buds, and trained instructors to advise on methods.

In summary, the inter-war period saw tremendous economic growth in Africa. There is, accordingly, no justification for the view of this period of African history as one of imperial neglect in contrast with Communist progress. True enough, development was uneven. Large areas of Africa were little affected by change; only South Africa, the oldest white-settled area on the continent, managed to build up substantial industries, while the continent as a whole remained a primary producer which devoted its resources to the export of minerals and crops. Africa did, however, see vast additions to its real resources in the shape of railway lines, roads, mines, plantations, hydroelectric plants, and other assets. These economic changes came about without large-scale liquidations and without forced labor of the Stalinist variety. Imperial rule indeed shielded sub-Saharan Africa from other foreign pressures and prevented internecine struggles; colonial Africa bore but a minor military burden; it operated with a relatively small and inexpensive state machinery, so that comparatively few resources were diverted into civil service and defense expenditure (the Gold Coast had fewer than 150 civil servants in the 1930s).

The new enterprise, by the very speed of its impact, created a host of social tensions. The clash of black peasant agriculture, white farming, and company ventures, for instance, might engender sharp competition for labor and natural resources. Competition, on the other hand, might also imply cooperation. Firestone's activities to a certain degree assisted indigenous Liberian rubber producers; white Rhodesian tobacco farmers bought native-grown maize. The various new enterprises in some ways complemented one another. Critics of existing colonial practices often erred, therefore, when they advocated reforms in terms of a rigid either-or choice and contrasted black with white farming or primary with secondary industries as mutually exclusive categories.

Contact with the white man, whether as merchant, mineowner, farmer, or manufacturer also brought about economic changes of a more intangible kind. Europeans taught African villagers the art of storing ideas. In the past, tradition had depended on memory and word of mouth; the old knew most and the young least. Now missionaries and others showed how words might be committed to paper and permanently preserved. Not only were labor migrants enabled to communicate with their fellow villagers back home by means of inky marks on paper, but also they were enabled to read books and newspapers. Of equal significance was the creation of a vernacular literature which began, as in Europe, with translations of the Scriptures and the compilation of hymnbooks in indigenous languages. Cash-books and catechisms both demand literacy of their users, and these skills in turn helped to speed up economic transformation.

In addition, economic change spread new ways of measuring time and space. The Africans, of course, could reckon time quite adequately for their purposes; they divided the year into months and seasons, or they used the growth cycle of a crop, with the day further subdivided by the sun's position or what people would normally be doing at that hour. But in villages there were neither printed calendars nor mechanical clocks. Time was an everlasting stream. The white man's beliefs, however, were very different. Time to the European was something that could be minutely subdivided, a commodity for sale. … The new space-time concept slowly influenced African thought in general and in turn contributed to the great economic transformation that was beginning to change the face of Africa.

THE MYTH OF ECONOMIC EXPLOITATION

By D.K. FIELDHOUSE[2]

The most commonly held and dangerous myth connected with the modern empires is that they were great machines deliberately constructed by Europe to exploit dependent peoples by extracting economic and fiscal profit from them. Its corollary is that the new states had a moral claim to be compensated for losses suffered in the past by being helped to become advanced industrial economies. None denied that it was desirable for wealthy industrial states to help those with primitive economies, but to base their claim to assistance on the premise that they were exploited in the past was wrong. The myth of imperial profit making is false.

To start with, the modern empires were not artificially constructed economic machines. The second expansion of Europe was a complex historical process in which political, social and emotional forces in Europe and on the periphery were more influential than calculated imperialism. Individual colonies might serve an economic purpose; collectively no empire had any definable function, economic or otherwise. Empires represented only a particular phase in the ever changing relationship of Europe with the rest of the world, analogies with industrial systems or investment in real estate were simply misleading.

Yet, though the colonial empires were undoubtedly functionless in origin, this is not to say that they did not later provide an economic return, a "profit," to their owners. Certainly many colonial enthusiasts in Europe alleged that they could and did. Were they right?

To answer this question requires a careful analysis of its meaning. It is, in fact, highly theoretical. An industrial company exists to produce profits, colonies were human societies belonging to a different order of things. It is really as meaningless to ask whether a colony such as Nigeria was "profitable" to Britain as to ask whether Wales or England was. In each case some form of "advantage" was obvious. But this was not necessarily economic; and if it was it cannot necessarily be called "profit" and need not result from "exploitation." In short, such concepts reflect a perverted form of thinking about colonies which derived from the "mercantile" theories of the first empires. The fact that they were commonly held does not make them true. The task of the historian is to analyze the various forms of "profit" Europe may have gained from her colonies; to compare these with countervailing disadvantages; and to decide whether on balance empire gave economic advantages which Europe would not otherwise have obtained.

The crux of the matter is to define what empire meant in economic terms. A colony differed from an independent state only in that it was governed by an alien power, colonial status was primarily a political phenomenon. This immediately limits the field of inquiry, for it excludes all those influences exerted by Europe which fell short of full political control: "economic imperialism" and "informal empire," for example. If empire generated "profit" this must be directly attributable to alien rule. The question can therefore be redefined: what economic advantages did Europe extract from her colonies which she could not have gained from other countries, however similar in other ways?

There were at least six obvious ways in which this might be done. The first was simply to loot an occupied country of its treasures. This was very rare in the modern empires. Few new colonies possessed hoarded wealth on the scale of Mexico, Peru or India in the past: there was little that could profitably be seized from African or Polynesian chiefs. Moreover, although "pacifying" armies were often barbarous in their methods, they were normally under direct

D. K. Fieldhouse, Selections from *The Colonial Empires: A Comparative Survey from the Eighteenth Century*, pp. 380-387, 389-394. Published by Delacorte Press, 1967. Copyright by D. K. Fieldhouse. Permission to reprint granted by the rights holder.

metropolitan control, and conquest was quickly followed by civilized methods of government. The rape of Bengal in the 1760s was not repeated after 1815.

A more sophisticated way of extracting profit before 1815 was to transfer colonial revenues to the metropolitan treasury. This also became very rare. From 1831 to 1877 the Dutch transferred Indonesian surpluses through the "Culture System"; the British East India Company and other chartered companies sometimes paid dividends out of colonial taxation; but no normal colonial government ever did so. Some demanded contributions to defence costs; the French confused things by integrating the accounts of some colonies with their own. But most colonies were left to use their own revenues and were more likely to receive subsidies than to be robbed of surpluses.

A third possible source of imperial advantage was to transfer money or goods from colony to metropolis as interest on loans, payment for services rendered, the pensions and savings of colonial officials and the profits made by business firms. Much has been made of this "drain," particularly by Indian historians; but the Indian case is misleading. The greater part—interest charges, profits of alien enterprises, etc.—would have been equally due from independent states which borrowed in the British capital market or in which British firms operated. The net "drain" was therefore the cost of services, such as the Indian army, which Britain controlled and which India might not otherwise have chosen to pay for, and the transferred salaries of alien officials. The damage to India was not the absolute cost but the loss of currency and international exchange by a country short of both.

A fourth possible form of exploitation was the imposition of "unfair" terms of trade on a colony. This had been the basic device of the "mercantile" empires, and, in its pre-nineteenth century form, may well have provided artificially high profit levels for metropolitan merchants and producers. But no modern empire operated a comparable system of monopoly. By the 1860s the old controls had been dismantled. Although tariff preferences, shipping subsidies, navigation acts and import quotas were soon disinterred, no country ever entirely closed colonial ports to foreign competition. Even the proportion of colonial trade which fell to the

parent states was unimpressive. Britain's share of her empire's trade fell from an average of 49 per cent in the decade after 1854 to 36 per cent in 1929–33, thereafter, even revived protection only increased it slightly. France kept a larger share, always more than half, of the trade of her colonies; even so, the proportion declined with time. Most other empires had a similar experience, only the United States and Russia, which entirely enclosed their colonies within domestic tariff systems, really had a commercial monopoly; and this probably benefitted the dependencies as much as the metropolis. Although modern protectionism harmed the interests of colonial subjects as much as it did metropolitan consumers, it was at least reasonably impartial and the losses of colonial consumers were compensated by guaranteed and preferential markets in Europe. It is therefore unlikely that "neo-mercantilism" produced substantial net "profits" for metropolitan countries.

By a curious paradox, however, it has been argued that during their era of free trade the British "exploited" colonies by making it impossible for them to protect their own industries against her exports, so holding back their industrial progress. This did not apply to the settlement colonies, which were allowed their own protectionist policies from 1859, but may have been true of others. India was again the test case, since she was the only British dependency in the nineteenth century with the evident capacity to develop large-scale mechanized industry. There is no doubt that free trade had serious consequences for her. In the early nineteenth century free import of British cottons destroyed Indian hand-loom weaving on a commercial scale, thereafter the British ban on protective tariffs held back mechanized cotton production and kept the market open for Lancashire. Indian cottons were not protected until about 1926, and textile imports from Britain then dropped significantly. India consumed £40,729,000 out of total British manufactured textile exports of £195,805,000 in 1913, but only £11,373,000 in 1934. To some extent enforced free trade may have had similar effects on other nascent Indian industries and on the economic growth of other British dependencies.

Yet it is impossible to be certain that these disadvantages were specifically the result of British imperial authority, for other and totally independent states were also forced, during the nineteenth century, to reduce or abolish import duties in the interests of British exports. China, for example, was restricted by treaty after 1842 to a maximum tariff of 5 percent on all imports. An "open door" might, in fact, have been imposed on any weak state by European powers, an independent India might have been as unable as China was to protect her own industries against foreign demands for freedom of access. Thus the "open door" was a typical product of Europe's general preponderance. Formal empire was one way of imposing it, but by no means the only way; and the benefits resulting from free commercial access to non-European states cannot be regarded as an exclusively imperial "profit."

The most commonly alleged form of imperial profiteering was to "exploit" the natural endowments of dependencies—oil, minerals, natural rubber, ivory, etc. If these were extracted without giving compensating advantages, an ex-colony might hypothetically find itself robbed of assets which might otherwise have financed the creation of a modern industrial economy. … Examples of "exploitation" on this scale are, however, difficult to find. Extractive industries were never entirely insulated from their environment. All had to use local labor. They paid wages lower than they paid to Europeans but vastly higher than those normal in subsistence economies. All had to build modern communications and other amenities which benefitted the colony as a whole. Some part of company profits were always spent locally, lubricating the colonial economy. Most overseas companies had to pay taxes to the colonial government. Thus no extractive industry failed to provide some advantages to the dependency in which it operated. The question is whether these were enough: whether an independent state could have gained more.

The question was pragmatic rather than moral. The value of natural endowments was for the most part created by demand elsewhere, in most cases only alien capital and skills could give them commercial value. What tax was due to the indigenous owners of the soil? The only useful yardstick was what happened in comparable independent countries; and evidence provided by states such as Persia and the Latin American republics suggests that this would have been small simply because their bargaining power also was small. Independence enabled ex-colonies to impose stricter terms on foreign companies, but these were matched by the higher demands also made by previously independent states after 1945. If neither was able to undertake such complex economic operations on its own account, its demands were limited by the fact that Europeans might cease to operate altogether.

It is impossible, therefore, to measure the "profit" Europe gained from "exploiting" the natural resources of her dependencies because they were formal colonies. By mid-twentieth-century standards Europeans showed a cavalier disregard for the interests of other societies, taking what was profitable and putting back only what was necessary. Yet this had little to do with political empire and was not limited to it. One-sided use of natural resources reflected an imbalance of power between the west and the nonindustrialized areas of the world; and while this lasted no non-European society had sufficient bargaining power to impose fully equitable terms.

The last and most sophisticated way in which empires have been alleged to give economic profit was through the higher return Europeans could obtain by investing capital in colonies than they could get at home. … This theory was based on the Marxist principle of "surplus value," and turned on the greater profitability of using capital in tropical lands where labor was cheaper than in industrialized Europe. Lenin, for example, argued in 1916 that the growth of industrial monopoly and "finance-capitalism" in western states created an enormous "superabundance of capital." This could not profitably be invested at home without raising wage levels, and therefore reducing profits, simply because the labor supply could not be expanded. The rest of the world lacked capital but had ample labor and raw materials. European capital could generate a higher surplus value there than at home, and this enabled metropolitan capital to go on accumulating. If it could not go abroad, capital would stagnate and capitalism would crack. Lenin predicted that in course of time the nonindustrial world would be entirely absorbed by European "imperialists" (finance-capitalists), and that this would lead to wars for imperial redivision which would destroy capitalist society and usher in the socialist revolution.

Shorn of its ideological trimmings, Lenin's theory simply asserted that the combination of cheap labor, political power to make it work at subsistence wages, and commercial monopoly to exclude foreign rivals, generated excess profits for European empires. The desire for these advantages led to tropical colonization. Was he right?

He was wrong on one point at least, for, as has already been seen, it is impossible to explain the expansion of European empires after 1815 in terms of economic need: there simply was no correlation between the time-scale of European "finance-capitalism" and imperial expansion, nor between colonies and areas of greatest investment.

The advantages which Lenin thought European capital engaged in the colonies received from imperial political power were in fact of little significance. Labor was certainly cheap by European standards: otherwise many of these enterprises would have been unprofitable. But low wages were not created by political power, they reflected the social environment of a subsistence economy. In the period before about 1906 many colonial governments provided forced or semi-forced labor; but this was also a period of generally low company profits. Thereafter colonial governments tended to impose restrictions on labor contracts and conditions of work, both tending to raise labor costs. Europeans could have "exploited" native labor more effectively if they had not been policed by imperial administrations sensitive to humanitarian public opinion at home, and they often did so in independent Latin America and the Middle East. Nor did empire provide a degree of commercial monopoly sufficient to enable capitalists to sell at monopolistic prices at home or in the colonies. European investors showed no marked preference for their own colonies, and often got higher returns by operating in foreign empires. Conversely, the really artificial prices were those set by agreement between companies of different nationalities, especially the oil companies, which transcended imperial systems. Thus, while colonial governments often provided a convenient framework of political security within which private companies could work satisfactorily, formal empire was in no sense necessary for profitable European activity overseas.

Second, the relative profitability of investment in Europe and in tropical dependencies was determined by many complex factors and varied immensely from time to time. Changing economic and political conditions within Europe sometimes encouraged investment at home, sometimes overseas. Another important influence was the relative demand for the products of the advanced economies and those of primary producing countries in which a large proportion of "colonial" investment was made. When the terms of trade favored primary producers, investment in tropical colonies was obviously more profitable than when the terms favored manufacturing states. During the half century before 1914 European demand for minerals, tropical vegetable oils, and food increased considerably, and the terms of trade normally favored primary producers. This enabled the more fortunate European companies producing such goods to make spectacular profits. Between 1914 and 1939, however, the terms of trade normally favored industrial producers, with the result that the relative advantage of investing in primary-producing countries was less. After 1939 the war and postwar demand for primary products again favored the overseas investor, though by the later 1950s his advantage was declining. Such trends cannot confidently be translated into statistics, but some indication of their importance can be gained from estimates of the relative percentage rate of profit gained from investment in industrial concerns operating in Britain and in British companies operating overseas between 1953 and 1961. In 1953 British industrialists gave an average net profit of 12.5 percent on their capital (ordinary capital plus capital and revenue reserves), as against 21.5 percent from overseas companies. In 1961 British industrials were yielding 12.4 percent but overseas companies only 13.7 percent. In the same years the terms of trade, taking 1937–8 as 100, had moved in Britain's favor from 119 to 103.

Such figures are far too limited to prove anything; but they do suggest, in conjunction with other evidence, that the profitability of investment in primary-producing non-European economies, many of which were colonies, depended more on international economic factors than on the special advantages which Lenin thought colonies provided for their masters. By comparison the political status of nonindustrialized countries was of little importance, and empire could not of itself generate super profit for European capital.

If Europe benefitted economically from other parts of the world by "exploiting" them, it was because of her immense military and economic preponderance. Empire in the formal sense was merely one form in which this was expressed, and had no colonial empires been created in the nineteenth century Europe would still have taken whatever economic assets she needed and dictated the terms on which she did so.

In fact, no meaningful balance sheet can be constructed, even in economic terms. One or two small or short-lived empires almost certainly cost their owners more than they repaid. Certainly the German and Italian empires did so, because their colonies lacked natural resources, and because they were in any case destroyed before high initial expenditure could be written off against long-term advantages. All other empires were too complex for such definite verdicts to be made. Most colonies were "unprofitable" during the period of initial conquest and while later internal rebellions lasted. But there were few such expenses between about 1920 and 1939; and apart from obvious metropolitan expenditure (grants-in-aid, payment for services in particular colonies, etc.) the cost of colonies depends on what proportion of total imperial expenditure (on defence, for example) is debited to them. Hence no one can determine whether the accounts of empire ultimately closed with a favorable cash balance.

This is unimportant, for the value of the colonial empires was not to be measured in money. Colonies were seldom deliberately acquired to produce wealth, and they were retained irrespective of their "profitability." Empire in the modern period was the product of European power: its reward was power or the sense of power. The end of empire did not mean economic loss to the onetime imperial states; on the contrary, it meant that the economic advantage of operating in other parts of the world was no longer offset by the cost and inconvenience of political responsibilities. Only the minority of private investors and others, whose assets or business concerns were hampered, destroyed, or taken over without proper compensation by the new states, actually lost through decolonization. The West retained its economic preponderance: some even held that the margin of wealth between advanced and "developing" countries widened as empire ended. If Europe in fact derived her wealth from her colonies, their loss made remarkably little difference to her.

Yet the West undoubtedly suffered from the end of empire, for Europe and America lost some part of their political power and self-assurance. The world no longer consisted of colonies unable to complicate international politics, the United Nations provided a forum in which the new states could challenge overwhelming power by appealing to alleged moral standards and the principle of one state one vote. The powers were no longer free to use their military power to support their interests, the Suez crisis of 1956–7 marked the end of "informal empire" in its nineteenth-century form. The world was no longer ringed by the western bases and colonial armies which had enabled it to impose its will on all continents. Europeans had lost the freedom of movement and economic activity which empire had given them. They were now dependent on a multiplicity of small and often chauvinistic states who needed western enterprise but also resented it and complicated its operations. But above all the end of empire deprived the West of status. The countries of Europe were no poorer than they had been before, but they were infinitely smaller. They had been the centers of vast empires, now they were petty states preoccupied with parochial problems. Dominion had gone and with it the grandeur which was one of its main rewards.

THE ECONOMIC IMPACT OF COLONIAL RULE IN WEST AFRICA

By MICHAEL CROWDE[3]

The economic impact of colonial rule on African society was much less profound than colonial administrators liked to think. The period 1919–39 was one of *immobilisme* in which what little change there was did not stand comparison with what was taking place in the outside world. The railway systems had for the most part been completed by 1918—only the introduction of the motor vehicle was a significant factor for change in this period. The African found himself the simple producer of raw materials for which Lebanese were the agents of sale and European companies the exporters. Conversely these same companies imported the goods which the African bought, mainly at the shops or through the agencies of Lebanese traders, with the money he earned from the sale of his crop. Only in rare cases did the African survive as an importer, almost never as an exporter, and in neither role was he significant after 1920. Except in the cocoa-producing areas of the Gold Coast and Nigeria, the African was squeezed out of his precolonial role of middleman between peasant producer and expatriate exporter by the Lebanese. This meant that the African's role in the colonial economy became almost exclusively that of petty trader and primary producer of cash crops on his own account or as labourer on the farms of others, African or European, in the case of the few plantations that existed in French West Africa. A small number were employed in mining industries in Ashanti, Jos, and Enugu on the railways and as casual labourers in the urban centers. The income they derived from the colonial economy was for the most part so low that it brought about no significant change in their standard of living.

Only cocoa and coffee fetched high enough prices to affect the traditional socioeconomic structure of the peoples producing it. The other cash crops, most of which had, like palm products, groundnuts and cotton, been exported before the imposition of colonial rule fetched such low prices that the peasant produced just enough to pay taxes and satisfy his immediate needs for imported cloths, utensils and foodstuffs like sugar. The narrow range of goods in the Lebanese stores was not substantially different from those which the African middleman used as the basis of barter in pre-colonial times.

For the African peasant the growing of cash crops during the colonial period was, except in the cocoa-and coffee-producing areas, primarily geared to paying taxes and supplementing the subsistence economy with imported luxuries. If the price for cash crops was low, his marginal propensity to produce cash crops for sale over and above those necessary for the purposes of paying taxes fell also. For the peasant could provide most of his basic needs from internal sources. Even when the price for crops was high, immense effort was required in labor terms to produce larger quantities. This problem was solved, partially, by the importation of labor from other areas. This migratory labor was available, as we have seen, because of taxes imposed on peoples inhabiting areas on which no cash crops would grow. In certain areas the peasant would involve himself in commitments based on the previous year's price for a crop, and be forced to produce greater quantities of his cash crop in order to meet them if it fell. Where immigrant labor was scarce, he would have to transfer labor from the subsistence crops to the cash crops. In parts of Senegambia this situation, aggravated by the long-standing dependence on imported goods, reached the point where peasants were importing rice which they could grow themselves, and going without food for nearly two months a year, because they had neglected the subsistence economy in favor of the cash crops. Counteracting the propensity of the peasant to abandon cultivation of the cash crop in favor of subsistence crops, was his tendency to incur debts to the Lebanese traders, who were quite aware that indebtedness was one of the only ways over and above taxation which could force him to produce for a low price. The French, however, resorted to the introduction of compulsory production of crops in areas where the peasant would otherwise have refused to grow them because of the low price. Thus, anxious to be independent of cotton supplies from outside the French empire, the administration in French West Africa forced the peasant to produce it under threat of imprisonment if the quality was not good enough or the quantity insufficient. The ease with which people moved out of the cash economy into a purely subsistence economy also related to the dependence their society had built up on imported goods. In Senegal, where by the time of the Depression many families had been involved in the export of groundnuts to Europe for over seventy years, imported cloths, utensils and rice had become part of their way of life. But even they, despite predictions of famine and political upheaval, were able to revert to subsistence production in 1932. Millet, manioc and taro were substituted for imported rice. Home-grown tobacco replaced imported varieties. Honey was gathered in place of sugar, and local soap and perfumes were produced again; thus stimulating the subsistence economy.

The extent of the involvement of the peasant in the cash crop economy was limited by the extent of the colonial transportation system. Vast areas, such as Bornu in Nigeria, remained largely untouched by it because no railway passed through them, and until after the Second World War long-distance road haulage of the low-priced cash crops did not pay. Even the term cash applied to these crops is inappropriate, for in many areas the exchange of "cash" crop for imported goods was largely by barter. It was the migrant labourer father than the peasant farmer who became the pioneer of currency as a means of exchange.

Just how little the bulk of the people were affected by the European-dominated import–export economy is brought out by Governor Clifford's report to the Nigerian Council in 1923:

> The vast majority of the indigenous population are still independent of the outside world for all their essential supplies. They can and do spin their own thread, weave their own garments, provide their own foodstuffs, and even, when the necessity arises, forge their own tools, and make their own pottery. For them imports from Europe are still, in the main, luxuries with which, if needs must, they can wholly dispense; and the sole exception to this in pre-war days, was imported spirits of European manufacture.

And for these latter they had "illicit" substitutes. Twenty years later, with regard to the whole of British West Africa, the Leverhulme Trust Commission reported that "all Africans are, to a very large extent, and very many of them wholly, outside the system of money economy which dominates the economic life of Europe and the rest of the world." The African, encouraged in times of good prices to produce cash crops, and ignorant of the fluidity of prices on the world commodity markets, was easily convinced that he was being robbed and deceived by the whites if they offered him a low price, and refused to continue production unless under pressure of taxation, indebtedness or force.

THE AFRICAN PEASANT AND NEW CROPS

The colonial regime did little to improve the growing techniques of low-value export crops: they remained the same as in precolonial times. For most peasants the European agricultural officers were an irrelevance. There was of course no attempt to improve the methods of production of subsistence crops, as the Germans had done in Togo. Thus the peasant, whether farming for himself or working on the farms of others, did not gain any new knowledge of agricultural techniques under colonial rule. Even the labourer in European plantations used for the most part his traditional instruments, and stayed there as short a time as possible, learning nothing about improvement. Rather the peasant was allowed to exhaust the land. In Senegal, for instance, large areas, like the Baol, have been reduced to semi-desert by the cultivation of groundnuts. As early as 1925 certain areas of Senegal like Thies and Diourbel were exhausted and the peasants had to move eastwards, following the railway to earn enough money to pay taxes and buy imported goods.

The colonial administration did nothing to prevent situations such as that in Gambia where rice that could have been grown by the peasant more cheaply was imported, and to pay for it he devoted more of his energies in the cultivation of groundnuts. Indeed it favored the colonial economic system, for French rice exporters in Indochina could find a market in Senegal. Only when Indochina became independent of France did France make efforts to develop Senegal's own rice potential. Similarly, Cardinall, commenting on the imports of foodstuffs in Gold Coast in 1930, noted that the country could have produced itself half "the fresh fish, rice, maize and other meal, beans, salted and fresh meat, edible oils, spices and fresh vegetables (imported), or in other words would have saved 200,000 pounds."

The only crops that did radically alter the standard of living of their producers were cocoa and coffee in the Gold Coast, Ivory Coast and Western Nigeria. For both these crops the price was consistently sufficiently high for the farmer safely to depend on imported goods in substitution for domestically produced goods. Under the stimulus of a crop whose value increased in the Gold Coast from £4,764,067 in 1921 to £11,229,000 in 1928 on the eve of the Depression, great tracts of new land were opened to cocoa cultivation by immigrant "rural capitalists" who used the profits from their first crops to purchase further farm land. It has often been thought that the revolutionary aspect of the Gold Coast cocoa industry was the fact that

Africans sold land which was supposed to have been communally owned. But … the sale of land had been common in some areas for fifty years or so before the introduction of cocoa into the Akwapim and Akim-Abuakwa area. What was an innovation was not the idea of sale of land itself but the intensity of its application.

In Ivory Coast the Abe found no difficulty in selling land, but the Agni strongly resisted it. The cocoa boom in the Gold Coast and later in the Ivory Coast stimulated migrations of farmers into new lands. Those who could not buy land, worked for the owners. In the case of the Gold Coast two systems of tenant–farmer relation have been [documented.] The first was that of *abusa*, whereby the labourer was paid one third of the cocoa he plucked for his employing farmer, the second that of *nto-tokano*, whereby the labourer was paid a fixed sum per load for the cocoa he plucked for his employing farmer.

The cocoa industry in Ghana created a rich class of farmers who were able to undertake social innovations at their own initiative, and who showed that the African peasant, if prices were good, did not have to be forced into production. … The same was true of the Ivory Coast cocoa industry which grew from a mere 1,000 tons in 1920 to 52,714 tons in 1938, and the coffee industry which grew from 248 tons in 1928 to 14,076 tons in 1938.

Of the peasant-farmers in West Africa, only those producing cocoa and coffee were significantly involved in the money economy and experienced substantial social change as a result. In Larteh, Akwapim, in Ghana, cocoa-farming and the wealth it brought had far-reaching effects on all aspects of economic and social life. The farmers of Larteh on their own initiative built roads and bridges to link their farms with the government road and the main cocoa-collecting centers. In 1914 they even employed a Swiss engineer to build a wooden bridge, still standing today, for which nine of them and one other subscribed £2,000. Between 1914 and 1930 the people of Akwapim spent at least £30,000 on roads to connect with the government-built road.

One such road, built entirely without government assistance, was actually opened in 1926 by the acting governor, to whom the chief responsible addressed a request for government assistance with the debt of £2,600 still outstanding to the contractor. The chief, the Benkumhene, also asked that government "appoint a town engineer to lay and carry out the construction of streets and other works of public utility" in Larteh. These demands for development were refused and a warning given against the construction of further roads. As it was, apart from the railway the communications system of the area was built by the local people with little or no assistance and encouragement from government.

Over half Larteh's completed houses in 1963—some 1,000—were built with profits from the cocoa trade before 1910. Apart from investment in communications, housing, education and funerals became the main items of expenditure of the cocoa farmers. Unfortunately, … the acquisition of wealth did not mean a necessary improvement in basic standards of living and nutrition, for far too much money was spent on luxuries, and at the same time concentration on cocoa farming led to neglect of subsistence farming. No other group was brought into the money economy in the way the cocoa and coffee farmers were. The migrant labourer depended on currency, but he earned very little, and most of it was taken in taxes and by his family on his return.

THE AFRICAN LABOURER

Those employed on the European plantations of the Ivory Coast or Guinea were little affected by their experience. Their terms of labor were seasonal for the most part, and they were not only underpaid, but not given, as we have seen in Ivory Coast, all that they earned in cash. No rural proletariat arose from among the workers on the European plantations. Before 1940 only the railways employed a large number of regular workers, among whom many were, or were trained as, skilled artisans. The only comparable industries to the railways as employers of labor were the mines. But much of the labor on

the mines was irregular. In Jos, the tin mines employed for the most part daily paid unskilled and illiterate labor to dig at the faces of the open mines. In the gold mines of Ashanti the main problems were the shortage of labor and its irregularity. And most of those employed were immigrants who intended returning home eventually. In Enugu labourers were press-ganged by unscrupulous chiefs into work on the coal mines in the early years from 1915 until 1922. After that labor flowed freely into the mines so that by 1930 the management, which was a government agency, was able to be selective in the employment policy. The peoples of the area in which the mines were situated tended to be less educated than those from neighboring divisions, and management deliberately pursued a policy of recruiting illiterate locals rather than their neighbors who were relatively more educated and could voice their grievances and were therefore regarded as trouble makers.

The mines, then, employed a labor force which was either of temporary immigrant nature as in the case of the Gold Coast gold mines, or, where locally recruited as in the case of the Jos and Enugu mines, largely illiterate. Wages on all three mines were low for the ordinary labourer: in the coal mines in 1929 they were about 7d.-1s. 6d. per day; in 1930 in the gold mines they were 1s. a day for unskilled surface labourers and between 1s. 3d. and 1s. 9d. for unskilled underground labourers; on the tin mines 1s. 6d. per day for unskilled labourers.

The wages for these labourers were too low to alter their standard of living significantly. Before 1940 none of the mine workers had organized themselves into effective trade unions, though wildcat strikes had taken place before that time. For instance in 1925, pit boys in the Enugu mines downed tools in protest against the failure of management to raise their pay to 1922 levels. They were dismissed. In 1937 after the recovery of the colliery from the Depression, workers undertook considerable but uncoordinated agitation for an increase in their rates of pay. In September of that year the tub boys struck when a European overman assaulted one of their fellows. In 1924 there was a strike at Obuasi on the Ashanti goldfields against the introduction of time clocks. None of these strikes were organized by a union. Indeed until the Second World War trade unions were of no real significance in either British or French West Africa. In the latter they were illegal until the advent of the Popular Front Government in 1937. In the former they were tolerated but not recognized until about the same time. Trade Union Ordinances were passed for Gambia in 1932, Sierra Leone in 1939, Nigeria in 1939 and Gold Coast in 1941. The attitude of the Sierra Leone Government to Trade Unions was not much different from that of the Southern Nigerian Government with respect to employment on the Enugu mines. In 1921 it refused to recognize a union on the grounds that:

> A tribal ruler is elected for each tribe in Freetown by the members of the tribe themselves. These tribal rulers are recognized by law and form the intermediaries between the members of the tribe and the government, and it is not possible for the government to deal with or recognize any rival authority introduced by strangers to the colony.

Only some ten trade unions of any importance seem to have been formed and to have survived any length of time in West Africa before 1940. Significantly of these five were African Civil Servants unions, and two were railway workers unions.

Civil servants and railway employees formed the only two major coherent groups of workers among whom there was an educated elite in any way capable of organizing workers against government. Thus in 1919 daily-paid workers on the Sierra Leone railway went on strike from 15th–22nd July, because they had not been paid their "war bonus." The railway was brought to a standstill, and work was only resumed when they were promised payment of their war bonus as soon as possible. Daily-paid staff of the Public Works Department also went on strike at the same time. In 1926 the unrecognized Sierra Leone Railway Workers' Union led a strike for improved conditions of service, which led to a slowdown

of service. Government took a very tough line against the strikers who returned to work on its terms. The 1926 strike, in contrast to those in 1919, had the active support of the Sierra Leone members of the National Congress of British West Africa.

In French West Africa the railways too were the main focus of strikes. In 1925 railway workers on the Dakar-St. Louis line went on strike, and in the same year Bambara conscripted for work on the Thies-Kayes line provoked a general strike after three of their leaders were arrested as a result of discontent among them. The troops, many of whom were Bambara, refused to be involved in any action against the strikers and the administration had to release the Bambara leaders to bring an end to the strike.

From a social point of view, then, the impact of the colonial economy was much less than has usually been supposed. Perhaps the most important effect was the ousting and consequent frustration of the African businessman from a share in the profits from the expansion of the economy that took place under colonial rule.

HOW EUROPE UNDERDEVELOPED AFRICA

By WALTER RODNEY[4]

The ... benefits from colonialism were small and they were not gifts from the colonialists, but rather fruits of African labor and resources for the most part. Indeed, what was called "the development of Africa" by the colonialists was a cynical shorthand expression for "the intensification of colonial exploitation in Africa to develop capitalist Europe." The analysis has gone beyond that to demonstrate that numerous false claims are made purporting to show that Europe developed Africa in the sense of bringing about social order, nationalism, and economic modernization. However, all of that would still not permit the conclusion that colonialism had a negative impact on Africa's development. In offering the view that colonialism was negative, the aim is to draw attention to the way that previous African development was blunted, halted, and turned back. In place of that interruption and blockade, nothing of compensatory value was introduced.

The decisiveness of the short period of colonialism and its negative consequences for Africa spring mainly from the fact that Africa lost power. Power is the ultimate determinant in human society, being basic to the relations within any group and between groups. It implies the ability to defend one's interests and if necessary to impose one's will by any means available. In relations between peoples, the question of power determines maneuverability in bargaining, the extent to which one people respect the interests of another, and eventually the extent to which a people survive as a physical and cultural entity. When one society finds itself forced to relinquish power entirely to another society, that in itself is a form of underdevelopment.

During the centuries of precolonial trade, some control over social, political, and economic life was retained in Africa, in spite of the disadvantageous commerce with Europeans that little control over internal matters disappeared under colonialism. Colonialism went much further than trade. It meant a tendency towards direct appropriation by Europeans of the social institutions within Africa. Africans ceased to set indigenous cultural goals and standards, and lost full command of training young members of the society. Those were undoubtedly major steps backward. The Tunisian, Albert Memmi, puts forward the following proposition:

> The most serious blow suffered by the colonized is being removed from history and from the community. Colonization usurps any free role in either war or peace, every decision contributing to his destiny and that of the world, and all cultural and social responsibility.

Sweeping as that statement may initially appear, it is entirely true. The removal from history follows logically from the loss of power which colonialism represented. The power to act independently is the guarantee to participate actively and *consciously* in history. To be colonized is to be removed from history, except in the most passive sense. A striking illustration of the fact that colonial Africa was a passive object is seen in its attraction for white anthropologists, who came to study "primitive society." Colonialism determined that Africans were no more makers of history than were beetles—objects to be looked at under a microscope and examined for unusual features.

The negative impact of colonialism in political terms was quite dramatic. Overnight, African political states lost their power, independence, and meaning—irrespective of whether they were big empires or small polities. Certain traditional rulers were kept in office, and the formal structure of some kingdoms was partially retained, but the substance of political life was quite different. Political power had passed into the hands of foreign overlords. Of course, numerous African states in previous centuries had passed through the cycle of growth and decline. But colonial rule was different. So long as it lasted, not a single African state could flourish.

To be specific, it must be noted that colonialism crushed by force the surviving feudal states of North Africa; that the French wiped out the large Moslem states of the Western Sudan, as well as Dahomey and kingdoms in Madagascar; that the British eliminated Egypt, the Mahdist Sudan, Asante, Benin, the Yoruba kingdoms, Swaziland, Matabeleland, the Lozi, and the East African lake kingdoms as great states. It should further be noted that a multiplicity of smaller and growing states were removed from the face of Africa by the Belgians, Portuguese, British, French, Germans, Spaniards, and Italians. Finally, those that appeared to survive were nothing but puppet creations. For instance, the Sultan of Morocco retained nominal existence under colonial rule which started in 1912; and the same applied to the Bey of Tunis; but Morocco and Tunisia were just as much under the power of French colonial administrators as neighboring Algeria, where the feudal rulers were removed altogether.

Sometimes, the African rulers who were chosen to serve as agents of foreign colonial rule were quite obviously nothing but puppets. The French and the Portuguese were in the habit of choosing their own African "chiefs"; the British went to Iboland and invented "warrant chiefs"; and all the colonial powers found it convenient to create "superior" or "paramount" rulers. Very often, the local population hated and despised such colonial stooges. There were traditional rulers such as the Sultan of Sokoto, the Kabaka of Buganda, and the Asantehene of Asante, who retained a great deal of prestige in the eyes of Africans, but they had no power to act outside the narrow boundaries laid down by colonialism, lest they find themselves in the Seychelles Islands as "guests of His Majesty's Government."

One can go so far as to say that colonial rule meant the effective eradication of African political power throughout the continent, since Liberia and Ethiopia could no longer function as independent states within the context of continent-wide colonialism. Liberia in particular had to bow before foreign political, economic, and military pressures in a way that no genuinely independent state could have accepted; and although Ethiopia held firm until 1936, most European capitalist nations were not inclined to treat Ethiopia as a sovereign state, primarily because it was African, and Africans were supposed to be colonial subjects.

The pattern of arrest of African political development has some features which can only be appreciated after careful scrutiny and the taking away of the blinkers which the colonizers put on the eyes of their subjects. An interesting case in point is that of women's role in society. Until today, capitalist society has failed to resolve the inequality between man and woman, which was entrenched in all modes of production prior to localism. The colonialists in Africa occasionally paid lip service to women's education and emancipation, but objectively there was deterioration in the status of women owing to colonial rule.

A realistic assessment of the role of women in independent precolonial Africa shows two contrasting but combined tendencies. In the first place, women were exploited by men through polygamous arrangements designed to capture the labor power of women. As always, exploitation was accompanied by oppression; and there is evidence to the effect that women were sometimes treated like beasts of burden, as for instance in Moslem African societies. Nevertheless, there was a countertendency to insure the dignity of women to greater or lesser degree in all African societies. Mother-right was a prevalent feature of African societies, and particular women held a variety of privileges based on the fact that they were the keys to inheritance.

More important still, some women had real power in the political sense, exercised either through religion or directly within the politico-constitutional apparatus. In Mozambique, the widow of an Nguni king became the priestess in charge of the shrine set up in the burial place of her deceased husband, and the reigning king had to consult her on all important matters. In a few instances, women were actually heads of state. Among the Lovedu of Transvaal, the key figure was the Rain-Queen, combining political and religious functions. The most frequently encountered role of importance played by women was that of "Queen Mother" or "Queen Sister." In practice, that post was filled by a female of royal blood, who might be mother, sister, or aunt of the reigning king in places such as Mali, Asante, and Buganda. Her influence was considerable, and there were occasions when the "Queen Mother" was the real power and the male king a mere puppet.

What happened to African women under colonialism is that the social, religious, constitutional, and political privileges and rights disappeared, while the economic exploitation continued and was often intensified. It was intensified because the division of labor according to sex was frequently disrupted. Traditionally, African men did the heavy labor of felling trees, clearing land, building houses, apart from conducting warfare and hunting. When they were required to leave their farms to seek employment, women remained behind burdened with every task necessary for the survival of themselves, the children, and even the men as far as foodstuffs were concerned. Moreover, since men entered the money sector more easily and in greater numbers than women, women's work became greatly inferior to that of men within the new value system of colonialism: men's work was "modern" and women's was "traditional" and "backward." Therefore, the deterioration in the status of African women was bound up with the consequent loss of the right to set indigenous standards of what work had merit and what did not.

One of the most important manifestations of historical arrest and stagnation in colonial Africa is that which commonly goes under the title of "tribalism." That term, in its common journalistic setting, is understood to mean that Africans have a basic loyalty to tribe rather than nation and that each tribe still retains a fundamental hostility towards its neighboring tribes. The examples favored by the capitalist press and bourgeois scholarship are those of Congo and Nigeria. Their accounts suggest that Europeans tried to make a nation out of the Congolese and Nigerian peoples, but they failed, because the various tribes had their age-long hatreds; and, as soon as the colonial power went, the natives returned to killing each other. To this phenomenon, Europeans often attach the word "atavism," to carry the notion that Africans were returning to their primitive savagery. Even a cursory survey of the African past shows that such assertions are the exact opposite of the truth.

All of the large states of nineteenth-century Africa were multi-ethnic, and their expansion was continually making anything like "tribal" loyalty a thing of the past, by substituting in its place national and class ties. However, in all parts of the world, that substitution of national and class ties for purely ethnic ones is a lengthy historical process; and, invariably there remains for long periods certain regional pockets of individuals who have their own narrow, regional loyalties, springing from ties of kinship, language, and culture. In Asia, the feudal states of Vietnam and Burma both achieved a considerable degree of national homogeneity over the centuries before colonial rule. But there were pockets of "tribes" or "minorities" who remained outside the effective sphere of the nation-state and the national economy and culture.

Colonialism blocked the further evolution of national solidarity, because it destroyed the particular Asian or African states which were the principal agents for achieving the liquidation of fragmented loyalties. Because ethnic and regional loyalties which go under the name of "tribalism" could not be effectively resolved by the colonial state, they tended to fester and grow in unhealthy forms. Indeed, the colonial powers sometimes saw the value of stimulating the internal tribal jealousies so as to keep the colonized from dealing with their principal contradiction with the European overlords—i.e., the classic technique of divide and rule. Certainly, the Belgians consciously fostered that; and the racist whites in South Africa had by the 1950s worked out a careful plan to "develop" the oppressed African population as Zulu, as Xhosa, and as Sotho so that the march towards broader African national and class solidarities could be stopped and turned back.

The civil war in Nigeria is generally regarded as having been a tribal affair. To accept such a contention would mean extending the definition of tribe to cover Shell Oil and Gulf Oil! ... What came to be called tribalism at the beginning of the new epoch of political independence in Nigeria was itself a product of the way that people were brought together under colonialism so as to be exploited. It was a product of administrative devices, of entrenched regional separations, of differential access by particular ethnic groups into the colonial economy and culture.

Pre-colonial trade had started the trend of the disintegration of African economies and their technological impoverishment. Colonial rule speeded up that trend. The story is often told that in order to make a telephone call from Accra in the British colony of the Gold Coast to Abidjan in the adjacent French colony of Ivory Coast it was necessary to be connected first with an operator in London and then with an operator in Paris who could offer a line to Abidjan. That was one reflection of the fact that the Gold Coast economy was integrated into the British economy, and the Ivory Coast economy was integrated into the French economy, while the neighboring African colonies had little or no effective economic relations. The following conclusion reached by the United Nations Economic Commission for Africa in 1959 goes directly to the point:

> The most outstanding characteristic of the transportation systems of Africa is the comparative isolation in which they have developed within the confines of individual countries and territories. This is reflected in the lack of links between countries and territories within the same geographical sub-region.

Africa was denied the opportunity of developing healthy trade links with parts of the world other than Europe and North America. Some trade persisted across the Indian Ocean, but on the whole it is fair to say that the roads in Africa led to the seaports and the sea lanes led to Western Europe and North America. That kind of lopsidedness is today part of the pattern of underdevelopment and dependence.

The damaging impact of capitalism on African technology is even more clearly measurable in the colonial period than in the earlier centuries. In spite of the slave trade and of the import of European goods, most African handicraft industries still had vitality at the start of the colonial period. They had undergone no technological advance and they had not expanded, but they had survived. The mass production of the more recent phase of capitalism virtually obliterated African industries such as cloth, salt, soap, iron, and even pottery-making.

In North Africa, handicraft industries had made the greatest advances before colonialism, in spheres ranging from brasswork to woolens. As in the towns of feudal Europe, craft workshops flourished in Algerian towns like Oran, Constantine, Algiers, and Tlemcen. But French colonialism destroyed the handicraft industries and threw thousands out of work. The same thing had happened in Europe itself when new machines had thrown artisans out of employment in places like Lancashire and Lyons, but in that instance the new machines became the basis of the prevailing mode of production, and formerly independent artisans returned to factories as proletarians to master different skills and expand the productive capacity of their society. In Africa it was simply destruction without redress. By the time political independence was achieved, surviving craftsmanship had been turned towards attracting tourists rather than meeting the real needs of African people.

Besides, as was true of the European slave trade, the destruction of technology under colonialism must be related to the barriers raised in the path of African initiative. The vast majority of Africans drawn into the colonial money economy were simply providing manual labor, which stimulated perspiration rather than scientific initiative. Africans connected to the trading sector were sometimes successful in a limited way. The resourcefulness of West African market women is well known, but it was put to petty purposes. The problem posed to capitalists and workers in Europe while making insecticide from African pyrethrum was one requiring that resourcefulness be expressed in a technical direction. But the problem posed to an African market woman by the necessity to make a penny more profit on every tin of imported sardines was resolved sometimes by a little more vigor, sometimes by a touch of dishonesty, and sometimes by resort to *juju*.

Colonialism induced the African ironworker to abandon the process of extracting iron from the soil and to concentrate instead on working scraps of metal imported from Europe. The only compensation for that interruption would have been the provision of modern techniques in the extraction and processing of iron. However, those techniques were debarred from Africa, on the basis of the international division of labor under imperialism. As was seen earlier, the non-industrialization of Africa was not left to chance. It was deliberately enforced by stopping the transference to Africa of machinery and skills which would have given competition to European industry in that epoch.

In the period of African development preceding colonialism, some areas moved faster than others and provided the nuclei for growth on a wide regional basis. Northern Nigeria was one of those; and it virtually went to sleep during the colonial period. The British cut it off from the rest of the Moslem world and fossilized the social relations, so that the serfs could not achieve any change at the expense of the ruling aristocracy.

Instead of speeding up growth, colonial activities such as mining and cash-crop farming speeded up the decay of "traditional" African life. In many parts of the continent, vital aspects of culture were adversely affected, nothing better was substituted, and only a lifeless shell was left. The capitalist forces behind colonialism were interested in little more than the exploitation of labor. Even areas that were not directly involved in the money economy exploited labor. In extracting that labor, they tampered with the factor that was the very buttress of the society, for African "traditional" life when deprived of its customary labor force and patterns of work was no longer "traditional."

During the colonial era, many thinly populated villages appeared in Central and Southern Africa, comprising women, children, and old men. They practiced subsistence agriculture which was not productive enough, and colonialists contrasted them with cash-crop areas, which in comparison were flourishing. However, it was precisely the impact of colonialism which left so many villages deserted and starving, because the able-bodied males had gone off to labor elsewhere. Any district deprived of its effective laboring population could not be expected to develop.

There were several spots within different colonies which were sufficiently far removed from towns and colonial administration that they neither grew cash crops nor supplied labor. In southern Sudan, for instance, there were populations who continued to live a life not dissimilar to that which they had followed in previous centuries. Yet, even for such traditional African societies the scope for development no longer existed. They were isolated by the hold which the colonialists had on the rest of the continent. They could not interact with other parts of Africa. They were subject to increasing encroachment by the money economy and were more and more to be regarded as historical relics. The classic example of this type of obstructed historical development is to be found in the U.S.A., where the indigenous population of Indians who survived slaughter by the whites were placed in reservations and condemned to stagnation. Indian reservations in North America are living museums to be visited by white tourists who purchase curios.

In South Africa and Rhodesia, the policy of establishing "native reserves" was openly followed. Inside a reserve, the major means of production was the land. But the quantity and fertility of the land allocated was entirely inadequate to support the numbers of Africans who were driven in. The reserves were reservoirs of cheap labor, and dumping grounds for those who could not be accommodated within the money economy of the racist southern section of Africa. Further north, there were no areas named as reserves except in colonial Kenya and to a very limited extent in Tanganyika. But the money economy was constantly transforming the traditional sector into one which was just as deprived as any reserve.

The money economy of colonialism was a growing sector. That is not to be denied. However, it has already been indicated how limited that growth was, viewed over the continent as a whole. The growth in the so-called modern sector exercised adverse effects on the non-monetary sector. What remains is to emphasize that the character of growth in Africa under colonialism was such that it did not constitute development—i.e. it did not enlarge the capacity of the society to deal with the natural environment, to adjudicate relations between members of the society, and to protect the population from external forces. Such a statement is already implicitly borne out in the inability of capitalism to stimulate skilled labor in colonial Africa. A system which must stand in the way of the accumulation of skills does not develop anything or anybody. It is implicit, too, in the manner in which Africa was cut into economic compartments having no relation one to another, so that, even though the volume of commercial activity within each compartmentalized colony may have increased, there was no development comparable to that which linked together the various states of the U.S.A.

In recent times, economists have been recognizing in colonial and postcolonial Africa a pattern that has been termed "growth without development." That phrase has now appeared as the title of books on Liberia and Ivory Coast. It means that goods and services of a certain type are on the increase. There may be more rubber and coffee exported, there may be more cars imported with the proceeds, and there may be more gasoline stations built to service the cars. But the profit goes abroad, and the economy becomes more and more a dependency of the metropoles. In no African colony was there economic integration, or any provision for making the economy self-sustained and geared to its own local goals. Therefore, there was growth of the so-called enclave import–export sector, but the only things which developed were dependency and underdevelopment.

A further revelation of growth without development under colonialism was the overdependence on one or two exports. The term "monoculture" is used to describe those colonial economies which were centered around a single crop. Liberia (in the agricultural sector) was a monoculture dependent on rubber, Gold Coast on cocoa, Dahomey and southeast Nigeria on palm produce, Sudan on cotton, Tanganyika on sisal, and Uganda on cotton. In Senegal and Gambia, groundnuts accounted for 85 to 90 percent of money earnings. In effect, two African colonies were told to grow nothing but peanuts!

Every farming people have a staple food, plus a variety of other supplements. Historians, agronomists, and botanists have all contributed to showing the great variety of such foods within the precolonial African economy. There were numerous crops which were domesticated within the African continent, there were several wild food species (notably fruits), and Africans had shown no conservatism in adopting useful food plants of Asian or American origin. Diversified agriculture was within the African tradition. Monoculture was a colonialist invention.

There was nothing "natural" about monoculture. It was a consequence of imperialist requirements and machinations, extending into areas that were politically independent in name. Monoculture was a characteristic of regions falling under imperialist domination. Certain countries in Latin America such as Costa Rica and Guatemala were forced by United States capitalist firms to concentrate so heavily on growing bananas that they were contemptuously known as "banana republics." In Africa, this concentration on one or two cash crops for sale abroad had many harmful effects. Sometimes, cash crops were grown to the exclusion of staple foods—thus causing famines. For instance, in Gambia rice farming was popular before the colonial era, but so much of the best land was transferred to ground-nuts that rice had to be imported on a large scale to try to counter the fact that famine was becoming endemic. In Asante, concentration on cocoa raised fears of famine in a region previously famous for yams and other foodstuff.

Yet the threat of famine was a small disadvantage compared to the extreme vulnerability and insecurity of monoculture. When the crop was affected by internal factors such as disease, that amounted to an overwhelming disaster, as in the case of Gold Coast cocoa when it was hit by swollen-shoot disease in the 1940s. Besides, at all times, the price fluctuations (which were externally controlled) left the African producer helpless in the face of capitalist maneuvers.

From a capitalist viewpoint, monocultures commended themselves most because they made colonial economies entirely dependent on the metropolitan buyers of their produce. At the end of the European slave trade, only a minority of Africans were sufficiently committed to capitalist exchange and sufficiently dependent upon European imports to wish to continue the relationship with Europe at all costs. Colonialism increased the dependence of Africa on Europe in terms of the numbers of persons brought into the money economy and in terms of the number of aspects of socio-economic life in Africa which derived their existence from the connection with the metropole. The ridiculous situation arose by which European trading firms, mining companies, shipping lines, banks, insurance houses, and plantations all exploited Africa and at the same time caused Africans to feel that without those capitalist services no money or European goods would be forthcoming, and therefore Africa was in debt to its exploiters!

The factor of dependency made its impact felt in every aspect of the life of the colonies, and it can be regarded as the crowning vice among the negative social, political, and economic consequences of colonialism in Africa, being primarily responsible for the perpetuation of the colonial relationship into the epoch that is called neocolonialism.

In the light of the prevailing balance-sheet concept of what colonial rule was about, it still remains to take note of European innovations in Africa such as modern medicine, clinical surgery, and immunization. It would be absurd to deny that these were objectively positive features, however limited they were quantitatively. However, they have to be weighed against the numerous setbacks received by Africa in all spheres due to colonialism as well as against the contributions Africa made to Europe. European science met the needs of its own society, and particularly those of the bourgeoisie. The bourgeoisie did not suffer from hunger and starvation. Bourgeois science therefore did not consider those things as needs which had to be met and overcome—not even among their own workers and least of all on behalf of Africans. This is just a specific application of the general principle that the exploitation of Africa was being used to create a greater gap between Africa and capitalist Europe. The exploitation and the comparative disadvantage are the ingredients of underdevelopment.

IMPERIALISM AND UNDERDEVELOPMENT IN NIGERIA

By BADE ONIMODE[5]

Free-trade imperialism under British hegemony was a system of international division of labor for global accumulation by Britain and her allies of Western Europe. Under this global division of labor, the imperialist metropoles monopolized manufacturing and forced the colonies to specialize in primary production of raw materials for their factories, and cheap food for their labor force. While this primary production chained the colonial population to the land in abysmal ignorance, poverty and backwardness, their cheap food supply helped to maximize the exploitation of the European labor force with low wages, while their abundant cheap raw materials ensured enormous profits for the exploiters who dumped shoddy manufactures on the colonies. This squalid fraud was wrapped in the intellectual garb of the so-called theory of comparative advantage and free trade.

This summary of the British economic philosophy of free-enterprise capitalism for the colonial economy reflects the classical economic thought of Adam Smith, whose reactionary ideas still dominated imperial thinking, even during the new-classical era of the 1920s. It explains why, throughout the colonial era, until 1946, when political circumstances forced it to embark on patched-up economic planning, the imperial administration neither directly undertook any large-scale productive enterprises, nor evolved a coherent development strategy for the colonies.

Consequently, the motives and processes of primary production in the colonial economy were dictated by private capitalist calculations for which the colonial administration provided a propitious environment. In Nigeria, the dominant motives were simply to use the country as an agricultural estate to produce raw materials for British factories, and thereby generate some purchasing power to enable Nigerians to buy the manufactured products of these same factories. Both objectives would ensure the transfer of economic surplus from Nigeria to Britain.

The actual process of primary production included cash-cropping, forestry and mining. The production of cash crops was left largely to peasant farmers, both because they were more efficient than the few plantation planters, and because Lugard's indirect rule required minimal disruption of traditional land tenure. But forestry and mining, which were less tedious, more lucrative and more capital intensive, were dominated by British imperialists.

The production of "cash crops" in Nigeria for export spearheaded the incorporation of the majority of Nigerians into the colonial capitalist economy, constituted the springboard for the series of factors that led to the entrenchment of capitalist relations of production and dominated the sources of transfer of economic surplus to Britain. The principal cash crops were palm oil and kernels, cocoa, cotton, groundnuts and rubber. Some hides and skins, citrus, kola nuts, beni-seed, shea butter and bananas were also produced for export, especially towards the end of the colonial era. Palm oil and kernels were required for soap, candles, tin plate, nut butters and cattle cake. Cocoa was needed for chocolate and confectionery, cotton for textiles, groundnuts for oils and soap, rubber for tires and other products, and hides and skins for leather. The introduction of taxes to be paid in cash, payment of money for these cash crops and direct government stimulus encouraged their production by peasants, almost to the neglect of food crops.

Huge export values represented only part of the economic surplus from capitalist agriculture in colonial Nigeria. The shamelessly unfavorable terms of trade for these exports, which fell as low as twenty-two, meant that much of the surplus was transferred to Britain through exploitively monopolistic pricing. Producer incomes associated with these export values under the Marketing Board system were generally much below world prices.

The use of money in payment for these export crops, the existence of produce-buying agents, plantations, plot registration, hired labor and monetary taxes meant that commercial agriculture was one of the critical bridgeheads for the infiltration of capitalist relations of production into Nigeria. This was particularly the case with the tree crop culture in palm produce, cocoa and rubber in the south. This in part explains the longer survival of feudal relations in the groundnut and cotton culture of the north.

Technologically, even though agrarian capitalism experienced some innovations involving new seeds, crop research, insecticides, harvesting and oil extraction machines, the basic techniques for land clearing and cultivation remained stagnated under the hoe-and-cutlass culture. Modern agricultural machinery like tractors, ploughs, harvesters, milk processors etc. of the Agrarian Revolution were never introduced into the country.

Food crops constituted the much maligned "traditional" or "subsistence" production. The production organization for these consisted of household peasant cultivation on small plots under a mixture of communal and feudal land tenure. Feudal land relations were reflected in payments called *isakole* in the western parts and *kurdin kasa* in the northern emirates. The extended family system provided most of the labor, seeds were provided by the peasants, while the production techniques consisted of the hoe and cutlass. After deducting the share for family consumption and feudal tribute, the surplus was sold in the local markets, and sometimes transported by head, canoes, donkeys, and later lorries and trains, to other parts of the country in the predominantly north–south trade.

The static nature of food production and its backward technology were part of the cumulative consequence of near total neglect of food production by the imperialists. Indeed, under such conditions, it was a miracle that the indigenous labour force was able to feed its rising population as well as pay oppressive taxes. This is particularly true after 1900, when the export boom led to an increasing transition from food to export production.

In terms of relative size, unexported agricultural production engaged some 85 percent of the Nigerian population during most of the colonial era, though the percentage dropped slightly from the beginning of the twentieth century. But even during the 1900–29 boom, food output rose by only about 10 percent, whereas agricultural export production rose by about 500 percent in this period. Consequently, in spite of huge differences in input employment, both the absolute and relative increase in the production of "cash crops" exceeded that of food products. By the 1950s, the performance gap was much wider, given the continuing innovations for export crops involving new seeds, planting instruction, research, processing machines, and so on.

The associated rising prices and incomes from export production led to a continuing switch from the largely static food production to commercial agriculture. These conversions were particularly frequent and significant during 1900–29 and 1945–60; the opposite switch, from commercial to food cropping, was much less, even during the slack years from 1929–45, because land under export tree crops could not easily be transferred to food production.

The colonial financial system was supposed to be self-sufficient, but in reality it was neither self-supporting nor autonomous. Throughout its existence, it was merely an appendage of the British imperialist financial structure. Consequently, it had neither the dynamism for internal growth, nor the external assistance for any international recognition. … In particular … the financial system was the organized purveyor of credit and the creator of money, which were the taproots of capitalist exchange and accumulation.

Seven fundamental characteristics distinguish the colonial financial system. First, it was a thoroughly exploitative conduit system designed specifically for the transfer of Nigeria's enormous economic surplus for the development of imperial Britain. This process was in turn facilitated by some critical features of the functioning of the system. One of these was the fact that the colonial government and the imperialist firms used this financial system for the continuous transfer of annual surpluses like those of the Marketing Boards and the so-called foreign profit—under frequently dubious practices. Another was the 100 percent external reserve demanded for colonial currency in Nigeria, which in effect meant continuous zero interest loans by Nigeria to Britain for several decades. Moreover, while export and budget surpluses at nominal interest rates were piled up by Nigeria for the development of Britain, Nigeria was forced by colonial administrators to borrow at a higher interest rate from the British capital market. This meant, on net, that Nigeria borrowed her own funds from Britain at a positive interest rate. Instead of employing the funds obtained from Nigeria to further development there the policy of colonial financial institutions was to invest abroad, or make loans to fellow expatriate exploiters.

Second, the colonial financial infrastructure was really an extension of the British financial system. Nigeria's colonial currency was tied to the Sterling Exchange Standard, external reserves were largely in sterling, held in London, and London determined the exchange rate. The main commercial banks were overseas branches of British multinational financial oligarchies like Bank of British West Africa (B.B.W.A.) and Barclays (now Union) Bank, while the credit offered by these financial houses went largely to Britain. Consequently, the colonial financial system was the nerve of the umbilical cord, which, until 1960, tied Nigeria bilaterally to British imperialism. Since then, the link has become increasingly multilateral with all the industrialized capitalist countries. Indeed, until the last year of its existence in 1959, the hub of this colonial financial apparatus was the extra-territorial West African Currency Board whose sole agent in West Africa was the B.B.W.A.

Third, foreign domination crippled the colonial financial system. Until 1929, there was no indigenous bank in Nigeria, and by 1945 there were only two indigenous financial institutions. In the same year, foreign balances due to other British banks accounted for over 80 percent of total assets of commercial banks in Nigeria whose foreign investment was 79 percent of total investment. By 1960, out of 195 commercial bank branches, 130 were owned by expatriate banking houses, while the imperialist banks controlled over 80 percent of all loans and advances. Thus, throughout the colonial era, these imperialist banks are accused of ruinous competition designed to destroy all indigenous banks and exclude Nigerians from the banking industry.

Fourth, the competitive structure of these financial institutions was distinctly monopolistic and oligopolistic at various times. Between 1894 and 1917 the B.B.W.A., which swallowed the Bank of Nigeria in 1912, was the only bank in the country. Then from 1917 to 1960, the B.B.W.A. and Barclays Bank controlled over 60 percent of commercial banking activities in the country, accounting for 118 of the 195 bank branches in the country. Moreover, from 1912 to 1959 the B.B.W.A. was the sole agent of the West African Currency Board and the colonial administration. This market control also enhanced the exploitative activities of these banks.

Fifth, unbridled *laissez-faire*, bordering on anarchy, was another characteristic of the colonial financial structure. There was no real central bank throughout the period, so there was no real control over the monetary system, especially over the predominantly expatriate commercial banks. Even when the Central Bank of Nigeria was established in 1959, it was required by its ordinance to cooperate with the commercial banks, rather than to control them. For this same reason, monetary policy rested largely on "moral persuasion." There was no banking examiner until 1959, no minimum liquid-asset reserve requirement for bank loans until 1958, no banking ordinance until 1952 after the bankruptcies of the "banking mania" of the late 1940s, and no published banking statistics until 1943. These facts meant that for several decades Nigerians had no protection against the excesses of the imperialist banks, thus constituting the country into a financial jungle for Adam Smith's avaricious "invisible hand." Hence, Nigeria had barely one decade of organized commercial banking "under law," during a total colonial tutelage of 100 exploitative years.

Sixth, financial conservatism, which imperialist scholars gleefully flog to demonstrate their "critical" view of colonial financial arrangements, was in reality only an offshoot of the predatory primitiveness and intellectual backwardness of capitalist economics and imperialist social thought generally, and of British empiricist philosophy in particular. Earl Grey's insistence on financial self-sufficiency, which was ignored in the accumulation of Nigerian surpluses in London, was pursued in the reactionary obsession with "sound money" and "balanced budgeting" was perverted into persistent budget surpluses, ... with surpluses for all but one year during 1946 to 1960. In spite of these surpluses, Nigeria was forced to borrow from London at exorbitant interest rates.

Finally, the collective consequence of these characteristics of the imperialist financial system in Nigeria was to burden the country with a weak, largely amorphous and ruthlessly exploitative set of financial institutions after 1960. With neither money nor capital market, no tradition of monetary control, and only a nominal Central Bank, this colonial financial apparatus was a veritable Trojan horse which performed only one function too well—to serve as a conduit for the transfer of Nigeria's economic surplus to develop imperialist Britain and simultaneously underdevelop Nigeria.

The colonial fiscal system was distinguished by nondevelopmental, oppressive, externally oriented, conservative and divisive features. Developmental expenditure, especially on capital projects, typically accounted for less than 30 percent of total annual budgets. Even during the exceptional railway construction era from about 1890 to 1920, revenue for the railways was usually raised externally, as if it were outside the annual budget. During 1943–45, for example, public works, education and agriculture were

allocated barely 10 percent, 5 percent and 5 percent each of the budget respectively. By contrast, the civil establishment involving colonial salaries, pensions and the coercive apparatus together swallowed up over 50 percent of the budget from 1860–90, and more than 40 percent thereafter. This was partly a consequence of capitalist *laissez-faire* policy.

Colonial taxes were usually oppressive and exploitative with respect to their absolute rates relative to Nigerian incomes, coercive methods of collection, their functional distribution among social classes and the minimal benefits of taxation. In an age when incomes were derived in kind for some 80 percent of the largely agricultural population, and when, even by 1947, wages were as low as 1s. 6d. per day, the imposition of regressive poll taxes on both men and women often led to anti-tax riots, such as the Aba women's riot of 1929. The violent tax-raids, together with the colonial objective of forcing peasants into the nascent capitalist labor force by imposing taxes to be paid in cash, were equally repressive. Multiple taxation of the peasantry through poll, income, produce, export, land and cattle taxes, etc., were really ruinous to the peasants and destroyed their productive energies.

In addition, the imperialist orientation of the colonial fiscal system was reflected in its heavy and continuous reliance on exploitative foreign loans, as well as import duties. Even when the country was piling up export surpluses in London at very low interest rates, especially during the export booms of 1900–29 and 1946–54, the colonialists imposed huge foreign debts on Nigeria at exorbitant interest rates. For example, the total loan of £24.9 million in 1946–47 was external, while in 1955–56, £16.8 million out of the total loan of £20.0 million was external. And, except for a small deficit in 1949, there were budget surpluses from 1946 to 1960. Import duties similarly accounted for about 45 percent of total revenue from 1930–45, and about 60 percent from 1946–60 with 78 percent in 1960. Such heavy reliance on import duties meant a built-in commitment to imperialist manufactures and the dominance of the foreign trade sector, both of which exposed the colony to further imperialist exploitation and negated any internal dynamics for manufacturing and development.

No indirect rule anchored to imperialism and feudalism could ever serve, or was even meant to serve, "the public interest." The dual fiscal system of the colonial administration and local authorities degenerated into a tripartite system under the explosively divisive and centrifugal regional system of government after 1951. That meant multiple tiers of taxation by different authorities with all the arbitrariness this implies, including the imposition of "warrant chiefs" in such areas as Eastern Nigeria where feudalism had no historical roots, regressive poll taxes levied lumpsum on whole communities, taxes without receipt, and similar abuses. Predictably, the revenue garnered through these repressive methods was frequently put to fraudulent use by the traditional rulers, and lapped up in expenditure on the "civil establishment" of the colonial D.O. and his cohorts.

SUGGESTED READINGS

Atmore, A.E. "The Credit Balance of Imperialism," A Review of L.H. Gann and Peter Duignan's *Burden of Empire*, in *The Journal of African History* 10, no. 2, (1969), 333–6.

Ausetn, Ralph, *African Economic History: Internal Development and External Dependency* (London: J. Currey, 1987). Davidson, Basil, *Modern Africa: A Social and Political History* (Long: Longman, 1989).

———, *Which Way Africa? The Search for a New Society* (Baltimore: Penguin Books, 1964).

Falola, Toyin, ed., *Britain and Nigeria: Exploitation or Development* (London: Zed Press, 1987).

Fannon, Frantz, *Wretched of the Earth* (New York: Grove-Weidenfeld, 1991).

Gann, L.H., and Duignan, Peter, *White Settlers in Tropical Africa* (Harmoundsworth: Penguin Books, 1962).

Howards, Rhoda, *Colonialism and Underdevelopment in Ghana* (London: Groom Helm, 1978).

Huttenback, Robert, *Mammon and the Pursuit of Empire: The Economics of British Imperialism* (New York: Cambridge Press, 1988).

Huxley, Elspeth, *Race and Politics in Kenya: A Correspondence between Elspeth Huxley and Margery Perham* (Westport: Greenwood Press, 1975).

Johnston, Sir Harry, *A History of Colonization of Africa by Alien Races* (London: Cambridge, 1913).

Kabwegyere, Tarris, *The Politics of State Formation: The Nature and Effects of Colonialism in Uganda* (Nairobi: East African Literature Bureau, 1974).

Kitching, Gavin, *Development and Underdevelopment in Historical Perspective* (London: Routledge, 1989).

Lloyd, Peter, *Africa in Social Change* (New York: Praeger, 1968).

———, *Classes, Crises and Coups* (London: MacGibbon and Kee, 1971).

McCarthy, Dennis, *Colonial Bureaucracy and Creating Underdevelopment: Tanganyika, 1919–1940* (Ames: Iowa State University Press, 1982).

Memmi, Albert, *The Colonizer and the Colonized* (Boston: Beacon Press, 1982).

Offiong, Daniel, *Imperialism and Dependency: Obstacles to African Development* (Washington, D.C.: Howard University Press, 1982).

Perham, Margery, *The Colonial Reckoning* (New York: Knopf, 1962).

———, *The Economics of Tropical Dependency* (London: Faber and Faber, 1946).

Strachey, John, *The End of Empire* (London: Gollancz, 1959).

Suret-Canale, Jean, *French Colonialism in Tropical Africa, 1900–1945* (New York: Pica Press, 1971).

Wallerstein, Immanuel, *African and the Modern World* (Trenton: Africa World Press, 1986).

Williams, Eric, *Capitalism and Slavery* (Chapel Hill: University of North Carolina Press, 1944).

Woddis, Jack, *Africa: The Roots of Revolt* (New York: Citadel Press, 1962).

Woolf, Leonard, *Empire and Commerce in Africa: A Study of Economic Imperialism* (New York: H. Fertig, 1968).

NOTES

1. Gann, L.H., and Duignan, Peter, *Burden of Empire: An Appraisal of Western Colonialism in Africa South of the Sahara* (New York: Frederick A. Praeger, 1967). Excerpts taken from pages v–vii, 229–31, 234, and 236–52. L.H. Gann and Peter Duignan are both senior fellows at the Hoover Institute. Together they have authored

many books on African history and have come to be renowned for their interpretations. Some of their many influential publications include *Africa and the World* (San Francisco: Chandler, 1972), the two volume edited collection of *Colonialism in Africa 1870–1960*, (Cambridge: Cambridge University Press, 1972), *White Settlers in Tropical Africa*, (London: Penguin, 1962), *The Rulers of British Africa* (Stanford: Stanford University Press, 1978), and *The Rulers of German Africa* (Stanford: Stanford University Press, 1977).

2. Fieldhouse, D.K., *The Colonial Empires: A Comparative Survey from the Eighteenth Century* (New York: Delacorte Press, 1967). Excerpts taken from pages 380–7 and 389–94. D.K. Fieldhouse received his M.A. and D.Litt. from Oxford University and is the Vere Harmsworth Professor of Imperial and Naval History and fellow of Jesus College, Cambridge University. He is recognized as a leading scholar on empire and colonialism. He is author of Colonialism, 1870–1945 (New York: St. Martin's Press, 1981), *Economics and Empire, 1830–1914* (Ithaca, NY: Cornell University Press, 1973), and *The Theory of Capitalist Imperialism* (New York: Barnes and Noble, 1967).

3. Crowder, Michael, *West Africa under Colonial Rule* (Evanston: Northwestern University Press, 1968). Excerpts taken from pages 345–53. Michael Crowder was a former professor of history at the University of Ibadan and fellow at the Commonwealth Institute. He is recognized as having been one of the leading historians of West Africa. He is author of *The Story of Nigeria* (London: Faber and Faber, 1978), *West African Resistance* (London: Hutchinson, 1978), *Senegal* (London: Oxford University Press, 1962), and *Revolt in Bussa* (London: Faber and Faber, 1973).

4. Rodney, Walter, *How Europe Underdeveloped Africa* (Washington, D.C.: Howard University Press, 1982). Originally published in 1972 by Bogle-L'Overture Publications, London and Tanzanian Publishing House. Excerpts taken from pages 223–238. Dr. Rodney's biography

is listed beneath his reading in the preceding problem on "Educating the African."

5. Onimode, Bade, *Imperialism and Under-development in Nigeria: The Dialectics of Mass Poverty* (London: Zed Press, 1982). Excerpts taken from pages 42–3, 48–9, 51–2, 91–3, and 103–4. Bade Onimode is an economist at the University of Ibadan and is one of Nigeria's foremost progressive scholars. He has written many works addressing the political economy of underdevelopment in Africa. These include *Economic Development in Nigeria* (Ibidin: Nigeria Academy of Arts, Sciences, and Technology, 1975), *MNC's in Nigeria: Multinational Corporations in Nigeria* (Ibidin: L. Shynden, 1983), *An Introduction to Marxist Political Economy* (London: Zed Books, 1985), and his most recent work, *A Political Economy of the African Crisis* (London: Zed Books, 1988).

AFRICAN HISTORY

PART FOUR

NATIONALISM AND DECOLONIZATION

NATIONALISM AND AFRICAN INTELLECTUALS

By Toyin Falola

[W]hen we review the years during which we have been numbered among the nations, and see how far behind we are in all the elements of abiding prosperity and usefulness; how little we have done in the cause of Africa's regeneration; how small the quota we have contributed to the comfort and happiness of mankind; this should be to us a day of earnest and solemn thoughtfulness. ...
—Edward Wilmot Blyden, 1865[1]

WESTERN EDUCATION AND THE NEW ELITE

Africa has always had its intellectuals, although my concerns are with those that have emerged during the nineteenth and twentieth centuries. The representatives of the previous intellectual traditions also remain, but they are often marginalized by the modern educated elite that controls power. We can talk of "traditional intellectuals" comprising priests, kings, chiefs, and merchants who generated knowledge and exercised considerable power and authority. While the knowledge of the "traditional elite" was usually oral, it constituted the foundations of politics, it could be esoteric, and there were specialists who handled the interpretations of complex religious ideas. An indigenous education system, informal and varied, existed partly to reproduce the traditional intellectuals and socialize everybody into the community. Diviners, griots, and priests contributed to the development of society by using their specialized knowledge to interpret reality, produce relevant histories for leaders, mediate in conflicts, and even predict the future. Modern intellectuals have tried to understand the "traditional elite" by studying its member's knowledge and using the results to show that Africa had sages and a long intellectual tradition before any contact with Europeans.[2]

We can also talk of an "Islamic intelligentsia," based on the practice of Islam and a formal Islamic educational system. Before the rise of Islam in the seventh century, writing had, of course, been invented, and schools had existed in various parts of the world. Reference has frequently been made to the monasteries and the Alexandria museum and library in Egypt developed in the third century B.C. This intellectual tradition continued to be improved upon in the Middle East, Europe, Asia, and North Africa. With the spread of Islam to Africa, a formal Islamic educational system followed in North, West, and East Africa, where the religion took roots. At the most elementary level, Islamic education involved the teaching of the Koran, the Arabic language, and religious knowledge by an Islamic scholar who received gifts and alms in lieu of payment. At the secondary level, advanced students took classes in language, philosophy, law, and other subjects. Students could also be organized into colleges, called *madrasa*, led by prominent scholars. The intelligentsia played a variety of roles in administration where learned people worked as clerks, tax collectors, diplomats, historians, and judges. Devoted scholars established colleges and monasteries where different interpretations of religious books were discussed.

Islamic education also reached the university level, and a few Islamic universities were created in Africa.[3] The first was at Karawiyyin, founded in 859 A.D., in the old city of Fez, from which prominent Islamic professors spread the Maliki code of law, religious brotherhoods, and other cultural ideas to the Maghreb and West Africa. In the tenth century A.D., Al-Azhar University in Cairo became very prominent. This was Ibn Khaldun's location from about 1382 to 1421, and the place where he produced his famous *Universal History*.[4] For many years before the sixteenth century, Sankore in Timbuktu (West Africa) housed a university, supported by kings and wealthy merchants, along with a variety of monasteries with distinguished teachers and priests. Timbuktu contributed to the spread of Islam in the West African region.

Generally, the spread of Islam went hand in hand with the spread of the Arabic language, thereby creating an intelligentsia that relied on writing. However, Islam was also oral, retaining an aspect of culture well established in the African continent. For instance, Swahili poetry reveals an oral tradition rich in history and culture. Similarly, the Fulani and Hausa of West Africa established a rich Islamic-cum-oral culture. A literate intelligentsia relied on the radicalism supplied by Islam to develop a vision of society in different parts of Africa. For instance, during the nineteenth and twentieth centuries, Islam became a tool to fight imperialism by resorting to radicalism and tradition, both already tested in previous years in reforming society.

Ethiopia was in a class of its own in the history of education and the creation of an intelligentsia at a time much earlier than in most other parts of the continent. From the twelfth to the sixteenth centuries, the Orthodox Church established three levels of schools for would-be monks and priests. The centers of excellence, supported by the emperors with land grants, were monasteries in remote places, to allow for serious meditation. Training was rigorous, involving examinations and diplomas to attest to success.

As important as all these antecedents are, they did not create the modern intellectuals that form the subject of this book. The modern intellectuals owe their origins to the spread of Western formal education, which began in some parts of Africa in the sixteenth century. The Portuguese initiated the contact with Africa during the fifteenth century and were soon joined by the British, Danes, French, Dutch, and Germans. As the slave trade became lucrative and widespread, more and more Europeans went to Africa. Trading stations were established along the coast in St. Louis and Goree in Senegal, Elmina, Accra, and Cape Coast on the Gold Coast, Benin in the area of modern Nigeria, and the Kingdom of the Congo. In these places, rudimentary elementary schools sprang up, to introduce a limited number of Africans to basic accounting as well as reading and writing European languages. A small scheme to produce teachers also started, sending Africans to Europe for further education. During this time of the slave trade and increasing racism, the students must have endured harsh study environments. Many of them overcame these conditions, and several became famous, notably Anton Amo of the Gold Coast who wrote a philosophy thesis for Martin Luther University in Halle, Germany, Philip Quaque, a schoolteacher, and Jacobis Capitein who justified slavery.

The production of an educated elite was a slow process, but the pace accelerated in the twentieth century as Africans insisted on change. In establishing elementary schools, the missionaries offered the basis for producing literate people. Euro-African relations during the nineteenth century called for the use of more literate Africans in commercial houses, churches, and government establishments. The African elite had to respond to the changing nature of Euro-African relations. The abolition of slavery led to trade in raw materials and later to colonial conquest. The "success" of Western education can be dated to the nineteenth century, when missionaries started arriving in large numbers. More and more Africans were receptive to conversion and secular education. Some governments, such as those of Egypt, and many individuals, notably liberated slaves, demanded education for Africans. The provision of Western education enabled the missionaries to propagate Christianity, campaign against the slave trade, and create a new, Western-oriented African intelligentsia. The missionaries used education to convert Africans to Christianity and assimilate them to a new way of life and thinking. Although the agendas of the missionaries tended to be similar, their methods, their achievements, and the limitations posed by the various European governments varied. For instance, the British allowed opportunities for missionary operation, except in Islamic areas; the French colonial authorities cooperated only slightly with the missionaries; and in South Africa, the emphasis was on the education of people of European descent. The missionaries and colonial powers both understood the relevance of education, and they tried to balance its provision with perceived need and the awareness of its power as a social agency. Higher education was completely neglected, as there was no need to produce educated Africans at that level. Only a few secondary schools were provided, and by and large, the education of Africans was restricted to the elementary level.

The self-interest of the missionaries made them front-runners in the provision of education. As long as education was the handmaiden of evangelization, they were ready to work for it. However, contrary to what many contemporaries thought, the missionaries did not set themselves up as enemies of the colonial state. Of course, there were numerous instances of tension between the missionaries and officials. For instance, the missionaries resented the restrictions on their activities in Islamic areas and what they interpreted as the official encouragement of the spread of Islam. However, the areas of collaboration were many. For instance, the colonial governments were not opposed to the creation of a new African "middle class" as long as the members of this class were pro-European, dedicated workers, and consumers. In the views of the colonial governments, education could be a means to create their local collaborators or to silence opposition forces. The missionaries were also useful in the "pacification" of African chiefs and rulers. Children and wards of chiefs and rulers were encouraged to go to school, to create a pool of well-connected citizens to work for the government. Through these children and their parents, the indigenous rulers accepted their new role as collaborators, earned their wages as the reward for keeping quiet, threatened no wars of resistance, and demanded no major reforms. If the nineteenth-century chiefs had seen in Europeans the allies that would give them guns and technology, their successors in the twentieth century simply supported the modernization agenda of missionaries and colonial officers. Education was one of the means to ensure their change of attitude. In some countries, notably the English-speaking ones, the missionaries received education grants from the government, a better source of revenues than tithes from church members. In the last quarter of the nineteenth century, relations changed in response to the imposition of colonial rule, a process that implicated a number of Africans who supported colonial rule in the hope that it would bring development to Africa. The colonial period saw an appreciable increase in the number of modern intellectuals, just enough to service the colonial system, but grossly inadequate for rapid transformation. Although always inadequate, many new schools were established during the colonial period, but they were still mostly elementary schools.

Both for Africans and colonizers, education was necessary for survival. For the colonizers, the system could not function without an elite or, at the very minimum, a group of people who could read and write. While a number of European administrators learned and used African languages, many others had to depend on interpreters to serve as intermediaries. Thus, the first major job of educated Africans was to mediate in all sorts of relations: to present the Bible on behalf of white missionaries, to relay instructions on behalf of European administrators, and to negotiate trade deals. As important as these roles were, the elites extended this to become also the mediators of history and culture. They presented European values to Africans, either as critics or as modernizers. Yet on the other hand, they presented Africa to the Europeans. As we shall see with regard to the writings of Wilmot Blyden and others, the intellectuals regarded this mediation as important to themselves and to the continent.

The colonizers and representatives of European firms also needed educated Africans as workers. The missionaries required native agents, mainly schoolteachers and priests. The firms needed clerks, cashiers, and others to facilitate the import–export trade. The government required clerks, tax collectors, police, soldiers, and many others to serve in different agencies. Where the colonial officers depended on local chiefs, as in the case of the British system of "indirect rule," the number of educated Africans required was small indeed. In other colonial systems, a selfish calculation was made that training Africans for positions that Europeans could occupy was in effect creating a revolution that would destroy the system. The number of Africans required was dependent on the nature of the colonial economy and politics, the extent to which a colonial government was willing to depend on European migrants and settlers, and the extent of exploitation or modernization underway. As new occupations became necessary, including nursing, teaching, law, and medicine, the system also needed qualified Africans to fill them. Nevertheless, colonial governments deliberately created an educational system that would make Africans subordinate to Europeans.[5]

For Africans, Western education was necessary. I have mentioned the mediation role of the elite, which was an exercise of power. Indeed, the voice of mediation was a source of great power for the court interpreters who profited from closeness to the judiciary, for the officers in the police and army who served as agents of coercion, and for the highly educated who were negotiating old and new cultures. Education was an agency of social change, indeed the most potent agency of change. Africans who wanted to join in the new sectors needed the knowledge of a European language and education.

Piecemeal measures never satisfied Africans, who understood the game that the missionaries and colonial governments were playing with them. Having realized that education brought many advantages, notably mobility and social status, the African beneficiaries of Western education in the nineteenth century wanted to retain their privileges, to consolidate their power, to educate their offspring, and to use education to transform the continent. Wherever a mission had established a school, the community ensured that education survived and expanded.

Africans also exerted pressure on the missionaries and governments to create secondary schools and universities. If education was confined to the elementary level, Africans could only work as subordinates to white superiors in all establishments. Creating an alliance with a Christian mission turned out to be the easiest way for Africans to ensure the creation of new secondary schools, as in the case of southern Nigeria where the Church Missionary Society (CMS) and the Baptist and Roman Catholic churches established secondary schools.[6] Those Africans who had received higher education and held positions of power (for example, as school principals) used their influence to persuade communities and congregations to contribute money to start new schools, which a mission or government could then acquire or subsidize. This was the case in a number of southwestern Nigerian towns in the first two decades of the twentieth century when six new secondary schools were created. In Ghana, the elite raised money from traditional leaders and businessmen to start new schools in Accra and Cape Coast. In order to obtain schoolteachers, pressure was also directed at creating teacher training colleges. While a number were established in different parts of the continent, so acute was the shortage of teachers that this became a factor in the expansion and creation of secondary schools. In South Africa, the churches began to make an important impact from the 1840s onward; following the leadership of the London Missionary Society, the Methodists and the Paris Evangelical Mission took an interest in teacher training colleges, secondary schools, and agricultural and industrial schools. As Fourah Bay College acquired fame in West Africa, so did the Lovedale Institution, established in 1841 by the Scottish Presbyterian Mission in South Africa. The objective of Lovedale was to train students in a variety of occupations (industrial, evangelical, teaching, and so on). It offered courses in carpentry, masonry, printing, and bookbinding.[8] Its academic offerings were equally diverse and rigorous. Lovedale provided the model and inspiration for the establishment of other secondary schools in South and East Africa after 1870.

Those who had enjoyed the opportunity of a secondary school education or who had such a school in their area sought to establish an institution of higher education or travel abroad for further education. In British West Africa, a few students went to Fourah Bay College, which was upgraded to a university in 1876. However, as theology dominated the training there, those seeking education in law, medicine, accountancy, and other fields had to seek opportunities in Europe. Others went to the United States; these included such men as Kwame Nkrumah of the Gold Coast (later Ghana) and Nnamdi Azikiwe of Nigeria. Slow to be accepted as possessing the same credentials as those trained in Europe, the graduates of American universities became strong advocates of the American system of higher education. The combination of academic, vocational, and technical training, as in Tuskegee Institute, was highly recommended for producing a new elite that would be able to think and invent.[9]

Where long-distance learning was possible, a number of Africans seized the opportunity. For instance, the first three Zambians to obtain degrees did so as external candidates, while a few Nigerians also acquired B.A. degrees as private students. Successful African entrepreneurs sent their children abroad to study and acquire diplomas in such professions as law, medicine, and accountancy. The missionaries also sent their priests and a few others to seminaries in Europe for advanced degrees. During the colonial period, communities often contributed money to sponsor a brilliant son. And there were enterprising people who simply struggled on their own, including a number of soldiers who served in the Second World War and went to Europe in search of greener pastures. In the late 1950s, Tom Mboya, a Kenyan trade unionist and Pan-Africanist, organized the journeys of many students to the United States for higher education, certainly the most successful effort of its kind during the colonial period. The quest for a university education became part of the African expression of nationalism.[10]

There were great variations and disparities in the growth of education in Africa. Only a brief history can be provided here, to indicate important phases, developments, and limitations. In West and East Africa, the mission house was both a school and church, and it used various means to attract Africans to both functions. The school system used European languages to teach reading and writing. The Sunday schools provided an opportunity to teach the Bible and provide adult education through reading and writing. The mission houses produced African pastors and teachers who served as native agents in evangelization and the spread of education. Varying degrees of success were recorded in different parts of the continent, except North Africa. In Madagascar, the Hova oligarchy that seized power in the 1860s used state power to introduce compulsory elementary education. In West Africa, Sierra Leone became a leading country in the growth of education. Indeed, Sierra Leone and Liberia, two countries that received large numbers of liberated slaves, provided leadership in missionary activities. In the case of Sierra Leone, the British government sought cooperation with the Church Missionary Society to rehabilitate freed slaves in the city of Freetown and its surrounding areas. Rapid evangelization and the establishment of schools followed after 1808, producing a new "middle class," known as the Krio (Creole). Unable to depend on European recruits because of a high mortality rate, the CMS decided to produce local workers. In 1827, the CMS established Fourah Bay College (FBC) to train its African auxiliaries. Fourah Bay later became the first modern institution of higher learning in Africa. In the 1840s, the CMS established two secondary schools along gender lines, while the Methodists also improved their educational systems. In addition, a number of Africans were sent to Europe for training, and many African parents seized the opportunity to train their children in law and medicine overseas. The Royal Navy also trained a few people who later worked for them, notably Africanus Horton, who is one of the heroes of this book, and Broughton Davis, who served as a medical doctor. In the 1870s, FBC became a college, with a narrow focus on the production of a B.A. in theology, under the supervision of Durham University. Fourah Bay College enjoyed its status as the only West African university until 1948. In West Africa, the CMS established two grammar schools in 1845 and a female secondary institution in 1849. The French established a "school for the sons of chiefs" in 1848 to teach language, administration, and law. Other secondary schools emerged in later years, in places such as Lagos, Onitsha, Bonny, Calabar, all in Nigeria, and Freetown in Sierra Leone. The trend continued during the colonial period, largely due to African pressure for more schools.

In the early years of colonial rule, British policy supported the missionaries with grants, and officials of the Government Inspectorate were used to ensure adherence to guidelines on quality and the adaptation of education to meet the needs of the colonial system.[11] The major decision was taken in 1923 to establish the Advisory Committee on Education in Tropical Africa, an agency that provided important guidelines on education. The committee arose partly as a consequence of the 1922 reports by the Phelps-Stokes Commission (PSC), which was sponsored by a charitable foundation based in the United States.

With the aim of improving the education of blacks in the United States and Africa, the PSC was sent to West, central, and South Africa to study the state of educational policies and recommend important changes. An African hero in the PSC was J. K. Aggrey of the Gold Coast.[12] The commission recommended that education should be adapted to the African situation and that more opportunities should be created. The PSC reports became the most important documents on educational reforms in Africa until 1940, although many colonial governments ignored them. The Advisory Committee used the reports to make changes or propose alternatives to elementary, secondary, vocational, and teacher training institutions. The committee always recommended adaptation and change, but continued to stress the issue of morality over professionalization:

> The first task of education is to raise the standard alike of character and efficiency of the bulk of the people, but provision must also be made for the training of those who are required to fill posts in the administrative and technical services, as well as of those who as chiefs will occupy positions of exceptional trust and responsibility. As resources permit, the door of advancement, through higher education, in Africa must be increasingly opened for those who by character, ability and temperament show themselves fitted to profit by such education.[13]

The key policies recommended by the Advisory Committee included the following: the government should continue to cooperate with communities and missionaries to support education but must retain the power of supervision; traditional rulers, as participants in the administration, should become more enlightened; the training of Africans should be based on their production as subordinate workers, at a level that could maintain the needs of the colonial system; more funds should be made available to school proprietors; additional schools should be built; and a number of secondary schools should be operated at different locations to offer academic and technical training in a number of subjects.[14] The leading secondary schools were affiliated with European universities, where their syllabi and examinations were approved and graded.[15] Indeed, the British successfully introduced a system of external examinations to Africa, examinations both dreaded and valued for their difficulty and the likelihood of failure. Usually of the same quality and standard as for students based in Europe, the examinations reminded Africans of the power of imperialism and the difficulty of adjusting education to the local environment. Successful Africans were able to use their results to enhance their social status or secure admission to European institutions of higher learning.

In the French-speaking areas, missionaries and governments did not necessarily collaborate. Governments were distrustful of the missionaries, while attempts to centralize policies tended to stifle local initiatives. If the missionaries were interested in evangelization, the French government was interested in secular French culture. Consequently, the missionaries were less active in providing elementary education, pressuring the government for grants or mobilizing communities to create schools. Dominated by the Roman Catholics, the missionaries promoted limited courses in French as a language. The French accepted the idea of a secular education, as long as it corresponded with the interests of the colonial authorities. Many French administrators believed that secular education would bring civilization to Africans and make them better workers. Courses at the elementary level included French language, culture, history, and literature. The Muslims were allowed to continue with their Quranic schools while French authorities assisted in the "secularization" of Islamic education at the elementary level. French scholars were sponsored in research to understand Islamic societies, an interest that helped lead to the creation in 1938 in Dakar of the Institut Français d'Afrique Noire (IFAN). In spite of this interest, the French discouraged the establishment of Islamic secondary education and pan-Islamic organizations, to prevent radical Islamic nationalism. Until 1939, only a few secondary schools existed in the French colonies. In French West Africa, the major schools included the Ecole Normale William Ponty, a teacher training college, two secondary schools in Senegal (one mainly for French settlers and children of French officials), a veterinary school and polytechnic in Bamako, and a number of trade and technical schools in other colonies, such as the Tananarive Medical Institute in Madagascar.

The extent of opportunities for higher education turned it into a desirable aim for many Africans. Those who managed to receive college diplomas were able to obtain good jobs. Among them were the évolués, who were committed to French culture and were encouraged to travel to France for more education. A number of Africans, notably from Togo, Cameroon, and Dahomey, traveled on their own to France for secondary and higher education, and many of them developed anticolonial ideas and supported the emerging ideas of Pan-Africanism. A number of others resisted what they perceived as the imposition of French culture, and they began to call for the study of African culture and customs.

Developments in the colonies controlled by the other European powers were not impressive. For example, Italy, which exercised power in Somalia and attacked Ethiopia in 1935, achieved very little. In Somalia, the attempt to cooperate with missionaries produced little result, due in part to the people's resistance. In Ethiopia, the Italian invasion disrupted the educational system until 1940. In the Belgian colony of the Congo, the government allowed the missions to establish elementary schools, supporting the Catholics financially while ignoring the Protestants. The state required the missions to limit severely the purpose of elementary schools, and the majority of African students were instructed in local languages. A few, selected for clerical duties as priests, had the opportunity of learning French. In a highly paternalistic arrangement, the elementary schools were like convents, and the colleges were like seminaries. The results of the system were that the Belgians occupied all the major technical and administrative jobs, that the brightest Africans were prepared for the priesthood and the others for subordinate positions, and that the majority of Africans ended up as workers and producers in the colonial system.

In the Portuguese colonies, the colonial government spent little on education, allowed the missionaries to operate, and supported the Portuguese settlers and company employees in providing a good education for their children. Except for a few people who were assimilated, education was not considered important for the majority of Africans. Opportunities for secondary and higher education were virtually nonexistent for the African population.

In the years after the Second World War, a number of changes were recorded throughout the continent. This was a time of reform in politics, the economy, and education, and it was the period of decolonization in a number of British and French colonies. The demands for higher education were met in some places,[16] and many new schools were established. When African countries obtained independence, a "revolution" occurred in the phenomenal spread of Western education, especially in higher education (discussed in a later chapter).

To reiterate: Western formal education in most of Africa has colonial origins, and for most of the colonial period it was in the service of the colonial system. Thus, the goal of education was focused: the production of a limited number of educated people to work in the modernizing sectors created by the colonial state. In some cases, education was dominated by the missionaries in alliance with the state. In such cases, evangelization was the major goal, with service to the state as a secondary goal. In places like the Belgian Congo (now the Democratic Republic of Congo), missionary education was opposed to elitism and vocationalism, as the elite was presumed to be dangerous and subversive, and producing them would destroy the foundations of the state. The majority of Africans did not have the opportunity to go to school, primarily because the facilities and teachers were not made available to them, and the majority of those who did were regarded as inferiors and fed with racist and/or colonial values. For most of the colonial era, higher education was underdeveloped. Until the Second World War, the objective of many colonial governments was simply to offer alternatives to degree-awarding institutions. After 1945, when universities were created, the faculty and staff were European, the disciplines were limited, the

curricula were approved by metropolitan universities, and control was exercised by representatives of the colonial authorities. Most African universities are new, less than fifty years old. With the exception of Fourah Bay College in Sierra Leone, universities in Anglophone tropical Africa date back only to 1948 when the first were established in Ibadan, Legon and Makerere. All the three were originally university colleges controlled by the University of London. These universities came into maturity and obtained their autonomy in the 1960s when African countries became independent. When African countries obtained their independence, the expansion of the education system became a top priority.

Western education created the new elite, invested it with power, and made it the most important participant in the modernizing sectors of society. The governments of postindependence Africa expanded facilities, created new schools at all levels, devoted considerable budgets to education, created opportunities to train girls and women, and developed African languages and literatures. Education became an important part of national politics. Where a section of a country had produced a larger proportion of the elite because of the advantage of having missionaries, the excluded sections feared the domination of this elite. For instance, in Nigeria this played out in the divisive south–north politics, largely because of the disproportionate production of the educated elite in the south. In virtually all countries, the challenge was to improve education— the quantity (by creating more schools), the quality (by overcoming the negative values implanted by colonialism and seeking the means to relate education to development), and the languages of instruction (the use of European languages in combination with indigenous ones).

In view of the slow and uneven development of Western education, the modern intellectuals showcased in this study exhibit the following features. For most of the period under consideration, their number was small, thereby constituting them as a minority. But this elite has always been a powerful minority, so successful that it inherited power from Europeans and has continued to generate ideas, in spite of the domination of politics by the military. The intellectuals have always invested in the notion of progress—the genuine hope that Africa would develop and that they would be the agency of the transformation. The notion of progress has intermeshed with that of nationalism: most demands in the nineteenth and twentieth centuries have been couched in the language of nationalism. The intellectuals have constructed or accepted not only the ideas of the nation-state, but also those of ethnicity and even the larger project of a continental identity for Africa. They participate in local and global cultures; their perspectives are drawn from local, national, continental, and international issues; they were originally resented by Europeans but later acquired power from them; they constitute essentially a public-sector elite, that is, they are not primarily "an economic bourgeoisie," which means that they have had to seek relevance and power in government and the apparatus of state. Let me now turn to the ideas that they generated.

THE INTELLECTUAL AGENDA

The question that has dominated intellectual thinking in Africa in the last two hundred years has been constant: against the background of Western incursion, how can Africa uplift itself? This is an intellectual confrontation with a modern world where continuity and change go hand in hand, compete and clash, reinforce and complement one another. Change, continuity with the past, and adaptations to new circumstances have all been part of the challenges that intellectuals have confronted as they make sense of modernity and reflect on what they perceive as their alienation in a world increasingly dominated by European values. As with the intelligentsia in other lands, Africans are not merely trying to understand the process of change and continuity, but they also have to experience the reality and insert themselves into the very process and society that they are analyzing. Theory can merge with practice, writing with experience. Knowledge is useful to the extent that writings can feed actions or simply suggest alternative lifestyles. Thus, we are

not dealing with an intelligentsia that primarily occupies an "ivory tower," disconnected from the rest of society. An "ivory tower," in its European sense, has not really existed in most of Africa. To say this is not to suggest that the intelligentsia is almost always connected with the society or that there is no distinction between the elite and other segments of society. To be excessively pro-modern is to create a distance from traditions. To be excessively pro-tradition is to despise modernization. To be elitist is to live apart from the generality of the people. And to be close to the people is to violate certain presumptions of elitism. From where should models and concepts be drawn? Should they be from the external world or from indigenous practices, or a blend of both? The intelligentsia is "no longer at ease," to borrow an appropriate title from one of Chinua Achebe's novels. It has to confront a variety of alternatives.

On all these issues, opinions have been divided along ideological and religious lines, and sometimes along gender and generational lines. There is much talk about class, but less about gender; more about religion, less about generation; more about sustaining values, less about self-destructive degeneracy. Thinkers may be variously labeled as pragmatist, traditionalist, assimilationist, or Afrocentrist, although the line is not always clear-cut. Some are radical, others are conservative. Lately, those who have come to be known as "Afro-pessimists" reflect anger and distrust about Africa or merely doubt what others see as the African genius and even the prospect of any future development. Both conservatism and radicalism are defined by the age, or even by the competing elite.

The fear and the appreciation of the West have created grave concerns, some bordering on alienation and others on excessive imitation. Academic and political thinkers have called for diverse strategies in overcoming these fears and/or excesses. All have been forced to address the impact of the West on Africa. While some have advocated isolationist paradigms, others have called for a more open response. But none has been able to move away from the framework of alienation, or what those in the literary world call the "conflict of culture," which has, in some circles, acquired a sinister meaning. When treated as the agent of alienation, the intelligentsia itself becomes part of the African crisis and requires decolonization or sanitization, as Frantz Fanon and Chinweizu argue.[17] When treated as victims of alienation, Africans are presented as helpless followers of modernity who, as some novelists have suggested, may require suicide—a transition to a cosmos where their souls may be at peace.[18] So sinister has the representation of alienation been that many have focused on combating it, developing confrontational strategies both in scholarship and lifestyle. Of course, there are those who warn about the dangers of such an obsession and who seek positive values in alienation, to release its energies, in such areas as science and technology, in order to develop Africa.[19] Is the fear of alienation or of the West so threatening as to continue to drive scholarship?

A moment of digression is in order here to comment on the politics of scholarship. Reading the works of Africans or listening to their lectures, you may form an impression that they are either angry or blaming their pathetic conditions on forces beyond their control. To be a bit more elegant, you can say that they are either polemical or defensive, bitter or apologetic. Yes, you are right! However, you need to know the reason for this. Scholarship in Africa has been conditioned to respond to a reality and epistemology created for it by outsiders, a confrontation with imperialism, the power of capitalism, and the knowledge that others have constructed for Africa. The African intelligentsia does not write in a vacuum but in a world saturated with others' statements, usually negative about its members and their continent. Even when this intelligentsia seeks the means to intrude itself into the modern world, modernity has been defined for it and presented to it in a fragmented manner. It should progress to resemble the history of Europe, many have opined over the years as part of the definition of this modernity. When Africa has radios, there will be no power or batteries to make them work, just to give one example of a fragmented modernity. When there are radios or batteries, there will be no local

news, to show how technology and information control may not be allies. When there is local news, its reliability may have to be authenticated by the British Broadcasting Service in London, yet another example of the manipulation of fragmentation. African discursive strategies and paradigms may tend to be confrontational or aggressive, but this is inevitable when the presentation of the continent by others has been negative and demeaning.

But Africans are more angry at themselves, as recent writings show, with some going as far as presenting the colonial period as the "golden age" of the twentieth century. In a consistent manner, the intelligentsia has criticized some of its own members as collaborators with imperialism who maintained the colonial power structures and who, after decolonization, plundered their nations. In recent times, so distrustful and alienated is the intelligentsia that most of its members do not trust their governments and regard the words of their political leaders as empty.

A legitimate question follows: Is there, then, an African scholarship if ideology intermeshes with the production of knowledge? The answer is that if the intention of scholarship is to uplift Africa, it cannot dissociate itself from challenging the representation that it seeks to correct. A counter-discourse, even when it is political or subversive, is still valid and legitimate scholarship. A counter-discourse may upset the mainstream, but it is not an intellectual anarchism lacking in rules and critical modes of evaluation. Bear in mind that the African intelligentsia is searching for truth, as it defines it, knowledge about itself and its continent, and a variety of alternative insights to solve a myriad of problems. There is a distinction between politicized scholarship and scholarship that recognizes the place of politics. There is also the issue of relevance—the right of the marginalized and poor people to demand of their intelligentsia solutions to their problems. Scholars have to be familiar with and be committed to the material world at the same time. Those who seek purity in scholarship, or Robert Nisbet's "academic dogma," should reflect on the role of the intelligentsia in a developing continent with many problems and limited resources to solve them. Here, I am not recommending that activism becomes the driving engine of scholarship; at the same time, I cannot say that all forms of scholarship should be divorced from political motives. The wise scholar seeks a blend, often ignoring current political concerns and challenges and refusing to make bogus, unverifiable claims in support of political objectives. Whether in Africa or the West, scholarship is not divorced from power, interest, and preferences.

In this chapter, I identify the issues that have dominated the thinking of the African intelligentsia and summarize the ideas of some of the leading schools of thought, focusing mainly on the scholars who came before the rise of the modern academy now associated with the formal university system. I will demonstrate that a profound intellectual orientation had long existed, that the concerns of this intelligentsia are similar even to those of the present era, and that a previous generation served as forebears to the contemporary academic intelligentsia. I will show that the success of this previous generation, instigated by nationalism, has been very empowering and liberating, and indeed has opened the minds of successive generations of Africans to issues posed by modernization. While raising issues of broad significance, I illuminate them with the writings of leading thinkers. By highlighting these leading thinkers, I celebrate the African genius as well as showing that scholarship has been deliberately constructed to serve the needs of the state and the nation, to create new souls whose minds will be decolonized or who, at least, will carefully edit received wisdom.

Scholarship has made a vigorous attempt to declare independence, both politically and culturally. Some struggle to search for an original African soul or mind, an affirmation of eagerness to be free of Western domination. The most astute among them do in fact accept the globalization of knowledge but nevertheless seek what is peculiarly African. Not many choose to disconnect from the global, from what they perceive as the threat posed by the Anglo-European academy or European values and ideas, but they reject intellectual imprisonment.

No matter how brilliant the external ideas are, scholars still want to domesticate them. Not all seek domestication, to be sure, but most desire it. In refocusing the global or domesticating the external, the African intelligentsia falls on the inherited tools of tradition, history, and culture, sometimes even of the recent history of European domination or capitalist penetration. Many ideas now appear confusing, neither consolidated nor brilliant enough, but let me reemphasize the urge to be independent. The obsession for intellectual independence, even when it is manifested in a caricatured imitation of the Western academy, shows creativity and a capacity to reflect, to turn our continent into a frontier. Even if the lack of success of the nation-state in Africa can partly be attributed to the failure of the intelligentsia, we also have to accept that this failure has long been anticipated by the continent's leading thinkers, the real heroes of the African intellectual community.

THE ISSUES

African intellectuals of the twentieth century and their predecessors have confronted a number of issues and posed a variety of questions on the necessity and strategy of uplifting Africa:

i.   Can Africa stand on its own? Tradition is needed to autonomize this and progress to enhance it, but ambiguity remains, and it calls into question the idea of universalism and globalism.

ii.   How can self-reliance be created? How can Africa develop? Seeking answers in tradition is inadequate. Changes are necessary in the following aspects: technology, unity of Africans in the new countries created for them by Europeans, and transnational cooperation to unite all blacks in Africa and the diaspora. If all these changes are desirable, how can modernization/Westernization be reconciled with the African past?

iii. How can Africans forge a racial identity in a world they view as racist and discriminatory? Can they minimize contacts with Europeans?

If not, how can they be autonomous and retain their personality? Euro-African dialogue is not based on equality; even many of the missionaries who converted Africans to Christianity and educated them in formal schools did not believe in a philosophy of equal dialogue.

iv. How should the traditional and educated elites distribute power? The assumption, at least from the point of view of the educated elite, is that the traditional elite can not handle modernization. From the point of view of the traditional elite, the modern educated elite has no legitimacy to govern in many communities.

v. Can the concept of an "African personality" be sustained in a changing world? Are Africans really different from others? Can uniqueness be retained in an age of globalization?

vi. How should it be demonstrated that, contrary to views expressed in influential European circles, Africa had science, poetry, philosophy, religion, and history? What sort of evidence, what sort of methods are appropriate?

vii. By the 1940s, it was clear that Africa would inherit the Western legacy of capitalism, liberal democracy, and the nation-state. Can African leaders manage the three, either individually or collectively? Are the three even reconcilable or desirable? If they are desirable, are there conditions and opportunities to achieve them? Can they all be redefined so that they will grow on African soil? Do they all create tensions between the "traditional" and the "modern"?

The list can be extended, but the issues keep revolving around the theme of African progress in a modern world. The fact that the issues appear constant should not be misread as an indication of intellectual poverty in thought and choices. Lately, some voices have been challenging Africans and Africanists to keep shifting their paradigms, as their Western counterparts manifest their own shifts, without considering the implications for the issues that drive intellectual production in Africa. My response is that if the issues have remained constant and unsolved, how can one theory replace another so fast, how can scholarship resemble fashion and weather, changing so rapidly? Why should scholars of Africa follow and accept all fast-changing academic trends, if their conditions are either constant or changing for the worse? Why should they keep replacing one mode of analysis with another if they are yet to overcome their own limitations, both practical and intellectual? They can do so in order to participate in the debate in a "global academy," but they must consider the consequences for Africa.

MODERNIZERS OF THE NINETEENTH CENTURY

Contrary to popular thinking in much of modernist and postmodernist literature, Africans did not begin reflecting on modernity and their adjustments to a new world order only during the twentieth century. Highlighting the issues above shows the continuity in the thinking of the intelligentsia.

There was a fear of crisis in the nineteenth century, remarkably similar to what obtains today. Many scholars have misleadingly regarded the colonial period as the origin of modernity, the beginning of that "ambiguous adventure," to use the title of the well known novel by Cheik Hamidou Kane (*L'Aventure ambigüe*), when Africa entered the phase of confusion between its past and present. Let me quickly show that this is not true by pointing to the trends that produced great intellectual ideas and to some of the themes that dominated the nineteenth century. During this period, a few Africans were able to foresee the consequences of European imperialism and to advance arguments about how Africans should respond to it. Where Christianity was already spreading and producing converts, conversion and/or the challenges to conversion unleashed an array of intellectual arguments about the role of culture, the impact of foreign culture on the indigenous, and how cultures found "uncivilized" or repugnant by the colonizers should be changed or abolished. There was also talk about civilization, often cast in the language of progress, and to a limited extent about technology.

Even as new institutions were adapted or created to respond to indigenous circumstances and to European contacts, local events also produced new thinkers who reflected on a dying society or one in transition. All the changes generated their own consequences, political as well as intellectual. When the slave trade was abolished and replaced with trade in raw materials, the business class had to adjust and reflect on the nature of the change: the extent to which they should continue with the older trade in slaves or profit from newer forms of commerce, the implications of the wealth they acquired, and the means of wielding political influence and authority in a way that would either undermine or complement existing power structures. Trade in raw materials enabled greater access to production and enlarged the scale of domestic exchange. While the slave trade was controlled by kings and chiefs, who had access to the means of violence, many more people benefited from the trade in produce. New merchants (including the so-called merchant princes), a rural bourgeoisie, and local traders were created, many with the resources to consume imported objects, send their children to school, and form a network in social communication that spread ideas over a wider region. The "intellectual minds" of the merchant class and emerging rural bourgeoisie have yet to receive the attention they deserve.

The abolition of the slave trade and the challenge of resettlement of freed slaves led to the creation of Libreville in Equatorial Africa, Liberia in 1787, and Sierra Leone in 1820. In the West African cases of Liberia and Sierra Leone, creative cultures and languages emerged. Americo-Liberian became an intellectual and subcultural identity in Liberia, while in Sierra Leone the Krio (Creole) culture developed. Krio was a brilliant mixture of Canadian (Nova Scotian), British, and African cultures, and its elite, the Krios, became the vanguard in the creation of a Christian community and a new intelligentsia in the West African region.[20]

There were massive migrations in different parts of the continent, followed by constitutional and political changes where migrants created new cities and villages, as among the Yoruba. The choice of new political systems was both pragmatic and intellectual, fiercely contested as a political discourse and in some cases resolved on battlefields.[21] If great empires collapsed, many new ones emerged to address a host of issues. The theocratic states in West Africa addressed intellectual concerns. The Nguni people, Buganda and such states as Ethiopia and Madagascar modernized themselves by a process of political centralization. The Imerina kingdom under King Andrianaimpoinimerina (1782–1810) and Ethiopia under King Menelik II (1889–1918) sought to use the power of culture and language to create hegemonic ideology to unify diverse groups.

The Islamic revolutions in northwestern Africa produced monumental political and social changes. Led by Fulani scholars, the jihad was an intellectual movement that produced many pamphlets and essays on issues such as injustice, taxation, and legal and political systems. Such leaders as Usman dan Fodio, El Kanemi, and Mohammed Bello were important thinkers, and the sources of their knowledge were broad and "international."

The encounter with Europeans predated colonial conquest. During the nineteenth century, the contacts reached beyond the coastal areas. The bigger picture of the loss of sovereignty and colonial conquest has obscured the slow but steady spread of European technology, including mirrors, guns, and a wide range of other items with transformative capacity—printing machines that served the needs of a literate group; new machinery that improved agriculture in some places; technical knowledge; the railway, the telegraph, and other innovations. None of these was ignored, and each entered the realm of intellectual discourse and even the practical politics of seeking the means either to import them or invent local substitutes. Military historians have shown how European objects and ideas led to changes in a number of African armies. Such kings as Samori Touré in West Africa and Tewedros and Menelik in Ethiopia modernized their armies. In North Africa, the changes went as where Tunisia established factories to produce weapons and Morocco founded an engineering school. While details may be scant on the extent of intellectual discourse, we are familiar with its result, the attempt to reorganize the military in Tunisia and Morocco along European lines. With respect to the economy, Muhammad Ali of Egypt promoted the establishment of sawmills, paper mills, textile mills, and the printing press. In the second half of the nineteenth century, printing presses emerged in many other parts of the continent, creating opportunities to publish. Not only was there a quest for education where this was available, but a country like Egypt undertook broad educational reform.

THE MODERN INTELLIGENTSIA

As my analysis unfolds, intellectual heroes such as Bishop Ajayi Crowther, the Reverend Samuel Johnson, Edward Blyden, Mojola Agbebi, Bishop James Johnson, and others will feature prominently. This prominence is in part an outcome of Christian missionary activities, the impact of the Bible on Africans, and the development of nationalism in Africa. During the nineteenth century, missionary evangelization in Africa was aggressive. With a philosophy combining the Bible, commerce, and the plough, an army of foreign and local Christian agents worked in different parts of sub-Saharan Africa to create Christian-cum-middle-class citizens. By the 1880s, Christianity had set itself on a course of phenomenal success in eastern and central Africa. In southern Africa, its success was unmistakable, and the missionaries there also became active in politics, diplomacy, and agriculture. In West Africa, about fifteen missionary organizations were active after 1840. Hand in hand with evangelization was the spread of Western education. The missionaries contributed to the study of African languages, transcribing many of them into the Roman alphabet; and also enabled the new African intelligentsia to use European as well as local languages.

Missionary education produced a new elite, different in its mode of thinking and skills from the indigenous and Islamic intelligentsia. Bookbinding, printing, carpentry, and smithing were some of the new skills associated with this elite. To some extent, a new "industrial class" was also being created.

Western architecture and medicine also began to define some of the demands of the Christian intelligentsia, thus arousing the notion of "social engineering," which was to become a common theme of discussion in the years ahead. There was the issue of tradition, as missionaries criticized polygamy, African gods, ancestor veneration, witchcraft, and what they chose to call superstition. There was also the question of power: to what extent should the new elite allow the traditional to continue to wield power?

Originally, the elite was concentrated in the coastal cities, notably in West and South Africa. As education expanded to the hinterland, so too the elite emerged in scattered locations. Educational growth manifested regional variations, caused by the extent to which the missionaries were successful in evangelization, the receptivity to conversion, and the colonial attitude toward the education of Africans. Perhaps the least developed areas were eastern and central Africa. The size of the elite in this region was small during the nineteenth century. However, missionary activities became pronounced after the 1880s, leading to the production of a first-generation elite that became prominent during the twentieth century and from which Jomo Kenyatta and a few others later emerged to distinguish themselves. In southern Africa, it was a different story—here the size of the intelligentsia was larger, but its significance was undermined by racist politics. As elsewhere, the church was influential, with schools and missions in Natal, the Cape Town, and elsewhere. One institution alone, the Lovedale Missionary Institution, trained close to 4,000 Africans between 1841 and 1896 for different careers. The elite took an active role in Christianity and politics. While the list of early pioneers was long, a number were truly outstanding, including men such as Tiyo Soga, the first Xhosa to become a minister of the Free Church of England in 1856, and John Tengo Javabu, a trained teacher, pioneer founder of the Bantu newspaper *Imvo Zabantsundu*, and a politician from the 1890s to the second decade of the twentieth century. West Africa was a special case, famous for producing an intelligentsia that was able to define its identity and reflect African conditions. In the lead were the Krios of Sierra Leone who served as pioneer teachers and missionaries in other parts of West Africa. Some were to make a notable impact on the church and education, for example, Samuel Ajayi Crowther, the first African bishop of the Anglican Church, and Bishop James Johnson, missionary and radical thinker. A number were famous for their ideas, including men such as James Africanus Horton, a medical doctor and philosopher, Edward Wilmot Blyden, a notable thinker, Mojola Agbebi (formerly T. B. Vincent), a cultural nationalist, and many more.

The significance of the emerging intelligentsia was not just in number but in the great diversity of new occupations. Many people worked as clergymen and schoolteachers, serving as local agents in the spread of Christianity. A number advanced to become professionals—lawyers, doctors, and surveyors. As the need for clerks in the colonial bureaucracy increased, many were drawn into this occupation. Many others took to trade, becoming a corps of educated entrepreneurs who behaved like their European counterparts in pursuing trade opportunities or working as agents of European firms.

All these acted as the vanguard of a "new civilization," defined by new lifestyles and intellectual vision. In adopting new lifestyles, they cultivated a taste for imported items. Almost everywhere, they promoted the importation of European goods, presented and consumed as objects of modernity. Many chose to accept Western civilization to as full an extent as possible, while others sought partial adaptation to it. How they would use the civilization, skills, and knowledge created ambiguity. The aims were pretty clear: they wanted progress for Africa, while defending it from exploitative Western predatorship. By the 1880s, many members of the elite saw the futility of resisting imperialism. The choice was in seeking the means to respond to it.

THE COLONIAL PHASE

To say that modernity preceded the twentieth century is in no way to underestimate the significance of the colonial moment. Not only did Western education expand during the colonial period, but the new African intelligentsia became consolidated, assertive, and prominent as well. Most aspects of society were transformed. Production expanded to meet increasing domestic and external demands, manifested in the proliferation of newspapers, printing houses, pamphlets, and books. Africans in the West also borrowed the strategies of their hosts, both in expanding production and injecting Africa into intellectual discourse. One respected figure in this careful expansion in the West was Alioune Diop (1910–80), a leader in the emergence of the modern African discourse in French. Born in Saint-Louis, Senegal, he rose to become a distinguished professor and a representative of Senegal in the French Senate. In 1947, he established *Présence Africaine*, then and now the leading journal on Africa published in French. To Alioune Diop, the journal and its publishing house was designed to redefine Africa, enhance its visibility, and empower it. Anticolonial in his thinking, Alioune Diop demanded a quiet revolution that would unite all blacks. He was also a Pan-Africanist and a believer in the idea of Négritude. In addition to establishing the Société Africaine de Culture, he played a leading role in the planning of the International Congress of Black Writers and Artists in 1956 and 1959 and the Festival of Black and African Arts in 1966 and 1967.

Africanus Horton and Edward Blyden had defined the intellectual agenda for the first decades of the nineteenth century—issues of race difference, progress, "African personality," and Pan-Africanism. Their notable successors included Léopold Sédar Senghor, Alioune Diop, and Cheikh Anta Diop, all from Senegal. Other issues were later added to this agenda, arising from the colonial context and its attendant political changes. A corpus of literature advanced the cause of progress, yet another example of anticolonial resistance and nationalism. The writing of town histories became a flourishing industry, motivated by a desire for urban improvements and the discovery of the past. Known variously as chroniclers, antiquarians, and local historians, the writers of these histories expanded the field, both as a complement to emerging colonial ethnography and as a corrective. In South Africa, John Henderson Soga (1860?–1941), son of Tiyo Soga, the first black South African ordained as a minister, was trained in Scotland as a missionary. Working in the Transkei and worried that the Xhosa were losing both their history and identity, he embarked on an endeavor to write history, define the Xhosa, promote the study of local language, and encourage reading. His endeavor resulted in two famous books, one of which he succeeded in publishing only after a great deal of difficulty.[22] His was a comprehensive project, beyond the usual production of pamphlets. However, his failure to publish in Xhosa limited his audience, and he failed to question many colonial ideas on race and migrations. Hundreds of other writers emerged in different parts of Africa, many with better luck in publishing than Soga and others with less, but all advancing the frontiers of knowledge through the genre of local histories.[23]

The academy grew more crowded than before as European ethnographers, anthropologists, ethnologists, colonial officers, and others joined the list of writers on Africa. From the point of view of many of the European writers, the central focus became the discussion of a society in transition, changing from the assumed "primitive" society dominated by slavery to a new one dominated by Westernization. To the extent that the goals of this scholarship were limited, its writings can be described as ideological tools of colonial exploitation. A limited vision of development, a denial of people's history, and a nugatory paternalistic attitude all ensured that while the information being collected was extensive, its value was limited. What should Europeans know about Africa? What information was necessary for administration? These were the sorts of questions that the leading authors posed.[24] African scholars had to confront these writings spending much of their time debunking them, to counteract the false distinction between an African society acting under the influence of tradition and that of the West acting allegedly under rational motivations. They had to deal with a series of denials popularized in colonial discourse—the idea of a continent without history,

poetry, science, and philosophy. In addition, they had to attack the "traditional" against the "rational" dichotomies in virtually all spheres of knowledge—the mythical against the scientific, the concrete against the abstract. Not all Africans are ordinary, proclaimed the pioneer academic intellectuals, who had to publicize African queens and kings to demolish an age-old portrayal of their people as lacking in great leadership and accomplishments.

Colonial policies contributed to shaping ideas and visions among the African elite. The consensus of opinion was that Africa was the "Other," the primitive, different from civilized Europe. The empire set out to tame and teach the primitive. In British colonies, administrators assumed a difference between European and African cultures, an attitude contributing to the establishment of government based on "indirect rule." Indeed, in some areas such as the Sudan and Nigeria, the British preferred the Islamic intelligentsia to the educated elite. However, British administrators were not all opposed to assimilation. With many pro-assimilationist white missionaries working everywhere, administrators were necessarily either ambivalent toward or supportive of the spread of British civilization. Thus, the British transferred their cultures overseas, in terms of legal and administrative institutions as well as material objects. The ambivalence of the British was matched by the ambivalence of the African intelligentsia. Some were assimilationists to the extreme, while most ranged from limited to general acceptance of British ideals.

Unlike the British, the French believed that their supposedly superior language and culture should be spread in their colonies, and sought to assimilate their subjects into French culture. While the assimilationist policy did not work in all French colonies and actually had to be abandoned in some places, the policy had an impact in some communes in Senegal, notably among the mixed race population. A number of assimilated French-Africans believed that the development of Africa would come with the ability to master French ideals and use French skills. According to them, African nationalism must not stand in the way of assimilation or advocate the rejection of European values; the advocacy of "African personality" or black identity must not precede membership of an international community as sanctioned by France.

The colonial period also witnessed the emergence of political activists who had to popularize their agenda. Thus a small elite of political theorists who doubled as political leaders emerged. In this rank can be found men such as Obafemi Awolowo and Nnamdi Azikiwe of Nigeria, Jomo Kenyatta of Kenya, Léopold Senghor of Senegal, Julius Nyerere of Tanzania, Kenneth Kaunda of Zambia, Sékou Touré of Guinea, and Félix Houphouë t-Boigny of Côte d'Ivoire. Thanks to Western education and colonial conditions, they were aware of the need to use ideas to fight for decolonization. Education made available to them Western political ideas, which they adapted to create a philosophy they believed could work in Africa. At the same time, they had to present the histories and cultures of their people to the outside world and draw on them to create a system for the contemporary world. Those who rejected certain ideas as alien countered by drawing on local traditions. Even when foreign ideas were found appealing, they still had to see the possibility of applying them to local situations.

POWER

African history is rife not just with intra-elite struggles for power but also with conflicts between an emerging elite and an older one. For instance, a class of merchants fought with the traditional elite in the Niger Delta, a similar class clashed with a ruling elite among the Joola, and the Fulani *ulama* overthrew the Hausa kings.

The modern educated intelligentsia also had to confront the issue of power, perhaps more aggressively than ever before, by moving from a strategy of negotiation to one of control. Education itself was a source of privilege and power, which the intelligentsia wanted to maximally exploit. The scenario unfolded from the very beginning of colonial penetration. On the one hand, they wanted either to share power with or wrest it from the traditional

power elite. Their main claim was to modernity, as the only agents who understood it enough to manipulate it for the good of Africa. On the other hand, they wanted to contest power with Europeans, at first sharing it and later taking complete control. Here, they claimed nationality as the authentic voice of the "natives." The ultimate victory came with decolonization, when the Europeans who took over power from the traditional elite handed it over to the educated elite. The tension remains—the traditional elite continues to use tradition to contest the legitimacy of the educated elite in many local settings, while the power of capitalism has subordinated the African educated elite to the West.

A pattern of power relations was established from the nineteenth century onward—a strategy of criticizing the power structure, demanding reform, and pressuring to create windows of opportunity for the elite to exercise power. Until the 1920s, the educated elite did not attempt to undermine the traditional arrangement or displace kings and chiefs. Rather, they offered intellectual justification for constitutional modifications to participate in politics. A few examples drawn from West Africa should suffice. In Abeokuta, a Yoruba city-state, the Egba United Board of Management (EUBM), an elite organization, wanted to manage local government in a way that would protect property, promote Christianity, and "forward Civilization."[25] In the case of the Fante, the 1874 Constitution of the Gold Coast made the king the president, but gave educated men such other offices as those of vice-president, secretary, under-secretary, treasurer, and assistant treasurer, all of whom would constitute a ministry.[26] This was an experiment in modernization, inspired by the ideas of Africanus Horton but aborted by the British. Further provisions in the constitution revealed the intellectual agenda of Horton and his associates. First, there was an emphasis on the introduction and spread of Western education and on development planning. To start with, the constitution stipulated that all children must go to school and be taught by "efficient school masters." Second, the education must have an industrial base, creating skilled carpenters, masons, lawyers, sawyers, joiners, agriculturists, smiths, architects, and builders. Third, the society must improve its infrastructure (notably creating and expanding roads, as much as fifteen feet wide and with an efficient drainage system), and economy by enhancing its agriculture, cultivating new plants, promoting commerce, and exploiting available mineral resources. Fourth, foreign policy must be defined by strengthening Fante unity, enabling the Fante to defend themselves against their enemies.

Although the idea of a constitution collapsed, the elite did not relent in asserting itself. One hero of the era was John Mensah Sarbah (1864–1910), an activist, political leader, lawyer, and publisher. Born of a wealthy father and politician, Sarbah himself rose to become the foremost Fante politician in the late nineteenth and early twentieth century. Intelligent and hardworking, he attended Lincoln's Inn, London, qualifying as an attorney at the age of twenty-three. He returned to the Gold Coast to practice. He was a reformer, leading the fight against the Municipal Ordinance in the Gold Coast in 1888. A year later he joined others to organize the Fante National Political Society to advocate the preservation of Fante culture, while modernizing it at the same time. He studied his culture and became one of the first writers on the subject, publishing two major books.[27] He continued to demand reforms, leading the opposition to the 1892 Land Bill, which sought to transfer the control of public land from the chiefs to the British Crown. The earliest Fante political party, the Aborigines' Rights Protection Society, was formed in 1897, to continue the opposition. Due to his influence and knowledge, he was appointed to the Legislative Council as an extraordinary member in 1901, and a year later he became an ordinary member. Also in 1901, he established the *Gold Coast Weekly Record*, his second newspaper. The newspaper publicized some of his reformist views, including his opposition to the 1906 Native Jurisdiction Bill, which proposed to institutionalize indirect rule by excluding the elite from the administration of local government. Sarbah contributed to the spread of missionary education by joining the Fante Public School Company,

which, in 1903, founded the Mfantsi National Education Fund, which raised the money to establish, in 1905, the Mfantsipim Secondary School. He died in November 1910, after a lifetime of reformist politics.[28] A host of other West African politicians were to follow in his footsteps.

Perhaps the issue of power is best revealed in the relations between the intelligentsia and Europeans. Relations with Europeans were based on conflicts, cooperation, or accommodation in order to benefit from colonialism in general and the new political arrangements, while protecting what the intelligentsia regarded as the interest of Africa. The conflicts played out in what is generally characterized as nationalism.

VARIETIES OF NATIONALISM

In seeking answers to the various issues highlighted above and creating the discourse on power, a number of "schools" can be identified. Some can be defined as "traditionalists," for insisting that the old ways are better and that Western civilization should be avoided. At the other extreme are the "assimilationists," who argue that change can come if Africans accept Western civilization. There are the "middle-roaders," who advocate embracing certain aspects of Western civilization while retaining many aspects of tradition. The members of these schools are variously known as "reformers," "modernizers," or "revivalists." These various divisions have appropriately been characterized as varieties of nationalism.[29] In what follows, I summarize the various responses, bringing out their essential elements and identifying the main opinion leaders.

"In the Image of the Other"

The early modern intelligentsia was fascinated with Europe and its ideas. Within Africa, education and Christianity had given them an edge in constructing a new Africa. The earliest ones among them were very grateful for conversion, with some even repudiating African culture and seeking to imitate Western civilization. This is precisely what the missionary project of creating an African middle class sought to achieve. This pioneer middle class began to occupy positions of influence in the church, commercial firms, and schools. Proudly, many called themselves "Black Englishmen," adopting English names, English dress, English entertainment, and English leisure habits. Their weddings were conducted in Victorian style, with partners carefully chosen from among the new middle class.[30]

This development was an interlude in the mid-nineteenth century, the abolitionist phase, when there was widespread discussion about humanitarian values, and how a new Christian philosophy and the work ethic could revolutionize Africa. The African middle class believed that Europeans regarded its members as equals, and were just in distributing rewards and wages to Africans relative to their qualifications and experience. Many among them reflected on how Africa could develop along European lines, by adopting Western education, technology, and even culture and religion. Their writings emphasized the need to educate Africans so that they could become "civilized." They argued that given the right circumstances and opportunities, Africans could succeed in the ways defined by Europeans. It is among this group that some African advocates of European imperialism can be found. By accepting the relevance of Western education and extolling the virtues of Western civilization, they were giving a humanitarian voice to European encroachment. Leading African missionaries such as Ajayi Crowther and Samuel Johnson looked forward to European control as a positive civilizing force.

This was the beginning of an accommodationist response, one that has lingered until the present but has also been constantly challenged. To be sure, accommodationists did not advocate a total surrender of Africa to Western civilization; rather, they sought an understanding of the West to discern what was valuable in it for Africans. Many institutions and ideas of the West were taken for granted—the judiciary, police, and bureaucracy. However, accommodationists sought to use these same institutions to develop Africa. They would borrow them, use them to fight the West, as latter-day nationalists were to do.

Accommodationists ran into many difficulties. To start with, there was no agreement as to how to edit Western civilization to reject what they disapproved of or choose whatever they approved of. Second, in modernizing and protecting Africa from exploitation, seeking a balance was likely—if they borrowed too much, the cultural extinction they wanted to avoid became difficult; if they borrowed little, the progress they wanted would not come. As editors of two cultures, they had to present an image of themselves as intellectual superiors, discerning learners and teachers, wise leaders of their people, and arrogant followers of Europeans. Wanting to assimilate without being assimilated was tricky. On the one hand, they did not want to ignore African cultures and identities. Yet, their education and acceptance of Western civilization meant that they could not totally accept African cultures or draw all references from them. On the other hand, they wanted to show that they totally understood Western culture and institutions in order to represent their people and gain the respect of Westerners. Many were to fail in this complicated balancing act. The failure came sooner than expected.

"Africa for Africans"

The hope and optimism of the "Black Englishmen" were soon shattered. As white missionaries criticized Ajayi Crowther, the first African to become a bishop, he was forced to resign. Other forms of discrimination ensued. African surveyors, lawyers, and other professionals found it hard to obtain jobs or social mobility. New rules introduced residential segregation in Freetown, Sierra Leone. In Lagos, an attempt to turn Christ Church, a leading pioneer church, into a "whites only" institution offended the African elite. Black entrepreneurs also complained of discrimination.[31]

An intellectual revolution occurred in the second half of the nineteenth century with the development of a movement known as Ethiopeanism, which began to undermine African respect for Europe and to create an assertive, patriotic elite with a desire for empowerment and for solutions in

African traditions and values. An impressive array of speeches, correspondence, pamphlets, and books emerged, with antiracist arguments and advocacy of race consciousness, support for African solidarity, and support for African autonomy, especially in the religious field. The "Black Englishman" now aspired to become the "Black African," identifying with local people and promoting African culture.

Both in West and South Africa, contemporaries have attributed this intellectual revolution to European racism. A number of analysts have noted the trend towards racism in mid-nineteenth-century Europe and the categorization of Africans as the lowest group in intelligence.[32] The racist scholarship of such figures as Arthur de Gobineau, Sir Richard Burton, and Winwood Reade was translated into practice in Africa, where white missionaries and colonialists regarded themselves as superior to Africans, defined themselves paternalistically as parents and teachers obliged to "civilize" Africans, and began to discriminate against educated Africans in the church and the bureaucracy. Missionary propaganda propagated the view of the "noble savage," and converts and the educated elite were regarded as "half devil, half child." Richard Burton had authoritatively asserted that the Negro "mentally remains a child," and a renowned European philosopher, Hegel, concluded that the continent was incapable of development or education.

"Ethiopia shall soon stretch out her hands unto God" was the biblical phrase that was converted into the ideology of Ethiopeanism—a belief that without African self-discovery, humiliation and discrimination at the hands of the white man would continue. Self-discovery must involve the interrogation of culture and tradition and the use of both (along with Western education) to empower Africans and to fight for their rights. This ideology produced the pioneer nationalists who struggled to create new religious and cultural movements.

Perhaps the most successful manifestation of Ethiopeanism was in the creation of independent churches, headed by Africans, and the adoption of African cultural features and institutions to distinguish them from European mission churches. The trend began in South Africa in the 1860s, and by the 1880s it had witnessed the emergence of Nehemiah Tile who established an independent church after breaking away from the Wesleyan ministry. According to Tile, the church must adapt itself to Africa, and the paramount chief of his Tembu people must be the head of the religious organization, just as "the Queen of England was the Head of the English Church."[33] Tile was to have more than a handful of successors and imitators in eastern and central Africa where independency became a revolution from the 1880s to the 1920s. Ethiopeanism enabled black South African intellectuals to oppose the government and to promote secession. More practically minded religious leaders, such as Isaiah Shembe, emerged later as part of this radical Ethiopean tradition. Shembe successfully adapted Christianity to Zulu culture, borrowing heavily from the Old Testament to create a Nazarite movement that continues to exist today.[34]

In West Africa in the 1880s, Nigerian church leaders broke away from the Southern American Baptist Mission. Echoing the deeds and words of Tile, a pioneer secessionist, Mojola Agbebi, changed his name from T. B. Vincent, created an independent church, and called for Africans to drop their foreign names and adopt local names, local clothes, "healthful native customs and habits," and the use of African languages in worship. He confidently asserted that

> to render Christianity indigenous to Africa, it must be watered by native hands, pruned with the native hatchet, and tended with native earth. ... It is a curse if we intend for ever to hold at the apron strings of foreign teachers, doing the baby for aye.[35]

If the church mobilized many people, literary works energized the elite. In combative speeches, small books, pamphlets, and newspaper articles, a radical elite created a notion of difference based on race consciousness, Pan-Africanism, and the idea of the "African personality." Because they were responding to discrimination and humiliation at the hands of the Europeans, race matters dominated their thinking.

A notable representative of this intellectual tradition was Surgeon-Major James Africanus Beale Horton (1835–83), the first black to be commissioned into the British army, a prolific author and radical intellectual.[36] Son of a liberated slave, he had a vision of a free, united Africa. As early as 1859, he remarked in his doctoral thesis that the Krumen, Yoruba, and Igbo would, through intermarriage, produce the leading race for Africa. For Horton, theories of black racial inferiority were misleading. While not denying differences in stage of civilization between blacks and whites, he attributed this not to race but to "external circumstances." To contemporaries who believed that white power would be a scourge leading to the extermination or permanent suppression of the black race, Horton replied that not only would this race increase in number, "no matter under what depressing and burdensome yoke they may suffer," they would endure, and their triumph would be similar to that of the abolition of the slave trade.[37]

Africa would progress, he asserted. He dismissed negative views that found Africans incapable and argued that the black race would take its place in the history of the civilized world. He compared African history with that of Europe and saw hope on the horizon:

> "Rome was not built in a day"; the proudest kingdom in Europe was once in a state of barbarism perhaps worse than now exists amongst the tribes chiefly inhabiting the West Coast of Africa; and it is an incontrovertible axiom that what has been done can again be done. If Europe, therefore, has been raised to her present pitch of civilization by progressive advancement, Africa too, with a guarantee of the civilization of the north, will rise into equal importance.[38]

He advocated policies for change: Africans must liberate themselves from the notion of inferiority; they must seek political independence, self-government that would enable them to govern themselves along a more orderly and progressive manner; and they must all unite. Horton was of the view that whatever inadequacies were to be found in Africa would be corrected by education.[39]

Edward Wilmot Blyden (1832–1912): "The Father of Cultural Nationalism"[40]

It would be the destiny of Edward Wilmot Blyden to become more famous than many of his contemporaries for his great ideas and his opportunities to deliver speeches in different countries and to diverse audiences. He was certainly far more radical than Horton and certainly much more prolific.[41] He consistently demanded self-pride and self-assertion for Africans, even if the process of achieving these presented him with a number of conflicting options. His sociology of race anticipated later works on Négritude, Pan-Africanism, and the African personality. His thinking influenced many other educated elites for decades, until the 1920s when Marcus Garvey became a new point of reference. Explaining his stature as the result of luck (as some people do) may in fact be a slight, for he was indeed the first famous African philosopher to fully grasp the ambiguities and complexities of modernization and tradition and to carefully reflect on how Africa could borrow European ideas while retaining its pride and identity. To put it in another way, he was a genius in creating a blend of progress with racial pride and dignity, thus qualifying to be described as the "father of African cultural nationalism." He also preceded Frantz Fanon in "psychologizing" the African encounter with Europeans and imperialism. On occasion, he took Africa's eventual freedom for granted, going further to elaborate a post-colonial theory of development.

His antecedents lay in slavery, as his ancestors were taken from West Africa, but he himself was born in the West Indies (St. Thomas). Denied the opportunity to be educated in the United States because of racism, he migrated to Liberia in 1851 where he went to school. He was introduced to the classics, and mastered Greek, Latin, and Hebrew. His skills were reflected in his editorship of the *Liberia Herald* in the 1850s. He became a teacher in his alma mater and its principal in 1858. In the same year, he became an ordained minister of the Presbytery of West Africa. In 1861, he traveled to the United States to seek African-Americans who would return to Liberia. A year later, he became a professor of Latin and Greek in the new Liberia College. He was a teacher, preacher, scholar, and diplomat. He held ambassadorial appointments (1877–78, 1892), was the president of Liberia College (1880–84), failed in his bid to become president of Liberia in 1885, and relocated to Freetown where he became interested in Islam and lived till his death.

His themes were like those of Horton, although he reflected more on culture. He condemned racism, and he asked Africans to be proud of their race. "I would rather be a member of this race," he maintained, "than a Greek in the time of Alexander, a Roman in the Augustine period, or an Anglo-Saxon in the nineteenth century."[42] Africa need not seek universalism, he opined:

> An African nationality is the great desire of my soul. I believe nationality to be an ordinance of nature and no people can rise to an influential position among nations without a distinct and efficient nationality. Cosmopolitanism never effected anything and never will.[43]

He advocated Pan-Africanism, the concept of the "African personality," and a slogan, "Africa for Africans." He believed that Islam and polygamy were good for Africa, he supported the idea of an African independent church, and he opposed mixed marriages so that blacks would retain their identity and racial purity. Development was certain, asserted Blyden. Where others saw gloom, he saw hope, great prosperity, and privileges. To uplift the race, however, Africans must work hard, achieve self-pride, and develop a concept of African personality:

> It is sad to think that there are some Africans, especially among those who

have enjoyed the advantages of foreign training, who are so blind to the radical facts of humanity as to say, "Let us do away with the sentiment of Race. Let us do away with our African personality and be if possible in another Race". ... Preach this doctrine as much as you like, no one will do it, for no one *can* do it, for when you have done away with your personality, you have done away with yourselves ... the duty of every man, of every race, is to contend for its individuality—to keep and develop it. ... Therefore, honour and love your Race. ... If you are not yourself, if you surrender your personality, you have nothing left to give the world. ...[44]

Blyden did not limit himself to theories. In pursuing intellectual liberation, a first step was the study of local history and cultures, from the "uncontaminated Africans" who knew the songs, traditions, and history of "the wonderful and mysterious events of their tribal and national life."[45] Educated Africans were advised by Blyden to return to the native soil, to the simple life of their ancestors. Next, the Christian Church must become indigenized, completely removing European control and influence. Education must also be localized, to avoid teaching Africans European history, European heroes, and European philosophy. As if anticipating academic historians of the 1950s, Blyden called for the study of African history to understand and appreciate past glories and to provide lessons on the dignity and achievements of his race.

Africans can only uplift their race in Africa, argued Blyden. He was an advocate of the return of Africans in the diaspora to Africa. For blacks to realize their genius, they had to return to their own native soil. They should seek nationality, not cosmopolitanism. His concept of the nation and nationality was tied to that of race. While he did not disagree with the concept of race difference, a popular European doctrine at the time, such differences, Blyden contended, owed not to intelligence but to environment. He rejected the prevailing

European notion that races could be organized in a pyramid on the basis of achievement, ability, and civilization, with the white man at the top. If the white man had constructed this pyramid and placed himself on top, another race could do the same, using a different set of criteria. For Blyden, each race excelled in certain things and lagged behind in others. Rather than regard races as competitive, he saw them as complementary, equal but different. He moved the argument away from biology to divinity, seeing every race as the creation of God, a "representation of the Deity … a different side of the Almighty."[46] This is a concept of God with many faces, each face representing a race, with no face superior to the other and all the faces forming a unitary godhead.

As controversial as this may be today, he attributed distinct qualities to each race. He saw the white race as driven by material accomplishments, as aggressive, science-oriented, and didactic. These values enabled it to introduce modern medicine to Africa (a knowledge of its science), end the slave trade (a didactic value), and contribute to economic development (a quality of material benefit). However, the negative values of the white race limited the outcome of its positive contributions: whites' aggressiveness led to destruction in Africa, to enslavement, to imperialism, and to exploitation.

If Africans were looking for a race to emulate, Blyden warned them against the white race. His reasons were devastating: white values were too materialist, too domineering, too ungodly. While whites practiced Christianity, Blyden believed that they had turned man, instead of God, into the sole attention of worship; materialism, rather than spiritualism, into the real focus; their objective was not to seek salvation but to seek temporal and material benefits. If the European doctrine of race had constructed Africa as inferior and different, Blyden used this to argue that the European race was not the model for Africans to aspire to. But whom should they emulate? Themselves, because they had their own unique defining characteristics. If they kept to their own qualities and sought improvements within themselves, Africa would

become "the conservatory of the world" to which others would come to learn:

> When the civilized nations, in consequence of their wonderful material development, shall have had their spiritual perceptions darkened and their spiritual susceptibilities blunted through the agency of a captivating and absorbing materialism, it may be, that they may have to resort to Africa to recover some of the simple elements of faith.[47]

By almost a century, Blyden anticipated modern sociologists and anthropologists in searching for the cultures that defined Africans. Blyden was one of the earliest to use the concept of "African personality" to distinguish Africans from others, a term that a later generation such as W. E. Abraham, Jomo Kenyatta, and John Mbiti would revist in a related concept of the community.[48] African community life, concluded Blyden, consisted of the elements of humanitarianism, communalism, and spirituality, all of which created harmony in African society.[49] The community was more important than the self, harvests belonged to the many, and land was communal. Rather than compete, individuals cooperated with one another to own and share property, to avoid antagonism, to prevent wealth accumulation at the expense of one another, to protect the weak members of society, and to check the aggressiveness of the ambitious. Blyden also anticipated the twentieth-century philosophers of "African socialism" by describing a concept of "African cooperative socialism," based on the family. This cooperative spirit, according to Blyden, suffered decline and destruction because of the slave trade and the negative impact of Christianity.

Blyden believed that Africans had other characteristics that distinguished them: respect for God, profound spirituality, and closeness to nature. To start with religion, having dismissed Europeans for not worshiping God in a proper manner, Blyden extolled the African virtue of communion with God. By refusing to differentiate between the spiritual and the temporal, Africans were able to place God at the center of world affairs. By developing a conception of creation and time that comprised the ancestor, the living, and the yet unborn, Africans created an unbroken chain between the past and the present, between humans and God. Worship had no Sabbath, with work taking over the remaining six days. Compassion is shown all the time, even to strangers, and tolerance is reflected in dealing with enemies and in receiving such other religions as Islam and Christianity. The activities of Africans reflect the aspirations of God: Africans and God wanted to serve, not to be masters like the Europeans. Drawing from the preaching of Jesus Christ, Blyden concluded that by being servants, Africans would ultimately become masters: "Africa's lot resembles Him also who made Himself of no reputation, but took upon Himself the form of a servant. He who would be chief must become the servant of all, then we see the position which Africa and Africans must ultimately occupy."[50]

Africa's communion with nature—a surrender to mother earth—completes Blyden's list of unique African features: Africans learned most things from nature, they imitated nature's nudity, love for the outside, and the industry of the termite. From the rhythm of creation and recreation, they embraced polygamy to expand their families and kinship groups. By serving humanity, obeying the wishes of God, and following the lead of nature, Africans ensured a place for themselves on earth. Africa's place, according to Blyden, is to teach other races a lesson as they destroy their own souls and seek wealth. By playing a complementary role in God's and nature's schemes, Africans would be ensured mastery of the worldly affairs, and equality with other races.

Blyden's logic was a powerful affirmation of self-esteem at a time of encroaching European power. European technology could subdue Africa, European leaders could govern or exploit Africa, but all this would be temporary and simply solidify the place of Africans as a race.

Blyden would, no doubt, deny any charge that he was a racist, but his views privilege racial segregation and "racial purity" to allow each race to fulfil its destiny. Unlike the contemporary German cultural nationalists, notably Johann von Herder who used language to construct a notion of cultural nationalism, Blyden resorted to race, accepting a notion that associated it with the evolution of history and culture. If some European philosophers such as Comte Arthur de Gobineau (1816–82) had condemned Africans as members of a primitive race, Blyden would use the same categorization to uplift them. Miscegenation, as found among the Creoles of Sierra Leone and African-Americans, was not good in the eyes of Blyden, as it tended to produce confused and misguided people. To him, an Africa uncontaminated by other races would develop along its own lines. Necessity, communion with nature and God, and the genius of the race were all adequate in fashioning creative institutions both to stabilize and to change society. Liberia, his adopted country, could serve as the new beacon.

No one could match Blyden in his powerful association of the black race with pride. "It will stand to his credit forever," concluded the *Sierra Leone Weekly News*, "that to Dr. Blyden it was due that the word Negro became shorn of the degrading associations which gathered around it in the fifties and sixties in Sierra Leone. It is due to the late Doctor that we today prize the word and are proud to call ourselves even niggers if need be."[51]

Bishop James Johnson

A third influential writer and leader was James Johnson (ca. 1836–1917), a radical preacher and patriot. Born in Sierra Leone, he attended the influential Freetown Grammar School and Fourah Bay College. He qualified as a teacher and evangelist and lectured at Fourah Bay College from 1860 to 1863. Then, he joined the CMS and in 1874 was posted to Nigeria where he worked in different capacities until he was ignominiously removed in 1880. The removal further radicalized him. Whether in the church as a preacher or in his writings, James Johnson was consistent in preaching Ethiopeanism. The past of the black race was noble, full of accomplishments. Underlying most of his ideas was the concept of "Africa for Africans." Africa must control the church, he argued, and play a prominent role in the civil service. Africans were intelligent enough to educate themselves and to convert others to Christianity. He rejected racism and saw in Christianity a liberating force. He envisioned an African Church, with a doctrine of uniting all of Africa and creating one African race, that would be independent, avoid sectarian rivalries, be staffed only by Africans, and promote African values. He called for the departure of Europeans from Africa since Europeans would never be able to identify with Africans or appreciate "African racial ambitions and idiosyncrasies." Indeed, to him, their presence was injurious. He described the Africans who had not come in contact with Europeans as better, independent in their thinking, self-reliant, courageous, daring, and brave. With European contact and interactions came disaster:

> With the missionaries of the present day an independent thought in an African and a clear enunciation of his convictions are a great crime. He has no right to them: he must always see with other people's eyes and swear by other people's opinions: he must not manifest any patriotic sentiments; he must denude himself of manhood and of every vestige of racial feeling and flinging away his individuality and distinctiveness to make peaceable existence with them possible and secure favorable recommendations to the Society.[52]

Johnson collaborated with Blyden in the 1870s to publish *The Negro*, a newspaper that called for an African university and called on Africans to develop race consciousness. Like Blyden, Johnson criticized his generation for being confused and hankering after false living and distorted tastes. He criticized white missionaries for destroying African traditions and the pride of Africans in their culture. As if the entire culture was already lost, he asked the whereabouts of African songs, history, language, parables,

modes of thought, poetry, manufactures, and social habits in a world dominated by whites. In a sorrowful manner, he concluded that the Africans of his generation who accepted Christianity and attended Western schools had lost their self-respect and love for Africa, and that they were inferior to the so-called "natives." God, asserted Johnson, did not intend to create Africans in the image of Europeans.

Assimilationism: Total Conversionists

Assimilationists were accommodationists, but their ranks were disorganized. A few advocated total assimilation, that is, full acceptance of European civilization. The trouble was not whether African culture was good or bad, but that progress could only come to the extent that Africa adopted Western civilization. Among the leading advocates of this idea were Abbé Boilat and Paul Holle of Senegal and Kitoye Ajasa of Nigeria. Thinkers such as Ajasa were in a hurry to see change; the more new ideas and institutions that could be introduced and take root, the better for Africa's progress. Why delay the spread of a superior culture? Ajasa's newspaper, *The Nigerian Pioneer*, supported colonial reforms, and contemporaries described it as reactionary.[53] Those who advocated a philosophy of assimilation to European cultures became unpopular in the first half of the twentieth century. To take the example of Ajasa, he was criticized by his contemporaries in very unpleasant words. One described his newspaper as "the guardian angel of an oligarchy of reactionaries."[54] Yet another wondered why "any man in Lagos, African by birth, race and descent … should be so wholly devoid of race consciousness, and utterly oblivious of appreciation of the duties, obligations and responsibilities devolving on him."[55]

Négritudists

Other assimilationists rejected the idea of total conversion. Not everything was good about the West, they argued. Indeed, some regarded Western civilization as corrupt and decadent, its society too alienating, and its technology too degrading of human values. Négritudists falling into this group were cultural nationalists who advocated respect for African identity while choosing what was valuable from Western civilization. Africa must develop along self-defined lines, while acquiring ideas and skills from Europe, useful for developing strategies against Europe and creating progress for Africa. What was black must be promoted and its contribution to civilization asserted.

The leaders of Négritude thought were Leopold Sédar Senghor of Senegal, Aimé Césaire of Martinique, and Lé on-Gontran Damas of Guyana. Their writings aided the decolonization movement and contributed to the ideological presentation of Africa as the beautiful "Other." Senghor combined the fame of a poet with that of a politician, as the first African to be elected into the Académie Française, the highest honor in France and the first president of Senegal (1960–81). He can be described as an eclectic personality: a scholar and a politician, an African and a French citizen, a reformer and a defender of culture. This set of dualities revealed itself very early in his history. His parents sent him to a Western school to be educated and become "civilized," but the tension between the indigenous and the foreign began to take root. Later he attended a seminary where he had to leave because of his anti-racist protests. After 1928 he went to France to study, and there he developed an ambition to become a "black-skinned Frenchman." According to him, he realized that this wish was misplaced, and the experience forced him instead to become conscious of his ancestry and his African foundations. He had to search for what he called his "Négritude," that is, his "Africanness." Writing poems about his soul and his childhood formed a major part of his intellectual self-discovery.

On the one hand, he pursued politics. Imprisoned by the Nazis during World War II, he was later elected to the French Assembly, serving from 1946 to 1958. He called for "Eurafrica," a Pan-Africanist version of a European-style federation. In anticipation of European disengagement, he called for a union of Francophone Africa, another Pan-Africanist idea. Competing nationalisms, however,

made his idea unrealistic. On the other hand, he pursued his scholarship. He fully emerged as an apostle of global multiculturalism, advocating a theory of civilization that would produce a universal culture.[56] Senghor's Négritude and its variants have been criticized on several grounds, not the least of which is erroneously thinking that the past can be reclaimed in all its essentials.[57]

Marxism and Socialism

A number of currents created a Marxist tradition in Africa. To start with, decolonization occurred during the Cold War, and the new African nations were born when superpower rivalry was intense. This rivalry presented choices since both the United States and the Soviet Union were aggressive in promoting their conflicting ideologies, capturing a number of minds in the process. Those who adopted the socialist option were partly offended by imperialism and the exploitation associated with it. The leading thinkers of the Left came much later, and the majority of them were associated with the academy. They found the goals that the nationalists set for Africa—political liberation and economic development—to be narrow and doubted whether they could in fact attain them. Also, if previous writers were obsessed with the paradigm of the colonizer and the colonized, Marxists added another: conflicts among the colonized, especially class rivalry between the intelligentsia and the masses. The Marxists also had to contend with such powerful thinkers as Léopold Senghor, who had ruled out Marxism as an option for Africa, and also those who accepted aspects of socialism but carefully found a place for religion (including Julius Nyerere of Tanzania). As I will later show, many intellectuals, dating back to the nineteenth century, have supported socialism primarily because of the resemblance of its ideas to an African kinship mode of production, distribution, and communal living.

African Marxist intellectuals did not challenge the notion of the nation-state, but they called into question the process and outcome of the transfer of power, and pointed out the limitations of independence and the backwardness of inherited structures. They accepted the universality of class analysis, including class struggle and "power to the people." Marxist converts were many, emerging among the ranks of teachers and students in the postindependence universities. Profound thinkers, however, were few, and among them Amilcar Lopes Cabral (1924–73) stands out. A revolutionary and political strategist, he derived his fame from the anti-Portuguese movement in his country, Guinea-Bissau. In his twenties, he witnessed the growing anti-imperialism of Africans, which radicalized him. In the 1950s he founded the Partido Africano da Independência da Guiné e Cabo Verde (PAIGC) with a commitment to the use of violence to dislodge the Portuguese. A strategy of underground activity followed; this recorded successes in the 1970s but ultimately led to Cabral's assassination in 1973. Theory cannot be divorced from practice, Cabral stressed, and active political participation must translate into both personal and collective renewal.[58] If Europeans had sought to dominate Africa by destroying its culture, Cabral argued that liberation should also involve the use of culture to regain the lost ground and create a new society.[59]

Socialism and Marxism are two of the most compelling ideas of the twentieth century, and both are connected with the rise of nationalism and the academy in Africa.

Pan-Africanism

Many of the ideas of Pan-Africanism emphasized the need for black unity to overcome racial discrimination and to empower blacks irrespective of where they might be living. Pan-Africanism also advocated the adoption of socialism. Only a passing reference need be made here since the subject occupies detailed attention in another chapter. W. E. B. Du Bois is a father figure, and Marcus Garvey, his contemporary, is also of considerable stature. A person who brought a commercial dimension to the movement was Duse Mohammed Ali (1886–1945), a journalist and entrepreneur. He exchanged ideas with Marcus Garvey and Winfried Tete-Ansa of

Ghana, and he combined the pragmatism of these two men with his own business skills. He believed in both the economic and the political liberation of the "black race." In his multiple locations of London, New York, and Lagos, Ali founded and edited newspapers from 1912 to 1945. Among the better known of his publishing career were the *West African Dictionary* and *Year Book, 1920–21*. The *Comet*, a newspaper Ali founded in 1933, survived his death. He gave business advice to African traders and farmers, all in the spirit of encouraging the growth of black enterprise at a time when all complained of the inability to compete with European and Asian merchants. For ten years, 1921–31, he was himself an entrepreneur, engaged in a number of marketing ventures. He was active in the African and Oriental Society, a business organization.[60]

Cheikh Anta Diop (1923–86) deserves both eulogy and evaluation in any discourse on the African intellectual tradition and Pan-Africanism. He and W. E. B. Du Bois received in 1966 an award at the first World Festival of Negro Arts in Dakar, which described them as "the scholars who exerted the greatest influence on Negro thought in the twentieth century." Numerous other honors went to Anta Diop. A man of both action and letters, Anta Diop sought a balance between virtually all types of ideas as they could serve to enhance Africa. Like Camara Laye, Léopold Senghor, and a few others, he traced the origins of his ideas to his upbringing and education. Born into a peasant Islamic background, he experienced the French educational system, collecting a first degree in Senegal. In 1946, he went to France to pursue graduate studies in physics. Activism and politics began shortly after, as he became the organizer of the pioneer Pan-African Student Congress in Paris in 1951. This was the time when the ideologies of Marxism, Négritude, and Pan-Africanism were circulating among African students. He took part in the first and second congresses of black writers of artists in Paris and Rome, and he became part of the anticolonial and antiracist movements.

His major impact began in the 1940s when he studied the contributions of the origins of ancient

Africa to civilization. Committed to demonstrating that Africa had a civilization, his doctoral thesis argued that Egypt was a black African civilization. Although he completed his thesis in 1951, a jury could not be assembled, and it took another nine years before he could defend his work and receive his degree. In 1960, he returned to Senegal to work at the Institut Fondamental d'Afrique Noire (IFAN) where he established a carbon-14 dating laboratory. Much later, in 1980, he became a professor of ancient history at the University of Dakar.

Equipped with a knowledge of history, archaeology, Egyptology, and linguistics, Anta Diop began a prodigious publishing career that led to four major interrelated books, all originally published in French but now widely available in English. Translated texts appeared as *The African Origin of Civilization* (1974); *The Cultural Unity of Black Africa: The Domains of Patriarchy and Matriarchy in Classical Antiquity* (1978); *Precolonial Black Africa: A Comparative Study of the Political and Social Systems of Europe and Black Africa, from Antiquity to the Formation of Modern States* (1987); and *Civilization or Barbarism: An Authentic Anthropology* (1991).[61]

He argued that Africans had contributed to the civilization of Egypt, to the link between Egypt and Greece, and to religions such as Judaism, Christianity, and Islam. If African and European civilizations were different, the explanation owes to race and gender, since these categories had been used to create political ideologies. Where matriarchy was important—and he attributed an African origin to it—civilization tended to be humane. Patriarchal regimes, such as those of Europe, were prone to ambitions of conquest and imperialism. He advocated a syllabus for African schools that would ground the study of Africa not in European classics but in Egyptian ones. The achievements of the past are repeatable, he confidently insisted. Diop was also one of the first to express the possibility of a black presence in pre-Columbian America.

Like Senghor, he moved beyond the particular to the general, searching for the means by which a unified global civilization could emerge from an agglomeration of cultures. Africans must be part of the agglomeration and must, as a prelude, transcend what he called the barbarism of imperialism and colonial plunder. In choosing Anta Diop as my case study to end this section, I connect the past to the present. Diop's ideas, together with those of Du Bois, continue to shape the orientation of scholarship today. The relevance of Egypt to Afrocentric studies and perspectives, most notably in the United States, derives in part from Anta Diop's work, which used the study of Egypt to challenge many Western assumptions about Egypt and other aspects of African civilization. Some of the issues he raised have become part of contemporary ideological battlegrounds, even cultural warfare. In his *Nations nègres et culture*, Diop dismissed the Western scholarship that rejected the evidence of the black origins of ancient Egyptians, calling this an attempt to insist on the inferiority of the black race, since the subtext is that an inferior race could not produce a grand civilization. He went on to assert that the Egyptian civilization was created by Africans, and that African civilization in turn affected others outside of the continent. Martin Bernal later took up this theme in *Black Athena*, and Molefi Asante also relied on Anta Diop and related ideas to create an Afrocentric school.[62] Afrocentrists regard Diop as an "intellectual ancestor." In fact, there is a Diopian School of Afrocentricity. There is more to Africa than Egypt, but the current extension of Anta Diops works and the various ideological battles around them show how scholarship and politics can meet and clash and how defining identity for Africa and searching for ideas to uplift it remain open to controversy.

TRADITION

I want to elaborate on the relevance of tradition to the African intelligentsia. As I have said (or implied) previously, all strands of opinions see tradition as crucial to the agenda, drawing from it or using it to define modernity. The Left believed that the idea of a classless and egalitarian society had a foundation in the African past and tradition. Cultural nationalists believed that tradition alone was sufficient to empower Africans. Reformers sought elements from tradition to add to aspects of modernity to create a new future for Africa. What did they all mean by tradition and what issues stand out in their various descriptions and applications?

If a number of Western thinkers have constructed Africa as static, some members of the African intelligentsia have constructed the West as lacking in tradition. This position may be at the root of a neat distinction between tradition and modernity. There is no society without "tradition," in such areas as established practices, pride in history, values, and identity. Even a modern society is at the same time an embodiment of tradition. But Westerners who use the concept of tradition for Africa repackage it in a negative manner, ascribing to it a connotation of barbarism and decay. In some intellectual circles, tradition connotes the poor village, the irrational mind, and resistance to change. The African intelligentsia certainly do not try to project their past in this way. However, they do buy into the notion that the opposite of the definition they reject constitutes the modern—a rational society, industrial, technological, urbanized, always receptive to change. Herein lies the contradiction—the acceptance of polar opposites, but with a different definition from that of Western critics. When African academic intellectuals joined in the discussion, they wasted a great deal of time and space demonstrating the obvious: that there is no society in Africa (or indeed elsewhere) where change does not occur. Again, many of them stumble, precisely because they are trying to explain the various changes, but the bulk of their evidence derives from the Western data on European contact after the fifteenth century or from the spread of Islam and Arab cultures, thereby privileging the very external world whose impact they seek to minimize. Africa is always in transition, as are all continents.

It is hard to contest the point made by most African intellectuals that several aspects of the past are useful. In talking about the past, the intelligentsia sees tradition as the combination of history and culture. The time line is long. The important code phrase, "the practices of our ancestors," is another

way of saying that tradition is a combination of deeply established values, practices, and beliefs that have been handed … down from one generation to another. The "battle" among the intelligentsia is over what is to be preserved from this legacy. Western education and Christianity brought rapid changes in religion, kinship, and occupations, but many aspects of the past have survived till the present, suggesting that successive generations of Africans have actually been preservers of tradition, even when they are making or advocating rapid changes. As preservers, they do refine traditions to suit the present; but the very process of refinement is a positive statement that modern Africa can function within the framework of refined inherited traditions.

In a sense, every member of the African intelligentsia can be described as a contributor to the refinement of tradition. A culturalist guru, Blyden was deeply committed to African tradition, but at the same time he called for a suitable form of Christianity and the spread of Western education. Blyden's ideas contain not contradictions but the germs of refinement and preservation. On the one hand, tradition is needed to determine which elements are necessary and which can be abandoned. No one ever says that everything is needed, but core values remain. On the other hand, change is recognized. In the case of Africa, external contact with Europe and the Islamic world have constituted the pressure for change. The changes may be forced, as with the colonial policies that revolutionized the economy and politics. They may be voluntarily accepted, as with foreign songs, dress, and food. But there is also a sense in which the accepted changes are interpreted according to the knowledge and experience supplied by tradition. Blyden accepted Christianity—a great change indeed—but called for its "Africanization," a way of reconnecting it to tradition, an effective framework.

One cannot talk about tradition without inevitably talking about modernity. The African intelligentsia often uses "progress," "civilization," and "development" to mean the same thing as modernity. I am more interested in the way the African intelligentsia has interrogated this notion than about its meaning in other places. In using words such as civilization, progress, and development, the intelligentsia is at the same time defining the complex notion of modernity, making it more precise for Africans to grapple with. In yet another way, modernity is defined by the intelligentsia in opposition to tradition. The Yoruba of West Africa have an umbrella phrase for it, "Aiye Oyinbo," that is, "the era of the white man, of change." Linking change and the white man is, of course, derived from the European encounter, most notably the colonial phase. However, it makes modernity easier to define and delineate. Modernity includes the notion of change—in practices and ideas that are new, from technology to consumption. It also connotes newness, an intergenerational or intercultural marker between a past and a present. To those with access to objects and ideas associated with modernity and who flaunt them as worth having, it also connotes prestige. The linkage with the white man is an unambiguous declaration that modernity is an import.

I have indicated that modernity is understood and discussed, both by those who accept it and by those who reject it, based on the assumption that the West is already fully modern and that its present stage constitutes the model to which to aspire. This is misleading, as modernity lacks precise boundaries. As every important technological innovation is sent to Africa or as an African visits the West, the exclamation is usually, "these people are restless, we cannot match them!" This elegant reaction is an understanding that modernity does not stop, to give way to the so-called postmodern. In Africa, modernity is yet to fully realize itself, to run its course (assuming that this is ever possible), to get to a stage of "crisis of modernity" that creates the postmodern. The attack on reason and the support for feelings that consume the postmodernists are important, to be sure, but not necessarily in lands and climates where the premodern is still as important as the modern.

If Africans are in awe of Western technology and economy, the intelligentsia is generally not in awe of its culture. Thus, there is sometimes an attempt to edit culture out of modernity, which raises a problem as they are clearly linked. On this, I will say something in a moment. For now, let it be proclaimed that the intelligentsia is unanimous in rejecting what is characterized as Western individualism. The code phrase, "ice people," refers to what the African intelligentsia perceives as a total lack of warmth, a lack of generosity, and a prevalence of self-centeredness in Western societies. Set in the context of kinship and community, with the expectation that the successful must help others, Africans may perceive Western individualism as rather strange and unworthy of emulation. How can a "big man" eat all by himself, in a mansion set apart from others, with only himself, one wife, and two children living there? To many, this would not be modernization but alienation

To return to the issue of dissociating culture from modernity, I think those who do so are unaware of the very philosophical and historical foundations that have been propelling modernity since the seventeenth century. Modernity is about technology, as all Africans agree, but it is also about values, ideas, philosophy, and concepts. Modernity and its culture are in a marriage where divorce cannot occur. Tracing the history of modernity in Europe, which has constituted the Mecca of modernity for Africans since the nineteenth century, one cannot ignore the cultural transformation from the medieval period in science and technology; the intellectual movement associated with the Renaissance; the idea that a single person can have abundant and supernatural ability to invent, and that all must enjoy freedom and rights; the idea of humanism; the expansion of the market; the rise of capitalism and what is called the Protestant ethic; and the great Industrial Revolution, to mention only a few examples. Still drawing from Europe, many of the aforementioned developments could be inherited from a previous generation or even borrowed from elsewhere, but the point is that they were all exploited in the service of change. Rather than worry about the origins of certain ideas, Africans may have to worry far more about the exploitation of ideas.

When modernity travels, it does so through culture. A wristwatch changes the concept of time; a television alters the practice of leisure; a car affects status. These and other items have reshaped Africa, even in ways that people attack as degenerate. However, since Africans have never fully abandoned their traditions, modernity among them also has to inherit their past, with new imports always added. This seems to me the reality reflected in the arguments of "reformers," who seem to have been proved right by African history. Africans must never abandon their community and spirituality, warned Blyden, but they have to travel in airplanes, ride cars, and use computers, as the assimilationists maintained. Africa is, of course, good for Africans, to paraphrase the Ethiopeaniast phrase, but there can be no de-linking from globalism, as imperialism very cruelly imposed itself on all cultural nationalists.

SHARED ASSUMPTIONS

I want to close this chapter by identifying a number of common elements in the various writings and reflections of the African intelligentsia, the predecessors and companions of the academics that I discuss in other chapters. To start with, their concerns were similar: the intelligentsia sought the means to bring progress to Africa, to free it from European domination and exploitation, to restore its dignity, and to question all negative assumptions and racist prejudices.

The context was similar, even if the dynamics were changing. They were interpreting reality and history in the milieu of European expansion and domination. The early writers in places like Liberia and Sierra Leone were dealing with freedom from slavery. The luxury of the ivory tower was not available to them as they reflected on lived reality, writing works of reflection that were at the same time read as manifestoes. Although the size of the educated elite was initially small, growing during the twentieth century, its influence was far more than the number would suggest, the most successful members acquiring influence well beyond their own lifetimes.

Their writings and reflections do not make any distinctions between scholarship and politics, academy and ideology. What we may call scholarship, an author could have primarily conceived as a document of political liberation. Thus, "Ethiopeanists" were writing, but their motive was to attain cultural liberation. Samuel Johnson was writing on the Yoruba, but he wanted to use his book to create a Yoruba nation that would seek progress under the British. Such writers were conscious of the need to respond to negative comments about Africans and the black race in general. Nineteenth-century Eurocentric theories presented Africans in animal forms, lacking the ability to think, to reflect, or to create philosophical works. Even the current social forms that were clearly visible or whose histories they heard were condemned or their creation attributed to non-Africans. In a sense, social conditions and European epistemologies created the intellectual orientation and the subjects for the pioneer African intelligentsia. The major ideas fall into four categories, as described below:

1. Western Domination, Imperialism, and Exploitation

Without exception, all the writers had the West in mind. During the nineteenth century, the abolition of the slave trade, the increasing contact with the West in all its ramifications, and the expanding frontier of Christianity and Western education were all major themes. During the twentieth century, the colonial factor and neocolonialism have been the two dominant issues. Without the colonial factor, Africa would have been different, they argued. No one knew how and in what ways, but speculation was inclined toward showing that things would have been better without colonialism,[63] although we have no way of confirming this. While some African thinkers justified colonialism as a civilizing mission, most rejected it on the grounds that it was exploitative and racist. The notion of a "superior" race conquering an "inferior" race has troubled the

African intelligentsia, and very justifiably, they have rejected it.

2. "African Personality"

The intelligentsia has sought to present Africans as different from other races, not inferior to any, but equal to all as achievers and creators of civilizations. If Aristotle talked about a "universal man" defined by "sociality," a number of African thinkers would argue that there is an "African being" different from this so-called universal being. Many thinkers have spent considerable time and space on defining the difference between an African and a European, between the African past and its traditional values and the modern European world and its moral decadence, and on creating a distance between them. Edward Blyden defined an "African," and a number of his successors did the same, under the rubric of "the African personality." For them, Africa is rooted in community, not just a social being creating a living, but an integral aspect of the whole—he suffers and celebrates in a collective. Decisions were reached by consensus, in such a way as to satisfy the community; what K. A. Busia of Ghana described as "talking till unanimity was reached." Society was regarded as egalitarian, lacking class antagonism. As Nyerere restated it, society was an extension of the family. An ideology of communism prevailed, leading Senghor and his admirers to talk of an African socialism and Nyerere to talk of *ujamaa*.

The "African personality" was destroyed by European contacts, as many writers such as Blyden and Horton lamented. Nkrumah concluded that foreign economic and political forces, in collaboration with Islam and Christianity, assaulted African values. If many believed that the essence of this personality can be reconstructed (as did Blyden and Busia), some wanted Africans to recognize that living with this synthesis (what Ali Mazrui later called the "triple heritage") would be the ideal way to go. In the words of Nkrumah,

> With true independence regained …
> a new harmony needs to be forged, a
> harmony that will allow the combined presence of traditional Africa, Islamic Africa and Euro-Christian Africa, so that this presence is in tune with the original humanist principles underlying African society. Our society is not the old society, but a new society enlarged by Islamic and Euro-Christian influences. A new emergent ideology is therefore required, an ideology which can solidify in a philosophical statement, but at the same time an ideology which will not abandon the original humanist principles of Africa. … Such a philosophical statement I propose to name *philosophical consciencism*.[64]

I have invoked Nkrumah in order to use this respected thinker to comment on the limitation of constructing the African personality on the selected criteria of past values. Such values have changed and been contaminated by agencies that Nkrumah identified. The assumption that culture always determines identity and lifestyle, without recognizing profound historical changes, may also be a bit exaggerated.

3. Identity

The search for the "African personality" is part of the broader agenda of seeking an African identity. Both for good and bad, but more for bad than good, the intelligentsia regards the experience of imperialism as brutalizing, destructive, violent, and racist. Combined with the slave trade, imperialism is treated as a tragedy in the African encounter with Europe, a tragedy that destroyed African values, a tragedy that should be resented. To continue to move along the path dictated by this tragedy, many argue, is to end in destruction. Yet there is an awareness that modernity is defined by the spread of Western civilization, and the intelligentsia itself is defined by its ability to draw from this civilization. Many are inclined not to overdraw, in order to retain an identity for Africa. Virtually all thinkers have had to deal with the association of Western civilization with imperialism and all the negative baggage that comes with it. They have also had to deal with the African past and traditions, and they see issues of tradition and Western civilization creating a dilemma in terms of retaining or constructing an African identity. Senghor's poetry or Achebe's novels are all part of the broad genre of the "pathology of alienation"—to borrow Abiola Irele's words—which describes all the losses and sufferings in the encounter with the West.

4. Alternatives for Africa

If Europe created problems for Africa, and if the "African personality" deserves to be restored, how should Africans effect the necessary changes? Most looked for answers in the restoration of indigenous institutions and later in capitalism and socialism.

Blyden is again a front-runner in packaging a model of transformation based on African values, an inward-looking set of ideas. Senghor and others were to advance this argument by emphasizing two elements of the African past: humanism and a communalistic society. According to Senghor and other Négritude thinkers, traditional African culture must be revitalized and regenerated as a basis for national development, the assumption being that there was a uniqueness to African culture that could be preserved.

They were great dreamers, some speaking as if new heroes would arise in a later generation. They dealt with what they assumed to be possible, not necessarily realizable. Many had grand visions for the future of Africa, using ideas and writings to create optimism. This optimism was itself liberating, for almost a century in many places, from the mid-nineteenth to the mid-twentieth century, primarily because they conceived of a better future for Africa. Some were realistic in their demands, and some were not. A few exaggerated the past, even thinking that a path could be created to reach back to it or that the past could be duplicated.

Agendas of cultural nationalism appear to be weakly grounded in history, assuming that the past can be neatly separated from the present. They

also tend to assume that the intelligentsia and the masses are different in their relation to modernity—that on the one hand, it is the intelligentsia, with investments in Western education and access to Western civilization, that is in trouble, but not the masses. While it is true that the degree of interaction with the West and its civilization does in fact vary according to education, travel, and occupation, there is no evidence that any segment of society is completely immune from new influences and ideas. Alien material objects and culture do spread, wreaking great havoc on traditions in many places. It can, of course, be argued that members of the intelligentsia (the people of two worlds) are indeed more troubled, more disoriented than the "ordinary Africans" who are less connected with the sites of culture conflict.

It is fair to say that the presentation of tradition as unchanging is unrealistic and contestable. Tradition always faces change, either resisting or adapting to it. Its totality is always hard to reconstruct, as many members of the intelligentsia attempted to do. And to assume that it does not change, as some argued in wanting to deploy it to create an identity or an "African personality," is to ignore the very process of change in society. Very few are able to interrogate the inadequacies of traditions in dealing with major political and social development, even in denying the intelligentsia the power it seeks, especially in the management of local administration. Can a wage earner in a colonial civil service, living in a city, minister unto a large network of social relationships, maintain many wives and raise many children? How can the intelligentsia crave Western material culture and at the same time promote local science?

Politics has always been part of the core ambitions of the intelligentsia. Not just studying reality, they wanted to shape events and the future. Most sought power, sometimes using their writings as part of the strategy of obtaining power. Thus, the elite in Liberia and Sierra Leone behaved as a dominant class in relation to the indigenous population, describing them in derogatory terms, similar to the words employed by Europeans in describing so-called primitive Africans. Cheikh Anta Diop established political opposition parties, Jomo Kenyatta, Léopold Senghor, and Kwame Nkrumah became leaders of their countries, while Azikiwe became a premier and Nigeria's first president. These examples were even latter-day cases of the transfer of power, when the European grip on Africa had weakened. Their predecessors had used their role as elites and their capacity to think to create the origins of nationalism during the nineteenth century. Thus, Samuel Johnson, Joseph E. Casely Hayford, and Edward Blyden were all patriots and nationalists, fostering the idea of a new community a new nation.

Most members of the intelligentsia can be regarded as idealistic in their readings of African history and culture. Even those who were well read among them, such as Blyden, went further to idealize biology and the social sciences. This idealism has to be understood as part of a deliberate effort to change the image of Africa. Missionaries, slave dealers, and alien conquerors had assaulted them mentally and physically, debased their cultures, and undermined their humanity. They had to correct these errors by presenting alternative facts, alternative interpretations of history, enduring indigenous legacies. There seems to have been a consensus on the African past—a consensus not always justified by historical evidence—that the past was the ideal moment for Africa, when traditions existed in their purity, when human beings and gods obeyed all the rules of nature and of the cosmos, when Africans were moral and happy. Africa's modern history may lack wealth and power, but not spirituality and humanity, both more precious than the gold and silver of the developed world. The present, defined by the encounters with the West, is alienating, humiliating, and depressing, and identity and happiness should be sought in the past. There is a great deal of romanticism in this line of thinking, but it also contains a philosophy of martyrdom and redemption. Presented as innocent people living their lives in accordance with the rules of God and nature, Africans became slaves to develop the rest of the world, victims crucified at the altar of capitalism.

Evoking the image of redemption, the intelligentsia believed in the resurrection of Africa, after a long period of suffering.

The intelligentsia was successful in its academic project of showing that Africans had history, culture, science, philosophy, art, and religion. The pride generated by the cultural nationalism of Ethiopeanism or Négritude and other movements cannot be denied, in spite of the limitations that I have identified. Against the background of colonial rule and a long history of exploitation, that pride was necessary. As I show in chapter six, the academics among them also succeeded in inserting Africa into mainstream knowledge and, together with their non-African colleagues, were able to promote multicultural studies in different parts of the world. As most of the members of the intelligentsia realized, the pen was not necessarily mightier than the sword—they had to mobilize by developing a strategy of resistance. This strategy found intellectual expression in both nationalism and Pan-Africanism. In chapter four, I explore nationalism more fully, as it began to shape ideas from the late nineteenth century onward, and in its connection to the larger project of Pan-Africanism.

CONNEXIONS BETWEEN 'PRIMARY RESISTANCE' MOVEMENTS AND MODERN MASS NATIONALISM IN EAST AND CENTRAL AFRICA

By Terence O. Ranger

In the first part of this article a number of possible connexions between 'the last-ditch resisters' and the 'earliest organizers of armed risings', and later leaders of opposition to colonial rule in East and Central Africa, were explored. It was argued that African 'primary' resistance shaped the environment in which later politics developed; it was argued that resistance had profound effects upon white policies and attitudes; it was argued that there was a complicated interplay between manifestations of 'primary' and of 'secondary' opposition, which often overlapped with and were conscious of each other. Then the argument turned to a more ambitious proposition, namely that 'during the course of the resistances, or some of them, types of political organization or inspiration emerged which looked in important ways to the future; which in some cases are directly and in others indirectly linked with later manifestations of African opposition'.

Half of the case for this assertion was set out in the first article, and the character of the organization and aspirations of the great resistance movements was discussed. It was argued that they attempted to create a larger effective scale of action; that they endeavoured to appeal to a sense of African-ness; that they displayed an ambiguous attitude to the material aspects of white colonial society, often desiring to possess them without at the same time abandoning the values of their own communities; that they attempted to assert African ability to retain control of the world by means of a millenarian message. In all these ways, it was asserted, they were *similar* to later mass movements. But the first part of this article ended by posing, rather than answering, the key question of whether they were also *connected* with later mass movements. It is to this question that we must now turn.

It has most often been argued, of course, that 'primary' resistances were *not* connected, either directly or indirectly, with later forms of opposition. Resistances were followed, it was held, by 'a period of calm', out of which emerged 'other leaders and other motives'. And it is unquestionably true that after, say, 1920 there were very few 'tribal' risings and that different sorts of political organization were developed by new men. To that extent periodization of African nationalist history is legitimate enough. But, as I suggested in the first part of this article, we need to look for continuity in mass emotion as well as for continuity in *élite* leadership, if we are to establish a satisfactory historiography of nationalism. It is obviously important to ask whether there was any continuity in terms of mass emotion between the sort of risings I have been discussing and modern nationalism.

The first part of an answer is that there is undoubtedly a link between these resistances and later

Terence O. Ranger, "Connexions Between 'Primary Resistance' Movements and Modern Mass Nationalism in East and Central Africa: II," from *The Journal of African History*, Vol. 9, No. 4, pp. 631–64 . Copyright © 1968 by Cambridge University Press. Permission to reprint granted by the publisher.

mass movements of a millenarian character. Nor is this link merely a matter of *comparing* the Shona-Ndebele or Maji-Maji risings with later prophet movements or witchcraft eradication cults. There is often a quite direct connexion. The millenarian movements of the twentieth century in East and Central Africa varied widely in character. Sometimes they remained frankly 'pagan', and are hard to distinguish from the Nyabingi type of movement. (Nyabingi itself, long enduring as it was, continued to operate into the 'secondary' opposition period, and gave the British administration in Kigezi, right up until the end of the 1920s and beyond, the same sort of bother that was being provided elsewhere by 'new' pagan cults or by semi-Christian or Christian-independent movements.) In other cases Christian elements entered to a greater or lesser degree, but this does not prevent direct or indirect connexions with primary resistance movements, as we shall see.[1]

The most direct connexions, of course, are provided by examples like that of Nyabingi, which provided the basis both of 'primary resistance' and of persistent twentieth-century millenarian manifestations. Next come movements like that of the Mumbo cult in Nyanza province, Kenya. The Mumbo cult has recently been examined in a very interesting paper by Audrey Wipper. It arose among the Gusii, apparently around 1913, after the defeat of various 'primary resistances'. It reached peaks of activity in 1919, in 1933, and to a lesser extent in 1938 and 1947; it was one of the movements banned in 1954. Thus in point of time it bridged the period between the suppression of the Gusii risings of 1904, 1908 and 1916 and the emergence of modern mass nationalism. In character it was strikingly similar to the sort of movement we have already discussed. Although arising among the Gusii, it was 'a pan-tribal pagan sect', creating its own society of true believers, whom it bound by its own codes of conduct and to whom it promised eventual triumph and reward. The colonial period, in its mythology, was merely a testing period devised by the God of Africa to sort out the true believers from the faint-hearted; before long those who remained true would enter into the wealth and power of the whites. Mumbo had the most direct links with the period of primary resistance. 'The Gusii's most venerated warriors and prophets, noted for their militant anti-British stance, were claimed by the movement,' Miss Wipper tells us. 'Zakawa, the great prophet, Bogonko, the mighty chief, and Maraa, the *laibon* responsible for the 1908 rebellion, became its symbols, infusing into the living the courage and strength of past heroes ... Leaders bolstered up their own legitimacy by claiming to be the mouth-piece of these deceased prophets.'

Indeed, if Miss Wipper is right, we are close here to the idea of an 'alternative leadership', stemming from traditions of resistance and opposed to officially recognized authority. 'Especially successful in effecting such claims were the descendants' of the prophets and chiefs concerned. 'Thus, with the progeny of the Gusii heroes supporting the sect, a physical as well as a symbolic link with the past was established. Here was a powerful symbolic group whose prestige and authority could well be used to arouse, strengthen and weld the various disunited cults into a solid anti-British opposition.' Miss Wipper makes the important point that the cult looked back only to those figures who themselves stood out from and tried to transform traditional small-scale society; 'it looks to the past for inspiration and to the future for living'. 'Its goals', she tells us, 'are Utopian and innovative rather than traditional and regressive', involving attacks upon small-scale traditional values as well as upon European values. It would seem that Professor Ogot has considerable justification for applying the word 'radical' to the cult, and in claiming that 'the history of African nationalism in the district must be traced back' to its emergence.[2]

An interesting later example of a movement in the same western district of Kenya in which the continuity with the tradition of primary resistance was 'symbolic' rather than 'physical' is provided by the Dini Ya Msambwa cult, of Elijah Masinde. Through this cult Masinde called for Bukusu and for wider African unity, meeting together with cult representatives from Uganda, Suk, North Nyanza and Kiambu to resolve 'that since they have similar traditional religions they must unite in Dini Ya Msambwa'. Masinde also made a millenarian appeal, and referred back emphatically to the heroic and traumatic experience of the resistances. Mr. Welime tells us that

> In September 1947 he led about 5,000 followers to Chetambe's, where in 1895 many Bukusu died in their campaign against Hobley. He wanted his followers to remember the dead in their prayers. One interesting thing about this meeting is that they were dressed as in readiness for the 1895 war. At this meeting it is alleged that he unearthed a skull in which a bullet was found buried in the mouth … The crowd became very emotional and destructive.[3]

Similar examples of direct 'physical' and indirect 'symbolic' connexion with primary resistances can be given for Christian independent church movements. In the first category comes, for instance, Shembe's Nazarite Church in Zululand, so vividly described by Professor Sundkler. This impressive manifestation of Zulu, rather than South African, nationalism referred back to 'one of the most dramatic occasions in the history of Zulu nationalism', the Bambata rising of 1906. It was physically linked to this rising through the person of Messen Qwabe, one of its leaders. Shembe himself proclaimed: 'I am going to revive the bones of Messen and of the people who were killed in Bambata's rebellion.' All five sons of Messen have joined the church, which was given posthumous spiritual approval by their dead father, and it is taken for granted that all members of the Qwabe clan will be members of it. In the second category comes Matthew Zwimba's Church of the White Bird, established in 1915 in the Zwimba Reserve in Mashonaland, which appealed to the memory of the 1896–7 rising by regarding all those who died in the fighting in the Zwimba area as the saints and martyrs of the new church. It is important to note also that Zwimba regarded himself as very much a modernizer and succeeded, at least

for a time, in establishing himself as the intermediary between the chiefs and people of Zwimba and representatives of the modern world.[4]

It can be shown, then, that some at least of the intermediary opposition movements of a millenarian character, which are usually by common consent given a place in the history of the emergence of nationalism, were closely linked, as well as essentially similar, to some movements of primary resistance. Can we go further than this? It would be possible to argue, after all, that whatever may be the interest of such millenarian movements in the history of African politics, they have not in fact run into the mainstream of modern nationalism and in some instances have clashed with it. A movement like Dini Ya Msambwa might be cultivated for short-term purposes by a political party—as KANU is said to have cultivated it in order to find support in an otherwise KADU area—but it can hardly be thought to have had much future within the context of modern Kenyan nationalism.

It seems to me that there are a number of things to be said at this stage. I have argued that modern nationalism, if it is to be fully successful, has to discover how to combine mass enthusiasm with central focus and organization. This does not mean that it needs to *ally* itself with movements of the sort I have been describing which succeeded, on however limited a scale, in arousing mass enthusiasm. Indeed, it will obviously be in most ways a rival to them, seeking to arouse mass enthusiasm for its own ends and not for theirs. But it would be possible to present a triple argument at this stage. In the first place, one could argue, where nationalist movements *do* succeed in achieving mass emotional commitment, they will often do it partly by use of something of the same methods, and by appealing to something of the same memories as the movements we have been discussing. In the second place, where nationalist movements are faced with strong settler regimes, as in southern Africa, they will tend to move towards a strategy of violence which is seen by them as springing out of the traditions of 'primary resistance'. And in the third place, where nationalist movements fail, either generally or in particular areas, to capture mass enthusiasm, they may find themselves opposed by movements of this old millenarian kind, some of which will still preserve symbolic connexions at least with the primary resistances.

Let us turn first to the question of the methods by which nationalist parties achieve mass emotional involvement. Here Dr. Lonsdale's comments on the history of politics in Nyanza Province—the home of both the Mumbo cult and of Dini Ya Msambwa—are pertinent. Having described how Christian independency in the Province had its roots in pre-colonial religious phenomena, and how the first and second generations of the *élite* could not come to terms with it, he notes that 'only after the start of popular, mass nationalism did the politicians court the independents'. In a sense, he suggests, the values of the independents triumphed in mass nationalism rather than those of the *élite* welfare associations and proto-nationalist parties. 'The independents' selective approach to Western culture has triumphed over the early politician's desire to be accepted by and participate in the colonial world. It is symbolic of the victory of the mass party over the intellectual and occupational *élite* of the inter-war years.'[5]

The new mass party in East and Central Africa, as it spreads to the rural districts, comes to embody much of the attitude which has hitherto been expressed in less articulate movements of rural unrest. It often appears in a charismatic, almost millenarian role—the current phrase, 'a crisis of expectations', which politicians from Kenya to Zambia employ to describe their relations with their mass constituents, is not a bad description of the explosive force behind all the movements we have described. Often the party locally—and nationally—appeals to the memories of primary resistance, and for the same reason as the millenarian cults did; because it is the one 'traditional' memory that can be appealed to which transcends 'tribalism' and which can quite logically be appealed to at the same time as tribal authorities are being attacked and undermined. My own experience of nationalist politics in Southern Rhodesia certainly bears out these generalizations. It was the National Democratic Party of 1960–1 which first really penetrated the rural areas and began to link the radical leadership of the towns with rural discontent. As it did so, the themes and memories of the rebellions flowed back into nationalism. 'In rural areas', writes Mr. Shamuyarira of this period, 'meetings became political gatherings and more ... the past heritage was revived through prayers and traditional singing, ancestral spirits were evoked to guide and lead the new nation. Christianity and civilization took a back seat and new forms of worship and new attitudes were thrust forward dramatically ... the spirit pervading the meetings was African and the desire was to put the twentieth century in an African context.' So Mr. George Nyandoro, grandson of a rebel leader killed in 1897, and nephew of a chief deposed for opposition to rural regulations in the 1930s, appealed in his speeches to the memory of the great prophet Chaminuka round whom the Shona rallied in the nineteenth century; so Mr. Nkomo, returning home in 1962, was met at the airport by a survivor of the rebellions of 1896–7, who presented him with a spirit axe as a symbol of the apostolic succession of resistance; so the militant songs copied from Ghana were replaced by the old tunes belonging to spirit mediums and rebel leaders.[6]

Again there are senses in which the Tanganyika African Peoples Union appeared to the people of southern Tanzania as the direct successor of the Maji-Maji movement. 'Many people took the water', runs an oral account of the spread of Maji-Maji collected in 1966.

You know this is how the water spread very quickly. Take for example the struggle for independence in Tanganyika. If you did not buy a TANU card you were considered as an enemy to independence by those around you ... The same thing with the 'maji', although this was more serious. If your wife took the water and you did not, you were considered an enemy to your fellow Africans, so you had to be removed. For how can anyone allow the life of one man who is dangerous to hazard the lives of the whole people.[7]

At any rate the continuity between Maji-Maji and TANU is a theme of some importance in contemporary Tanzanian politics.

The people fought [so Julius Nyerere told the Fourth Committee of the United Nations in December 1956] because they did not believe in the white man's right to govern and civilize the black. They rose in a great rebellion, not through fear of a terrorist movement or a superstitious oath, but in response to a natural call, a call of the spirit, ringing in the hearts of all men, and of all times, educated and uneducated, to rebel against foreign domination. It is important to bear this in mind in order to understand the nature of a Nationalist movement like mine. Its function is not to create the spirit of rebellion but to articulate it and show it a new technique.

Today, as TANU strives to retain and to develop its character as a radical mass movement, the appeal back to Maji-Maji has become more frequent. 'On the ashes of Maji-Maji' writes the *Nationalist*, 'our new nation was founded.'[8]

A caution and clarification is perhaps in order here. Obviously the *Nationalist* writer quoted above is being very selective in his use of the pre-TANU political tradition. In this paper I am anxious to show that in some ways the radical, millenarian tradition of mass protest *does* run into modern nationalism, but I certainly do not wish to claim that it is the *only* tradition that runs into modern nationalism. TANU has as its background not only Maji-Maji and the Hehe wars, but also the centralizing *élite* associations—the Tanganyika African Civil Servants Association; the Tanganyika African Association—led by the men of what Dr. Iliffe has called 'the Age of Improvement'. There is obviously a danger in the nationalist historiography which sees an exclusive line of ancestry running from one episode of violent resistance to another, excluding the accommodators and the pioneers of modern political organization. Yet the fact that today Maji-Maji is seen in this way as the most significant predecessor to TANU, even if this is a myth in some respects, is in itself a fact which influences contemporary nationalist politics in Tanzania.

This brings us to the second point. It is natural that a nationalist movement which is still engaged in an increasingly violent struggle for independence will turn even more exclusively to the tradition of resistance. This has certainly happened in Southern Rhodesia, for example. The present phase of guerrilla activity in Rhodesia is called by the nationalists 'Chimurenga', the name given by the Shona to the 1896 risings. 'What course of action will lead to the liberation of Zimbabwe?' asks a Zimbabwe African National Union writer. 'It is not the path of appeasement. It is not the path of reformism. It is not the path of blocking thirds. It is the path of outright fearless defiance of the settler Smith fascist regime and fighting the current war for national liberation. It is the path of direct confrontation. It is the path of Chimurenga.' Here, within the Rhodesian movement, there is not only an attempt to stress the mass, radical characteristics of the nationalist parties as with TANU, but in many ways a repudiation of the party as an organizational form in favour of a return to the older tradition.

The nationalist movement has failed to mobilize these disparate Africans of Rhodesia into an effective revolutionary force [writes Davis Mugabe] because it has moved uncertainly from one European model to another, without ever sinking its roots deep into the African soil ... For almost three decades, the nationalist leaders based their operations and their pronouncements on the myth that they spoke for an integrated political community. Although we tried to paper over the differences for the sake of appearances, no real attempt was made to build bridges between the vaShona, the amaNdebele, and the immigrant groups, or even between the city politicians and the peasant farmer. In the anger and bitterness of the past year, however, a new sense of unity can be detected. It has little connexion with the personality feuds of earlier times, for the old game of constitutional politics has run its fruitless course ... From now on the only political leaders who will matter are those who are working 24 hours a day with the people in the countryside—not those in city offices with party names on the door, or in jail, or manning governments in exile. Somewhere in Rhodesia is our Mao or our Castro. His ideology and past affiliations are unimportant; but he must be a man who can become one with the people of the village and with the guerrillas preparing for war in the mountains. Bridges will fall into place between Rhodesia's divergent peoples when they are organized to fight acre by acre for what is most important to them—'the land on the hill'.[9]

Once again it is time for a caution. Mr. Mugabe is appealing back to Chimurenga, 'the first war of independence', as an example of a war fought for the things people understand—land and cattle—and as an example of how best to unite the African people of Rhodesia. I have written about the 1896–7 uprisings in terms of the attempts then made to find such a basis of action and unity. To the extent that the risings took place and presented so formidable a challenge, this attempt was successful. But one should not forget that the success of the leaders of the 1896–7 movement did not last long. Defeat broke up unity; it remains an unproven question whether unity would have survived victory. In the event it was probably true of 1896–7, as Dr. Iliffe has written of Maji-Maji, that the collapse of all the high hopes resulted immediately in greater disunity and tensions. The Ndebele and the Shona joined together for a time under the leadership of the prophets; but the Ndebele, or most of them, made a separate peace while the Shona fought on. The unity gave way to Shona attacks on surrendering Ndebele. After 1896 the whites managed Ndebele society by playing upon the triple division into 'loyalists', rebels who negotiated, and rebels who vainly opposed negotiation. After 1897 Shona society was divided in a similar way. These great movements of mass resistance are important as *attempts* at unity.

It is time to move to the third point—that these traditions of resistance can sometimes be used *against* nationalist movements as well as *by* them. Indeed the whole question of African resistance to *African* pressures is one which urgently needs investigation before we can obtain a balanced view of the significance of resistance as a whole.

A number of preliminary points, however, can already be made. In the first place, of course, the extension of the concept of resistance to include African resistance to African pressures reminds us that historical discussion of the role of resistance as a force for change cannot be restricted to the period of the Scramble and the Pacification. This is true even if we limit the idea of resistance to European-African confrontations: the Shona, for instance, had a long tradition of rebellion against the Portuguese which served as the background to their rebellion against the British. But it is even more importantly true if we consider African resistance to African pressures. During the nineteenth century, East and Central Africa were exposed to a number of powerful African intrusions which threatened the very existence of certain societies. Partly in response to these intrusions, the existing secular authorities in some African societies attempted to build up new powers; sometimes this attempt also provoked resentment and resistance within the society.

Some at least of these resistances to external African invaders or to the expansion of internal central authority took the form of the reactions to European rule which I have described above. The prophetic and witchcraft eradication traditions were as available to movements of this kind as to later movements of protest against the whites; certain features of the later movements which historians have felt to be characteristic of response to colonialism as such were almost certainly present in these earlier manifestations. Thus the Nyabingi movement, which we have seen already as a focus of integrative opposition to colonial rule and as a continuing messianic cult in the twentieth century, originated as a movement of opposition to Tutsi control of northern Rwanda and served as a rallying point for Hutu resistance from the middle years of the nineteenth century onwards. Thus the hierarchy of Shona spirit mediums, which we have seen involved in the 1896 risings, also provided a focus for Shona reactions to earlier Ndebele raids; the hero-figures of nineteenth-century central Shona history are the two great mediums of the Chaminuka spirit who rallied the western and central Shona and who were killed at Lobengula's orders.

Then again, during the colonial period itself, a good deal of what we can properly call African resistance, in the sense of movements similar to those categorized as 'primary resistance' movements, has taken the form of protest against dominance or sub-imperialism by other African peoples. A few examples may be given. The violent opposition, once more using the Nyabingi cult as its vehicle, of the Kiga clans to the control of the Ganda agents of British overrule; the rebellion in 1916 of the Konjo people against Toro control, which is being followed up at the present time by a second rebellion of the Konjo for the same reasons; the disturbances in Balovale and elsewhere against the control of local government by the Lozi; these are all instances of resistance which clearly have to be fitted into any general discussion of the topic.

Finally there is the problem of African resistance, again in the same sense of violent 'primary' style reaction, to African governments after the attainment of territorial independence. I am thinking here of events like the clashes between the followers of Alice Lenshina and members of UNIP in Zambia; of the upheavals organized by the Parmehutu association in Rwanda; above all of the Congo rebellions, particularly of the Kwilu rising. The atmosphere of these events is very similar in many ways to that of the 'primary resistances'.[10]

Let us take the Kwilu example. The Kwilu rebellion seems to fit neatly enough into the category already mentioned, in which the nationalist movement fails to retain the confidence of the mass and is faced with a millenarian style resistance. In a recent study of the Kwilu rising, a convincing argument is stated for the thesis that the inspiration for resistance came not from alien ideas but from 'frustrations profoundly Congolese'. What was being aimed at, so the authors hold, was 'an inherently Congolese social revolution' which must be seen in the long line of millenarian integrative attempts so characteristic of Congolese history in the nineteenth and twentieth centuries. The Kwilu rising must be seen in the context of preceding movements in that area: the Bapende revolt of 1931, in which, 'the Bapende reached a magico-religious belief in their own invulnerability'; The Great Serpent sect of 1932, which predicted 'the collective rising of the dead, the eclipse of the sun, and the coming of a Man, part white and part black' who would institute a new order; the Nzambi Malembe movement of 1945, which appealed to the memory of the old empire of the Kongo and which outlawed all fetishes and witchcraft; the Dieudonne movement of the 1950s, which again ordered the destruction of all fetishes and general baptism in its own holy water.

Into this background modern nationalism arrived in 1959 with the creation of the Parti Solidaire Africain, which promised in its election campaign 'total reduction of unemployment, work for all, multiplication of schools, free primary and secondary education, a rise in salaries for all, improvement in housing, free medical care'. 'Independence', the tribesmen were told, 'would be an era of leisure, plenty and happiness.' They found it instead a time of firm government by the progressive *élite* of the moderate P.S.A., and the authors quote what they hold to be a typical reaction. 'Before independence we dreamed that it would bring us masses of marvellous things. All of that was to descend from the sky ... Deliverance and Salvation ... But here it is, more than two years we have been waiting, and nothing has come. On the contrary our life is more difficult, we are more poor than before.' And so, the argument concludes, the masses turned to a 'this-worldly-oriented messianic movement, headed by a compelling leader-saviour', Mulele.

This analysis may be greeted with some scepticism, but it rests on more than an easy comparison of Socialist idealism with millenarian panaceas. Mulele, it is generally accepted, has acquired the characteristics of previous prophet figures in the minds of his followers—he is regarded as invulnerable to bullets; his followers hope to share his invulnerability and explain death in battle as punishment for 'having transgressed certain norms and practices of the movement'. Rebels take *mai Mulele*, the water of the rebellion, as a sign of commitment and guarantee of invulnerability. Mulele lays down new rules of conduct for his fighters as strict as, and strikingly similar to, the prohibitions of the Shona mediums in 1896—his followers must live communally, must not loot, must not use European goods. As the authors comment, these rules, in addition to creating the sense of the new society, are as essential in 1966 as they were in 1896 to preserve discipline among irregular rebel forces. According to the authors, many of those who support the movement draw a quite conscious parallel between the colonial rule against which their fathers revolted in 1931 and the present regime in Kwilu province. But the authors, also make the point that, like Miss Wipper's followers of Mumbo, the rebels look to the past for inspiration and to the future for living. The revolt is no rejection of modern goods and advantages, but rather an attempt to obtain them on a 'just' basis and within a 'good' society defined in African communalist terms. 'The new society is conceived of as a gigantic village made up of thousands of small villages in which the people find their own authenticity.'[11]

I should perhaps say in conclusion about the Mulelist movement something which applies to all the others discussed in this paper. I have no intention of maligning or mocking the Mulelist movement by stressing its character as a successor to other millenarian Congolese cults. However strange their mythologies and structures may appear to us, these movements require to be taken seriously and with sympathy as consistent expressions of aspirations which in the end have to be met in one way or another by the rulers of East and Central Africa, whether white or black. The aspiration to 'put the twentieth century in an African context'; the aspiration towards a new society 'conceived of as a gigantic village made up of thousands of small villages in which the people find their own authenticity'; the aspiration towards gaining control of their own world without surrendering its values; all these are still characteristic of the rural masses of East and Central Africa. It is, of course, true that these movements have not offered lasting or effective solutions; to extend the already cited description of Nyabingi to all of them, they have been 'revolutionary in method' but also 'anarchic in effect'. It is the task of the nationalist movements of East and Central Africa, therefore, to maintain mass enthusiasm for their own solutions. It is their task to demonstrate that they can institutionalize and make permanent their answers to the problem of how to increase effective scale without destroying African communalist values more successfully than the primary resistance leaders or the millenarian cults.

NOTES

1. Bessell, op. cit. 'Nyabingi' *Uganda Journal*, 6, no. 2 (1938).

2. A. Wipper, 'The cult of Mumbo', East African Institute Conference paper, January 1966; B. A. Ogot, 'British administration in the Central Nyanza district of Kenya', *J. Afr. Hist.* IV, no. 2 (1963).

3. J. D. Welime, 'Dini ya Msambwa', Research Seminar Paper, Dar es Salaam (1965).

4. B. G. M. Sundkler, *Bantu Prophets in South Africa* (London, 1961); T. O. Ranger, 'The early history of independency in Southern Rhodesia', *Religion in Africa*, ed. W. Montgomery Watt (Edinburgh, 1964), 54–7.

5. J. M. Lonsdale, 'A political history of Nyanza, 1883–1945', Cambridge University Ph.D. thesis (1964), chaps. 11 and 12.

6. N. S. Shamuyarira, *Crisis in Rhodesia* (London, 1965), 68–9.

7. Interview between Mr. G. C. K. Gwassa and Mzee Hassan Mkape, Kilwa Kivinje, June 1966.

8. Speech by J. K. Nyerere, 20 December 1956 to the 578th meeting of the Fourth Committee of the United Nations; editorial comment, *The Nationalist*, 18 September 1967.

9. 'Spotlight on Zimbabwe', *The Nationalist*, 18 July 1967; Davis Mugabe, 'Rhodesia's African majority', *Africa Report*, February 1967.

10. Andrew Roberts, 'The Lumpa Church of Alice Lenshina and its antecedents', mimeo. (Dar es Salaam, 1967). Dr. Roberts argues that the clash between the Lumpa Church and the United National Independence Party arose because both organizations were making claims to exclusive emotional commitment in the same area. The Church reacted against the loss of many of its numbers to the later secular mass movement.

11. R. C. Fox, W. de Cramer and J. M. Ribeaucourt, 'The second independence: a case study of the Kwilu Rebellion in the Congo', *Comparative Studies in Society and History*, VIII, no. 1 (October 1965).

TRENDS AND PATTERNS IN AFRICAN NATIONALISM

BY EHIEDU E. G. IWERIEBOR

This chapter examines the movement that sought to liberate Africa from colonial domination, overthrow European colonial governments, and achieve independence. The focus is on the evolution of African nationalism, especially the emergence of mass nationalism and the drive to independence between the 1940s and the 1960s. This struggle, though countered by the colonialists' divisive actions and the creation of disabling conditions for postcolonial development, ultimately resulted in a major victory. It created the opportunity for African peoples to, once again, be acknowledged as a history-making people. African independence was, therefore, a major contribution to the global quest for freedom.

* * *

INTRODUCTION

African nationalism involved the collective effort of many anticolonial African groups. These included groups that were political, ideological, cultural, and labor-related. Their purpose in working together was to overthrow European colonial domination, achieve independence, and build new nation-states out of the various peoples and societies that comprised the European colonial territories. While the focus here is on the period of the concerted drive toward independence between the 1940s and the 1960s,

African struggles for freedom from European colonial domination started much earlier. This later phase was a culmination of all previous struggles.

The first section of this chapter outlines the emergence of African nationalism in the context of the imposition and consolidation of European colonial domination from the late nineteenth century onward. The political, economic, and cultural forces that this domination set in motion are noted. The exploitative and oppressive conditions generated various protests and freedom struggles; these included political, ideological, cultural, and economic resistance. The colonial enterprise also motivated the human and social forces, the educated elite, the intelligentsia, the labor unions, various social and cultural groups, and the activated masses to fight against colonialism. This led to the growth of various proto-nationalist pressure groups and movements whose political and ideological activities formed the seedbed of incipient anticolonial nationalism from the late nineteenth century to the late 1920s.

African nationalism continued to grow from the early 1930s onward. Other developments, global and internal, laid the groundwork for the rise of militant mass nationalism from the 1940s to the 1960s. The catalytic events of the 1930s and 1940s included the world depression; the formation of African social, cultural, and labor groups; the rise of a new nationalist intelligentsia and more militant movements; and

Ehiedu E. G. Iweriebor; Toyin Falola, ed., "Trends and Patterns in African Nationalism," from *Africa, Volume 4: The End of Colonial Rule: Nationalism and Decolonization,* pp. 3–27. Copyright © 2002 by Carolina Academic Press. Permission to reprint granted by the publisher.

the Italo-Ethiopian conflict. These issues, examined in the second section, created the conditions in which the African freedom movements evolved, matured, and became more focused and directed toward the achievement of independence. World War II (1939–1945) also had a decisive impact on the course of political developments in Africa. The conditions which led to the emergence of mass nationalism in the postwar period are outlined in the third section. The fourth section examines the drive to independence in the different regions which used various practical strategies as dictated by their conditions. Whatever their different strategies and paths to independence, all regions had to contend with the colonizers' objective to retain indirect control after independence.

The conclusion highlights the forces that contributed to the emergence and maturation of the struggles for freedom and independence. It emphasizes the significance of the political and ideological concepts and practical strategies African freedom movements used and the challenges they faced politically and practically in their long struggles for the recovery of political independence.

BACKGROUND: EUROPEAN COLONIAL DOMINATION AND THE ORIGINS OF AFRICAN NATIONALISM

The Imposition of European Colonial Domination

European colonial domination over Africa was established in the early twentieth century. Colonies were established in an especially frenzied fashion after the Berlin Conference of 1884–1885 by seven imperial powers: Britain, France, Germany, Italy, Belgium, Portugal, and Spain.[1] The European quest for colonies in Africa followed the decline of the profitability of the slave trade. The abolition of the slave trade coincided with the development of a need for steady supplies of raw materials and markets for Europe's expanding industries. The initial European commercial strategy, known as free trade

imperialism, was to establish commercial relations with African societies as suppliers of raw materials and market outlets. This attempt to structure African societies into producers of raw materials and importers of manufactured goods did not quite succeed. This was primarily because these societies still had their sovereignty; therefore, European traders, merchants, companies, cultural agents, and missionaries had to operate partly on terms imposed by sovereign African leaders and societies.

However, the imperative of Europe's industrial production and capitalist economic calculations could not tolerate relations of equality and equal exchange with African societies. This was the context and impetus of the European movement for the colonization of Africa. Equipped with superior military technology provided by industrial development and spurred politically by inter-European power struggles for preeminence, the aspirant European imperialists embarked on the colonization of Africa. In the confrontation between European forces and African forces—even though African societies in different parts of the continent valiantly resisted—the imperial forces ultimately won; and in the late nineteenth and early twentieth centuries, they imposed colonial domination over all of Africa except Ethiopia and Liberia.

Thereafter, the European imperial powers began establishing the political and administrative machinery to facilitate the realization of colonialism's basic objective, that is, the exploitation of African resources for European industrial production, economic development, and prosperity. The various administrative systems that the European powers established reflected their national administrative traditions, their imperial ideologies, and the conditions they met in African societies. Whatever their formal differences, they were all bureaucratic, authoritarian colonial state systems which were organized to extract resources and labor to build the administrative, social, and physical infrastructures needed to facilitate economic exploitation. In practice, Africans experienced colonial domination through forced labor, low wages, heavy taxation, land expropriation, social segregation, racial discrimination in employment and services, racist colonial education, and the vassalization and diminution of the traditional political leaders and institutions. It was these oppressive and exploitative colonial political, administrative, cultural, and economic institutions and processes that generated the African human and social forces that began the quest for freedom in various spheres of life: political, social, economic, cultural, and religious. This culminated in the emergence of African nationalism and the eventual attainment of independence.

THE EMERGENCE OF AFRICAN NATIONALISM, 1880S–1920S

African nationalism was part of the broader struggles of African peoples for political, economic, cultural, and religious freedom from European colonial domination.[2] The movement for political freedom, or nationalism, did not initially emerge as a fully formed movement. It went through various phases and struggles over different aspects of life affected by colonialism. African nationalism can be defined as the movement that sought to overthrow European colonial domination, achieve independence, and build new nation-states out of the peoples who composed the colonial territories. The aim of building new nation-states is analytically important, as it distinguishes postcolonization nationalist freedom struggles from the resistance struggles of the precolonial African societies against the imposition of colonial domination. The African societies that faced colonial pressures and subsequent military invasions included organically different political and social entities organized as empires, kingdoms, chiefdoms, and decentralized societies (the so-called stateless societies). They struggled to resist the colonial invasions, maintain their political sovereignty, and retain the precolonial political and social order.

On the other hand, African nationalist movements were struggles for freedom in the postcolonization phase, occurring specifically within the new colonial territories. As the ruling global, political, and social entities of the era were nations and nation-states, not surprisingly, African freedom movements also aimed to achieve power and independence as new nations. Hence, the nationalist struggles for independence and the objective of building new nation-states were products partly of living in new colonial territories and partly of the global prevalence of nation-states as the dominant political forms of the time. Consequently, the historiography of African nationalism attempts to identify the resistance of precolonial African societies as primary resistance and the African nationalism of the postcolonization phase as secondary resistance, implying they shared substantively similar goals. This is misleading. While African nationalists undoubtedly derived inspiration and examples from the anticolonial resistance to the imposition of colonial domination, postcolonization African nationalism was a new and substantively different movement which aimed not to restore the old political order, but to win independence for the colonized territories and to transform these territorial shells into new political and cultural communities, that is, postcolonial nation-states.

Thus, it is common for those who subscribe to a Hamitic view of African history to believe that external impulsion was required for the development of nationalism. This, again, is misleading. The primary and irreducible fact about African nationalism is that it was an internally generated, internally organized, and internally directed movement for freedom. Nationalists struggled against powerful imperialist forces that expected to keep their colonies permanently. The colonizers did not believe that African colonial territories could emerge as nations. They perceived and treated people within their territories as distinct, incompatible, and unrelated "tribes" who were so culturally different that they could not possibly form nations. In this context, the chief achievement of the African nationalists was to perceive their colonial territories as potential nations, struggle to achieve independence, and, in the process, create the ideological, cultural, and political consciousness that aided in converting the colonial territorial shells into vital new political-cultural communities. In the light of this fact, the significance ascribed to external ideas in the development of African nationalism has to be reduced. Struggles for freedom originated from a variety of conditions: the actual responses of Africans to the experiences of colonial oppression and exploitation, Africans' desire for freedom, their ideological formulations, their psychological motivations, and their practical nationalist activities. Hence, African nationalism was the product of the imaginative conceptions and practical struggles of Africans for freedom—not the result of copied ideas or external stimulation.

African nationalism evolved in different phases between the 1880s and the attainment of independence. Three main phases of the freedom struggles may be distinguished according to the following time periods: 1880s–1920s, 1930s–1940s, and 1940s–1960s.

The period from the 1880s to the 1920s saw the emergence of the nationalist intelligentsia and the rise of early protest movements in political, economic, cultural, and religious spheres. The early manifestations of African anticolonial resistance included pressure group protests against specific abuses such as forced labor, administrative malfeasance, and racial discrimination.

In terms of the development of colony-wide or territorial nationalism, while various groups such as farmers, workers, market women, traders, and youth and community associations organized the protection and advancement of their own group interests and thereby contributed to the general stream of nationalism, it was the nationalist intelligentsia that played the decisive coordinating role which converted these discrete and diverse movements into territorial ones. The members of the intelligentsia were products of the colonial or Western educational systems. They rebelled against education for subservience, detached themselves in varying degrees from colonial ideological acculturation, and began to raise the banner of freedom. These members of the intelligentsia were often economically and professionally independent and included lawyers, surveyors, merchants, traders, doctors,

newspaper publishers, and employed groups such as teachers, clerks, and labor union leaders.

The members of this small educated elite were very politically and socially active. They struggled for political and social change through frameworks of ideas and ideological constructs. For instance, to the colonial views about African inferiority and the necessity for African subjection and external guidance, the intelligentsia counterposed and propagated ideas of cultural nationalism, political capacity, self-determination, independence, and nationhood. Petitions, the press, organizational activity, and other methods were used to disseminate these views.

The intelligentsia were responsible for bringing together and mobilizing the various nationalist groups, articulating and propagating nationalist ideas, and formulating preliminary visions of postcolonial nation-building. They spearheaded the formation of political pressure groups, cultural nationalist associations, and broad nationalist parties and movements. Thus, they provided the general leadership for the freedom movement, and some of them went on to become leaders of the independent nation-states. Examples include Gamal Nasser of Egypt, Habib Bourguiba of Tunisia, Ben Bella of Algeria, Nnamdi Azikiwe of Nigeria, Kwame Nkrumah of Ghana, Jomo Kenyatta of Kenya, Milton Obote of Uganda, Julius Nyerere of Tanzania, Kamuzu Banda of Malawi, Felix Houphouet-Boigny of the Ivory Coast, Leopold Sedar Senghor of Senegal, Sékou Touré of Guinea-Conakry, Robert Mugabe of Zimbabwe, Samora Machel of Mozambique, Amilcar Cabral of Guinea-Bissau, Agostinho Neto of Angola, and Nelson Mandela of South Africa.

The intelligentsia evolved historically and ideologically throughout the colonial period. Some of its members were moderate reformist nationalists who preferred a nonmilitant strategy of struggle, advocated gradual change and negotiations with the colonial powers, and even accepted colonialist ideas of postindependent African development. Others evolved into radical nationalists, advocating radical strategies of struggle which included politicized strikes, civil disobedience, and armed insurrection. They often broached ideas of national liberation as a composite of political independence and social and economic revolution. Yet, despite their political and ideological differences, the members of the intelligentsia were united by ideas of African freedom and independence.

The early protest movements focused on ameliorating conditions of political disempowerment, economic exploitation, social oppression, and cultural denigration. They campaigned for the protection of land rights, the expansion of educational facilities and opportunities, civil and political rights, participation in colonial political institutions and processes, and the dignity and integrity of indigenous leaders and political institutions. They campaigned against forced labor, heavy taxation, and colonial racism, and also against their vassalization, misuse, corruption, and diminution as adjuncts of the colonial authorities.

This small group of elites spearheaded the early expressions of nationalist resistance and organization in the form of cultural and religious nationalism. Cultural nationalism was an attempt by the intelligentsia to assert the integrity, validity, and normalcy of African culture, practices, values, and institutions such as languages, orature (i.e., the literature of predominately oral societies), dance, music, cuisine, style of dress, historical achievements, and social and political thought. Religious nationalism asserted the validity of indigenous religions. In the non-Muslim parts of Africa, African Christians also attempted to establish independent churches under African control. In Muslim parts of Africa, such as Egypt, Morocco, Somalia, and Tunisia, Islam and syncretic, indigenous, Islamic cultural forms provided coherent and unified cultural and religious traditions which the nationalists used to defend their social order and cultural heritage.

Major cultural and religious nationalists included Simon Kimbangu of the Belgian Congo; Nehemiah Tile of South Africa; Edward Blyden of Liberia, Sierra Leone, and Nigeria; Casely Hayford and Mensah Sarbah of the Gold Coast; Patriarch Campbell and Mojola Agbebi of Nigeria; and others.

Cultural and religious nationalist activities were also important in the psychological re-empowerment of the colonized. Nationalist attempts at cultural and religious rebirth provided the colonized with the cultural resources and psychological confidence to organize nationalist movements, challenge colonial certitudes, and struggle for freedom and independence.

The intelligentsia also spearheaded the formation of the early political pressure groups, associations, and later nationalist parties and movements. The early political pressure groups and movements in North Africa included the Wafd of Egypt (1918); the Young Tunisian Party and the Destour (1920) of Tunisia; and the Etoile Nord Africain (the North African Star) formed by a group of Algerian migrants in France in 1926. In West Africa, these movements included the Aborigines Rights Protection Society of the Gold Coast (1897); the People's Union in Lagos (1908); the Nigerian National Democratic Party in Nigeria (1923); and the interterritorial nationalist movement—the National Congress of British West Africa (1920) which embraced nationalists from Nigeria, the Gold Coast, Gambia, and Sierra Leone. Another expression of regional Pan-Africanism was the West African Students Union which was formed in London in 1925 by students led by Nigerian Ladipo Solanke. It was also in the 1920s that the militant Pan-Africanism of Marcus Garvey spread through the establishment of Garvey's Universal Negro Improvement Association in various parts of Africa, especially West and South Africa.

In South Africa, African political nationalism was partially stimulated by Britain's withdrawal and the assumption of power by British and Boer settlers under the Union Constitution of 1910. The new white power structure began to systematically deprive Africans of political, civil, social, and economic rights and impose wide-ranging racially discriminatory laws and policies. This systematic deprivation was epitomized by the Land Act of 1913 which reserved eighty-seven percent of the land for whites and thirteen percent of the land for the African majority. These developments led to the emergence of organized African political activity as expressed in the South African Native National Congress, formed in 1912, which later became the African National Congress in 1923. Led by Pixley Seme, John Jabavu, John Dube, and Sol Plaatje, the Congress campaigned against the removal of political and civil rights and economic and social discrimination.

In general, the early African nationalist groups can be described as reformist. This is because they demanded gradual reform of defective aspects of the colonial systems. Their demands included the review of expropriatory land policies, the maintenance of civil liberties, a universal franchise, African representation in colonial legislative and executive councils, the liberalization of colonial rule, the abolition of racial discrimination in employment and social relations, the maintenance of traditional institutions, and the provision of mass education. Thus, while the early nationalist groups were still dominated by the elite and by elite concerns and had not yet evolved into mass movements as they would after World War II, they also championed the social causes of other groups like workers, farmers, traders, market women, and youth and advocated policies that would have mass consequences and ultimately undermine colonial power.

THE GESTATION AND GROWTH OF AFRICAN NATIONALISM, 1930S–1940S

During the second phase of the African freedom struggles, in the 1930s and the 1940s, African nationalism was affected by developments in the colonial political economy, internal developments in the colonies, and other events within and outside Africa.

The nature of nationalism began to change in the early 1930s. This was partly due to the Great Depression and its impact, the emergence of a new generation of young militant nationalists and youth movements, the growth of social, cultural, ethnic, and community associations, the Italo-Ethiopian conflict of 1935–1941, and World War II and its simultaneously destabilizing and liberating effects.[3]

In the economic sphere, by the 1920s, African economies and their production patterns had been structured in such a way that they exported their primary commodities to Europe and imported manufactured goods. This meant that Africa had been effectively integrated into the global capitalist commercial network. As a result, African economies began to be subjected to the economic cycles of the Western world. Consequently, when the crash of 1929 occurred and set off the Great Depression, Africa was automatically affected. The demand for Africa's primary commodities, mineral and agricultural, fell precipitously and the impact of this was felt in the export and import dependent sectors. At the same time, the importation of manufactured goods and items like soap, medicines, sugar, oil, rice, bicycles, cars, trucks, and other goods on which the colonies now depended was severely affected. The consequences of this massive economic contraction in African colonies included the closure of import and export companies, the disruption of distributive networks, a reduction in plantation production, and a reduced demand for the products of peasant and large-scale farmers. These developments all generated unemployment, hardship, deprivation, and general impoverishment, leading to labor and social protests which the colonial governments tried to contain.

Although labor organization and action was still in its incipient phase during this period, labor activism did occur. For example, workers organized strikes in the mines in Sierra Leone, Guinea, and the Gold Coast in the 1920s and in the copperbelt of Northern Rhodesia in the period from 1935 to 1940. This led to colonial repression, but labor consciousness and activism continued to evolve. Various social, community, self-help, ethnic, and economic interest groups also emerged to protect and advance their interests.

In the political sphere, three important events took place. The first was the emergence of a new, young intelligentsia and of youth nationalist movements. Most members of this intelligentsia had been born in the early colonial period and received their early education and socialization in colonial schools. As they matured, these young Africans often found the political movements, activities, and ambitions of their elders too reformist, too gradualist, too inadequately focused on independence, and therefore too "tame" and generally unsatisfactory as challenges to colonialism. They consequently adopted a more militant stance and a populist orientation, becoming more focused on speedy political reform and advancement toward some form of self-rule. The vehicles they created were energetic youth political movements. Among them were the Gold Coast Youth Conference led by J. B. Danquah (1930), I.T.A. Wallace-Johnson's West African Youth League (1935), the Nigerian Youth Movement (1934), and Habib Bourguiba's New Destour of Tunisia (1934). These movements directly demanded self-government and pushed their demands militantly. They also began mobilizing the people, which gradually led to the expansion of nationalism beyond the elite, a development which intensified after World War II.

The Italo-Ethiopian crisis of 1935–1941 intensified the political militancy of the youth and anticolonial nationalism. The Italians had invaded and occupied Ethiopia following an incident in 1934 in which the Ethiopians attacked an Italian garrison. For the Italians, this was a godsend, an event with which to redeem their national "honor" which had been sullied by Ethiopia's decisive defeat of Italian forces at the Battle of Adowa in 1896 during the Scramble for Africa. It was also an opportunity for the Italians to satisfy the fascist objectives of imperial expansion. Despite militant protest and the actions of the League of Nations, the Italians occupied Ethiopia between 1935 and 1941.

This event had a great impact on African political consciousness and the growth of nationalism. It generated massive anti-imperialist and anticolonial sentiments throughout the African world, both within the continent and in the African diaspora in the Americas and Europe. This was because Ethiopia, Liberia, and Haiti were seen by African and black nationalists as islands of African freedom and independence and as exemplars of the African political capacity for self-rule in a sea of white colonial domination. From different parts of Africa and the black world including the U.S., Britain, and the West Indies, Africans provided funds, arms, ammunition, and other support for the Ethiopian resistance. This was a classic expression of practical Pan-Africanism. Partly as a result of this mobilization, Pan-African sentiments, views, and activities spread beyond the elite to the masses of Africans.

All these developments aroused a mass political consciousness and made the nationalist intelligentsia and their movements more geared to political militancy. This was aided by the third major political event of this period: World War II.

THE EMERGENCE OF MASS NATIONALISM: CONDITIONS AND CONSTRAINTS

The period after World War II saw the emergence of mass nationalism, the intensification of freedom struggles, labor agitation, popular protests, and armed struggles in some colonies. In other colonies, constitutional struggles and negotiations between nationalists and colonial authorities preceded the restoration of African independence. These developments were facilitated by a number of factors, including the emergence and maturation of the nationalist intelligentsia; the impact of World War II; the economic prostration of the imperial countries; the weakening of the political and moral confidence of the imperial powers; the formation of broader nationalist parties and movements; and the activation, incorporation, and participation of the masses in the nationalist struggles for independence.[4]

During World War II, European colonial powers intensified their exploitation of African human, agricultural, and mineral resources for the furtherance of the war. Large numbers of Africans were recruited into colonial armies and served in various parts of the world including Africa, Europe, and Asia. For instance, the British recruited 280,000 people from East Africa and 167,000 from West Africa. The French conscripted over 100,000 from West Africa alone. Thus, between these two colonial powers, nearly 500,000 Africans were recruited.

The war also required the increased production of export crops such as cocoa, palm products, rubber, timber, peanuts, iron ore, and coal. This intensified demand led to the construction or expansion of railroads, seaports, and airfields and the general expansion of economic activities in the African colonies. The labor for these activities was sometimes forced or involuntarily procured through colonial chiefs. The recruitment of soldiers, expansion of raw materials production, and construction of physical infrastructure generated employment opportunities and a small economic boom in the colonies. They also led to rapid urbanization by means of migration to towns where, despite all the economic activities, employment was still inadequate and social facilities, health care, and housing infrastructures were largely unavailable. Thus, those attracted to the opportunities in the town actually faced social deprivation and hardship. This situation was exacerbated by a shortage of food due to the focus on production of export crops and restrictions on the use of foreign exchange for the importation of consumer goods on which the colonized had become dependent. Consequently, there were shortages of foods and basic necessities like soap, oils, sugar, salt, and medicines in the urban centers and even rural areas. This situation led to scarcities and price inflation. Faced with these hardships, the people, especially the growing labor unions, organized popular protests and strikes. Labor activism expanded rapidly after the war.

In fact, after the war ended in 1945 and for the next few years, there were numerous strikes in various parts of Africa. These included the 1945 General Strike in Nigeria; the railway workers' strike in French West Africa in 1946; the mine and railway workers' strike in Zambia in 1945; the strikes in Tanganyika in 1947; the coal miners' strike in Enugu, Nigeria in 1949, in which twenty-one miners were killed; and several others in Kenya and Sierra Leone. There were also popular protests by the laboring classes, a prominent example being the Gold Coast demonstrations of 1948 during which protesters were killed. These actions often elicited colonial repression, but they also often won some concessions—no matter how small and grudging—from the colonial states which, in the postwar situation, were concerned about mobilizing African people and resources to pay for the reconstruction of their devastated societies. The strikes revealed the emergence of the working class as a powerful social and political force that would play a significant part in the postwar freedom struggles.

The war experience and postwar activities of the returning ex-servicemen also contributed to the growth of political consciousness and political militancy that fed into the nationalism of the period. These soldiers had seen service across the world; they had seen free and independent peoples, and they had seen Japan, a powerful non-European country, fighting against Europeans. They had also observed the nationalist freedom struggles in places like India, Pakistan, Ceylon, and Burma. All these experiences stimulated their desire for freedom.

In the actual theaters of war, they saw European soldiers and officers express normal human fear and saw them killed by African soldiers fighting in opposing armies. Thus, they began to see Europeans as normal human beings and not as superior or invincible beings, as they had been constructed and projected in the colonies. Also, living in European countries the soldiers saw all classes of Europeans: the unemployed, the poor, the middle classes, and the upper classes. This helped to destroy the erroneous impression that all Europeans were rich and authoritative as they seemed in the colonies. Lastly, the war itself, along with its destructiveness and savagery, raised questions about the alleged superiority of the Europeans who had clearly demonstrated their inability to resolve their conflicts without recourse to war. Taken together, these experiences were profoundly liberating psychologically, intellectually, and politically for the war veterans and the colonized in general. Consequently, when the soldiers returned home and began to face hardships due to the failure of the colonial governments to provide jobs and the promised entitlements, they often joined the nationalist movements and adopted a militant approach.

Internationally, the Atlantic Charter's declaration for the right of all peoples to determine the governments they will live under, the formation of the United Nations and its anticolonial orientation, and the emergence of the U.S. and the Soviet Union as superpowers with their own national political and economic agendas for global ascendancy—which differed from those of the European colonial powers—all helped to create a context in which the direct colonialism of the European variety began to seem less tolerable.

The nationalist forces of this period mobilized the labor movements, peasant farmers, war veterans, youth, market women, traders, and other interest groups with grievances against the colonial system. By attempting to advance and incorporate the social concerns of these groups and reaching out to various groups in different parts of the country, these political parties enlarged the ideological platforms of the nationalist struggles and became mass nationalist movements. These activities led to the expansion of the scope of nationalism in terms of territorial reach and social composition, which now became broader and more representative of the populace. Thus, even though they were still led by the reformist intelligentsia, mass nationalist movements were emerging. The nationalists used the enlarged constituency to intensify their struggles for political independence.

IMPEDIMENTS TO THE STRUGGLE FOR INDEPENDENCE

Although this period saw more concerted direct freedom struggles, it did not see a painless or one-way drive to independence. It saw all the twists and turns of major historical events, including heightened organization and forward movement; but it also saw uncertainties, hesitations, and deliberately-generated reactionary forces. In the anticolonial nationalist movement, this was exemplified by the emergence of competing political currents of divisive and subversive natures, including all manner of regional, ethnic, and religious movements. This often happened when a pan-territorial nationalist movement had become better organized and emerged as the ascendant political force and, therefore, a more formidable challenge against the colonial state. Ethnic, sectional, and religious groups that had no previous political agenda or direct involvement in the nationalist struggles were "suddenly" manufactured and brought into the political scene to compete against the pan-territorial nationalist movements and leaders. Since territorial national consciousness was still inchoate and evolving, it was easy to mobilize the primordial parochialisms of ethnicity, sectionalism, and religion against the broader nationalist movements. These new anti-national forces constituted major obstacles to the drive to unfettered independence. Indeed, they became constraints on the movements and to the postindependence nation-building processes.

A second profound challenge in the period leading up to independence was caused by counter-nationalist actions and by the terms of independence set by the colonial powers. On the one hand, the primary colonial powers in Africa, Britain and France, were shaken and weakened politically, economically, and morally by World War II. This removed the imperialist certitudes and confidence of the period of colonial conquest, domination, and consolidation up to the early 1930s. Weakened by the war, these imperial powers now directed their attention to the economic and social reconstruction of their devastated nations. Therefore, for them, the colonies became extremely important as sources of primary commodities, agricultural and mineral, for capital accumulation for national economic and social reconstruction.

This led the colonial powers, during the negotiations for independence, to insist on and require the protection of their economic interests by the maintenance of the African societies as captive suppliers of raw materials and importers of manufactured goods. The territorial nationalist movements and the mobilized masses were geared toward the recovery of independence as the all-consuming passion and fundamental concern. However, these groups were somewhat less focused on regaining total freedom—not only political, but also economic, social, and cultural. They therefore paid less than adequate attention to the full terms for the recovery of political independence. Hence, the colonial powers were able to create and insist on conditions in which African states won political independence without economic freedom. The African states were to pay a heavy price for this oversight. This was the origin of the neocolonial condition under which African states won independence but found themselves in conditions of economic dependency.

Despite these challenges, there is no question that the recovery of independence was an important victory and historic achievement for African peoples. It was a major contribution to the growth of freedom globally.

THE DRIVE TO INDEPENDENCE

As noted earlier, the period from the 1940s onward saw the rise of mass nationalist movements and focused nationalist struggles, which led to the emergence of numerous free African states in the 1960s—an era which can be rightly called the age of African political independence. However, as African countries were colonized at different times and nationalist movements emerged at different times, they also achieved their independence at different times.[5] This section outlines the main highlights of the drive to independence in selected countries chronologically, beginning with the earliest victories in North Africa.

NORTH AFRICA

The first major African colony to achieve independence was Egypt in 1922. This followed the struggles of the various secular and religious nationalist and protest groups which eventually formed a nationalist party, the Wafd, in 1918 under Zaghlul Pasha. Yet this independence was only nominal, since Britain had set conditions that made it the effective ruler of Egypt even though Egyptians now formally governed their state. This continued until the 1940s, when there was a revival of Egyptian nationalism. It was best illustrated by the coup d'etat led by Colonel

Gamal Abdel Nasser in 1952. The senior officer whom the young military nationalists installed as head of government, General Naguib, was removed in 1954. Colonel Gamal Nasser assumed leadership and expressed a radical nationalism that was strongly resented by the Western powers such as Britain, the U.S., France, and the new state of Israel. These powers came into conflict with Nasser. They sought to destroy him, the independence which he had shown, and the national pride which he had generated. Seeking to defend their revolution and to promote their nation's economic development, the Egyptians became allies of the Soviet Union, which provided them with military and economic support. Determination to destroy the Egyptian revolutionary government led to an invasion by Israeli forces, supported by Britain and France, in November 1956. While Egypt suffered considerable losses, it resisted valiantly and, hurt by international denunciations of their unprovoked aggression, the aggressors withdrew. Thereafter, Egypt emerged as a truly independent state.

Libya was the second North African colony to achieve independence. Libya was a former Italian colony, and arguments arose among the major powers over who should assume UN trusteeship over it after World War II. Britain and the U.S. made their interests known during these deliberations. The British, working with the aristocracy, granted Libyan independence in 1951 under King Idris, head of the Sanusiyya Brotherhood. This was clearly a compromised, incomplete, and unsatisfactory independence. Libyan middle-class nationalists campaigned for fuller independence and political modernization, which was partially realized in 1969, when young military nationalists under Colonel Muammar Gaddafi overthrew King Idris, established effective independence, and initiated a populist, Islam-based social revolution.

In Morocco, which was occupied by many French settlers and administered through the indirect rule system, the upsurge of nationalism was partly due to an informal alliance of Sultan Mohammed and the nationalist forces led by the Istiqlal (Independence) Party (1943). The

French, enraged by the sultan's alliance with the nationalists, deposed the sultan and exiled him to Madagascar. However, the sultan's popularity continued to soar, and France returned him after being pressured by the Algerian liberation war. Morocco became independent in 1956.

In Tunisia, the nationalist struggle, led by Habib Bourguiba and the Neo-Destour Party, grew stronger after the war. The movement received mass support from both urban and rural people who felt that independence was necessary for social betterment. The French, in typical fashion, resorted to oppression and violence. The Neo-Destour Party was banned in 1952, Bourguiba was detained, and attempts were made to destroy the trade unions. These actions stiffened Tunisian nationalist resolve and led to an armed struggle. Although organized by small groups, the struggle was sufficiently effective that the French brought in a large army. Due to the strength of the resistance and pressures on France in its other colonies in Africa and Asia, France was compelled to negotiate with Bourguiba and the Neo-Destour Party. In 1956, Tunisia won her independence.

The fiercest struggle for independence in North Africa took place in Algeria, as the French established it as a settler colony and considered it a province of France. The settlers, who were over one million strong by 1945, also received the best land, from which Algerians were expelled. Much land was also devoted to the cultivation of grapes for wine. This reduced the land available for food crops and made food supplies inadequate and expensive. All these conditions, combined with the settlers' intransigence, forced the Algerians to resort to armed struggle. Beginning in 1945, Algerian reformist nationalists campaigned unsuccessfully for civil, political, and social rights. Consequently, young nationalists formed the National Liberation Front (FLN). Led by war veterans like Ahmed Ben Bella, the FLN launched an armed struggle in 1954 and won mass support. The French eventually mobilized a large army that checkmated the FLN

African nations, with dates of independence.

in battle but did not defeat it. The FLN's popularity remained strong. The stalemate in the war, despite the French massive military presence, convinced the French of the need to negotiate. The settlers, feeling betrayed, engaged in terrorist acts in France, convincing Charles de Gaulle to negotiate seriously with the FLN. A cease-fire was declared in March 1962. After elections, which the FLN won resoundingly, Algeria became independent in July 1962.

WEST AFRICA

In British West Africa, there was a fairly common pattern in the advancement toward independence from the 1940s onward. Following nationalist agitation, the colonialists usually formulated constitutions that were often rejected by nationalists as inadequate, because they provided insufficient room for African "participation" in government. After further struggles and negotiations, "responsible" government was often conceded to the nationalists before independence was eventually won.

The first British West African colony to win independence was the Gold Coast in 1957. Independence was preceded by efforts of a reformist nationalist movement, the United Gold Coast Convention (UGCC), which was founded in 1946 by Dr. J. B. Danquah. The UGCC was a conservative and moderate elite party which was temperamentally, ideologically, and politically out of tune with the radicalized political attitudes of the times. The party was eventually displaced by a radical nationalist party, the Convention People's Party (CPP), led by Kwame Nkrumah, the UGCC's former secretary. Nkrumah had studied in the United States and was influenced by Marcus Garvey's militant Pan-Africanist ideas and activities. Nkrumah had had a distinguished Pan-African career in London and was involved in the Pan-African Conference in Manchester in 1945. The CPP had a populist political and ideological orientation, and it expanded to embrace the working class, the war veterans, the youth, the market women (traders), and even the unemployed youth derisively described by the elite as "Singlet Boys," referring to the inexpensive

V-necked T-shirts they commonly wore. With this broad social base, the CPP became a formidable challenge to the colonial authorities who blamed the political, economic, and social challenges of any organized group on CPP incitement. Consequently, following the violent general strike of 1950, Nkrumah was imprisoned. This merely increased his popularity and his reputation as a committed and fearless radical nationalist. In the 1951 elections, the CPP won resoundingly, gaining most of the seats in the legislature. Nkrumah was released and became a leader of government business. He led the Gold Coast to independence in 1957. The country's name was later changed to Ghana, in honor of the great empire of ancient Ghana.

The next colony to gain its independence was Nigeria. Its most important nationalist movement in the years after World War II was the National Council of Nigeria and Cameroon (NCNC), which was founded in 1944 at the instigation of younger activists who were tired of their elders debilitating intra-elite conflicts and of the neglect of the colonial enemy. It was led by veteran nationalist Herbert Macaulay and a younger militant reformist nationalist, Nnamdi Azikiwe. The NCNC spread nationalism across Nigeria. It mobilized the labor movement, war veterans, ethnic communities, town associations, social and cultural clubs, market women, other women's groups, urban elites, and politicized youths. Its Pan-Nigerian Tour of 1946, which took it to virtually all the provinces of colonial Nigeria, was the most extensive effort to propagate nationalism in the history of colonial Nigeria. Another major nationalist movement, which aided the expansion of Nigerian nationalism and added a dimension of radical militancy to the nationalist struggle, was the Zikist Movement, founded in 1946. This was the primary radical political movement of the early postwar period. It gradually transformed itself from a Pan-Nigerian militant nationalist movement into a radical populist, socialist-oriented movement. The Zikists used a strategy of "positive action," which included politicized strikes, civil disobedience, and sabotage. Its militant agitations, along with the NCNC's struggles, compelled the colonial government to draft a constitution in 1951. New regional parties emerged under this constitution: the Northern Peoples Congress (NPC) in the North and the Action Group in the West. The emergence of these sectional parties weakened the Pan-Nigerian drive to independence, as their sectionalist claims had to be accommodated. This undoubtedly delayed Nigeria's progress toward independence. Eventually, after several constitutional conferences, all the parties agreed on Nigeria's freedom, and the country became independent in October of 1960.

Sierra Leone, after similar constitutional struggles from the 1950s onward, became independent in 1961, led by the Sierra Leone Peoples Party (SLPP). Gambia, led by the People's Progressive Party (PPP), was the last British colony in West Africa to gain its independence, which was achieved in 1965.

FRENCH WEST AFRICA

The path to independence in the French West and Equatorial (Central) African territories was complicated by the French doctrine of assimilation and the French view of the colonies as being part of a Greater France that would ultimately be assimilated into French culture and society. While some African politicians subscribed to these views, others began to organize the political movements that eventually led to independence.

The major political movement in these territories was the Rassemblement Democratique Africain (RDA), formed in Bamako, French Soudan (Mali), in 1946. It was an inter-territorial movement that covered French West and Equatorial Africa. It was led by Felix Houphouet-Boigny of the Ivory Coast, Mamadou Konate of Mali, Leopold Senghor of Senegal, Sékou Touré of French Guinea, and Barthelemy Boganda of Central Africa (Ubangi Shari). The RDA struggled for basic political and civil rights such as the right to form trade unions, establish newspapers, form political parties, and end forced labor. French settlers and businessmen, supported by the French government, reacted strongly against this upsurge of African nationalism and tried to destroy the RDA.

The RDA continued the struggle, however, and demanded that French West Africa (with eight territories) and French Equatorial Africa (with four territories) emerge as two federated states with strong central governments. The French refused, since it was clear that such federations with large populations and territories would be difficult to control. In 1956, under the *loi cadre* or enabling law, the French transferred power from the central capitals in Brazzaville and Dakar to the individual territories that then controlled local affairs. This action weakened the drive to federation and encouraged the growth of territorial nationalism—both of which suited France's objectives.

Despite this setback, African nationalists continued the struggle, while France remained determined to prevent full independence. In 1958, the French president, General Charles de Gaulle, came up with the idea of a French Community under which the twelve territories would be given self-governments and responsibility for local affairs like education, health, and agriculture. France would remain responsible for such critical areas as finance, defense, and foreign affairs.

This plan proved attractive to some African nationalists. Those who accepted the plan would vote "yes" and become autonomous republics within the community, and those who opposed the plan would vote "no" and become fully independent nations while losing all French support. De Gaulle campaigned extensively for the "yes" vote and largely succeeded; all the colonies except one voted for the plan. French Guinea, led by the radical nationalist and labor leader Sékou Touré and his well organized political party, the PDG, voted "no." The French reaction was swift and spiteful. The French removed all mechanical and electrical fixtures, typewriters, tables, chairs, and file cabinets. They also stopped all aid in hopes of crippling the new state.

But Guinea survived with support from the new government of Ghana and the Soviet Union. Guinean independence came in 1958 in spite of French tantrums, and it affected the course of political developments in the region. Soon, all the countries that had voted "yes" demanded independence.

By 1960, all had gained independence, but the countries remained under the indirect control of France, as they had all signed agreements giving France supervision over their finances and foreign and military affairs, thereby creating a situation of neocolonialism. By the mid-1960s, all the West African colonies had become independent states. The Portuguese colonies were the only exception.

EAST AND CENTRAL AFRICA

In the British East and Central African colonies of Tanganyika, Uganda, Kenya, Nyasaland, and Southern and Northern Rhodesia, struggles for independence were complicated by the presence of European and Asian minority settlers. Together, these settlers controlled much of the best land and much of the economic life of the colonies. The European settlers also saw themselves as potential political successors to the colonial powers. Nevertheless, African movements for freedom emerged.

The first colony to recover its independence was Tanganyika. Its early proto-nationalist group was the Tanganyika African Association (TAA), which struggled for political and civil rights. In the postwar period, the TAA supported a general strike of the port workers, teachers, and salt and sisal workers. It also had close links with African cooperative societies, farmers, and pastoralists. The TAA was succeeded by a broader-based nationalist movement, the Tanganyika African National Union (TANU), formed in 1954 and led by the modest but astute and effective leader, Julius Nyerere. TANU established its presence across the country and applied the Nkrumaist strategy of positive action which served to increase activism. It attracted repressive responses from the colonial government, which banned TANU in eleven districts in 1958.

This merely increased the party's popularity. Nyerere also exploited Tanganyika's status as a UN trusteeship territory to advance the goal of independence. He sent proposals to a visiting UN delegation in 1954 and visited the UN headquarters to make his case. With TANU established as the uncontested nationalist party, the colonial government, in a classic display of colonialist bad faith, deployed the divide-and-rule tactic of promoting a so-called "multiracial" constitution which was intended to dilute TANU's power at the district and national levels. But this ploy failed; in the parliamentary elections of 1958, under the "multiracial" constitution, TANU won decisively, capturing all the African seats and some European and Asian seats. In 1961, Tanganyika won its independence.

In 1964, Tanganyika and Zanzibar formed the loose political union of Tanzania. This was after the island of Zanzibar recovered her independence from the British in 1963 and the African majority there carried out a military revolution that overthrew the Arab sultan. The new Tanzanian union was a testimony to Nyerere's commitment to Pan-African unity.

Uganda's path to independence was complicated by the heightened level of political, cultural, and religious divisions in the colony. In addition to the continued existence of precolonial entities, especially Buganda, whose king had received special treatment as a junior partner and collaborator with the British, the colony was afflicted with religious divisions and conflicts that impeded united action by nationalist politicians. These included differences between Muslims and Christians and between Catholics and Protestants. Thus, the nationalist parties that emerged in the 1950s, the Uganda National Congress (UNC) and the Democratic Party (DP), were sectional groups, even though the UNC had a broader national base. They could not agree on a form of government for postindependence-Uganda. Yet, in any event, the UNC—which had become the Uganda Peoples Congress (UPC) led by Milton Obote—aligned with the Bugandan royalist party to lead Uganda to independence in 1962. This compromise could not last long, however. The King and Kingdom of Buganda had been granted the right to operate a separate government distinct from the national government (in effect, a state within a state). This was clearly a recipe for future political conflict. Not surprisingly, as the government of Obote became more powerful, it dislodged the leadership and Kingdom of Buganda. Thus, Uganda achieved independence with major unresolved political and administrative problems.

The Kenyan struggle for independence involved a peasant armed struggle and negotiations between moderate African nationalists and the British government. The armed faction, known as Mau Mau, was led by the Kenya Land and Freedom Army and was a reaction against the economic exploitation and social deprivation perpetrated by the large European settlers who had expropriated African lands and turned the Kikuyu, Meru, and Embu into landless "squatters" and low-paid wage laborers so as to prevent African peasant farmers from competing with the settlers. This led to violent protests beginning in the 1940s, including labor strikes and the destruction of farm buildings, crops, and livestock intended to scare white farmers into leaving the country. As revolutionary actions intensified in the 1950s, the colonial government declared a State of Emergency, arrested well-known African nationalists, including Jomo Kenyatta, and brought in British troops. The Mau Mau struggles continued, though the movement suffered significant losses, and the British detention of Africans in concentration camps weakened the movement militarily. Yet the force of the resistance persuaded the British to accept the principle of majority rule. The State of Emergency was lifted in 1959, and the British negotiated with two new African parties, the Kenya African National Union (KANU) led by Jomo Kenyatta and the Kenyan African Democratic Union (KADU) founded by the radicals Oginga Odinga and Tom Mboya. Kenya became independent in 1963 under the moderate leadership of Kenyatta, its economic and social problems unresolved.

In the Central African colonies of Nyasaland, Northern Rhodesia, and Southern Rhodesia, the British and the white settler population attempted to prevent the emergence of African nationalism, majority rule, and independence by creating a large, rich, settler-dominated Central African Federation in 1956. This was used to entrench discriminatory laws and the disempowerment of Africans. The colonialist hope of African acquiescence and depoliticization was not realized. Instead, African political activism was reactivated and concerted struggles began. These were led in Nyasaland by the Nyasaland African National Congress, later the Malawi Congress Party under the physician and nationalist Dr. Kamuzu Banda, and in Northern Rhodesia by the Northern Rhodesia African National Congress, later the Zambia African National Congress led by Harry Nkumbula. Both parties intensified their struggles through strikes, demonstrations, and protests, which persuaded the British to accept the inevitability of independence. Following constitutional conferences, Nyasaland (Malawi) and Northern Rhodesia (Zambia) became independent in 1964.

In Southern Rhodesia, where Africans were faced with a determined white settler regime, the nationalist struggle was led by the African National Congress and later the Zimbabwe African National Union and the Zimbabwe African People's Union. These groups continued their struggles beyond the 1960s, and their full story belongs to the second wave of African nationalism.

The other Central African territories, including the Belgian Congo, Rwanda, and Urundi, were Belgian colonies. The Belgians did not expect or plan that these colonies would become independent in the foreseeable future. In the Congo, Belgium's primary colony, Africans had experienced the full weight of colonial depredations: economic exploitation, cultural domination, and racial discrimination. There was no political progress, and Africans worked only in the lowest levels of the civil service.

The small African intelligentsia of teachers, clerks, priests, and traders began to demand political liberalization and an end to racial discrimination. The Belgians responded with repression and then tried to channel the rising African activism into political participation in elections for town councils in the major cities. The elections spurred African political activity and the formation of numerous, mostly regional, parties such as the ABAKO of the

Bakongo led by Joseph Kasavubu, the CONAKAT of Katanga led by Moise Tshombe, and the MNC (Congolese National Movement) led by Patrice Lumumba which, although locally based, attempted to develop a colony-wide following. In this state of political and popular activation, popular protests exploded in Leopoldville in 1959 and included attacks on colonial institutions, Catholic missions, and European property. The Belgian government, shaken by these events, negotiated with the nationalists, and Congo became independent in 1960, with the conflict between regionalism and centralism unresolved.

The UN-mandated territories of Rwanda and Burundi, which has been under Belgian control, gained their independence in 1962. Accumulated intergroup antipathies, partly historical and partly fostered by colonial divide-and-rule policies, led to conflicts after independence.

SOUTHERN AFRICA

In southern Africa, the colonies included South Africa, the British protectorates of Basutoland, Bechuanaland, and Swaziland, and the UN Trusteeship Territory of South West Africa. The nationalist struggles in South Africa, as noted earlier, began early in the twentieth century. However, due to the British transfer of power to the settlers and the subsequent emergence of the apartheid state in 1948, the African struggles continued through the 1990s, when democratic majority rule was finally established. The character and strategies of the struggles changed during this long period. The details of these struggles and those of South West Africa against the white South African state belong to the second wave of African nationalism, from the 1960s to the 1990s.

In the case of Bechuanaland, Basutoland, and Swaziland, the British assumption was that they would ultimately be absorbed by South Africa. Yet the emergence of the apartheid state and its vigorous and unapologetic repression of the African majority, brutally manifested in the Sharpeville massacre of 1960, changed British political calculations. Thereafter,

political parties emerged in the territories, and negotiations led to the achievement of independence by Bechuanaland (Botswana) and Basutoland (Lesotho) in 1966 and by Swaziland in 1968.

CONCLUSION

The struggles of the various nationalist movements led to the achievement of independence by about forty African countries by the late 1960s. It has been shown that African nationalism began with political, economic, cultural, and religious protests by groups like the intelligentsia, laborers, farmers, traders, market women, and youth. These subsequently gelled into colony-wide nationalist movements led by the nationalist intelligentsia. The freedom movements derived their ideas from internal responses to colonial domination and from external sources including Pan-Africanism, Western liberalism, and Marxist radicalism. But the primary intellectual and ideological achievement of the nationalist intelligentsia was that, though they logically accepted Western ideas of the nation-state as the organizational form of postindependence polities, their nationalist assumptions and conceptions of the possibilities of nationhood differed fundamentally from the colonizers' assumptions and expectations. The colonizers saw and administered their colonies as incompatible agglomerations of discrete "tribal" entities that could not possibly emerge as nations. It was the nationalists who envisioned the fusion, political and cultural, of the various precolonial societies into coherent nation-states. Equally crucially, these African freedom movements that had organized colony-wide campaigns against colonialism began to arouse a common consciousness of colonial oppression and to infuse these colonial territorial shells with the cultural, social, and emotive aspects of nationhood.

As the imperial powers also had their designs, they countered the nationalist upsurge with violent repression and containment strategies. They created fissiparous social and political forces (ethnic, sectional, and religious) and disabling economic conditions that affected the freedom struggles and constrained the future of Africa. But the forceful pull of freedom compelled the nationalists to proceed to independence with these disabilities and without adequate preparation or vigilance, probably hoping to address the challenges of nationhood subsequently. Yet, limited as political independence was, the struggle was hard fought and hard won; and its historic significance in the annals of global struggles for human freedom should not be minimized. Frantz Fanon summarizes the extent and limits of any generation's understanding of the context and resources for its struggles:

Each generation must out of relative obscurity discover its mission, fulfil it, or betray it. In underdeveloped countries the preceding generations have both resisted the work of erosion carried out by colonialism and also helped in the maturing of the struggles of today. We must rid ourselves of the habit … of minimizing the actions of our fathers or of feigning incomprehension … They fought as well as they could, with the arms that they possessed then.[6]

REVIEW QUESTIONS

1. What is African nationalism and how did it evolve during the early phase of colonialism between the 1880s and 1920s?

2. Identify the various groups that contributed to the emergence of African nationalism and assess their relative contributions.

3. What forces and developments affected the growth of nationalism during the interwar years?

4. What internal and external factors contributed to the emergence of mass nationalism in the post-World War II period? How was this new mass nationalism expressed?

5. Describe in detail the struggles for independence in one region of Africa with particular attention to movements, strategies, leaders, and responses of the colonial states.

ADDITIONAL READING

Boahen, Adu, ed. *UNESCO General History of Africa, VII: Africa under Colonial Domination, 1880–1935.* Paris: UNESCO, 1990.

Davidson, Basil. *Modern Africa: A Social and Political History.* New York: Longman, 1989.

Hodgkin, Thomas. *Nationalism in Colonial Africa.* New York: New York University Press, 1957.

Frantz Fanon, *The Wretched of the Earth* (New York: Grove Press, 1968), 206–7.

Mazrui, Ali, ed. *UNESCO General History of Africa VIII: Africa Since 1935.* Paris: UNESCO, 1999.

NOTES

1. For the imposition of colonial domination and African resistance, see Adu Boahen, ed., UNESCO General History of Africa VII: Africa under Colonial Domination, 1880–1935 Abridged Edition, (Paris: UNESCO, 1989), Chapters 2–10; 1–19.

2. For the emergence and development of African nationalism, see Thomas Hodgkin, Nationalism in Colonial Africa (New York: New York University Press, 1957); J. Ayo Langley, Ideologies of African Liberation, 1856–1970: Documents on Modern African Political Thought from Colonial Times to the Present (London: Rex Callings, 1979); Basil Davidson, Africa in Modern History: The Search for a New Society (Harmondsworth: Penguin Books, 1978); Basil Davidson, Modern Africa: A Social and Political History 2nd ed. (New York: Longman, 1989).

3. For the political and economic developments of this period, see Boahen, ed., UNESCO General History of Africa VII: chapters 14, 22–27; Davidson, Modern Africa, 47–95; Kevin Shillington, History of Africa rev. ed., (New York: St. Martin's Press, 1995), 347–62.

4. For developments during and after World War II, see Davidson, Modern Africa, 62–95; Shillington, History of Africa, 364–72.

5. For exhaustive discussions of the drive to independence in the various regions and

countries of Africa, see Ali Mazrui, *UNESCO General History of Africa, VIII: Africa since 1935* (Paris: UNESCO, 1999), Chapters 5–10; Davidson, *Modern Africa* 101–64; Shillington, *History of Africa*, 373–397; Richard Olaniyan, *African History and Culture* (Lagos: Longman, 1982), 81–110; Ehiedu Iweriebor, *Radical Politics in Nigeria, 1945–1950: The Significance of the Zikist Movement* (Zaria: Ahmadu Bello University Press, 1996).

THE APARTHEID ERA, 1948–1978

BY LEONARD THOMPSON

After its initial victory in 1948, the National party consolidated its power. In that year it created new parliamentary seats for representatives of white voters in South West Africa (six in the House of Assembly and four in the Senate) who were elected to support the government. Then, step by step, it eliminated every vestige of black participation in the central political system. In 1956, after a long political and legal struggle, it dealt the Coloured votes in the Cape Province, most of whom had supported the United party, the same blow as the Hertzog government had dealt the African voters in 1936: it placed them on a separate roll and gave them the right to elect Whites to represent them in Parliament. Fourteen years later, it abolished the parliamentary seats of the white representatives of both African and Coloured voters.

For three decades, the National party had the support of the overwhelming majority of the Afrikaner people. In the election of 1966, it also began to win substantial support from English-speaking Whites, who were attracted by the government's determination to maintain control in the face of increasing black unrest and foreign criticism. It won successive elections by increasing majorities. The United party never recovered from its defeat in 1948. Once in 1959 its leaders actually tried to outbid the Nationalists in racism by rejecting the purchase of more land for Africans, whereupon its relatively liberal members broke ranks and founded the Progressive party. In 1977, a shadow of its former self, the United party dissolved. In the general election that year, the Nationalists won 134 seats in the House of Assembly, whereas the major opposition, the Progressive Federal party, won a mere 17 seats.

The National party used its control of the government to fulfill Afrikaner ethnic goals as well as white racial goals. It achieved a major ethnic objective in 1961 when, after obtaining a narrow majority in a referendum of the white electorate, the government transformed South Africa into a republic, thereby completing the process of disengagement from Great Britain. The government had intended to follow the precedent whereby India remained a member of the British Commonwealth when it became a republic. At a conference of Common wealth countries, however, the African members, supported by Canada as well as India, sharply criticized apartheid, and South Africa then withdrew from that loose association.

The government meanwhile Afrikanerized every state institution, appointing Afrikaners to senior as well as junior positions in the civil service, army, police, and state corporations. Medical and legal professional associations, too, came increasingly under Afrikaner control. The government also assisted Afrikaners to close the economic gap between themselves and English-speaking white South Africans. It directed official business to Afrikaner banks and allotted valuable state contracts to Afrikaners. Afrikaner businesspeople channeled Afrikaner capital into ethnic banks, investment houses, insurance companies, and publishing houses. By 1976, Afrikaner entrepreneurs had obtained a firm foothold in mining, manufacturing, commerce, and finance—all previously exclusive preserves of English-speakers. Whereas in 1946 the average Afrikaner's income had been 47 percent that of an English-speaking white South African, in 1976 it had risen to 71 percent and continued to rise thereafter.

The political successes of the National party were due in part to the rising standard of living of white South Africans of all classes. Except for recessions in the early 1960s and the late 1970s, the South African economy was buoyant. The value of South African output at 1970 prices grew from R 4,434 million in 1950 to R 15,474 million in 1979. The Whites were the principal beneficiaries. White farmers, most of whom were Afrikaners, received massive state support. They mechanized their farms and trebled their output, while the government assisted them to obtain and keep black wage laborers and to eliminate the vestiges of black occupation of white land as sharecroppers or renters.

The Nationalist government also gave fierce expression to its determination to maintain white supremacy in postwar South Africa. Much of its early legislation coordinated and extended the racial laws of the segregation era and tightened up the administration of those laws. The term *apartheid*, however, soon developed from a political slogan into a drastic, systematic program of social engineering. The man largely responsible for that development was Hendrik Frensch Verwoerd.

Verwoerd was born in the Netherlands in 1901 and migrated to South Africa in 1903 with his pro-Boer Dutch parents. Brought up in Cape Town, Southern Rhodesia, and the Orange Free State, he identified passionately with the Afrikaners. In private life he was charming; in public affairs, dogmatic,

intolerant, domineering, and xenophobic. After acquiring a doctorate in psychology at Stellenbosch, the premier Afrikaner university, and spending 1927 visiting German universities, he became professor of applied psychology at Stellenbosch. In the mid-1930s, he promoted the cause of the Poor Whites and opposed Jewish immigration from Nazi Germany. In 1937, he became founding editor of *Die Transvaler*, created with nationalist funds for the express purpose of rallying Transvaal Afrikaners to the party. By 1948, he was widely known as a fiery republican. Malan then made him an appointed senator and in 1950 minister of native affairs. He was prime minister of South Africa from 1958 until September 6, 1966, when, as he was about to make a major speech in Parliament, a deranged attendant stabbed him to death.

During Verwoerd's premiership, apartheid became the most notorious form of racial domination that the postwar world has known. The cabinet, with enthusiastic support from the rank-and-file members of the National party, tried to plug every gap in the segregation order. The process continued under Verwoerd's successor, B. J. Vorster, prime minister from 1966 to 1978. The Smuts government had interned Vorster during World War II because he was a general in the extra parliamentary Ossewa Brandwag (Oxwagon Sentinel), which opposed South Africa's participation in the war. Since 1962, he had been minister of justice in Verwoerd's cabinet.

The National party government applied apartheid in a plethora of laws and executive actions. At the heart of the apartheid system were four ideas. First, the population of South Africa comprised four "racial groups—White, Coloured, Indian, and African—each with its own inherent culture. Second, Whites, as the civilized race, were entitled to have absolute control over the state. Third, white interests should prevail over black interests; the state was not obliged to provide equal facilities for the subordinate races. Fourth, the white racial group formed a single nation, with Afrikaans- and English-speaking components, while Africans belonged to several (eventually ten) distinct nations or potential nations—a formula, that made the white nation the largest in the country.

Soon after coming to power in 1948, the government began to give effect to those ideas. The Population Registration Act (1950) provided the machinery to designate the racial category of every person. Its application led to the breaking up of homes; for example, where one parent was classified White and the other was classified Coloured. The Prohibition of Mixed Marriages Act (1949) and the Immorality Act (1950) created legal boundaries between the races by making marriage and sexual relations illegal across the color line. In 1953, after a court had ruled that segregation was not lawful if public facilities for different racial groups were not equal (as in waiting rooms at railroad stations), Parliament passed the Reservation of Separate Amenities Act to legalize such inequality.

As mentioned above, the National party used its majority in Parliament to eliminate the voting rights of Coloured and African people. During the 1950s, when the Nationalist party's majority in Parliament was still short of two-thirds, it enforced its will by a stratagem that circumvented the Constitution by packing the Senate (the upper house of Parliament) and the Appellate Division of the Supreme Court—South Africa's highest court. In 1951, it passed an act by the ordinary legislative procedure (that is, by simple majorities in each house, sitting separately) to remove Coloured voters from the common electoral rolls. The Appellate Division ruled that the law was invalid, because the Constitution required such an act to be passed by a two-thirds majority of both houses in a joint sitting. Parliament then passed another act by the ordinary procedure, purporting to transform Parliament into a High Court with the power to review and override such judgments of the Appellate Division. The Appellate Division ruled, however, that that act, too, was invalid, on the ground that the High Court was Parliament under another name. Foiled in that maneuver, in 1955 Parliament passed two more acts by the ordinary procedure: one adding sufficient nominated members to the Senate to give the government a two-thirds majority in a joint sitting, the other increasing the number of appellate judges from five to eleven. Finally, in 1956, a new act to revalidate the act of 1951 and deny the courts the power to inquire into its validity received a two-thirds majority in a joint sitting (thanks to the packed Senate), and the enlarged Appellate Division agreed that the act was valid. The government had used a blend of legalism and cunning to remove Coloured voters from the common roll.

The government also transformed the administration of the African population. In 1951, it abolished the only official countrywide African institution, the Natives Representative Council. Then it grouped the reserves into eight (eventually ten) territories. Each such territory became a "homeland" for a potential African "nation," administered under white tutelage by a set of Bantu authorities, consisting mainly of hereditary chiefs. In its Homeland, an African "nation" was to "develop along its own lines," with all the rights that were denied it in the rest of the country. The legislative framework, foreshadowed by Verwoerd, was completed in 1971, when the Bantu Homelands Constitution Act empowered the government to grant independence to any Homeland. Government propaganda likened this process to the contemporaneous decolonization of the European empires in tropical Africa (map 8).

The Transkei was the pacesetter for this process. The government made it "self-governing" in 1963 and "independent" in 1976. Bophuthatswana followed in 1977, Venda in 1979, and Ciskei in 1981. As they became "independent," their citizens were deprived of their South African citizenship. The Pretoria government also ensured that collaborative chiefs such as the Matanzima brothers in the Transkei controlled all the Homelands. KwaZulu, the most populous Homeland, was a partial exception. There, Chief Mangosuthu Buthelezi created a powerful political organization, Inkatha, refused to accept "independence" on the South African government's terms, and developed an ambiguous relationship with Pretoria.

Although the South African economy burgeoned in the 1950s and 1960s, the Homelands remained economic backwaters. Nearly every Homeland consisted of several pieces of land, separated by white-owned farms. Bophuthatswana had nineteen fragments, some hundreds of miles apart; KwaZulu comprised twenty-nine major and forty-one minor fragments. Verwoerd forbade white capitalists from investing directly in the Homelands, and the governments of the Homelands depended on subsidies from Pretoria. Under apartheid the condition of the Homelands continued to deteriorate. They could provide full subsistence to a smaller and smaller proportion of the African people. Consequently, the economic incentives for Africans to leave the Homelands, either as migrant laborers or permanently, grew more powerful than ever. The African people relied on wage labor in the great industrial complexes of the southern Transvaal and the Durban, Port Elizabeth, and Cape Town areas. Moreover, no foreign country recognized the sovereignty of the "independent" Homelands.

Apartheid included rigid and increasingly sophisticated controls over all black South Africans. The government tried to herd into the Homelands nearly all Africans, except those whom white employers needed as laborers. In 1967, the Department of Bantu Administration and Development stated this policy quite bluntly in a general circular: "It is accepted Government policy that the Bantu are only temporarily resident in the European areas of the Republic for as long as they offer their labour there. As soon as they become, for one reason or another, no longer fit for work or superfluous in the labour market, they are expected to return to their country of origin or the territory of the national unit where they fit ethnically if they were not born and bred in their homeland." To give effect to this policy in the towns, the government intensified its predecessors' attempts to limit the influx of rural Africans by prohibiting them from visiting an urban area for more than seventy-two hours without a special permit and by authorizing officials to arrest any African who could not produce the requisite documents. Every year, more than 100,000 Africans were arrested under the pass laws; the number peaked at 381,858 in the year 1975–76. The government also removed African squatters

from unauthorized camps near the cities, placing those who were employed in segregated townships, and sending the rest either to the Homelands or to farms where the white owners required their labor.

The government also began to eliminate "black spots" in the countryside—that is to say, land owned or occupied by Africans in the white areas. And since white farming was becoming largely commercial and mechanized, Africans lost their last land rights on white farms and many Blacks became redundant to the labor needs of farmers. The "surplus" Africans were expelled from the white rural areas, and, because they could not enter the towns, most were obliged to resettle in the Homelands, even if they had never been there before. In several cases, the government started new townships alongside existing urban complexes and treated them as parts of Homelands, as in Mdantsane in the Ciskei outside East London and Umlazi in KwaZulu outside Durban. In other cases, displaced people were congregated so densely in Homelands, far from the existing urban complexes, that they formed new townships. In 1980, in the tiny Sotho Homeland called QwaQwa, 157,620 Africans were trying to survive on 239 square miles.

In the cities outside the Homelands, the government transferred large numbers of Coloureds and Indians, as well as Africans, from land they had, previously occupied to new segregated satellite townships. Under the Group Areas Act (1950) and its many subsequent amendments, the government divided urban areas into zones where members of one specified race alone could live and work. In many cases, areas that had previously been occupied by Blacks were zoned for exclusive white occupation. Of the numerous removals effected under this act, one of the most notorious was Sophiatown, four miles west of Johannesburg center. Sophiatown was one of the few townships where Africans had owned land since before the Urban Areas Act (1923) put an end to African purchases. In 1955, the government removed the African inhabitants to Meadowlands, twelve miles from the city. Sophiatown was rezoned for Whites and renamed Triomf (Triumph). Another notorious removal was District Six, adjacent to the center of Cape Town, which had been the home of a vibrant Coloured community since at least the early nineteenth century. The homes were razed and the inhabitants relocated to the sandy, wind-swept Cape flats. In Durban, many Indians also suffered severely, losing homes and businesses, in areas zoned for Whites.

The government claimed that these removals were voluntary. In fact, it intimidated the victims and when they resisted used force. An African woman who had been moved to a Homeland told an interviewer: "When they came to us, they came with guns and police. ... They did not say anything, they just threw our belongings in [the government trucks]. ... We did not know, we still do not know this place. ... And when we came here, they dumped our things, just dumped our things so that we are still here. What can we do now, we can do nothing. We can do nothing. What can we do?"

One cannot know for sure how many Blacks were uprooted by those measures. The number was certainly vast. The Surplus People Project, which made a thorough study of the removals, estimated that 3,548,900 people were removed between 1960 and 1983: 1,702,400 from the towns, 1,129,000 from farms, 614,000 from black spots, and 103,500 from strategic and developmental areas.

The removals resulted in a great intensification of the overpopulation problem in the Homelands. At the time of the 1950 census, 39.7 percent of the African population of South Africa lived in the areas that became Homelands; in 1980, 52.7 percent was there. The Homeland population increased by 69 percent between 1970 and 1980, by which time the density of population in the Homelands was 23.8 per square mile, compared with 9.1 for all of South Africa, including the Homelands. In spite of all those removals, the African population of the towns continued to increase rapidly under apartheid, and so did the Coloured and Asian urban populations. By 1980, the towns were occupied overwhelmingly by Blacks. Their 4 million white inhabitants were greatly outnumbered by 6.9 million Africans, 2 million Coloureds, and 700,000 Indians.

By that time, the black urban settlements of the war years had expanded into vast "townships" adjacent to the major white "cities"—Johannesburg, Durban, Port Elizabeth, Pretoria, and even Cape Town where previously few Africans had lived. Hundreds of thousands of Africans had been born and bred in the towns, and nearly as many African women as men were living there. Still the government persisted in treating all urban Africans as visitors whose real homes were in the Homelands and whose real leaders were "tribal" chiefs. Moreover, the material gap between employed Africans and employed Whites increased significantly between 1948 and 1970, by which time white manufacturing and construction workers were earning six times as much as Africans and white mineworkers were earning no less than twenty-one times as much as Africans. In 1971 the real wages of African mineworkers were less than they had been in 1911. During the 1970s, African wages began to rise in response to competition among employers for experienced workers and vigorous African trade union activity—even though African trade unionism was illegal. The gap was down to 4.4 in manufacturing and construction and 5.5 in mining by 1982. But wage rates do not provide a complete picture of the condition of the Africans. Unemployment, always high among black South Africans, increased during the 1970s. South African economist Charles Simkins estimated that African unemployment almost doubled from 1.2 million to 2.3 Billion between 1960 and 1977, by which time perhap. 26 percent of Africans were unemployed. Consequently, Blacks experienced high levels of poverty, undernutrition, and disease, especially tuberculosis.

The government also intensified its control of the educational system. Although it treated Whites as a single entity in politics, in defense of Afrikaans culture it insisted on separation between Afrikaners and other Whites in the public schools. Building on the policy that J. B. M. Hertzog had initiated in the Orange Free State, the government maintained parallel sets of white public schools throughout the country and made it compulsory for a white child to attend a public school that used the language of the child's home—Afrikaans or English.

Previously, as we have seen, the government had left African education almost entirely to the mission institutions, whose capacity to meet the needs of the large African population was constrained by lack of funds, despite increasing public subsidies. This was unsatisfactory to the Nationalist government. It considered that the mission schools were transmitting dangerous, alien ideas to their African students and turning them, in Verwoerd's words, into Black Englishmen. As the economy expanded and became more sophisticated, moreover, industry required more literate workers than the mission schools could produce. Under the Bantu Education Act (1953) the central government thus assumed control of public African education from the provincial administrations, made it virtually impossible for nongovernmental schools to continue, and proceeded to expand African education while controlling it firmly. During the 1960s the government also assumed control over the education of Coloured and Asian children. Verwoerd was frank on the subject of African education" Native education should be controlled in such a way that it should be in accord with the policy of the state. ... If the native in South Africa today in any kind of school in existence is being taught to expect that he will live his adult life under a policy of equal rights, he is making a big mistake. ... There is no place for him in the European community above the level of certain forms of labour."

Under government control, the number of black children at school increased considerably. By 1979, 3,484,329 African children in the entire country including the Homelands (21.41 percent of the African population of the country) were officially listed as attending school. Substantial differences remained in the quality of education provided for different "races," however. Education was compulsory for white but not black children. White children had excellent school buildings and equipment; black children, distinctly inferior facilities. Most African children were in the pre-primary and the primary classes. In 1978, when there were five times as many African children as white children in South Africa, only 12,014 Africans passed the matriculation examination or its equivalent (similar to American graduation from high school), whereas three times as many Whites did so. The government spent ten times as much per capita on white students as on African students, and African classes were more than twice as large as white ones. Moreover, most teachers in African schools were far less qualified than the teachers in white schools; African teachers were paid less than Whites even when they did have the same qualifications; and they had to teach African schoolchildren from textbooks and to prepare for examinations that expressed the government's racial views. The white schools were also superior to the Coloured and Indian schools, though to a lesser extent.

The government imposed segregation in higher education as well. When the National party came to power in 1948, there were in South Africa four English-language universities, four Afrikaans-medium universities, one bilingual correspondence university, and the small South African Native College at Fort Hare. Though autonomous, all were largely dependent on government subsidies. The Afrikaans-medium universities and English-medium Rhodes University admitted white students only. Twelve percentof the students at the University of Cape Town and 6 percent of the studentsat the University of the Witwatersrand were black and were taught in integrated classes; 21 percent of the students in the University of Natal were black and were taught in segregated classes.

In 1959, brushing aside large-scale student and faculty opposition in the English-medium universities, Parliament passed the Extension of University Education Act, which prohibited the established universities from accepting black students except with the special permission of a cabinet minister and led to the foundation of three segregated colleges under tight official control for Coloured, Indian, and Zulu students and another one for African students in the Transvaal. At the same time, the government took over the South African Native College at Fort Hare, fired the principal and seven senior staff members, and made it a college for Xhosa students, Subjecting it to the same controls as the other black colleges. By 1978, nearly 150,000 students were enrolled in universities in South Africa, 80 percent of them White.

From 1948 on, "Whites Only" notices appeared in every conceivable place. Laws and regulations confirmed or imposed segregation for taxis, ambulances, hearses, buses, trains, elevators, benches, lavatories, parks, church halls, town halls, cinemas, theaters, cafes, restaurants, and hotels, as well as schools and universities. It was also official policy to prevent interracial contacts in sport: no integrated teams and no competitions between teams of different races in South Africa, and no integrated teams representing South Africa abroad. Although no legislation was specifically designed to give effect to this policy, the government was able to keep sports segregated under other legislation, such as the Group Areas Act. Verwoerd even tried to prohibit Blacks from attending church services in white areas and moderated his demands only when Geoffrey Clayton, Anglican archbishop of Cape Town, died of a heart attack after signing a letter saying he could not counsel members of his church to obey such legislation.

The government also established tight controls over the communications media. The South African Broadcasting Corporation (SABC), a public corporation controlled by government appointees, had a monopoly on radio broadcasting and on television when it began to operate in South Africa in 1976. Chaired by Piet J. Meyer, who had been interned as an Ossewa Brandwag leader during World War II, the SABC became an instrument of official propaganda. Other government-appointed bodies exercised wide powers of censorship. In 1977, for example, they banned 1,246 publications, 41 periodicals, and 44 films. Most of those banned publications were books and pamphlets dealing with such radical opposition movements as the African National Congress, so that it became difficult

for South Africans to find out what opposition movements were doing and thinking.

The impact of the Nationalist regime on the mentality of Afrikaners was profound. Their language was unique, and most Afrikaners experienced little but the Nationalist world perspective from cradle to grave: at home, in Afrikaans-language schools and universities, in Dutch Reformed churches, in social groups, on radio and television, and in books and newspapers. In particular, their schools imbued them with a political mythology derived from a historiography that distorted the past for nationalist purposes. For example, it made heroes out of the border ruffians who were responsible for the Slagtersnek rebellion in 1815, and it associated God with the victory of the Afrikaner commando over the Zulu at the battle of Blood River on December 16, 1838.

The Nationalist government inherited a substantial coercive apparatus from its predecessors. It expanded that apparatus prodigiously. Among its first punitive laws was the Suppression of Communism Act (1950), which defined communism in sweeping terms and gave the minister of justice summary powers over anyone who in his opinion was likely to further any of the aims of communism. The minister could "ban" a person and prevent him or her from joining specified organizations, communicating with another banned person, or publishing anything at all; or he could confine the person to his or her house without the right to receive visitors. The minister did not have to give reasons for his decision, and the victim had no legal means of challenging it.

The repressive legislation escalated from the mid-1950s onward. The catalog includes the Riotous Assemblies Act (1956), the Unlawful Organizations Act (1960), the Sabotage Act (1962), the General Law Amendment Act (1966), the Terrorism Act (1967), and the Internal Security Act (1976). That mass of legislation gave the police vast powers to arrest people without trial and hold them indefinitely in solitary confinement, without revealing their identities and without giving them access to anyone except government officials. The government could ban any organization, prohibit the holding of meetings of any sort, and prevent organizations from receiving funds from abroad. There were also laws giving the government special powers over Africans, such as the Bantu Laws Amendment Act 1964), which empowered the government to expel any African from any of the towns or the white farming areas at any time. The Public Safety Act (1953) included a provision that empowered the government to declare a State of emergency in any or every part of the country and to rule by proclamation, if it considered that the safety of the public or the maintenance of public order was seriously threatened and that the ordinary law was inadequate to preserve it. Most of those repressive laws barred the courts from inquiring into the ways in which officials used their delegated powers. Although some judges sought to protect individuals by finding humane interpretations in the laws, their capacity to do so was very limited. To administer the laws of apartheid, the bureaucracy grew enormously. By 1977, about 540,000 Whites were employed in the public sector (including the central, provincial, and homeland governments, the local authorities, the statutory public bodies, the railways and harbors service, and the postal service), and Afrikaners occupied more than 90 percent of the top positions. The vast majority of the white bureaucrats were ardent supporters of apartheid. Most of the black bureaucrats, numbering about 820,000 were reliable servants of the regime on which they depended for their livelihood.

To enforce the laws of apartheid, the government had powerful resources. Few black civilians were licensed to carry firearms, whereas most white men and many white women possessed firearms and were experienced in using them. The South African police force was well trained and equipped. In 1978, it had 3 5,000 members (55 percent of them white) and 31,000 reserves. The police force included a security branch, which was responsible for interrogating political suspects and frequently resorted to torture.

Whereas the police were relatively few in proportion to the population, the Nationalist government embarked on a massive program of military expansion. In 1978, defense absorbed nearly 21 percent of the budget and 5.1 percent of the gross national product. By that time, every young white man was subject to two years' compulsory military service, and the active duty defense force comprised 16,600 permanent members (about 5,000 c whom were black) and 38,400 white conscripts. There were also 2,55,000 white citizen reserves. The police and the army, navy, and air force were well armed. ARMSCOR, a state corporation, and its subsidiaries manufactured a high proportion of the country's military needs, including armored cars, mortars, guns, bombs, mines, fighter aircraft, missiles, and tear gas and napalm. Local production was supplemented by military hardware and technology imported from Europe, the United States, Israel, and Taiwan. The flow continued, mainly from Taiwan and Israel, despite the international arms embargo imposed by the United Nations in 1977. South African armed forces were far the most powerful and disciplined in Africa south of the Sahara.

APARTHEID SOCIETY

South Africa in the apartheid era was unique. It became increasingly distinctive from other countries as decolonization and desegregation spread elsewhere. South Africa was a partly industrialized society with deep divisions based on legally prescribed biological criteria. As the economy expanded, industry absorbed more and more black workers, but racial categories continued to define the primary social cleavages.

Possessing privileged access to high-level jobs and high wages, white South Africans were as prosperous as the middle and upper classes in Europe and North America. Characteristically, they owned cars and lived in substantial houses or apartments in segregated suburbs, with black servants. The state provided them with excellent public services: schools and hospitals; parks and playing fields; buses and trains; roads, water, electricity, telephones, drainage, and sewerage. Social custom, reinforced by the official radio and television and the controlled press, sheltered them from knowing how their black compatriots lived. Few Whites ever saw an African, a Coloured, or an Asian home. Fewer still spoke an African language. Wherever White encountered Black, White was boss and Black was servant. Indeed, Whites were conditioned to regard apartheid society as normal, its critics as communists or communist-sympathizers.

Public services for Blacks were characteristically inadequate or nonexistent. In the Homelands, women still walked miles every day to fetch water and firewood; in the towns, people crowded into single-sex compounds, leaky houses, or improvised shacks. Schools, hospitals, and public transport for Blacks were sharply inferior. Electricity, running water, public telephones, sewage systems, parks, and playing fields were rare.

Besides their common lot as victims of apartheid, Blacks had varied experiences. Black residents of the cities, the white farming areas, and the African Homelands had vastly different lives. The government accentuated black ethnic differences, favoring Coloureds and Indians over Africans and encouraging internal ethnic divisions among Africans. The government also promoted class divisions among Blacks. It supported collaborators and provided relative security of urban residence for some Africans, whereas it kept African laborers tied to white farms and made it illegal for Africans to leave their Homelands, except as temporary migrant workers.

There is a story to be told by social historians of the ways in which black people not only survived under apartheid but also created their own social and economic worlds. In the urban ghettos, Africans mingled, regardless of ethnicity. For example, they ignored the government's attempt to carve up the townships into ethnic divisions; they married across ethnic lines; and members of the younger generation identified themselves as Africans (or even, comprehensively, as Blacks, thus including Coloureds and Indians) rather than as Xhosa, Zulu, Sotho, Pedi, or Tswana. The story will also emphasize the achievements of African women, who were particularly insecure, since the

law codified the inferior status that they had had in precolonial custom and applied it to the very different circumstances of a capitalist state. Under apartheid, African women, many of them heads of households as a result of the persistence of male migrant labor, held the fabric of African society together.

Social historians will also record the experiences of African children under apartheid. In a report for the United Nations Children's Fund, Francis Wilson, an economic historian, and Mamphela Ramphele, a doctor, drew attention to the fact that "children may be socialized into vandalism or find themselves having to adopt violent measures as a matter of survival and, in the process, losing any sense of right and wrong. The impact on children's minds and values of the physical violence that they witness and erience, not least at the hands of the police, is a matter of grave concern." Wilson and Ramphele also emphasized "the widespread disorganization of family life due to the migratory labour system" and the political, economic, and social powerlessness experienced by a large proportion of black South African men, which engenders a frustrated rage that all too often manifests itself in domestic violence, particularly against women.

These generalizations can be illustrated in the fields of wealth and health. As we have seen, under apartheid there were huge differentials in the wage rates of white and black workers, and although those began to narrow in the 1970s, they remained high, and black unemployment rose to extraordinary levels. Economic inequality has existed everywhere in the modern world, but nowhere was it as great and as systematic as in apartheid South Africa. A University of Cape Town economist stated in 1980 that of ninety countries surveyed by the World Bank, South Africa had the most inequitable distribution of income. Estimates by the World Bank and the Ford Foundation showed that the top 10 percent of the population received 58 percent of the national income and the lowest 40 percent received 6 percent.

The Second Carnegie Inquiry into Poverty and Development in South Africa revealed that nearly two-thirds of the African population had incomes below the Minimum Living Level (MLL), defined as the lowest sum on which a household could possibly live in South African social circumstances. African conditions were worst in the places where the government had relocated the largest number of displaced people—notably, QwaQwa, with a population density of 777 per square mile in 1980. Throughout the Homelands, the land was eroded, people were deriving little income from agriculture, and over four-fifths of the people lived below the MLL. In the white farming areas, most black men, women, and children worked for a pittance. In the cities, the wages of some employed Africans were actually below the MLL, and unemployment was high and rising. There was also a vast shortage of housing for Blacks. In Soweto, with a population of over one million by 1978, seventeen to twenty people were living in a typical four-room house; in Crossroads, outside Cape Town, there were more than six people to a bed.

Under apartheid, there were intense contrasts in the health of the different sections of the South African population. White South Africans, like Europeans and North Americans, had a low infant mortality rate (14.9 per thousand live births in 1978) and a long life expectancy (64.5 years for males and 72.3 years for females in 1969–71). Their diseases were those of the industrialized countries—including the highest rate of coronary heart disease in the world—and they enjoyed some of the highest standards of health care in the world. Ninety-eight percent of the medical budget was spent on curative rather than preventive services, and most of it was consumed by white patients. Doctor Christiaan Barnard performed the world's first heart transplant operation at Groot Schuur Hospital in Cape Town in 1968, and there were many transplants in later years, almost exclusively for white recipients. Medical education concentrated on the problems of the white population. The vast majority of doctors were white, and the medical schools were not substantially changing the balance. At the end of 1980, 657 white, 52 African, 62 Indian, and 18 Coloured medical students qualified as doctors.

The government did not keep detailed medical statistics for Africans. In urban areas, black infant mortality rates and life expectancies improved substantially during the 1960s and 1970s, but there was no discernible improvement in the Homelands. The official estimate of the African infant mortality rate in South Africa as a whole in 1974 was 100 to 110 per 1,000, which was worse than every country in Africa except Upper Volta (now Burkina Faso) and Sierra Leone. In South Africa as a whole, the Coloured infant mortality rate was 80.6 per 1,000 and the Indian rate was 15.3 per 1,000 in 1978. Mortality rates for both African and Coloured children aged one to four years old were thirteen times as high as for Whites. The principal cause of these exceptional infant and child mortality rates was inadequate nutrition. An Institute of Race Relations survey revealed in 1978 that 50 percent of all the two- to three-year-old children in the Ciskei were undernourished and that one in ten Ciskeian urban children and one in six Ciskeian rural children had kwashiorkor (a severe protein deficiency disease) and/or marasmus (a wasting disease ultimately induced by contaminated food and water). Official life expectancy figures for Africans were not available in the apartheid period, but official estimates (almost certainly overestimates) put them at 51.2 for males and 58.9 for females in 1965–70.

The principal African diseases were those common in third world countries: pneumonia, gastroenteritis, and tuberculosis (TB). Apart from kwashiorkor, TB, which is closely associated with poor socioeconomic conditions, was the most important cause of severe morbidity and death for the African population. According to official statistics, in 1979 there were 45,000 reported cases of TB in South Africa, 78.5 percent of them African, 18.5 percent Coloured, 1.5 percent Indian, and 1.5 percent White. Unofficial estimates are much higher. The head of the Community Health Department at the South African medical school for Africans said that in 1982, 110,000 people had active TB in South Africa, while about 10 million had it in dormant form, and that 82 percent of these were Africans.

Moreover, though TB was decreasing among Whites (whose children were routinely inoculated against it), it was increasing among Blacks. Other infectious diseases included typhoid fever (more than three thousand cases reported annually), typhus, measles (which was often fatal among under-nourished children), and rheumatic fever. Venereal diseases were prevalent. There were also epidemics of cholera, polio, and bubonic plague, while trachoma was endemic in the northern Transvaal. Many mine workers suffered disabling injuries or contracted lung diseases. In all these cases, the incidence was higher among Africans than among Coloureds and Asians, and far higher than among Whites.

Apartheid society was also ridden with mental stress and violence. Suicides were exceptionally frequent among white South Africans. Murder was a frequent cause of death among Africans and Coloureds. South African society was very different from the benign picture produced by the government's information services and presented by official guides to foreign visitors.

ADAPTATION AND RESISTANCE TO APARTHEID

There were always some members of the enfranchised population of South Africa who sought to arouse the conscience of their fellow Whites against apartheid. They focused on the gulf between the theory of apartheid (separate freedoms) and its practice (discrimination and inequality) and on the brutality of the apartheid state—the pass laws, forced removals, house arrests, and detentions without trial.

Soon after the election of 1948, leaders of all the white South African churches except the Dutch Reformed churches issued statements criticizing apartheid. In following years, many clergy came into conflict with the government. In 1968, the South African Council of Churches labeled apartheid a pseudo-gospel in conflict with Christian principles. Initially, nearly all the Afrikaner clergy were united in support of apartheid. But in 1962, C. F. Beyers Naude, a leading Broederbonder and former moderator of the principal Dutch Reformed church in the Transvaal, broke ranks and founded the Christian Institute, which brought black and white Christians of various denominations together, launched a Study Project on Chris-tianity in Apartheid Society (SPROCAS), and espoused increasingly radical responses to official policies. The government banned Naudé and the institute in 1977, but by that time apartheid was a controversial issue within the Dutch Reformed churches, and in 1978 a group of Afrikaner clergy produced a radical critique of apartheid.

The English-medium universities, especially the Universities of Cape Town and the Witwatersrand, were foci of opposition to apartheid. The National Union of South African Students (NUSAS), founded in 1924, organized a series of spectacular demonstrations in 1959 against the closure of the established universities to black students and in 1966 arranged for a visit by Sen. Robert Kennedy, who denounced apartheid in rousing speeches. In 1973, the government banned eight NUSAS leaders on the ground that they endangered internal security, and the following year it prohibited NUSAS from receiving funds from abroad. Nevertheless, NUSAS continued to introduce fresh generations of white (predominantly English-speaking) students to critical thinking about South African politics andsociety. In the late 1970s, NUSAS organized conferences on the theme "education for an African future."

Apartheid also brought into being a women's organization, the Black Sash. The white, mainly English-speaking, middle-class members of the Black Sash devised a skillful method of embarrassing Nationalist politicians and attracting media attention. Wearing white dresses with black sashes, they stood silently with heads bowed in places where politicians were due to pass, such as the entrance to Parliament buildings. The government banned such demonstrations in 1976, but the Black Sash remained in existence, running offices that gave legal advice to Africans who fell foul of the apartheid laws.

Authors, too, were exposing the effects of apartheid. Alan Paton, who in 1947 had written the best-selling *Cry, the Beloved Country*, calling for humane race relations, published a series of pungent criticisms of apartheid in the 1950s and 1960s. "God save us all," he wrote, "from the South Africa of the Group Areas Act, which knows no reason, justice, or mercy." By the 1970s, such authors as Andre Brink, Nadine Gordimer, J. M. Coetzee, and Athol Fugard were demonstrating the destructive effects of South African racism in perceptive novels and plays. Other white critics included lawyers who deplored the disregard for human rights and the rule of law; historians who recalled that apartheid was an attempt to reverse the process of economic integration that had operated in South Africa for over three hundred years; and an archaeologist who declared, "Science provides no evidence that any single one of the assumptions underlying South Af-rica's racial legislation is justified." Furthermore, the "Native Representatives" who sat in Parliament until that form of representation was abolished in 1960 and Helen Suzman, the only Progressive party member of Parliament from 1961 to 1974, vigorously opposed every racially opressive bill.

Nevertheless, before the late 1970s no powerful economic interest was fundamentally opposed to apartheid. White industrial workers benefited from an economic system that gave them a virtual monopoly not only of skilled jobs and high wages but also of workers' legal participation in the industrial bargaining process. White bureaucrats depended on a system that provided them with sheltered employment. Farmers, too, had reason to be satisfied with a government that gave them generous subsidies and ensured their supply of cheap black labor, and then helped them to dispose of it when there was a surplus.

The relation between mining and industrial capitalism and apartheid is a highly controversial subject. Some have argued that capitalism was inexorably opposed to apartheid and that economic growth was bound to erode and destroy it; others have charged capitalists with being the real creators and sustainers of apartheid. Each argument draws attention to one part of the complex reality. On the one hand, it was white South African politicians, organized in an ethnic party that excluded most major capitalists, who devised and enforced apartheid. On the other hand, though apartheid imposed costs on the different sectors of business, also benefited all of them, and although they criticized specific actions of the government, all sectors accommodated apartheid before 1978.

The behavior of Harry Oppenheimer, the South African financial giant, was most ambiguous. In 1957, he succeeded his father as head of the great global "empire" that included the Anglo American Corporation and De Beers Consolidated Mines. "It controlled forty percent of South Afrca's gold, eighty percent of the world's diamonds, a sixth of the world's copper and it was the country's largest producer of coal." He subsidized the Progressive party, which was launched in 1959, recommended the incorporation of educated Africans into the political system, and through the Urban Foundation, established in 1976, contributed to welfare projects in African urban areas. Yet he had no respect for African culture and, though admitting that the migrant labor system was bad in principle, treated it as essential for the gold-mining industry.

The behavior of manufacturing industrialists, too, was most equivocal. As manufacturing became more diversified and sophisticated, it was increasingly hampered by the small size of the domestic market for its products, by the shortage of skilled workers, and by the inefficiency of black workers through their lack of education. By the late 1960s, not only the Federated Chamber of Industries, which represented the English-speaking manufacturers, but also the Afrikaanse Handelsinstituut, the organization of Afrikaner businesspeople, were criticizing aspects of influx control, the industrial color bar, and the black educational system as obstacles to the creation of a skilled black work force. Nevertheless, manufacturing was expanding and making substantial profits throughout the period in spite of the: constraints imposed by apartheid. Industry, moreover, had relatively little influence in government circles, compared with mining, agriculture, and white labor, and its leaders, like other white South Africans, believed in white supremacy. Consequently, although they pressed for economic reforms within the apartheid framework, even the manufacturing industrialist stopped short of working for changes in the political system before 1978.

Lacking substantial support from the other side of the color line, black South Africans continued to face immense odds in coping with their erstwhile conquerors. Poor, unarmed, and insecure, most experienced life as a continuous struggle for survival. For many Africans, success involved adapting to apartheid by circumventing the law, living in the informal economy, or acquiring a powerful patron—a chief or a white person. Other Africans found a niche in the formal economy as teachers, nurses, or industrial workers. Such people ceased to be marginal. They formed the nucleus of an African middle class and an African working class.

Needled by the increasing brutality of the government and inspired by contemporary events in tropical Africa and other parts of the world, black leaders gradually transcended their regional, ethnic, and class divisions and devised more effective means of mobilizing the masses and confronting the regime. Soon after the National party came to power, a new generation took control of the African National Congress, spurred by the wartime protests in Johannesburg and the miners' strike of 1946. In 1949, the nnual conference elected three members of the Youth League to the national executive: Walter Sisulu (b. 1912), Oliver Tambo (b. 1917), and Nelson Mandela (b. 1918). All three were from the Transkei and had attended mission schools. Both Tambo and Mandela had been expelled from Fort Hare, but they had later qualified as lawyers by correspondence at the University of South Africa and shared a practice in Johannesburg. Mandela was the dominant personality in the group. A member of the Thembu ruling family in the Transkei, he was a man of powerful physique, commanding bearing, sharp intelligence, and deep commitment

to the cause of African liberation. Three years later, the conference elected Albert Lutuli as president-general of the ANC. Born in about 1898, Lutuli bridged the old and new elites. He was the elected chief of a small Zulu community in Natal, a teacher at Adams College (the leading African high school in Natal), a polished orator in English and in Zulu, a devout Christian, and a man of impeccable moral character.

In 1952, the ANC and the South African Indian Congress, which had undergone a similar change of leadership, launched a passive resistance campaign that attracted wide support. Large numbers of volunteers defied discriminatory laws and eight thousand were arrested. The ANC called off that campaign early in 1953, however, after rioting had broken out in Port Elizabeth, East London, Cape Town, and Johannesburg and Parliament had enacted severe penalties for civil disobedience.

In 1955, the ANC formed a coalition representing a broad spectrum of South African society to organize a campaign designed to enlist the participation of the black masses and win the sympathy of the outside world. With the cooperation of the South African Indian Congress, the South African Coloured People's Organisation, the small, predominanty white Congress of Democrats, and the multiracial South African Congress of Trade Unions, the ANC convened a Congress of the People. On June 26, 1955, 3,000 delegates (over 2,000 Africans, 320 Indians, 230 Colóureds, and 112 Whites) met in an open space at Kliptown near Johannesburg and adopted a Freedom Charter before the crowd was broken up by the police.

The Freedom Charter was destined to endure as the basic policy statement of the ANC. It was drafted by a small committee, including white members of the Congress of Democrats, after numerous individuals and committees in various parts of the country had submitted lists of grievances. The charter started with the ringing assertion that "South Africa belongs to all who live in it, black and white, and that no government can justly claim authority unless it is based on the will of the people." It then set out a list of basic rights and freedoms, derived largely from ideas then current in liberal circles in Britain, continental Europe, and the United States: equality before the law; freedom of movement, assembly, religion, speech, and the press; the right to vote and to work, with equal pay for equal work, a forty-hour work week, a minimum wage, annual leave, and unemployment benefits; free medical care and free, compulsory, and equal education. The Freedom Charter also included some socialist ideas: "The mineral wealth beneath the soil, the banks and monopoly industry shall be transferred to the ownership of the people as a whole," and "Restriction of land ownership on a racial basis shall be ended, and all the land re-divided amongst those who work it." But it made a concession to advocates of group rights: "There shall be equal status in the bodies of the state, in the courts, and in the schools for all national groups and races." Critics noted the inconsistencies in the document. Liberals as well as government supporters raised the specter of communism; radicals deplored the concession to "national groups."

The government responded by enacting further repressive legislation, and in December 1956 it arrested 156 people and charged them with high treason, in the form of a conspiracy to overthrow the state by violence and replace it with a state based on communism. The court was not persuaded that any of the accused had planned to use violence, but the trial dragged on, preoccupying the leadership, until March 1961, when the last thirty were found not guilty.

Though the ANC and its allies in the Congress movement were all male-dominated organizations, Lilian Ngoyi and other women had formed the Federation of South African Women, which organized protests against the decision of the government to extend the pass laws to African women. The demonstrations culminated on August 9, 1956, when 20,000 African women assembled outside the Union Buildings—the national administrative headquarters in Pretoria—delivered a petition to the empty prime minister's office, and stood in silence for thirty minutes. Two years later the police arrested two thousand African women for refusing to accept passes. Nevertheless, the government stood by its decision and from 1961 African women were obliged by law to carry passes. Other protests were reactions against specific local events. African men and women in the townships around Johannesburg and Pretoria, for example, boycotted the bus company for raising the fares and walked up to twenty miles a day to and from their work between January and April 1957.

Failure to modify government policy caused frustration and divisions of opinion among politically conscious black South Africans. Whereas Lutuli, Mandela, and their colleagues continued to work for a reconciliation between the races in South Africa, others contended that the alliance with the white-dominated Congress of Democrats had impeded the ANC, as is shown by what they regarded as a concession to white interests in the Freedom Charter. They wanted a purely African movement, dedicated to the emancipation of the African population. An African journalist struck a popular note when he wrote: "The masses do not hate an abstraction like 'oppression' or 'capitalism'. … They make these things concrete and hate the oppressor—in South Africa the White man." With such forces behind him, Robert Sobukwe emerged as an alternative to the Lutuli-Man-dela leadership. Sobukwe, a powerful orator, was born in Graaff-Reinet in the eastern Cape Province in 1924. He was educated at Fort Hare and was a Bantu language instructor at the University of the Withwaterand. He did not hold the extreme views of some of his followers. Ultimately, according to Sobukwe, Whites might become genuine Africans; but since they benefited from the existing social order, they could not yet identify with the African cause.

Failing to gain control of the ANC, the Africanists under Sobukwe broke away in 1959 and founded the Pan-Africanist Congress (PAC). On March 21, 1960, upstaging the ANC, they launched a campaign against the pass laws. Large numbers of Africans assembled at police stations without passes, inviting arrest in the hope of clogging the machinery of justice. At the police station at Sharpeville, near

Johannesburg, the police opened fire, killing 67 Africans and wounding 186, most of whom were shot in the back. In the following weeks there were widespread work stoppages, and disturbances in various parts of the country. In Cape Town, on March 30, a crowd of Africans, estimated at between 15,000 and 30,000, marched in orderly procession to the center of the city, near Parliament, which was in session; but the police assured their leader, a twenty-three-year-old university student named Philip Kgosana, that the minister of justice would receive him that evening if he would persuade the people to return home. He told them to go, and they did so. That evening, when Kgosana reported, the police arrested him.

As the disturbances mounted, the government struck back fiercely. It declared a state of emergency, mobilized the army reserves, outlawed the ANC and the PAC, and arrested 98 Whites, 90 Indians, 36 Coloureds, and 11,2,79 Africans. The police jailed another 6,800 people, including the PAC leaders, as well as beating hundreds of Africans and compelled them to return to work. These measures broke up the campaign. They also deprived Africans of the last chance of organizing lawful, peaceful, countrywide opposition to apartheid and forced the ANC leaders underground to reconsider their strategy and goals.

The year 1960 was a watershed in modern South African history. Previously, nearly every ANC leader had been deeply committed to non-violence. But nonviolent methods had achieved nothing except a series of defeats at the hands of a violent state. In those circumstances, the ANC concluded, and the PAC agreed, that South Africa was not like India, where passive resistance had persuaded the British to quit. As Mandela put it in 1964, when he was on trial for sabotage after his eventual arrest: "We of the ANC had always stood for a non-racial democracy, and we shrank from any policy which might drive the races further apart than they already were. But the hard facts were that fifty years of non-violence had brought the African people nothing but more and more repressive legislation, and fewer and fewer rights. … [I]t would be unrealistic and wrong for African leaders to continue preaching non-violence

at a time when the Government met our peaceful demands with force."

The first attempts to meet state violence with revolutionary violence were not successful. Umkhonto we Sizwe (The Spear of the Nation, the militant wing of the ANC), Poqo (Pure, the militant wing of the PAC), and the African Resistance Movement (a multiracial organization consisting mainly of young white professionals and students) made over two hundred bomb attacks on post offices and other government buildings and on railroad and electrical installations near the main industrial centers. The government succeeded in breaking the three organizations, however. The police forces achieved a major coup in July 1963, when they arrested seventeen Umkhonto leaders in a house near Johannesburg. By the end of 1964, the first phase of violent resistance was over, and for another decade the country was quiescent. Mandela and Sisulu were serving life sentences on Robben Island four miles from Cape Town. Sobukwe, too, was jailed on Robben Island until 1969, when the government released him but kept him politically impotent by banning him; he lived in Kimberley until his death in 1978. Tambo escaped the net and settled in Lusaka, Zambia, where he became acting president-general of the ANC after the death of Lutuli in 1967.

Quiescence did not mean acquiescence. Three significant developments fueled a spirit of resistance until it broke out in massive confrontations in 1976. First, there was a vigorous movement in the arts. During the late 1950s and early 1960s, the Johannesburg magazine *Drum* was a vehicle for black criticism of apartheid. During the late 1960s and early 1970s, copies of books that were published overseas, such as Bloke Modisane's *Blame Me on History* and Alex La Guma's *A Walk in the Night*, and the poetry of Dennis Brutus, evaded the censors and brought a strong liberationist message to the townships. A popular black theater movement made a strong impact on the Witwatersrand and in Durban. As Nomsisi Kraai wrote in the newsletter of the People's Experimental Theatre, "Black theatre is a dialogue of confrontation, confrontation with the Black situation."

Second, the rapid growth of the economy, involving a vast increase in the number of black semiskilled as well as unskilled workers, led to the development of class consciousness among black workers and the creation of an effective black trade union movement, despite its exclusion from the formal bargaining process. The year 1973 marked the beginning of a wave of strikes with demands for higher wages and improved working conditions.

Third, the government's attempt to mold the minds of young black people through tight control over their education boomeranged. Black students were profoundly frustrated by the conditions in their schools and colleges. In 1968 Steve Biko, a twenty-two-year-old student, led a secession from the white-controlled National Union of South African Students to found the exclusively black South African Students Organisation (SASO). SASO declared that all the victims of white racism should unite and cease to depend on white organizations that claimed to work for their benefit. As Biko wrote in 1971:

> Black consciousness is in essence the realisation by the black man of the need to rally together with his brothers around the cause of their subjection—the blackness of their skin—and to operate as a group in order to rid themselves of the shackles that bind them to perpetual servitude. It seeks to demonstrate the lie that black is an aberration from the "normal" which is white. … It seeks to infuse the black community with a new-found pride in themselves, their efforts, their value systems, their culture, their religion and their outlook to life. The interrelationship between the consciousness of self and the eman cipatory programme is of paramount importance. Blacks no longer seek to reform the system because so doing implies acceptance of the major points around which the system revolves.

Blacks are out to completely transform the system and to make of it what they wish.

The ideology of Black Consciousness penetrated the urban schools. On June 16, 1976, thousands of black schoolchildren in Soweto demonstrated against the government's insistence that half of their subjects be taught in Afrikaans—as they saw it, the language of the oppressor. The protests became nationwide after the police shot and killed a thirteen-year-old African student during the demonstration. The government reacted brutally. By February 1977, according to an official commission of inquiry, at least 575 people had been killed, including 494 Africans, 75 Coloureds, 5 Whites, and 1 Indian. Of the victims, 134 were under age eighteen. During 1977, the government also banned SASO and all its affiliated organizations. and jailed numerous black leaders. Police arrested and killed Steve Biko. He died from brain damage caused by injuries to his skull. After inflicting the injuries, police transported Biko naked in the back of a van for 750, miles on the night before he died.

After those events, thousands of young black South Africans fled the country and received military training in camps in Tanzania and Angola. The militant wings of the ANC and the PAC planned to infiltrate trained men and women into South Africa from the north, attack police stations, ex plode bombs in public places, deposit caches of arms, and, ultimately, launch a guerrilla war.

SOUTH AFRICA IN THE WORLD

The postwar world was quite a different place from the imperialist world of the 1930s. While apartheid was taking root in South Africa, political power was flowing in the opposite direction in the rest of Africa. In 1957, following the decolonization of its Asian territories, Britain transferred power to African nationalists in the Gold Coast (Ghana), soon to be followed by the other British territories in West Africa— Sierra Leone, Nigeria, and the Gambia. In 1960, the French relinquished political control over their two federations of colonies in west and central

Africa, and the Belgians withdrew from the Congo (Zaire), their vast territory in central Africa.

By that time, African nationalism had swept eastward and southward into the British territories where there were significant pockets of white settlers. Early in 1960, Prime Minister Harold Macmillan of Britain toured tropical Africa and then visited South Africa. On February 3, in the Parliament in Cape Town, he spoke of "the wind of change" that was sweeping over the continent and made it clear that Britain would not support South Africa if it tried to resist African nationalism. Over the next four years, the British transferred power to local nationalist parties in Tanganyika (Tanzania), Uganda, Kenya, Malawi, and Northern Rhodesia (Zambia). In 1965, the white settler government of Rhodesia postponed a similar outcome by asserting sovereignty over the colony and making a unilateral declaration of independence. No country recognized Rhodesian independence, however, and local Africans resorted to guerrilla warfare against the regime. Between 1966 and 1968 Britain transferred power to Africans in three other neighbors of South Africa—Basutoland (Lesotho), Bechuanaland Protectorate (Botswana), and Swaziland. Successive governments in Pretoria had tried to persuade London to allow South Africa to incorporate those three territories, as had been envisaged by the South Africa Act of 1909. But after 1961, when South Africa became a republic and left the Commonwealth, incorporation was no longer possible.

African nationalism continued to transform the Southern African region. In 1974, African resistance to Portuguese colonialism led to a coup in Lisbon, and the following year Angola and Mozambique gained independence. By 1978, the white settler regime in Rhodesia was barely surviving a fierce civil war and international sanctions, and South Africa was controlling Namibia only by defying the United Nations.

The United Nations differed from its predecessor, the League of Nations. Whereas the European powers had dominated the League of Nations, which the United States never joined, the Soviet Union and China, as well as France, Britain, and the United States, had permanent seats and vetoes in the U.N. Security Council, and other countries, including third world countries, served in turn on the Security Council and formed a majority in the General Assembly. From 1952 onward, the General Assembly passed annual resolutions condemning apartheid. Then, as the number of independent Asian and African states increased, each with a seat in the General Assembly, the United Nations devoted more and more attention to racism in South Africa. By 1967, the General Assembly had created both a Special Committee on Apartheid and a Unit on Apartheid, which issued a stream of publications exposing and denouncing the effects of South Africa's racial policies. The General Assembly also declared that South Africa's mandate over South West Africa (Namibia) was terminated and established a U.N. Council for Namibia. In 1971, the International Court of Justice gave an advisory opinion to the effect that South Africa's control of Namibia was illegal. Two years later, the General Assembly declared apartheid to be "a crime against humanity." In 1977, after South Africa's police were known to have killed Steve Biko and its government had suppressed numerous anti-apartheid movements, the Security Council unanimously voted a mandatory arms embargo against South Africa. That was the first time the United Nations had done that to a member state.

In 1963, meanwhile, independent African states founded the Organization of African Unity (OAU), which set up a Liberation Committee with headquarters in Dar es Salaam, Tanzania. The Liberation Committee established camps for refugees from South Africa and provided them with education and military training. But although the new African regimes earnestly desired to eradicate apartheid, they lacked the means to do so. They were weak regimes, preoccupied with survival. Singly or in combination, they could not match South Africa's military power. In varying degrees all of South Africa's neighbors were economically dependent on South Africa. Lesotho was exceptionally vulnerable. Entirely surrounded by South Africa, its main source of income came from the wages its peoplearned in white South African mines and factories and on white South African farms. Even Zambia imported food from South Africa and ex ported half of its copper—the source of 95 percent of its export earnings—via South African rail roads and South African ports.

Down to 1978, international opposition to apartheid, though strong in rhetoric, was weak in substance. The South African government mustered an effective response to the challenges resulting from changes in the world order. The response included skillfully formulated ideological components. As decolonization swept through tropical Africa, Verwoerd present ed his Homelands policy as an analogous process. In 1961, he told a London audience:

> We do not only seek and fight for a solution which will mean our survival as a white race, but we seek a solution which will ensure survival and full development—political and economic— to each of the other racial groups. ... We want each of our population groups to control and to govern themselves, as is the case with other Nations. ... In the transition stage the guardian must teach and guide his ward. That is our policy of separate development. South Africa will proceed in all honesty and fairness to secure peace, prosperity and justice for all, by means of political independence coupled with economicinterdependence.

Above all, South African foreign propaganda was well tuned to the cold war fears and prejudices of Europeans and Americans. It portrayed South Africa as a stable, civilized, and indispensable member of the "free world" in its unremitting struggle against international communism. Moscow's aim was world domination. The imperial powers were leaving tropical Africa open to communist infiltration. The ANC was a communist organi zation, directed by Moscow. Communists were responsible for the uprisings of 1960 and 1976—77. For domestic consumption, this formula was accompanied by the assurance that the interests of the white population were the first priority of the government. "Our motto," said Verwoerd, "is to maintain white supremacy for all time to come over our own people and our own country, by force if necessary."

How real was the "communist menace"? The Soviet Union and its Eastern European satellites, especially East Germany, did indeed cham pion the interests of the third world against Western imperialism. They supplied arms to resistance movements in colonial Angola, Mozambique, and Rhodesia. In Rhodesia, however, the Soviets supported the weaker of the two African movements, whereas its communist rival, China, supported Robert Mugabe's Zimbabwe African National Union (ZANU), which triumphed in the election held on the eve of the independence of what had been Rhodesia in 1980.

When the Portuguese left Angola in 1975, the Soviet Union armed and transported Cuban troops to help the Popular Movement for the Liberation of Angola (MPLA) consolidate its control over rival African nationlist organizations and to resist an invasion launched by the South African army in collusion with the United States. The Soviet Union and its allies also had close links with the ANC. They provided education and military training for South African refugees, and they were the main suppliers of arms for the military wing of the ANC that began to infiltrate guerrillas into South Africain the late 1970s. Moreover, the ANC included communists in its ranks and among its leaders.

Yet Southern Africa never had high priority on the Soviet agenda. Moscow was mainly concerned with preserving its hegemony in Eastern Europe, defending its border with China, and increasing its influence in Southeast Asia and the Horn of Africa. It was not practicable for Moscow to risk a military confrontation with the Western powers in distant Southern Africa. The level of Soviet trade with Southern Africa was insignificant: so was the level of its aid to the black Southern African states. The ANC, moreover, was an open organization and its top leaders—Nelson Mandela and Oliver Tambo—were not communists. At minimal cost, the Soviet Union was deriving advantages from the equivocation of the Western powers in the face of the rampant racism and discriminatory state cap italism of South Africa. Pretoria's rhetoric against communism was a skill ful attempt to divert attention from the domestic causes of black resistance in South Africa. Black South Africans needed no foreign indoctrination to oppose apartheid.

The South African regime also benefited from material factors. After World War II, technological developments were drawing the world to gether and the capitalist world economy was becoming increasingly integrated. South Africa possessed a distinctive place in it as the producer of a wide range of valuable minerals, which accounted for about three-quarters of South Africa's foreign exchange earnings. In 1979, according to the U.S. Bureau of Mines, besides producing 60 percent of the world's annual sup ply of gold, South Africa produced significant quantities of four minerals that were essential for Western industry and defense: 47 percent of the world's platinum group of metals (which are used as catalytic agents for refining petroleum and for reducing automobile emissions) and 33 percent of the world's chromium, 21 percent of the world's manganese, and 42 percent of the world's vanadium (some of which are indispensable in the production of steel). South Africa was known to contain vast reserves of all those minerals. And South Africa was still the world's major producer of gem diamonds and a producer of significant quantities of asbestos, coal, copper, iron, nickel, phosphates, silver, uranium, and zinc.

The South African economy was extremely attractive to American and European business and defense interests. In 1948, Britain, the former colo nial power, had far the largest foreign stake in the South African economy, put in the 1950s and, particularly, during the boom years of the 1960s and early 1970s, American and continental European trade and investments grew spectacularly. By 1978, the United States had surpassed Britain as South Africa's principal trading partner and the Japanese as well as the Europeans were trading with South Africa on an increasing scale. By then, too, $26.3

billion of foreign capital was invested in South Africa. About 40 percent of the total was British capital, 20 percent was American, and 10 percent was West German, while the Swiss and the French contributed about 5 percent each. About 40 percent of the total consisted of direct investment in the South African subsidiaries or affiliates of American companies, such as Ford, General Motors, Mobil, and Caltex Oil, and 60 percent of the total consisted of indirect investment—American and European bank loans, and shares in South African gold-mining and other stock.' The returns on foreign investment were high. American returns averaged over 15 percent in 1970–74, declined to 9 percent in 1975, and rose again to 14 percent in 1976—78.

The South African economy was not autarchic. It was vulnerable in three respects. First, it required considerable infusions of foreign capital. Second, except in mining, South Africa did not possess the latest technology and needed to import heavy machinery and electronic and transportation equipment. Third, South Africa produced no natural oil. Nevertheless, except for brief periods after the disturbances following the Sharpeville killings in 1960 and the Soweto uprising in 1976, the United States and Western Europe provided the necessary capital and equipment, and although the Organization of Petroleum Exporting Countries (OPEC) imposed an oil embargo on South Africa in 1973, it was unable to enforce it, and most of South Africa's oil came from Iran until the fall of Reza Shah Pahlavi in 1979. To reduce its dependence on imports, the government meanwhile created a stockpile of petroleum products, and by 1978 it was producing more than 10 percent of South Africa's domestic consumption of gasoline in two large oil-from-coal plants created by a state corporation, the South African Coal, Oil and Gas Corporation (SASOL).

In those circumstances, powerful interests in the United States and Western Europe were loath to disturb the status quo in South Africa. With their cold war perspective they were prone to exaggerate the communist menace, and with their business perspective they tended to assume that economic growth was bound to erode apartheid.

Great Britain had especially close ties with South Africa, even after 1961, when South Africa became a republic and left the Commonwealth Tens of thousands of white South Africans were born in Britain, hundreds of thousands had relatives and close friends there, and the culture or English-speaking white South Africans was oriented toward Britain. The South African economy also meant far more to Britain than to any other country. In 1978, Britain was responsible for about 40 percent of all foreign investment in South Africa and a considerable share of the trade. About 10 percent of British overseas direct investment was in South Africa, and British banks—Standard Chartered and Barclays International—controlled 60 percent of South African bank deposits. Some South African émigrés, white as well as black, organized a vigorous antiapartheid movement in Britain, but from 1965 until 1980 Britain's concern in SouthernAfrica was focused on the Rhodesian problem, since white Rhodesa's unilateral declaration of independence was an act of rebellion. British administrations, Conservative as well as Labour, joined in the antiapar-theid rhetoric, but even Labour vetoed resolutions for sanctions in the Security Council, except in 1977, when Britain abstained on the resolution for an arms embargo against South Africa. South Africa's other major European trading partners— West Germany, France, and Switzerland—were also disinclined to risk their growing trade and investments in SouthAfrica by taking action against apartheid.

Relations between South Africa and the United States became more important as British power ebbed. The South African economy meant far less to the United States than to Britain and accounted for only about 1percent of American foreign trade and investment. Nevertheless, some sectors of American business were profitably involved in South Africa, and the Pentagon deemed it essential to have access to South Africa's strategic minerals. Although few South Africans had American origins, as the civil rights movement registered gains in the United States, black American leaders began to identify with black South Africans and to lobby against apartheid.

Under Dwight D. Eisenhower (1953–61), the United States continued to treat South Africa as an ally regardless of its racial policies. The Pen tagon and the Central Intelligence Agency (CIA) had contacts with South Africa's military and security services. As a producer of uranium, South Africa became a member of the International Atomic Energy Board and joined the United States in nuclear research, and an American firm built South Africa's first nuclear reactor. The adverse effects of the Sharpeville episode of 1960 were short-lived. The United States voted for U.N. con demnation of apartheid, but business quickly resumed as usual, and that December the National Aeronautics and Space Administration (NASA) ob tained an agreement to set up three tracking stations in South Africa. The Kennedy and Johnson administrations (1961—69) were more critical of apartheid and committed the United States to stop selling arms to South Africa, but they continued to reject proposals for economic sanctions, and the implications for South Africa of Lyndon Johnson's support for civil rights at home were overshadowed by the Vietnam War.

Under Richard Nixon and Gerald Ford (1969–77) there was a distinct tilt away from the antiapartheid lobby and the relatively liberal Africa Bureau in the State Department toward the Pentagon and big business. In1969, Henry Kissinger, Nixon's national security adviser, ordered a review of American policies throughout the world. The administration chose thesecond of five options outlined in the Southern African review, National Security Study Memorandum 39, which reasoned,

The whites are here [that is, in Southern Africa] to stay and the only way that constructive change can come about is through them. There is no hope for the blacks to gain the political rights they seek through violence, which will only lead to chaos and increased opportunities for the communists. We can, through selective relaxation of our stance toward the white regimes, encour age some modification of their current racial and colonial policies and through more substantial economic assistance to the black states ... help to draw the two groups together and exert some influence on both for peaceful change. Our tangible interests form a basis for our contacts in the region, and these can be maintained at an acceptable political cost.

That memorandum led to increased official contacts with white South African officials, pro-South African U.N. votes, and the appointment of an ambassador to South Africa who showed minimal concern for the lot of black South Africans and was reported to have gone hunting on Robben Island with political prisoners as beaters.

The Carter administration (1977–81) tilted in the opposite direction. It considered South Africa to be a liability to the Western alliance rather than an ally. It believed that the future lay with black nationalists and that the United States had an interest in coming to terms with them. Vice-President Walter Mondale would even tell Prime Minister John Vorster that America supported the principle of majority rule with universal suffrage—the ANC formula—one person, one vote.

THE RISE OF THE APARTHEID STATE, 1936–1976

By John A. Williams

The course of South African history from 1936 to 1976 is one of sweeping and complex transformation. At the beginning of the period, South Africa had begun to industrialize, yet it was basically a poor country. The African majority had lost a large proportion of its traditional land and resources and was only partially integrated into the modern wage economy. Many Africans had to participate in both modern and traditional economic sectors to earn even an inadequate living. The few who had gained a prosperous foothold in the modern economy were increasingly undermined by hostile government legislation. But poverty also touched large elements of the white population. By 1976 South African destitution had not been eliminated but redistributed. Poverty among whites had substantially vanished, but it had deepened among wide segments of the burgeoning black population.

Meanwhile, a vast bureaucratic state had grown up, one dedicated to broad control of the entire society. This surge to centralized wealth and power was accompanied by intensifying white domination. Although segregation, racial prejudice, and oppression had long been a fact of life, white rule in the second half of the twentieth century became efficient, thorough, and often brutal. In particular, whites increasingly denied the aspirations of the small but growing African elite.

We can cast such changes in terms of the defeat of liberalism. White liberals took a paternalist, gradualist, legalist, and optimistic approach to defending African interests. Their paternalism led them to counsel Africans against militant action, lest African protest inflame white opinion and frustrate the liberals' task. Their gradualism offered token political and social rights for Africans only after a long, slow process of acculturation. Their admonishment to Africans, "not now," did not immediately differ from what the supporters of baaskap told Africans: "Never." Their emphasis on legal procedures revealed a determination to work within the system, no matter how biased it was against nonwhites. Their optimism led them to accept such defeats as the passage of the Native Trust and Land Act and Representation of Natives Act in 1936, even though these measures segregated South Africa more thoroughly than ever, further closed the land market to Africans, and repealed the limited African vote in the Cape Province.

Despite these setbacks, the period of the Second World War (1939–1945) gave liberals a glimmer of hope. Faced with wartime labor needs, the government dropped some restrictions on African economic opportunity, and African movement into urban jobs accelerated. Segregation, said Prime Minister Jan Smuts, had fallen on evil days. But white liberals in the United party—the coalition party that had formed in 1934 out of Smuts's South African party and Hertzog's National party—could not sustain these advantages after the war.

By the mid-1940s, the old African National Congress alliance with white liberals had come under heavy attack from within ANC ranks. A new generation of activists, led by Nelson Mandela and Oliver Tambo, founded the Congress Youth League and challenged the older leadership. In 1949 a compromise candidate, Dr. J. S. Moroka, replaced the old-guard figure, Dr. A. B. Xuma, as president of the ANC; three years later, Chief Albert Luthuli began his fifteen-year presidency committed to decisive protest action. By then the ANC had fully rejected the gradualist and legalist counsels of white liberals, though it retained its full commitment to nonviolence. It sought full exercise of political and civil rights for all Africans. At the same time, a strong strain of "Africanism" in the Congress Youth League implied that Africans might reject the universalist principle of liberalism that presumed a common basis for the rights of all human beings. Throughout the 1950s, a struggle between Africanism and universalism would rage within the ANC. The group's 1955 Freedom Charter signaled a decisive victory for universalism, as the ANC remained committed to an alliance between like-minded people of all races. The opponents of this universalist commitment seceded in 1959 and formed the Pan Africanist Congress (PAC).

During these years, Afrikaner nationalists had grown more militant. When the National and South African parties fused in 1934, not all Nationalists had agreed to this merger. A small group instead formed the "Purified" National party. Closely associated with it were other Afrikaner organizations, especially the secret Afrikaner Broederbond and the Ossewa Brandwag (Oxwagon Sentinel), which later became a quasimilitary, profascist organization. During the Second World War, Afrikaners in the Broederbond and Ossewa Brandwag worked for the victory of Nazi Germany. (A number of leaders within the two groups, including Hendrik Verwoerd, had been educated in Nazi Germany and admired Nazi ideas.)

In 1948 the National party stunned South Africa by taking power in that year's general elections. The key campaign slogan of the election encapsulated in a new word, apartheid. At first no one fully knew what the term would mean, but planners and theorists at Afrikaner universities and within the Broederbond were working to define it. In the forty-two turbulent years from 1948 to 1990, apartheid became synonymous with racist oppression. It was that and much more: a complex system of social engineering created by a vast network of laws and bureaucratic mechanisms. Apartheid provided for systematic racial separation to be applied to all imaginable aspects of life. Based on a version of Calvinist theology, apartheid ostensibly offered Afrikaners—and, theoretically, peoples such as the Zulu or Sotho—a free space to enjoy full national rights within South Africa.

As enacted in legislation in the thirty years after 1948, the apartheid system enveloped all aspects of South African life. The keystone of the system was the Group Areas Act of 1950, which built on earlier land legislation and separated the entire country into unequal black and white areas. The forcible relocation of people under its provisions formed one of the most oppressive aspects of the system. A second crucial piece of legislation came with the Population Registration Act of 1950, which required every person over the age of sixteen to register and carry an identity card as a member of a particular race. A huge bureaucracy carried out and enforced this system.

The secret to enforcing this system of racial groups and group areas lay in the pass laws, which required Africans to carry a reference book to prove their right to be in areas of the country set aside for whites. Africans found in white urban areas without passes were sent back to the countryside, or "endorsed out"; the government carried out three hundred thousand or more pass-law prosecutions annually during the height of apartheid. In addition, an elaborate system of job allocation reserved skilled and highly paid jobs for whites.

In the quest for thorough separation of the races, the government between 1951 and 1956 attacked and destroyed the remaining common-roll franchise of the Cape Coloured people. At the same time, the National party government abolished remaining indirect representation of Aricans in the government by proposing to give Africans full political rights outside the white-dominated state. The administration proceeded to develop the African reserves into homelands, which would eventually become separate independent nations for Africans. Thus members of African nations, such as Xhosa or Zulu, would lose their South African citizenship and become citizens of their homeland nations. The chief architect of this plan, Henrik Verwoerd, first as native minister (1948–1958) and then as prime minister (1958–1966), contended that this policy would provide liberty and justice for all. Critics pointed out the fraudulent nature of this independence, which established "countries" for over 80 percent of the population on only 13 percent of the land area of South Africa.

The social engineers of apartheid took over the entire system of mission education of Africans and consigned it to the Bantu Affairs department. Bantu education sought primarily to give Africans sufficient training so that they could satisfy the labor needs of the white-dominated economy. Nevertheless, primary education—and eventually secondary and higher educational institutions— were extended on a "tribal" basis to serve the needs of the "independent" nations being developed in the homelands.

The apartheid system also regulated interracial social contacts. The Immorality Act of 1950, which strengthened an earlier law, proscribed interracial sexual relations, and the Prohibition of Mixed Marriages Act (1949) outlawed marriages between individuals with different racial classifications. These laws were an important expression of white fears, but for Africans they proved relatively minor irritants in the overall system of oppressive legislation. In the mixed neighborhoods of the Western Cape, however, where racial identities were ambiguous, these laws at times inflicted considerable personal hardship.

Apartheid's creators defended the system as a manifestation of the will of God and dealt with their opponents harshly. Under a sequence of mandates— the Suppression of Communism Act (1950), the Terrorism Act (1967), the Internal Security Act (1976), and others—all avenues of legal recourse were closed off for anti-apartheid organizations. The first act not only outlawed the Communist party but created a vague standard for the prosecution of individuals whom the government deemed to be furthering the goals of communism. Later provisions established the principle of banning for individuals and organizations and repeatable six-month imprisonment in solitary confinement without charges. Eventually, the enforcers of apartheid went beyond such oppressive rulings to assume powers with no basis at all in statute law.

Despite such harsh and determined measures, apartheid did not go unchallenged. The ANC-led Defiance Campaign of 1952 ended with the government's enacting draconian punishments for any symbolic breaking of the law. After 1952 the struggle continued in many arenas: resistance to the destruction of urban neighborhoods, such as Sophiatown, Cato Manor, and District Six; bus boycotts; demonstrations against the application of the pass system to women; and protest against the repeal of the Cape Coloured vote in the Cape Province. When the ANC-led Congress Alliance met in 1955 to draft the Freedom Charter, the fundamental statement of principle for the anti-apartheid movement, the government responded immediately by accusing one hundred and sixty-two people of high treason. Even though they were all acquitted, the trial tied down the opposition in legal battles for six years.

In 1960, following the split between the ANC and the PAC, the PAC launched its anti-pass campaign. The government responded with force, killing sixty-eight demonstrators at Sharpeville on March 21. But the campaign pressed on, quickly swamping the prisons and straining the capacity of the state to control the unrest. The government was forced to suspend the pass laws. At first the protest seemed to succeed, but the government quickly turned the tables by banning the PAC and ANC and by assuming new powers. In secret deliberations after being banned, both the ANC and PAC, deprived of all legal means of protest, reluctantly decided to initiate armed struggle. Neither organization had much success in their early sabotage campaigns, and when the government caught and arrested some important ANC leaders at their hideout in Rivonia farm in 1964, the government gained the upper hand decisively. Resistance ground on throughout the 1960s and early 1970s, but to no avail.

The official version of Afrikaner history in this period emphasized triumph. It focused on the progressive defeat and scattering of the enemies of apartheid, the successive electoral successes of the National party by increasing majorities, the burgeoning prosperity of South Africa, the phasing out of "poor whiteism," and finally, the achievement of the long-sought Republic with South Africa's separation from the British Commonwealth.

Another version of South African history would emphasize neither the antiapartheid opposition's struggle nor government victories but simply life under apartheid and the emerging contradictions of the system. Verwoerd had predicted that by the mid-1970s the movement of Africans to urban areas would see substantial reversal. But with rapid population growth and the surging labor needs of the growing economy, quite the opposite happened. More and more Africans moved toward the cities, and full-time efforts to "endorse out"—to send back to the countryside—"surplus" Africans had little impact. By the early 1970s, the growing light-manufacturing sector needed African workers and wanted the freedom to negotiate with responsible union leaders; it also desired African consumers with purchasing power. The old assumptions of baaskap were becoming obsolete for an increasing proportion of the white public, including the ruling Nationalist elite.

In the meantime, a generation and more of Africans had grown up under apartheid and had been educated by the Bantu education system. Deprived of the role models of the banned, imprisoned, exiled leaders of the ANC, the new generation started over. In student organizations and church discussion groups, young Africans worked out a philosophy of "black consciousness." They had no intention of challenging the government's policies immediately, but instead hoped to pursue projects of consciousness raising, self-help, identity, and pride. Would the government allow them this? It incessantly reassured its critics around the world that Africans had free space for such development. The black consciousness movement called its bluff.

The government quickly demonstrated its unwillingness to allow Bantu Education to produce independent thinkers. In 1976 students violently rejected new government educational policies that required that certain subjects be taught in Afrikaans. After more than a decade of quiescence, African opposition exploded in 1976. It was not the older, banned, and exiled organizations who took the lead this time, but the township dwellers, especially the schoolchildren, who rose up spontaneously against the new government regulations. The disturbances started in Soweto in June and halted Bantu Education all over South Africa for the next two years. Although not inspired or led by the ANC, these events provided the occasion for the organization to recover its strength and resume effective leadership in the anti-apartheid struggle.

Another piece of the South African puzzle in this period concerns the country's international standing and reputation. In the 1930s, South Africa had been virtually in step with the colonial policies of the rest of the Western world. The major colonial powers—Britain, France, Belgium, and the Netherlands—were still committed to long-term colonial "responsibilities," which they pursued in ways not markedly different from those of South Africa. But after the Second World War, Britain moved toward colonial development and rapid decolonization while South Africa proceeded in the opposite direction. In the United Nations, newly independent India quickly became a critic of South Africa, and South Africa's application to move from League of Nations Mandate to United Nations Trusteeship authority over South West Africa was refused.

The beginnings of the Cold War had coincided with the victory of the vigorously anticommunist National party in 1948. Indeed, the Western powers and South Africa were concerned about growing communist influence in Africa and the colonial world in general. Britain pursued a policy of preempting communists by transferring power to responsible nationalist leaders. The South African government tended to believe, by contrast, that nationalist leaders were the communists and that decolonization constituted an abject surrender to the enemies of "Western civilization." Thus, as decolonization proceeded and African states became independent, a gap in policy toward the Third World widened between South Africa and the Western powers. Nevertheless, although Western powers criticized apartheid, they did not yet seek to punish or isolate South Africa. South Africa, in fact, was an important ally of the West in the Cold War.

From 1948 to the 1970s, both the South African government and the growing anti-apartheid movement in Western countries waged major campaigns for support from opinion. Government propaganda trumpeted economic progress for all South Africans, the region's value as a trading partner producing scarce resources, the supposed benefits to Africans of homeland self-government, and South Africa's role as a bulwark against communism.

At the same time, the Western countries gradually became acquainted with oppression in South Africa through books. Leading the way in fostering outside awareness of conditions in South Africa was Alan Paton's Novel, *Cry, the Beloved Country* (1947). Father Trevor Huddleston's *Naught for Your Comfort* (1956) recounted the destruction of Sophiatown. Journalists' records, especially works by Basil Davidson ("Report on Southern Africa," 1952) and Anthony Sampson ("Drum," 1956) also played a major role in spreading news about apartheid. The novels of Andre Brink and the works of Nadine Gordimer also awakened Western interest in South Africa, though both authors were far from anti-apartheid polemicists.

The reporting of the events of 1960, especially the Sharpeville massacre, reflected a quantum jump in international criticism of South African racial policies. UNESCO and International Defense and Aid Fund publications on the sufferings of Africans under apartheid quickly garnered increased circulation. Organizations tied to the American civil-rights movement kept South African issues alive, and apartheid became a continuous concern rather than an occasional issue linked to big news stories. The 1976 Soweto disturbances received prime-time news coverage across the globe. Soon international concern about apartheid seemed powerful enough to shape conditions within South Africa. The tensions within that country and the mounting chorus of international criticism combined to make 1976 a decisive turning point, as the end of the apartheid regime drew near.

BLACK SOULS IN WHITE SKINS?

By Steve Biko

A *t the 1st General Students Council of SASO in July 1970 Steve was succeeded as President by Barney Pityana. Steve was elected Chairman of SASO Publications. The following month the monthly SASO Newsletter began to appear carrying articles by himself called "I write what I like" and signed Frank Talk. At the BPC/ SASO Trial the Judge at one point interjected: Isn't (accused) number 9 [Strini Moodley] Frank Talk?" to which Steve replied, "No, no, he was never Frank Talk, I was Frank Talk" (see p. 108). This article and the one that follows, from the August and September 1970 issues of the Newsletter respectively, give an authentic exposition of the philosophy of Black Consciousness.*

I WRITE WHAT I LIKE

The following is the first of a series of articles under the above topic, that will appear regularly in our Newsletter.

BLACK SOULS IN WHITE SKINS?

Basically the South African white community is a homogeneous community. It is a community of people who sit to enjoy a privileged position that they do not deserve, are aware of this, and therefore spend their time trying to justify why they are doing so. Where differences in political opinion exist, they are in the process of trying to justify their position of privilege and their usurpation of power.

With their theory of "separate freedoms for the various nations in the multinational state of South Africa" the Nationalists have gone a long way towards giving most of white South Africa some sort of moral explanation for what is happening. Everyone is quite content to point out that these people—meaning the blacks—will be free when they are ready to run their own affairs in their own areas. What more could they possibly hope for?

But these are not the people we are concerned with. We are concerned with that curious bunch of nonconformists who explain their participation in negative terms: that bunch of do-gooders that goes under all sorts of names—liberals, leftists etc. These are the people who argue that they are not responsible for white racism and the country's "inhumanity to the black man." These are the people who claim that they too feel the oppression just as acutely as the blacks and therefore should be jointly involved in the black man's struggle for a place under the sun. In short, these are the people who say that they have black souls wrapped up in white skins.

The role of the white liberal in the black man's history in South Africa is a curious one. Very few black organisations were not under white direction. True to their image, the white liberals always knew what was good for the blacks and told them so. The wonder of it all is that the black people have believed in them for so long. It was only at the end of the 50s that the blacks started demanding to be their own guardians.

Nowhere is the arrogance of the liberal ideology demonstrated so well as in their insistence that the problems of the country can only be solved by a bilateral approach involving both black and white. This has, by and large, come to be taken in all seriousness as the *modus operandi* in South Africa by all those who claim they would like a change in the *status quo*. Hence the multiracial political organisations and parties and the "nonracial" student organisations, all of which insist on integration not only as an end goal but also as a means.

The integration they talk about is first of all artificial in that it is a response to conscious manoeuvre rather than to the dictates of the inner soul. In other words the people forming the integrated complex have been extracted from various segregated societies with their in-built complexes of superiority and inferiority and these continue to manifest themselves even in the "nonracial" set-up of the integrated complex. As a result the integration so achieved is a one-way course, with the whites doing all the talking and the blacks the listening. Let me hasten to say that I am not claiming that segregation is necessarily the natural order; however, given the facts of the situation where a group experiences privilege at the expense of others, then it becomes obvious that a hastily arranged integration cannot be the solution to the problem. It is rather like expecting the slave to work together with the slave-master's son to remove all the conditions leading to the former's enslavement.

Secondly, this type of integration as a means is almost always unproductive. The participants waste lots of time in an internal sort of mudslinging designed to prove that A is more of a liberal than B. In other words the lack of common ground for solid identification is all the time manifested in internal strifes inside the group.

It will not sound anachronistic to anybody genuinely interested in real integration to learn that blacks are asserting themselves in a society where they are being treated as perpetual under-16s. One does not need to plan for or actively encourage real integration. Once the various groups within a given community have asserted themselves to the point that mutual respect has to be shown then you have the ingredients for a true and meaningful integration. At the heart of true integration is the provision for each man, each group to rise and attain the envisioned self. Each group must be able to attain its style of existence without encroaching on or being thwarted by another. Out of this mutual respect for each other and complete freedom of self-determination there will obviously arise a genuine fusion of the life-styles of the various groups. This is true integration.

From this it becomes clear that as long as blacks are suffering from inferiority complex—a result of 300 years of deliberate oppression, denigration and derision—they will be useless as co-architects of a normal society where man is nothing else but man for his own sake. Hence what is necessary as a prelude to anything else that may come is a very strong grass-roots build-up of black consciousness such that blacks can learn to assert themselves and stake their rightful claim.

Thus in adopting the line of a nonracial approach, the liberals are playing their old game. They are claiming a "monopoly on intelligence and moral judgement" and setting the pattern and pace for the realisation of the black man's aspirations. They want to remain in good books with both the black and white worlds. They want to shy away from all forms of "extremisms", condemning "white supremacy" as being just as bad as "Black Power!" They vacillate between the two worlds, verbalising all the complaints of the blacks beautifully while skilfully extracting what suits them from the exclusive pool of white privileges. But ask them for a moment to give a concrete meaningful programme that they intend adopting, then you will see on whose side they really are. Their protests are directed at and appeal to white conscience, everything they do is directed at finally convincing the white electorate that the black man is also a man and that at some future date he should be given a place at the white man's table.

The myth of integration as propounded under the banner of liberal ideology must be cracked and killed because it makes people believe that something is being done when in actual fact the artificial integrated circles are a soporific on the blacks and provide a vague satisfaction for the guilty-stricken whites. It works on a false premise that because it is difficult to bring people from different races together in this country, therefore achievement of this is in itself a step forward towards the total liberation of the blacks. Nothing could be more irrelevant and therefore misleading. Those who believe in it are living in a fool's paradise.

First the black–white circles are almost always a creation of white liberals. As a testimony to their claim of complete identification with the blacks, they call a few "intelligent and articulate" blacks to "come around for tea at home", where all present ask each other the same old hackneyed question "how can we bring about change in South Africa?" The more such tea-parties one calls the more of a liberal he is and the freer he shall feel from the guilt that harnesses and binds his conscience. Hence he moves around his white circles—whites-only hotels, beaches, restaurants and cinemas—with a lighter load, feeling that he is not like the rest of the others. Yet at the back of his mind is a constant reminder that he is quite comfortable as things stand and therefore should not bother about change. Although he does not vote for the Nats (now that they are in the majority anyway), he feels quite secure under the protection offered by the Nats and subconsciously shuns the idea of a change. This is what demarcates the liberal from the black world. The liberals view the oppression of blacks as a problem that has to be solved, an eye sore spoiling an otherwise beautiful view. From time to time the liberals make themselves forget about the problem or take their eyes off the eyesore. On the other hand, in oppression the blacks are experiencing a situation from which they are unable to escape at any given moment. Theirs is a struggle to get out of the situation and not merely to solve a peripheral problem as in the case of the liberals. This is why blacks speak with a greater sense of urgency than whites.

A game at which the liberals have become masters is that of deliberate evasiveness. The question often comes up "what can I do?" If you ask him to do something like stopping to use segregated facilities or dropping out of varsity to work at menial jobs like all blacks or defying and denouncing all provisions that make him privileged, you always get the answer—"but that's unrealistic!" While this may be true, it only serves to illustrate the fact that no matter what a white man does, the colour of his skin—his passport to privilege—will always put him miles ahead of the black man. Thus in the ultimate analysis no white person can escape being part of the oppressor camp.

"There exists among men, because they are men, a solidarity through which each shares responsibility for every injustice and every wrong committed in the world, and especially for crimes that are committed in his presence or of which he cannot be ignorant."

This description of "metaphysical guilt" explains adequately that white racism "is only possible because whites are indifferent to suffering and patient with cruelty" meted out to the black man. Instead of involving themselves in an all-out attempt to stamp out racism from their white society, liberals waste lots of time trying to prove to as many blacks as they can find that they are liberal. This arises out of the false belief that we are faced with a black problem. There is nothing the matter with blacks. The problem is WHITE RACISM and it rests squarely on the laps of the white society. The sooner the liberals realise this the better for us blacks. Their presence amongst us is irksome and of nuisance value. It removes the focus of attention from essentials and shifts it to ill-defined philosophical concepts that are both irrelevant to the black man and merely a red herring across the track. White liberals must leave blacks to take care of their own business while they concern themselves with the real evil in our society—white racism.

Secondly, the black-white mixed circles are static circles with neither direction nor programme. The same questions are asked and the same naiveté exhibited in answering them. The real concern of the group is to keep the group going rather than being useful. In this sort of set-up one sees a perfect example of what oppression has done to the blacks. They have been made to feel inferior for so long that for them it is comforting to drink tea, wine or beer with whites who seem to treat them as equals. This serves to boost up their own ego to the extent of making them feel slightly superior to those blacks who do not get similar treatment from whites. These are the sort of blacks who are a danger to the community.

Instead of directing themselves at their black brothers and looking at their common problems from a common platform they choose to sing out their lamentations to an apparently sympathetic audience that has become proficient in saying the chorus of "shame!" These dull-witted, self-centred blacks are in the ultimate analysis as guilty of the arrest of progress as their white friends for it is from such groups that the theory of gradualism emanates and this is what keeps the blacks confused and always hoping that one day God will step down from heaven to solve their problems. It is people from such groups who keep on scanning the papers daily to detect any sign of the change they patiently await without working for. When Helen Suzman's majority is increased by a couple of thousands, this is regarded as a major milestone in the "inevitable change." Nobody looks at the other side of the coin—the large-scale removals of Africans from the urban areas or the impending zoning of places like Grey Street in Durban and a myriad of other manifestations of change for the worse.

Does this mean that I am against integration? If by integration you understand a breakthrough into white society by blacks, an assimilation and acceptance of blacks into an already established set of norms and code of behaviour set up by and maintained by whites, then YES I am against it. I am against the superior–inferior white–black stratification that makes the white a perpetual teacher and the black a perpetual pupil (and a poor one at that). I am against the intellectual arrogance of white people that makes them believe that white leadership is a *sine qua non* in this country and that whites are the divinely appointed pace-setters in progress. I am against the fact that a settler minority should impose an entire system of values on an indigenous people.

If on the other hand by integration you mean there shall be free participation by all members of a society, catering for the full expression of the self in a freely changing society as determined by the will of the people, then I am with you. For one cannot escape the fact that the culture shared by the majority group in any given society must ultimately determine the broad direction taken by the joint culture of that society. This need not cramp the style of those who feel differently but on the whole, a country in Africa, in which the majority of the people are African must inevitably exhibit African values and be truly African in style.

What of the claim that the blacks are becoming racists? This is a favourite pastime of frustrated liberals who feel their trusteeship ground being washed off from under their feet. These self-appointed trustees of black interests boast of years of experience in their fight for the 'rights of the blacks.' They have been doing things for blacks, on behalf of blacks, and because of blacks. When the blacks announce that the time has come for them to do things for themselves and all by themselves all white liberals shout blue murder!

"Hey, you can't do that. You're being a racist. You're falling into their trap."

Apparently it's alright with the liberals as long as you remain caught by *their* trap.

Those who know, define racism as discrimination by a group against another for the purposes of subjugation or maintaining subjugation. In other words one cannot be a racist unless he has the power to subjugate. What blacks are doing is merely to respond to a situation in which they find themselves the objects of white racism. We are in the position in which we are because of our skin. We are collectively segregated against—what can be more logical than for us to respond as a group? When workers come together under the auspices of a trade union to strive for the betterment of their conditions, nobody expresses surprise in the Western world. It is the done thing. Nobody accuses them of separatist tendencies. Teachers fight their battles, garbagemen do the same, nobody acts as a trustee for another. Somehow, however, when blacks want to do their thing the liberal establishment seems to detect an anomaly. This is in fact a counter-anomaly. The anomaly was there in the first instance when the liberals were presumptuous enough to think that it behoved them to fight the battle *for* the blacks.

The liberal must understand that the days of the Noble Savage are gone; that the blacks do not need a go-between in this struggle for their own emancipation. No true liberal should feel any resentment at the growth of black consciousness. Rather, all true liberals should realise that, the place for their fight for justice is within their white society. The liberals must realise that they themselves are oppressed if they are true liberals and therefore they must fight for their own freedom and not that of the nebulous "they" with whom they can hardly claim identification. The liberal must apply himself with absolute dedication to the idea of educating his white brothers that the history of the country may have to be rewritten at some stage and that we may live in "a country where colour will not serve to put a man in a box." The blacks have heard enough of this. In other words, the liberal must serve as a lubricating material so that as we change the gears in trying to find a better direction for South Africa, there should be no grinding noises of metal against metal but a free and easy flowing movement which will be characteristic of a well-looked-after vehicle.

FRANK TALK

AFRICAN HISTORY

PART FIVE

POSTCOLONIAL AFRICA

THE COLONIAL IMPACT

By Adu Boahen

As we saw in the previous chapter, only forty-five years after the Italian occupation of Ethiopia, all African states except a few in southern Africa had been liberated politically from the yoke of colonialism, and Africans had regained their sovereignty and independence. In other words, nowhere in African did the colonial system last more than a hundred years—from the 1880s to the 1970s. In the history of a continent, a hundred years is a very brief span indeed, a mere episode or interlude in the life of the peoples. Yet, short and episodic as it was, there is no doubt that colonialism made an impact on the continent. In this final chapter, I would like to examine the nature of the legacies that colonialism has bequeathed to Africa, as well as assess the significance of colonialism for Africa and Africans.[1]

Nothing has become more controversial now than the question of the nature of the impact of colonialism on Africa. Many European and Eurocentric historians—such as L. H. Gann, P. Duignan, Margery Perham, P. C. Lloyd, and more recently D. K. Fieldhouse—have contended that the impact was both positive and negative, with positive aspects far outweighing the negative ones. Gann and Duignan, who appear to have devoted themselves to the defense of colonialism in Africa, concluded in 1967 that "the imperial system stands out as one of the most powerful engines for cultural diffusion in the history of Africa; its credit balance far outweighs its debit account."[2]

Other historians—mainly African, black, and Marxist scholars and especially the development and the underdevelopment theorists—have maintained that colonialism made no positive impact on Africa. The great exponents of this rather extreme position are Walter Rodney, the black Guianese historian and activist, and the Ugandan historian T. B. Kabwegyere. According to the former, "the argument suggests that, on the one hand, there was exploitation and oppression but on the other hand colonial governments did much for the benefit of Africans and they developed Africa. It is our contention that this is completely false. Colonialism had only one hand—it was a one-armed bandit."[3] Before deciding one way or the other, let us examine the colonial balance sheet in the political, social, and economic fields.

The first obvious positive political legacy was undoubtedly the establishment of continuous peace and stability in Africa, especially after the First World War. Let me hasten to add, first, that Africa was certainly not in a Hobbesian state of nature at the dawn of the colonial era and, secondly, that the first three decades of the colonial era, as should be obvious from the two previous chapters, introduced into Africa far more violence, instability, anarchy, and loss of African lives than probably any other period in its history. The population of the Belgian Congo fell by 50 percent, and that of the Herero by 80 percent, as a result of the oppressive and inhuman treatment of the Africans by the colonizers during the period. There is no doubt, however, that after the wars of occupation and the repression of African opposition and resistance, an era of continuous peace, order, and stability set in. This certainly facilitated and accelerated the economic and social changes that occurred on the continent during the colonial period.

The second positive political impact has been the very appearance of the independent African states of today. The partition of Africa by the imperial colonial powers led ultimately to the establishment of some forty-eight new states, most of them with clearly defined boundaries, in place of the existing innumerable lineage and clan groups, city-states, kingdoms, and empires without any fixed boundaries. It is significant that the boundaries of these states have been maintained ever since independence.

However, the creation of the states has proved to be more of a liability than an asset to the present independent African nations. Had the boundaries of these states been laid down in accordance with any well-defined, rational criteria and in full cognizance of the ethnocultural, geographical, and ecological realities of Africa, the outcome would have been wholesome. Unfortunately, many of these boundaries were arbitrarily drawn on African maps in the chancelleries of the imperial powers in Europe. The result has been that most of these states are artificial creations, and this very artificiality has created very serious problems, many of which have still not been solved. One of these problems is that of nation-state building. Because of the artificiality of these boundaries, each independent African state is made up of a whole host of different ethnocultural groups and nations having different historical traditions and cultures and speaking different languages. One can imagine, then, how stupendous the problem of developing the independent states of Africa into true nation-states is.

A second problem has been that of interstate boundary disputes. Not only did these artificial boundaries create multi-ethnic states, but worse still, they often run across preexisting nations, ethnicities, states, kingdoms, and empires. The Bakongo, for instance, are divided by the boundaries of the Congo, Zaire, Angola, and Gabon. Some of the Ewe live in Ghana, some in Togo, and others in Benin, while the Akan are found in the Ivory Coast and Ghana. The Somali are shared among Ethiopia, Kenya, and Somalia. The Senufo now live in Mali, the Ivory Coast, and Burkina Faso. Is it surprising, then, that there have been boundary disputes between Ghana and the Ivory Coast, Ghana and Togo, Burkina Faso and Mali, Nigeria and Cameroons, Somalia and Ethiopia, Kenya and Somalia, Sudan and Uganda?

A third problem has been the uneven sizes and unequal natural resources and economic potentialities of these states. Some of the states that emerged from the partition were really giants, like the Sudan, with an area of approximately 967,000 square miles, Zaire with 906,000, Algeria with 920,000, and Nigeria with 357,000; others were midgets, like the Gambia, with a total area of 4,000 square miles, and Lesotho and Burundi with 11,000 each. Moreover, some states have miles and miles of coastline, while others are landlocked, with no access to the sea. The latter include Mali, Burkina Faso, Niger, Chad, the Central African Republic, Uganda, Malawi, Zambia, Zimbabwe, and Botswana. Some have very fertile lands and several mineral resources, but others—such as Niger, Chad, and most of the Sudan, Algeria, and Egypt—are mere desert. Finally, while some states, like the Gambia and Somalia, have only a border or two to police, others have four or more, and Zaire has seven. Here, again, how can such handicapped states solve their problems of development? How can a state without access to the sea or without fertile land really develop? Can one imagine the problems of security and of smuggling confronting these states with so many borders to patrol?

The third positive political impact of colonialism was its introduction into Africa of two new institutions—a new bureaucracy of civil servants and a new judicial system. On the first score, the contribution of the Europeans was uneven: the British bequeathed a far better trained and numerically stronger civil service to its former colonies than the French, while the record of the Belgians and the Portuguese is the worst in this field. However, the judicial systems, bequeathed by the colonial administrations, have not undergone any fundamental changes in any of the independent African states.

Another positive colonial impact was the generation of a sense of nationalism as well as the intensification of the sprit of Pan–Africanism. The colonial system generated a sense of identity and consciousness among the different ethnic groups of each colonial state, while the anticolonial literary activities of some of the educated Africans and more especially the Fascist attack on Ethiopia and the connivance of the other European imperial powers diffused and strengthened the spirit of Pan–Africanism throughout the black world.

But it should be immediately pointed out that African nationalism was one of the accidental by-products of colonialism. No colonial power ever deliberately set out to generate or promote that consciousness. Moreover, the nationalism that was generated by colonialism was not a positive but a negative one, arising out of the sense of anger, frustration, and humiliation produced by the oppressive, discriminatory, and exploitative measures and activities of the colonial administrators. It is rather unfortunate that with the overthrow of colonialism, this negative sentiment of nationalism or, rather, anticolonialism has almost lost its cohesive force. Independent African states are therefore now saddled with the crucial problem of how to forge a new and more positive force of nationalism in place of the negative one generated by colonialism, or, as Ali Mazrui and M. Tidy have recently put it, how to move "from modern nationalism to modern nationhood."[4]

Another political legacy bequeathed to independent African states was the professional army. In traditional Africa, there were hardly any full-time, standing armies. In the whole of West Africa, it was probably only the kings of Dahomey and Samori Ture who developed real full-time, well-trained armies. However, all the imperial powers developed professional armies, which they used first to occupy and police their colonies, then in the First and Second World Wars, and finally in the campaigns against African independence; and these armies were among the most conspicuous legacies apart from physical structures bequeathed to independent African states. And what a legacy these armies have turned out to be! In retrospect, they have become nothing but a chronic source of instability, confusion, and anarchy as a result of their often unnecessary and unjustifiable interventions in the political processes of African countries. Indeed, African armies are the greatest millstones around the necks of African leaders, and the future of the continent is going to be determined very much on how these armies are dealt with.

The final political impact—and a very negative and regretable one—is the delay that colonialism caused in the political development and maturity of African states. If colonialism meant anything at all politically, it was the loss of sovereignty and independence by the colonized peoples. This loss of sovereignty, in turn, implied the loss of the right of a state to control its own destiny; to plan its own development; to decide which outside nations to borrow from or associate with or emulate; to conduct its own diplomacy and international relations; and above all, to manage or even mismanage its own affairs, derive pride and pleasure from its successes, and derive lessons, frustrations, and experience from its failures. As Rodney has pointed out, the seventy-year colonial era was one of the most dynamic and scientific periods in world history. It was the period, for instance, that witnessed Europe's entry into the age of the motor vehicle, of the airplane, and finally of nuclear power. Had African states been in control of their own destinies—as say, Japan was, or as South Africa became after 1910—there is no reason why, judging from the very healthy and promising trends which were outlined in the first chapter, they could not also have followed the Japanese model, as indeed some of their educated sons, like Mensah Sarbah and the Malagasi scholar Ravelojaona, were advocating.[5] But colonialism completely isolated and insulated Africa from all these changes. It is in this loss of sovereignty and the consequent isolation from the outside world that one finds one of the most pernicious impacts of colonialism on Africa and one of the fundamental causes of its present underdevelopment and technological backwardness.

The impact of colonialism in the economic field, as in the political field, was clearly a mixed one. The most important economic benefit was the provision of an infrastructure of roads, railways, harbors, the telegraph and the telephone. The basic infrastructure of every modern African state was completed during the colonial period, and in most countries, not even a mile of railroad has been constructed since independence. A second important economic impact was the development of the primary sector of Africa's economy. It was during this period that the mineral potential of many African countries was discovered and modern scientific mining introduced. Above all, it was during this period that the production of such cash crops as cotton, peanuts, palm oil, coffee, tobacco, rubber, and cocoa, became the main feature of the political economy of many an African state.

These fundamental economic changes, in turn, had some far reaching consequences. In the first place, land acquired great commercial value and assumed far greater importance than it had ever had before. Secondly, the spread of cash-crop agriculture enabled Africans of whatever social status, and especially rural Africans in many regions, to acquire wealth and raise their standard of living. Another significant impact was the spread and consolidation of the money economy in Africa and with it not only a change in the traditional standards of wealth and status but also a phenomenal increase (as will be seen below) in the class of wage earners and salaried persons. In the wake of the money economy came the banking activities which have become such a feature in the economies of independent African states. The sum total of all these colonial economic reforms was what has been described by economists as the completion of the integration of the African economy into the world economy in general and into the capitalist economy of the former colonial powers in particular.[6]

But the economic changes introduced by colonialism had a negative side also. First, the transportation and communications infrastructure that was provided was not only inadequate but was also very unevenly distributed in nearly all the colonies. The roads and railways were by and large constructed to link areas with the potential for cash crops and with mineral deposits with the sea or the world commodity market. In other words, the infrastructures were meant to facilitate the exploitation of the natural resources but not to promote the accessibility and development of all regions of the colony. The outcome of this has been uneven regional economic development in most African countries, still a major stumbling block in the way of nation-building in Africa today.[7]

Secondly, the colonial system led to the delay of industrial and technological developments in Africa. As has been pointed out already, one of the typical features of the colonial political economy was the total neglect of industrialization and of the processing of locally produced raw materials and agricultural products in the colonies. It should not be forgotten that before the colonial period, Africans were producing their own building materials, their pottery and crockery, their soap, beads, iron tools, and especially cloth; above all, they were producing the gold that was exported to Europe and the Mediterranean world.[8] Had the traditional production techniques in all these areas been modernized and had industrialization been promoted, African industrial and technological development would have commenced much earlier than it did. But they were not. Instead, preexisting industries almost all eradicated by the importation of cheap and even better substitutes from Europe and India, while Africans were driven out of the mining industry as it became an exclusive preserve of Europeans. This neglect of industrialization, destruction of the existing industries and handicrafts in Africa, and elimination of Africans from the mining field further explain Africa's present technological backwardness.

Thirdly, colonialism saddled most colonies with monocrop economies. During the colonial period, as may be recalled, each colony was made to produce a single cash crop or two, and no attempts were made to diversify the agricultural economy. The habit of producing these single cash crops appears to have become so ingrained that it has not been changed to any appreciable degree since independence. The other consequence of this concentration on the production of cash crops for export was the neglect of the internal sector of the economy and, in particular, of the production of food for internal consumption, so that rice, maize, fish, and other foods had to be imported. Thus, during the colonial period, Africans were encouraged to produce what they did not consume and to consume what they did not produce, a clear proof of the exploitative nature of the colonial political economy. It is lamentable that this legacy has not changed materially in most African countries. To this day, they have to rely on the importation of rice, maize, edible oil, flour, and other food-stuffs to survive.

Nor did the commercialization of land turn out to be an unqualified asset. In its trail followed a whole series of litigations over the ownership of land, which caused widespread poverty, especially among the ruling houses and land-owning families. Again, litigation over land has continued to this day.

Colonialism also put an end to inter-African trade. I pointed out in the first chapter that on the eve of the imperial scramble and occupation, the commercial unification of the African continent had been completed. There is no doubt that Africans would have continued to trade among themselves as they had been doing from time immemorial. One of the consequences of this inter regional and intraregional trade would have been the continuing spread of, say, the Swahili language and culture in eastern and central Africa, the Hausa language and culture in western Africa, and the Arabic language and culture in northern Africa. What a beneficial development this would have been for the whole continent! But colonialism put an end to all this. The new artificial boundaries not only divided peoples but also blocked the centuries-old transregional and regional caravan routes. Trading between even members of the same ethnic group on either side of new borders suddenly became no longer trading but smuggling, which was heavily punished. On the contrary, the flow of trade in each colony was now oriented to the relevant metropolitan country. The sad thing is that even after twenty years of independence, this orientation has not ended, thanks to the neocolonialist activities of the former metropolitan countries and their African allies.

Finally, the monetary policies pursued by all the colonial powers must be held partly responsible for the present underdeveloped state of the continent. Under these policies, all the colonial currencies were tied to those of the metropolitan countries, and all their foreign exchange earnings were kept in the metropolitan countries and not used for internal development. The expatriate commercial banks and companies were also allowed to repatriate their deposits, savings, and profits instead of reinvesting them in the colonies for further development. The consequence of all this was that at the time of independence, no African state apart from the Union of South Africa had the strong economic or industrial base needed for a real economic takeoff. And if this base could not be provided during the eighty-year period of colonial rule, should we expect it to have been done in twenty years of independence, especially in the light of the changing international economic order?

What about the impact in the social field? Here again, there are both credit and debit sides. In the first place, there is no doubt that after the initial decline, population growth resumed after the First World War. Caldwell has estimated that the population of Africa increased by 37 percent during the colonial period. The increase was undoubtedly due to some of the policies and activities of the colonial administrators—such as the provision of roads and railways, which made for mobility; the campaign launched against such epidemic diseases as sleeping sickness, bubonic plagues, yellow fever, and yaws; and the provision of some medical facilities.

A second important benefit was urbanization. Not only did preexisting towns expand, but completely new urban centers emerged following the establishment of the colonial system. The new cities included Abidjan in the Ivory Coast, Takoradi in Ghana, Port Harcourt and Enugu in Nigeria, Nairobi in Kenya, Salisbury (now Harare) in Zimbabwe, Lusaka in Zambia, and Luluabourg in Zaire. All these new urban centers were created either as ports or harbors, mining centers, administrative centers, or railway centers or terminuses. The population of Nairobi, which was founded in 1896 as a transit depot for the construction of the Uganda railway, rose from 13,145 in 1927 to over 25,000 by 1940; that of Accra jumped from 17,892 in 1901 to 135,926 in1948; and that of Casablanca, from 2,026 in 1910 to 250,000 in1936.[9] There is no doubt that the quality of life for Africa's population was relatively improved through the provision of piped water, hospitals and dispensaries, better housing and sanitary facilities.

A third important social benefit of colonialism was the spread of Christianity and Islam and especially of Western education. During the colonial period Christianity gained far more converts and penetrated farther, especially in East and Central Africa, than it had in all the previous three or four centuries put together. Islam also gained a lot of ground thanks to the patronage especially of the French and British colonial administrators. It should be emphasized that traditional African religion maintained its position in the face of all the inroads by these foreign religions.

The spread of Western education was due mainly to the activities of the Christian missionaries. By the 1930s, there were very few areas in Africa where elementary education was not being provided, while a few secondary schools and, from the 1940s onwards, even universities began to appear everywhere except in the Portuguese and Belgian colonies. The impact of Western education on African societies is too well-known to be discussed here. Suffice it to say that it was mainly responsible for producing the educated African elite which not only spearheaded the overthrow of the colonial system but also constitutes the backbone of the civil service of independent African states.

The other beneficial result of the spread of Western education was the provision of a lingua franca for each colony or cluster of colonies. In all the colonies, the mother tongue of the metropolitan country became the official language as well as the main medium of communication among the multi-ethnic populations of each colony. With very few exceptions (Tanzania, Kenya, Madagascar, and the states of North Africa), the metropolitan languages to this day the official and business languages in Africa.

The final social benefit was the new social order that emerged in Africa as a result of the operation of the colonial system. Though there was social mobility in the traditional African social order, undue weight was given to brith. The colonial system, on the other hand, emphasized individual merit and achievement rather than birth, and this is greatly facilitated social mobility. Moreover, as a result of Western education, employment opportunities, the production of cash crops, the abolition of slavery, and many other new avenues for advancement, all introduced by colonialism, a new social structure emerged. In place of the traditional structure of ruling aristocracy, ordinary people, and slaves, by the 1930s a new structure had developed, divided, first, into rural and urban dwellers, and then further subdivided. The urban dwellers became stratified into three main subgroups: namely, the elite, or, as others would term them, the administrative-clerical-professional bourgeoisie; the nonelite, or subelite; and the urban proletariat, or workers. The rural population became subdivided into rural proletariat, or landless peasantry, especially in southern and eastern Africa, and peasants. The social order produced by the colonial system has been maintained, and the stratification has been, if anything, sharpened even further since independence. I regard this new social structure as an asset because membership is based on individual effort and achievement rather than on birth.

It would appear that the positive contribution of colonialism in the social field was quite considerable. Unfortunately, so also—and probably more so—was the negative impact. In the first place, it was the colonial system that initiated the gap that still exists between the urban and rural areas. All of the modern facilities—schools, hospitals, street lights, radio, postal services—and above all most of the employment opportunities were concentrated in the urban centers. The combination of modern life and employment pulled rural dwellers, especially the young ones and those with schooling, in the direction of the cities.

Secondly, the social services provided by colonialism were grossly inadequate and unevenly distributed. For instance, while in Nigeria by the 1930s, twelve modern hospitals had been built for Europeans, who numbered only 4,000, there were only fifty-two for Africans, numbering 40 million. In Dar es Salaam the ratio of beds to population by 1920 was approximately 1 to 10 for the European hospital and 1 to 400–500 for the African hospital.

There was even greater deficiency, uneven distribution, and in this case even misdirected orientation in the educational facilities that were provided in colonial Africa. University education was totally ignored in all the colonies until the 1940s, and only one university was subsequently established for each colony. In Portuguese Africa, there were no universities. Moreover, most of the secondary schools were in the major cities and the coastal areas of the colonies and seldom in the interior and rural regions. Thirdly, in no colony was the demand for education at all levels ever adequately met. In practically every colony, only a very small percentage of school-age children could gain admission into schools. Educational facilities were so limited and so unevenly distributed simply because education was not really meant for the benefit of the Africans themselves but primarily "to produce Africans who would be more productive for the [colonial] system."[10] Nor were the curricula provided by these educational institutions of real relevance to the needs and aspirations of Africans. Most of the curricula were in fact carbon copies of those of the metropolitan countries.

The effects of colonial education were really unfortunate. First, because of its inadequacy, large numbers of Africans remained illiterate, and illiteracy is still widespread. Secondly, the elite produced by these colonial educational institutions were with few exceptions people who were alienated from their own society in terms of their dress, outlook, and tastes in food, music, and even dance. They were people who worshiped European culture, equating it with civilization, and looked down upon their own culture. Radical African scholars are now talking of colonial miseducation rather than education. Unfortunately, it is this very alienated and badly oriented elite that have dominated both the political and the social scene in Africa since independence. Above all, the neglect of technical education and the emphasis on liberal education created in educated Africans a contempt for manual work and an admiration for white-collar jobs which have still not left them. Finally, the use of the metropolitan language as the lingua franca also had the most regrettable effect of preventing the development of an official African language as a lingua franc in each colony or even in a cluster of colonies. This question has become so sensitive that only a few African states have been able to tackle it since independence.

Another negative social impact of colonialism was the downgrading of the status of women in Africa. During the colonial period, there were far fewer facilities for girls than for boys. Women could therefore not gain access into the professions—medicine, law, the civil service, and the bench. Very few women were ever appointed to any "European post," while there was never a female governor of a colony. The colonial world was definitely a man's world, and women were not allowed to play any meaningful role in it except as petty traders and farmers.

The colonial administrators and their allies, the European missionaries, condemned everything

African in culture—African names, music, dance, art, religion, marriage, the system of inheritance—and completely discouraged the teaching of all these things in their schools and colleges. Even the wearing of African clothes to work or school was banned. All this could not but retard the cultural development of the continent. One of the greatest achievements of independent African governments has been the revival of and the generation of pride in African culture and its propagation in the outside world.

But the last and the most serious negative impact of colonialism has been psychological. This is seen, first, in the creation of a colonial mentality among educated Africans in particular and also among the populace in general. This mentality manifests itself in the condemnation of anything traditional, in the preference for imported goods to locally manufactured goods (since independence), and in the style of dress—such as the wearing of three-piece suits in a climate where temperatures routinely exceed eighty degrees Fahrenheit. Above all, it manifests itself in the belief so prevalent among Africans, both literate and illiterate, that government and all public property and finance belong, not to the people, but to the colonial government, and could and should therefore be taken advantage of at the least opportunity, a belief which leads to the often reckless dissipation and misuse of public funds and property.

Another psychological impact is apparent in ostentatious and flamboyant life-styles, especially on the part of the elite and businessmen. All this arose from the fact that while the colonialists taught their colonial subjects the Protestant work ethic, the drive for worldly success, and the acquisitive instinct, they did not, for obvious reasons, inculcate in them the puritanical spirit which emphasized frugality and very little consumption. In other words, colonialism taught its subjects only part of the puritanical lesson of "make money," not the full one of "make money but do not spend it," which, according to Ali Mazrui, "seemed to be the ultimate commercial imperative operating within the Protest antethic."[11] Thus, while in Europe this full ethic led to the rise of capitalism,

as both Weber and Tawney have clearly shown, and with it the scientific and technological break through, in the African colonies it only generated the ostentatious consumption habits which are still very much with us.

The final and worst psychological impact has been the generation of a deep feeling of inferiority as well as the loss of a sense of human dignity among Africans. Both complexes were surely the outcome not only of the wholesale condemnation of everything African already referred to but, above all, of the practice of racial discrimination and the constant humiliation and oppression to which Africans were subjected throughout the colonial period. The sense of human dignity seems to have been regained, but the feeling of inferiority has not entirely disappeared even after two decades of independence.

It should be obvious from the above, then, that all those historians who see colonialism as a "one-armed bandit" are totally wrong. Equally guilty of exaggeration are those colonial apologists who see colonialism as an unqualified blessing for Africa as well as those who see its record as a balanced one. Colonialism definitely did have its credit and debit sides, but quite clearly the debit side far outweighs the credit side. Indeed, my charge against colonialism is not that it did not do anything for Africa, but that it did so little and that little so accidentally and indirectly; not that the economy or Africa under colonialism did not grow but that it grew more to the advantage of the colonial powers and the expatriate owners and shareholders of the companies operating in Africa than to the Africans; not that improvements did not take place in the lives of the African peoples but that such improvements were so limited and largely confined to the urban areas; not that education was not provided but that what was provided was so inadequate and so irrelevant to the needs and demands of the Africans themselves; not that there was no upward social mobility but that such a relatively small number of Africans did get to the top. In short, given the opportunities, the resources, and the power and influence of the colonial rulers, they could and should have done far more than they did for Africa. And it is for this failure that the colonial era will go down in history as a period of wasted opportunities, of ruthless exploitation of the resources of Africa, and on balance of the underdevelopment and humiliation of the peoples of Africa.

What then is the real significance of colonialism for Africa? Was it just a mere interlude that did not and will not affect the course of African history, or has it left an indelible imprint on Africa which is destined to influence its future? This topic has become a very controversial one. To a majority of historians, colonialism, though a short period in the history of Africa, is of great significance and bound to affect the future course of events. As Oliver and Atmore contend, "Measured on the time-scale of history, the colonial period was but an interlude of comparatively short duration. But it was an interlude that radically changed the direction and momemtum of African history." To Gann and Duigan, the colonial era was "the most decisive for the future of Africa."[12]

The other school of thought, championed by scholars such as Ajayi and Hopkins, regards the impact of colonialism on Africa as skin-deep, seeing colonialism as a mere episode that did not constitute any break with the African past. Ajayi has argued out this case in a series of articles, while Hopkins has also maintained that "colonial rule itself had a less dramatic and a less pervasive economic impact than was once supposed," that colonialism did "not create modernity out of backwardness by suddenly disrupting a traditional state of low-level equilibrium," and that "the main function of the new rulers was to give impetus to a process of economic development which was already under way."[13] Ali Mazrui has recently placed his enormous weight behind this school of thought. As he and Tidy have recently concluded, "The impact of the West may now turn out to be more short-lived than many have expected."[14]

I believe that the issue at stake is not as clear-cut and simple as both schools of thought have made it look. In some respects the impact of colonialism was deep and certainly destined to affect the future course of events, but in others, it was not. For instance, the colonial impact in the economic field was on the whole decisive and fundamental and affected both the rural and urban areas. In virtually all parts of Africa, the money economy completely and permanently replaced the barter economy. With the use of cash, the status of the individual in society came to be and is still determined by the amount of money or personal property that he has been able to accumulate, not by his birth or age or the number of his wives and children. Likewise, the commercialization of land which followed the introduction of cash crops and the modern mining industry has remained and is growing in intensity each day. Again, the integration of the economy of Africa into the world economy in general and into that of the former colonial powers in particular is destined to remain forever in the case of the world economy and for a very long time in the case of the European economies.

Many aspects of the political impact of colonialism are going to be even more lasting. In the first place, the very appearance of the present political map of Africa is a direct product of colonialism, and with the adoption of the principle of the sanctity of national boundaries by the Organization of African Unity (OAU), this appearance is going to endure. Secondly, the fundamental shift of the focus of political authority and power from the old ruling aristocracy of kings and priests to the educated elite (or, as Chinweizu insists on calling them, the petite bourgeoisie)[15] is also going to remain. Finally, the colonial armies which were bequeathed to African states have been and are certainly going to be maintained for a considerable length of time. These armies have already played crucial and in many cases disastrous and negative roles in the political processes in independent African states, and it appears that their role is not yet ended. In all these ways, then, the impact of colonialism in the political field was crucial and will prove of lasting consequence.

In the cultural field, the colonial impact has already proved to be superficial and ephemeral. Most of the changes that were introduced in this area, such as racial discrimination and the condemnation of African culture, have disappeared with the attainment of independence. Today, African art, music, and dance are recognized and taught in most of the institutions of higher learning both in and outside Africa, and exhibitions of African art have taken place in most of the capitals and major cities of the world since independence.

Finally, some aspects of the social impact will also endure. The foreign linguae francae are going to remain with us for a very long time if not forever. The new social classes produced by colonialism are bound to remain and will probably grow in complexity. Indeed, two new groups have already emerged since independence. The first consists of the new political elite of the leading members of the political parties that mushroomed in Africa during and since the independence revolution. Members of this group include former and current presidents, prime ministers, ambassadors, and high commissioners. The second is the military elite of the present and former officers of the armed forces of each independent state. Finally, the formation of independent African churches which began during the colonial era has continued and in fact has greatly intensified since independence.

In the light of all the above, we may safely conclude that though colonialism was a mere episode lasting no more than a hundred years anywhere in Africa, it was nonetheless an extremely important one. It marks a clear watershed in the history of the continent, and Africa's subsequent development is bound to be very much determined by some of its legacies. Ali Mazrui has recently speculated that "African culture may reclaim its own and help Africa retreat back to its ancestral authenticity, or Africa may struggle to find a third way."[16] I do not agree with the first alternative, since any such retreat is exceedingly unlikely if not utterly impracticable. I find the second alternative more realistic, but even here, I am convinced that any third way that would be found would still bear some of the impregnations and scars of colonialism. It would be most expedient, then, for African leaders to take the colonial impact very much into account

in the formulation of their future development programs and strategies.

THE COLONIAL IMPACT

1. This chapter is based mainly on the final chapter of Boahen, *UNESCO History*, vol. 7.
2. Gann and Duignan, *Burden of Empire*, p. 382.
3. Rodney, *How Europe Underdeveloped Africa*, p. 223.
4. A. A. Mazrui and M. Tidy, *Nationalism and New States in Africa* (London: Heinemann, 1984), p. xxii.
5. See Chapter 3, above, at n. 17.
6. Hopkins, *An Economic History of West Africa*, p. 235.
7. W. A. Lewis, *Politics in West Africa* (London: Allen and Unwin, 1965), pp. 24–25.
8. T. Garrard, *Akan Weights and the Gold Trade* (London: Longman, 1980), pp. 127–66.
9. Boahen, *UNESCO History*, 7:440, 484–85.
10. T. B. Kabwegyere, *The Politics of State Formation* (Nairobi: East African Publishing House, 1974).
11. A. A. Mazrui, *The Moving Cultural Frontier*, World Order Model Project, working paper no. 18, (New York: Institute of World Order, 1982).
12. R. Oliver and A. Atmore, *Africa since 1800*, 2d ed. (Cambridge: Cambridge University Press, 1972), p. 275; Gann and Duignan, *Colonialism in Africa*, 1:23.
13. J. F. A. Ajayi, "Colonialism: An Episode in African History," in Gann and Duignan, *Colonialism in Africa*, 1:497–509; J.F.A. Ajayi, "The Continuity of African Institutions under Colonialism," in Ranger, *Emerging Themes of African History*,; Hopkins, *An Economic History of West Africa*, pp. 167, 206, 235.
14. Mazrui and Tidy, *Nationalism and the New States in Africa*, p. xii.
15. Chinweizu, *The West and the Rest of Us*, pp. 80–187.
16. Mazrui and Tidy, *Nationalism and the New States in Africa*, p. xii.

BIBLIOGRAPHY

Ajayi, J. F. A., and M. Crowder, eds., *History of West Africa.* Vol. 2. London: Longman, 1974.

_____. "Colonialism: An Episode in African History." In Gann, and Duignan Colonialism in Africa, 1897–1960.

_____. "The Continuity of African Institutions under Colonialism." In Ranger, Emerging Themes of African History.

Ajayi, J. F. A., and M. Crowder, eds. *History of West Africa.* Vol. 2. London: Longman, 1974.

Akpan, M. B., "Ethiopia and Liberia." In Boahen, *UNESCO History,* vol. 7.

Asante, S. K. B. *Pan-African Protest: West Africa and the Italo-Ethiopian Crisis,* 1939–1941. London: Longman, 1977.

Asiwaju, A. I. "Migrations as Revolt: The Example of the Ivory Coast and Upper Volta before 1945." *Journal of African History* 17 (1976): 577–94.

Ayandele, E. *The Missionary Impact on Modern Nigeria,* 1842–1914: *A Political and Social Analysis.* London: Longman, 1966.

Azikiwe, N. *Liberia in World Politics.* London: A. H. Stockwell, 1934.

_____. *Renascent Africa.* 1937; repr. London: Frank Cass, 1968.

Barrett, D. B. *African Initiatives in Religion. Nairobi: East African Publishing House,* 1971.

Blyden, E. W. Christianity, Islam, and the Negro Race. New Ed. Edinburgh: Edinburgh University Press, 1967.

Boahen, A. Adu. *Britain, the Sahara, and Western Sudan.* Oxford: Clarendon Press, 1964.

_____. *Ghana: Evolution and Change.* London: Longman, 1975.

_____. "Towards a New Categorization and Periodization of African Responses and Reactions to Colonialism." Seminar paper, Department of History, University of Ghana, 1976.

_____. "Prempeh in Exile." *Research Review* (Legon) 8, no. 3 (1977): 3–20.

_____, ed. *General History of Africa.* Vol. 7. UNESCO. London: Heineman, 1985.

Casely Hayford, J. E. *Gold Coast Native Institutions.* ed. London: Frank Cass, 1970.

THE COLD WAR COMES TO AFRICA

Cordier and the 1960 Congo Crisis[1]

By Carole J. L. Collins

The spectacle is of the working of the political fate of human beings: the veiled logic which requires from political men actions which are the function of what they represent—and to a lesser extent of what they are—in circumstances which they cannot ever have wholly foreseen.

The movement of this logic, toward the mutual destruction of Dag Hammarskjold and of Patrice Lumumba, is the movement of Murderous Angels. The angels are the great and noble abstractions represented by the protagonists: Peace in the case of Hammarskjold, Freedom in the case of Lumumba. That the idea of Freedom can be murderous is obvious. ... To connect Peace with murder seems. ... shocking, yet the reality of the connection can be demonstrated.

—*Conor Cruise O'Brien, former representative of the U.N. Secretary-General to Katanga, in the preface to his 1968 play* Murderous Angels.[2]

Since its founding, the United Nations has sought to defuse tensions between member states that have threatened international peace and security. In the past five years, however, the U.N. Security Council has increasingly authorized intervention in civil conflicts including those in Angola, Bosnia and Croatia, Cambodia, El Salvador, Mozambique, Somalia and Western Sahara. U.N. operations in Cambodia and the Balkans are reported to be the largest such operations since the United Nations' 1960 intervention in the former Belgian Congo (now Zaire). A measure of this growing interventionist role in civil conflicts has been the price tag: Such U.N. operations cost member states a mere $200 million in 1987, but close to $3 billion by 1992.

U.N. members have increasingly supported intervention in civil conflicts for humanitarian reasons—to assist famine victims and halt widespread violence against civilians—as well as to forestall wider regional strife and to monitor democratic elections aimed at restoring peace. While the United Nations has been reluctant to become too deeply involved in these complex local conflicts, the mounting human toll from inter-ethnic and sectarian violence has multiplied demands for U.N. action. The central dilemma of such intervention, however, lies in the risk that the United Nations itself may become a player in the local conflict, sacrificing its ostensible role as a nonpartisan mediator. The neutrality and impartiality of a U.N. intervention has been challenged, fairly or not, as far back as the 1960 Congo crisis and as recently as its current interventions in Angola, Bosnia, Cambodia and Somalia.

Carole J. L. Collins, "The Cold War Comes to Africa: Cordier and the 1960 Congo Crisis," *Journal of International Affairs*, vol. 47, no. 1, pp. 243-269. Copyright © 1993 Journal of International Affairs. Permission to reprint granted by the publisher.

Indeed the 1960 United Nations Operation in the Congo (UNOC) presents a classic example of the risks of U.N. crisis intervention and attempted mediation in a civil conflict. UNOC looms large in U.N. institutional memory because, until recently, it was the largest U.N. peacekeeping operation ever, involving over 20,000 troops and logistical support from 30 countries;[3] it marked one of the first U.N. attempts to intervene in a civil conflict, albeit one involving many external powers, and set major precedents for future interventions; it further polarized already acute East-West tensions and paralyzed U.N. decision-making for years afterward; it served as an unconscious midwife to the arrival of the Cold War in Africa; and it inadvertently aborted the Congo's transition from colonial to democratic rule.

In analyzing the U.N. intervention in the Congo, this paper focuses on a *pivotal man*, a *pivotal period* and a *pivotal decision*. While most studies of the Congo crisis concentrate on Dag Hammarskjold—the charismatic U.N. Secretary-General who directed the overall intervention in the Congo until his death in a suspicious 1961 plane crash[4]—this study focuses on Andrew W. Cordier, who worked for the United Nations from its inception in 1946 until 1961, and later went on to a distinguished career at Columbia University. As Hammarskjold's executive assistant from 1952 until soon after the Secretary-General's death, Cordier became a pivotal diplomatic player early in the Congo crisis.[5]

Although UNOC lasted nearly four years, from July 1960 to June 1964, this paper focuses on the operation's first eight months. This pivotal period began with an international agreement on the need to intervene in the Congo to maintain the peace. By the end of the period, in February 1961, that consensus had shattered, and East and West were locked in a diplomatic confrontation that effectively paralyzed the United Nations' capacity to maintain international peace and security. During the pivotal period, the United Nations was transformed from a would-be mediator to a *de facto* player in the political dynamics of both the Congo and the Cold War, seriously compromising its efforts to restore peace. Alienated by U.N. leaders' actions, many African and other non-aligned members gradually withdrew their political support—and troops—from UNOC.

The resulting discord was heightened as a result of pivotal decisions taken by Cordier in early September 1960, while filling in as the Secretary-General's interim special representative to the Congo after the departure of the African-American diplomat Ralph Bunche and before the arrival of Bunche's successor, Indian General Rajeshwar Dayal. Cordier's barely three week stay in the Congolese capital of Leopoldville (now Kinshasa) coincided with a constitutional crisis: the reciprocal efforts of the Congo's President Joseph Kasavubu and its Prime Minister Patrice Lumumba to dismiss each other from office. Cordier's decisions effectively threw U.N. support behind Kasavubu and reinforced U.S. and Belgian efforts to oust Lumumba—seriously compromising the United Nations' impartiality. Some scholars argue that Cordier's actions ultimately served to help abort the Congo's transition to democracy, set in motion a series of events culminating in the murder of Lumumba—the Congo's first democratically elected prime minister—and facilitated the rise to power of a young Congolese army officer, Joseph Désiré Mobutu, whose more than a quarter century of rule has been marked by widespread human rights abuses and kleptocratic government.[6]

The Zairian people are still grappling to this day with the tragic legacy of these decisions. Likewise the United Nations has continued to struggle, both during the 1991 Persian Gulf War and the more recent U.N. interventions—such as in Somalia—undertaken in the unipolar post–Cold War era, with a central dilemma of the Congo crisis: how to maintain its credibility as a mediator when its acts, ostensibly based on multilateral consensus, appear to serve the unilateral policy objectives of one or a few U.N. member-states.

HISTORICAL CONTEXT OF THE CRISIS

The origins of the crisis can be found in the Congo's history as a Belgian colony, a history of exploitation of African labor and extraction of wealth by Belgian and other foreign economic interests. This history began with the European slave trade, in which perhaps 30 million people were killed or abducted, and which depopulated large tracts of Zaire, decimating the indigenous societies. In the late nineteenth century, Belgium's King Leopold II imposed the first central administrative authority to tax the Congolese people, as well as a forced labor system for collecting rubber and ivory that proved to be even more brutal than slavery.[7] Such harsh practices sparked one of the first international human rights campaigns, in which Mark Twain played a prominent role. Although blood flowed less freely when the Belgian government took over administration of the Congo after 1908, the Belgian colonial state did little more than modernize Leopold's system. It retained Leopold's coercive tax structure and used the First World War as a pretext to reimpose forced cash cropping and conscription, practices which lasted well into the 1950s.[8] It also imposed a system of rigid repression, racial segregation and white privilege—modelled after South Africa's apartheid system—that aroused intense resentment among virtually all Congolese and helped ignite the mutiny of Congolese soldiers against Belgian officers that broke out only days after independence in1960.

The Belgians did virtually nothing to prepare the Congolese for self-rule.[9] Compared to other colonial powers, Belgium went to extremes in barring Africans from most educational opportunities and from all but the most menial positions in the colonial government. The Congolese were also prohibited from voting or forming political parties until 1957, barely three years before independence and, even then, such activities were largely restricted to urban areas.[10] Colonial prohibitions on free speech, assembly and travel—maintained until the eve of independence—made political discussion and coalition-building beyond local levels all but impossible.

In addition, Belgian mining, agricultural and commercial interests fostered extremely uneven economic development, creating regional antagonisms and political fragmentation along ethnic lines. Recruitment of workers on a tribal basis sowed further social tensions, as did the colony's systematic deployment of Congolese soldiers to areas outside their home regions, where they could not speak any of the local languages. These factors led to horrendous fragmentation when Belgium legalized political activity in the late 1950s. Belgian suppression of trade unions deprived the Congolese of an important institution that nurtured multi-ethnic independence movements elsewhere in Africa.[11] Whereas years of anti-colonial agitation in other African countries often led to unified independence movements—or at most the establishment of only two or three major parties—in the Congo over 100 political ethnic, geographic or personality-based micro-parties rapidly formed in the year preceding independence. United only in their demand for immediate independence, they quickly became mired in political infighting once Belgium suddenly conceded the issue in early 1960.[12] Seventy-five years under a colonial government, which had deliberately divided in order to rule, had prevented the Congo's diverse peoples—speaking more than 200 languages and dialects—from melding into a nation.

ELEMENTS OF A COMPOSITE CRISIS

The suddenness with which Belgium acquiesced to Congolese demands for independence contributed to the series of crises that began just days after the new Congolese government assumed power on 30 June 1960. In January 1960, Belgium had unexpectedly agreed to grant independence to the Congo by the end of June, following national elections to be held in May. In those elections, Lumumba—the most charismatic leader in the Congolese independence movement—and his Stanleyville-headquartered Mouvement National Congolais (MNC) won a plurality over all other Congolese parties, including the ethnically based Association des Bakongo

(ABAKO) party headed by Joseph Kasavubu, a long-time advocate of independence.[13] Barely a week before independence, the newly elected parliament chose Lumumba to be prime minister and Kasavubu to be the largely figurehead president and chief of the army.

A key characteristic of the Congo crisis was its complex sequence of events, a product of multiple political actors—nationalist and secessionist politicians; external powers such as Belgium, the United States, the Soviet Union, France and various African and other Third World countries; and multilateral agencies like the United Nations—stalking the Congo's political landscape. In addition, these actors tended to be non-unitary and often changed their positions;[14] and the Congolese and Belgian governments in particular suffered from frequent internal divisions. U.N. intervention was ultimately sabotaged by this complexity.

The Congo crisis was actually a composite of several smaller but interrelated crises, three of which initially caused the new Congolese government to request U.N. assistance between 10 and 13 July 1960. First, a spontaneous mutiny of Congolese soldiers against their remaining Belgian officers that broke out between 4 and 5 July led to a *crisis in public order*. The mutiny reflected the pent-up grievances of Congolese soldiers against the remaining Belgians, many of whom still retained privileged positions in the post-colonial bureaucracy and army. The mutiny quickly spread and led to riots, looting and—to a lesser extent—attacks on Europeans, although the latter became the major focus of Western media coverage. For Belgium, this crisis provided the ideal pretext to justify introducing Belgian troops to support Katanga's secession.[15] The mutiny was the primary precipitant to Lumumba's and Kasavubu's joint appeal for U.N. assistance.

Second, a *crisis of secession* erupted in the province of Katanga when Moise Tshombe—then president of the provincial government—declared the copper-rich province independent on 11 July. Provincial government leaders in the diamond-rich province of Kasai quickly followed suit. The secessions, largely instigated by Belgian settlers and

business interests remaining in the Congo—but also backed by Rhodesian (now Zimbabwean) and South African elements—played on ethnic and regional divisions and threatened to dismember the Congo. The loss of Katanga and Kasai would have deprived the central government of most of its revenue, and left it unable to pay for routine government functions let alone development.

Third, Brussels' dispatch of troops to the Congo between 9 and 10 July to protect Belgian citizens and economic interests, as well as to support indirectly Belgian-backed Kasai and Katanga secessionist movements, led to a *crisis of direct external intervention*. The Belgian deployment violated the provisions of a treaty signed on the eve of Congolese independence which required the new central government to approve any such troop movements. Belgium's intervention was driven by its economic dependence on Congo investments; both its government and private interests wanted to maintain Belgian control of the Congolese economy. They were also determined to oppose any central government headed by Lumumba, whose radical-sounding anti-colonial sentiments, calls to diversify the Congo's external economic ties and willingness to accept aid from the Soviet bloc were anathema to them.[16]

Two subsequent crises quickly emerged to further complicate U.N. mediation efforts. First, President Kasavubu's decision, in early September 1960, to dismiss Prime Minister Lumumba, and Lumumba's reciprocal efforts in kind provoked a *constitutional political crisis*. Allied after independence despite strong personality clashes and political differences, their working relationship had begun to unravel in August because of diverging views on how to handle the Katanga secession. This dispute polarized their respective supporters in the legislature and throughout the country. The crisis was compounded by the ambiguity of constitutional arrangements inherited from the Belgians. Second, disagreements between U.N. member-states over the organization's efforts to resolve the conflict and Hammarskjold's and Cordier's actions—which had the effect of strengthening Kasavubu in his conflict with Lumumba—led to a *spinoff crisis* within the United Nations.[17] Growing splits among the East, the West and the Non-Aligned Movement over the legitimacy of those actions shattered the body's initial consensus on how to respond to the crisis and immobilized the Security Council for six months. For the first time, the U.N. General Assembly was asked to make decisions on a U.N. peacekeeping operation; it soon became equally mired in vitriolic debate.

While each of these smaller crises retained its own distinctive political dynamic, they influenced each other in various ways. Although such linkages can sometimes facilitate mediation, in this case their very multiplicity doomed U.N. attempts to synchronize subsidiary negotiations around these smaller crises. Given that various actors disagreed as to which crises were most critical, U.N. mediation efforts failed to resolve the overall crisis. In fact, the Congo situation gradually evolved into a more or less *continual crisis* that flared up repeatedly in following years and on which U.N. mediation efforts and troops had very little effect. Linkage effects generated an impasse rather than providing a basis for a diplomatic breakthrough.

VIEWS OF U.N. MEDIATION: CORE ISSUES AT STAKE

Congolese Leaders

Lumumba, Kasavubu and other Congolese nationalist leaders were divided by competing personal ambitions, ethnic loyalties and political ideologies that shaped their divergent views of the U.N. mediation effort. Initially, Lumumba and Kasavubu jointly requested the intervention of U.N. troops to preserve the Congo's territorial integrity, national unity and sovereignty. Lumumba evidently believed that U.N. troops would join with Congolese forces to help end the Katangan secession. His acceptance of the U.N. role was tacitly but clearly predicated on its assumed willingness to help the new government exert control over all national

territory and counter the secessionists.[18] When in late July, it became clear that the Secretary-General would not order U.N. troops to do so, Lumumba began to oppose the U.N. presence and to solicit Soviet military assistance in ending the Katangan succession. Lumumba's anti-U.N. stance intensified in August when Hammarskjold effectively ignored Lumumba's legal government and flew to Katanga to negotiate directly with Tshombe.

U.N. Member-States

UNOC was intended to restore civil order, which had collapsed in urban areas following the mutiny of Congolese troops in early July. Multilateral intervention was also designed to exclude external actors—explicitly Belgium and implicitly the Soviet Union—from becoming further involved. As consensus on how to maintain the peace collapsed, U.N. members soon formed competing coalitions reflecting their increasingly divergent goals and the larger Cold War-era divide between Western and Soviet blocs. While African and Third World members, supported by the Soviet bloc, wanted the United Nations to induce Belgian troops to withdraw and help end secessions threatening the Congo's sovereignty and unity, the United States, Belgium and other Western allies emphasized the need to halt the growing Soviet presence in this strategically located nation. These coalitions increasingly disagreed on the legitimacy of U.N. objectives and actions in the Congo. Even U.N. officials differed on how best to resolve the crisis, as Cordier did with his more neutralist successor Rajeshwar Dayal.

U.N. Officials

Senior U.N. officials were motivated to intervene, quite apart from any Congolese request, because they feared that the crisis—on the heels of the U.S.-Soviet U-2 incident, Cuba's turn to the left and simmering East-West tensions in Indochina—might escalate into a major global conflict.[19] For Hammarskjold and Cordier, the core issue was always maintenance of global peace in a world deeply split by the Cold War. They believed that Congolese issues were of subordinate importance to the risk that the Congo crisis might intensify East-West tensions and ultimately spark a nuclear showdown. This fear blinded them to the fact that many Congolese and other Africans perceived their actions as so skewed to Western priorities as to render the neutrality of their actions suspect, especially in relation to Belgium. Further, neither Hammarskjold nor Cordier saw any contradiction between their anti-communist stances and their roles as international, ostensibly neutral and nonpartisan civil servants. While both criticized Belgian intervention, they saw the Soviet Union as a possibly greater irritant in the Congo crisis and the primary threat to global peace. Cordier's comments on the Soviets at the United Nations reflects this sweeping anti-communism: "I know that their fundamental aim is one of the destruction of Western civilization."[20]

Because Cordier and Hammarskjold shared the Western anti-Soviet worldview, they felt little discomfort in collaborating with Western interests and strategies, including those of the U.S. Department of State and the Central Intelligence Agency.[21] Several sources, including Madeleine Kalb's study based on declassified diplomatic cable traffic, document the extent to which Cordier continually briefed and was briefed by U.S. diplomats and collaborated with them on Congo policy.[22] At one point Cordier noted that U.S. assistance, especially financial, was essential to the U.N.'s presence in the Congo: "It is always necessary to keep the leadership firmly in our hands, providing thus a basis for support from the mass of the U.N. membership. Washington has been giving excellent support at all times."[23] Cordier provided $1 million— money supplied to the United Nations by the U.S. government—to Mobutu in early September to pay off restive and hungry Congolese soldiers and keep them loyal to Kasavubu during his attempt to oust Lumumba as prime minister.[24] Such U.S.-U.N. cooperation became a highly contentious issue for African and Third World states, some of whom felt

the United Nations had become "the transmission belt for American policy."[25]

Given the primacy of the Cold War in his calculations, Cordier was particularly incensed that Lumumba "has been playing a game of bilateral competition and has therefore opened the door quite wide to Soviet influence in the Congo."[26] Cordier and Hammarskjold shared the assumption that there were no valid grounds for Lumumba to seek Soviet assistance. Both felt, seemingly *a priori*, that any Soviet aid to the Congo was both an expansion of Soviet influence into Africa and a "provocation" they feared could ignite an East-West crisis. That Lumumba would take such aid indicated that he was either ultimately a Communist sympathizer or a dupe, both equally illegitimate in their eyes. As Cordier wrote:

> One of the extraordinary features of their [Soviet] tactics is the feverish support that they give to people like Castro and Lumumba, persons who are themselves destroyers and who therefore not only become the symbols of Russian influence abroad but the outposts of their effort.[27]

The dangers of such aid legitimated almost any actions needed to forestall it. Hammarskjold and Cordier were willing to undermine any leader, like Lumumba, whom they thought served Soviet aims in the Congo.

Still, Cordier was no simplistic admirer of the Belgians: "The world is now reaping the whirlwind of Belgian misrule" in the Congo, he wrote, adding that after 80 years of colonial rule the Congolese "people were left in a state of illiteracy and poverty and were used as pawns in the Belgian game of profit seeking."[28] He consistently saw the presence of Belgian troops as a central irritant in the crisis: "The presence of Belgian troops in the Congo was a most disturbing element in the preservation of peace. There was simply no alternative except to seek their complete removal from the country."[29]

Brussels initially saw support for Katangan secession as an ideal means to maintain its economic interests and protect its settlers in the Congo. But Belgian ministries and politicians became increasingly divided throughout 1960 and 1961, however, over the extent to which Belgium should become involved in Congolese internal affairs, or support or oppose U.N. mediation and Katangan secession. Brussels' policies and resolve varied accordingly. At times Brussels actively supported Tshombe's Katanga; at other times it sought an accommodation with Leopoldville and the United Nations. Yet Brussels resisted U.N. pressure to cut all support for the secessionist movements.

The United States—particularly sensitive to newly Communist Cuba and a more assertive Communist China—was obsessed with preventing the Soviet Union from using its championing of anti-colonial struggles to expand its influence in Africa. London and Paris soon joined Washington in backing U.N. mediation as a more politically acceptable way to pre-empt Soviet intervention without open alliance with the discredited Belgians, although the Eisenhower administration tended to view Brussels as a stabilizing force in the Congo. Whenever the United Nations put greater emphasis on issues other than containing Soviet influence, as it tended to do after Dayal replaced Cordier in September 1960, the U.S. and other Western powers tended to reduce their support for U.N. mediating efforts. While Cordier sought American support for the U.N. role in the Congo, it is equally clear that Washington sought to use the United Nations to pursue its own policy objectives. Nominally neutral, UNOC could not have operated without the roughly $100 million a year it received in U.S. funds, and was thus heavily influenced by Washington.[30] U.S. influence was especially strong during the first months of Congolese independence, when Bunche and Cordier served as Hammarskjold's representatives in Leopoldville.[31]

For Hammarskjold and Cordier, Lumumba became the central factor blocking U.N. mediation efforts. Of all the characters on the Congolese political stage, none so fueled the fears of political opponents, Western powers and U.N. diplomats as this charismatic, abrasive and mercurial man. His anti-colonial passion, his grip on the popular imagination, his growing international following and his advocacy of non-alignment raised—in the Cold War-clouded minds of U.N., Belgian and especially American policy makers—the specter of a socialist Congo with strong links to the Soviet bloc.[32] Cordier and Hammarskjold consistently discounted Lumumba's legitimacy and sincerity, and failed to distinguish him from his Soviet supporters. They failed to grasp what he symbolized—or, in death, came to symbolize—for millions of ordinary Africans. As O'Brien noted:

> To say that millions of Africans are affected by some event, or impressed by some personality is usually an exaggeration … But the name and fate of Patrice Lumumba have really reached the minds and hearts of millions of Africans. The thousands of "Cafe Lumumba" and "Lumumba Chop Bar" signs scattered through countless bush villages in tropical Africa are a more impressive tribute to his memory than the Patrice Lumumba University in Moscow. …[33]

Given his fiery oratory, Lumumba's efforts to be privately charming and conciliatory with Westerners, instead of soothing their fears, made him seem all the more unpredictable and duplicitous. The Belgian government's unrelenting hostility toward Lumumba—mainly due to his trenchant criticism of their remaining economic interests in the Congo and his desire to eliminate their continuing lock on Congolese export markets—largely motivated their decision to back the secessionist movements in Kasai and Katanga.

Early in the crisis, both Hammarskjold and Cordier came to distrust and dislike Lumumba.[34] Cordier's antagonism towards Lumumba was evident. He saw the Congolese leader as the precipitant of the crisis:

> Since July 10 … we have surmounted several crises already [including getting Belgium to start withdrawing its troops in the Congo] but now we are in the middle of a new one centering around the person of Mr. Lumumba, the Prime Minister. He is completely irresponsible—if not a mad man.[35]

Cordier seemed only bemused by the fact that Lumumba was the democratically elected and legitimate leader of the Congo government, who had received significantly more votes than Kasavubu in the May elections and commanded predominant support in the Congolese parliament. Rather than accepting Lumumba's legitimate claim to political authority, Cordier believed that "all these Lumumba explosions"[36] were dangerous developments that needed to be countered, circumvented and neutralized:

> He is wildly ambitious, lusting for power and strikes fear into anyone who crosses his path. There is really no such thing as a Congolese Government. Several weeks ago I sent a cable to Dag suggesting that he see someone in the Government about a certain matter. He replied, "But who can I see?" There is a cabinet, but Lumumba uses it as his tool. Some members of the Cabinet share his vision and lust for power, while the few moderates … are understandably fearful to take any positive line.[37]

In his letters to Schwalm, Cordier consistently portrays Lumumba as corrupt. He recounted Belgian tales of Lumumba's conviction on embezzlement, alleges that Lumumba "got away" with some $400,000 while working for a soft drink company in the capital, and says that "there are those … who say that he is a drug addict," though he never cites any hard evidence or sources.[38] In general, Cordier seems to have little sympathy for African nationalists, characterizing—in one startling passage—then Ghanaian president Kwame Nkrumah as "a madly ambitious man," and then going on to assert that "Nkrumah is the Mussolini of Africa while Lumumba is its little Hitler."[39]

Cordier seems blind to any U.N. obligation to mediate between contending politicians or defend the Congolese people's right to choose their leaders without fear of foreign intervention. Cordier's dislike of Lumumba seems to have prevented him from pushing for a reconciliation—a more traditional mediator's goal—between Kasavubu and Lumumba in early to mid-September, when their rift might still have been resolved.[40] Rather, he identifies Lumumba's personality as the problem to be circumvented:

> The only real solution of the problem is a change of leadership. It will not be easy, however, to remove Lumumba from his position. Furthermore there are limits to our own capacity to bring about a change of leadership. We can produce such a situation in the international climate as to affect political pressures within the country, but we are excluded under the Charter from direct action of a political character which would affect the political balance of leadership within the country. In various ways the Secretary-General has given encouragement to the moderates and they are also receiving encouragement from other powerful political sources.[41]

In his search for alternatives to Lumumba, Cordier initially saw Kasavubu as a "reasonable man who has often been at odds with Lumumba but … is ineffective since he is unwilling to use the same rash methods as those used by Lumumba."[42] By early 1961, however, Cordier was commenting that "Kasa-Vubu's [sic] ineptness, inaction and incompetence continue to this day."[43] Cordier found Kasavubu's inaction particularly frustrating, especially when compared with Lumumba's energy and initiative:

> The whole situation ... is a story out of Gilbert and Sullivan. Each day brings its own extraordinary surprises of ineptitude, inexperience and futility. For example, to my amazement, after the President returned from the radio station [after dismissing Lumumba] he went to bed around midnight and assumed I guess that his job had been done. There were most essential contacts that he should have made in the early hours of Tuesday morning but he was unavailable. On the other hand Lumumba ... worked around the clock without regard for sleep or meals, ... rounding up support and generally beating down efforts made by the President and his few active supporters.[44]

PIVOTAL MOMENT, PIVOTAL DECISIONS

In September 1960, while still in Leopoldville, Cordier made several key decisions that effectively aligned the United Nations with Kasavubu in his dispute with Lumumba. Cordier's 15 September letter to Schwalm reveals that he had advance notice of Kasavubu's intent to dismiss Lumumba, and that he welcomed the move but wanted to ensure that the United Nations not appear too blatantly partial to Kasavubu. Cordier notes he met four times with Kasavubu, at the latter's request, to discuss the firing of Lumumba, and "explained to him in detail the extent, as well as the limitations of the role of the United Nations force in a national emergency."[45] When Kasavubu announced his dismissal of Lumumba from office on the radio on Monday, 5 September, Cordier—at Kasavubu's request—made his "two most important decisions:" to send U.N. troops to close the airport and to seize the radio station.

These nominally neutral actions, ostensibly taken "to keep the crisis within bounds and especially to avoid bloody civil outbreaks," primarily hurt Lumumba because only Kasavubu enjoyed access to radio facilities in the neighboring state of Congo (Brazzaville).[46] Similarly, Kasavubu's allies were allowed to use the ostensibly closed airport to travel into the Congolese interior to mobilize support for the president while Lumumba's supporters were grounded. Both U.N. actions entrenched Kasavubu's control of the capital and helped him silence his charismatic rival.[47] The legal fiction that the United Nations was acting only to preserve the peace was for the international audience; it convinced no Congolese. As a result of Cordier's decision, the United Nations lost both credibility and leverage over the Lumumbist forces and contributed to the spread of civil unrest. As U.S. Ambassador Timberlake noted following a 7 September 1960 speech by Lumumba to parliament:

> Lumumba ... attacked the UN saying the country was not really free if arms, airports and radio facilities were controlled by the UN. How could the UN justify this interference if it refused to liberate Katanga?[48]

Cordier was uninterested in having the United Nations try to reconcile Kasavubu and Lumumba; for instance, he made himself "unavailable" when Lumumba "demanded" to see him early on the morning of 6 September.[49] His letters reflect an obvious but surprising disdain for the Congo's one most democratic institution, its parliament. He saw it as little more than a tool for Lumumba—because its members supported Lumumba. Unhappy at Lumumba's persuasiveness among his fellow parliamentarians, Cordier actually opposed its meeting. Only in his 3 October letter did he reluctantly concede that "it appears that we must encourage the parliament to meet."[50]

Cordier noted on 15 September that he "knew full well that these decisions would have profound repercussions in all the capitals of the world and indeed this has been the case." He must have found it all the more disconcerting that Lumumba's "talent and dynamism" continued to bedevil his opponents, as a CIA operative ruefully noted.[51] On 12 September, Lumumba managed to elude arrest and his MNC government went on to win a parliamentary vote of confidence. A frustrated Timberlake complained: "Kasavubu acts more like a vegetable everyday while Lumumba continues to display brilliant broken field running."[52]

Near the end of his three-week stay in early September, Cordier sought to "immobilize" the Congolese Army so that it could not be used by Lumumba. Drawing on the "brilliant assistance of General Kettani, a Moroccan General," Cordier authorized the United Nations to offer "food and pay to the Congolese Army which was a very important factor in the maintenance of their neutrality."[53] This action was far from neutral as it allowed Mobutu—a one-time Lumumba aide who had been appointed chief-of-staff of the army by Kasavubu just days earlier—to win credit for paying the soldiers their past-due salaries, to buy their loyalty for Kasavubu and himself and to pave the way for his coup attempt a few days later.[54] Although Cordier had noted that "regrettably Mobutu is anything but the strongman as described by American newspapers, but nevertheless, backed by the Belgians, took over political power," the combination of U.N. and U.S. support was pivotal for Mobutu's subsequent seizure of power.[55]

Efforts by the United States, the United Nations and Belgium to isolate Lumumba by co-opting Mobutu-doomed democracy in the Congo, cementing the army's loyalty to Mobutu. On 14 September, Mobutu seized power, ostensibly to protect the Congo "from Communist colonialism and from Marxist-Leninist imperialism." Mobutu suspended the nation's first—and last—democratically elected parliament.[56] Throughout this tumultuous week, all accounts agree, Cordier cooperated closely with U.S. Ambassador Timberlake and avoided consulting with Hammarskjold, who was at U.N. headquarters in New York.[57] Mobutu, after ostensibly acting to neutralize both Kasavubu and Lumumba, gradually allowed President Kasavubu to resume most powers of his office, while imprisoning Lumumba.[58]

In the end, Cordier's actions served to fuel the Congolese civil war. They deepened the estrangement between Lumumba and Kasavubu, and so compromised the United Nations's professed neutrality that many Congolese—and Third World U.N. members—questioned its allegedly disinterested role in the Congo onwards. Cordier had to admit that Lumumba retained significant popular support:

> … [T]ragically, if Lumumba came into power we could not work with him and many governments would oppose him. If KasaVubu [sic] succeeded in getting the upper hand and established a firm government, we could work with him but many governments, including the Communists, Ghana, Guinea, India and others would oppose him.[59]

After his dismissal by Kasavubu, Lumumba was placed under virtual house arrest, but even this failed to dampen his popular or legislative support. When, in January 1961, he was killed through the coordinated efforts of Mobutu, Kasavubu, Tshombe and the CIA, his stature continued to increase and bedevil his opponents.[60]

The explicit intent behind Cordier's actions remains hard to judge and his letters to Schwalm are circumspect, as one might expect, on this point. Dayal insists that—at worst—Cordieri inadvertently abetted an anti-Lumumba plot conceived and directed by Western embassies.[61] O'Brien—the conservative Irish diplomat and essayist who had represented the United Nations in Katanga in 1961 and his closely followed Congo politics for many years since then—believes that Cordier deliberately helped Washington plot Lumumba's ouster, and may have done so with Hammarskjold's plausibly deniable approval.[62]

REFLECTIONS ON U.N. MEDIATION

The United Nations performed many of the formal mechanics of mediation, especially as a *facilitator of communication* among parties, in the Congo. Over several years its officials shuttled between Katanga and Leopoldville with various proposals and counter-proposals. In July and August 1960, both Hammarskjold and Cordier tried to persuade Lumumba to be less adamant in his hostility to Tshombe and the Belgians, using meetings to convey aspects of their talks with both. They also tried to act as *formulators of solutions*, suggesting various strategies. Their imagination and capacity to innovate breakthroughs was limited, however, by their Cold War presumptions and priorities. They never succeeded in seeing the conflict from a Congolese point of view even though, in Hammarskjold's case, he at one point presumed to speak for the Congolese people.[63] Many Congolese rightly saw this as patronizing and a reflection of these diplomats' inherent contempt for the Congolese and Africans.

The predominant U.N. mediating style was as a *manipulator*: trying to move parties to adopt its favored solution, using U.N. troops and the supposed intolerability of a political stalemate as leverage. Intolerability, however, is in the eye of the beholder: the stalemate of continued Katangan secession, intolerable to the United Nations because it increased the risk of Soviet meddling, was tolerable to Lumumba if the only alternative was to accept the secession, which he regarded as little more than capitulation to continued Belgian colonial rule.

The Congo crisis illustrates the primary role of personalities such as Lumumba and Cordier in influencing the course of multilateral intervention. As mediators, Hammarskjold and Cordier obviously had many of the personal qualities often considered to be keys to success: intelligence, commitment, perseverance, persuasiveness and imagination. Hammarskjold was even noted for his charisma. But these qualities were more effectively utilized in the U.N. arena than in the Congo itself. In retrospect one is struck by how consistently Cordier and Hammarskjold both discounted Lumumba's legitimacy and sincerity and failed to distinguish him from his Soviet supporters. Very early in the crisis, Cordier screened out information that contradicted his pre-formed view of Lumumba.[64] This was facilitated by his extensive reliance on Western embassies and intelligence services. Sharing his Cold War preconceptions, their information on and views of Lumumba tended to be mutually reinforcing.

The Congo crisis moves one to question how effective mediation can be when the mediators lack detailed knowledge of the local situation, and sensitivity toward expressing their considerable qualities in culturally appropriate and hence persuasive ways. In fact, both Hammarskjold and Cordier failed to persuade Lumumba to modify his negotiating stance and make concessions to defuse the volatile situation. Indeed, his adamancy combined with their anti-communism to create *de facto* diplomatic gridlock.

In trying to ensure the success of the U.N. mission as they conceived it in the Congo, Cordier and other top U.N. leaders took steps which constituted *de facto* intervention in internal Congolese affairs. In effect, they played kingmaker, albeit within certain constraints of deniability. They threw their backing behind their preferred Congo leader in a manner that created longterm suspicions among many Congolese and Africans about U.N. motivations.

THE COLD WAR COMES TO AFRICA

The Congo crisis has had profound implications for Africa, the first case of Cold War-driven superpower intervention in the sub-Saharan region. The long-term consequences of superpower intervention have been devastating, marked by Africa's limited democracy and arrested self-determination, extensive militarization, large refugee movements, declining food production and economies that have been shattered by the weight of civil wars fought with hardware supplied by East and West. It is both ironic and sobering that the United Nations and its officials—in their efforts to prevent an East-West confrontation in the Congo—contributed to making Africa one of the Cold War's most deadly killing fields.

Perhaps the ultimate irony is that the Congo crisis precipitated exactly what Cordier and Hammarskjold tried urgently to prevent: a sharpening of East-West conflict at a time when the risk of nuclear confrontation was high. Because of Hammarskjold and Cordier's actions to forestall the escalation of East-West rivalry in the Congo, Hammarskjold himself became so much the focus of controversy that the Security Council was effectively immobilized for six months while debating the issue. The Congo crisis ultimately became the United Nations' own: its capacity to confront other threats to international peace and security, such as in Laos, quickly eroded as the political fallout from its actions in the Congo spread to other issue areas.[65] The Congo's immediate crisis became a permanent crisis for the United Nations—which stretched well into the following decades.

Cordier squarely blamed the Congo debacle on the Soviets and their supporters, absolving those Western actors—and indeed himself—who intervened in the Congo's first steps toward democracy. There is nothing to indicate that Cordier ever explicitly regretted or felt the need to further defend his decision to back Kasavubu and ultimately Mobutu. But Cordier did lament the sharpening of Cold War antagonisms that followed that decision. Several times he expressed growing despair at the course of events, most notably when he remarked, in a 3 October letter to Schwalm that "The world has clearly fallen into a profound crisis and I feel it necessary to guard myself against the odor of atomic and hydrogen bombs and of dying masses."[66]

The tragedy of the Congo crisis was that the U.N. leadership—personified by Cordier and Hammarskjold—was so preoccupied with global East-West concerns that it remained blind to the implications of its actions for the decolonization and democratization of Africa. O'Brien's "veiled logic" is the logic of global politics within an anti-communist framework that Cordier and Hammarskjold accepted without question. For Lumumba, on the other hand, the logic was a white man's logic that denied the Congo real sovereignty:

In the opposition between Hammarskjold and Lumumba, it is no accident that the white man is the hero of Peace, the black man the hero of Freedom. ... Hammarskjold ... welcomed ... the accession of new nations to freedom. ... But Peace, not Freedom, was his primary concern, and calculations about world peace had necessarily to be mainly about the positions of those who could make world war. ...

From Hammarskjold's point of view this seemed a legitimate subordination of the part to the whole, the subordination of the demands of a particular set of people to the universal and overriding requirement of world peace. From Lumumba's point of view it was yet another example of the continued subordination of black to white. The calculations of the political conjuncture were white calculations and Peace—if it were to be Peace without Freedom—was a white vested interest. Lumumba's summoning of Russian aid is a defiant inversion of Hammarskjold's values; he is willing to risk general war for the sake of his concept of Freedom, expressed in the sovereignty of a black state. This is not allowed. ...[67]

Today Zaire is struggling to navigate the passage from over a quarter century of dictatorship under Mobutu to democratic rule. The outcome is far from certain. As in Yugoslavia and the rest of East Central Europe, past ethnic and political tensions are resurfacing in new forms, accelerated by the collapse of the economy, transport and communications infrastructure, and Mobutu's strategic marginalization in a post–Cold War era. Many of the over 200 political parties that have participated since 1991 in Zaire's Sovereign National Conference resurrect or mirror the traditional political factions that developed at and following the Congo's independence in 1960.

From 1991 on, Mobutu—like King Leopold before him—has become increasingly isolated and discredited. Yet with the help of his stolen wealth, an abundance of printed banknotes and the bought loyalty of the presidential guard, he has clung to power. The Bush administration was reluctant to end decisively diplomatic support for this longtime friend of U.S. strategic interests. The Clinton administration has proved equally reluctant to back fully its rhetorical support for Zaire's democratization process by taking concrete steps to isolate politically and financially this last of the old-time dictators[68]

But a decision to abandon Mobutu may not necessarily presage a wiser U.S. policy toward the Congo, or a wiser U.N. role in the future should it, as some Zairian politicians have urged, be asked to intervene in the current Mobutu-orchestrated spread of ethnic conflict. Will it again be the case where, as O'Brien commented on Western support for Tshombe: "the white political leader chooses to bypass the political leader of the blacks, in order to arrange matters with a black man who has been chosen by whites"?[69]

The Congo's past experience suggests that outside attempts to impose a political outcome on a people's transition to democracy, however sincere the motives, will likely endanger rather than enhance peace and security. Let us hope that the Zairian people will be spared the agony of again facing—due to outside manipulation—"the odor … of dying masses."[70]

NOTES

1. An earlier version of this article appeared as "Fatally Flawed Mediation: Cordier and the Congo Crisis of 1960," *Africa Today* 39, no. 3 (3rd Quarter 1992) pp. 5–22. Parts of this paper draw on research conducted jointly with a colleague, Steve Askin, for a forthcoming book on Zaire.

2. Conor Cruise O'Brien, *Murderous Angels: A Political Tragedy and Comedy in Black and White* (Boston, MA: Atlantic Monthly Press, 1968) pp. xix–xx.

3. Both the Korean conflict and the 1991 Persian Gulf War involved more troops, but were essentially U.S.-initiated military coalitions that won U.N. Security Council approval. UNOC forces were drawn from such countries as Burma, Sri Lanka, Egypt, Ethiopia, Ghana, India, Indonesia, Ireland, Liberia, Malaya, Mali, Morocco, Nigeria, Pakistan, Sierra Leone, Sudan, Sweden and Tunisia. The United States, the Soviet Union, Britain and Canada provided funding and air transport. The total cost of the four-year operation was $400 million.

4. Some believe Hammarskjold's plane may have been shot down by white mercenaries fighting with Katanga secessionists. See "Ex-U.N. Officials Question Hammarskjold Crash," *New York Times*, 13 September 1992, p. 21, a letter by Conor Cruise O'Brien and George Ivan Smith alleging evidence of probable mercenary involvement in Hammarskjold's death. A subsequent report by the Swedish foreign ministry claims the crash was accidental (Bengt Rösiö, "The Plane Crash at Ndola: A Re-examination," English translation from the Swedish Information Service, 4 March 1993, p. 26).

5. My discussion of Cordier's role in the Congo crisis draws extensively on his correspondence with his close friend and college mentor, Dr. V.F. Schwalrn, an emeritus professor at Manchester College in Indiana. These papers are in the A.W. Cordier Collection deposited with the Rare Book and Manuscript Library at Columbia University, New York, NY. I thank the library for its generous cooperation. Cordieris virtually the only key diplomatic player not to have published his memoirs about the Congo crisis. This correspondence forms a most remarkable and revealing, if informal, diary that sheds much light on his perception of events and personalities in the Congo.

6. For various accounts of the Congo crisis and Mobotu's rise to power, see in particular

Madeleine G. Kalb, The Congo Cables: *The Cold War in Africa—From Eisenhower to Kennedy* (New York: Macmillan, 1982); David Gibbs, "Private Interests and International Conflict: A Case Study of Intervention in the Congo," unpublished doctoral dissertation (Cambridge, MA: Massachusetts Institute of Technology, 1989); David Gibbs, *The Political Economy of Third World Intervention: Mines, Money and U.S. Policy in the Congo Crisis* (Chicago, IL: University of Chicago Press, 1991); Stephen R. Weissman, *American Foreign Policy in the Congo 1960-64* (Ithaca, NY: Cornell University Press, 1974); Catherine Hoskyns, *The Congo Since Independence* (London: Oxford University Press, 1965); and Richard D. Mahoney, *JFK: Ordeal in Africa* (New Oxford, UK: Oxford University Press, 1983).

7. Peter Duignan and L.H. Gann, *The Rulers of Belgian Africa: 1884-1914* (Princeton, NJ: Princeton University Press, 1979) p. 96.

8. Jean-Philippe Peemans argues there was "no real break between the Leopoldian state and the Belgian colonial regime." See his "Capital Accumulation in the Congo Under Colonialism: The Role of the State," in Peter Duignan and L.H. Gann, eds., *Colonialism in Africa 1870-1960: The Economics of Colonialism*, 4 (London: Cambridge University Press, 1975) p. 180. See also Crawford Young, *Politics in the Congo: Decolonization and Independence* (Princeton, NJ: Princeton University Press, 1965) p. 219.

9. For details of the colonial legacy, see: Rene Lemarchand, *Political Awakening in the Belgian Congo* (Berkeley, CA: University of California Press, 1964) pp. 25–74 *passim;* and Young, *Politics in the Congo*, pp. 33–161 *passim*.

10. Lemarchand, pp. 72–3; Young, *Politics in the Congo*, p. 296.

11. Lemarchand, pp. 103–4, 167–84.

12. Young, *Politics in the Congo*, p. 298.

13. Patrice Lumumba, *Congo My Country* (London: Pall Mall Press, 1962) p. 162.

14. For a discussion of unitary and non-monolithic diplomatic actors, see Gilbert Winham, "Practitioner's View of International Negotiations," *World Politics* 32, 1 (October 1979) pp. 111–35; and Howard Raiffa, *The Art and Science of Negotiation* (Cambridge, MA: Harvard University Press, 1982) pp. 11–19.

15. For further discussion of the "justification of hostility," see Richard Ned Lebow, *Between War and Peace: The Nature of International Crisis* (Baltimore, MD: Johns Hopkins University Press, 1981) pp. 29–40.

16. Until independence, the Congo was a major source of revenue for Belgian corporations. In the 1950s, firms in Belgium averaged an 8 to 9 percent return on capital while those in the Congo averaged about 20 percent, according to Conor Cruise O'Brien in *To Katanga and Back: A UN Case History* (New York: Simon and Schuster, 1962) p. 173. As late as 1958, foreign—mostly Belgian—residents in the Congo, barely one percent of the colony's population, controlled 95 percent of its total assets, 88 percent of private savings, 47 percent of its cattle stocks and 35 percent of agricultural output. This huge economic stake motivated Brussels' post-independence efforts to retain its economic lock on the Congo's economy, despite competition from French and U.S. interests, and to help Belgian settlers retain their holdings in the vast, resource-rich land. See Peemans, "Capital Accumulation," in Duignan and Gann, eds., p. 181.

17. Lebow, pp. 25, 41–6 *passim*.

18. See I.B. Ekpebu, *Zaire and the African Revolution* (Ibadan, Nigeria: Ibadan University Press, 1989) pp. 31–8 *passim*.

19. For a general discussion of mediators' defensive reasons for intervening, see Saadia Touval and I.W. Zartman, eds., *International Mediation in Theory and Practice* (Boulder, CO: Westview Press, 1985).

20. Cordier letter to Schwalm, 11 January 1961, p. 3.

21. On the extent to which U.N. and U.S. policies towards the Congo coincided, despite occasional divergences, see especially: Rajeshwar Dayal,

Mission for Hammarskjold: The Congo Crisis (Princeton, NJ: Princeton University Press, 1976) pp. 34, 65–6; Gibbs, *Private Interests*, pp. 143–92 *passim;* Kalb, pp. 1–196 passim; Mahoney, pp. 34–88 *passim* and Weissman pp. 60, 77, 86–90.

22. To give one example, Kalb cites cables from the U.S. Mission to the United Nations, to the Department of State, indicating Cordier's agreement with Secretary of State Christian Herter on the need to prevent the routing of aid through the Soviet Union and Cordier's willingness to raise the issue with Lumumba. Kalb, pp. 42, 74–5; Gibbs, *Private Interests*, p. 167; and Weissman, pp. 89–91.

23. Cordier letter to Schwalm, 18 August 1960, p. 8.

24. See Dayal, pp. 34, 65–6; Kalb, pp. 93–6. Also, Dayal, Weissman, pp. 86–95 *passim*, and other sources indicate Mobutu received extensive funding from the CIA.

25. Weissman, p. 77. See also pp. 86–90.

26. Cordier letter to Schwalm, 15 September 1960, p. 5.

27. Cordier letter to Schwalm, 11 January 1961, p. 3.

28. Cordier letter to Schwalm, 18 August 1960, p. 1.

29. *ibid.*, p. 3.

30. See Crawford Young, "The Zairian Crisis and American Foreign Policy," in Gerald Benderetal., eds., *African Crisis Areas and U.S. Foreign Policy* (Berkeley, CA: University of California Press, 1985) pp. 211–2; and Weissman, p. 60. For contrasting views of the U.N. role in the Congo, see the memoirs of three key participants: Major General Carl von Horn, *Soldiering for Peace* (New York: David MacKay Co., 1966); Dayal; and O'Brien, *To Katanga and Back*. General Von Horn, a fierce anti-communist, commanded UNOC forces in 1960; Dayal, a neutralist, was the U.N. Congo representative from September 1960 to May 1961; and O'Brien was U.N. representative to Katanga in 1961.

31. As O'Brien points out, Hammarskjold's three closest advisors during this period were American and "Washington paid most of the bills, was the heaviest contributor to the organization's budget and by far the heaviest contributor to the Congo operation, which would be brought to a standstill by a withdrawal of American support." (*To Katanga and Back*, p. 56.) See also Gibbs, *Private Interests*, pp. 166–7; and Gibbs, *Political Economy*, p. 93.

32. For a good review of how Lumumba was viewed by various analysts and U.S. officials, see Mahoney, pp. 43–5.

33. O'Brien, *Murderous Angels*, p. xxii.

34. See Dayal, pp. 296–7, 309–10.

35. Cordier letter to Schwalm, 18 August 1960, p. 1.

36. *ibid.*, p. 8.

37. *ibid.*, p. 4.

38. *ibid.*, p. 5. See also Cordier letter to Schwalm, 15 September 1960, p. 3. This charge is repeated by Ernest W. Lefever in *Crisis in the Congo: A United Nations Force in Action* (Washington, DC: The Brookings Institution, 1965). Mahoney notes, however, that "both his admirers and antagonists seemed to agree … that Lumumba … unlike his Congolese contemporaries, cared for something more than his own remuneration." (Mahoney, p. 43).

39. *ibid.*, p. 7.

40. See Ekpebu, pp. 31–8 *passim*. Ekpebu believes this was a real option and notes that Congolese efforts to bring the two sides together received no encouragement from the United Nations.

41. Cordier letter to Schwalm, 18 August 1960, p. 6.

42. *ibid.*, p. 4.

43. Cordier letter to Schwalm, 11 January 1961, p. 3.

44. Cordier letter to Schwalm, 15 September 1960, p. 3.

45. *ibid.*, p. 1.

46. *ibid.*, pp. 1–2. See also Mahoney, p. 47.

47. Weissman, pp. 91–2; O'Brien, *Murderous Angels*, pp. 198–9; Cordier letter to Schwalm, 15 September 1960, p. 2.

48. Mahoney, p. 47.

49. Cordier letter to Schwalm, 15 September 1960, p. 3.

50. Cordier letter to Schwalm, 3 October 1960, p. 4.

51. See Kalb, p. 87.

52. *ibid.*, pp. 85–7.

53. Cordier letter to Schwalm, 15 September 1990, p. 4.

54. Dayal, pp. 34, 65; and Kalb, p. 96. Dayal believes the timing of the U.N. payment to Mobutu was an innocent coincidence, but notes that large additional sums of money flowed to Mobutu from the CIA and other Western sources.

55. Cordier letter to Schwalm, 11 January 1961, p. 3. Cordier initially viewed Mobutu as politically weak, especially after Mobutu and the Belgians made the political mistake, in December 1960, of landing their troops—while vainly attempting to seize control of the Congolese province of Kivu from Lumumbist forces—in Burundi, then a U.N. Trust Territory (Cordier letter to Schwalm, 11 January 1961, p. 4).

56. P. Alan Merriam, *Congo: Background of Conflict* (Evanston, IL: Northwestern University Press, 1961) p. 267; Jonathan Kwitny, *Endless Enemies: The Making of an Unfriendly World* (New York: Congdon & Weed, 1984) pp. 65–6. On Cordier's role, see also O'Brien, *Murderous Angels*, pp. 93–6.

57. See Dayal, p. 33–5; Kalb, p. 74–5; O'Brien, *Murderous Angels*, p. 93–4; Weissman, p. 91.

58. Kasavubu resumed formal control of the government in February 1961. See Kalb, p. 224.

59. Cordier letter to Schwalm, 21 October 1960, p. 4.

60. On the CIA role in the assassination of Lumumba see the "Church Commission Report," named for the chair of the U.S. Senate investigative committee, Senator Frank Church. (Senate Select Committee to Study Governmental Operations with Respect to Intelligence Activities, *Interim Report: Alleged Assassination Plots Involving Foreign Leaders*, 94th Cong., 1st sess., 20 November 1975.) Also Kalb, pp. 53–5, 63–6, 101–3, 128–33, 149–52, 158–9, offers an excellent detailed account. See also Gibbs, *Private Interests*, pp. 168–74; Mahoney, pp. 52–3, 57–67 *passim*, 69–74; and Weissman, pp. 88–90.

61. Dayal, p. 65.

62. O'Brien, *Murderous Angels*, p. 198–201.

63. See Ekpebu concerning Hammarskjold's remarkable statement, in a 13 July 1960 report, that "I am the one who is closest to speaking for the Government of the Congo at this table." (Ekpebu, p. 51).

64. U.S. policy makers made the same mistake in the waning days of the Eisenhower administration (Mahoney, pp. 43–5). For a discussion of *cognitive dissonance* and how negotiators tend to filter out information that contradicts their early preconceptions, see Lebow, pp. 101–19.

65. Cordier to Schwalm, 29 April 1961, p. 3.

66. Cordier letter to Schwalm, 3 October 1960, p. 3.

67. O'Brien, *Murderous Angels*, p. xxii-xxvi passim.

68. For current U.S. policy towards Zaire, see Secretary of State Warren Christopher's address to the African-American Institute at their May 1993 annual meeting, and Assistant Secretary of State for African Affairs George Moose's testimony before the U.S. Senate Foreign Relations Subcommittee on African Affairs on 9 June 1993.

69. O'Brien 1968, p. xxviii.

70. Cordier letter to Schwalm, 3 October 1960, p. 3.

CHINA'S AFRICAN POLICY IN THE POST-COLD WAR ERA

By Joseph Y. S. Cheng and Huangao Shi

ABSTRACT: *As China's economy continues to grow, it wants to expand its markets and secure reliable supplies of resources in support of its economic development. Resource diplomacy therefore becomes a prominent feature of its modernisation diplomacy. In turn, many African governments perceive political and economic ties with China to be an important asset, which strengthens their international bargaining power, especially vis-à-vis Western governments. African countries are also depicted as China's reliable political and economic partners, though one can hardly afford to be optimistic regarding Africa's peace and development in the future. Many small African governments have been switching diplomatic recognition between Taipei and Beijing for economic assistance too. Chinese leaders have no intention of engaging in diplomatic and strategic competition with the USA and the European Union in Africa, but they certainly will not co-operate with Western governments in helping Africa because they want to push for multipolarity.*

KEY WORDS: Foreign aid, human rights, oil, resource diplomacy, Forum on China-Africa Co-operation

Africa has been seen as probably the most important part of the developing world in the Chinese leadership's worldview. And, yet, despite occasional major encounters, such as the Tanzania-Zambia railway project in the late 1960s, China's contacts with and influence on Africa remained limited until recent years in view of its constraints in resources and power projection capability (Larkin, 1971: 1–14).

Today, Chinese leaders pursue a "major power diplomacy," based on the assumption that China is a major power and should be accorded the status and influence of one. China's impressive economic growth also involves an expansion of

Contemporary China Research Project, City University of Hong Kong, Kowloon, Hong Kong,

**Department of Government and International Studies, Hong Kong Baptist University, Kowloon, Hong Kong*

Correspondence Address: Joseph Y. S. Cheng, Contemporary China Research Project, City University of Hong Kong, 83 Tat Chee Avenue, Kowloon, Hong Kong. Email: rcccrc@cityu.edu.hk

ISSN 0047-2336 Print/ 1752-7554 Online/09/010087-29 © 2009 *Journal of Contemporary Asia*
DOI: 10.1080/00472330802506840

trade and investment activities, as well as efforts to ensure a reliable supply of resources in support of its development. Africa, therefore, is no longer an element of the abstract "Third World" concept in China's diplomacy; it has become significant politically in international organisations, as well as an increasingly important trade partner and supplier of energy resources. In this context, China and Egypt established a strategic co-operation relationship facing the twenty-first century in 1999; and China and South Africa established a strategic partnership in 2004 (Policy Research Department, 2005: 107, 222).

Traditionally, the Ministry of Foreign Affairs (MFA) of the People's Republic of China (PRC) covers Africa by the West Asia and North Africa Department and the African Department. The former deals mainly with the Arab world, while the latter with sub-Saharan Africa. This article examines China's African policy in the post Cold War era from a continental perspective. It briefly reviews China's African policy in the past decades, analyses China's political and economic interests in Africa, and considers the opportunities and challenges in Sino-African relations at this stage.

CHINA'S AFRICAN POLICY IN RETROSPECT

The Bandung Conference in 1955 placed Africa firmly in the "intermediate zone" between the socialist camp and the imperialist camp in Mao Zedong's worldview and strategic considerations, with internationalism and world revolution being the main themes. This initial contact was followed by a period of ideological radicalism in the context of the Sino-Soviet split, the Vietnamese War and China's isolation in international affairs, as well as the Cultural Revolution in the domestic scene. The commitment to build the Tanzania-Zambia railway, costing more than US$450 million, was made at the height of the Cultural Revolution (Yu, 1980: 170–2). Pragmatic considerations gradually entered the picture in the 1970s, and became predominant in the 1980s (Lin, 1989).

A major issue of contention between the Communist Party of China (CPC) and other communist parties in the period of ideological radicalism was whether or not any Third World country, irrespective of its politico-social system, should be accepted as part of the main force against imperialism and hegemonism. The Chinese leaders' position was that the nature of the Third World countries' politico-social systems could not alter the fundamental contradiction between the Third World on one hand and imperialism and hegemonism on the other. They also presented a three-stage revolutionary process in the Third World, as summarised by the following slogan: countries want independence, nations want liberation and the people want revolution. All Third World countries should, therefore, be included in the anti-imperialist united front; and, in the struggle against imperialism and hegemonism, the people's political consciousness would be raised and revolutionary forces would grow. Since revolution could not be exported, the success of revolution would be determined by the accumulation and expansion of revolutionary forces and the domestic conditions within each individual country (Van Ness, 1970).

In many ways, China in the Maoist era was probably the major power that was most forthcoming in supporting the Third World's demands. China was the only bilateral aid donor in the world whose foreign aid often went to countries with a higher per capita gross national product (GNP) than its own (Lin, 1996). Strengthening its distinction from the two superpowers, while fully realising its limited military and economic capabilities, China's support for non-alignment and neutralisation served its purpose well. In the field of arms control and disarmament, China's declaration neither to be the first to use nuclear weapons, nor to use them against non-nuclear countries certainly won support in the Third World (Cheng, 1989: 190–4).

In the late 1960s and 1970s, a serious controversy in China's African policy was which national liberation movements to support. In those years, Chairman Mao Zedong certainly considered that Soviet social-imperialism was more dangerous than US imperialism; and this consideration guided the Chinese leadership's choices of national liberation movements for support. In South Africa, for example, Beijing supported the Pan Africanist Congress (of Azania) against the African National Congress during the political struggles led by Nelson Mandela. In Mozambique, it backed the Mozambique Revolutionary Committee against the Liberation Front of Mozambique. In Angola, China supported the National Front for the Liberation of Angola (which was also supported by the US's Central Intelligence Agency and the South African apartheid regime) against the Popular Movement for the Liberation of Angola-Party of Labour. Unfortunately, the Chinese leadership backed the wrong horse in all three cases; and the Chinese position generated considerable resentment in many independent African countries as well (Rubinstein, 1975).

Regarding foreign aid, China in 1977 offered US$1.5 billion to 49 countries. After the termination of aid to Vietnam and Albania in 1978, China's foreign aid had probably been reduced by more than one third. The post-Mao leadership did not like to see foreign aid drain too many resources away from China's Four Modernisations programme. Though China's foreign aid was maintained at a much lower level, its terms were generally much more favourable than those of other aid donors; in this way, it was still welcomed by the Third World because of its demonstration effect. After all, China was not able to compete with the major aid donors in terms of the amount of aid provided.

In the 1980s, China devoted considerable attention to South-South co-operation, and this emphasis on co-operation helped to cover the Chinese reduction in foreign aid. In his tour of Africa at the end of 1982 and the beginning of 1983, the then Premier Zhao Ziyang put forward four principles on strengthening South-South co-operation, namely, equality and mutual benefit, stress on practical results, diversity in form and attainment of common progress (*Beijing Review*, 24 January 1983: 19). This was in sharp contrast to Zhou Enlai's eight principles on Chinese foreign aid enunciated 19 years earlier, again during his African tour. Zhou's principles practically guaranteed that Chinese aid would be the most generous in the world (Armstrong, 1977).

China had been firmly supporting the establishment of a New International Economic Order since the 1970s; in the 1980s, however, it became more specific in its proposals. Moreover, it became quite active in supporting the United Nations (UN) and its specialised agencies in organising projects, seminars and so on, for the benefit of the developing countries. Premier Zhao's African tour and his later trip to South America in October and November 1985 demonstrated the Chinese leaders' efforts to cultivate important areas of the Third World, which hitherto had been neglected (Mu, 1985: 4).

Table 1 provides statistical data on China's foreign aid to Africa in the 1980–92 period, which largely stayed at the same level. Meanwhile, China's gross domestic product (GDP) more than doubled, and its annual trade grew from US$4.4 billion in 1981 to US$10.3 billion in 1988 (Taylor, 1998). Philip Snow (1994: 306) observed that China's retreat from aid commitments to Africa was camouflaged by the rhetoric of South-South co-operation, while the African countries concerned were expected to contribute to the maintenance of many of the aid projects. While China itself began to receive foreign aid from Japan and some Western European countries from 1979 onwards, Africa's strategic value in the 1980s was more and more

Table 1. China's foreign aid to Africa, 1980–92 (US$ million)

Year	1980	1981	1982	1983	1984	1985	1986	1987	1988	1989	1990	1991	1992
Amount	157	412	390	309	223	262	230	306	60	224	375	303	345

Source: Statistical data for 1980–87 from Bartke (1992: 8–9); for 1988–89 from Editorial Board of the Yearbook of China's Foreign Economic Relations and Trade (1989–90); and, for 1990–92, from Lin (1996).

rhetorical in nature as the Chinese leadership could not see much economic significance in a remote and impoverished continent (Harding, 1984: 184).

The post-Mao leaders in theory affirmed the Third World's important role, but in the actual implementation of their foreign policy, their focus had been on the handling of China's relations with the two superpowers and the developed countries. This, in fact, was the case throughout the 1970s, though such trends became more conspicuous in the pursuit of the leadership's modernisation diplomacy. Taking a long-term view, the progress of a global socialist revolution could not rely too much on the exploitation of the contradictions among the imperialist powers and the expansion of the anti-imperialist united front; these were but tactical measures in the short run. Long-term progress of a global socialist revolution ultimately had to rely on the accumulation and strengthening of revolutionary forces, and priorities among the components of the anti-imperialist united front had to be defined clearly. This was why the post-Mao leaders still emphasised the important role of the Third World from a theoretical, long-term point of view: the ultimate judgement as to whether or not their foreign policy line had violated the obligations of a socialist country had to depend on whether or not it had contributed to the accumulation and strengthening of revolutionary forces in the long run. This was the implicit ideological defence of Deng Xiaoping's foreign policy line, though it did not appear to be convincing in the eyes of the African governments (Cheng, 1989: 190–4).

The Tiananmen protests and state crackdown in June 1989 altered the balance between the conservatives and the reformers in the Chinese collective leadership: Zhao Ziyang fell from power, and the conservative older generation gained influence. Chinese leaders felt the pressure of sanctions initiated by the Bush administration and other Western governments (McGurn, 1990). The Political Bureau of the CPC made the following observation after the Tiananmen events: China in the past had been too close to the West and the rich countries, and had neglected the Third World and

the old friends in Africa. In crucial moments, as had been demonstrated in the recent disturbance, it was old friends and the Third World that had shown China sympathy and support. China, therefore, should strive to resume and develop relations with these old friends (Lo, 1989: 8).

Soon after the 1989 Tiananmen events, the then Chinese foreign minister, Qian Qichen, visited Africa in August and the Middle East in September (*South China Morning Post*, 9 September 1989). These visits were designed to raise China's international profile among Third World countries and reassure them of its renewed commitment in view of its recent setbacks. No dramatic results were achieved, but they symbolised a significant shift away from Beijing's pro-Western tilt from 1978, a policy that had disappointed many of China's Third World friends (Cheng, 1990).

During Foreign Minister Qian's visit to Africa, he noted at a press conference in Harare, Zimbabwe, that of the 137 countries that had established diplomatic relations with China, only some 20 had reacted adversely to the Tiananmen events. The majority, including African countries, neighbouring Asian countries, Latin American countries and socialist countries, considered it China's internal affair and that other countries should not interfere (Chang, 1989: 10).

In line with China's impressive economic growth in the 1990s, the Chinese leadership expected China to be taken seriously as a "major power" and accorded its "rightful place" in the international community (Cheng and Zhang, 2002). Michael D. Swaine (1995: 87) argued that China's foreign policy in the 1980s exploited "the development of common interests with most Third World (and especially Asian) states, to raise China's global stature and increase Beijing's bargaining leverage with the United States." ... In the post-Cold War era, the world was perceived as a unipolar one. Chinese leaders wanted to contain US hegemonism, as reflected by the then Premier Li Peng's comment in 1990 that Western countries should not be allowed "to interfere in the internal affairs of the developing countries, or pursue power politics in the name of 'human rights, freedom and democracy'" (*Xinhua Domestic Service*, 12 March 1990).

China's relations with the Third World were not without difficulties. Despite its claim of being a developing country belonging to the Third World, it was not a member of the Group of 77 or the Non-Aligned Movement. Partly because of its pledge not to become a superpower and probably because of its shortage of seasoned diplomats, China adopted a low profile regarding any leadership of the Third World and had, until recently, few initiatives or concrete proposals to offer.

In diplomatic competition with Taiwan, China sometimes encountered difficulties too. In the aftermath of the 1989 Tiananmen events, Taiwan hoped that the offer of generous economic aid and the international revulsion at the bloody suppression of the Chinese students' democracy movement would encourage some Third World countries to re-establish diplomatic relations with Taipei. The first breakthrough came in July 1989, when Grenada announced the establishment of diplomatic relations with Taipei, while trying to maintain formal ties with Beijing. China responded by breaking off diplomatic relations with Grenada (*South China Morning Post*, 8 August 1989). Grenada was followed by Liberia and Belize (*South China Morning Post*, 11 and 14 October 1989) and Nigeria and Senegal were seen as next. While diplomatic competition with Taiwan was related to the legitimacy of the Chinese communist regime in both the international and domestic arenas, the actual foreign policy impact was limited.

In the first decade or so after the Chinese leadership had adopted its economic reforms agenda and opened to the external world, and with its admission of the failure of the Maoist development strategy, China could no longer claim to be an attractive model of socio-economic progress offering a successful alternative to the Third World. In its new guise, China's economic development strategy was similar to that of other developing countries in East and Southeast Asia; it developed export-orientated industrialisation strategies and competed with other Third World

countries for aid and loans from international organisations and from the Western and Japanese governments. As China joined the Multi-Fibre Arrangement and began to negotiate to participate in the General Agreement on Tariffs and Trade (and later the World Trade Organisation; WTO), it also entered into hard bargaining for export quotas from the developed countries and into competition with the developing countries.

In this period, the impact of China's development on Africa remained very limited. However, as the Chinese economy achieved respectable growth, China's economic ties with Africa have strengthened. Africa has been an important target in China's "resources diplomacy" in recent years. China, as a major power, has assumed a greater role in providing aid to the developing world, and Africa has become a significant recipient. For example, in 2005, China began to offer tariff-free treatment to part of its imports from the 25 least developed African countries and 16 African countries qualified as official Chinese tourist destinations. China engages in co-operation with African countries on environmental protection and population development and has initiated a Young Volunteers Programme similar to the US's Peace Corps, with the first batch of volunteers being posted to Ethiopia. Human resources development programmes have been one of Beijing's priority areas, and it claimed that more than 4000 African participants received training in China in 2005. The Forum on China-Africa Co-operation (FOCAC) held a summit meeting and its third ministerial meeting in Beijing in November 2006 (Policy Research Department, 2006: 30–3).

The first ministerial meeting of FOCAC was held in Beijing in 2000 at the initiative of the then Chinese President Jiang Zemin. In contrast with the previous Third World meetings, which were heavily political in orientation, this forum was business-orientated, with the Chinese Minister of Foreign Trade and Economic Co-operation (now Minister of Commerce) Shi Guangsheng as the honorary president. The forum focused on two topics: how to push ahead with the establishment of a new international political and economic order that is fair and just in the twenty-first century; and how to promote Sino-African economic and trade co-operation (*People's Daily Online*, 9 October 2000). The second ministerial meeting of FOCAC took place in Addis Ababa, Ethiopia in 2003. It had concentrated mainly on the implementation of the Beijing Declaration and the programme for China-Africa co-operation in economic and social development, two programmes adopted in the first ministerial meeting. It was noteworthy that a China-Africa business conference was held during this forum to facilitate exchanges among entrepreneurs, and between entrepreneurs and officials. The new foci in this ministerial meeting were China-Africa co-operation in human resources development, promotion of African exports to China, and increases in exchanges in the fields of tourism and culture (*China Daily*, 30 November 2003).

At the international organisation level, China is grateful for support from African governments on the issues of Taiwan's representation and China's human rights situation. On issues such as reform of the UN and negotiations at the WTO, China and Africa have also had mutual interests. China has become involved in a number of peacekeeping operations in Africa under UN auspices, including those in Congo (Kinshasa), Liberia and Darfur in Sudan. At the end of 2005, Chinese personnel involved in peacekeeping operations in Africa numbered 843. Beijing also offers the African Union grants for material and specific peacekeeping operations, and China's ambassador to Ethiopia also serves as ambassador to the African Union. After the December 2004 Indian Ocean tsunami impacted East Africa as well, China was involved in disaster-relief operations in the affected African countries (Policy Research Department, 2006: 32–3).

In September 2005, President Hu Jintao announced a package of aid measures in support of developing governments in a fund-raising conference of the UN. First, China offered the 39 least developed countries with diplomatic relations with China tariff-free treatment for most of their exports to China. Secondly, China expanded its

assistance for poor countries with heavy debts and the least developed countries. It also offered to waive the remaining repayments of all low-interest and interest-free governmental loans from China which were due at or before the end of 2004. Thirdly, over the following three years, China offered developing countries US$10 billion of preferential loans and preferential export buyer credits to support their infrastructural development and to promote bilateral joint ventures among enterprises. Fourthly, over the same period, China agreed to increase its medical assistance to developing countries, especially those in Africa, including the provision of pharmaceutical supplies (in particular those against malaria), the establishment and improvement of medical facilities, and the training of medical personnel; these medical assistance programmes were to rely on mechanisms, such as FOCAC and bilateral channels. Fifthly, over the same period, China committed to providing various types of training to 30,000 people from developing countries, in support of their human resources development (Zhang and Huang, 2006: 283). Africa was to be the main beneficiary of these aid programmes, reflecting China's enhanced input to Sino-African ties. As a symbolic gesture of the significance China attached to Africa, since 1989, the foreign minister has visited African countries in his first foreign visit every year. In 2005, the Ministry of Foreign Affairs organised its first open day for the public on the theme of Africa and the promotion of understanding of Africa and Sino-African relations.

The year 2006 marked the fiftieth anniversary of the beginning of China's diplomatic relations with Africa; and, on 12 January 2006, the government formally released a document on "China's African Policy" (Ministry of Foreign Affairs, 2006). This was the first document of its kind; and the Chinese Assistant Foreign Minister, Lui Guozeng stated: "Our objective is to show the international community the importance China accords to Africa, and to demonstrate China's strong will to develop friendly relations with African countries" (Zhang and Huang, 2006: 284). The document is divided into six sections: Africa's position and role, China's relations with Africa, China's African policy, the enhancement of all-round co-operation between China and Africa, FOCAC and its follow-up actions, and China's relations with African regional organisations.

The document states that China will establish and develop a new type of strategic partnership with Africa, featuring political equality and mutual trust, economic "win-win" co-operation, and cultural exchanges. Several measures were proposed to strengthen Sino-African economic co-operation, including: the setting up of a China-Africa Joint Chamber of Commerce and Industry; initiating of negotiations for free trade agreements with African countries and African regional organisations; the provision of preferential loans and buyer credits to encourage Chinese investment and business in Africa; the conclusion of agreements on bilateral facilitation and protection of investment and agreements on avoidance of double taxation with African countries; agricultural co-operation in technology, training courses, experimental and demonstration agricultural technology projects, and the formulation of a China-Africa Agricultural Co-operation Programme; co-operation in transportation, communications, water conservation, electricity and other infrastructural projects; resources co-operation; human resources development through Beijing's African Human Resources Development Foundation and an increase in the number of government scholarships to promote student exchange; science and technology co-operation; and medical and health co-operation (Ministry of Foreign Affairs, 2006).

Sino-African trade grew from less than US$10 million per annum in the 1950s to almost US$40 billion in 2005. In the past half a century, China offered about 800 aid projects to African countries, and Chinese enterprises had contracted construction and labour service projects amounting to US$38.9 billion by October 2005. Mutual investment flows, however, remain limited: China's investment in Africa was about US$1.075 billion by October 2005, and only a few African countries, such as South Africa, have investments in China. China has basically fulfilled its pledge made at the second FOCAC ministerial meeting in December

2003 to offer training for 10,000 African personnel in 2004–06. Since China first dispatched its medical team to Algeria in 1963, Beijing claims to have sent 14,000 medical personnel in various missions to 37 African countries up to the end of 2005 (Zhang and Huang, 2006: 284–5).

In the Beijing summit, under the auspices of the third FOCAC ministerial meeting in November 2006, the Chinese leadership made further offers of aid which amounted to US$10 billion. Such aid commitments have considerably enhanced China's influence in Africa in support of its strategic partnership with the continent. In addition, as an aid donor, China gradually can compete with the USA and France on the continent. The pledges made by the Chinese government during the 2006 summit expanded earlier commitments and included: doubling the amount of aid to Africa by 2009; a US$3 billion offer of preferential loans and US$2 billion in preferential export credits for purchasers to African countries in the 2006–09 period; establishing a China-Africa Development Fund of up to US$5 billion to promote investment in Africa by Chinese enterprises; construction of the African Union Convention Centre at the headquarters of the African Union in Addis Ababa, Ethiopia; waiving the repayment of interest-free government loans, which were due at or before the end of 2005 for all highly indebted African countries and least developed countries in Africa with formal diplomatic relations with China; as a gesture to open the China market to Africa, tariff-free treatment for more than 440 import items (up from 190 items) to the least developed African countries with formal diplomatic relations with China; the establishment of three to five offshore economic and trade co-operation zones in African countries within three years; the provision of training for 15,000 Africans over three years; and 300 million *yuan* for the prevention of malaria, as well as the construction of medical, agricultural and educational facilities in Africa (*Ming Pao*, 5 November 2006). The summit also facilitated the conclusion of US$1.9 billion of contracts between African countries and Chinese enterprises (*Ming Pao*, 6 November 2006).

CHINA'S POLITICAL INTERESTS IN AFRICA

Chinese leaders understand that catching up with the most advanced developed countries in the world will take a considerable time. Hence, they feel a need to maintain a peaceful international environment so that China can concentrate on economic development. As China's economy grows, heavy industries have become more significant and, in recent years, China's heavy industries have enjoyed a higher growth rate than light industries, and China has become a net exporter of steel, aluminium, auto parts and other machinery products (Anderson, 2007: 18). This development demands more raw materials and energy resources from abroad. China's expanding exports also call for new markets. From the first half of 2004 to the first half of 2007, China's monthly trade surplus jumped by nearly US$20 billion, of which only US$6 billion came from exports to the USA (Anderson, 2007: 16).

China's impressive economic development enhances its "comprehensive national strength." Chinese foreign policy adopts a considerably higher profile and the leadership engages in "major power diplomacy" to strengthen China's influence in international affairs. Such efforts are part of its grand design to promote multipolarity based on the idea of "peaceful rise."

These two trends imply that China will be more involved in African affairs; it will seek recognition of its interests in the continent as a world power and will attempt to resist US "unilateralism" in Africa. However, China has no intention of confronting the USA, including in its approach to Africa. In Africa, while there is a "resource diplomacy" element, it will promote African solidarity and the strengthening of the Africa Union (China Institutes of Contemporary International Relations, 2006: 193–214). At the same time, in the early summer of 2007, Beijing responded to Western demands and appointed a special envoy and began to exert some pressure on the government of Sudan on Darfur (see Holbrooke, 2007: A25).

Chinese leaders realise China's limited power projection capabilities. They, therefore, have attempted to develop a loosely organised multilateral forum to gradually enhance China's influence on the continent, as they believe that time is on China's side. It is expected that economic ties will strengthen, accompanied by increased foreign aid from China, which will be designed to achieve maximum publicity. Beijing is obviously interested in establishing a good image, and it will continue to articulate a pro-developing world position on African affairs. The Darfur crisis is an example. The Chinese government has insisted on reaching a solution through political and diplomatic means, without coercion, discouraging major power intervention and arguing that there are local and regional interests that need to be respected as far as possible. This approach was not particularly well-received in the West, but as China has become more inclined to take part in UN peacekeeping operations and offer financial and other types of assistance, the pressure on China has been reduced (He, 2007).

As China becomes more active in international organisations, it views African countries as natural allies. Upon re-establishment of diplomatic relations with Chad in early August 2006, China had formal ties with 48 of the 53 African countries. Many African governments respond positively to Beijing's appeal to unite together to withstand the pressures from imperialism and neo-colonialism. Some resent Western criticisms of their lack of democracy and allegations of human rights abuses. They perceive such criticisms as an interference in domestic affairs and support Beijing's position that "the right of survival" and "the right of development" should take precedence over individual human rights. The Chinese leadership probably considers that there have been important diplomatic achievements from its African policy, including some African support for China against condemnation of China's human rights record and for its position to deny Taiwan representation in international organisations (Policy Research Department, 2006).

The issue of human rights has been an area of contention in Sino-American relations, especially after the Tiananmen events. American presidents have been under substantial domestic pressure to condemn China's human rights violations in multilateral forums. The Chinese leadership perceives this as a matter of "face" or prestige, and treats voting processes as competitions for support from the international community. The UN Commission on Human Rights is a major battlefield, as reflected by the following comment of the former US Assistant Secretary of State for Democracy, Human Rights and Labour, John Shattuck: "the [UN Commission on Human Rights] is probably the most important tool to condemn China's human rights violations" (Office of the Spokesman, 1997). From 1990 to 2006, the USA and its allies initiated motions to condemn China's human rights violations, including the 1989 Tiananmen events, Tibet and the suppression of Falun Gong, 11 times at the UN Commission on Human Rights annual conferences, and China typically countered with "no action" motions. China was able to avoid condemnation through securing majority support for its "no action" motions; and, as shown by Tables 2, 3 and 4, China owed much of its success to support from African governments. The African Group delivered 120 supporting votes throughout these years, compared with 137 votes from the rest of the world. The annual ratio of African supporting votes to total supporting votes averaged 46.6%, ranging from a low of 35.3% to a high of 51.9%. There were only eight votes opposing the eleven "no action" motions from African governments, compared with 182 from the rest of the world. There were no opposing votes from Africa in the respective votes in 1992, 1993, 2001 and 2004 (see Tables 2–4).

In the competition between Beijing and Taipei for diplomatic recognition, Africa also figures prominently. Since the PRC's entry into the UN in 1971, the number of countries recognising the Republic of China (ROC) dropped from approximately 70 to about 22 by the early 1980s. Under such circumstances, Taiwan pursues its "pragmatic diplomacy" consisting of de jure recognition by a small number of countries and de facto economic and informal linkages with most countries of the world. Taiwan values its "international space" and its "pragmatic diplomacy" was said by Jason Hu, Taiwan's foreign minister, to be "like the sun, the air and the water for a person."[1] Taiwan is also ready to engage in "dollar diplomacy" to raise its international profile; and given its substantial foreign exchange reserves, it has been able to induce a few small and poor African, Central American and South Pacific governments to establish formal diplomatic relations with it (Anon., 1997; Taylor, 1998).

The Chinese leadership treats the prevention of Taiwan's independence as a high priority national goal, partly because isolating Taiwan internationally and defeating it in diplomatic competition are linked strongly to the Chinese leadership's exploitation of nationalism and its attempt to preserve and strengthen its legitimacy. Hence, Beijing allocates considerable resources to winning the diplomatic recogni-tion of small states in Africa, Central America and the South Pacific (Christensen, 1996). This competition has often been criticised by the

Table 2. Regional distribution of seats in the UN Commission on Human Rights (1980–present)

	Regional Group									
	African Group		Eastern European Group		Latin American Group		Asian Group		Western Group	
Period	Seats	% of total	Seats	% of total	Seats	% of total	Seats	% of total	Seats	% of total
1980–91	11	26	5	11	8	19	9	21	10	23
1992–present	15	28	5	9	11	21	12	23	10	19

Source: Comission on Human rights (n.d.).

Table 3. African countries' votes on the "no action" motions concerning condemnation of China's human rights situation at UN Human Rights Conferences

	Supporting votes				Opposing votes				Abstention votes			
Year	Total	African votes	% of total supporting votes	% of African group total	Total	African votes	% of total opposing votes	% of African group total	Total	African votes	% of total abstention votes	% of African group total
1990	17	6	35.3	54.5	15	1	6.7	9.1	11	4	36.4	36.4
1992	27	13	48.1	86.7	15	0	0	0	11	2	18.2	13.3
1993	22	11	50.0	73.3	17	0	0	0	12	2	16.7	13.3
1994	20	10	50.0	66.7	16	1	6.3	6.7	17	4	23.5	26.7
1995	20	11	55.0	73.3	21	1	4.8	6.7	12	3	25.0	20.0
1996	27	14	51.9	93.3	20	1	5.0	6.7	6	0	0	0
1997	27	14	51.9	93.3	17	1	5.9	6.7	9	0	0	0
1999	22	8	36.4	53.3	17	2	11.8	13.3	14	5	35.7	33.3
2000	22	9	40.9	60.0	18	1	5.6	6.7	12	5	41.7	33.3
2001	23	10	43.5	66.7	17	0	0	0	12	4	33.3	20.0
2004	28	14	50.0	93.3	16	0	0	0	9	1	11.1	6.7
Average	23.2	10.9	46.6	74.0	17.2	0.7	4.2	5.1	11.4	2.7	22.0	18.5

Source: Various reports from *Renmin Ribao [People's Daily]*; and Xiao (2002: 39). In case of discrepancies in statistics, *Renmin Ribao* data are used.

Table 4. Regional votes on the "no action" motions concerning condemnation of China's human rights situation at UN Human Rights conferences

Regional Group

Year	African Group			Eastern European Group			Latin American Group			Asian Group			Western Group		
	Supporting	Opposing	Abstentions	Supporting	Opposing	Abstentions	Supporting	Opposing	Abstentions	Supporting	Opposing	Abstentions	Supporting	Opposing	Abstentions
1990	6	1	4	3	2	0	1	1	6	7	1	1	0	10	0
1992	13	0	2	1	3	1	2	1	7	11	1	0	0	10	0
1993	11	0	2	0	5	0	1	1	9	10	1	1	0	10	0
1994	10	1	4	0	3	2	1	1	9	9	1	2	0	10	0
1995	11	1	3	0	5	0	2	4	5	9	2	1	0	10	0
1996	14	1	0	2	2	1	2	6	3	9	1	2	0	10	0
1997	14	1	0	2	2	1	2	3	6	9	1	2	0	10	0
1999	8	2	5	1	3	1	4	1	6	9	1	2	0	10	0
2000	9	1	5	1	3	0	3	3	5	9	1	2	0	10	0
2001	10	0	4	1	4	0	2	2	7	10	1	1	0	10	0
2004	14	0	1	2	2	0	2	3	6	10	1	2	0	10	0
Total	120	8	30	13	34	6	22	26	69	102	12	16	0	110	0

Barbados (Latin American Group) did not vote in 1992; Togo and Mauritius (African Group) did not vote in 1993; Romania (Eastern European Group) was absent in 2000; and Congo (Kinshasa) (African Group) was absent in 2001.

Source: Various reports from *Renmin Ribao*; and Xiao (2002: 39). In case of discrepancies in statistics, *Renmin Ribao* data are used.

overseas Chinese communities as meaningless and wasteful, as reflected by reports and commentaries in newspapers in Hong Kong and China. When the Democratic Progressive Party was in opposition in Taiwan, it also criticised the Kuomintang government for its "dollar diplomacy." But, when it came to power in 2000, it has not deviated from its predecessor's practice (Payne and Veney, 2001).

The re-establishment of diplomatic relations between Chad and the PRC is a typical example. In 1972, Chad abandoned Taiwan to establish diplomatic relations with the PRC, after the PRC secured UN membership. In August 1997, Taiwan was able to persuade the Chadian government to switch recognition back to the ROC. At that time, Chad needed investment to develop its oil resources and foreign aid to relieve it of its economic difficulties, and the government badly needed money to fight the rebel forces. Since 1997, the Idriss Déby regime, which had seized power in a military *coup* in 1990, had been seeking money from Taiwan, although Taipei was increasingly reluctant to accept the financial burden (*Ming Pao*, 7 August 2006).

Finally, the prospects of expanding trade with and attracting investment from the PRC induced Chad's government to revert to supporting the PRC in August 2006. Apparently, economic assistance from Beijing was an important consideration too.[2] Beijing's diplomatic victory in Chad was interpreted as a deliberate attempt to insult the Taiwanese government as the news was released on the eve of Taiwanese Premier Su Tseng-chang's formal visit to Chad.[3]

Reflecting Beijing's increasing diplomatic clout, it was alarming to Taipei that Chad was the seventh country to switch diplomatic recognition to Beijing since 2000, when Chen Shui-bian had become president (Table 5). Earlier, Lesotho in 1994, Niger in 1996, and the Central African Republic and Guinea-Bissau in 1998 had switched their diplomatic recognition from Taipei to Beijing. In 2008 there were only four African countries maintaining formal diplomatic ties with the ROC (Burkina Faso, Gambia, Sao Tome and Principe, and Swaziland).

Table 5. African countries' diplomatic switches between Taiwan and China (as of 2008)

Country	Year of establishing diplomatic relations with Taiwan	Year of establishing diplomatic relations with China
Current diplomatic relations with Taiwan		
Burkina Faso	1961, 1994	1973
The Gambia	1968, 1995	1974
Sao Tome and Principe	1997	1975
Swaziland	1968	
Current diplomatic relations with PRC		
Central African Republic	1962, 1968, 1991	1964, 1976, 1998
Chad	1962, 1997	1972, 2006
Guinea-Bissau	1990	1974, 1998
Lesotho	1966, 1990	1983, 1994
Liberia	1957, 1989, 1997	1977, 1993, 2003
Malawi	1966	2008
Senegal	1960, 1969, 1996	1964, 1971, 2005
South Africa	1976	1998

Source: Ministry of Foreign Affairs, Republic of China (Taiwan) (2001–06).

This diplomatic competition between Beijing and Taipei is expected to continue. This is because the Chinese government has allocated a very high priority and more resources to it, and because of Taiwan's refusal to give up the competition. Since 1993, Taipei has been actively promoting its re-entry into the UN; and, beginning from 1997, it has been working hard to secure at least observer status at the World Health Organisation (WHO). The African states maintaining diplomatic relations with Taiwan have been key supporters in such diplomatic offensives. Meanwhile, Gambia has often served as the lead sponsor of Taipei's applications to re-join the UN.

Again, using Chad, the competition between Taiwan and China can be examined in terms of Taiwan's "dollar diplomacy." In 1995, total foreign aid commitments to Chad amounted to US$238.3 million, and Taipei won its diplomatic recognition with a remarkable offer of US$125 million in August 1997. In the same year, Taipei offered an aid package of US$30 million to win over Sao Tome and Principe, exceeding 50% of its total foreign aid commitments of US$57.3 million. Earlier in 1992, Taipei also succeeded in winning over Niger, with a loan package of US$50 million. Between 1988, when Taipei stepped up its "dollar diplomacy" and quietly accepted the dual recognition of Beijing and Taipei, and 1996, it managed to win diplomatic recognition from three states in the Caribbean, one in Central America, and eight in Africa before the end of 1996. But between 1994 and the end of 1998, four of these African states re-established diplomatic relations with Beijing, reflecting the severity of the diplomatic competition in Africa (Cheng, 1992; Liu, 2001; Taylor, 2002).[4]

When the provisional government of Liberia resumed diplomatic relations with the PRC in 1993, the Taiwan authorities refused to accept defeat. From 1993 to 1997, both Beijing and Taipei maintained embassies in Monrovia, Liberia's capital, creating the first "two Chinas" precedent. The dual recognition principle did not work because Beijing refused to accept it. Although Chinese leaders routinely denounced Taipei's "dollar diplomacy" as "bribery,"

they also offered financial rewards to consolidate Beijing's diplomatic ties with the African countries. For example, when Li Peng, the then chairman of the Standing Committee of the National People's Congress, visited Africa in 2001, he offered US$24 million worth of grants and interest-free loans to Tanzania and a US$3.6 million grant to Zambia (Taylor, 2002). According to Philip Snow (1994: 297), Beijing "routinely use[s] aid as an inducement to African governments which have established ties with Taiwan to switch their diplomatic allegiance, undertaking for good measure to finish off any project which Taiwanese technicians might have begun in the countries involved."

As mentioned above, when Chinese President Hu announced a package of aid measures in support of developing countries in a UN fundraising conference in September 2005, he specifically excluded countries without formal diplomatic ties with the PRC. Hu was, in fact, following the precedent set by Jiang Zemin. In the first FOCAC hosted by Jiang in Beijing in 2000, he offered debt-waivers to the poor indebted African countries in the following two years amounting to US$1.2 billion. At that time, the then Chinese foreign minister Tang Jiaxuan made it clear that those countries maintaining official ties with Taiwan would be excluded. None the less, Taipei's African friends were strongly encouraged by Beijing to join the forum. Two of them, Liberia and Malawi, did attend; Liberia subsequently resumed diplomatic relations with the PRC in October 2003 (Liu, 2001); and Malawi, later on, in January 2008.

A new aspect of Africa's significance in China's efforts to enhance its international status is seen in the election of Margaret Chan Fung Fu-chun, a former Hong Kong health official, as the director-general of WHO in November 2006. Her election demonstrated the critical weight of the votes from African governments.[5] China would like to secure a fair share of the important positions of international organisations through intensive lobbying of governments of developing countries, partly as compensation for its contributions to the specific organisations and to the international community, and partly as a symbol of its rising international status and influence. African countries' support will be sought keenly in subsequent competitions for leading positions in the international civil service.[6]

In the eyes of China's experts on Africa, the latter's strategic significance has been on the rise because of the issues of oil supply, anti-terrorism, poverty alleviation and UN reforms; and they see that competition for influence has emerged. Western countries have demonstrated an increasing interest in the continent and a willingness to expand their inputs. The British initiative of the so-called African Marshall Plan launched during its hosting of the G-8 summit in 2005 is a good example. The plan asks developed countries to double their aid to Africa, to set a timetable to realise their pledge of delivering 0.7% of their respective GDP for official development assistance, and to waive all debts of African countries heavily in debt (Commission for Africa, 2005). The USA, Japan and many European countries have all been presenting their respective new programmes of aid for Africa. China has also offered generous aid packages for Africa, implying that China is prepared to take part in this competition as a major power.

Interestingly China's increased interest in Africa and its approach to Africa have been followed by some other Asian countries. The successful East Asian economic development experiences and the increasing trade between the two regions have generated a demonstration effect on Africa. Since 2005, some African sub-regional organisations have established multilateral co-operation mechanisms with Malaysia, Japan, India and Vietnam. In April 2005, South Africa and Indonesia co-hosted the Second Asian-African Summit in Jakarta, which had participation from more than 100 government leaders. The summit released a Declaration on the New Asian-African Strategic Partnership (China Institutes of Contemporary International Relations, 2006: 204).

CHINA'S ECONOMIC INTERESTS IN

As China embraces economic globalisation and expands the reach of its trade and investment activities, Africa has emerged as an increasingly important economic partner. At the end of 2000, there were 499 Chinese enterprises in Africa, with a total contractual investment of US$990 million, of which US$680 million was Chinese capital (Ministry of Foreign Affairs, 2001). Since 1995, China has been establishing Investment, Development and Trade Promotion Centres in Africa.

China's economic interests in Africa have been based on certain assumptions. Importantly, Beijing believed that the macro-economic situation in Africa began to turn around at the beginning of this century. The PRC embassy in Zimbabwe in 2000, for example, observed that African countries had "adopted a set of active measures to push forward the pace of privatisation, open up international trade and reform based on bilateral and multilateral trade agreements;" as a result, many African countries had improved their macro-economic situation (Embassy of the People's Republic of China, 2000).

In contrast to the Maoist era's emphasis on Third World solidarity, China's economic ties with most African countries are based on objective evaluation of the perceived economic benefits. Li Peng's statement in Ghana in September 1997 that Africa was a "continent with great development potential and hope" genuinely reflected the Chinese authorities' confidence in its future economic progress (Agence France Presse, 14 September 1997). A China Daily (9 January 1998) commentary asserted that "as more African countries improve political stability and make headway in economic growth, the continent will have more say in international affairs." China supports this development as it believes that it shares with Africa, in the words of Shi Guangsheng, then Minister of Foreign Trade and Economic Co-operation at the first FOCAC, "identical and similar options on many major international affairs as well as common interests" (Renmin Ribao [People's Daily], 11 October 2000). According to the International Monetary Fund, Africa as a whole achieved an economic growth rate of 5.3% in 2004 and 4.5% in 2005. Its fiscal deficit of 0.2% of GDP in 2004 transformed into a surplus of 0.6% in the following year; and its current account surplus improved from 0.1% of its GDP to 1.6% in the same period. In 2005, Africa's exports rose 26.5%, and imports, 19.5%; while its total foreign debt declined from US$293.2 billion in 2004 to US$285.8 billion in 2005 (International Monetary Fund, 2005: 193–281).

Further, Chinese businesspeople believe that China's export structure, with its strength in household electrical appliances, garments and other household goods, meets demand in Africa where price is of more concern than quality (Lafargue, 2005). Leading Chinese telecom service provider Zhongxing Telecom Company, for example, has been spreading its outlets in Africa, including being responsible for renovating the telephone network in Djibouti. There is a view in the telecommunications industry that the cheap Chinese mobile telephones may corner a substantial segment of the 900 million people African market (Lafargue, 2005). As in

Europe and North America, enterprises from China make good use of the local Chinese communities in French-speaking West African countries and in East Africa to establish their business networks, especially in the initial stage of their business development.[7]

Finally, Africa is perceived as rich in natural resources, especially in oil, non-ferrous metals and fisheries. China's increasing demand for oil and new materials has been the most important factor supporting the impressive expansion of Sino-African trade and the flow of investment funds from China to Africa since the beginning of this century (Table 6). The oil trade especially has attracted much attention. In 1993, China became a net oil importer; and it is expected to depend on imports to meet 45% of its oil consumption by 2010 (Troush, 1999: 2–4). According to the Energy Information Administration of the US Department of Energy, China accounted for 40% of the growth in global demand for oil from 2002 to 2004. In 2003, China surpassed Japan as the second largest

Table 6. Sino-African trade, 1990–05 (US$ million)

Year	Imports from Africa	Exports to Africa	Total trade
1990	5	660	665
1991	426	1,000	1,426
1992	504	1,302	1,806
1993	1,003	1,527	2,530
1994	894	1,749	2,643
1995	1,427	2,494	3,921
1996	1,464	2,567	4,031
1997	2,464	3,207	5,671
1998	1,477	4,060	5,537
1999	2,375	4,109	6,484
2000	5,555	5,043	10,598
2001	4,790	5,970	10,760
2002	5,430	6,960	12,390
2003	8,360	10,140	18,500
2004	15,650	13,820	29,470
2005	21,060	18,680	39,740

Source: Statistics for 1990–04 are from Editorial Board of the Yearbook of China's Foreign Economic Relations and Trade (1991–06). Statistics for 2005 are from the Department of Western Asian and African Affairs (2006).

oil importer, after the USA (Zweig and Bi, 2005). This demand explains the close ties between China and the oil-rich African countries, such as Angola, Nigeria and Sudan, in recent years. China's "resource diplomacy" means that it has adapted its foreign policy to support its domestic development strategy to an unprecedented level by encouraging state-controlled companies to conclude exploration and supply contracts with countries that produce oil, gas and other resources (Zweig and Bi, 2005).

In its initial years as an oil importer, China depended mainly on Asia and the Middle East. Since 1995, the Chinese authorities have been trying to reduce dependence on the latter because it is politically unstable and China has limited influence in the region. This trend has been accelerating after the 11 September attacks (Pan, 2006). Crude oil from the Middle East accounted for 52.9% of China's imports in 1996 but dropped to 46.2% in 1999 (Anon, 2000: 17) (Table 7).[8]

Russia, Central Asia and Africa are obvious sources in China's attempts to diversify its oil suppliers. Africa's oil reserves represent 8.9% of the world total, and it accounts for 11% of the world production (International Energy Agency, 2006). Algeria, Libya and Nigeria are among the 11 members of the Organisation of Petroleum Exporting Countries. The experts in China estimate that the six major Western oil companies (ExxonMobil, British Petroleum, Shell, Total, Chevron and ConocoPhillips) already control over 80% of the world's quality oil and gas reserves, so Africa is an important source where China, as a latecomer, still has a chance to secure a substantial share of the remaining reserves (Zhang and Huang, 2006: 169). Moreover, the average production cost of African oil is relatively cheap, at about US$3.73 per barrel, roughly equivalent to that in the Middle East, in comparison with US$4.6 in Latin America, US$7.17 in Canada, US$8.29 in Europe, US$9 in

Table 7. Regional shares of China's crude oil imports, 1993–04 (percentages)

| Year | Region | | | |
	Middle East	Africa	Asia-Pacific	Europe, North and South Americas
1993	56.5	18.4	14.9	10.3
1994	39.7	4.1	48.4	7.3
1995	45.4	12.8	39.5	4.3
1996	52.9	8.5	29.8	4.4
1997	47.3	16.7	25.6	10.4
1998	61.0	8.0	19.3	11.7
1999	46.2	15.5	18.3	9.8
2000	53.6	24.2	13.4	7.8
2001	56.2	22.5	12.8	7.0
2002	46.3	22.3	13.1	4.8
2003	50.9	24.3	15.2	9.6
2004	45.3	28.7	11.5	14.3

Source: Statistics for 1993–02 are calculated from data in Editorial Board of the Yearbook of China's Foreign Economic Relations and Trade (1994–03); and statistics for 2003 and 2004 are from Zweig and Bi (2008: 28).

China, and US$13.3 in the USA (Shu and Chen, 2004; Taylor, 2004: 93).

In 2004, Africa supplied 28.7% of China's crude oil imports (Table 7). This share was a result of many years of Beijing's diplomatic efforts. In his visit to Nigeria in 1997, Premier Li Peng signed two oil exploration agreements for the Chad River Basin and the Niger River delta. Foreign Minister Tang Jiaxuan went to Abuja in January 2000 to negotiate the purchase of Nigerian oil. China became involved in many projects in the country, including the restoration of the Nigerian railway network. In January 2004, President Hu Jintao toured Egypt, Gabon and Algeria to increase China's oil suppliers. In Gabon, Hu concluded an agreement with President Omar Bongo on the exploration and production of oil. The Total-Gabon Co. and the China Petroleum and Chemical Corporation (Sinopec) also signed a contract in 2004 to export to China one million tons of crude oil (Lafargue, 2005).

China's state-owned enterprises (SOEs) have been firmly supported by the Chinese authorities' offers of aid and various forms of development assistance in their search for resources. In the first ten months of 2005, SOEs invested US$175 million in African countries, mainly in oil exploration and infrastructural projects. In January 2006, China National Offshore Oil Corporation (CNOOC) announced that it would acquire a 45% stake in an offshore oilfield in Nigeria for US$2.27 billion. By then, China already had a significant economic presence in a number of African countries. For example, in 2005, 50% of Sudan's oil exports went to China, which satisfied 5% of China's oil needs (Pan, 2006).

Before 1992, Angola was the only African energy supplier to China, and the volume of exports was not significant. From 1993 onwards, China increased its oil imports from Angola substantially; and it became the fourth largest oil supplier for China in that year (*Renmin Ribao*, 4 March 1997).[9] In 1997, China National Petroleum Corporation entered into partnership with the Malaysian company Petronas and the Canadian firm Talisman to conclude an agreement with Sudapet, the state oil company of Sudan, to engage in oil exploration and production, as well as the construction of pipelines from the Muglad basin in southern Sudan. This project, amounting to US$1 billion, was the first major investment of this type by a Chinese SOE in Africa (Jiang, 2004; *Renmin Ribao*, 4 March 1997).[10] In 2000, the Muglad Field produced 2.4 million tons of crude oil, or 144,000 barrels a day. China received

Table 8. Chinese enterprises' major investment in Africa, 2002–06

Year	Name of Company	Nature of business	Recipient country	Amount of investment (US$ million)
2002	Sinopec	Energy	Algeria	420
2002	China State Farms Group	Agriculture	Tanzania	15
2003	Sinohydro Corporation	Construction	Sudan	650
2003	Alcatel Shanghai Bell	Telecom	Nigeria	99
2004	Huawei Tech Co. Ltd.	Telecom	Nigeria	400
2005	Ghana Gold Mining Co.	Mining	Ghana	12
2006	CNOOC	Energy	Nigeria	2268

Source: Statistical data from *Converge! Network Digest* (2004), Economic and Commercial Office (2006), Goodman (2006), Lafargue (2005), Ministry of Commerce of People's Republic of China (2002), *Sudan Tribune* (2006). For earlier data, see Ministry of Commerce of People's Republic of China (2002).

its share of 60,000 barrels a day, which amounted to 5% of its oil imports and 50% of its foreign production in that year (Downs, 2000: 53; *Renmin Ribao*, 21 December 2000; Ruan, 2000).

China's economic interests in Africa are not limited to oil. Since the 1990s, there has been an increasing number of joint ventures and investment projects, as well as rapid trade expansion (Table 6). From 1990 to 2005, Sino-African trade increased from US$665 million to US$39,740 million. China has long enjoyed a substantial surplus in bilateral trade. However, because of Africa's rising oil exports, China experienced its first trade deficit in 2000; and there were deficits in 2004 and 2005 as well.

China's increasing trade surpluses and foreign exchange reserves support China's investment overseas, which has been encouraged by the Chinese authorities too. Such investment aims to ensure China's supply of energy and raw materials, and to expand China's market shares for its products and services. As shown by Tables 8 and 9, there have been some substantial Chinese investments in Africa since from 2000. At the end of 2005, there were 750 enterprises from China operating in 49 African countries. They are concentrated in the mining, telecom, fishing and timber sectors, but they have also been moving into sectors perceived to be less profitable and abandoned by Western countries, such as retail trade (*Converge! Network*

Digest, 2004; Economic and Commercial Office, 2006; Goodman, 2006; Lafargue, 2005; Ministry of Commerce of People's Republic of China, 2002; *Sudan Tribune*, 30 January 2006).

In July 2004, Jinchuan Group, China's largest nickel producer, established an office in Johannesburg in South Africa to acquire cobalt, copper, nickel and platinum from countries in southern Africa (*Reuters*, 14 December 2005). China National Machinery and Equipment Import and Export Corporation soon afterwards concluded an agreement with Gabon to exploit untapped iron ore at Belinga. According to the Gabon Minister of Mines, Energy, Oil and Hydraulic Resources, Richard Onouviet, the reserves in Belinga are at least one billion tons, 60% of which is rich iron ore. Chinese companies have investment in Zambia where they are involved in a copper project. In South Africa, the China Iron and Steel Industry and Trade Group Company invested US$70 million in chromite mining and processing (Anon., n.d). Other Chinese enterprises, like Shanghai Industrial, Hisense, Huawei and ZTE Corporation, have set up manufacturing facilities in Africa to produce electrical household appliances, including refrigerators, washing machines and television sets (Table 8).

Though China is the second largest recipient of foreign direct investment (FDI) in the world, it has

Table 9. China's major investment in Africa (end of 2005)

Country	Amount (US$ million)	Share (%)
Sudan	351.5	22.0
Algeria	171.2	10.7
Zambia	160.3	10.0
South Africa	112.3	7.0
Nigeria	94.1	5.9
Tanzania	62.0	3.9
Kenya	58.3	3.7
Total in Africa	1595.3	100

Source: Department of Foreign Economic Co-operation (2006).

also been an increasingly important source of FDI, utilising its over US$1 trillion of foreign exchange reserves. In 2003, China ranked fifth for FDI origin world-wide, after the USA, Germany, the UK and France. In 2005, China's total overseas investment amounted to US$12.26 billion, of which 52.6% was in Latin America, 35.6% in Asia, 4.2% in Europe, 3.3% in Africa, 2.6% in North America and 1.7% in Australia (Department of Foreign Economic Co-operation, 2006). The main recipients of Chinese investment in Africa have been Sudan, Algeria, Zambia, South Africa, Nigeria, Tanzania and Kenya (Table 9).

African companies have been investing in China too, but to a more limited extent. SAB Miller, the world's second largest brewer, has acquired more than 30 breweries in China, and is competing vigorously with popular local brands. A South African company invested US$72 million in establishing the Hongye Aluminum Plant in Inner Mongolia Autonomous Region. Moreover, South African technologies are used in the Chinese government campaign to connect all villages to a radio and television transmission network (Liu, 2003).

Chinese investment in Africa, however, has generated resentment. Whereas China was hailed for creating jobs and saving industries, more recently Chinese investors have been accused of discriminatory employment practices. Some of the more common complaints against Chinese firms in Africa include poor pay, lack of safety protection for workers in the textiles, copper and coal mining industries, and the use of short-term contracts. In 2004, the Zambian government asked the Chinese managers at Zambia-China Mulungushi Textiles in northern Kabwe to stop locking workers in the factory at night. In June 2006, the Zambian authorities shut down Collum Coal Mining Industries in southern Zambia, indicating that miners had been forced to work underground without safety clothing and boots. Union officials in Chambishi Mining, a copper producer in Zambia, complained that miners there were the lowest paid in the country's entire mining sector, with the least paid earning US$100 a month, compared with US$424 in Konkola Copper Mines, the largest copper producer in Zambia. Chambishi Mining was sold to Chinese investors in 2003, and was the scene of violent workers' protests in July 2006 (Dickson, 2006).

Chinese enterprises have been active in infrastructural projects in Africa, such as the construction of roads, railways and housing. The major difference in operating styles between the Chinese companies and their Western counterparts is that the former often bring their own labourers. The arrival of tens of thousands of Chinese workers naturally creates ill feeling in African countries with very high unemployment rates. There are complaints against the contracts concerned, which normally require the successful bidders to contract only 30% of their work to local companies. Typical examples are the road and railway rehabilitation projects in Angola funded by Chinese credit backed by oil exports to China (Zafar, 2007).

There are many complaints regarding cheap Chinese products flooding the African continent, as they sometimes force local industries to close, with severe job losses. In Lesotho, Chinese operators are licensed to operate only big retail shops or supermarkets, but locally owned grocery stores have largely disappeared. It was said that the local people had rented their shops to the Chinese because "they get a better profit from rent than from running the shops themselves" (*South China Morning Post*, 14 August 2006).

CHALLENGES FOR CHINA'S APPROACH TO AFRICA

Traditional solidarity, China's rising international status and influence, the attraction of China's development experience and complementary economic and trade structures will likely contribute to closer Sino-African co-operation. Even so, China's leaders will certainly face challenges emanating from changes within Africa and from Western competition for influence on the African continent.

In the 1960s and 1970s, China's first-generation revolutionary leaders established highly symbolic friendship with their counterparts in Africa. Today, Beijing intends to substantiate this friendship with trade, investment and aid. Some Chinese scholars observe that China and Africa have no historical disputes and only common interests (Kong, 2003). In the post–Cold war era, both China and Africa share the objective of establishing a more egalitarian and equitable international political and economic order. However, the Chinese government has yet few concrete policy programmes to offer in important international organizations.

In more concrete terms, China's veto at the UN Security Council is a valuable asset often sought by African governments to ensure that Western governments cannot impose sanctions against them through international organisations. China as a trade partner and source of investment will enhance African countries' bargaining power *vis-á-vis* the European Union and other developed countries, which tend to take a common stand regarding demands on democracy, human rights and the rule of law. China's demand for energy and raw materials has been a significant factor in driving up their prices in international markets, which has benefited many African countries in recent years. Some Chinese experts consider that China can be an important source of intermediate technology, which is cost-effective and appropriate for the stage of development of many African countries. China has yet to demonstrate that it can serve as a generous and effective source of technology transfer for Africa in household electrical appliance industries, textiles and apparel industries, infrastructure construction, and so on.

Establishing networks through education, both by sending teachers to Africa and providing scholarships to African students to study in Chinese universities, are effective ways to strengthen China's "soft power." From the mid-1950s to 2000, 5582 African students had enrolled in tertiary institutions in China. These students typically took two years learning the Chinese language, then pursued technical subjects, especially in the engineering disciplines. In 2003, about half of the African students in China were studying for postgraduate degrees. The Chinese government's hope is that these education exchanges will improve China's image in Africa, establish grassroots support in local communities, and cultivate networks and goodwill among the future elites. In the foreseeable future, these African talents are expected to contribute to the expansion of Sino-African economic ties in the high-tech fields (Gao, 2006; Ni, 2008).

To succeed in the cultivation of goodwill, the Chinese authorities have to work hard to ensure that African students in university campuses in China do not suffer from discrimination and racist attitudes from Chinese students. The latter often value the friendship of their counterparts from the developed countries more than that of classmates from Africa. Discipline of African students is occasionally a problem. In the past, there were protests against discrimination among the African students, which were an embarrassment to the Chinese authorities.[11]

While China's ventures in Africa have attracted considerable attention in the Western media, the Chinese authorities are well aware of China's limitations in its competition with the leading Western countries (Idun-Arkhurst and Laing, 2007: 22). The oil situation is a good illustration. In recent years, there are many reports on China trying hard to acquire oil in Africa. Chinese experts estimate that the West's six leading oil companies control over 30% of the world's industrial output value of petroleum products, more than a 50% share of the oil technical services market, over 65% of the international oil trade and direct investment in oil projects, as well as more than 80% of the advanced technology in the oil and petrochemicals sectors. In comparison, China controls less than 4% of the world's oil resources, and has been attempting to achieve breakthroughs from the margin (Cui, 2005).[12]

In April 2006, the US administration initiated a plan to promote "African economic growth and opportunity partnership" to encourage US companies to develop African markets. European countries, such as France, have always regarded Africa as their traditional market. France remains the largest aid donor to African countries, as over half of its foreign aid goes to the continent (Zhong, 2002). French investment also accounts for 20% of total foreign investment in Africa (Marchal, 1998). Given their traditional market ties, advanced technology and substantial aid programmes, the USA and the European Union still enjoy a substantial edge over China in Africa. Africa experts in China estimated that 70% of the African market was still in the hands of Western countries; and that China had to overcome its disadvantages in language and culture, as well as those of a latecomer (*Guoji Shangbao*, 22 September 2007; Jiang, 1997).

China's aggressive oil diplomacy has generated Sino-American competition in Africa (Bartholomew, 2005: 48).[13] Angola is, perhaps, a good example. American oil companies have been active in the country for more than two decades; and half of Angola's oil goes to the USA, making it that country's sixth largest oil supplier (Energy Information Administration, 2008). China has emerged as a major player in Angola in recent years, buying a third of total production. In October 2004, China secured a 50% share of the Block 18 oilfield, a cross-regional area spanning several administrative regions, previously held by Royal Dutch/Shell (Lafargue, 2005). In the following February, Chinese Vice-Premier Zeng Peiyan visited Angola and finalised several contracts with Sonagol, Angola's national oil company.[14] A report by the US Council on Foreign Relations highlighted China's oil diplomacy in Africa and urged a robust response from the Bush administration (Pan, 2007), Congressional hearings on China's influence in Africa, and strong criticisms from the Congress effectively blocking CNOOC's bid to acquire Unocal. The strategic consideration argument reinforced the belief among Chinese people that the USA did not want to see a strong China (Wilson, 2006).

Following the 9/11 terrorist attacks, the USA has also been making efforts to diversify its oil imports, reducing its heavy dependence on the Middle East and turning its attention to Africa. In June 2002, President George W. Bush visited Africa. During his visit, Bush attended the US-African Energy Ministerial Conference in Morocco, and met leaders of oil-exporting countries, including Angola, Cameroon, Equatorial Guinea and Chad. In the following UN General Assembly session, Bush had another round of meetings with African leaders. One result was an agreement to increase daily oil imports from Nigeria from 0.9 million barrels to 1.8 million barrels (*Africa Research Bulletin*, 16 June-15 July 2002).

China's economic activities in Africa today remind us of those of Japan in Southeast Asia in the 1960s and early 1970s. Premier Tanaka Kakuei's visit to Southeast Asia in 1974 encountered massive protests; this taught the Japanese leadership a lesson and Premier Fukuda Takeo returned in 1977 with the proposal of a "heart to heart diplomacy." However, China differs from Japan in two important aspects. The People's Republic of China throughout its history has strongly identified itself with the Third World; and this remains an important theme of Chinese foreign policy at this stage. A bad image of Chinese economic activities abroad goes against the Chinese leadership's efforts to enhance China's soft power, especially that in the Third World. China differs from Japan too in that it does not trust the international market dominated by multinational corporations based in Western countries. The pursuit of economic security and the potential competition with the USA mean that Chinese leaders are willing to spend more and pay higher than market prices to secure autonomous supplies of energy and other natural resources.

In China's recent approach to Africa, the "ugly Chinese" syndrome has emerged, even when Beijing offers generous aid packages to the continent. The Chinese authorities, while directing SOEs to expand and invest in Africa, do not direct these SOEs to operate as "model business partners" on the continent. However, some of China's aid money can go to the SOEs so that they will be able to behave as "model employers" and contribute to community projects. It requires effective co-ordination at the central government level and new mechanisms have to be built to achieve the desirable outcomes. However, the Chinese leadership is obviously aware of the emerging adverse publicity and will try to reverse the trend. This is one of the major challenges to the Chinese leadership's attempt to enhance China's soft power (Deng and Wang, 2005).

CONCLUSION

Multipolarity has become a significant goal of China's foreign policy in the post Cold War era. Chinese leaders have adopted this as a long-term objective; and, given the dominant position of the USA, China strives to maintain good relations with America, avoiding any sharp deterioration in the bilateral relationship. The Chinese government has established various strategic partnerships with other major powers, emphasising the promotion of common interests, while abandoning the Maoist united front strategy (Cheng and Zhang, 2002). Meanwhile, China seeks to maintain a peaceful international environment and concentrate on its modernisation programme, while building its comprehensive national power. In many ways, China has been pursuing a modernisation diplomacy in the era of economic reforms and opening to the outside world since the end of 1978 (Cheng, 1989); and developed countries play a more important role than developing countries in terms of markets as well as sources of investment, advanced management and technology, and so on. Ideology and revolution the main Maoist objectives—now have a limited role in this modernisation diplomacy.

Sanctions from Western governments in the aftermath of the Tiananmen protests and violent crackdown reminded Chinese leaders of the significance of the Third World, especially African countries. This was reinforced by the depreciation of China's strategic weight in the eyes of the Western world, with the disappearance of the "strategic triangle" in the context of the break up of the Soviet Union and the dramatic changes in Eastern Europe. Diplomatic support from the African countries has thus become indispensable when China comes under criticisms for its human rights record in international organisations, and when it chooses to exert pressure on Taiwan. The cultivation of a network of friendly supporters on the African continent therefore becomes a significant task in China's diplomacy. The strategic co-operation relationship with Egypt, the strategic partnerships with Nigeria and South Africa, and the Forum on China-Africa Co-operation are landmarks in the building of this network.

As China's economy continues its impressive growth, it wants to expand its markets and secure reliable supplies of resources in support of its economic development. Resource diplomacy, therefore, becomes a prominent feature of its modernisation diplomacy. China's rising economic status also means that it has more resources at its disposal to ensure success in its African policy. In turn, many African countries perceive political and economic ties with China to be an important asset, which strengthens their international bargaining power, especially with Western governments. These new features of Sino-African ties have attracted the attention of the Bush administration and the international media. Their criticisms are against the Chinese authorities' intention to present China as a responsible major power in the international community and to enhance its soft power in the Third World, while neglecting co-operation and co-ordination with Western governments in its approach to Africa.

In view of the substantial resources spent in support of Beijing's African policy, the Chinese leadership, China's foreign policy think-tanks and the official media tend to present Africa as a lucrative market and an important source of badly needed raw materials. African countries are also depicted as reliable political and economic partners. In fact, however, a large part of the continent still suffers from domestic instability, poverty, AIDS, rampant corruption and a range of other developmental problems, so optimism regarding Africa's peace and development in the near future may be misplaced. Many small African countries have been switching diplomatic recognition between Taipei and Beijing, playing the two off against each other for economic assistance, and so they are obviously not reliable political partners. Regime changes take place often in some African countries, too. Hence, setbacks for China's African policy will not be surprising.

Chinese leaders would like to avoid engaging in open and ongoing diplomatic and strategic confrontation with the USA and the European Union in Africa, but they certainly want to push for multipolarity and to ensure a reliable supply of resources from Africa in support of domestic economic development. Whether China can achieve this balance remains a fundamental dilemma of its African policy, which exacerbates the risks of its foreign policy and commercial initiatives in Africa.

NOTES

1. "Pragmatic Diplomacy for Taiwan is like the Sun, the Air, and the Water for a Person," release by the Taipei Liaison Office in South Africa, Pretoria, 8 November 1997.

2. See all the major newspapers in Hong Kong published on 7 August 2006.

3. At the time, the head of Taipei's Mainland Affairs Council, Joseph Wu Jau-shieh, indicated that the plan for Chen Yunlin, Director of the Taiwan Affairs Office of Beijing's State Council, to visit Taiwan would almost certainly be denied (*South China Morning Post*, 7 August 2006). This was not an isolated incident. Earlier in May 2006, Premier Su had to abandon a scheduled visit to Haiti as the president's special envoy to take part in the inauguration ceremony of the Haitian president because of pressure from Beijing. Observers noted that Su was considered a moderate within the Democratic Progressive Party, and his position on relations across the Taiwan Straits was said to be "pragmatic." In 2002, when President Chen Shui-bian became Chairman of the Democratic Progressive Party, the occasion was compromised by the news of Nauru establishing diplomatic relations with

the PRC on the same day (*Ming Pao*, 7 August 2006).

4. See also the website of the Ministry of Foreign Affairs, Republic of Taiwan at http://www.mofa.gov.tw; and the web site of the Ministry of Foreign Affairs of the PRC at http://www.fmprc.gov.cn.

5. See all the leading newspapers in Hong Kong published on 10 November 2006.

6. China's success in securing such support is acknowledged in the country reports in Policy Research Department (2001–07).

7. Chinese populations are extremely small in the Maghreb countries but they are larger in Senegal, Kenya and Tanzania.

8. The high sulphur content of some Middle Eastern oil is a consideration too. At the end of the last century, China's short-term maximum daily refining capacity was estimated to be 4.35 million barrels of low-sulphur crude, 0.16 million barrels of medium-sulphur crude and 0.24 million barrels of high-sulphur crude (Anon., 1999: 25).

9. In 1993, the top five oil suppliers to China were: Oman (26%), Indonesia (25%), Yemen (10.6%), Angola (7.8%) and Papua-New Guinea (5%).

10. CNPC invested US$700 million and secured a 40% share of the project; the shares of Petronas, Talisman and Sudapet were 30%, 25% and 5%, respectively.

11. These observations are based on the authors' frequent visits to universities in China.

12. China's national oil firms have been particularly handicapped by their backward technology in tapping oil from deeper ocean floors (Houser, 2008).

13. Bartholomew, who was Commissioner, US-China Economic Security Review Commission, argued that China's direct investment into energy production would not contribute to the overall energy security of energy-importing countries.

14. Sonagol is the sole concessionaire for oil exploration and production, and the only way a foreign company can enter the market

is via joint ventures and production-sharing agreements with it.

REFERENCES

Anderson, J. (2007) "China Should Speed Up the Yuan's Rise," *Far Eastern Economic Review*, 170, 6, pp. 14–20.

Anon. (1997) "Ambassador I-Cheng Loh's Address at ROC National Day Reception," Pretoria: Taipei Liaison Office in South Africa, 10 October.

Anon. (1999) "China's Oil Imports Rise Possible Boon for U.S.," *Oil and Gas Journal*, 97, 23, 7 June, pp. 24–6.

Anon. (2000) "China Accelerates Shift in Energy Policy, Restructuring of State Petroleum Firms," *Oil and Gas Journal*, 98, 2, 10 January, pp. 14–19.

Anon, (n.d.) "Sino-African Relations," *News-Africa* (United Kingdom), http://www.newsafrica.net/ articles. php?action=view&id=191 (downloaded 5 January 2007).

Armstrong, J.D. (1977) *Revolutionary Diplomacy*: Chinese Foreign Policy and the United Front Doctrine, Berkeley: University of California Press.

Bartholomew, C. (2005) "China's Influence in Africa," hearing before the Subcommittee on Africa, Global Human Rights and International Operations of the Committee on International Relations, House of Representative, First Session of the 109th Congress, Washington, D.C.: U.S. Government Printing Office, 28 July, Serial No. 109-74, http://www.house. gov/international_relations (downloaded 5 January 2007).

Bartke, W. (1992) *The Agreements of the People's Republic of China with Foreign Countries, 1949–1990*, Munich: K.G. Saur.

Chang, Q. (1989) "Chinese Foreign Minister Tours Africa," *Beijing Review*, 32, 35, p. 10.

Cheng, J.Y.S. (1989) "The Evolution of China's Foreign Policy in the Post-Mao Era: From Anti-Hegemony to Modernization Diplomacy," in J.Y.S. Cheng (ed.), *China: Modernization in the 1980s*, Hong Kong: The Chinese University Press, pp. 161–201.

Cheng, J.Y.S. (1990) "China's Post-Tiananmen Diplomacy," in G. Hicks (ed.), *The Broken Mirror: China After Tiananmen*, Chicago: St. James Press, pp. 401–16.

Cheng, J.Y.S. and W.K. Zhang (2002) "Patterns and Dynamics of China's International Strategic Behaviour," *Journal of Contemporary China*, 11, 31, pp. 235–60.

Cheng, T.Y. (1992) "Foreign Aid in ROC Diplomacy," *Issues and Studies*, 28, 9, pp. 67–84.

China Institutes of Contemporary International Relations (2006) *Guoji Zhanlue yu Anquan Xingshi Pinggu 2005–06 [Strategic and Security Review 2005/2006]*, Beijing: Shishi Chubanshe, pp. 193–214.

Christensen, T.J. (1996) "Chinese Realpolitik," *Foreign Affairs*, 75, 5, pp. 37–52.

Commission for Africa (2005) *Our Common Interest: Report of the Commission for Africa*, http://www. commissionforafrica.org/english/report/introduction. html (downloaded 5 January 2007).

Commission on Human Rights (n.d.) "Membership," Office of the United Nations Higher Commissioner for Human Rights, http://www.unhchr.ch/html/menu2/2/ chrmem.htm (downloaded 5 January 2007).

Converge! Network Digest (2004) "Huawei Announces US$400 million in African Contracts," 12 November, http://www.convergedigest.com/Daily/daily.asp?vn=vl ln219&fecha=11%2F15%2F2004#Huawei%20 Announces%20US$400%20million%20in%20 African%20Contracts (downloaded 1 April 2008).

Cui, D.H. (2005) "Daguo Nengyuan Zhanlue Boyixia de Zhongguo Shiyou Qiye Quanqiuhua Jingying Zhanlue" [The Global Business Strategy of China's Oil Enterprises in the Context of Major Powers' Energy Strategic Game], *Shijie Jingji Yanjiu* [World Economic Study], Shanghai, 11 November, pp. 37–43.

Deng, Y. and F.L. Wang (eds) (2005) *China Rising: Power and Motivations in Chinese Foreign Policy*, Lanham: Rowman & Littlefield Publishers.

Department of Foreign Economic Co-operation (2006) *2005niandu Zhongguo Duiwai Zhijie Touzi Tongji Gongbao (Feijinrong Bufen) [2005 Statistical Bulletin of China's Outward Foreign Investment (Non-financial)]*, Ministry of Commerce of the People's Republic of China, 8 September, http://hzs.mofcom. gov.cn/aarticle/date/200609/20060903095437.html (downloaded 5 January 2007).

Department of Western Asian and African Affairs (2006), "2005nian Zhong Fei Maoyi Bijin 400yi Meiyuan" [Trade between China and Africa Approaches US$40

Billion], Ministry of Commerce of the People's Republic of China, 16 January, http://xyf.mofcom.gov.cn/aarticle/date/200601/20060101369686.html (downloaded 5 January 2007).

Dickson, R. (2006) "Africans Lash Out at Chinese Employers," *Los Angeles Times*, 6 October.

Downs, E.S. (2000) *China's Quest for Energy Security*, Santa Monica: Rand Corporation.

Economic and Commercial Office (2006) "Zhongguo Qiye Kaituo Niriliya Tongxun Shichang de Xianzhuang, Cunzaiwenti ji Jianyi" [The Current Situation, Existing Problems and Suggestions for Chinese Enterprises Establishing Business in Nigeria's Communications Market], Consulate General of the People's Republic of China in Lagos, 26 March, http://ng.mofcom.gov.cn/aarticle/slfw/200603/20060301752083.html (downloaded 1 April 2008).

Editorial Board of the Yearbook of China's Foreign Economic Relations and Trade (eds) (1989–2006) *Almanac of China's Foreign Economic Relations and Trade*, Beijing: China Foreign Economic Relations and Trade Publishing House, 1989–2006.

Embassy of the People's Republic of China in the Republic of Zimbabwe (2000) *Actively Carrying out International Exchanges and Co-operation in the Realm of Human Rights*, Harare: Embassy of the People's Republic of China in the Republic of Zimbabwe.

Energy Information Administration (2008) "Country Analysis Briefs: Angola: Oil," http://www.eia.doe.gov/emeu/cabs/Angola/Oil.html, US Department of Energy (downloaded 28 March 2008).

Gao, Q.F. (2006) "Old Friends, New Partners," *Beijing Review*, 49, 22, http://www.bjreview.com.cn/expert/txt/2006–12/10/content_50411.htm (downloaded 27 March 2008).

Goodman, P.S. (2006) "Cnooc Buys Oil Interest In Nigeria: Overseas Deal First Since Unocal Bid," *The Washington Post*, 10 January.

Harding, H. (1984) "China's Changing Role in the Contemporary World," in H. Harding (ed.), *China's Foreign Relations in the 1980s*, New Haven: Yale University Press, pp. 177–223.

He, W.P. (2007) "The Future of Darfur: The World Awaits," *Beijing Review*, 50, 23, http://www.bjreview.com/quotes/txt/2007-06/04/content_65207.htm (downloaded 26 March 2008).

Holbrooke, R. (2007) "China Lends a Hand," *The Washington Post*, 28 June, p. A25.

Houser, T. (2008) "The Roots of Chinese Oil Investment Abroad," *Asia Policy*, 5, pp. 141–66.

Idun-Arkhurst, I. and J. Laing (eds) (2007) *The Impact of the Chinese Presence in Africa*, London: africapractice, http://www.davidandassociates.co.uk/davidandblog/newwork/China_in_Africa_5.pdf (downloaded 5 January 2007).

International Energy Agency (2006) "Oil in Africa in 2005," http://www.iea.org/textbase/stats/oildata.asp?COUNTRY_CODE=11&Submit=Submit (downloaded 22 March 2008).

International Monetary Fund (2005) *World Economic Outlook*, Washington, D.C.: International Monetary Fund.

Jiang, C.L. (2004) "Oil: A New Dimension in Sino-African Relations," *African Geopolitics*, 14, pp. 65–77.

Jiang Q.H. (1997) "Feizhou Duiwai Maoyi yu Shichang de Zhuyao Tedian" [The Basic Features of Africa's Foreign Trade and Market], *Xiya Feizhou [West Asia and Africa]*, Beijing: Institute of West Asian and African Studies, Chinese Academy of Social Sciences, 5, pp. 69–71.

Kong, M.H. (2003) "Sino-African Relations and China's Policy towards Africa," Bureau of International Co-operation of the Chinese Academy of Social Sciences, 13 May, http://bic.cass.cn/english/infoShow/Arcitle_Show_Conference_Show.asp?ID=32&Title=&strNavigatio (downloaded 5 January 2007).

Lafargue, F. (2005) "China's Presence in Africa," *China Perspectives*, 61, pp. 2–9.

Larkin, B.D. (1971) *China and Africa 1949–70: The Foreign Policy of the People's Republic of China*, Berkeley: University of California Press.

Lin, T.C. (1996) "Beijing's Foreign Aid Policy in the 1990s: Continuity and Change," *Issues and Studies*, 32, 1, pp. 32–56.

Lin, Y.L. (1989) "Peking's African Policy in the 1980s," *Issues and Studies*, 25, 4, pp. 76–96.

Liu, G.J. (2003) "Great Prospects for Sino-African Cooperation," China Internet Information Centre, 11 December 2003, http://china.org.cn/english/features/

China-Africa/82197.htm (downloaded 5 January 2007).

Liu, P. (2001) "Cross-Strait Scramble for Africa: A Hidden Agenda in China-Africa Co-operation Forum," *Harvard Asia Quarterly*, 5, 2, http://www.fas.harvard.edu/-asiactr/haq/200102/0102a006.htm (download 5 January 2007).

Lo, B. (1989) "Zhonggong Waijiao de Da Zainan" [The Big Disaster in Chinese Communist Diplomacy], *Cheng Ming* (Hong Kong), 144, October, p. 8.

Marchal, R. (1998) "France and Africa: The Emergence of Essential Reforms?," *International Affairs*, 74, 2, pp. 335–72.

McGurn, W. (1990) "The US and China: Sanctioning Tiananmen Square," in G. Hicks (ed.), The Broken Mirror: *China After Tiananmen*, Chicago: St. James Press, pp. 233–45.

Ministry of Commerce of People's Republic of China (2002) "Zhongguo yu Feizhou yi Shishi de Hezuo Xiangmu Yilanbiao" [List of Co-operation Projects Implemented between China and Africa), 16 July, http://www.mofcom.gov.cn/aarticle/bg/200207/20020700032349.html (downloaded 5 January 2007).

Ministry of Foreign Affairs (2001–06) *Waijiao Tongji Nianbao* [Ministry of Foreign Affairs Statistics Yearbook], Republic of China (Taiwan), http://www.mofa.gov.tw/webapp/lp.asp?CtNode=1123&CtUnit=58&BaseDSD=7&mp=1 (downloaded 30 October 2008).

Ministry of Foreign Affairs of the People's Republic of China (2001) "Sun Guangxiang Fubuzhang zai Zhongfei Hezuo Luntanhou Xu Xingdong Tongbao ji Cuoshanghui shang de Jianghua" [Speech of Sun Guangxiang (Vice-Minister of Foreign Trade and Economic Co-operation) at the Conference on post-Forum on China-Africa Co-operation's Follow-up Action, Reporting and Consultation], 9 February 2001, http://big5.fmprc.gov.cn/gate/big5/www.mfa.gov.cn/chn/ziliao/wzzt/2355/2388/t11249.htm (downloaded 5 January 2007).

Ministry of Foreign Affairs of the People's Republic of China (2006) "China's African Policy," 12 January, http://www.fmprc.gov.cn/eng/zxxx/t230615.htm (downloaded 5 January 2007).

Mu, Y.L. (1985) "Premier Zhao's S. America Trip," Beijing Review, 28, 43, p. 4.

Ni, Y.S. (2008) "Confucius Around the World," Beijing Review, 51, 10, http://www.bjreview.com.cn/print/txt/2008-03/04/content_102849.htm (download 27 March 2008).

Office of the Spokesman (1997) "Press Briefing: 1996 Country Reports on Human Rights Practices," Washington, D.C.: US Department of State, 30 January, http://secretary.state.gov/www/statements/970130.html (downloaded 26 January 2007).

Pan, E. (2006) "Q&A: China, Africa, and Oil," *New York Times*, 18 January.

Pan, E. (2007) "China, Africa, and Oil," Council on Foreign Relations Backgrounder, updated 26 January, http://www.cfr.org/publication/9557/ (downloaded 23 March 2008).

Payne, R.J. and C.R. Veney (2001) "Taiwan and Africa: Taipei's Continuing Search for International Recognition," *Journal of Asian and African Studies*, 36, 4, pp. 437–50.

Policy Research Department, Ministry of Foreign Affairs, People's Republic of China (ed.) (2001–07) Zhongguo *Waijiao* [*China's Foreign Affairs*], Beijing: Shijie Zhishi Chubanshe.

Ruan, C.S. (2000) "Tan Zhongguo zai Feizhou de Liyi" [On China's Interests in Africa], *Lianhe Zaobao* [Singapore], 7 September.

Rubinstein, A.Z. (ed.) (1975) *Soviet and Chinese Influence in the Third World*, New York: Praeger.

Shu, X.L. and S.L. Chen (2004) "Feizhou Shiyou yu Zhongguo Nengyuan Anquan" [African Oil and China's Energy Security]), *Shiyou Daxue Xuebao (Shehui Kexueban) [Journal of the University of Petroleum (Social Sciences Edition)]*, 20, 5, pp. 5–9.

Snow, P. (1994) "China and Africa: Consensus and Camouflage," in T. Robinson and D. Shambaugh (eds), *Chinese Foreign Policy: Theory and Practice*, Oxford: Clarendon Press, pp. 283–321.

Swaine, M.D. (1995) China: Domestic Change and Foreign Policy, Santa Monica: Rand Corporation.

Taylor, I. (1998) "China's Foreign Policy Towards Africa in the 1990s," The Journal of Modern African Studies, 36, 3, pp. 443–60.

Taylor, I. (2002) "Taiwan's Foreign Policy and Africa: The Limitation of Dollar Diplomacy," *Journal of Contemporary China,* 11, 30, pp. 125–40.

Taylor, I. (2004) "The 'All-Weather Friend'?: Sino-African Interaction in the Twenty-First Century," in I. Taylor and P. Williams (eds), *Africa in International Politics,* London: Routledge, pp. 83–101.

Troush, S. (1999) "China's Changing Oil Strategy and Its Foreign Policy Implications," Washington, D.C.: Brookings Institution, Center for Northeast Asian Policy Studies Working Paper.

Van Ness, P. (1970) *Revolution and Chinese Foreign Policy: Peking's Support for Wars of National Liberation,* Berkeley: University of California Press.

Wilson, E. (2006) "China, Africa & the U.S.: Something Old, Something New," TPM Cafe, 30 January 2006, http://tpmcafe.talkingpointsmemo.com/2006/01/30/ china_africa_the_us_something (downloaded 26 March 2008).

Xiao, W.L. (2002) "Zhongmei Renquan Jiaoliangzhong Feizhou dui Zhongguo de Zhichi" [Africa's Support for China in Sino-American Human Rights Contests], *Xiya Feizhou [West Asia and Africa],* 2, pp. 37–40.

Yu, G.T. (1980) "Sino-Soviet Rivalry in Africa," in D.E. Albright (ed.), *Communism* in Africa, Bloomington: Indiana University Press, pp. 168–88.

Zafar, A. (2007) "The Growing Relationship Between China and Sub-Saharan Africa: Macroeconomic, Trade, Investment, and Aid Links," *The World Bank Research Observer,* 22, 1, pp. 103–30.

Zhang, Y.W. and R.W. Huang (2006) 2006 *Zhongguo Guoji Diwei Baogao* [*China's International Status Report* 2006], May, Beijing: Renmin Chubanshe.

Zhong, W.Y. (2002) "Feizhou zai Guoji Tixizhong de Diwei" [Africa's Place in the International System], *Xiya Feizhou [West Asia and Africa],* 2, pp. 16–21.

Zweig D. and J.B. Bi (2005) "China's Global Hunt for Energy," *Foreign Affairs,* 84, 5, pp. 25–38.

BACKGROUND TO GENOCIDE: RWANDA

By Catharine Newbury*

Readers of *Issue* know better than to accept the images of tribalism and ancient hatreds propagated in much of the American press during the early days and weeks of the genocide in Rwanda. And the media (or at least some journalists) came around eventually to a recognition that far from mindless tribal violence, this was planned and calculated genocide. Still, in North America it is the deaths and brutality that have most mesmerized public attention; there has been too little discussion of the political, social, and economic context in which the genocide occurred.

We know now, and many observers of Rwanda knew from early on in the conflict, that the massacres that began during the night of April 6–7, 1994 had been carefully planned. Although generated at the level of the state, the genocide was mostly carried out by "militias," the *Interahamwe* (associated with the ruling party, MRND), and the *Impuzamugambi* (associated with the CRD party, a hardline, extremistally of the MRND). These units worked together with and were directed by the Presidential Guard, certain elements in the army, various gendarmes, and in many cases, civilian administrative authorities.

The goal was to liquidate Tutsi and any moderate Hutu who were seen as opposed to the Habyarimana government. The carnage resulted in the deaths of between five hundred thousand and one million men, women, and children. We will probably never know the exact numbers. It was organized and directed by a small group of people bent on keeping power. In addition to the normal chain of command through the army, police, administration, and militias, they used radio broadcasts to emit hate messages, encouraging Rwandans to kill fellow citizens. The horrific results testify in part to the penetration of state power in this society. But they also raise the question: Why did the extremist appeals of these leaders find resonance among at least some sectors of the population? In other words, why did some Rwandans support the genocidal project, and why did many others go along with it? There are no easy answers, and individual testimony may not be the most reliable guide on such issues. We can, however, explore some of the underlying social, economic, and political conditions which interacted to create a pervasive climate of insecurity and fear among the population.

It is an understatement to say that these tragic events occurred at a time when Rwanda's state and society were in severe crisis. External and internal factors combined during the five years preceding 1994 to create an extremely volatile mix. Among these were the nature of the postcolonial state in Rwanda and the changing configuration of regional, class, and ethnic divisions; the growing militarization of state and society in the country as the

Catharine Newbury, "Background to Genocide: Rwanda," from *Issue: A Journal of Opinion*, Vol. 23, No. 2, Pp. 12–17. Copyright © 1995 by African Studies Association. Permission to reprint granted by the publisher.

Habyarimana regime responded to military attacks by the Rwandan Patriotic Front; and the effects of a process of political liberalization and multipartyism truncated from the concerns of ordinary citizens. These processes occurred in a context of sharply deteriorating economic conditions internally. The Arusha Peace Accords of 1993 served to heighten anxieties further, while events in neighboring Burundi increased fears and insecurities among many in Rwanda. This analysis will review the role of these different factors in creating the conditions for genocide, but it must be remembered that these were not discrete factors; each operated in a climate created by the intersection of multiple pressures, different in their kaleidoscopic combination, perhaps, for each individual.

THE PATRIMONIAL STATE AND BIPOLAR ETHNIC POLITICS

The ways in which history is defined, imagined, and articulated are important in shaping competing visions of power and mobilization of ethnic identities within a particular power context. This has been particularly true in the case of Rwanda. It is customary to speak of Rwandan society as divided into three groups, Hutu (85% of the population), Tutsi (about 14%), and Twa (less than 1%). These are not racial groups, nor are they really ethnic groups in the conventional sense. Indeed the meaning of the terms and the categories they describe have changed over time, influenced in important ways by changing contexts of power, and particularly by the role of the state.[1]

Rwandans share one language, Kinyarwanda, and common membership within a set of state structures that long predated the arrival of Europeans at the end of the 19th century. At the time of European imposition, high office in the monarchy ruling Rwanda was dominated by a Tutsi minority. Colonial policy helped to intensify bipolar differentiation between Tutsi and Hutu, by inscribing "ethnic" identification on identity cards, by relegating the vast majority of Hutu to particularly onerous forms of forced cultivation and corvée, and

by actively favoring Tutsi in access to administrative posts, education, and jobs in the modern sector.

By the end of the colonial period in Rwanda, though not all Tutsi were wealthy and powerful, most of those who were wealthy and powerful were Tutsi. To many Hutu in Rwanda the Revolution of 1959 was an important watershed, because it marked the end of domination of the state by Tutsi and the accession to power of Hutu. But the Revolution also resulted in the deaths of many Tutsi and tens of thousands of Tutsi left the country as refugees, to seek asylum in neighboring countries and elsewhere.

Thus over the years, partisans from both sides have called on history to claim the rightness of their cause. Hutu have cited a history of oppression and exploitation under a Tutsi-dominated monarchy; Tutsi have pointed both to the waves of refugees driven from the country (in 1959–1961, 1963–64, and 1972–1973) and to the multiple forms of discrimination experienced both by Tutsi in Rwanda and by the exiles outside the country.

A coup d'état brought Juvénal Habyarimana to power in 1973; from that time the structure of political institutions within Rwanda permitted the extensive concentration of power in the office of the president, in the organ of the single party (MRND), and in the security services. Nevertheless, within the postcolonial state, dominated by Hutu from the central regions during the First Republic and by Hutu from the northwest after 1973, relations between the groups changed significantly; among other indices, intermarriage between Hutu and Tutsi became increasingly common in areas outside the north. For a variety of reasons, the Habyarimana regime faced serious economic and political problems, from the mid-1980s. It is important to recognize, however, that during this period the main axis of conflict was based on region and class, and for the most part these were conflicts between Hutu factions.

The Habyarimana regime adopted increasingly harsh measures against its political opponents; many were eliminated, including imprisoned leaders from the First Republic, and the late 1980s saw a rash of political assassinations, often in the guise of car accidents. The targets of these murders were usually people seen as too critical of the regime, such as the courageous editor of *Kinyamateka*, a widely-read newspaper written in Kinyarwanda (and important also in the revolution of 1959–62), and an outspoken and popular woman deputy. But it was only after the attack of the RPF at the beginning of October in 1990 that the Habyarimana regime made personal targets of Tutsi within the country.

Patrimonial states are found elsewhere in Africa and so is the manipulation of ethnicity. Within these political contexts, losing power entails heavy costs and therefore, to retain contol, those in power often go to extreme lengths to undermine all opposition. One of the most common political tools at their disposal is to revivify ethnic identities and try to set ethnically-defined categories in opposition against each other. But ethnic conflict is not automatic, it is a response to certain conditions. So when it happens, it raises questions; it is not a self-explanatory factor. In Rwanda, the intensification of ethnic conflict was not therefore the result of a "collapsed" state, as many superficial analyses aver. Rather, in this case ethnic conflict served to illustrate state power in action; in Rwanda, the "ethnic conflict" of 1994 was simply state-sponsored terrorism against its own citizens. The situation was rendered all the more volatile because of the history of ethnic conflict between Tutsi and Hutu, the numerical imbalance between them, the popular remembered histories highlighting antagonism along ethnic lines, and the association of ethnicity and power. (Twa were discriminated against by both groups, but because of their lack of demographic weight or political resources, they had little political voice.)

THE OCTOBER WAR OF 1990

The Habyarimana government had long recognized the problem of demographic pressures on land in Rwanda, where more than 90 percent of the population depend on agriculture for their livelihood. In fact the government had explored settlement schemes elsewhere, and had seriously proposed programs which would have exported Rwandans not only to neighboring countries like Zaire and Tanzania, but even to places as far away as—and as different in ecological and epidemiological terms as—Gabon. Claiming that there was insufficient land for the population currently in the country, Habyarimana took the position that Rwanda could not accommodate large numbers of additional people, and on those grounds the government refused to allow the repatriation of refugees, often the children of Tutsi who had fled the country in previous episodes of violence.

The total number of Rwandan refugees residing in countries neighboring Rwanda was estimated to be between 400,000 and 600,000; a significant proportion of that number may include the descendants of people who had left Rwanda during colonial rule or had been excluded by colonial boundaries. Many of these "Rwandans abroad" were treated as second class citizens, as if they were all refugees. In 1982 these pressures reached a peak in Uganda when thousands of Rwandans were expelled by the second Obote government. Many fled to northeastern Rwanda, where they were crowded into refugee camps for up to three years. The Rwandan government refused to acknowledge the right of these people to live in the country, and eventually most were sent back to Uganda. There, many supported the National Resistance Movement led by Yoweri Museveni, and significant numbers joined the National Resistance Army which eventually overthrew the second Obote regime.

Rwandan refugees were well placed in the new Ugandan administration, and this in part accounts for tense relations between Rwanda and Uganda at the time. The RPF was composed of two segments: those in high political positions, and those who had been excluded by Ugandan society. But in the eyes of many Ugandans, these two categories overlapped; it became common to ask why so many foreigners occupied influential positions in their government. So the Rwandan refugee community, formerly a military asset to the National Resistance Movement of Uganda, now became a political liability.

Thus the RPF attack of 1990 can be seen as having resulted from the convergence of multiple interests:

many refugees (both elite and non-elites, for different reasons) may have felt that this provided an escape from the burden of discrimination they felt in Uganda; Museveni may have been concerned to divest his government of an increasing liability within the Ugandan political arena. The timing of the invasion, however, may have been more affected by initiatives within Rwanda, as the Habyarimana regime moved—very cautiously—towards a more open political system and a new position on refugee issues.[2] Both policies—the move to "political liberalization" and the move to address the "refugee problem"—undercut RPF claims to moral superiority. So the RPF attack on October 1, 1990, carries the appearance of an attempt to pre-empt two issues on which the Rwanda government had indicated a wilingness to act. By attacking when they did, the RPF seemed intent on maintaining the moral "high ground."

Whatever the motives behind the timing of the attack, the RPF incursions of October and the war which resulted had very important repercussions within Rwanda. The extreme right factions in the government, including elements in the military, seized on the invasion to promote a significant expansion of the security forces, and to brand all Tutsi as internal supporters of the RPF. In this version, the conflict was not just a war, but an ethnic war. Tutsi living inside Rwanda were indiscriminately categorized as potential accomplices of the RPF, and therefore as "suspect." The military took on a more central role in politics, and the size of the army grew from 5,000 to more than 30,000; but many of the new recruits were poorly trained and poorly disciplined. Within this context, the proliferation of arms became a critical factor, both at the international level, in building up the army, and at the local level, for arming the general population and militias. By the end of 1993, for example, grenades were easily available in Rwanda's open air markets for the equivalent of a few dollars apiece.

Following the October invasion Habyarimana pursued a two-track policy. On the one hand, responding to pressure from western donors, he permitted a gradual process of political liberalization

and made concessions to an active internal pro-democracy movement. Simultaneously Habyarimana permitted (or pursued) a policy of internal repression as part of the war strategy, and he allowed (or encouraged) a proliferation of human rights abuses. The main targets were Tutsi—from 1990 to 1993 an estimated 2,000 Tutsi were killed in massacres and murders in several different regions. But outspoken critics of the regime and advocates of human rights were also targetted, regardless of ethnic categories. It is important to note that these were not simply rogue incidents of populist militance; an international commission of inquiry that visited Rwanda in January 1993 found evidence that these attacks were directed from the security services in the office of the President. The RPF invasion did not cause these to happen; the regime in power did that. But it nonetheless provided a pretext, a context, and a means for engaging in such abuses.

It became clear that resources that were needed to alleviate increasingly desperate economic difficulties were going instead to the purchase of weapons and to other expenses of the war effort. Fear and insecurity intensified, as generalized hardship, hunger, and everyday violence became increasingly common experiences for ordinary citizens.

THE SOCIAL CONSEQUENCES OF ECONOMIC DECLINE

During the first decade of his rule, Habyarimana could point to important achievements of his government in several sectors: in the development of infrastructure (roads in particular), in the expansion of schools and health centers, in reforestation programs, and in attempts to promote increased agricultural production. But by the mid-1980s the economy faced serious difficulties; austerity measures were introduced, and the gap between rich and poor widened markedly.[3]

The vagaries of the commodities markets also took their toll on Rwandan peasant producers. The world price of coffee, Rwanda's main export, showed worrisome price fluctuations towards the end of the 1980s, and in the summer of 1989 the price plummeted by about 50 percent. The repercussions for rural dwellers were severe; it is not accidental that a serious famine wracked the south and southwest areas of the country in the fall of 1989 (the first such famine since 1943). Then in November 1990 Rwanda devalued the currency as part of a stabilization program mandated by the International Monetary Fund. Devaluation meant that prices increased drastically, even for non-imported items. Fuel for trucks and other vehicles became more expensive, and this affected trade, raising the price of food products and other merchandise—Rwanda's agricultural plan was premised on regional production, and the marketing of food crops through internal transport flows. An increase in transport costs also meant that coffee producers (mostly small-holders) received less for their product. At the same time, with the drop in world coffee prices, the government reduced the statutory minimum price which smallholder coffee producers received for a kilo of coffee, even while transport costs rose and inflation translated into higher prices for other goods.[4]

Declining income for rural producers had a multiplier effect, as traders and merchants depended on peasant coffee earnings for much of their sales. Furthermore, a disease affecting coffee trees had already reduced yields in some areas of the country, heightening rural resentment against the rules governing coffee production. Because of the overwhelming importance of coffee exports for government revenues, it was illegal for farmers to cut down coffee trees. Yet with declining returns on coffee beans, peasants preferred to use the land for producing food, often sold on the market for greater return than coffee provided; farmers uprooted an estimated 300,000 coffee trees, thus still further reducing coffee production and government revenues.

The war effort created additional economic hardships, and the economic reform package prescribed by the IMF and the World Bank served to exacerbate poverty and insecurity. Programs were introduced to require increased "cost-sharing" on the part of citizens; this required them to pay higher fees for public services such as primary school education, health care, and even access to water.

All these factors contributed significantly to social tensions and fear. But most important for later political developments, the harsh IMF measures exacerbated the already difficult conditions which youth faced. In some areas population densities exceeded 400 people per square kilometer—over 1000 per square mile. In many parts of the country, the average family had scarcely half a hectare of land, while increasing amounts of land were being taken over by the wealthy. Youths faced a situation where many (perhaps most) had no land, no jobs, little education, and no hope for the future. It was increasingly difficult for young men to acquire the wherewithal to get married; hence the path to social adulthood was blocked, for the minimum legal requirement for marriage was that a young man have a house where he and his bride could live. We know from studies elsewhere what a dangerous condition such social circumstances create.

Careful studies carried out by Danielle de Lame in southern Rwanda show the extent of class polarization and rural resentment at the local level.[5] I share her conclusion that grinding poverty and class divisions were an important factor in the conflicts. In sum, there was in Rwanda of the late 1980s and early 1990s growing regional polarization in political access, social polarization between rich and poor, and a strong awareness of increasing marginalization among urban poor and the majority of rural dwellers.

POLITICAL LIBERALIZATION, THE ARUSHA PEACE ACCORDS, AND EVENTS IN BURUNDI

In the midst of war and growing economic austerity, Rwanda was also making gradual steps toward political liberalization. A National Commission of Synthesis was established by Habyarimana in September 1990 to prepare a new constitution; the new constitution was adopted in June 1991; and multiparty competition was legalized from July of that year. In 1992 Habyarimana was pressured to accept inclusion of the major opposition parties in the cabinet, with a prime minister from the Democratic Republican Movement party (MDR).

Meanwhile, as opposition political parties organized, newspapers proliferated and many political and professional organizations formed. But this apparent resurgence of civil society was fragile. There were only weak linkages between political parties and organizations in civil society.[6] Moreover, town residents showed greater interest in the new political parties than rural dwellers—perhaps because there was no strong and committed voice among peasants to represent their concerns. While eager to see improvements in the daily difficulties they faced in their lives, a substantial proportion of rural dwellers doubted elections would achieve this. To them, multiparty competition meant mainly a changing of the guard in the capital. Widening splits among leaders in the major opposition parties did little to reassure the citizenry.

Negotiations to end the war were shaped significantly by internal pressures from opposition parties calling on Habyarimana to accept power sharing with the RPF so as to end the war. External pressures from Tanzania, the Organization of African Unity, and donors such as the U.S. and Belgium—as well as the negotiating skills of the RPF—were also important factors pushing the government towards a political resolution. In the end, the Arusha Peace Accords ending the war between the RPF and the Rwandan army were signed on August 4, 1993. These accords, along with other protocols signed previously, constituted the blueprint for a power-sharing arrangement between the former single party (MRND), the internal opposition parties, and the RPF.

According to the peace agreement, an interim transitional government with an expanded base, and an interim parliament were to be put in place after the installation of a UN Peacekeeping force in the country. Seats on the cabinet and in the national assembly were apportioned among the RPF and the political parties; occupants of these seats were to be selected in each case by the parties they represented.

The UN peacekeeping force reached Rwanda in November 1993. But there followed delay after delay in setting up the interim government and parliament. Manipulations by Habyarimana and his entourage accounted for some of the delays, but in addition several of the major political parties were unable to agree on a slate of representatives to occupy seats in the national assembly. The deepening fissures in these parties were exacerbated by events in Burundi—the assassination of the first Hutu president of the country and the slaughter of up to 100,000 people in its wake being the most prominent; and these events were exploited by Habyarimana and the MRND. On April 6, when Habyarimana's plane crashed and the genocide began, there still was no interim parliament in place.

Three aspects of the Arusha Accords seem to have contributed to polarization of political tensions within Rwanda. First, hardliners in the government insisted that Habyarimana had given up too much to the RPF. According to the Arusha Accords, the RPF were to receive five ministries out of 20, including the important Ministry of the Interior; they were to receive 11 posts of deputies in the Parliament (of 70 total).

Second, provisions on merging the two armies stipulated that in the new army RPF elements would fill 40% of the rank and file positions and 50% of the officer corps. As a result, few RPF personnnel would be dismissed, while large numbers of Rwandan government soldiers faced demobilization, with no alternatives; already, in 1992, there had been mutinies in the army related to concerns over demobilization. Inadequate provision for demobilization and the effective integration of former soldiers into civilian society (with jobs and some means of subsistence) must be seen as a serious lacuna in the Arusha Accords.

A third aspect of the Arusha Accords which heightened tensions was the stipulation of a right to return for refugees. This was, of course, a critical issue—it was one of the key concerns that the RPF was fighting for, and it became an integral part of the peace agreement. Yet here again, inadequate provision had been made to allay real fears and anxieties among the population as to the impact of this policy. How would the returning refugees be accommodated? Would they be allowed to reclaim land they (or their parents or other relatives) had lost when they fled thirty years ago? According to the peace agreement, no one who had been gone 10 years or more could reclaim property, but few rural dwellers knew of or believed this stipulation. Given the severe land shortages in most regions of the country, anxieties over land rights were a serious concern to rural dwellers. Here also, the economic crisis only exacerbated such fears and concerns. Meanwhile, instead of trying to allay fears the hardliners in the regime spread misinformation, and helped to promote and heighten such anxieties.

Events in neighboring Burundi only exacerbated the deep fears and anxieties in Rwanda.[7] In October 1993 President Melchior Ndadaye of Burundi and several other high officials were killed in an attempted coup. This tragedy sent a shock wave through Rwanda's political elite. Here was the first Hutu president of Burundi, elected in a free and fair election (June 1993), assassinated by elements in the Burundi army, which was Tutsi-dominated. Opponents of the Arusha Accords within Rwanda held up the death of Ndadaye as an example of what might happen in Rwanda if the "Inkotanyi" were allowed to take power (i.e., participate in the government through the RPF).

The death of Ndadaye was followed by widespread violence in Burundi. Hutu attacked Tutsi, and the Tutsi army retaliated against Hutu. Tens of thousands of people were killed; thousands more fled the country. In April 1994, there were some 400,000 refugees from Burundi, mostly Hutu, crowded into refugee camps in southern Rwanda. As noted above, these violent events in Burundi served to deepen cleavages in the political parties within Rwanda, but they also introduced a large population of highly politicized and bitter potential recruits to the Rwandan militias. Some Burundians from the refugee camps in southern Rwanda apparently served as active participants in the massacres of Rwandan Tutsi, acting in some cases as the shock troops for local militias during the genocide in Rwanda.

Another regional consideration that inspired distrust of the RPF was the widespread belief that the RPF could not have carried out its initial attack and continued the war over several years without the support of Uganda's president, Yoweri Museveni. Critics of the Habyarimana government, on the other hand, pointed to its heavy dependence on French military assistance and other aid. To many Rwandans, and to people in the surrounding countries, this conflict was represented as a struggle between anglophone and francophone influence in the region, a reprise of colonial jousting from early in this century.

EXTERNAL ACTORS: ARMS, AND INACTION

The international community was shocked by what happened in Rwanda. We should be equally shocked by the distortions in the media and the dithering of the western powers in formulating a response. Political violence was not entirely unforeseen, although the scale of the tragedy was simply unthinkable. In February 1994, tensions in Rwanda intensified noticeably as the paralysis in the government dragged on. The leader of one of the opposition parties, the Social Democratic Party (PSD) was killed in February; PSD supporters, believing the Coalition for the Defense of the Republic (CDR, a party of militant proponents of hard-line action) to be responsible for this assassination, then killed the leader of the CDR. There followed numerous killings, burnings, and lootings in Kigali. It was a trial run, an opportunity for the militias to practice their "work."

The UNAMIR force in Rwanda did nothing; it became clear to those in the Habyarimana regime planning the liquidation of opponents that they could act with impunity. Tensions were rising in March: there is evidence that the UN forces in Rwanda were warned that militias were being armed and that there was a plan to re-start the war.

What did the UN do? We are told that the UN force was not given the mandate and forces it needed. If not, why not? If the U.S., Belgium, and France did not know what was going on, why not? At the least, this bespeaks a blatant failure of intelligence. But even after the slaughter began the actions of the west seemed almost to acquiesce in—and perhaps even further—the killings: western governments sent in troops only to save whites, then they withdrew. Nothing was done to protect those clearly at risk. The UN did not reinforce their contingent, nor even change their mandate to defend themselves and save the lives of perhaps thousands of innocent civilians: many were killed right in front of UN troops, who stood aside and let it happen. Instead, the UN all but pulled out, leaving behind a derisory force of about 450 soldiers (down from 2500, and in the face of the Secretary-General's request for increasing the numbers to 5500).

The lack of any rapid, efficacious international response when the killings began is one reason the death toll from the genocide was so great. Rwanda is a compact country with an excellent and easily accessible road network; the few troops that were there showed that by their very presence, in many instances lives could be saved. Many more could have been saved by judicious timely response on a scale appropriate to the genocide. But Rwanda was portrayed as Africa, and Africa was Somalia; the west was unwilling to take the political initiatives (the military risks were very small) to save hundreds of thousands of lives. The instant chorus of news media that this was just another tribal war rendered meaningless any call for assistance; the press and the TV reports in the U.S. (including *Nightline* and *Sixty Minutes*) persistently portrayed this as simply the continuation of ancient tribal animosities—in spite of the empirical record (a record they were informed of) which cast a very different light on the killings. And from the left, the condemnation of any intervention left the genocide a free track to proceed on its way.

CONCLUSIONS

Far from tribal warfare erupting in the vacuum created by the collapse of the state, genocide in Rwanda resulted from the machinations of state actors seeking to extend and consolidate their power. It occurred in a context of escalating political, economic, and social tensions within civilian society, at a time of massive popular withdrawal from the political process. Civil war, devastating economic conditions, anxieties over the consequences of implementing the Arusha Accords, class polarization, intense power struggles linked with democratization initiatives—all of this in a country where leaders could (and did) manipulate ethnic rivalries and fears which had strong historical resonance.

Having taken power in July 1994, the leaders of the Rwandan Patriotic Front and the government they have established in Rwanda face many difficult challenges. Not the least of these is how to prevent future pogroms and ethnic violence in a deeply factionalized political environment. The scars of war and genocide run deep; hopes for reconciliation compete with calls for vengeance. To construct a different future will require enormous reserves of political will, creativity, tolerance, and courage on all sides—and a firm focus on societal well-being. It will not be easy; it may demand putting aside factional bickering and personal ambitions. Yet to fail in such a project is to condemn the people of Rwanda to continuing cycles of violence in the future.

Yet while the lives of many Rwandans have been lost, there are a few terrible lessons to be learned. They are obvious, but they have been too often ignored. First and foremost, it is imperative to stop the proliferation of arms across the African continent. Second, "democratization" programs—often devised in the west—need to be rethought; in Rwanda they contributed to, rather than alleviated, the crisis. Similarly, structural adjustment programs, also devised in the west to conform to western ideologies and assumptions—and which remove culture, class, and gender from any meaningful planning process—need be themselves restructured, if not abolished. In Rwanda, as elsewhere across Africa, their toll has been incalculable and their contribution to both global and national class divisions and social stress unconscionable. Furthermore, women and youth need special attention, care, and hope in any societal healing process[8] at the least, that requires meaningful, accessible education and reliable employment with dignity. And finally, the international community needs to be prepared to act decisively when genocide is threatened.

These will be dismissed as impossible demands. To the contrary: we have dismissed them for too long; it is western power, with its structural adjustment programs and its capricious terms of trade, that makes these simple goals impossible. It is the west that has for too long turned a deaf ear to the cry for help, and that has for too long provided comfort and resources to "leaders" without followers, only clients. And it is the west which insists on minimizing commodity prices and maximizing arms profits, that makes such a vision impossible. To be sure, it was not the west that carried out the genocide in Rwanda: the leaders of those atrocities are well known. But in this interdependent global community the west did help create the conditions which allowed such horrors to occur—and then walked away when they did. To state these needs is not to call for recolonization—in fact, it is to confront the recolonization processes already underway; it is instead to call for realisitic support for internal initiatives, and opposition to those who will oppress and exploit and deny basic justice to the people of Africa.

NOTES

Among our many Rwandan friends and acquaintances killed during the genocide was Joseph, a colleague and close friend of many years. He perished in the massacre at the Bishopric of Kibungo that began on April 17, 1994. I dedicate this paper to the memory of Joseph, a lover of history; his intelligence, his calm demeanor, his absolute integrity, and his kind and gentle manner touched many lives. There are many others. With this work, I offer my profound sympathy and condolences to all the people of Rwanda for the terrible tragedy they have experienced.

1. Catharine Newbury, *The Cohesion of Oppression: Clientship and Ethnicity in Rwanda, 1860-1960* (New York: Columbia University Press, 1988).
2. Filip Reyntjens, *L'Afrique des Grands Lacs en crise: Rwanda, Burundi, 1988-1994* (Paris: Karthala, 1994).
3. Fernand Bézy, *Rwanda: Bilan socio-économique d'un régime (1962-1989)* (Louvain: Institut d'études des pays endéveloppement; 1990).
4. See Catharine Newbury, "Rwanda: Recent Debates over Governance and Rural Development," in Goran Hyden and Michael Bratton, eds., *Governance and Politics in Africa* (Boulder and London: Lynne Rienner, 1992), 193–219.
5. Danielle de Lame, personal communication.
6. See Timothy Longman, "Democratization and Civil Society: The Case of Rwanda," in *The Democratic Challenge in Africa: Discussion Papers from a Seminar on Democratization* (Atlanta: The Carter Center of Emory University, 1994), 61–69.
7. For analyses of postcolonial political conflicts in Burundi, see René Lemarchand, *Burundi: Ethnocide as Discourse and Practice* (Cambridge and New York: Cambridge University Press, 1994); and Reyntjens, *L'Afrique des Grands Lacs en crise.*
8. On the particular burdens that war, genocide, and life in refugee camps have placed on Rwandan women, and on the importance of women for promoting reconciliation, see Clotilde Twagiramariya, "Women as Victims of Power Conflict: The Case of Rwanda," *ACAS Bulletin*, Nos. 44/45 (Winter/Spring 1995), 13–18.

*Catharine Newbury
University of North Carolina
Chapel Hill, NC, USA*

GENESIS OF PEACE EDUCATION IN AN ERA OF XENOPHOBIA AND TERRORISM: THE CASE OF AFRICA

By Dr. Nana Adu-Pipim Boaduo FRC (Principal),
Dr. Kazamula S. Milondzo, Mr. Alex Adjei

ABSTRACT: The 21st century ushered in new political developments in Africa of which civil strife, xenophobia and terrorism, as new political cultures stand supreme. In the 1940s, Hitler initiated both xenophobic and terroristic actions against the Jews that led to World War II. During the Cold War era, both the East and the West initiated xenophobic and terroristic activities against each other's interests worldwide, resulting in human, material and financial losses. Hence, Africa suffered the maximum blunt of these activities through economic and political sabotage (coup d'etats). When the USSR disintegrated in 1990, Africa and the rest of the developing world breathed a sigh of relief believing that the biblical peace on earth had come. However, the collapse of the USSR and the death of East-West economic, ideological and political competition ushered in a new surge of civil and ethnic conflicts in many parts of the world as xenophobia and terrorism and new political cultures replaced the East and West sabotage of rival interests in Africa, and other parts of the world.

Presently, Africa stands at the centre of precarious civil and ethnic conflicts leading it to the edge of a precipitous cliff of disaster, inhibiting it from all forms of development—industrial, social, economic and education. Therefore, this paper attempts to provide a brief epistemological interpretation of the xenophobia and terrorism that have threatened peace in the world by providing empirical evidence supported by scholarly discussion, and a proposal to initiate peace in Africa, and throughout the world.

Key words/concepts: world peace, terrorism, xenophobia, political culture, ideological sabotage, epistemological, investment in conflict prevention

INTRODUCTION

In the summary of chapter five of Our Common Interest: Report of the Commission for Africa (2005:157) it states that: "The right to life and security is the most basic human right. Without increased investment in conflict prevention, Africa will not make the rapid acceleration in development that its people seek. Investing in development is itself an investment in peace and security, but there is much more that should be done directly to strengthen conflict prevention".

An unknown African philosopher once stated that world peace rests on a number of things—"social and economic development, ability of a government to sustain its citizens, cultural respectability

Dr. Nana Adu-Pipim Boaduo FRC, Dr. Kazamula S. Milondzo, and Mr. Alex Adjei, "Genesis of Peace Education in an Era of Xenophobia and Terrorism: The Case of Africa," from *The Journal of Pan African Studies*, Vol. 2, No. 9; March 2009, pp. 260–274. Copyright © 2009 by The Journal of Pan African Studies. Permission to reprint granted by the publisher.

and integration, justice and truth". According to this philosopher, these things are one and the same because if a society is socially and economically self-reliant, and the government is able to sustain the people progressively, and the people respect each other's culture and there is absolute truth, then justice is done. In this way peace will naturally be firmly established.

The pressure on the international community to undertake peace operations worldwide stems exclusively from humanitarian concerns about massive human suffering depicted in any international headline news—Darfur, Somalia, and DR Congo. Generally, the moral impulse to alleviate suffering does not constitute sufficient basis for action (Badat, 1997; Avis, 1996). The theoretical orientation, however, is that external interventions have to be based on a pragmatic assessment of their potential need and effectiveness. Such assessment depends, to a large extent, on the circumstances of each specific case. Less importantly, it may also depend on the manner in which the conflict or the problem, and the peace or the desired outcome, are understood at a more general level by the interventionists who see the need to intervene (Pizam & Mansfeld, 1996).

What is being stated here is not a matter of abstract theorising, because theory leads to planning, and every planned action is based on some kind of theoretical analysis; whether or not the analysis is specific, particular, generalised, conscious and sound? Therefore, if the problem or the desired outcome is misconceived, the peace endeavours will be ineffectual and counterproductive (Maila & Loubser, 2003).

And since the efforts of the international community to promote peace in Africa has not yielded great success, we suggest that theoretically, every conflict and/or crises can be traced to a certain level of xenophobic attitude of a cultural group which normally imposes its authority through acts of terror. Consequently, xenophobic actions are always pepped up by terroristic activities so as to be able to tame the revolting group, and a brief trace of all conflicts and/or crises will reveal this element; for instance World War II, The Palestinian-Israelis crisis, Somalia political ferment and the Burundi-Rwanda genocide, USA-UK joint invasion of sovereign Iraq and Afghanistan, and even the Falkland Islands occupation by Argentina.

Thus, this paper adopts a radical theoretical stance both in the sense of questioning conventional wisdom and in the sense of shifting focus from the symptoms of the causes of the crises to providing the epistemological background of the crises and possible actions to take to resolve them. Furthermore, attempts are made to present theoretical qualitative analytical synthesis for understanding conflicts and peace in Africa, and the rest of the world and explore the implications for peace-making and peace-building through peace education in the context of state and intrastate crises in Africa. Accordingly, the content of this discussion is based on the following theories:

- That ethnic conflicts and military operations have limited utility in the context of real peace making.
- That the emphasis on policies for peace in Africa should lie with the broader dimensions of peace initiatives through protracted peace education for the entire population of the continent.
- That building the capacity of African states and societies to prevent and manage conflicts can only succeed by tackling the root causes.
- That the steps to take to make aids more effective at building the foundations for durable peace to improve the management of natural resources and revenues and to tackle the trade in arms and conflict resources need reappraisal.
- That strengthening African regional organisations and the UN's ability to prevent and resolve conflicts through more effective early warning, mediation and peace-making efforts should be made a priority.
- That reframing the "sovereignty clause" in the UN Charter to allow the Security Council to intervene militarily without the

consent of governments before lives are wasted needs immediate ratification.

- That it is important to improve the co-ordination and financing of post-conflict peacebuilding and development, so that countries emerging from violent conflict do not slide back into it.

Hence, we believe that this will be consistent with the African comparative advantages, which derive from the success of a traditional communal past before the advent of colonialism, not from its military capacity.

Further, in using the concepts like "Africa", the "international community", "local actors", "xenophobia" and "terrorism" this paper obscures significant differences within each category of the concepts. However, there may consequently be important exceptions to this generalization and therefore suggest that our discussion should be accompanied by country-and-actor-specific analyses when determining appropriate strategies in a particular case. Lastly, apart from the section on military operations, this paper draws on the experiences of practitioners at the various centres for conflict resolution and its partner organizations in Africa, as well as the document Our Common Interest: Report of the Commission for Africa (2005).

EPISTEMOLOGY OF CONFLICT IN AFRICA

In theory, we must understand the conflicts and crises that has engulfed Africa from a broader perspective and that the starting point must be from traditional Africa society before the advent of colonial intrusion to the time the colonialists hacked their culture and tradition into African societies. Furthermore, another theoretical postulation is that during the African independence struggle, the colonialists left us with but conflicts, which they nurtured through their cunning strategies of partitioning and divide and rule. The most significant of them all are their tactics of 'divide and rule' and 'partitioning of Africa' where ethnic communities were cut into pieces by an imaginary boundary which was generally not based on ethnic sentiments, which they fomented to work to their advantage, which still continues today.

Thus, we ask, what is going on in Africa, dubbed as conflict prone continent, is the harvesting of the 'divide and rule' and 'partitioning of Africa', crops planted by the colonialists eternal? And unfortunately, despite the problems created by these crops, African governments allow them to grow and produce uncontrollable seeds, spreading like wild fire throughout the continent, heralding xenophobia and terrorism in their midst. And we are all witnesses of this dilemma, but are helpless to curb its spread, and know that in theory, divide and rule breeds xenophobia which gives birth to terrorism (Shillington, 1995; Curtin, Feierman, Thompson & Vansina, 1998).

Conflicts are intrinsically an integral negative dynamic implicit in much of the academic and policy literature on peace operations where the concepts 'conflict' and 'conflict prevention' typically refer to situations of crises characterized by actual or potential outbreak of widespread violence. Yet, in all cases of violence, certain levels of xenophobia and terrorism are inherent, but it is analytically limited and misleading when considered in total isolation. Violent conflicts have killed and displaced more people in Africa than in any other continent in recent decades (Commission for Africa, 2005). This has driven poverty and exclusion, undermined growth and development, and deprived many of their right to life, liberty and security as enshrined in Article 3 of the Universal Declaration of Human Rights.

Accordingly, how we understand conflict in Africa at a general level has a critical bearing on our response in specific situations; if we regard the phenomenon as inherently destructive. The theory of ethnic sentiments, (also called native sentiments by the colonialists) has had a deep root in African communities as a result of a systematic colonial hammering of the ethnic sentiments through the divide and rule strategy. In this way, our efforts would be directed towards eliminating it. However, this has been a feature of authoritarian regimes in the continent, for instance the Idi Amin regime in Uganda, Siad Barre in Somalia, the upheaval in Ivory Coast, and more recently in the Darfur region of Sudan which may heighten rather than reduce tension as has been the case in the Democratic Republic of the Congo and Chad. And if in theory conflict can be viewed as a means to change or at least, a desire for change, then something has to be done to bring that change about, especially in eradicating the ethnic sentiments and applying a negotiation strategy. Thus, an assessment of whether conflict is positive or negative depends on a contextual judgement of what is to be changed, to what end, and by what methods, and theoretically, acts of xenophobia and terrorism do not contribute to peace-making and peacebuilding.

Nonetheless, the implicitly theory is that if we view conflict as normal and inescapable, then the challenge is to manage it in constructive ways. The indication is that states which are stable are not free from conflicts, but instead portray mature sentiments and are able to deal with its various manifestations in a manner which is generally acceptable to the parties involved. Africa has not come to that stage yet either because some do not want to give in to communal welfare or somebody is behind all of what is going on in the continent and thus benefits from the conflict, and therefore will do everything possible to see that conflict continues, unabated.

In theory and from the national context, constructive conflict management is the essential, and an on-going business of good governance; which is the formal responsibility of the executive, parliament, provincial, regional and local authorities, the police and the judiciary. And in all cases where conflicts and crises occur, and the lack of capacity to resolve them, conflicts loom. Therefore in the absence of creditable institutional means of addressing disputes and grievances by the state, individuals and groups may grab the opportunity and resort to violence, and careful examination in this scenario will reveal that instances of xenophobia and terrorism will reign in all cases.

As indicated above, as a result of the dissection of ethnic communities by colonial boundaries, some ethnic/religious communities are excluded from state institution formation, and the mainstream political and social life via ethnic cleansing. Hence hostilities may be intense because the issues at stake are fundamental to physical security, the protection and advancement of interests and rights, and psychological needs regarding cultural identity as seen in the Democratic Republic of Congo, Somalia, Ivory Coast, the Darfur region in the Sudan, Burundi, and Rwanda which relate as much to perceptions as to material conditions, and thus important to the ruling group as to the marginalised. Therefore, crisis resolution is further inhibited by entrenched cultural stereotypes and deep feelings of animosity, such as fear, uncertainty and mistrust which triggers a violent explosion of tempers laced in elements of xenophobia and terrorism as has seen in the case of Burundi and Rwanda.

In other instances, where diversity is a source of strife, stability might be sought through the physical separation of antagonistic groups as seen in Somalia. But since that is seldom feasible throughout, the most viable alternatives are structural arrangements which accommodate the aspirations of the majority and the fears of the minority through the institution of basic rights for citizens as seen in Ghana, Botswana and South Africa wherein democratic forms of majority rule and structural diversity accommodation incorporate exclusivity and respect for diversity in the constitution, the government, the political system, and in state institutions.

Besides, many of the crises in Africa, if critically analysed, have common, deep-rooted causes which include the lack of cultural identification between nation and ethnicity resulting in ethnic tension (the grounds for xenophobia to germinate) coupled with the suppression of minority groups, corrupt and dictatorial regimes, and the support for these regimes by the Western world which supply the arms and trade in technical support systems cumulating in unstable civil military relations, chronic underdevelopment, poverty, and an inequitable economic system (debt burden, the imbalance in trade and financial relations between the West and the developing world) via the Structural Adjustment

Programme of the West that has made millions un-employed, again exacerbating underdevelopment, creating frustration and consequently sparking violence, at the least provocation.

It is very unfortunate to note that within and outside of Africa, the attention paid to these for-midable problems is largely rhetorical, especially by the developed countries, because the resources and energy of the international community are mo-bilised mainly around these symptoms, especially when they reach catastrophic proportions like civil war, genocide and mass starvation. This is not to undermine the importance of emergency action by the international community, but rather to make the point that the symptoms will persist, and the crises will recur for as long as the underlying causes prevail.

Yet, apart from what have been painted, the theoretical origins and dynamics of state and intrastate conflicts in Africa differ markedly from country to country as a result of historical, political, cultural, geographical and other factors. However, xenophobia and terrorism are the key elements that help to inflame conflicts in Africa. Therefore, broad generalizations about a continent characterised by diversity are not helpful in addressing this crisis. And at the risk of undermining the propositions advanced in this paper, it must also be stressed that different cultures perceive conflict and conflict management differently (Salem, 1993).

However, this position is not widely appreciated by foreign governments who intervene in African crises, and even where they have good intentions, their interests, ethnocentric world view and preoc-cupation with quick-fix solutions result in superfi-cial analysis and a profound lack of respect for the local actors. And generally, they regard Africans as villains or victims, and therefore as the objects rather than the subjects of development and peace initiatives. It is, therefore, not surprising that these initiatives are frequently ineffective. However, it is prime opportunity for the international community to change its approach in support of African efforts to promote peace and security. Thus, Africa and the developed world should invest in the prevention of violent conflicts in Africa, because, prevention is better than cure, as the old adage goes.

CULTURE OF PEACE: UNDERSTANDING THE CONCEPT

Our theoretical understanding of conflict informs the nature of peace as well as our concept of peace. Yet, for all the governments and citizens of stable Western democracies, the concept is unproblematic and defined as the absence of widespread physical violence, and peace is held to be an unqualified good in terms of orderly politics and the sanctity of life. However, in Africa, where large numbers of people are being killed in civil wars, it becomes obvious that the paramount goal is to end hostilities. And from the context of these civil wars, this perspective may have very little relevance when generally, oppressed groups in any part of the world may prize freedom and dignity more than peace and may be prepared to provoke and endure a high level of violence to achieve the rights of citizenship. But in all these cir-cumstances, authoritarian regimes and the foreign powers which sustain them are interested in peace only in so far as popular resistant threatens the sta-tus quo, and as a result, the cessation of hostilities is less a goal in its own right than an outcome of the antagonists' willingness to reach a settlement which addresses the substantive causes of the violence (Commission for Africa, 2005).

Theoretically speaking, the absence of justice is frequently the major reason for the absence of peace in Africa. Thus, the theory of acute injustice, in all respects, gives rise to popular struggles which, in all cases, are met by systematic repression. The Somali people saw Siad Barre as such, and they rose against him. However, at the helm of conflicts when no one has taken up leadership, chaos reigns after the over-throw of a dictator as is the case in Somalia. And we know that foreign powers which support dicta-tors for the sake of stability as was the case in the former Zaire; are simply postponing the inevitable and other manifestations of injustice when they are themselves forms of violence usually termed as structural violence (Galtung, 1969).

Ethically and analytically, the primary objective of external and local efforts to prevent and resolve African crises should be about the establishment of peace with justice (Galtung, 1969). Hence, a formulation that helps to explain why the termination of civil wars is so complicated and difficult for the antagonists; and where the disputant parties have a common interest in peace, they will have significant different perspectives on the constituent elements of justice in a post-settlement dispensation wherein the major differences may derive from cultural norms, historical experience, or in the case of minorities who have a need for special protection against discrimination and exclusion depending on the balance of power, and where in some cases, the parties would have to compromise their position in order to accommodate those of their opponents.

It is very important to add that during transition from authoritarian rule to democracy, the imperative of peace and justice may be in conflict with each other. This tension is always acute when groups and leaders responsible for oppression have to accommodate the new order because of their popular support or capacity to thwart the transition as a related debate concerns the alternatives of prosecution and indemnity in respect to previous violations of human rights, although prosecution would be consistent with justice, the prospect of war trials may heighten the perpetrators' resistance to a settlement as has been seen in Uganda, Burundi, Liberia and Sudan.

Furthermore, international bodies which view justice and human rights in absolute terms tend to enter such debate with a hard-line position. Thus, in the complex and tenuous process of forging a democracy, the tensions between peace and justice are better understood as dilemmas, which have no easy resolution and may entail trade-offs, without detracting from the importance of international human rights standards, yet it meets the requirements of a settlement regarded by the disputant parties and their constituencies as sufficiently just.

STRATEGIC FRAMEWORK FOR CULTURE OF PEACE IN AFRICA

Attempts have been made to provide a brief schematic overview from the above discussion that reveals some implications for the provision of a strategic framework for lasting peace in Africa. At this point, it would be ideal to highlight the distinction between conflict and crisis that underlines the significance of managing the former and addressing the causes of the latter. As conflict is ever-present and the causes of crises are numerous, complex and structural; both processes have to be undertaken in a sustained and systematic manner. There is no single, simple or short-term approach to resolving crises. Peace operations should, therefore, be viewed as a component of long-term endeavours rather than as an end in themselves.

It is also very important to note that preventive diplomacy, peacemaking and post-conflict peace-building are not inherently sequential activities. According to Boutros-Boutros Ghali (Agenda for Peace, 1992) preventive diplomacy is to avoid a crisis and post-conflict peace-building is to prevent a recurrence. Thus, peace-building encompasses entrenching respect for human rights and political pluralism; accommodation of diversity; building the capacity of state institutions; and economic growth and equity. Correspondingly, these measures are the most effective means of preventing crises; they are consequently as much pre-crisis priorities which juxtapose the concept of 'post-conflict peace-building' which is inapt since peace-building has everything to do with the on-going management of social and political conflict through good governance.

Conversely, an important issue in this discussion is that the international community should abandon the delusive notion that it is responsible for resolving crises and managing conflict in Africa, and what must be identified and recognised is that the functions of crises resolution can be properly performed only by local actors involved in the crises. Hence, peace-making and peace-building are not sustainable unless their form and content are shaped by these actors, and thus, the international community's contribution should be reoriented from the delivery of products to the facilitation of the processes.

What is being advocated here is that the context of peace-making should entail supporting local negotiations and problem-solving rather than prescribing outcomes based on Western experiences. In the case of peace-building, efforts should be directed towards strengthening the capacity of government and civil society through the transfer of skills and knowledge. Literally and metaphorically, teaching people to build bridges is more useful than building bridges for them; and more useful still if the education draws on their expertise and experiences, and thus, not reliant on foreign technology.

Second, the greatest need for capacity-building is in the area of national and local governance. In the post-crisis reconstruction, sectors of the international community are preoccupied with democratic governance; a condition which they believe is met through free and fair elections, and thus less emphasis is placed on efficient and effective governance. Yet without viable systems and the principles of democracy, such efforts cannot become operational. For instance, it is hard to imagine how President Robert Mugabe of Zimbabwe could hold free and fair elections by giving the opposition a fair share in campaigning through the government media and not rig the process during the election at the polls, as expected by the international community.

Furthermore, the adherence to the rule of law presupposes the existence of a competent and fair judiciary, police service and criminal justice system. And the requirement that police personnel respect human rights is unrealistic if they have not been trained in methods other than use of force. Hence, stable civil military relations depend not only on the values of the armed forces but also on the functional expertise of departments of defence and parliamentary defence committees (in each of these areas, capacity can be built only through long-term programmes).

And again, one of the most significant contributions the international community could make would be to attend to the ways in which foreign powers and institutions deliberately or inadvertently provoke and exacerbate conflict in Africa which include excessive and injudicious arms sales; political and economic support for authoritarian regimes, the debt crises and the structural adjustment programmes as well as international trade relations. And with respect to development aids and humanitarian relief, their desire to do well should be secondary to the imperative of not causing harm. Hence, the efforts of the international community should address the causes of African crises, prioritise long-term capacity-building, especially in the area of governance; be grounded in a sound analysis of national and regional dynamics, be based on real respect for local parties and communities and seek to support and empower them.

In short, against the above background, we can now consider the strategy of peace education, mediation, the utility of military operations, and the contributions of the UN and African nations in the peace-making and peace-building process in Africa.

CULTURE OF PEACE EDUCATION

When we talk about the theory of the culture of peace, the first most important ingredient that comes to mind is education. Specifically, education is the only means through which people can be brought together to deliberate on issues that affect their general well being. Education forms the base of every development—political, industrial, economic and social. Education buttresses successful governance of nations. Education eliminates ignorance and dictatorship.

In short, education opens up whole new vistas of understanding enabling people to learn to tolerate others, what they believe in, and what they would want to achieve collectively. It is both theoretical and practical and it is impossible to talk about a culture of peace if people lack the basic understanding of that very culture and the role it can play in bringing about peace. In brief, education liberates. And the basic significant aim of any form of education, be it formal or informal, is it to transform the educated into responsible, progressive, dynamic and reasonable individuals who would be able to play a role in the advancement of humankind; through the transfer of societal, traditional and cultural norms and values.

Education, therefore, serves as the only single weapon that can be used to change and liberate society and direct its activities in a positive direction. If people have received relevant, applicable and responsible education, it is expected, therefore, that they will exhibit an advanced level of change in attitudes, values, knowledge and skills; and generally, they will display advance behavioural attitudes compatible to the level of education received. Furthermore, due to the level of education that people have received they are expected to think and reason better, know and argue better so they are able to contribute positively to bringing about meaningful changes in society that will benefit the immediate and distant communities, which should reflect their understanding of events, issues, people, places and things. Thus, their level of interaction, tolerance, judgement and above all cooperation and sacrifice should be at a stage pertinent to their level of education, therefore establishing the main ingredients for peace, an ingredient very important to survival, advancement and development in a time perspective (Binn, 1993).

And we content that whoever receives peace education should be able to use the acquired knowledge, skills and the expertise to live better, contribute better to human advancement, interact better with other cultural groups (thereby eliminating xenophobia), tolerate still better and help to bring about the ever-awaiting positive societal changes thereby leading humankind closer to the allegorical Biblical heaven; when such an ideal is achieved through peace education, when cultures are fused and the globalised world has been realised, then the peace we so badly need could be ushered in throughout the world.

It is very surprising, if not incredible, to observe that many of the so-called civilised world leaders who are supposed to have received peace education and are supposed to know better and do better

to uplift human expectations to new heights, use the same education to suppress, subjugate and undermine the progress of others, thereby eluding humankind of the peace we badly need (President Bush and Prime Minister Blair are two of such leaders; they have used their position and education to place the whole world into crises unparalleled in the history of humankind).

PEACE EDUCATION: A MULTIPLICITY OF APPROACHES

Geography is a subject that must be looked at seriously if global peace is to be attained, thus geographical literacy can help buttress peace initiatives. Nature knows why the locations of areas on earth are what they are. Probably, it is nature's way of refinement of humankind which leads to excellence and excellence leads to perfection, and what is very important in this analogy is that perfection can find solace in geographical education because it helps to orientate human acts of ignorance to acts of informed mind (Fairhurst, 1993). Informed minds always think about peace and how to bring it about, and make it available to the rest of humanity. Thus, geographical education paves the way for people to study the relationships among people and culture including the environments they manifest (Harper, 1992). Furthermore, geography, with its integrative emphasis provides the logical vehicle for bringing together diverse natural and social worlds (Simmons, 1990). And last, geographic education helps individuals and groups to recognise differences from diverse perspectives leading to the understanding of the concept of diversity in unity, which in turn, helps individuals and groups recognise each other as part of a whole, despite their cultural differences.

After the end of World War I, the noble minds of the world came together to form what came to be known as the League of Nations whose sole mandate was to see to it that another world war did not materialise. In doing that all peace-loving nations of the world were invited to become members of the League of Nations. Unfortunately, the provisions in the documentations of the organisation did not put effective and efficient mechanisms in place that would help in the achievement of the aims and objectives of the organisation. For this short-sightedness, the Second World War surfaced, and countless millions of innocent people suffered the blunt of the holocaust, including dedicated combatants who were roped into the war by their colonial masters. However, the conversion of the League of Nations to the United Nations Organisation (now known as the United Nations or UN) identified the shortcoming of the League of Nations, but up till today, they can't seem to stamp out the tide of conflicts in many parts of the world, and one wonders about the exact reasons for the failure of the UN, in our modern era, to bring about world peace. For example, in the provision of the UN Charter, the "sovereignty" clause needs revalidation and reframing, because while states should be accorded their sovereign rights, there are times when non-delay in action is required to save millions of lives, i.e., the Bosnia-Herzegovina, Burundi-Rwanda and the Darfur region in Sudan crises required intervention, but the UN was delayed by the sovereignty clause. Therefore member states of the UN should be required to surrender part of such sovereignty in times of need to save lives; such surrender will thus enable the UN to intervene in good time when conflicts are imminent so as to be able to save lives, indeed, this idea needs considering if world peace could be forged in the 21st century.

Next in our effort to advance peace education, we must also remember that in the course of state conflicts, the parties may come to believe that the cost of perpetuating hostilities is too high and that their interests would be better served through a political settlement, and thus the initiation of negotiations may nevertheless be inhibited by intense animosity and fear of a disadvantageous outcome. In these circumstances, a skilled mediator can help to create a climate of confidence, facilitate talks and guide the parties through setbacks in the negotiating process.

However, many mediators make serious mistakes by believing that their authority and mandate derive from their personal stature or the body which appointed them, rather than from the disputant parties. Mediators need to promote or impose a particular solution rather than assist the parties to reach a collectively acceptable settlement. Most seriously, they disregard the cardinal principle that mediators should be non-partisan; if they display an overt bias, they are likely to lose the trust of one or more of the disputants and become a party to the conflict. Such has been the case of Zimbabwe where President Mbeki played silent diplomacy at the expense of several Zimbabweans lives, but nevertheless, this perspective does not negate the necessity for advocacy and enforcement action in certain circumstances. In the case of Zimbabwe, the international community should oppose authoritarian rule and support the cause of oppressed communities. Yet in other situations, the use or threat of diplomatic and economic sanctions may constitute effective pressure on minority regimes and push hard-line groups to engage in negotiations and abide by their agreements. Hence, in many cases economic sanctions achieve the opposite effect as in Zimbabwe wherein advocacy and enforcement may complement mediation, however they should not be pursued by the mediator, because by definition, a mediator is something like an umpire, and certainly not a player.

And when conflict escalates to the point of imminent violence on a large scale, the international community is sometimes, though not always, moved to consider the option of military intervention. The cases in Darfur and Somalia are examples. The objectives might include containing hostilities, establishing safe havens, protecting refugees and ensuring the delivery of emergency aid. In order to expedite the deployment of a multi-national force at the speed at which crises break, a United Nations standby arrangement system should be launched together with the African Crisis Response Initiative. And as indicated already, part of the sovereignty of the nation (you may question what percentage which is not part of the debate here) should be surrounded to the UN to be able to act decisively and promptly.

Henceforth, in all cases, the deployment of the military should occur after the consent of all the parties involved in the conflict. If this is not the case, the possibility of the ineffective action by the military will be excessive and a waste of resources (the use of excessive force would always lead to loss of civilian lives); and it must be indicated that military interventions cannot address the causes of conflicts and therefore cannot be a substitute for a negotiated settlement between the antagonists, suggesting that specific peace-keeping has been more successful than quasipeace enforcement, because it takes place with the consent of the disputant parties; subsequent to a cessation of hostilities and as a result, not reliant on force to fulfil the mission.

CONCLUSION

This paper has addressed the problem of peace in Africa in particular and the world in general by providing the epistemological basis for the conflicts and crises in Africa. Second, it has discussed the necessity of looking into conflicts and crises from different perspectives, especially xenophobia and terrorism; and provided a framework for conflict resolution through the provision of protracted peace education, geographical education, the change of mindset of African leaders, partial surrender of sovereignty by states to the UN, mediation and military intervention. Hence, in a full disclosure posture, conflict and crises in Africa can and should be managed by Africans themselves, because they know the causes and for that reason they should be able to abate them through their own efforts, and not through external efforts; except when they can be useful with the consent of the parties involved in the conflict, in order to bring about peace.

REFERENCES

Avis, J. (1996). Knowledge and nationhood education, politics and work. London: Cassell.

Badat, S. (1997). Education politics in the transition period. In P. Kallaway, G. Krus, A. Fataar & G. Donn (eds.) Education after Apartheid: South African Education in Transition. Cape Town: University of Cape Town Press.

Binn, T. (1993). Geography and education: UK Perspective. *Progress in Human Geography.* Volume 17, Number 1, pp. 101–110.

Commission for Africa (2005). Our Common Interest: Report of the Commission for Africa. March 2005. Chapter 5, pp. 157–178.

Curtin, P., Feierman, S., Thompson, L., & Vansina, J. (1998). African History: From Earliest Times to Independence (2nd ed.). London: Longman.

Fairhurst, U.J. (1993). The Humanities, demise and dilemma: Addressing the challenge. *Africa 2001: Dialogue with the future,* Volume 2, Number 1, p. 66.

Galtung, J. (1969). Violence, Peace and Peace Research. *Journal of Peace Research,* 1969, Volume 6, pp. 167–191.

Harper, R.A. (1992). At issue: What is Geography's contribution to general education? *Journal of Geography.* May/June, pp. 124–125.

Maila, M.W. & Loubser, C.P. (2003). Emancipator Indigenous Knowledge Systems: Implications for Environmental Education in South Africa. In South African Journal of Education, 23 (4): 276–280.

Pizam, A. & Mansfeld, Y. (Eds.) (1996). Tourism, Crime and International Security issues. New York: Wiley & Sons Ltd.

Salem, P. (1993). A Critique of Western Conflict Resolution from a Non-Western Perspective. *National Journal,* October, 1993, pp 361–369.

Shillington, K. (1995). History of Africa (Revised ed.). London: Macmillan.

Simmons, I.G. (1990). Ingredients of a Green Geography. *Geography 327.* Volume 75, Number 2 pp. 98-105.

United Nations (1992). Agenda for Peace. New York.